Criminological Perspectives
Essential Readings
2nd Edition

Criminological Perspectives
Essential Readings
2nd Edition

**Edited by Eugene McLaughlin, John Muncie
and Gordon Hughes**

SAGE Publications
London ● Thousand Oaks ● New Delhi

SAGE Publications Ltd
1 Oliver's Yard
55 City Road
London EC1Y 1SP

SAGE Publications Inc
2455 Teller Road
Thousand Oaks
California 91320

SAGE Publications India Pvt. Ltd
B–42 Panchsheel Enclave
PO Box 4109
New Delhi 110 017

British Library Cataloguing in Publication data
A catalogue record for this book is available from the British Library

ISBN-10 0-7619-4143-6   ISBN-13 978-0-7619-4143-9
ISBN-10 0-7619-4144-4 (pbk)   ISBN-13 978-0-7619-4144-6 (pbk)

Printed on paper from sustainable sources

Typeset by Mayhew Typesetting, Rhayader, Powys
Printed and bound in Great Britain by
Cromwell Press Limited, Trowbridge, Wiltshire

Contents

Preface for second edition

At the beginning of the twenty-first century, criminology is an increasingly important field of study. New criminology departments have been established, reflecting increased student demand for criminology courses and degrees; national and international criminology conferences of a variety of hues are burgeoning; most academic presses have at least one thriving criminology series and a generation of new journals; and a multitude of sub-specialisms have been established. We are also being offered a choice of criminological discourses, some old, some re-works, some genuinely new, some reassuring and some troubling, about what criminology is and might be in the new century. Some believe that we are in need of major criminological reinvention and redrawing of boundaries, yet others are endeavouring to get to grips with various aspects of the archaeology of the criminological and indeed *pre*-criminological knowledge, and criminology's 'wisemen', who have learned to live with or ignore passing fads, remain wedded to criminology's 'tried and true' empirical project.

It is therefore, we feel, an appropriate moment to publish a second edition of *Criminological Perspectives* which reflects the diverse lines of theoretical enquiry that constitute contemporary criminology. The overall aim of this new edition is two-fold: to provide an accessible set of edited readings which familiarises students with the eclectic nature of 'criminological knowledge' and to prompt readers to gaze critically upon the constituent elements of the unfolding criminological enterprise. In compiling this second edition we recognize that we have been unable (not least because of the constraints of space) to cover every aspect of criminological theory. Like all editors, we have been forced to make some difficult choices and uneasy compromises. Uppermost in our minds were the needs of our primary audience, Open University students studying criminology. By choosing original readings, rather than depending on existing textbook summaries, commentaries and reviews, we hope to encourage our students to acquire a critical appreciation of the distinctiveness of criminological theorising. As far as possible, we have chosen readings for each part which are to some extent in conversation with each other. To do so, we have concentrated on pieces which provide expositions of key theoretical positions. We ask our students to study the multiple origins of criminological theory, but to avoid reading or mapping subsequent developments as some readily identifiable linear, uncontested progression. We prefer them to see the ever-present historical traces, thematic survivals, empirical residues, unresolved lines of dispute and to reflect upon the reality that no one theoretical perspective can lay sole claim to the empirical referents of crime. Criminology in our view is a 'site' of contested meaning where competing theoretical perspectives meet. Sometimes they are able to speak to, listen to and understand each other, at others they appear not to share any common discourse. There is, therefore, no one criminology to be found in this reader but a multitude of criminological perspectives which in the main depend and draw upon knowledges generated from elsewhere. To illustrate this point we have included pieces that depart from traditional agendas, and point to new points of departure and fruitful avenues for cross-discipline development.

The Reader is in six parts. Part I focuses on the origins of criminology as expressed through a wide variety of subject positions and theoretical arguments. It reveals a number of 'starting-points' from classicist interpretations of the function of law, positivist interrogations of the causes of crime and quantitative studies of crime statistics, through to Marxist, sociological and anarchist critiques of the problems of crime, law, and the state and social order. We have also included Bentham's 'panopticon', the plan for a 'new model prison' that was to exert such an influence on Foucault's 'discipline and punish' thesis.

Part II concentrates on criminology's historic concern to discover the causes of crime. Again, a wide variety in type of explanation and level of analysis is notable. The readings illustrate some of the key *contemporary* attempts to tackle the issue of crime causation and include discussion of genetic factors, personality traits, social disorganization, consumption patterns, illegitimacy and the underclass, relative deprivation, masculinity, the moral and expressive attractions of the preference for crime over non crime and crime as 'routine activity'. A number of competing theoretical positions and paradigms are at work in these chapters, from individual and sociological variants of positivism to neo-classicism, left realism and gender studies. Also included is a feminist critique of criminology's traditional representation of female criminality.

Part III reveals that understanding the 'problem of crime' does not simply involve trying to account for why certain individuals transgress moral and legal codes whilst others do not, but also necessitates interrogation of how and why it is that only certain behaviours seem to be subjected to criminal sanction whilst other harmful acts may go unnoticed, unpoliced or are even socially approved. Key readings from interactionist, labelling, Marxist and critical criminology perspectives are included to show how the subject matter of criminology has been significantly broadened to encompass issues of social order and power, and the ability of the state and powerful groups in society to confer and enforce the label of criminality on others. Collectively these readings encourage a critical reading and deconstruction of traditional and populist notions of what constitutes 'crime', 'criminality' and 'criminal behaviour'.

Part IV examines a number of competing rationales for systems of crime control, from deterrence, just deserts and rehabilitation through to crime prevention. Critiques of existing crime control systems – emanating from left realist, abolitionist and feminist perspectives – are also included. The part concludes by looking at how far informal systems of control – based on notions such as shaming and policing – can offer a more equitable vision of the future of crime control.

Part V explores how individuals and populations are controlled not simply through the formal processes of criminal justice, but through the imposition of forms of regulation, surveillance and 'government'. Foucault's vision of a 'carceral society' is assessed as is his governmentality thesis. The other readings examine the various techniques, practices, rationales and strategies that are constitutive of the governance of crime in what has been defined as the 'post social' moment.

Part VI poses a number of questions concerning the futures of criminology and its potential for theoretical development. A range of perspectives and issues are explored and compared. Some of these appear to herald new openings for the criminological enterprise; others rework to more traditional forms of analysis. At one and the same time they underline the past failings of criminology, its continuing diversity and the remaining potential to shed new light on new forms of crime and criminalization, harm and harm reduction and social control. Readers will soon become aware that however well established the debate and however numerous the perspectives, none of the central criminological questions highlighted can stand as resolved. As is nearly always the case in the social sciences all of them constitute perennial problems which are always open to further research and debate. And the most perplexing questions concerning 'crime' will never be fully resolved.

We are indebted to many people in putting this text together, not least the thousands of students who have studied criminology with the Open University. Their response to, and ability to engage with, previous course materials has been central in our decisions of what to include and in guiding our assessment of what is accessible and appropriate for study. We have also had the benefit of working with a team of assessors, academics and tutors at the Open University who have continually reminded us to keep the needs of students uppermost in our minds. In compiling the first edition of *Criminological Perspectives*, informal discussions with Pat Carlen, Stan Cohen, Richard Sparks, Loraine Gelsthorpe and Karim Murji were more influential than they may have realized. In the process of assembling the second edition we have benefitted from the advice of John Braithwaite, Lynn Chancer, David Garland, Tony Jefferson, Pat O'Malley, Ken Pease, Joe Sim, Kevin Stenson, Sandra Walklate and Jock Young. Hilary Canneaux, Pauline Hetherington, Donna Collins and Dianne Cook have been invaluable in providing administrative and secretarial support. At Sage we are indebted to Gillian Stern for her unwavering belief that *Criminological Perspectives* was a worthwhile project and to Miranda Nunhoffer for ensuring that a second edition is now available for the next generation of criminology students.

Eugene McLaughlin
John Muncie
Gordon Hughes
June 2002

Introduction: Theorizing crime and criminal justice

Whilst the transgression of moral and legal codes has probably always raised concerns for the maintenance of social order, 'crime' and 'criminology' have not always been with us. The first generally recognized school of criminology, the classical school of the eighteenth century, was less concerned with understanding the nature of 'the criminal' and more with developing rational and systematic means of delivering justice. In essence, classicism was, and remains, a plea for the supremacy of law, rather than of religion, superstition and arbitrary justice. Crime is understood as a product of a rational free will; a course of action freely chosen through calculations of the pain and pleasure involved. Its control is assumed to lie in better and more efficient carefully calculated means of punishment. Establishing specific causes of crime or trying to understand its meaning is of little or no concern.

It was not until the early nineteenth century that crime became an object of scientific enquiry in its own right. In important respects, a concept of 'crime' only came to replace a concept of 'sin' when a burgeoning legal apparatus, designed to protect property and the interests of the nation-state, evolved out of the social, economic and cultural transformations of the industrial revolution. As concern over the 'problem of crime' intensified, so crime became the object of more systematic observance and measurement. Analysis of its extent and causes was first made possible through the publication of national criminal statistics in France in the 1820s. Regularities in the occurrence of crime were then explained with reference to such factors as age, sex, climate and economic conditions. If crime rates were regular and predictable, it was assumed that the causes of crime must lie outside of each individual's control. It was not a simple matter of individual choice.

Such was the cornerstone of a positivist criminology which radically proposed that crime was a non-rational and determinate product of undersocialization and could be studied, via clinical and statistical methods, in much the same way as scientists studied the natural world. Typically, positivist conceptions of crime – whether they be individually or socially based – focus on isolating specific causes. The Italian *scuola positiva* of the late nineteenth century maintained that criminality had multi-factor explanations. In its earliest form, biological causes were prioritized. The criminal, it was argued, was a throwback to a more primitive form of human being, distinguishable through such physiological characteristics as large jaw and ears and facial asymmetry. Such a conclusion was based on the painstaking measurement of the skulls and skeletons of 'known criminals'. As a result it has been heralded as the first *scientific* study of crime. And it is probably no coincidence that it is also from this time that the term 'criminology' is widely assumed to have originated.

The impact of positivism on subsequent developments within criminology cannot be overstated. By searching for the causes of *criminal* behaviour as opposed to other human behaviours, positive criminology assumes that such behaviour has its own peculiar set of characteristics. The aim is to isolate key differences between criminals and non-criminals. Some theorists focus on biological and psychological factors, attempt to isolate specific genetic or personality causes and thus locate the sources of crime primarily within the individual. Other theorists argue that more insights can be gained by studying the social context external to individuals and maintain that crime is better explained with reference to such factors as levels of economic consumption, sites of social disorganization and types of urban structure. The origins of all such social approaches can be traced to the insistence that social phenomena, such as crime and law, have an objective existence of their own and exist independently of the individuals who experience them.

Positivist criminologies – whether individual or sociological in focus – remain influential because they prolong the modernist concern to account for crime with reference to some quantifiable and objective criteria. They also hold on to the hope that because people are propelled into crime through a range of determining factors, then it will always remain possible to treat or neutralize the underlying causes. Such treatments may range from individual rehabilitation through to social economic and policy reform.

Positivism, however, has always stood uneasily against the key principle of classicism that every individual is, and should be made, responsible for their actions. The development of criminology as governmental practice, for example, has meant that the advocacy of positivist treatment methods has always been contested by dominant classicist assumption of free will and rationality.

Almost from its inception, scientific positivism was also under attack from radicals for failing to take a more critical stance towards the nature of the social order in which crime and criminality are located. They warned that crime cannot be analysed outside of the social and economic circumstances in which it occurs. The propositions that law is a tool of state repression and that crime is a product of exploitative labour relations challenged the key positivist assumptions that crime is something abnormal and only practised by identifiable, pathological 'others'. Rather, such analyses (with differing ideological and political emphases) maintained that crime was widespread and ubiquitous – a defining characteristic of any social order based on inequality and social division.

Despite pragmatic, theoretical and political misgivings, it was not until the mid twentieth century that the conventional wisdom of positivism was subjected to sustained intellectual challenge. Whilst positivism tends to deny that criminality involves any element of choice, creativity or meaning, interactionism is more concerned to grant authenticity to deviant actions by recording the motives and meanings of the deviant actors themselves. Interactionism produced an epistemological break by radically shifting the object of criminological inquiry away from trying to isolate the presumed factors propelling a pathological few to break the rules of an assumed social consensus, to an analysis which rested on a conflict or pluralist conception of society in which deviance was ubiquitous and where 'crime' was constructed through the partial and pernicious practices of social reaction and social control. The adages of social reaction theory that 'there can be no crime without law' and that 'social control leads to deviance' effectively turned the time-honoured premises of positivism on their head. By the early 1970s this critical paradigm effectively placed a number of counter propositions on the criminological agenda.

Criminology was under challenge from a more comprehensive sociology of crime and deviance. Here questions of social control, rather than crime causation, are the central matters of concern. A determination to 'appreciate' (and some would say 'celebrate') deviance in terms of its subjective meaning for particular actors takes precedence over the scientific assertions that criminal behaviour is determined by a mix of innate, genetic or physiological incapacities (born bad) or instances of ineffective child rearing, family pathology and social disorganization (made bad). By focusing on processes of criminalization and law formation, rather than crime and criminal behaviour, whole new areas of research and empathies have been opened up, in which definitional rather than behavioural issues are central.

It is in this context that we can account for the emergence in the 1970s of *The New Criminology*. Despite its title, its originality lay not so much in innovation, but in the attempt to synthesize several different old traditions. The concern to respect the authenticity of the diverse and unique worlds of everyday life continued a tradition established by the Chicago School of the 1930s and the social interactionists; whilst dimensions of power and social control were appropriated from social reaction theory. The New Criminology, however, attempted to ground this anti-positivist radicalization by taking the world of personal meanings and social reaction back into a critique of the history and structure of society. This was achieved through locating definitions of crime and modes of control in the precise context of the social relationships and institutional arrangements emanating from particular modes of economic production. Clearly what this work was advocating was that the key subject of the new criminology was not crime and deviance as behaviours, but a critical understanding of the social order and the power to criminalize and control. When the task of criminology was defined as one of creating a society 'in which the facts of human diversity are not subject to the power to criminalize', it was clear that the aim was to transform criminology from a science of social control and into a fully politicized struggle for social justice. Part of this also relied on a reworking of the theoretical premises of Marxism. Following the supposition that laws perpetuate a particular mode of economic production, it is argued that bourgeois law not only acts to preserve existing unequal forms of property ownership, but also punishes the property offences of the poor whilst maintaining stable conditions for the exploitation of their labour. The subject matter of criminology has, as a result, been considerably broadened from its previous narrow focus of attempting to discover why those lowest in the social order appeared to exhibit the highest rate of criminality. Investigating the policies and crimes of the powerful and the human rights violations of the state, for example, have become legitimate forms of enquiry. Similarly, it is argued that more can be discovered about crime by examining how certain individuals and communities become subject to processes of criminalization, rather than by trying to identify particular causes.

In this way criminology has also become more critical of functioning of the agencies of criminal justice, and suggests that law and its enforcement are the key instruments by which 'race', class and gender power can be 'legitimately' exercised. The scientific objectivity and political neutrality of previous criminology is called into question; and the complex question of the relationship between knowledge and power is posed. Reliance on official statistics as 'real' indicators of where in society crime is committed and the rate at which it is committed is questioned. A critical approach not only argues that a greater number of 'crimes' are committed than official statistics suggest, but also that criminality is to be found at all points in the social formation. The key questions are directed not so much at the criminal act in isolation but at the dynamics of social institutions which construct crime and their ability to convey such social constructions to the public. The study of crime necessitates a much wider study of the agencies, processes and structures of social control.

These theoretical developments, originating from the mid 1970s, however, took place against the political backdrop of a resurgence in popular law and order politics and authoritarianism. In the UK and the United States the rhetoric of a resurgent radical Right revived a neo-classical vision of criminality as voluntaristic – a course of action willingly chosen by calculating individuals, lacking in self-control and with a potential for communal contamination and moral degeneracy. New 'realist' theorists of the Right disengaged from existing criminological agendas – whether they be positivist or critical – by claiming that crime emanates from rationally calculating individuals who are insufficiently deterred from the actions by a criminal justice system deemed to be chaotic and ineffective or lacking in 'just deserts'. Both remind us of the potency and endurance of classicist and neo-classicist formulations of the 'crime problem'. The key concern is with developing efficient means of control rather than with questions of causality. Against a backdrop of perennially growing official statistics of crime and the presumption of increases in a rational public fear, the extension of police powers, the erosion of civil liberties and the expansion of imprisonment to unprecedented levels have all been justified. The public/political debate has come to be dominated by images of violent crime, lawlessness, disorder and declining morality. In the early twenty-first century it seems that authoritarianism, law and order policies have the political potency to undermine welfare and rehabilitation discourses. However, the 'tough on crime' discourse has also been tempered by an apparent failure to prevent escalating crime rates. Within the developing ethos of 'what works' in all public services, it appears to be acknowledged that all that can be realistically hoped for is to implement more pragmatic means of managing crime through situational opportunity preventative measures and developing ever more cost-effective and efficient methods of managing criminal justice.

The New Right colonization of almost the whole terrain of law and order politics in the late 1970s forced sections of the Left to rethink their position and to move closer to the mainstream in a pragmatic attempt to counter some of its more reactionary policies. The self-styled left realists gradually disassociated themselves from the 'new' and 'critical' criminologies in an effort to find a new criminology for new times. Left realism, initiated its programme through virulent attacks directed as much to the Left as to the Right. Labelling its former bed fellows as idealist, it argues that the Left has traditionally either romanticized or underestimated the nature and impact of crime and largely 'speaks to itself' through its lack of engagement with the day-to-day issues of crime control and social policy. With empirical support from a series of victim surveys, left realism is able to assert that the fear of crime is indeed growing and that, in particular, property and street crimes are real issues that need to be addressed, rather than dismissed as social constructions. In short it concurs with right realism that people's fear of crime is rational and a reflection of inner city social reality. However, it differs from the Right in its insistence that the causes of crime need to be once more established and theorized; and a social justice and welfare programme initiated to tackle social and economic inequalities, under the rubric of 'inclusive citizenship'.

Clearly this marks a distinct break with the critical agenda of *The New Criminology*. It invokes many themes (such as crime causation) which are grounded in positivist criminology, with, for example, street crime being portrayed as caused by relative deprivation. In this respect it appears to reflect and indeed mirror New Right and media-driven definitions of what constitutes serious crime and consequently downplays corporate crime and crimes of the state. Analyses of the relationship between the public, criminal justice agencies, offenders and victims are largely restricted to street crime and fail to capture the harm caused, for example, by workplace injury, occupation-related diseases and environmental pollution. Left realism's dismissal of critical criminology idealist ignores the interventionist role that critical criminologists have played since the 1970s in developing a politics of support for marginalized groups such as black youth, prisoners, gypsies and women, as well as establishing independent inquiries into aspects of state authoritarianism and monitoring police practices.

Equally, critical criminology has not ignored the necessity of developing new theoretical frameworks in which to further an understanding of processes of criminalization. It believes that the para-Marxist heritage need not be totally abandoned but can be refined and developed; to deliver not a sealed doctrine, but a new set of provisional hypotheses or frames of conceptual resources/deposits. For example, it has become common to find a more complex set of analyses which move away from a restricted chain of criminological references – state, law, crime, criminals – to the examination of other arenas of social regulation. By recognizing and working within the Foucauldian concept of 'governance' it has become possible to study how networks of power and resistance are diffuse and governed more by their own internal logics and knowledge than by the definite intentions of particular classes or oppressive states. This direction in turn has opened up work on a variety of semi-autonomous realms, such as informal justice, local communities, privatized organizations and families in which notions of policing and control are present, but whose relation to the state is by no means direct and unambiguous. It is in these areas too that interest in the potential of often neglected processes of informal networks of order and control has been awakened, albeit sometimes from different theoretical starting points.

In this context the issues of idealism vs realism becomes something of a red herring. It is surely just as 'real' to unearth the complexities of processes of criminalization, resistance and control, as it is to be bound to public perceptions and victim surveys. Whilst the mainstream of criminology increasingly appears to be simply involved in a technocratic 'what works' exercise to evaluate the effectiveness of criminal justice procedures and practices, the critical paradigm continues to expose the discriminatory powers and outcomes and retains a space in which alternative visions of social justice can be created. Such visions remain important for they enable us to rethink social conditions in terms of them not simply being made bearable (as in left realism or social democratic reformism) but transformed into a vehicle for emancipation.

A key failing of all criminologists up to the 1970s was to acknowledge the 'presence of absence' in the form of critical analysis of gender relations and women and crime. The development of feminist inroads into the male bastion of criminology initially took the form of a comprehensive critique of the discipline firstly for its neglect even to study women's involvement in crime and criminal justice and secondly for its distortion of women's experiences as essentially biologically driven.

Since the mid 1970s a burgeoning literature has revealed that women's crimes are committed in different circumstances to men's and that the response to women's law breaking is constituted within sexist assumptions of femininity which have only further added to women's oppression. This body of knowledge has now successfully demonstrated how criminology has traditionally been driven by male assumptions and interests, how criminalized women are seen as doubly deviant and how assumptions about appropriate gender roles mean that women are judged less on the nature of their offences and more on their 'deviant' lifestyles. As a result some feminists have drawn more on sociologies of gender, than any pre-existing criminological knowledge, to explore their subject of matter, with the important message for male criminology that the object of their enquiry is essentially 'masculine' and that as much can be learned about processes of control and criminalization by focusing on those structures and processes that create conformity and social order, as on a sole concern with those that produce deviance and criminality. Others have gone further by questioning whether the focus on female lawbreakers is a proper concern for feminism and indeed whether a feminist criminology is theoretically possible or even politically desirable. Latterly this relation between feminism and criminology has been further problematized by a deconstructionist of postmodern twist which claims that the signifiers of 'women', 'crime' and 'criminology' trap any investigation in essentialist categories that obstruct the production of new knowledge. It is perhaps no surprise that the deconstruction of criminology has gathered most strength in some feminist perspectives, for it is they that were first alerted to the need for criminology to deconstruct itself if it was to break out of its gender essentialism.

The tendency of the social sciences to deconstruct and question their own internal logic is slowly permeating the discipline of criminology. As some feminist critics have warned, the discipline will remain forever self-justifying unless it is prepared to adopt a more critical stance towards the key referents of 'crime' and 'deviance'. The process of deconstruction also has its origins in the work of Foucault and his location of the discourse of criminology in the combination of knowledge and power that evolved with the modern state and the emergence of the social sciences. Foucault's acknowledgement of a multiplicity of power relations and the diverse settings in which they are activated, in particular, questioned the ability of any total theory (Marxism, for example) to answer all questions. This disenchantment with a priori claims to the 'truth', as represented in stark form by the way criminology has progressed through paradigmatic construction and contestation, is substantiated in the postmodern insistence that we should break with the rational and totalizing (modernist) intellectual movements of the past. Whilst modernism (of which criminology is but one element) attempts to ratify knowledge so that the social can be made an ordered totality, postmodernism views the world as replete with an unlimited number of models of order, each generated by relatively autonomous and localized sets of practices. Modernism strives for universality, postmodernism accepts relativity as a defining feature of the world. In essence postmodernism challenges the logic of 'referential finalities' as the foundation of western society. Rather it stresses the diversity and particularity of social life and accordingly asserts that no one theoretical paradigm is capable of making sense of the social world.

This post-criminological sensibility implies an abandonment of the concept of crime and its replacement by a new language to designate objects of censure and codes of conduct. By definition this would mean that criminology would lose its very *raison d'être*. Exactly what form such a project might take remains unclear, but the challenge of postmodernism is one that urges us continually to address the limitations of accepted knowledge's, to avoid dogmatism and to recognize the existence of a wide variety of subjectivities.

Unsurprisingly, this rejection of totalizing theory and of 'objective' criteria for establishing truth and meaning, can be viewed as intellectually liberating or as intrinsically nihilistic and conservative. For example, at present it is far from clear how a total rejection of established concepts might further an understanding of the relations between criminalization, poverty, inequality, racism, sexual violence and repressive state practices. The failure to replace existing concepts with alternative visions may only leave us with a series of dislocated and fragmented positions. Whilst we may sympathize with the postmodernist objection to the colonization of the intellectual world by a single all-encompassing meta-narrative, does this also mean that we can dispense with the imaginative purchase provided by critical and Utopian visions?

As we noted previously, several principles guided our selection of articles for this book. The first is that within the disciplinary space constituted by and for criminology the intellectual and the political are indivisible. Most obviously, from its origins, for a variety of reasons, criminologists have, despite all claims to neutrality and objectivity, sought to make themselves and their knowledge indispensable to governmental interests. The second is that criminological perspectives are not constructed in a vacuum but only acquire meaning in specific socio-cultural contexts. Although the basic concepts, methods and concerns have remained more or less the same, the discipline has, often in spite of itself, at key moments experienced a number of important transformations as the social world that it claims to represent and comprehend has altered. These principles are thrown into stark relief at the beginning of the twenty-first century and as a result sociologically inspired criminologists find themselves working within an unsettled, insecure disciplinary space. Underpinning many of the chapters in the last two sections of this reader is a realization that present conditions pose unprecedented challenges to criminologists who privilege 'the social' as their starting point.

First, there is the need for criminologists of 'the social' to engage in what we might describe as high definition widescreen analysis. A general consensus across the social sciences declares that we are in the midst of unprecedented global transformation defined variously as: post-modernity; late modernity; post-fordism; disorganized capitalism; turbo-capitalism; the information age; risk society; market society; network society; consumer society etc. Most recently, we have been informed of the need to think about the nature of the new global (dis)order that will emerge in the aftermath of the attacks on New York and Washington on 11 September 2001. Such shifts transform the task of all the social sciences. However, a significant part of criminology seems to have been caught unaware of the intellectual requirement to make sense of what is happening, why and with what consequences. In many respects, criminology has yet to face up to the possibility that notions such as fragmentation, difference, plurality and contingency are radically unsettling the established modernist categories, assumptions and models that have served it so well. For sociologically inspired criminology the very idea of 'the social' has been thrown into serious question. To date, sociologists of crime have struggled to articulate visions of this 'post-social' world. Some seem content to either wearily deny that anything really significant is happening whilst others wish to play the siren role of issuing doom-laden pronouncements about the 'dark' criminogenic side of the changes. There is a flourishing nostalgia-laden social democratic criminological literature that is saturated with images of the disorderly, fragmenting, disintegrating, ungovernable 'social'. Criminologists have engaged in the relatively easy part of narrating the new levels and forms of insecurity and risks and highlighting new modes of soft surveillance and hard control. What we do not have – at least at the moment – is a criminological imagination that provides us with a more nuanced, attuned understanding of the open-textured, multi-dimensional 'remaking of the social' currently in play. This will require criminologists to overcome their knee-jerk suspiciousness of theoretical developments that originate 'outside' of the discipline and indeed to 'fold' themselves however uncomfortably within these scholarly debates.

Second, we are witnessing the latest and perhaps most significant reconstitution of criminology as a self-declared governmental practice. Sociology's hegemony over criminology has been challenged by the demand for an applied criminology that generates 'evidence-based' policy and practice. Across a variety of jurisdictions, we can witness the consolidation of the presence of 'administrative criminology' whose self declared task is to close the gap between theory and criminal justice practice in order to design out crime. Its practitioners now seem to be in a strategic position to transform themselves into 'crime scientists'. This development heralds the re-emergence of what might be described as 'anti-social criminologies' which: accept dominant definitions of the 'problem of crime'; are seemingly willing to rule in any strategy that might control crime; and are resurrecting links with a new wave of socio-biologists and geneticists. We need to not only pay attention to but research how the ideas most closely associated with administrative criminology are implicated in the reordering of core governmental technologies and practices across many jurisdictions.

Third, as a result of the hyper-politicization of law and order and the ratchetting of public fears and anxieties we have witnessed what might be described as a highly unstable and unpredictable democratic or perhaps more accurately populist crimino-logical imagination. The proliferation of public and private fears, anxieties and fantasies can only be addressed via a psycho-social criminology. At the same time, paradoxically, sitting alongside what we might define as the 'fear complex' is a popular cultural criminological imagination that is constituted by a mass of hyper-fictional and hyper real representations of the 'mind of the criminal' and fascinated by all aspects of law enforcement and criminality. Instead of merely adopting a realist attitude that presents 'fascination' as the antithesis of 'fear' we need to develop a provocative cultural criminology that is able to recognize and explore the interconnectedness and closeness of these two fundamental manifestations of the human/inhuman condition. We also need to examine how and why conventional criminological understandings are in danger of being overwhelmed by (a) images of crime and crime control gleaned from novels, magazine, films, music, cyberspace and computer game simulations and (b) tabloid news media representations that can generate sharp swings in the politics of law and order.

We do not claim to have a unanimously held view on how to incorporate these concerns onto the formal criminological agenda. The problem for criminologists is that 'crime' as social fact, social construct and media spectacle, saturates everyday life of contemporary society. Its sites of production are diverse and multiplying, 'high' and 'low', bizarre and commonplace, shocking and thrilling, intimate and distant, desperate and exploitative, deeply damaging and potentially progressive. To grasp the complex variety of its subject matter, criminology must remain an intellectual space that rejects a theoretically correct version of itself. As a matter of urgency, it has to generate reflexive perspectives and practices that are capable of speaking and listening to local, national and global concerns.

Part I

Past tense: Criminological formations

INTRODUCTION

This collection of essays is designed to introduce the reader to the diverse origins of the study of crime and the law. It includes some of the now classic formulations of the nature and problem of crime as expressed by such eighteenth century philosophers as Cesare Beccaria and Jeremy Bentham, early nineteenth century mathematicians such as Adolphe Quetelet, late nineteenth century physicians such as Cesare Lombroso and sociological theorists such as Emile Durkheim. The eight classic readings reproduced here cover a period that stretches from 1764 to 1916. It is a period in which many of the debates about the function of law, the nature of crime, the causes of crime and the extent of crime, with which we are now familiar, were first given intellectual and public expression. The readings are not simply of historical curiosity. Each, in different ways continues to influence contemporary understandings and formulations of the 'crime problem'.

It is perhaps of some significance that the origins of modern criminological theory can be traced, not to the study of crime and criminals, but to Enlightenment philosophers, particularly in France and Italy, reflecting on the nature and functions of criminal law. Beccaria's *On Crimes and Punishments* (1764) set out a then controversial programme for criminal law reform. Critical of the barbarism, irregularity and ad hoc nature of eighteenth century criminal justice, he urged that social order be based on law, rather than religion or superstition; that the machinery of justice be answerable to rules of due process; that sentencing policies be formulated to 'fit the crime'; and that punishment be prompt and certain. At the time, Beccaria's work was condemned for its extreme rationalism, but within his recommendations are the seeds of policies present in most criminal justice systems around the world today. Above all he is now recognized as the founding father of a *classical* school of criminology (a term he never himself used, but was so described by later theorists) characterized by the key doctrines of rationality, free will and the social contract. Plans for 'the panopticon' were presented by Jeremy Bentham, the founder of English 'utilitarianism' or 'philosophical' radicalism. Bentham's 'new prison' was designed to ensure that the prisoner could never know when he was being watched. Visibility and surveillance would function as a rational cost effective instrument of discipline and control. Foucault's work spells out the wider implications of Bentham's utilitarian determination to 'grind rogues honest.'

In contrast a *positivist* criminology, which emerged from the mid nineteenth century onwards, was concerned less with the content and implementation of criminal law and more with establishing the causes of law breaking. In 1827 the French government published the first national statistical tables of crime, the annual *Compte général*. Whilst acknowledging the limitations of such statistics in revealing the true extent of crime in society, Quetelet discovered a remarkable constancy in recorded crime in France between 1826 and 1829. He thus argued that, even if individuals have free will, criminal behaviour appears to obey the same scientific laws that govern the natural world. Of note was the regularity with which young males and those in lowly employment had a greater propensity toward crime. The two factors most strongly associated with criminality were age and sex, but the rates of property and personal crime were also found to fluctuate according to the seasons and with the state of the economy. As a result, Quetelet formulated the then remarkable proposition that criminality is not freely chosen or that it is a sign of human wickedness, but that it is an inevitable and resultant feature of social organization. It was thus society that caused crime.

By the 1870s the impact of positivism on the doctrine of free will was underlined in Lombroso's key text *Criminal Man*. After studying anatomy and pathology, Lombroso argued that a significant proportion of criminals had cranial and other physiological defects which suggested that they were born to criminality and represented a throwback to primitive forms of social evolution. The extract reproduced here from his work with fellow collaborator William Ferrero applies this reasoning to establish a criminal type in women. Although female criminality increases with advances in civilization, most women are deemed non-criminal because biological factors predispose them to be more conservative and socially withdrawn. The physical characteristics of female criminals, such as prostitutes, however resemble those of male criminals, and their criminality is often more cruel, wicked and vindictive. In an exceptional, and subsequently highly controversial, series of statements Lombroso and Ferrero claimed that the female born criminal, when a complete type, is more terrible than the male'.

Lombroso's insistence on the accurate and deliberate measurement of the physical anomalies of known criminals has for many established him as first 'scientific' criminologist. And whilst his particular theory of crime causation was eventually to be discredited through the weight of counter argument, the principles of the Italian school of positivism (of which Lombroso is usually lauded as the founder) were gradually to become influential not only in intellectual circles but in the development of less uniform and more individually oriented forms of penal treatment. By the turn of the century, classicists and positivists were engaged in a series of bitter arguments about the nature of criminal responsibility and the objectives of punishment. The extract from one of three lectures given by Enrico Ferri at the University of Naples in 1901 clearly illustrates the divergencies between these two schools of thought and the depth of feeling by which the exponents of positivism sought to deliver their message.

In contrast the extracts from Bonger and Durkheim, whilst sharing some features with the fundamentals of positivism, mark something of a return to the principles of Quetelet in the insistence that the causes of crime lie not in individual abnormalities, but in the nature of economic conditions and social structures. Bonger was the first to apply the Marxist inspired notions of class conflict and capitalist exploitation to the concept of crime. In a scathing attack on the egoistic and competitive tendencies of capitalism, Bonger argued that most crime could be accounted for by a lack of common ownership of property and the brutalized conditions of existence endured by all classes in a society characterized by unfettered forms of capitalist exchange and labour exploitation. Durkheim's work in general adopts a less conflict-based analysis of society, preferring to view the social structure as characterized above all by consensus or a collective conscience. Durkheim, who is lauded as the founder of a sociological criminology, once more remarked on the regularity and constancy of crime rates in particular societies, and insisted that social phenomena (such as crime and law) have an objective existence irrespective of how they are experienced by individuals. This led to the now famous and perpetually controversial propositions that crime is normal, crime is inevitable and that crime is useful to society. The extract reproduced here from his 1895 work *The Rules of Sociological Method* marks a radical departure from the then prevailing notions of classical free will and positivist ideas of individual abnormality. Rather crime performs a vital function for society in establishing clear moral boundaries and in paving the way for social innovation and change.

Kropotkin's contribution, originally published in 1898, offers a more strident critique of bourgeois law from an anarchist perspective. In terms echoed some seventy years later by some abolitionist and critical criminologists (see Parts III and IV), Kropotkin roundly condemns the role of law in facilitating the accumulation of property in the hands of the few and in perpetuating barbaric forms of repression and control. For him the real criminals in society are not those 'unfortunates' who populate the prisons, but those figures of authority who, through their self-interested formulation and implementation of criminal law, have served to put them there.

1

On crimes and punishments

Cesare Beccaria

[. . .]

If we glance at the pages of history, we will find that laws, which surely are, or ought to be, compacts of free men, have been, for the most part, a mere tool of the passions of some, or have arisen from an accidental and temporary need. Never have they been dictated by a dispassionate student of human nature who might, by bringing the actions of a multitude of men into focus, consider them from this single point of view: the *greatest happiness shared by the greatest number*. Happy are those few nations that have not waited for the slow succession of coincidence and human vicissitude to force some little turn for the better after the limit of evil has been reached, but have facilitated the intermediate progress by means of good laws. And humanity owes a debt of gratitude to that philosopher who, from the obscurity of his isolated study, had the courage to scatter among the multitude the first seeds, so long unfruitful, of useful truths.

The true relations between sovereigns and their subjects, and between nations, have been discovered. Commerce has been reanimated by the common knowledge of philosophical truths diffused by the art of printing, and there has sprung up among nations a tacit rivalry of industriousness that is most humane and truly worthy of rational beings. Such good things we owe to the productive enlightenment of this age. But very few persons have studied and fought against the cruelty of punishments and the irregularities of criminal procedures, a part of legislation that is as fundamental as it is widely neglected in almost all of Europe. Very few persons have undertaken to demolish the accumulated errors of centuries by rising to general principles, curbing, at least, with the sole force that acknowledged truths possess, the unbounded course of ill-directed power which has continually produced a long and authorized example of the most cold-blooded barbarity. And yet the groans of the weak, sacrificed to cruel ignorance and to opulent indolence; the barbarous torments, multiplied with lavish and useless severity, for crimes either not proved or wholly imaginary; the filth and horrors of a prison, intensified by that cruellest tormentor of the miserable, uncertainty – all these ought to have roused that breed of magistrates who direct the opinions of men.

From *On Crimes and Punishments*, pp. 8–19; 55–9; 62–4; 93–9. (New York: Bobbs-Merrill, 1963. First published 1764.)

The immortal Montesquieu has cursorily touched upon this subject. Truth, which is one and indivisible, has obliged me to follow the illustrious steps of that great man, but the thoughtful men for whom I write will easily distinguish my traces from his. I shall deem myself happy if I can obtain, as he did, the secret thanks of the unknown and peace-loving disciples of reason, and if I can inspire that tender thrill with which persons of sensibility respond to one who upholds the interests of humanity.

[. . .]

THE ORIGIN OF PUNISHMENTS, AND THE RIGHT TO PUNISH

[. . .]

No man ever freely sacrificed a portion of his personal liberty merely in behalf of the common good. That chimera exists only in romances. If it were possible, every one of us would prefer that the compacts binding others did not bind us; every man tends to make himself the centre of his whole world.

The continuous multiplication of mankind, inconsiderable in itself yet exceeding by far the means that a sterile and uncultivated nature could offer for the satisfaction of increasingly complex needs, united the earliest savages. These first communities of necessity caused the formation of others to resist the first, and the primitive state of warfare thus passed from individuals to nations.

Laws are the conditions under which independent and isolated men united to form a society. Weary of living in a continual state of war, and of enjoying a liberty rendered useless by the uncertainty of preserving it, they sacrificed a part so that they might enjoy the rest of it in peace and safety. The sum of all these portions of liberty sacrificed by each for his own good constitutes the sovereignty of a nation, and their legitimate depositary and administrator is the sovereign. But merely to have established this deposit was not enough; it had to be defended against private usurpations by individuals each of whom always tries not only to withdraw his own share but also to usurp for himself that of others. Some tangible motives had to be introduced, therefore, to prevent the despotic spirit, which is in every man, from plunging the laws of society into its original chaos. These tangible motives are the punishments established against infractors of the laws. I say 'tangible motives' because experience has shown that the multitude adopt no fixed principles of conduct and will not be released from the sway of that universal principle of dissolution which is seen to operate both in the physical and the moral universe, except for motives that directly strike the senses. These motives, by dint of repeated representation to the mind, counterbalance the powerful impressions of the private passions that oppose the common good. Not eloquence, not declamations, not even the most sublime truths have sufficed, for any considerable length of time, to curb passions excited by vivid impressions of present objects.

It was, thus, necessity that forced men to give up part of their personal liberty, and it is certain, therefore, that each is willing to place in the public fund only the least possible portion, no more than suffices to induce others to defend it. The aggregate of these least possible portions constitutes the right to punish; all that exceeds this is abuse and not justice; it is fact but by no means right.

Punishments that exceed what is necessary for protection of the deposit of public security are by their very nature unjust, and punishments are increasingly more just as the safety which the sovereign secures for his subjects is the more sacred and inviolable, and the liberty greater.

CONSEQUENCES

The first consequence of these principles is that only the laws can decree punishments for crimes; authority for this can reside only with the legislator who represents the entire society united by a social contract. No magistrate (who is a part of society) can, with justice, inflict punishments upon another member of the same society. But a punishment that exceeds the limit fixed by the laws is just punishment plus another punishment; a magistrate cannot, therefore, under any pretext of zeal or concern for the public good, augment the punishment established for a delinquent citizen.

The second consequence is that the sovereign, who represents the society itself, can frame only general laws binding all members, but he cannot judge whether someone has violated the social contract, for that would divide the nation into two parts, one represented by the sovereign, who asserts the violation of the contract, and the other by the accused, who denies it. There must, therefore, be a third party to judge the truth of the fact. Hence the need for a magistrate whose decisions, from which there can be no appeal, should consist of mere affirmations or denials of particular facts.

The third consequence is this: even assuming that severity of punishments were not directly contrary to the public good and to the very purpose of preventing crimes, if it were possible to prove merely that such severity is useless, in that case also it would be contrary not only to those beneficent virtues that spring from enlightened reason which would rather rule happy men than a herd of slaves in whom a timid cruelty makes its endless rounds; it would be contrary to justice itself and to the very nature of the social contract.

INTERPRETATIONS OF THE LAWS

A fourth consequence: Judges in criminal cases cannot have the authority to interpret laws, and the reason, again, is that they are not legislators. Such judges have not received the laws from our ancestors as a family tradition or legacy that leaves to posterity only the burden of obeying them, but they receive them, rather, from the living society, or from the sovereign representing it, who is the legitimate depositary of what actually results from the common will of all [. . .]

Nothing can be more dangerous than the popular axiom that it is necessary to consult the spirit of the laws. It is a dam that has given way to a torrent of opinions. This truth, which seems paradoxical to ordinary minds that are struck more by trivial present disorders than by the dangerous but remote effects of false principles rooted in a nation, seems to me to be fully demonstrated. Our understandings and all our ideas have a reciprocal connection; the more complicated they are, the more numerous must the ways be that lead to them and depart from them. Each man has his own point of view, and, at each different time, a different one. Thus the 'spirit' of the law would be the product of a judge's good or bad logic, of his good or bad digestion; it would depend on the violence of his passions, on the weakness of the accused, on the judge's connections with him, and on all those minute factors that alter the appearances of an object in the fluctuating mind of man. Thus we see the lot of a citizen subjected to frequent changes in passing through different courts, and we see the lives of poor wretches become the victims of the false ratiocinations or of the momentary seething ill-humours of a judge who mistakes for a legitimate interpretation that vague product of the jumbled series of notions which his mind stirs up. Thus we see the same crimes differently punished at different times by the same court, for having consulted not the constant fixed voice of the law but the erring instability of interpretation.

The disorder that arises from rigorous observance of the letter of a penal law is hardly comparable to the disorders that arise from interpretations. The temporary inconvenience of the former prompts one to make the rather easy and needed correction in the words of the law which are the source of uncertainty, but it curbs that fatal licence of discussion which gives rise to arbitrary and venal controversies. When a fixed code of laws, which must be observed to the letter, leaves no further care to the judge than to examine the acts of citizens and to decide whether or not they conform to the law as written; when the standard of the just or the unjust, which is to be the norm of conduct for the ignorant as well as for the philosophic citizen, is not a matter of controversy but of fact; then only are citizens not subject to the petty tyrannies of the many which are the more cruel as the distance between the oppressed and the oppressor is less, and which are far more fatal than those of a single man, for the despotism of many can only be corrected by the despotism of one; the cruelty of a single despot is proportioned, not to his might, but to the obstacles he encounters. In this way citizens acquire that sense of security for their own persons which is just, because it is the object of human association, and useful, because it enables them to calculate accurately the inconveniences of a misdeed. It is true, also, that they acquire a spirit of independence, but not one that upsets the laws and resists the chief magistrates; rather one that resists those who have dared to apply the sacred name of virtue to that weakness of theirs which makes them yield to their self-interested and capricious opinions.

These principles will displease those who have assumed for themselves a right to transmit to their inferiors the blows of tyranny that they have received from their superiors. I would, indeed, be most fearful if the spirit of tyranny were in the least compatible with the spirit of literacy.

OBSCURITY OF THE LAWS

If the interpretation of laws is an evil, another evil, evidently, is the obscurity that makes interpretation necessary. And this evil would be very great indeed where the laws are written in a language that is foreign to a people, forcing it to rely on a handful of men because it is unable to judge for itself how its liberty or its members may fare – in a language that transforms a sacred and public book into something very like the private possession of a family. When the number of those who can understand the sacred code of laws and hold it in their hands increases, the frequency of crimes will be found to decrease, for undoubtedly ignorance and uncertainty of punishments add much to the eloquence of the passions. What are we to make of men, therefore, when we reflect that this very evil is the inveterate practice of a large part of cultured and enlightened Europe?

One consequence of this last reflection is that, without writing, a society can never acquire a fixed form of government with power that derives from the whole and not from the parts, in which the laws, which cannot be altered except by the general will, are not corrupted in their passage through the mass of private interests. Experience and reason have shown us that the probability and certainty of human traditions diminish the further removed they are from their source. For, obviously, if there exists no enduring memorial of the social compact, how are the laws to withstand the inevitable pressure of time and of passions?

[. . .]

PROMPTNESS OF PUNISHMENT

The more promptly and the more closely punishment follows upon the commission of a crime, the more just and useful will it be. I say more just, because the criminal is thereby spared the useless and cruel torments of uncertainty, which increase with the vigour of imagination and with the sense of personal weakness; more just, because privation of liberty, being itself a punishment, should not precede the sentence except when necessity requires. Imprisonment of a citizen, then, is simply custody of his person until he be judged guilty; and this custody, being essentially penal, should be of the least possible duration and of the least possible severity. The time limit should be determined both by the anticipated length of the trial and by seniority among those who are entitled to be tried first. The strictness of confinement should be no more than is necessary to prevent him from taking flight or from concealing the proofs of his crimes. The trial itself should be completed in the briefest possible time. What crueller contrast than the indolence of a judge and the anguish of a man under accusation – the comforts and pleasures of an insensitive magistrate on one side, and on the other the tears, the squalor of a prisoner? In general, the weight of punishment and the consequence of a crime should be that which is most efficacious for others, and which inflicts the least possible hardship upon the person who suffers it; one cannot call legitimate any society which does not maintain, as an infallible principle, that men have wished to subject themselves only to the least possible evils.

I have said that the promptness of punishments is more useful because when the length of time that passes between the punishment and the misdeed is less, so much the stronger and more lasting in the human mind is the association of these two ideas, *crime and punishment*; they then come insensibly to be considered, one as the cause, the other as the necessary inevitable effect. It has been demonstrated that the association of ideas is the cement that forms the entire fabric of the human intellect; without this cement pleasure and pain would be isolated sentiments and of no effect. The more men depart from general ideas and universal principles, that is, the more vulgar they are, the more apt are they to act merely on immediate and familiar associations, ignoring the more remote and complex ones that serve only men strongly impassioned for the object of their desires; the light of attention illuminates only a single object, leaving the others dark. They are of service also to more elevated minds, for they have acquired the habit of rapidly surveying many objects at once, and are able with facility to contrast many partial sentiments one with another, so that the result, which is action, is less dangerous and uncertain.

Of utmost importance is it, therefore, that the crime and the punishment be intimately linked together, if it be desirable that, in crude, vulgar minds, the seductive picture of a particularly advantageous crime should immediately call up the associated idea of punishment. Long delay always produces the effect of further separating these two ideas; thus, though punishment of a crime may make an impression, it will be less as a punishment than as a spectacle, and will be felt only after the horror of the particular crime, which should serve to reinforce the feeling of punishment, has been much weakened in the hearts of the spectators.

Another principle serves admirably to draw even closer the important connection between a misdeed and its punishment, namely, that the latter be as much in conformity as possible with the nature of the crime. This analogy facilitates admirably the contrast that ought to exist between the inducement to crime and the counterforce of punishment, so that the latter may deter and lead the mind toward a goal the very opposite of that toward which the seductive idea of breaking the laws seeks to direct it.

Those guilty of lesser crimes are usually punished either in the obscurity of a prison or by transportation, to serve as an example, with a distant and therefore almost useless servitude, to nations which they have not offended. Since men are not induced on the spur of the moment to commit the gravest crimes, public punishment of a great misdeed will be regarded by the majority as something very remote and of improbable occurrence; but public punishment of lesser crimes, which are closer to men's hearts, will make an impression which, while deterring them from these, deters them even further from the graver crimes. A proportioning of punishments to one another and to crimes should comprehend not only their force but also the manner of inflicting them.

THE CERTAINTY OF PUNISHMENT: MERCY

One of the greatest curbs on crimes is not the cruelty of punishments, but their infallibility, and, consequently, the vigilance of magistrates, and that severity of an inexorable judge which, to be a useful virtue, must be accompanied by a mild legislation. The certainty of a punishment, even if it be moderate, will always make a stronger impression than the fear of another which is more terrible but combined with the hope of impunity; even the least evils, when they are certain, always terrify men's minds, and hope, that heavenly gift which is often our sole recompense for everything, tends to keep the thought of greater evils remote from us, especially when its strength is increased by the idea of impunity which avarice and weakness only too often afford.

Sometimes a man is freed from punishment for a lesser crime when the offended party chooses to forgive – an act in accord with beneficence and humanity, but contrary to the public good – as if a private citizen, by an act of remission, could eliminate the need for an example, in the same way that he can waive compensation for the injury. The right to inflict punishment is a right not of an individual, but of all citizens, or of their sovereign. An individual can renounce his own portion of right, but cannot annul that of others.

As punishments become more mild, clemency and pardon become le
Happy the nation in which they might some day be considered pernicious*sary.*
therefore, that virtue which has sometimes been deemed a sufficient sub*ncy,*
sovereign for all the duties of the throne, should be excluded from perfect*y,*
where the punishments are mild and the method of judgment regular a*a*
tious. This truth will seem harsh to anyone living in the midst of the diso
criminal system, where pardons and mercy are necessary to compensate
absurdity of the laws and the severity of the sentences. This, which is in
noblest prerogative of the throne, the most desirable attribute of sovereignty,
however, the tacit disapprobation of the beneficent dispensers of public happin
a code which, with all its imperfections, has in its favour the prejudice of cen
the voluminous and imposing dowry of innumerable commentators, the we
apparatus of endless formalities, and the adherence of the most insinuating and
formidable of the semi-learned. But one ought to consider that clemency is a virtu
the legislators and not of the executors of the laws, that it ought to shine in the c
itself rather than in the particular judgments. To make men see that crimes can
pardoned or that punishment is not their necessary consequence foments a flattering
hope of impunity and creates a belief that, because they might be remitted, sentences
which are not remitted are rather acts of oppressive violence than emanations of
justice. What is to be said, then, when the ruler grants pardons, that is, public
security to a particular individual, and, with a personal act of unenlightened beneficence, constitutes a public decree of impunity? Let the laws, therefore, be inexorable,
and inexorable their executors in particular cases, but let the legislator be tender,
indulgent, and humane. Let him, a wise architect, raise his building upon the
foundation of self-love and let the general interest be the result of the interests of
each; he shall not then be constrained, by partial laws and tumultuous remedies, to
separate at every moment the public good from that of individuals, and to build the
image of public well-being upon fear and distrust. Wise and compassionate philosopher, let him permit men, his brothers, to enjoy in peace that small portion of
happiness which the grand system established by the First Cause, by that *which is,*
allows them to enjoy in this corner of the universe.
[. . .]

PROPORTION BETWEEN CRIMES AND PUNISHMENTS

It is to the common interest not only that crimes not be committed, but also that they
be less frequent in proportion to the harm they cause society. Therefore, the obstacles
that deter men from committing crimes should be stronger in proportion as they are
contrary to the public good, and as the inducements to commit them are stronger.
There must, therefore, be a proper proportion between crimes and punishments.

If pleasure and pain are the motives of sensible beings, if, among the motives for
even the sublimest acts of men, rewards and punishments were designated by the
invisible Legislator, from their inexact distribution arises the contradiction, as little
observed as it is common, that the punishments punish crimes which they themselves
have occasioned. If an equal punishment be ordained for two crimes that do not
equally injure society, men will not be any more deterred from committing the
greater crime, if they find a greater advantage associated with it.

ever sees the same death penalty, for instance, decreed for the killing of
nt and for the assassination of a man or for forgery of an important writing,
ike no distinction between such crimes, thereby destroying the moral senti-
, which are the work of many centuries and of much blood, slowly and with
difficulty registered in the human spirit, and impossible to produce, many
eve, without the aid of the most sublime of motives and of an enormous appar-
us of grave formalities.

It is impossible to prevent all disorders in the universal conflict of human
passions. They increase according to a ratio compounded of population and the
crossings of particular interests, which cannot be directed with geometric precision to
the public utility. For mathematical exactitude we must substitute, in the arithmetic
of politics, the calculation of probabilities. A glance at the histories will show that
disorders increase with the confines of empires. National sentiment declining in the
same proportion, the tendency to commit crimes increases with the increased interest
everyone takes in such disorders; thus there is a constantly increasing need to make
punishments heavier.

That force, similar to gravity, which impels us to seek our own well-being is
restrained in its operation only to the extent that obstacles are set up against it. The
effects of this force are the confused series of human actions. If these clash together
and disturb one another, punishments, which I would call 'political obstacles', prevent the bad effect without destroying the impelling cause, which is that sensibility
inseparable from man. And the legislator acts then like an able architect whose
function it is to check the destructive tendencies of gravity and to align correctly
those that contribute to the strength of the building.

Given the necessity of human association, given the pacts that result from the
very opposition of private interests, a scale of disorders is distinguishable, the first
grade consisting of those that are immediately destructive of society, and the last, of
those that do the least possible injustice to its individual members. Between these
extremes are included all the actions contrary to the public good that are called
crimes, and they all descend by insensible gradations from the highest to the lowest. If
geometry were applicable to the infinite and obscure combinations of human actions,
there ought to be a corresponding scale of punishments, descending from the greatest
to the least; if there were an exact and universal scale of punishments and of crimes,
we would have a fairly reliable and common measure of the degrees of tyranny and
liberty, of the fund of humanity or of malice, of the various nations. But it is enough
for the wise legislator to mark the principal points of division without disturbing the
order, not assigning to crimes of the first grade the punishments of the last.
[. . .]

HOW TO PREVENT CRIMES

It is better to prevent crimes than to punish them. This is the ultimate end of every
good legislation, which, to use the general terms for assessing the good and evils of
life, is the art of leading men to the greatest possible happiness or to the least possible
unhappiness.

But heretofore, the means employed have been false and contrary to the end
proposed. It is impossible to reduce the turbulent activity of mankind to a geometric

order, without any irregularity and confusion. As the constant and very simple laws of nature do not impede the planets from disturbing one another in their movements, so in the infinite and very contrary attractions of pleasure and pain, disturbances and disorder cannot be impeded by human laws. And yet this is the chimera of narrow-minded men when they have power in their grasp. To prohibit a multitude of indifferent acts is not to prevent crimes that might arise from them, but is rather to create new ones; it is to define by whim the ideas of virtue and vice which are preached to us as eternal and immutable. To what should we be reduced if everything were forbidden us that might induce us to crime! It would be necessary to deprive man of the use of his senses. For one motive that drives men to commit a real crime there are a thousand that drive them to commit those indifferent acts which are called crimes by bad laws; and if the probability of crimes is proportionate to the number of motives, to enlarge the sphere of crimes is to increase the probability of their being committed. The majority of the laws are nothing but privileges, that is, a tribute paid by all to the convenience of some few.

Do you want to prevent crimes? See to it that the laws are clear and simple and that the entire force of a nation is united in their defence, and that no part of it is employed to destroy them. See to it that the laws favour not so much classes of men as men themselves. See to it that men fear the laws and fear nothing else. For fear of the laws is salutary, but fatal and fertile for crimes is one man's fear of another. Enslaved men are more voluptuous, more depraved, more cruel than free men. These study the sciences, give thought to the interests of their country, contemplate grand objects and imitate them, while enslaved men, content with the present moment, seek in the excitement of debauchery a distraction from the emptiness of the condition in which they find themselves. Accustomed to an uncertainty of outcome in all things, the outcome of their crimes remains for them problematical, to the advantage of the passions that determine them. If uncertainty regarding the laws befalls a nation which is indolent because of climate, its indolence and stupidity are confirmed and increased; if it befalls a voluptuous but energetic nation, the result is a wasteful diffusion of energy into an infinite number of little cabals and intrigues that sow distrust in every heart, make treachery and dissimulation the foundation of prudence; if it befalls a brave and powerful nation, the uncertainty is removed finally, but only after having caused many oscillations from liberty to slavery and from slavery back to liberty.

Do you want to prevent crimes? See to it that enlightenment accompanies liberty. Knowledge breeds evils in inverse ratio to its diffusion, and benefits in direct ratio. A daring impostor, who is never a common man, is received with adorations by an ignorant people, and with hisses by an enlightened one. Knowledge, by facilitating comparisons and by multiplying points of view, brings on a mutual modification of conflicting feelings, especially when it appears that others hold the same views and face the same difficulties. In the face of enlightenment widely diffused throughout the nation, the calumnies of ignorance are silenced and authority trembles if it be not armed with reason. The vigorous force of the laws, meanwhile, remains immovable, for no enlightened person can fail to approve of the clear and useful public compacts of mutual security when he compares the inconsiderable portion of useless liberty he himself has sacrificed with the sum total of liberties sacrificed by other men, which, except for the laws, might have been turned against him. Any person of sensibility, glancing over a code of well-made laws and observing that he has lost only a baneful liberty to injure others, will feel constrained to bless the throne and its occupant.

[. . .]

Another way of preventing crimes is to direct the interest of the magistracy as a whole to observance rather than corruption of the laws. The greater the number of magistrates, the less dangerous is the abuse of legal power; venality is more difficult among men who observe one another, and their interest in increasing their personal authority diminishes as the portion that would fall to each is less, especially in comparison with the danger involved in the undertaking. If the sovereign, with his apparatus and pomp, with the severity of his edicts, with the permission he grants for unjust as well as just claims to be advanced by anyone who thinks himself oppressed, accustoms his subjects to fear magistrates more than the laws, [the magistrates] will profit more from this fear than personal and public security will gain from it.

Another way of preventing crimes is to reward virtue. Upon this subject I notice a general silence in the laws of all the nations of our day. If the prizes offered by the academies to discoverers of useful truths have increased our knowledge and have multiplied good books, why should not prizes distributed by the beneficent hand of the sovereign serve in a similar way to multiply virtuous actions? The coin of honour is always inexhaustible and fruitful in the hands of the wise distributor.

Finally, the surest but most difficult way to prevent crimes is by perfecting education – a subject much too vast and exceeding the limits I have prescribed for myself, a subject, I venture also to say, too intimately involved with the nature of government for it ever to be, even in the far-off happy ages of society, anything more than a barren field, only here and there cultivated by a few sages. A great man, who enlightens the world that persecutes him, has indicated plainly and in detail what principal maxims of education are truly useful to men: they are, that it should consist less in a barren multiplicity of things than in a selection and precise definition of them; in substituting originals for the copies of the moral as well as physical phenomena which chance or wilful activity may present to the fresh minds of youths; in leading them toward virtue by the easy way of feeling, and in directing them away from evil by the infallible one of necessity and inconvenience, instead of by the uncertain means of command which obtains only simulated and momentary obedience.

CONCLUSION

From what has thus far been demonstrated, one may deduce a general theorem of considerable utility, though hardly conformable with custom, the usual legislator of nations; it is this: *In order for punishment not to be, in every instance, an act of violence of one or of many against a private citizen, it must be essentially public, prompt, necessary, the least possible in the given circumstances, proportionate to the crimes, dictated by the laws.*

As punishments become more mild, clemency and pardon become less necessary. Happy the nation in which they might some day be considered pernicious! Clemency, therefore, that virtue which has sometimes been deemed a sufficient substitute in a sovereign for all the duties of the throne, should be excluded from perfect legislation, where the punishments are mild and the method of judgment regular and expeditious. This truth will seem harsh to anyone living in the midst of the disorders of a criminal system, where pardons and mercy are necessary to compensate for the absurdity of the laws and the severity of the sentences. This, which is indeed the noblest prerogative of the throne, the most desirable attribute of sovereignty, is also, however, the tacit disapprobation of the beneficent dispensers of public happiness for a code which, with all its imperfections, has in its favour the prejudice of centuries, the voluminous and imposing dowry of innumerable commentators, the weighty apparatus of endless formalities, and the adherence of the most insinuating and least formidable of the semi-learned. But one ought to consider that clemency is a virtue of the legislators and not of the executors of the laws, that it ought to shine in the code itself rather than in the particular judgments. To make men see that crimes can be pardoned or that punishment is not their necessary consequence foments a flattering hope of impunity and creates a belief that, because they might be remitted, sentences which are not remitted are rather acts of oppressive violence than emanations of justice. What is to be said, then, when the ruler grants pardons, that is, public security to a particular individual, and, with a personal act of unenlightened beneficence, constitutes a public decree of impunity? Let the laws, therefore, be inexorable, and inexorable their executors in particular cases, but let the legislator be tender, indulgent, and humane. Let him, a wise architect, raise his building upon the foundation of self-love and let the general interest be the result of the interests of each; he shall not then be constrained, by partial laws and tumultuous remedies, to separate at every moment the public good from that of individuals, and to build the image of public well-being upon fear and distrust. Wise and compassionate philosopher, let him permit men, his brothers, to enjoy in peace that small portion of happiness which the grand system established by the First Cause, by that *which is*, allows them to enjoy in this corner of the universe.

[. . .]

PROPORTION BETWEEN CRIMES AND PUNISHMENTS

It is to the common interest not only that crimes not be committed, but also that they be less frequent in proportion to the harm they cause society. Therefore, the obstacles that deter men from committing crimes should be stronger in proportion as they are contrary to the public good, and as the inducements to commit them are stronger. There must, therefore, be a proper proportion between crimes and punishments.

If pleasure and pain are the motives of sensible beings, if, among the motives for even the sublimest acts of men, rewards and punishments were designated by the invisible Legislator, from their inexact distribution arises the contradiction, as little observed as it is common, that the punishments punish crimes which they themselves have occasioned. If an equal punishment be ordained for two crimes that do not equally injure society, men will not be any more deterred from committing the greater crime, if they find a greater advantage associated with it.

Whoever sees the same death penalty, for instance, decreed for the killing of a pheasant and for the assassination of a man or for forgery of an important writing, will make no distinction between such crimes, thereby destroying the moral sentiments, which are the work of many centuries and of much blood, slowly and with great difficulty registered in the human spirit, and impossible to produce, many believe, without the aid of the most sublime of motives and of an enormous apparatus of grave formalities.

It is impossible to prevent all disorders in the universal conflict of human passions. They increase according to a ratio compounded of population and the crossings of particular interests, which cannot be directed with geometric precision to the public utility. For mathematical exactitude we must substitute, in the arithmetic of politics, the calculation of probabilities. A glance at the histories will show that disorders increase with the confines of empires. National sentiment declining in the same proportion, the tendency to commit crimes increases with the increased interest everyone takes in such disorders; thus there is a constantly increasing need to make punishments heavier.

That force, similar to gravity, which impels us to seek our own well-being is restrained in its operation only to the extent that obstacles are set up against it. The effects of this force are the confused series of human actions. If these clash together and disturb one another, punishments, which I would call 'political obstacles', prevent the bad effect without destroying the impelling cause, which is that sensibility inseparable from man. And the legislator acts then like an able architect whose function it is to check the destructive tendencies of gravity and to align correctly those that contribute to the strength of the building.

Given the necessity of human association, given the pacts that result from the very opposition of private interests, a scale of disorders is distinguishable, the first grade consisting of those that are immediately destructive of society, and the last, of those that do the least possible injustice to its individual members. Between these extremes are included all the actions contrary to the public good that are called crimes, and they all descend by insensible gradations from the highest to the lowest. If geometry were applicable to the infinite and obscure combinations of human actions, there ought to be a corresponding scale of punishments, descending from the greatest to the least; if there were an exact and universal scale of punishments and of crimes, we would have a fairly reliable and common measure of the degrees of tyranny and liberty, of the fund of humanity or of malice, of the various nations. But it is enough for the wise legislator to mark the principal points of division without disturbing the order, not assigning to crimes of the first grade the punishments of the last.
[. . .]

HOW TO PREVENT CRIMES

It is better to prevent crimes than to punish them. This is the ultimate end of every good legislation, which, to use the general terms for assessing the good and evils of life, is the art of leading men to the greatest possible happiness or to the least possible unhappiness.

But heretofore, the means employed have been false and contrary to the end proposed. It is impossible to reduce the turbulent activity of mankind to a geometric

2

Panopticon, or, the inspection-house, &C.

Jeremy Bentham

[. . .]

LETTER I

Idea of the inspection principle

[. . .]
 . . . It will be found applicable, I think, without exception, to all establishments whatsoever, in which, within a space not too large to be covered or commanded by buildings, a number of persons are meant to be kept under inspection. No matter how different, or even opposite the purpose: whether it be that of *punishing the incorrigible, guarding the insane, reforming the vicious, confining the suspected, employing the idle, maintaining the helpless, curing the sick, instructing the willing* in any branch of industry, or *training the rising race* in the path of *education*: in a word, whether it be applied to the purposes of *perpetual prisons* in the room of death, or *prisons for confinement* before trial, or *penitentiary-houses*, or *houses of correction*, or *work-houses*, or *manufactories*, or *mad-houses*, or *hospitals*, or *schools*.

It is obvious that, in all these instances, the more constantly the persons to be inspected are under the eyes of the persons who should inspect them, the more perfectly will the purpose of the establishment have been attained. Ideal perfection, if that were the object, would require that each person should actually be in that predicament, during every instant of time. This being impossible, the next thing to be wished for is, that, at every instant, seeing reason to believe as much, and not being able to satisfy himself to the contrary, he should *conceive* himself to be so [. . .]

LETTER II

Plan for a penitentiary inspection-house

Before you look at the plan, take in words the general idea of it.
 The building is circular.

The apartments of the prisoners occupy the circumference. You may call them, if you please, the *cells*.

These *cells* are divided from one another, and the prisoners by that means secluded from all communication with each other, by *partitions* in the form of *radii* issuing from the circumference towards the centre, and extending as many feet as shall be thought necessary to form the largest dimension of the cell.

The apartment of the inspector occupies the centre; you may call it if you please the *inspector's lodge*.

It will be convenient in most, if not in all cases, to have a vacant space or *area* all round, between such centre and such circumference. You may call if it you please the *intermediate* or *annular* area.

About the width of a cell may be sufficient for a *passage* from the outside of the building to the lodge.

Each cell has in the outward circumference, a *window*, large enough, not only to light the cell, but, through the cell, to afford light enough to the correspondent part of the lodge.

The inner circumference of the cell is formed by an iron *grating*, so light as not to screen any part of the cell from the inspector's view.

Of this grating, a part sufficiently large opens, in form of a *door*, to admit the prisoner at his first entrance; and to give admission at any time to the inspector or any of his attendants.

To cut off from each prisoner the view of every other, the partitions are carried on a few feet beyond the grating into the intermediate area: such projecting parts I call the *protracted partitions*.

It is conceived, that the light, coming in in this manner through the cells, and so across the intermediate area, will be sufficient for the inspector's lodge. But, for this purpose, both the windows in the cells, and those corresponding to them in the lodge, should be as large as the strength of the building, and what shall be deemed a necessary attention to economy, will permit.

To the windows of the lodge there are *blinds*, as high up as the eyes of the prisoners in their cells can, by any means they can employ, be made to reach.

To prevent *thorough light*, whereby, notwithstanding the blinds, the prisoners would see from the cells whether or not any person was in the lodge, that apartment is divided into quarters, by *partitions* formed by two diameters to the circle, crossing each other at right angles. For these partitions the thinnest materials might serve; and they might be made removable at pleasure; their height, sufficient to prevent the prisoners seeing over them from the cells. Doors to these partitions, if left open at any time, might produce the thorough light. To prevent this, divide each partition into two, at any part required, setting down the one-half at such distance from the other as shall be equal to the aperture of a door.

These windows of the inspector's lodge open into the intermediate area, in the form of *doors*, in as many places as shall be deemed necessary to admit of his communicating readily with any of the cells.

Small *lamps*, in the outside of each window of the lodge, backed by a reflector, to throw the light into the corresponding cells, would extend to the night the security of the day.

To save the troublesome exertion of voice that might otherwise be necessary, and to prevent one prisoner from knowing that the inspector was occupied by another prisoner at a distance, a small *tin tube* might reach from each cell to the inspector's lodge, passing across the area, and so in at the side of the correspondent window of the lodge. By means of this implement, the slightest whisper of the one might be heard by the other, especially if he had proper notice to apply his ear to the tube.

With regard to *instruction*, in cases where it cannot be duly given without the instructor's being close to the work, or without setting his hand to it by way of example before the learner's face, the instructor must indeed here as elsewhere, shift his station as often as there is occasion to visit different workmen; unless he calls the workmen to him, which in some of the instances to which this sort of building is applicable, such as that of imprisoned felons, could not so well be. But in all cases where directions, given verbally and at a distance, are sufficient, these tubes will be found of use. They will save, on the one hand, the exertion of voice it would require, on the part of the instructor, to communicate instruction to the workmen without quitting his central station in the lodge; and, on the other, the confusion which would ensue if different instructors or persons in the lodge were calling to the cells at the same time. And, in the case of hospitals, the quiet that may be insured by this little contrivance, trifling as it may seem at first sight, affords an additional advantage.

A *bell*, appropriated exclusively to the purposes of *alarm*, hangs in a *belfry* with which the building is crowned, communicating by a rope with the inspector's lodge.

The most economical, and perhaps the most convenient, way of *warming* the cells and area, would be by flues surrounding it, upon the principle of those in hot-houses. A total want of every means of producing artificial heat might, in such weather as we sometimes have in England, be fatal to the lives of the prisoners; at any rate, it would often times be altogether incompatible with their working at any sedentary employment. The flues, however, and the fire-places belonging to them, instead of being on the outside, as in hot-houses, should be in the inside. By this means, there would be less waste of heat, and the current of air that would rush in on all sides through the cells, to supply the draught made by the fires, would answer so far the purpose of ventilation. . . .

[. . .]

LETTER V

Essential points of the plan

It may be of use, that among all the particulars you have seen, it should be clearly understood what circumstances are, and what are not, essential to the plan. The essence of it consists, then, in the *centrality* of the inspector's situation, combined with the well-known and most effectual contrivances for *seeing without being seen*. As to the *general form* of the building, the most commodious for most purposes seems to be the circular: but this is not an absolutely essential circumstance. Of all figures, however, this, you will observe, is the only one that affords a perfect view, and the same view, of an indefinite number of apartments of the same dimensions: that affords a spot from which, without any change of situation, a man may survey, in the same perfection, the whole number, and without so much as a change of posture, the half of the whole number, at the same time: that, within a boundary of a given extent, contains the greatest quantity of room: – that places the centre at the least distance from the light: – that gives the cells most width, at the part where, on account of the light, most light may, for the purposes of work, be wanted: – and that reduces to the greatest possible shortness the path taken by the inspector, in passing from each part of the field of inspection to every other.

You will please to observe, that though perhaps it is the most important point, that the persons to be inspected should always feel themselves as if under inspection, at least as standing a great chance of being so, yet it is not by any means the *only* one. If it were, the same advantage might be given to buildings of almost any form. What is also of importance is, that for the greatest proportion of time possible, each man should actually *be* under inspection. This is material in *all* cases, that the inspector may have the satisfaction of knowing, that the discipline actually has the effect which it is designed to have: and it is more particularly material in such cases where the inspector, besides seeing that they conform to such standing rules as are prescribed, has more or less frequent occasion to give them such transient and incidental directions as will require to be given and enforced, at the commencement at least of every course of industry. And I think, it needs not much argument to prove, that the business of inspection, like every other, will be performed to a greater degree of perfection, the less trouble the performance of it requires.

Not only so, but the greater chance there is, of a given person's being at a given time actually under inspection, the more strong will be the persuasion – the more *intense*, if I may say so, the *feeling*, he has of his being so. How little turn soever the greater number of persons so circumstanced may be supposed to have for calculation, some rough sort of calculation can scarcely, under such circumstances, avoid forcing itself upon the rudest mind. Experiment, venturing first upon slight transgressions, and so on, in proportion to success, upon more and more considerable ones, will not fail to teach him the difference between a loose inspection and a strict one.

It is for these reasons, that I cannot help looking upon every form as less and less eligible, in proportion as it deviates from the *circular*.

A very material point is, that room be allotted to the lodge, sufficient to adapt it to the purpose of a complete and constant habitation for the principal inspector or head-keeper, and his family. The more numerous also the family, the better; since, by this means, there will in fact be as many inspectors, as the family consists of persons, though only one be paid for it. Neither the orders of the inspector himself, not any interest which they may feel, or not feel, in the regular performance of his duty, would be requisite to find them motives adequate to the purpose. Secluded oftentimes, by their situation, from every other object, they will naturally, and in a manner unavoidably, give their eyes a direction conformable to that purpose, in every momentary interval of their ordinary occupations. It will supply in their instance the place of that great and constant fund of entertainment to the sedentary and vacant in towns – the looking out of the window. The scene, though a confined, would be a very various, and therefore, perhaps, not altogether an unamusing one.

LETTER VI

Advantages of the plan

I flatter myself there can now be little doubt of the plan's possessing the fundamental advantages I have been attributing to it: I mean, the *apparent omnipresence* of the inspector (if divines will allow me the expression,) combined with the extreme facility of his *real presence*.

A collateral advantage it possesses, and on the score of frugality a very material one, is that which respects the *number* of the inspectors requisite. If this plan required more than another, the additional number would form an objection, which, were the difference to a certain degree considerable, might rise so high as to be conclusive: so far from it, that a greater multitude than ever were yet lodged in one house might be inspected by a single person; for the trouble of inspection is diminished in no less proportion than the strictness of inspection is increased.

Another very important advantage, whatever purposes the plan may be applied to, particularly where it is applied to the severest and most coercive purposes, is, that the *under* keepers or inspectors, the servants and subordinates of every kind, will be under the same irresistible controul with respect to the *head* keeper or inspector, as the prisoners or other persons to be governed are with respect to *them*. On the common plans, what means, what possibility, has the prisoner of appealing to the humanity of the principal for redress against the neglect or oppression of subordinates in that rigid sphere, but the *few* opportunities which, in a crowded prison, the most conscientious keeper *can* afford – but the none at all which many a keeper *thinks* fit to give them? How different would their lot be upon this plan!

In no instance could his subordinates either perform or depart from their duty, but he must know the time and degree and manner of their doing so. It presents an answer, and that a satisfactory one, to one of the most puzzling of political questions – *quis custodiet ipsos custodes?* And, as the fulfilling of his, as well as their, duty would be rendered so much easier, than it can ever have been hitherto, so might, and so should, any departure from it be punished with the more inflexible severity. It is this circumstance that renders the influence of this plan not less beneficial to what is called *liberty*, than to necessary coercion; not less powerful as a controul upon subordinate power, than as a curb to delinquency; as a shield to innocence, than as a scourge to guilt.

Another advantage, still operating to the same ends, is the great load of trouble and disgust which it takes off the shoulders of those occasional inspectors of a high order, such as *judges* and other *magistrates*, who, called down to this irksome task from the superior ranks of life, cannot but feel a proportionable repugnance to the discharge of it. Think how it is with them upon the present plans, and how it still must be upon the best plans that have been hitherto devised! The cells or apartments, however constructed, must, if there be nine hundred of them (as there were to have been upon the penitentiary-house plan,) be opened to the visitors, one by one. To do their business to any purpose, they must approach near to, and come almost in contact with each inhabitant; whose situation being watched over according to no other than the loose methods of inspection at present practicable, will on that account require the more minute and troublesome investigation on the part of these occasional superintendents. By this new plan, the disgust is entirely removed, and the trouble of going into such a room as the lodge, is no more than the trouble of going into any other.

Were *Newgate* upon this plan, all Newgate might be inspected by a quarter of an hour's visit to Mr. Akerman.

Among the other causes of that reluctance, none at present so forcible, none so unhappily well grounded, none which affords so natural an excuse, nor so strong a reason against accepting of any excuse, as the danger of *infection* – a circumstance which carries death, in one of its most tremendous forms, from the seat of guilt to the seat of justice, involving in one common catastrophe the violator and the upholder of the laws. But in a spot so constructed, and under a course of discipline so insured, how should infection ever arise? or how should it continue? Against every danger of this kind, what private house of the poor, one might almost say, or even of the most opulent, can be equally secure?

Nor is the disagreeableness of the task of superintendence diminished by this plan, in a much greater degree than the efficacy of it is increased. On all others, be the superintendent's visit ever so unexpected, and his motions ever so quick, time there must always be for preparations blinding the real state of things. Out of nine hundred cells, he can visit but one at a time, and, in the meanwhile, the worst of the others may be arranged, and the inhabitants threatened, and tutored how to receive him. On this plan, no sooner is the superintendent announced, than the whole scene opens instantaneously to his view.

In mentioning inspectors and superintendents who are such by office, I must not overlook that system of inspection, which, however little heeded, will not be the less useful and efficacious: I mean, the part which individuals may be disposed to take in the business, without intending, perhaps, or even without thinking of, any other effects of their visits, than the gratification of their own particular curiosity. What the inspector's or keeper's family are with respect to *him*, that, and more, will these spontaneous visitors be to the superintendent, – assistants, deputies, in so far as he is faithful, witnesses and judges should he ever be unfaithful, to his trust. So as they are but there, what the motives were that drew them thither is perfectly immaterial; whether the relieving of their anxieties by the affecting prospect of their respective friends and relatives thus detained in durance, or merely the satisfying that general curiosity, which an establishment, on various accounts so interesting to human feelings, may naturally be expected to excite.

You see, I take for granted as a matter of course, that under the necessary regulations for preventing interruption and disturbance, the doors of these establishments will be, as, without very special reasons to the contrary, the doors of all public establishments ought to be, thrown wide open to the body of the curious at large – the great *open committee* of the tribunal of the world. And who ever objects to such publicity, where it is practicable, but those whose motives for objection afford the strongest reasons for it?

[. . .]

I hope no critic of more learning than candour will do an inspection-house so much injustice as to compare it to *Dionysius' ear*. The object of that contrivance was, to know what prisoners said without their suspecting any such thing. The object of the inspection principle is directly the reverse: it is to make them not only *suspect*, but be *assured*, that whatever they do is known, even though that should not be the case. Detection is the object of the first: *prevention*, that of the latter. In the former case the ruling person is a spy; in the latter he is a monitor. The object of the first was to pry into the secret recesses of the heart; the latter, confirming its attention to *overt acts*, leaves thoughts and fancies to their proper *ordinary*, the court *above*.

When I consider the extensive variety of purposes to which this principle may be applied, and the certain efficacy which, as far as I can trust my own conceptions, it

promises to them all, my wonder is, not only that this plan should never have hitherto been put in practice, but how any other should ever have been thought of . . .
[. . .]
What would you say, if by the gradual adoption and diversified application of this single principle, you should see a new scene of things spread itself over the face of civilized society? – morals reformed, health preserved, industry invigorated, instruction diffused, public burthens lightened, economy seated as it were upon a rock, the gordian knot of the poor-laws not cut but untied – all by a simple idea in architecture?

3

Of the development of the propensity to crime

Adolphe Quetelet

OF CRIMES IN GENERAL, AND OF THE REPRESSION OF THEM

Supposing men to be placed in similar circumstances, I call the greater or less probability of committing crime, the *propensity to crime*. My object is more especially to investigate the influence of season, climate, sex, and age, on this propensity.

I have said that the circumstances in which men are placed ought to be similar, that is to say, equally favourable, both in the existence of objects likely to excite the propensity and in the facility of committing the crime. It is not enough that a man may merely have the intention to do evil, he must also have the opportunity and the means. Thus the propensity to crime may be the same in France as in England, without, on that account, the *morality* of the nations being the same. I think this distinction of importance.

There is still another important distinction to be made; namely, that two individuals may have the same propensity to crime, without being equally *criminal*, if one, for example, were inclined to theft, and the other to assassination.

Lastly, [. . .] our observations can only refer to a *certain number of known and tried offences, out of the unknown sum total of crimes committed.* Since this sum total of crimes committed will probably ever continue unknown, all the reasoning of which it is the basis will be more or less defective. I do not hesitate to say, that all the knowledge which we possess on the statistics of crimes and offences will be of no utility whatever, unless we admit without question that *there is a ratio, nearly invariably the same, between known and tried offences and the unknown sum total of crimes committed.* This ratio is necessary, and if it did not really exist, every thing which, until the present time, has been said on the statistical documents of crime, would be false and absurd. We are aware, then, how important it is to legitimate such a ratio, and we may be astonished that this has not been done before now. The ratio of which we speak necessarily varies according to the nature and seriousness of the crimes: in a well-organized society,

From *A Treatise on Man*, pp. 82–96; 103–8. (Edinburgh: Chambers, 1842.)

where the police is active and justice is rightly administered, this ratio, for murders and assassinations, will be nearly equal to unity; that is to say, no individual will disappear from the society by murder or assassination, without its being known: this will not be precisely the case with poisonings. When we look to thefts and offences of smaller importance, the ratio will become very small, and a great number of offences will remain unknown, either because those against whom they are committed do not perceive them, or do not wish to prosecute the perpetrators, or because justice itself has not sufficient evidence to act upon. Thus, the greatness of this ratio, which will generally be different for different crimes and offences, will chiefly depend on the activity of justice in reaching the guilty, on the care with which the latter conceal themselves, on the repugnance which the individuals injured may have to complain, or perhaps on their not knowing that any injury has been committed against them. Now, if all the causes which influence the magnitude of the ratio remain the same, we may also assert that the effects will remain invariable. This result is confirmed in a curious manner by induction, and observing the surprising constancy with which the numbers of the statistics of crime are reproduced annually – a constancy which, no doubt, will be also reproduced in the numbers at which we cannot arrive: thus, although we do not know the criminals who escape justice, we very well know that every year between 7,000 and 7,300 persons are brought before the criminal courts, and that 61 are regularly condemned out of every 100; that 170,000 nearly are brought before courts of correction, and that 85 out of 100 are condemned; and that, if we pass to details, we find a no less alarming regularity; thus we find that between 100 and 150 individuals are annually condemned to death, 280 condemned to perpetual hard labour, 1,050 to hard labour for a time, 1,220 to solitary confinement (*à la réclusion*), etc.; so that this budget of the scaffold and the prisons is discharged by the French nation, with much greater regularity, no doubt, than the financial budget; and we might say, that what annually escapes the minister of justice is a more regular sum than the deficiency of revenue to the treasury.

I shall commence by considering, in a general manner, the propensity to crime in France, availing myself of the excellent documents contained in the *Comptes Généraux de l'Administration de la Justice* of this country; I shall afterwards endeavour to establish some comparisons with other countries, but with all the care and reserve which such comparisons require.

During the four years preceding 1830, 28,686 accused persons were set down as appearing before the courts of assize, that is to say, 7,171 individuals annually nearly; which gives 1 accused person to 4,463 inhabitants, taking the population at 32,000,000 souls. Moreover, of 100 accused, 61 persons have been condemned to punishments of greater or less severity. From the remarks made above with respect to the crimes which remain unknown or unpunished, and from mistakes which justice may make, we conceive that these numbers, although they furnish us with curious data for the past, do not give us any thing exact on the propensity to crime. However, if we consider that the two ratios which we have calculated have not sensibly varied from year to year, we shall be led to believe that they will not vary in a sensible manner for the succeeding years; and the probability that this variation will not take place is so much the greater, according as, all things being equal, the mean results of each year do not differ much from the general average, and these results have been taken from a great number of years.

After these remarks, it becomes very probable that, for a Frenchman, there is 1 against 4,462 chances that he will be an accused person during the course of the year; moreover, there are 61 to 39 chances, very nearly, that he will be condemned at the time that he is accused. These results are justified by the numbers of the following table [Table 2.1]:

[Table 2.1]

Years	Accused persons present	Condemned persons	Inhabitants to one accused person	Condemned in 100 accused persons	Accused of crimes against		Ratio between the numbers of the two kinds of crime
					Persons	Property	
1826	6,988	4,348	4,557	62	1,907	5,081	2.7
1827	6,929	4,236	4,593	61	1,911	5,018	2.6
1828	7,396	4,551	4,307	61	1,844	5,552	3.0
1829	7,373	4,475	4,521	61	1,791	5,582	3.1
Total	28,686	17,610	4,463	61	7,453	21,233	2.8

Thus, although we do not yet know the statistical documents for 1830, it is very probable that we shall again have 1 accused person in 4,463 very nearly, and 61 condemned in 100 accused persons; this probability is somewhat diminished for the year 1831, and still more for the succeeding years. We may, therefore, by the results of the past, estimate what will be realized in the future. This possibility of assigning beforehand the number of accused and condemned persons which any country will present, must give rise to serious reflections, since it concerns the fate of several thousand men, who are driven, as it were, in an irresistible manner, towards the tribunals, and the condemnations which await them.

These conclusions are deduced from the principle [. . .] that effects are proportionate to their causes, and that the effects remain the same, if the causes which have produced them do not vary. If France, then, in the year 1830, had not undergone any apparent change, and if, contrary to my expectation, I found a sensible difference between the two ratios calculated beforehand for this year and the real ratios observed, I should conclude that some alteration had taken place in the causes, which had escaped my attention. On the other hand, if the state of France has changed, and if, consequently, the causes which influence the propensity to crime have also undergone some change, I ought to expect to find an alteration in the two ratios which until that time remained nearly the same.

It is proper to observe, that the preceding numbers only show, strictly speaking, the probability of being accused and afterwards condemned, without rendering us able to determine any thing very precise on the degree of the propensity to crime; at least unless we admit, what is very likely, that justice preserves the same activity, and the number of guilty persons who escape it preserves the same proportion from year to year.

In the latter columns of the preceding table [Table 2.1], is first made the distinction between crimes against persons and crimes against property: it will be remarked, no doubt, that the number of the former has diminished, whilst the latter has increased; however, these variations are so small, that they do not sensibly affect the annual ratio; and we see that we ought to reckon that three persons are accused of crimes against property to one for crimes against person.

[. . .]

OF THE INFLUENCE OF KNOWLEDGE, OF PROFESSIONS [. . .] ON THE PROPENSITY TO CRIME

It may be interesting to examine the influence of the intellectual state of the accused on the nature of crimes: the French documents on this subject are such, that I am enabled to form the following table [Table 2.2] for the years 1828 and 1829; to this table I have annexed the results of the years 1830 and 1831, which were not known when the reflections which succeed were written down.

[Table 2.2]

Intellectual state of the persons accused	1828–9: accused of crimes against		Ratio of crimes against property to crimes against persons	1830–1: accused of crimes against		Ratio of crimes against property to crimes against Persons
	Persons	Property		Persons	Property	
Could not read or write	2,072	6,617	3.2	2,134	6,785	3.1
Could read and write but imperfectly	1,001	2,804	2.8	1,033	2,840	2.8
Could read and write well	400	1,109	2.8	408	1,047	2.6
Had received a superior education to this 1st degree	80	206	2.6	135	184	1.4
	3,553	10,736	3.0 aver.	3,710	10,856	2.9 aver.

Thus, all things being equal, the number of crimes against persons, *compared with the number of crimes against property*, during the years 1828 and 1829, was greater according as the intellectual state of the accused was more highly developed; and this difference bore especially on murders, rapes, assassinations, blows, wounds, and other severe crimes. Must we thence conclude that knowledge is injurious to society? I am far from thinking so. To establish such an assertion, it would be necessary to commence by ascertaining how many individuals of the French nation belong to each of the four divisions which we have made above, and to find out if, proportion being considered, the individuals of that one of the divisions commit as many crimes as those of the others. If this were really the case, I should not hesitate to say that, since the most enlightened individuals commit as many crimes as those who have had less education, and since their crimes are more serious, they are necessarily more criminal; but from the little we know of the diffusion of knowledge in France, we cannot state any thing decisively on this point. Indeed, it may so happen, that individuals of the enlightened

part of society, while committing fewer murders, assassinations, and other severe crimes, than individuals who have received no education, also commit much fewer crimes against property, and this would explain what we have remarked in the preceding numbers. This conjecture even becomes probable, when we consider that the enlightened classes are presupposed to possess more affluence, and consequently are less frequently under the necessity of having recourse to the different modes of theft, of which crimes against property almost entirely consist; whilst affluence and knowledge have not an equal power in subduing the fire of the passions and sentiments of hatred and vengeance. It must be remarked, on the other hand, that the results contained in the preceding table only belong to two years, and consequently present a smaller probability of expressing what really is the case, especially those results connected with the most enlightened class, and which are based on very small numbers. It seems to me, then, that at the most we can only say that the ratio of the number of crimes against persons to the number of crimes against property varies with the degree of knowledge; and generally, for 100 crimes against persons, we may reckon fewer crimes against property, according as the individuals belong to a class of greater or less enlightenment.
[. . .]

The following details, which I extract from the *Rapport au Roi* for the year 1829, will serve to illustrate what I advance:

'The new table, which points out the professions of the accused, divides them into nine principal classes, comprising,

The *first*, individuals who work on the land, in vineyards, forests, mines, etc., 2,453.

The *second*, workmen engaged with wood, leather, iron, cotton, etc., 1,932.

The *third*, bakers, butchers, brewers, millers, etc., 253.

The *fourth*, hatters, hairdressers, tailors, upholsterers, etc., 327.

The *fifth*, bankers, agents, wholesale and retail merchants, hawkers, etc., 467.

The *sixth*, contractors, porters, seamen, waggoners, etc., 289.

The *seventh*, innkeepers, lemonade-sellers, servants, etc., 830.

The *eighth*, artists, students, clerks, bailiffs, notaries, advocates, priests, physicians, soldiers, annuitants, etc., 449.

The *ninth*, beggars, smugglers, strumpets, etc., 373.

Women who had no profession have been classed in those which their husbands pursued.

Comparing those who are included in each class with the total number of the accused, we see that the first furnishes 33 out of 100; the second, 26; the third, 4; the fourth, 5; the fifth, 6; the sixth, 4; the seventh, 11; the eighth, 6; the ninth, 5.

If, after that, we point out the accused in each class, according to the nature of their imputed crimes, and compare them with each other, we find the following proportions:

In the first class, 32 of the 100 accused were tried for crimes against persons, and 68 for crimes against property. These numbers are 21 and 79 for the second class; 22 and 78 for the third; 15 and 85 for the fourth and fifth; 26 and 74 for the sixth; 16 and 84 for the seventh; 37 and 63 for the eighth; 13 and 87 for the ninth.

Thus, the accused of the eighth class, who all exercised liberal professions, or enjoyed a fortune which presupposes some education, are those who, relatively, have committed the greatest number of crimes against persons; whilst 87-hundredths of the accused of the ninth class, composed of people without character, have scarcely attacked any thing but property.'

These results, which confirm the remark made before, deserve to be taken into consideration. I shall observe that, when we divide individuals into two classes, the one of liberal professions, and the other composed of journeymen, workmen, and servants, the difference is rendered still more conspicuous.

[. . .]

ON THE INFLUENCE OF SEASONS ON THE PROPENSITY TO CRIME

The seasons have a well-marked influence in augmenting and diminishing the number of crimes. We may form some idea from the following table [Table 2.3], which contains the number of crimes committed in France against persons and property, during each month, for three years, as well as the ratio of these numbers. We can also compare the numbers of this table with those which I have given to show the influence of seasons on the development of mental alienation, and we shall find the most remarkable coincidences, especially for crimes against persons, which would appear to be most usually dependent on failures of the reasoning powers:

[Table 2.3]

Months	Crimes against		Ratio: 1827–28	Crimes against		Ratio 1830–31
	Persons	Property		Persons	Property	
January	282	1,095	3.89	189	666	3.52
February	272	910	3.35	194	563	2.90
March	335	968	2.89	205	602	2.94
April	314	841	2.68	197	548	2.78
May	381	844	2.22	213	569	2.67
June	414	850	2.05	208	602	2.90
July	379	828	2.18	188	501	2.66
August	382	934	2.44	247	596	2.41
September	355	896	2.52	176	584	3.32
October	285	926	3.25	207	586	2.83
November	301	961	3.20	223	651	2.95
December	347	1,152	3.33	181	691	3.82
Total	3,847	11,205	2.77	2,428	7,159	2.94

First, the epoch of maximum (June) in respect to the number of crimes against persons, coincides pretty nearly with the epoch of minimum in respect to crimes against property, and this takes place in summer; whilst, on the contrary, the minimum of the number of crimes against persons, and the maximum of the number of crimes against property, takes place in winter. Comparing these two kinds of crimes, we find that in the month of January nearly four crimes take place against property to one against persons, and in the month of June only two to three. These differences are readily explained by considering that during winter misery and want are more especially felt, and cause an increase of the number of crimes against property, whilst the violence of the passions predominating in summer, excites to more frequent personal collisions.

[. . .]

ON THE INFLUENCE OF SEX ON THE PROPENSITY TO CRIME

[. . .]

At the commencement, we may observe that, out of 28,686 accused, who have appeared before the courts in France, during the four years before 1830, there were found 5,416 women, and 23,270 men, that is to say, 23 women to 100 men. Thus, the propensity to crime in general gives the ratio of 23 to 100 for the sexes. This estimate supposes that justice exercises its duties as actively with regard to women as to men; and this is rendered probable by the fact, that the severity of repression is nearly the same in the case of both sexes; in other words, that women are treated with much the same severity as men.

We have just seen that, in general, the propensity to crime in men is about four times as great as in women, in France; but it will be important to examine further, if men are four times as criminal, which will be supposing that the crimes committed by the sexes are equally serious. We shall commence by making a distinction between crimes against property and crimes against persons. At the same time, we shall take the numbers obtained for each year, that we may see the limits in which they are comprised [Table 2.4]:

[Table 2.4]

Years	Crimes against persons			Crimes against property		
	Men	Women	Ratio	Men	Women	Ratio
1826	1,639	268	0.16	4,073	1,008	0.25
1827	1,637	274	0.17	4,020	998	0.25
1828	1,576	270	0.17	4,396	1,156	0.26
1829	1,552	239	0.15	4,379	1,203	0.27
Averages	1,601	263	0.16	4,217	1,091	0.26
1830	1,412	254	0.18	4,196	1,100	0.26
1831	1,813	233	0.13	4,567	993	0.22
Averages	1,612	243	0.15	4,381	1,046	0.24

Although the number of crimes against persons may have diminished slightly, whilst crimes against property have become rather more numerous, yet we see that the variations are not very great; they have but little modified the ratios between the numbers of the accused of the two sexes. We have 26 women to 100 men in the accusations for crimes against property, and for crimes against persons the ratio has been only 16 to 100. In general, crimes against persons are of a more serious nature than those against property, so that our distinction is favourable to the women, and we may affirm that men, in France, are four times as criminal as women. It must be observed, that the ratio 16 to 26 is nearly the same as that of the strength of the two sexes. However, it is proper to examine things more narrowly, and especially to take notice of individual crimes, at least of those which are committed in so great a number, that the inferences drawn from them may possess some degree of probability. For this purpose, in the following table [Table 2.5] I have collected the numbers relating to the four years before 1830, and calculated the different ratios;

the crimes are classed according to the degree of magnitude of this ratio. I have also grouped crimes nearly of the same nature together, such as issuing false money, counterfeits, falsehoods in statements or in commercial transactions, etc.

[Table 2.5]

Nature of crimes	Men	Women	Women to 100 men
Infanticide	30	426	1,320
Miscarriage	15	39	260
Poisoning	77	73	91
House robbery (*vol domestique*)	2,648	1,602	60
Parricide	44	22	50
Incendiarism of buildings and other things	279	94	34
Robbery of churches	176	47	27
Wounding of parents (*blessures envers ascendans*)	292	63	22
Theft	10,677	2,249	21
False evidence and suborning	307	51	17
Fraudulent bankruptcy	353	57	16
Assassination	947	111	12
False coining (*fausse monnaie*, counterfeit making, false affirmations in deeds etc.	1,669	117	11
Rebellion	612	69	10
Highway robbery	648	54	8
Wounds and blows	1,447	78	5
Murder	1,112	44	4
Violation and seduction	685	7	1
Violation on persons under 15 years of age	585	5	1

As we have already observed, to the commission of crime the three following conditions are essential – the will, which depends on the person's morality, the opportunity, and the facility of effecting it. Now, the reason why females have less propensity to crime than males, is accounted for by their being more under the influence of sentiments of shame and modesty, as far as morals are concerned; their dependent state, and retired habits, as far as occasion or opportunity is concerned; and their physical weakness, so far as the facility of acting is concerned. I think we may attribute the differences observed in the degree of criminality to these three principal causes. Sometimes the whole three concur at the same time: we ought, on such occasions, to expect to find their influence very marked, as in rapes and seductions; thus, we have only 1 women to 100 men in crimes of this nature. In poisoning, on the contrary, the number of accusations for either sex is nearly equal. When force becomes necessary for the destruction of a person, the number of women who are accused becomes much fewer; and their numbers diminish in proportion, according to the necessity of the greater publicity before the crime can be perpetrated: the following crimes also take place in the order in which they are stated – infanticide, miscarriage, parricide, wounding of parents, assassinations, wounds and blows, murder.

With respect to infanticide, woman has not only many more opportunities of committing it than man, but she is in some measure impelled to it, frequently by misery, and almost always from the desire of concealing a fault, and avoiding the shame or scorn of society, which, in such cases, thinks less unfavourably of man. Such is not the case with other crimes involving the destruction of an individual: it is not the degree of the crime which keeps a woman back, since, in the series which we have given, parricides and wounding of parents are more numerous than assassinations, which again are more frequent than murder, and wounds and blows generally; it is not simply weakness, for then the ratio for parricide and wounding of parents should be the same as for murder and wounding of strangers. These differences are more especially owing to the habits and sedentary life of females; they can only conceive and execute guilty projects on individuals with whom they are in the greatest intimacy: thus, compared with man, her assassinations are more often in her family than out of it; and in society she commits assassination rather than murder, which often takes place after excess of drink, and the quarrels to which women are less exposed.

If we now consider the different kinds of theft, we shall find that the ratios of the propensity to crime are arranged in a similar series: thus, we have successively house robbery, robbery in churches, robberies in general, and, lastly, highway robbery, for which strength and audacity are necessary. The less conspicuous propensity to cheating in general, and to fraudulent bankruptcy, again depend on the more secluded life of females, their separation from trade, and that, in some cases, they are less capable than men – for example, in coining false money and issuing counterfeits.

If we attempt to analyse facts, it seems to me that the difference of morality in man and woman is not so great as is generally supposed, excepting only as regards modesty; I do not speak of the timidity arising from this last sentiment, in like manner as it does from the physical weakness and seclusion of females. As to these habits themselves, I think we may form a tolerable estimate of their influence by the ratios which exist between the sexes in crimes of different kinds, where neither strength has to be taken into consideration, nor modesty – as in theft, false witnessing, fraudulent bankruptcy etc.; these ratios are about 100 to 21 or 17, that is to say, about 5 or 6 to 1. As to other modes of cheating, the difference is a little greater, from the reasons already stated. If we try to give a numerical expression of the intensity of the causes by which women are influenced, as, for example, the influence of strength, we may estimate it as being in proportion to the degree of strength itself, or as 1 to 2 nearly; and this is the ratio of the number of parricides for each sex. For crimes where both physical weakness and the retired life of females must be taken into account, as in assassinations and highway robberies, following the same plan in our calculations, it will be necessary to multiply the ratio of power or strength ½ by the degree of dependence 1–5, which gives 1–10, a quantity which really falls between the values 12–100 and 8–100, the ratios given in the table [Table 2.5]. With respect to murder, and blows and wounds, these crimes depend not merely on strength and a more or less sedentary life, but still more on being in the habit of using strong drinks and quarrelling. The influence of this latter cause might almost be considered as 1 to 3 for the sexes. It may be thought that the estimates which I have here pointed out, cannot be of an exact nature, from the impossibility of assigning the share of influence which the greater modesty of woman, her physical weakness, her dependence, or rather her more retired life, and her feebler passions, which are also less frequently excited by liquors, may have respectively on any crime in particular. Yet, if such were the characters in which the sexes more particularly differ from each other, we might, by analyses like those now given, assign their respective influence with some probability of truth, especially if the observations were very numerous.

[. . .]

OF THE INFLUENCE OF AGE ON THE PROPENSITY TO CRIME

Of all the causes which influence the development of the propensity to crime, or which diminish that propensity, age is unquestionably the most energetic. Indeed, it is through age that the physical powers and passions of man are developed, and their energy afterwards decreases with age. Reason is developed with age, and continues to acquire power even when strength and passion have passed their greatest vigour. Considering only these three elements, strength, passion, and judgment (or reason), we may almost say, a priori, what will be the degree of the propensity to crime at different ages. Indeed, the propensity must be almost nothing at the two extremes of life; since, on the one hand, strength and passion, two powerful instruments of crime, have scarcely begun to exist and, on the other hand, their energy, nearly extinguished, is still further deadened by the influence of reason. On the contrary, the propensity to crime should be at its maximum at the age when strength and passion have attained their maximum, and when reason has not acquired sufficient power to govern their combined influence. Therefore, considering only physical causes, the propensity to crime at different ages will be a property and sequence of the three quantities we have just names, and might be determined by them, if they were sufficiently known. But since these elements are not yet determined, we must confine ourselves to seeking for the degrees of the propensity to crime in an experimental manner; we shall find the means of so doing in the *Comptes Généraux de la Justice*. The following table [Table 2.6] will show the number of crimes against persons and against property, which have been committed in France by each sex during the years 1826, 27, 28, and 29, as well as the ratio of these numbers; the fourth column points out how a population of 10,000 souls is divided in France, according to age; and the last column gives the ratio of the total number of crimes to the corresponding number of the preceding column; thus there is no longer an inequality of number of the individuals of different ages.

[Table 2.6]

Individuals' age	Crimes against Persons	Crimes against Property	Crimes against property in 100	Population according to age	Degrees of the propensity to crime
Less than 16 years	80	440	85	3,304	161
16 to 21	904	3,723	80	887	5,217
21 to 25	1,278	3,329	72	673	6,816
25 to 30	1,575	3,702	70	791	6,671
30 to 35	1,153	2,883	71	732	5,514
35 to 40	650	2,076	76	672	4,057
40 to 45	575	1,724	75	612	3,757
45 to 50	445	1,275	74	549	3,133
50 to 55	288	811	74	482	2,280
55 to 60	168	500	75	410	1,629
60 to 65	157	385	71	330	1,642
65 to 70	91	184	70	247	1,113
70 to 80	64	137	68	255	788
80 and upwards	5	14	74	55	345

This table gives us results conformable to those which I have given in my *Recherches Statistique* for the years 1826 and 1827. Since the value obtained for 80 years of age and upwards is based on very small numbers, it is not entitled to much confidence. Moreover, we see that man begins to exercise his propensity to crimes against property at a period antecedent to his pursuit of other crimes. Between his 25th and 30th year, when his powers are developed, he inclines more to crimes against persons. It is near the age of 25 years that the propensity to crime reaches its maximum.

[. . .]

If, instead of taking crimes collectively, we examine each in particular in proportion to age, we shall have a new proof that the maximum of crimes of different kinds takes place between the 20th and 30th years, and that it is really about that period that the most vicious disposition is manifested. Only the period of maximum will be hastened or retarded some years for some crimes, according to the quicker or slower development of certain qualities of man which are proportioned to those crimes. These results are too curious to be omitted here: I have presented them in the following table [Table 2.7], according to the documents of France, from 1826 to 1829 inclusively, classing them according to the periods of maxima, and taking into account the population of different ages. I have omitted the crimes which are committed in smallest number, because the results from that alone would have been very doubtful.

Thus the propensity to theft, one of the first to show itself, prevails in some measure throughout our whole existence; we might be led to believe it to be inherent to the weakness of man, who falls into it as if by instinct. It is first exercised by the indulgence of confidence which exists in the interior of families, then it manifests itself out of them, and finally on the public highway, where it terminates by having recourse to violence, when the man has then made the sad essay of the fullness of his strength by committing all the different kinds of homicide. This fatal propensity, however, is not so precocious as that which, near adolescence, arises with the fire of the passions and the disorders which accompany it, and which drives man to violation and seduction, seeking its first victims among beings whose weakness opposes the least resistance. To these first excesses of the passions, of cupidity, and of strength, is soon joined reflection, plotting crime; and man, become more self-possessed and hardened, chooses to destroy his victim by assassination or poisoning. Finally, his last stages in the career of crime are marked by address in deception, which in some measure supplies the place of strength. It is in his decline that the vicious man presents the most hideous spectacle; his cupidity, which nothing can extinguish, is rekindled with fresh ardour, and assumes the mask of swindling; if he still uses the little strength which nature has left to him, it is rather to strike his enemy in the shade; finally, if his depraved passions have not been deadened by age, he prefers to gratify them on feeble children. Thus, his first and his last stages in the career of crime have the same character in this last respect: but what a difference! That which was somewhat excusable in the young man, because of his inexperience, of the violence of his passions, and the similarity of ages, in the old man is the result of the deepest immorality and the most accumulated load of depravity.

[. . .]

[Table 2.7]

Nature of the crimes	Under 16 years	16–21	21–25	25–30	30–35	35–40	40–45	45–50	50–55	55–60	60–65	65–70	70–80	80 and upwards
Violations on children under 15 years	4	120	71	96	73	39	34	45	22	18	26	17	21	2
House robbery	54	965	845	766	528	351	249	207	112	56	61	34	14	–
Other thefts	332	2,479	2,050	2,292	1,716	1,249	1,016	707	433	263	190	98	65	10
Violation and seduction	9	155	156	148	99	38	40	27	9	5	3	1	2	–
Parricide	6	13	12	13	6	3	2	1	4	2	–	–	–	–
Wounds and blows	6	180	300	359	219	129	101	95	55	35	23	10	7	1
Murder	15	139	198	275	172	103	84	49	48	30	25	17	9	–
Infanticide	1	40	99	134	76	44	30	8	7	1	8	4	2	–
Rebellion	5	67	129	156	115	51	51	35	29	16	16	5	5	–
Highway robbery	21	80	111	149	107	60	62	46	22	21	8	6	4	1
Assassination	10	90	144	203	183	100	104	89	53	32	24	13	15	–
Wounding parents	2	47	64	73	72	40	30	16	8	2	1	–	–	–
Poisoning	5	6	17	30	27	15	20	12	6	2	5	4	1	–
False witnessing and suborning	2	23	46	48	44	42	42	35	23	15	15	11	7	–
Various misdemeanours	8	86	202	276	312	244	207	185	129	78	75	28	28	2

CONCLUSIONS

In making a summary of the principal observations contained in this chapter, we are led to the following conclusions.

(1) Age (or the term of life) is undoubtedly the cause which operates with most energy in developing or subduing the propensity to crime.

(2) This fatal propensity appears to be developed in proportion to the intensity of the physical power and passions of man: it attains its maximum about the age of 25 years, the period at which the physical development has almost ceased. The intellectual and moral development, which operates more slowly, subsequently weakens the propensity to crime, which, still later, diminishes from the feeble state of the physical powers and passions.

(3) Although it is near the age of twenty-five that the maximum in number of crimes of different kinds takes place, yet this maximum advances or recedes some years for certain crimes, according to the quicker or slower development of certain qualities which have a bearing on those crimes. Thus, man, driven by the violence of his passions, at first commits violation and seduction; almost at the same time he enters on the career of theft, which he seems to follow as if by instinct till the end of life; the development of his strength subsequently leads him to commit every act of violence – homicide, rebellion, highway robbery still later, reflection converts murder into assassination and poisoning. Lastly, man, advancing in the career of crime, substitutes a greater degree of cunning for violence, and becomes more of a forger than at any other period of life.

(4) The *difference of sexes* has also a great influence on the propensity to crime: in general, there is only one woman before the courts to four men.

(5) The propensity to crime increases and decreases nearly in the same degrees in each sex; yet the period of maximum takes place rather later in women, and is near the thirtieth year.

(6) Woman, undoubtedly from her feeling of weakness, rather commits crimes against property than persons; and when she seeks to destroy her kind, she prefers poison. Moreover, when she commits homicide, she does not appear to be proportionally arrested by the enormity of crimes which, in point of frequency, take place in the following order: infanticide, miscarriage, parricide, wounding of parents, assassination, wounds and blows, murder: so that we may affirm that the number of the guilty diminishes in proportion as they have to seek their victim more openly. These differences are no doubt owing to the habits and sedentary life of woman; she can only conceive and execute guilty projects on individuals with whom she is in constant relation.

(7) The *seasons*, in their course, exercise a very marked influence on crime: thus, during summer, the greatest number of crimes against persons are committed, and the fewest against property; the contrary takes place during winter.

(8) It must be observed that age and the seasons have almost the same influence in increasing or diminishing the number of mental disorders and crimes against persons.

(9) *Climate* appears to have some influence, especially on the propensity to crimes against persons: this observation is confirmed at least among the races of southern climates, such as the Pelasgian race, scattered over the shores of the Mediterranean and Corsica, on the one hand; and the Italians, mixed with

Dalmatians and Tyrolese, on the other. We observe, also, that severe climates, which give rise to the greatest number of wants, also give rise to the greatest number of crimes against property.

(10) The countries where frequent mixture of the people takes place; those in which industry and trade collect many persons and things together, and possess the greatest activity; finally, those where the inequality of fortune is most felt, all things being equal, are those which give rise to the greatest number of crimes.

(11) Professions have great influence on the nature of crimes. Individuals of more independent professions are rather given to crimes against persons; and the labouring and domestic classes to crimes against property. Habits of dependence, sedentary life, and also physical weakness in women, produce the same results.

(12) *Education* is far from having so much influence on the propensity to crime as is generally supposed. Moreover, moral instruction is very often confounded with instruction in reading and writing alone, and which is most frequently an accessory instrument to crime.

(13) It is the same with *poverty*; several of the departments of France, considered to be the poorest, are at the same time the most moral. Man is not driven to crime because he is poor, but more generally because he passes rapidly from a state of comfort to one of misery, and an inadequacy to supply the artificial wants which he has created.

(14) The higher we go in the ranks of society, and consequently in the degrees of education, we find a smaller and smaller proportion of guilty women to men; descending to the lowest orders, the habits of both sexes resemble each other more and more.

(15) Of 1,129 murders committed in France, during the space of four years, 446 have been in consequence of quarrels and contentions in taverns; which would tend to show the fatal influence of the use of *strong drinks*.

(16) In France, as in the Low Countries, we enumerate annually 1 accused person to 4,300 inhabitants nearly; but in the former country, 39 in 100 are acquitted, and in the second only 15; yet the same code was used in both countries, but in the Low Countries the judges performed the duty of the jury. Before correctional courts and simple police courts, where the committed were tried by judges only, the results were nearly the same for both countries.

(17) In France, crimes against persons were about one-third of the number of crimes against property, but in the Low Countries they were about one-fourth only. It must be remarked, that the first kind of crimes lead to fewer condemnations than the second, perhaps because there is a greater repugnance to apply punishment as the punishment increases in severity.

I cannot conclude this chapter without again expressing my astonishment at the constancy observed in the results which the documents connected with the administration of justice present each year.

'Thus, as I have already had occasion to repeat several times, we pass from one year to another, with the sad perspective of seeing the same crimes reproduced in the same order, and bringing with them the same punishments in the same proportions.' All observations tend likewise to confirm the truth of this proposition, which I long ago announced, that *every thing which pertains to the human species considered as a whole, belongs to the order of physical facts*: the greater the number of individuals, the more does the influence of individual will disappear, leaving predominance to a series of general facts, dependent on causes by which society exists and is preserved. These causes we now want to ascertain, and as soon as we are acquainted with them, we shall determine their influence on society, just in the same way as we determine effects by their causes in physical sciences.

[. . .]

[M]an commits crime with at least as much regularity as is observed in births, deaths, or marriages, and with more regularity than the receipts and expenses of the treasury take place. [. . .] since the crimes which are annually committed seem to be a necessary result of our social organization, and since the number of them cannot diminish without the causes which induce them undergoing previous modification, it is the province of legislators to ascertain these causes, and to remove them as far as possible: they have the power of determining the budget of crime, as well as the receipts and expenses of the treasury. Indeed, experience proves as clearly as possible the truth of this opinion, which at first may appear paradoxical, viz., that *society prepares crime, and the guilty are only the instruments by which it is executed.* Hence it happens that the unfortunate person who loses his head on the scaffold, or who ends his life in prison, is in some manner an expiatory victim for society. His crime is the result of the circumstances in which he is found placed: the severity of his chastisement is perhaps another result of it. [. . .]

4

The criminal type in women and its atavistic origin

Cesare Lombroso and William Ferrero

[. . .] [A] comparison of the criminal skull with the skulls of normal women reveals the fact that female criminals approximate more to males, both criminal and normal, than to normal women, especially in the superciliary arches in the seam of the sutures, in the lower jaw-bones, and in peculiarities of the occipital region. They nearly resemble normal women in their cheek-bones, in the prominence of the crotaphitic line, and in the median occipital fossa. There are also among them a large proportion (9.2 per cent) of virile crania.

The anomalies more frequent in female criminals than in prostitutes are: enormous pterygoid apophisis; cranial depressions; very heavy lower jaw; plagiocephalia; the soldering of the atlas with the occiput; enormous nasal spine; deep frontal sinuses; absence of sutures; simplicity of sutures; wormian bones.

Fallen women, on the other hand, are distinguished from criminals by the following peculiarities: clinoid apophisis forming a canal; tumefied parietal prominences; median occipital fossa of double size; great occipital irregularity; narrow or receding forehead; abnormal nasal bones; epactal bone; prognathous jaw and alveolar prognathism; cranial sclerosis; a virile type of face; prominent cheek-bones. [. . .] More instructive than a mere analytical enumeration of the characteristics of degeneration is a synthesis of the different features peculiar to the female criminal type.

We call a *complete type* one wherein exist four or more of the characteristics of degeneration; a *half-type* that which contains at least three of these; and *no type* a countenance possessing only one or two anomalies or none.

Out of the female delinquents examined 52 were Piedmontese in the prison of Turin, and 234 in the Female House of Correction were natives of different Italian provinces, especially from the South. In these, consequently, we set aside all special characteristics belonging to the ethnological type of the different regions, such as the brachycephali of the Piedmontese, the dolichocephali of the Sardinians, the oxycephali.

From *The Female Offender*, pp. 28; 103–13; 147–52; 190–1. (London: Fisher Unwin, 1895.)

We studied also from the point of view of type the 150 prostitutes whom we had previously examined for their several features; as well as another 100 from Moscow whose photographs Madame Tarnowsky sent us.
[. . .]

The results of the examination may be thus summarized:

1   The rarity of a criminal type in the female as compared with the male delinquent. In our homogeneous group (286) the proportion is 14 per cent, rising, when all other observations are taken into account, to 18 per cent, a figure lower almost by one-half than the average in the male born criminal, namely, 31 per cent.

In normal women this same type is only present in 2 per cent.
[. . .]

2   Prostitutes differ notably from female criminals in that they offer so much more frequently a special and peculiar type. Grimaldi's figures are 31 per cent (of anomalies), Madame Tarnowsky's 43 per cent, our own 38 per cent; making a mean of 37.1 per cent. These results harmonize with the conclusions to which we had already arrived in our study of particular features, and our survey of the various types of born prostitutes as distinguished from ordinary female offenders.

3   In the differentiation of female criminals, according to their offences, our last observations on the 286 criminals (made first without knowing the nature of their crimes and classified afterwards) give the prevalence of the criminal type among thieves as 15.3 and 16 per cent; among assassins as 13.2 per cent, and as rising to 18.7 per cent in those accused of corruption, among whom were included old prostitutes.

The least frequency was among swindlers, 11 per cent, and infanticides, 8.7 per cent, such women being indeed among the more representative of occasional criminals.
[. . .]

Here we see the crescendo of the peculiarities as we rise from moral women, who are most free from anomalies, to prostitutes, who are free from none, and we note how homicides present the highest number of multiple anomalies.

All the same, it is incontestable that female offenders seem almost normal when compared to the male criminal, with his wealth of anomalous features.
[. . .]

The remarkable rarity of anomalies (already revealed by their crania) is not a new phenomenon in the female, nor is it in contradiction to the undoubted fact that atavistically she is nearer to her origin than the male, and ought consequently to abound more in anomalies.

We saw, indeed, that the crania of male criminals exhibited 78 per cent of anomalies, as against 27 per cent in female delinquents and 51 per cent in prostitutes; but we also saw that the monstrosities in which women abound are forms of disease, consequent on disorder of the ovule. But when a departure from the norm is to be found only in the physiognomy, that is to say, in that portion of the frame where the degenerative stamp, the type declares itself, then even in cases of idiotcy, of madness, and, what is more important for our purpose, of epilepsy, the characteristic face is far less marked and less frequent in the woman. In her, anomalies are extraordinarily rare when compared with man; and this phenomenon, with a few exceptions among lower animals, holds good throughout the whole zoological scale.
[. . .]

Atavism helps to explain the rarity of the criminal type in woman. The very precocity of prostitutes – the precocity which increases their apparent beauty – is primarily attributable to atavism. Due also to it is the virility underlying the female criminal type; for what we look for most in the female is femininity, and when we find the opposite in her we conclude as a rule that there must be some anomaly. And in order to understand the significance and the atavistic origin of this anomaly, we have only to remember that virility was one of the special features of the savage women.

[. . .]

The criminal being only a reversion to the primitive type of his species, the female criminal necessarily offers the two most salient characteristics of primordial woman, namely, precocity and a minor degree of differentiation from the male – this lesser differentiation manifesting itself in the stature, cranium, brain, and in the muscular strength which she possesses to a degree so far in advance of the modern female.

[. . .]

The analogy between the anthropology and psychology of the female criminal is perfect.

Just as in the mass of female criminals possessing few or unimportant characteristics of degeneration, we find a group in whom these features are almost more marked and more numerous than in males, so while the majority of female delinquents are led into crime either by the suggestion of a third person or by irresistible temptation, and are not entirely deficient in the moral sense, there is yet to be found among them a small proportion whose criminal propensities are more intense and more perverse than those of their male prototypes.

'No possible punishments,' wrote Corrado Celto, an author of the fifteenth century, 'can deter women from heaping up crime upon crime. Their perversity of mind is more fertile in new crimes than the imagination of a judge in new punishments.'

'Feminine criminality,' writes Rykère, 'is more cynical, more depraved, and more terrible than the criminality of the male.'

'Rarely is a woman wicked, but when she is she surpasses the man' (Italian Proverb).

'The violence of the ocean waves or of devouring flames is terrible. Terrible is poverty, but woman is more terrible than all else' (Euripides).

'The perversity of woman is so great,' says Caro, 'as to be incredible even to its victims.'

[. . .] Another terrible point of superiority in the female born criminal over the male lies in the refined, diabolical cruelty with which she accomplishes her crime.

[. . .] We may assert that if female born criminals are fewer in number than the males, they are often much more ferocious.

What is the explanation? [. . .] [T]he normal woman is naturally less sensitive to pain than a man, and compassion is the offspring of sensitiveness. If the one be wanting, so will the other be.

We also saw that women have many traits in common with children; that their moral sense is deficient; that they are revengeful, jealous, inclined to vengeances of a refined cruelty.

In ordinary cases these defects are neutralized by piety, maternity, want of passion, sexual coldness, by weakness and an undeveloped intelligence. But when a morbid activity of the psychical centres intensifies the bad qualities of women, and induces them to seek relief in evil deeds; when piety and maternal sentiments are wanting, and in their place are strong passions and intensely erotic tendencies, much muscular strength and a superior intelligence for the conception and execution of evil, it is clear that the innocuous semi-criminal present in the normal woman must be transformed into a born criminal more terrible than any man.

What terrific criminals would children be if they had strong passions, muscular strength, and sufficient intelligence; and if, moreover, their evil tendencies were exasperated by a morbid psychical activity! And women are big children; their evil tendencies are more numerous and more varied than men's, but generally remain latent. When they are awakened and excited they produce results proportionately greater.

Moreover, the born female criminal is, so to speak, doubly exceptional, as a woman and as a criminal. For criminals are an exception among civilized people, and women are an exception among criminals, the natural form of retrogression in women being prostitution and not crime. The primitive woman was impure rather than criminal.

As a double exception, the criminal woman is consequently a monster. Her normal sister is kept in the paths of virtue by many causes, such as maternity, piety, weakness, and when these counter influences fail, and a woman commits a crime, we may conclude that her wickedness must have been enormous before it could triumph over so many obstacles.

[. . .]

M. R., a case described by Ottolenghi, was a thief, a prostitute, a corrupter of youth, a blackmailer, and all this at the age of 17. When only 12 she robbed her father in order to have money to spend among her companions. At 15 she fled from home with a lover, whom she left almost at once for a career of prostitution. With a view to larger gains, when only 16 she organized a vast system of prostitution, by which she provided young girls of 12 and 15 for wealthy men, from whom she exacted large sums, of which only a few sous went to the victims. And by threats of exposure she managed to levy costly blackmail on her clients, one of whom, a highly placed functionary, was dismissed from his post in consequence of her revelations. She was extremely vindictive, and committed two crimes of revenge which serve to show the strange mixture of ferocity and cunning composing her character. One of her companions having spoken evil of her, she (who was then only 16 years of age) let a little time pass, then coaxed her enemy to accompany her outside the gates of the town. They reached a deserted spot as evening fell, and M. R. suddenly threw the other girl on the ground, and while recalling her offence proceeded to beat her violently with a pair of scissors and a key, nor desisted until her victim had fainted; after which she quietly returned to town. 'You might have killed her,' somebody said. 'What did that matter?' she replied; 'there was nobody to see.' 'You might have employed a hired assassin.' 'I am afraid of those,' was the answer. 'Besides, on principle one should do things oneself.' 'But with a key you could never have killed her' (went on the other). 'If one beats the temples well,' M. R. replied, 'it is quite possible to kill a person even with a key.'

She conceived on another occasion such a violent hatred to a brilliant rival that, enticing her into a café, she furtively poisoned her coffee and thus caused her death.

It would be difficult to find greater wickedness at the service of a vindictive disposition and an unbridled greed. We may regard M. R. as an instance in which the two poles of depravity were united. That is to say, she was sanguinary (for she went about always with a dagger in her pocket, and stabbed anybody who offended her in the least) and at the same time inclined to commit the more cautious and insidious crimes, such as poisoning, blackmail, etc. And we consequently find in her an example of the law we have already laid down, to the effect that the female born criminal, when a complete type, is more terrible than the male.

5

Causes of criminal behavior

Enrico Ferri

When a crime is committed in some place, attracting public attention either through the atrocity of the case or the strangeness of the criminal deed – for instance, one that is not connected with bloodshed, but with intellectual fraud – there are at once two tendencies that make themselves felt in the public conscience. One of them, pervading the overwhelming majority of individual consciences, asks: How is this? What for? Why did that man commit such a crime? This question is asked by everybody and occupies mostly the attention of those who do not look upon the case from the point of view of criminology. On the other hand, those who occupy themselves with criminal law represent the other tendency, which manifests itself when acquainted with the news of this crime. This is a limited portion of the public conscience, which tries to study the problem from the standpoint of the technical jurist. The lawyers, the judges, the officials of the police, ask themselves: What is the name of the crime committed by that man under such circumstances? Must it be classed as murder or patricide, attempted or incompleted manslaughter, and, if directed against property, is it theft, or illegal appropriation, or fraud? And the entire apparatus of practical criminal justice forgets at once the first problem, which occupies the majority of the public conscience, the question of the causes that led to this crime, in order to devote itself exclusively to the technical side of the problem, which constitutes the juridical anatomy of the inhuman and antisocial deed perpetrated by the criminal.

In these two tendencies you have a photographic reproduction of the two schools of criminology. The classic school, which looks upon the crime as a juridical problem, occupies itself with its name, its definition, its juridical analysis, leaves the personality of the criminal in the background and remembers it only so far as exceptional circumstances explicitly stated in the law books refer to it: whether he is a minor, a deaf-mute, whether it is a case of insanity, whether he was drunk at the time the crime was committed. Only in these strictly defined cases does the classic school occupy itself theoretically with the personality of the criminal. But ninety times in one hundred these exceptional circumstances do not exist or cannot be

From *The Positive School of Criminology; Three Lectures by Enrico Ferri* (ed. S.E. Grupp), pp. 70–94. (Pittsburgh, PA: University of Pittsburgh Press, 1968. First published 1901.)

shown to exist, and penal justice limits itself to the technical definition of the fact. But when the case comes up in the criminal court, or before the jurors, practice demonstrates that there is seldom a discussion between the lawyers of the defense and the judges for the purpose of ascertaining the most exact definition of the fact, of determining whether it is a case of attempted or merely projected crime, of finding out whether there are any of the juridical elements defined in this or that article of the code. The judge is rather face to face with the problem of ascertaining why, under what conditions, for what reasons, the man has committed the crime. This is the supreme and simple human problem. But hitherto it has been left to a more or less perspicacious, more or less gifted, empiricism, and there have been no scientific standards, no methodical collection of facts, no observations and conclusions, save those of the positive school of criminology. This school alone makes an attempt to solve in every case of crime the problem of its natural origin, of the reasons and conditions that induced a man to commit such and such a crime.

For instance, about 3,000 cases of manslaughter are registered every year in Italy. Now, open any work inspired by the classic school of criminology, and ask the author why 3,000 men are the victims of manslaughter every year in Italy, and how it is that there are not sometimes only as many as, say, 300 cases, the number committed in England, which has nearly the same number of inhabitants as Italy; and how it is that there are not sometimes 300,000 such cases in Italy instead of 3,000?

It is useless to open any work of classical criminology for this purpose, for you will not find an answer to these questions in them. No one, from Beccaria to Carrara, has ever thought of this problem, and they could not have asked it, considering their point of departure and their method. In fact, the classic criminologists accept the phenomenon of criminality as an accomplished fact. They analyse it from the point of view of the technical jurist, without asking how this criminal fact may have been produced, and why it repeats itself in greater or smaller numbers from year to year, in every country. The theory of a free will, which is their foundation, excludes the possibility of this scientific question, for according to it the crime is the product of the fiat of the human will. And if that is admitted as a fact, there is nothing left to account for. The manslaughter was committed, because the criminal wanted to commit it; and that is all there is to it. Once the theory of a free will is accepted as a fact, the deed depends on the fiat, the voluntary determination, of the criminal, and all is said.

But if, on the other hand, the positive school of criminology denies, on the ground of researches in scientific physiological psychology, that the human will is free and does not admit that one is a criminal because he wants to be, but declares that a man commits this or that crime only when he lives in definitely determined conditions of personality and environment which induce him necessarily to act in a certain way, then alone does the problem of the origin of criminality begin to be submitted to a preliminary analysis, and then alone does criminal law step out of the narrow and arid limits of technical jurisprudence and become a true social and human science in the highest and noblest meaning of the word. It is vain to insist with such stubbornness as that of the classic school of criminology on juristic formulae by which the distinction between illegal appropriation and theft, between fraud and other forms of crime against property, and so forth, is determined, when this method does not give to society one single word which would throw light upon the reasons that make a man a criminal and upon the efficacious remedy by which society could protect itself against criminality.

[. . .]

The method which we, on the other hand, have inaugurated is the following. Before we study crime from the point of view of a juristic phenomenon, we must study the causes to which the annual recurrence of crimes in all countries is due. These are natural causes, which I have classified under the three heads of anthropological, telluric and social. Every crime, from the smallest to the most atrocious, is the result of the interaction of these three causes, the anthropological condition of the criminal, the telluric environment in which he is living, and the social environment in which he is born, living, and operating. It is a vain beginning to separate the meshes of this net of criminality. There are still those who would maintain the one-sided standpoint that the origin of crime may be traced to only one of these elements, for instance, to the social element alone. So far as I am concerned, I have combatted this opinion from the very inauguration of the positive school of criminology, and I combat it today. It is certainly easy enough to think that the entire origin of all crime is due to the unfavorable social conditions in which the criminal lives. But an objective, methodical, observation demonstrates that social conditions alone do not suffice to explain the origin of criminality, although it is true that the prevalence of the influence of social conditions is an incontestable fact in the case of the greater number of crimes, especially of the lesser ones. But there are crimes which cannot be explained by the influence of social conditions alone. If you regard the general condition of misery as the sole source of criminality, then you cannot get around the difficulty that out of one thousand individuals living in misery from the day of their birth to that of their death only one hundred or two hundred become criminals, while the other nine hundred or eight hundred either sink into biological weakness, or become harmless maniacs, or commit suicide without perpetrating any crime. If poverty were the sole determining cause, one thousand out of one thousand poor ought to become criminals. If only two hundred become criminals, while one hundred commit suicide, one hundred end as maniacs, and the other six hundred remain honest in their social condition, then poverty alone is not sufficient to explain criminality. We must add the anthropological and telluric factor. Only be means of these three elements of natural influence can criminality be explained. Of course, the influence of either the anthropological or telluric or social element varies from case to case. If you have a case of simple theft, you may have a far greater influence of the social factor than of the anthropological factor. On the other hand, if you have a case of murder, the anthropological element will have a far greater influence than the social. And so on in every case of crime, and every individual that you will have to judge on the bench of the criminal.

The anthropological factor. It is precisely here that the genius of Cesare Lombroso established a new science, because in his search after the causes of crime he studied the anthropological condition of the criminal. This condition concerns not only the organic and anatomical constitution, but also the psychological, it represents the organic and psychological personality of the criminal. Every one of us inherits at birth, and personifies in life, a certain organic and psychological combination. This constitutes the individual factor of human activity, which either remains normal through life, or becomes criminal or insane. The anthropological factor, then, must not be restricted, as some laymen would restrict it, to the study of the form of the skull or the bones of the criminal. Lombroso had to begin his studies with the anatomical conditions of the criminal, because the skulls may be studied most easily in the museums. But he continued by also studying the brain and the other physiological conditions of the individual, the state of sensibility, and the circulation of matter. And this entire series of studies is but a necessary scientific introduction to the study of the psychology of the criminal, which is precisely the one problem that is of direct and immediate importance. It is this problem which the lawyer and the public prosecutor should solve before discussing the juridical aspect of any crime, for this reveals the causes which induced the criminal to commit a crime. At present there is no methodical standard for a psychological investigation, although such an investigation was introduced into the scope of classic penal law. But for this reason the results of the positive school penetrate into the lecture rooms of the universities of jurisprudence, whenever a law is required for the judicial arraignment of the criminal as a living and feeling human being. And even though the positive school is not mentioned, all profess to be studying the material furnished by it, for instance, its analyses of the sentiments of the criminal, his moral sense, his behavior before, during, and after the criminal act, the presence of remorse which people, judging the criminal after their own feelings, always suppose the criminal to feel, while, in fact, it is seldom present. This is the anthropological factor, which may assume a pathological form, in which case articles 46 and 47 of the penal code remember that there is such a thing as the personality of the criminal. However, aside from insanity, there are thousands of other organic and psychological conditions of the personality of criminals, which a judge might perhaps lump together under the name of extenuating circumstances, but which science desires to have thoroughly investigated. This is not done today, and for this reason the idea of extenuating circumstances constitutes a denial of justice.

This same anthropological factor also includes that which each one of us has: the race character. Nowadays the influence of race on the destinies of peoples and persons is much discussed in sociology, and there are one-sided schools that pretend to solve the problems of history and society by means of that racial influence alone, to which they attribute an absolute importance. But while there are some who maintain that the history of peoples is nothing but the exclusive product of racial character, there are others who insist that the social conditions of peoples and individuals are alone determining. The one is as much a one-sided and incomplete theory as the other. The study of collective society or of the single individual has resulted in the understanding that the life of society and of the individual is always the product of the inextricable net of the anthropological, telluric and social elements. Hence the influence of the race cannot be ignored in the study of nations and personalities, although it is not the exclusive factor which would suffice to explain the criminality of a nation or an individual. Study, for instance, manslaughter in Italy, and, although you will find it difficult to isolate one of the factors of criminality from the network of the other circumstances and conditions that produce it, yet there are such eloquent instances of the influence of racial character, that it would be like denying the existence of daylight if one tried to ignore the influence of the ethnical factor on criminality.

In Italy there are two currents of criminality, two tendencies which are almost diametrically opposed to one another. The crimes due to hot blood and muscle grow in intensity from northern to southern Italy, while the crimes against property

increase from south to north. In northern Italy, where movable property is more developed, the crime of theft assumes a greater intensity, while crimes due to conditions of the blood are decreasing on account of the lesser poverty and the resulting lesser degeneration of the people. In the south, on the other hand, crimes against property are less frequent and crimes of blood more frequent. Still there also are in southern Italy certain cases where criminality of the blood is less frequent, and you cannot explain this in any other way than by the influence of racial character. If you take a geographical map of manslaughter in Italy, you will see that from the minimum, from Lombardy, Piedmont, and Venice, the intensity increases until it reaches its maximum in the insular and peninsular extreme of the south.
[. . .]

Let this be enough so far as the anthropological factor of criminality is concerned. There are, furthermore, the telluric factors, that is to say, the physical environment in which we live and to which we pay no attention. It requires much philosophy, said Rousseau, to note the things with which we are in daily contact, because the habitual influence of a thing makes it more difficult to be aware of it. This applies also to the immediate influence of the physical conditions on human morality, notwithstanding the spiritualist prejudices which still weigh upon our daily lives. For instance, if it is claimed in the name of supernaturalism and psychism that a man is unhappy because he is vicious, it is equivalent to making a one-sided statement. For it is just as true to say that a man becomes vicious because he is unhappy. Want is the strongest poison for the human body and soul. It is the fountain head of all inhuman and antisocial feeling. Where want spreads out its wings, there the sentiments of love, of affection, of brotherhood, are impossible. Take a look at the figures of the peasant in the far-off arid Campagna, the little government employe, the laborer, the little shopkeeper. When work is assured, when living is certain, though poor, then want, cruel want, is in the distance, and every good sentiment can germinate and develop in the human heart. The family then lives in a favorable environment, the parents agree, the children are affectionate. And when the laborer, a bronzed statue of humanity, returns from his smoky shop and meets his white-haired mother, the embodiment of half a century of immaculate virtue and heroic sacrifices, then he can, tired, but assured of his daily bread, give room to feelings of affection, and he will cordially invite his mother to share his frugal meal. But let the same man, in the same environment, be haunted by the spectre of want and lack of employment, and you will see the moral atmosphere in his family changing as from day into night. There is no work, and the laborer comes home without any wages. The wife, who does not know how to feed the children, reproaches her husband with the suffering of his family. The man, having been turned away from the doors of ten offices, feels his dignity as an honest laborer assailed in the very bosom of his own family, because he has vainly asked society for honest employment. And the bonds of affection and union are loosened in that family. Its members no longer agree. There are too many children, and when the poor old mother approaches her son, she reads in his dark and agitated mien the lack of tenderness and feels in her mother heart that her boy, poisoned by the spectre of want, is perhaps casting evil looks at her and harboring the unfilial thought: 'Better an open grave in the cemetery than one mouth more to feed at home!'

It is true that want alone is not sufficient to prepare the soil in the environment of that suffering family for the roots of real crime and to develop it. Want will weaken the love and mutual respect among the members of that family, but it will not be strong enough alone to arm the hands of the man for a matricidal deed, unless he should get into a pathological mental condition, which is very exceptional and rare. But the conclusions of the positive school are confirmed in this case as in any other. In order that crime may develop, it is necessary that anthropological, social and telluric factors should act together.

[. . .]

We have now surveyed briefly the natural genesis of crime as a natural social phenomenon, [. . .] which in any determined moment [acts] upon a personality standing on the cross road of vice and virtue, crime and honesty. This scientific deduction gives rise to a series of investigations which satisfy the mind and supply it with a real understanding of things, far better than the theory that a man is a criminal because he wants to be. No, a man commits crime because he finds himself in certain physical and social conditions, from which the evil plant of crime takes life and strength. [. . .]

[. . .] To sum up, crime is a social phenomenon, due to the interaction of anthropological, telluric, and social factors. This law brings about what I have called criminal saturation, which means that every society has the criminality which it deserves, and which produces by means of its geographical and social conditions such quantities and qualities of crime as correspond to the development of each collective human group.

Thus the old saying of Quetelet is confirmed: 'There is an annual balance of crime, which must be paid and settled with greater regularity than the accounts of the national revenue.' However, we positivists give to this statement a less fatalistic interpretation, since we have demonstrated that crime is not our immutable destiny, even though it is a vain beginning to attempt to attenuate or eliminate crime by mere schemes. The truth is that the balance of crime is determined by the physical and social environment. But by changing the condition of the social environment, which is most easily modified, the legislator may alter the influence of the telluric environ- ment and the organic and psychic conditions of the population, control the greater portion of crimes, and reduce them considerably. It is our firm conviction that a truly civilized legislator can attenuate the plague of criminality, not so much by means of the criminal code, as by means of remedies which are latent in the remainder of the social life and of legislation. And the experience of the most advanced countries confirms this by the beneficent and preventive influence of criminal legislation resting on efficacious social reforms.

We arrive, then, at this scientific conclusion: in the society of the future, the necessity for penal justice will be reduced to the extent that social justice grows intensively and extensively.

6

Criminality and economic conditions

Willem Bonger

[. . .] [I]t is certain that man is born with social instincts, which, when influenced by a favorable environment can exert a force great enough to prevent egoistic thoughts from leading to egoistic acts. And since crime constitutes a part of the egoistic acts, it is of importance, for the etiology of *crime in general*, to inquire whether the present method of production and its social consequences are an obstacle to the development of the social instincts, and in what measure. We shall try in the following pages to show the influence of the economic system and of these consequences upon the social instincts of man.

After what we have just said it is almost superfluous to remark that the egoistic tendency does not *by itself* make a man criminal. For this something else is necessary. It is possible for the environment to create a great egoist, but this does not imply that the egoist will necessarily become criminal. For example, a man who is enriched by the exploitation of children may nevertheless remain all his life an honest man from the legal point of view. He does not think of stealing, because he has a surer and more lucrative means of getting wealth, although he lacks the moral sense which would prevent him from committing a crime if the thought of it occurred to him. We shall show that, as a consequence of the present environment, man has become very egoistic and hence more *capable of crime*, than if the environment had developed the germs of altruism.

The present economic system is based upon exchange. [. . .] such a mode of production cannot fail to have an egoistic character. A society based upon exchange isolates the individuals by weakening the bond that unites them. When it is a question of exchange the two parties interested think only of their own advantage even to the detriment of the other party. In the second place the possibility of exchange arouses in a man the thought of the possibility of converting the surplus of his labor into things which increase his well-being in place of giving the benefit of it to those who are deprived of the necessaries of life. Hence the possibility of exchange gives birth to cupidity.

The exchange called simple circulation of commodities is practiced by all men as consumers, and by the workers besides as vendors of their labor power. However,

From *Criminality and Economic Conditions*, pp. 402–5; 667–72. (London: Heinemann, 1916.)

the influence of this simple circulation of commodities is weak compared with that exercised by capitalistic exchange. It is only the exchange of the surplus of labor, by the producer, for other commodities, and hence is for him a secondary matter. As a result he does not exchange with a view to profit (though he tries to make as advantageous a trade as possible), but to get things which he cannot produce himself.

Capitalistic exchange, on the other hand, has another aim – that of making a profit. A merchant, for example, does not buy goods for his own use, but to sell them to advantage. He will, then, always try, on the one hand, to buy the best commodities as cheaply as possible, by depreciating them as much as he can; on the other hand, to make the purchaser pay as high a price as possible, by exaggerating the value of his wares. *By the nature of the mode of production itself* the merchant is therefore forced to make war upon two sides, must maintain his own interests against the interests of those with whom he does business. If he does not injure too greatly the interests of those from whom he buys, and those to whom he sells, it is for the simple reason that these would otherwise do business with those of his competitors who do not find their interest in fleecing their customers. Wherever competition is eliminated for whatever cause the tactics of the merchant are shown in their true light; he thinks only of his own advantage even to the detriment of those with whom he does business. 'No commerce without trickery' is a proverbial expression (among consumers), and with the ancients Mercury, the god of commerce, was also the god of thieves. This is true, that the merchant and the thief are alike in taking account *exclusively* of their own interest to the detriment of those with whom they have to do.

The fact that in our present society production does not take place generally to provide for the needs of men, but for many other reasons, has important effects upon the character of those who possess the means of production. Production is carried on for profit exclusively; if greater profits can be made by stopping production it will be stopped – this is the point of view of the capitalists. The consumers, on the other hand, see in production the means of creating what man has need of. The world likes to be deceived, and does not care to recognize the fact that the producer has only his own profit in view. The latter encourages this notion and poses as a disinterested person. If he reduces the price of his wares, he claims to do it in the interest of the public, and takes care not to admit that it is for the purpose of increasing his own profits. This is the falsity that belongs inevitably to capitalism.

In general this characteristic of capitalism has no importance for the morality of the consumer, who is merely duped, but it is far otherwise with the press, which is almost entirely in the power of the capitalists. The press, which ought to be a guide for the masses, and is so in some few cases, in the main is in the hands of capitalists who use it only as a means of making money. In place of being edited by men who, by their ability and firmness, are capable of enlightening the public, newspapers are carried on by persons who see in their calling only a livelihood, and consider only the proprietor of the sheet. In great part the press is the opposite of what it ought to be; it represents the interests of those who pay for advertisements or for articles; it increases the ignorance and the prejudices of the crowd; in a word, it poisons public opinion.

Besides this general influence upon the public the press has further a special place in the etiology of crime, from the fact that most newspapers, in order to satisfy the morbid curiosity of the public, relate all great crimes in extenso, give portraits of the victims, etc., and are often one of the causes of new crimes, by arousing the imitative instinct to be found in man.

As we have seen above the merchant capitalist makes war in two directions; his interests are against those of the man who sells to him, and of the man who buys from him. This is also true of the industrial capitalist. He buys raw materials and sells what he produces. But to arrive at his product he must buy labor, and this purchase is 'sui generis.'

Deprived as he is of the means of production the working-man sells his labor only in order not to die of hunger. The capitalist takes advantage of this necessitous condition of the worker and exploits him. [. . .] Little by little one class of men has become accustomed to think that the others are destined to amass wealth for them and to be subservient to them in every way. Slavery, like the wage system, demoralizes the servant as well as the master. With the master it develops cupidity and the imperious character which sees in a fellow man only a being fit to satisfy his desires. It is true that the capitalist has not the power over the proletarian that the master has over his slave; he has neither the right of service nor the power of life and death, yet it is none the less true that he has another weapon against the proletarian, a weapon whose effect is no less terrible, namely enforced idleness. The fact that the supply of manual labor always greatly exceeds the demand puts this weapon into the hands of every capitalist. It is not only the capitalists who carry on any business that are subjected to this influence, but also all who are salaried in their service.

Capitalism exercises in still a third manner an egoistic influence upon the capitalistic 'entrepreneur'. Each branch has more producers than are necessary. The interests of the capitalists are, then, opposed not only to those of the men from whom they buy or to whom they sell, but also to those of their fellow producers. It is indeed claimed that competition has the effect simply of making the product better and cheaper, but this is looking at the question from only one point of view. The fact which alone affects criminality is that competition forces the participants, under penalty of succumbing, to be as egoistic as possible. Even the producers who have the means of applying all the technical improvements to perfect their product and make it cheaper, are obliged to have recourse to gross deceits in advertising, etc., in order to injure their competitors. Rejoicing at the evil which befalls another, envy at his good fortune, these forms of egoism are the inevitable consequence of competition. [. . .]

What are the conclusions to be drawn from what has gone before? When we sum up the results that we have obtained it becomes plain that economic conditions occupy a much more important place in the etiology of crime than most authors have given them.

First we have seen that the present economic system and its consequences weaken the social feelings. The basis of the economic system of our day being exchange, the economic interests of men are necessarily found to be in opposition. This is a trait that capitalism has in common with other modes of production. But its principal characteristic is that the means of production are in the hands of a few, and most men are altogether deprived of them. Consequently, persons who do not possess the means of production are forced to sell their labor to those who do, and these, in consequence of their economic preponderance, force them to make the exchange for the mere necessaries of life, and to work as much as their strength permits.

This state of things especially stifles men's social instincts; it develops, on the part of those with power, the spirit of domination, and of insensibility to the ills of others, while it awakens jealousy and servility on the part of those who depend upon them. Further the contrary interests of those who have property, and the idle and luxurious life of some of them, also contribute to the weakening of the social instincts.

The material condition, and consequently the intellectual condition, of the proletariat are also a reason why the moral plane of that class is not high. The work of children brings them into contact with persons to associate with whom is fatal to their morals. Long working hours and monotonous labor brutalize those who are forced into them; bad housing conditions contribute also to debase the moral sense, as do the uncertainty of existence, and finally absolute poverty, the frequent consequence of sickness and unemployment. Ignorance and lack of training of any kind also contribute their quota. Most demoralizing of all is the status of the lower proletariat.

The economic position of woman contributes also to the weakening of the social instincts.

The present organization of the family has great importance as regards criminality. It charges the legitimate parents with the care of the education of the child; the community concerns itself with the matter very little. It follows that a great number of children are brought up by persons who are totally incapable of doing it properly. As regards the children of the proletariat, there can be no question of the education properly so-called, on account of the lack of means and the forced absence of one or both of the parents. The school tends to remedy this state of things, but the results do not go far enough. The harmful consequences of the present organization of the family make themselves felt especially in the case of the children of the lower proletariat, orphans, and illegitimate children. For these the community does but little, though their need of adequate help is the greatest.

Prostitution, alcoholism, and militarism, which result, in the last analysis, from the present social order, are phenomena that have demoralizing consequences.

As to the different kinds of crime, [. . .] the very important group of economic criminality finds its origin on the one side in the absolute poverty and the cupidity brought about by the present economic environment, and on the other in the moral abandonment and bad education of the children of the poorer classes. Then, professional criminals are principally recruited from the class of occasional criminals, who, finding themselves rejected everywhere after their liberation, fall lower and lower. The last group of economic crimes (fraudulent bankruptcy, etc.) is so intimately connected with our present mode of production, that it would not be possible to commit it under another.

The relation between sexual crimes and economic conditions is less direct; nevertheless these also give evidence of the decisive influence of these conditions. We have called attention to the four following points.

First, there is a direct connection between the crime of adultery and the present organization of society, which requires that the legal dissolution of a marriage should be impossible or very difficult.

Second, sexual crimes upon adults are committed especially by unmarried men; and since the number of marriages depends in its turn upon the economic situation, the connection is clear; and those who commit these crimes are further almost exclusively illiterate, coarse, raised in an environment almost without sexual morality, and regard the sexual life from the wholly animal side.

Third, the causes of sexual crime upon children are partly the same as those of which we have been speaking, with the addition of prostitution.

Fourth, alcoholism greatly encourages sexual assaults.

As to the relation between crimes of vengeance and the present constitution of society, [. . .] it produces conflicts without number; statistics have shown that those who commit them are almost without exception poor and uncivilized, and that alcoholism is among the most important causes of these crimes.

Infanticide is caused in part by poverty, and in part by the opprobrium incurred by the unmarried mother (an opprobrium resulting from the social utility of marriage).

Political criminality comes solely from the economic system and its consequences.

Finally, economic and social conditions are also important factors in the etiology of degeneracy, which is in its turn a cause of crime.

Upon the basis of what has gone before, we have a right to say that the part played by economic conditions in criminality is preponderant, even decisive.

This conclusion is of the highest importance for the prevention of crime. If it were principally the consequence of innate human qualities (atavism, for example), the pessimistic conclusion that crime is a phenomenon inseparably bound up with the social life would be well founded. But the facts show that it is rather the optimistic conclusion that we must draw, that where crime is the consequence of economic and social conditions, we can combat it by changing those conditions.

However important crime may be as a social phenomenon, however terrible may be the injuries and the evil that it brings upon humanity, the development of society will not depend upon the question as to what are the conditions which could restrain crime or make it disappear, if possible; the evolution of society will proceed independently of this question.

What is the direction that society will take under these continual modifications? This is not the place to treat fully of this subject. In my opinion the facts indicate quite clearly what the direction will be. The productivity of labor has increased to an unheard of degree, and will assuredly increase in the future. The concentration of the means of production into the hands of a few progresses continually; in many branches it has reached such a degree that the fundamental principle of the present economic system, competition, is excluded, and has been replaced by monopoly. On the other hand the working class is becoming more and more organized, and the opinion is very generally held among working-men that the causes of material and intellectual poverty can be eliminated only by having the means of production held in common.

Supposing that this were actually realized, what would be the consequences as regards criminality? Let us take up this question for a moment. Although we can give only personal opinions as to the details of such a society, the general outlines can be traced with certainty.

The chief difference between a society based upon the community of the means of production and our own is that material poverty would be no longer known. Thus one great part of economic criminality (as also one part of infanticide) would be rendered impossible, and one of the greatest demoralizing forces of our present society would be eliminated. And then, in this way those social phenomena so productive of crime, prostitution and alcoholism would lose one of their principal factors. Child labor and overdriving would no longer take place, and bad housing, the source of much physical and moral evil, would no longer exist.

With material poverty there would disappear also that intellectual poverty which weighs so heavily upon the proletariat; culture would no longer be the privilege of some, but a possession common to all. The consequences of this upon criminality would be very important, for [. . .] even in our present society with its numerous conflicts, the members of the propertied classes, who have often but a veneer of civilization, are almost never guilty of crimes of vengeance. There is the more reason to admit that in a society where interests were not opposed, and where civilization was universal, these crimes would be no longer present, especially since alcoholism also proceeds in large part from the intellectual poverty of the poorer classes. And what is true of crimes of vengeance, is equally true of sexual crimes in so far as they have the same etiology.

A large part of the economic criminality (and also prostitution to a certain extent) has its origin in the cupidity excited by the present economic environment. In a society based upon the community of the means of production, great contrasts of fortune would, like commercial capital, be lacking, and thus cupidity would find no food. These crimes will not totally disappear so long as there has not been a redistribution of property according to the maxim, 'to each according to his needs', something that will probably be realized, but not in the immediate future.

The changes in the position of woman which are taking place in our present society, will lead, under this future mode of production, to her economic independence, and consequently to her social independence as well. It is accordingly probable that the criminality of woman will increase in comparison with that of man during the transition period. But the final result will be the disappearance of the harmful effects of the economic and social preponderance of man.

As to the education of children under these new conditions it is difficult to be definite. However, it is certain that the community will concern itself seriously with their welfare. It will see to it that the children whose parents cannot or will not be responsible for them, are well cared for. By acting in this way it will remove one of the most important causes of crime. There is no doubt that the community will exercise also a strict control over the education of children; it cannot be affirmed, however, that the time will come when the children of a number of parents will be brought up together by capable persons; this will depend principally upon the intensity that the social sentiments may attain.

As soon as the interests of all are no longer opposed to each other, as they are in our present society, there will no longer be a question either of politics ('a fortiori' of political *crimes*) or of militarism.

Such a society will not only remove the causes which now make men egoistic, but will awaken, on the contrary, a strong feeling of altruism. [. . .] In a larger measure this will be realized under a mode of production in common, the interests of all being the same.

In such a society there can be no question of crime properly so called. The eminent criminologist, Manouvrier, in treating of the prevention of crime expresses himself thus: 'The maxim to apply is, act so that every man shall always have more interest in being useful to his fellows than in harming them.' It is precisely in a society where the community of the means of production has been realized that this maxim will obtain its complete application. There will be crimes committed by pathological individuals, but this will come rather within the sphere of the physician than that of the judge. And then we may even reach a state where these cases will decrease in large measure, since the social causes of degeneracy will disappear, and procreation by degenerates be checked through the increased knowledge of the laws of heredity and the increasing sense of moral responsibility.

'It is society that prepares the crime', says the true adage of Quetelet. For all those who have reached this conclusion, and are not insensible to the sufferings of humanity, this statement is sad, but contains a ground of hope. It is sad, because society punishes severely those who commit the crime which she has herself prepared. It contains a ground of hope, since it promises to humanity the possibility of some day delivering itself from one of its most terrible scourges.

7

The normal and the pathological

Emile Durkheim

[. . .]

If there is any fact whose pathological character appears incontestable, that fact is crime. All criminologists are agreed on this point. Although they explain this pathology differently, they are unanimous in recognizing it. But let us see if this problem does not demand a more extended consideration.

[. . .] Crime is present not only in the majority of societies of one particular species but in all societies of all types. There is no society that is not confronted with the problem of criminality. Its form changes; the acts thus characterized are not the same everywhere; but, everywhere and always, there have been men who have behaved in such a way as to draw upon themselves penal repression. If, in proportion as societies pass from the lower to the higher types, the rate of criminality, i.e., the relation between the yearly number of crimes and the population, tended to decline, it might be believed that crime, while still normal, is tending to lose this character of normality. But we have no reason to believe that such a regression is substantiated. Many facts would seem rather to indicate a movement in the opposite direction. From the beginning of the [nineteenth] century, statistics enable us to follow the course of criminality. It has everywhere increased. In France the increase is nearly 300 per cent. There is, then, no phenomenon that presents more indisputably all the symptoms of normality, since it appears closely connected with the conditions of all collective life. To make of crime a form of social morbidity would be to admit that morbidity is not something accidental, but, on the contrary, that in certain cases it grows out of the fundamental constitution of the living organism; it would result in wiping out all distinction between the physiological and the pathological. No doubt it is possible that crime itself will have abnormal forms, as, for example, when its rate is unusually high. This excess is, indeed, undoubtedly morbid in nature. What is normal, simply, is the existence of criminality, provided that it attains and does not exceed, for each social type, a certain level [. . .]

Here we are, then, in the presence of a conclusion in appearance quite paradoxical. Let us make no mistake. To classify crime among the phenomena of normal sociology is not to say merely that it is an inevitable, although regrettable

From *The Rules of Sociological Method*, pp. 65–73. (New York: Free Press, 1964. First published 1895.)

phenomenon, due to the incorrigible wickedness of men; it is to affirm that it is a factor in public health, an integral part of all healthy societies. This result is, at first glance, surprising enough to have puzzled even ourselves for a long time. Once this first surprise has been overcome, however, it is not difficult to find reasons explaining this normality and at the same time confirming it.

In the first place crime is normal because a society exempt from it is utterly impossible. Crime [. . .] consists of an act that offends certain very strong collective sentiments. In a society in which criminal acts are no longer committed, the sentiments they offend would have to be found without exception in all individual consciousnesses, and they must be found to exist with the same degree as sentiments contrary to them. Assuming that this condition could actually be realized, crime would not thereby disappear; it would only change its form, for the very cause which would thus dry up the sources of criminality would immediately open up new ones.

Indeed, for the collective sentiments which are protected by the penal law of a people at a specified moment of its history to take possession of the public conscience or for them to acquire a stronger hold where they have an insufficient grip, they must acquire an intensity greater than that which they had hitherto had. The community as a whole must experience them more vividly, for it can acquire from no other source the greater force necessary to control these individuals who formerly were the most refractory. For murderers to disappear, the horror of bloodshed must become greater in those social strata from which murderers are recruited; but, first it must become greater throughout the entire society. Moreover, the very absence of crime would directly contribute to produce this horror; because any sentiment seems much more respectable when it is always and uniformly respected.

One easily overlooks the consideration that these strong states of the common consciousness cannot be thus reinforced without reinforcing at the same time the more feeble states, whose violation previously gave birth to mere infraction of convention – since the weaker ones are only the prolongation, the attenuated form, of the stronger. Thus robbery and simple bad taste injure the same single altruistic sentiment, the respect for that which is another's. However, this same sentiment is less grievously offended by bad taste than by robbery; and since, in addition, the average consciousness has not sufficient intensity to react keenly to the bad taste, it is treated with greater tolerance. That is why the person guilty of bad taste is merely blamed, whereas the thief is punished. But, if this sentiment grows stronger, to the point of silencing in all consciousnesses the inclination which disposes man to steal, he will become more sensitive to the offenses which, until then, touched him but lightly. He will react against them, then, with more energy; they will be the object of greater opprobrium, which will transform certain of them from the simple moral faults that they were and give them the quality of crimes. For example, improper contracts, or contracts improperly executed, which only incur public blame or civil damages, will become offenses in law.

Imagine a society of saints, a perfect cloister of exemplary individuals. Crimes, properly so called, will there be unknown; but faults which appear venial to the layman will create there the same scandal that the ordinary offense does in ordinary consciousnesses. If, then, this society has the power to judge and punish, it will define these acts as criminal and will treat them as such. For the same reason, the perfect and upright man judges his smallest failings with a severity that the majority reserve for acts more truly in the nature of an offense. Formerly, acts of violence against persons were more frequent than they are today, because respect for individual dignity was less strong. As this has increased, these crimes have become more rare; and also, many acts violating this sentiment have been introduced into the penal law which were not included there in primitive times.

In order to exhaust all the hypotheses logically possible, it will perhaps be asked why this unanimity does not extend to all collective sentiments without exception. Why should not even the most feeble sentiment gather enough energy to prevent all dissent? The moral consciousness of the society would be present in its entirety in all the individuals, with a vitality sufficient to prevent all acts offending it – the purely conventional faults as well as the crimes. But a uniformity so universal and absolute is utterly impossible; for the immediate physical milieu in which each one of us is placed, the hereditary antecedents, and the social influences vary from one individual to the next, and consequently diversify consciousnesses. It is impossible for all to be alike, if only because each one has his own organism and that these organisms occupy different areas in space. That is why, even among the lower peoples, where individual originality is very little developed, it nevertheless does exist.

Thus, since there cannot be a society in which the individuals do not differ more or less from the collective type, it is also inevitable that, among these divergences, there are some with a criminal character. What confers this character upon them is not the intrinsic quality of a given act but that definition which the collective conscience lends them. If the collective conscience is stronger, if it has enough authority practically to suppress these divergences, it will also be more sensitive, more exacting; and, reacting against the slightest deviations with the energy it otherwise displays only against more considerable infractions, it will attribute to them the same gravity as formerly to crimes. In other words, it will designate them as criminal.

Crime is, then, necessary; it is bound up with the fundamental conditions of all social life, and by that very fact it is useful, because these conditions of which it is a part are themselves indispensable to the normal evolution of morality and law.

Indeed, it is no longer possible today to dispute the fact that law and morality vary from one social type to the next, nor that they change within the same type if the conditions of life are modified. But, in order that these transformations may be possible, the collective sentiments at the basis of morality must not be hostile to change, and consequently must have but moderate energy. If they were too strong, they would no longer be plastic. Every pattern is an obstacle to new patterns, to the extent that the first pattern is inflexible. The better a structure is articulated, the more it offers a healthy resistance to all modification; and this is equally true of functional, as of anatomical, organization. If there were no crimes, this condition could not have been fulfilled; for such a hypothesis presupposes that collective sentiments have arrived at a degree of intensity unexampled in history. Nothing is good indefinitely and to an unlimited extent. The authority which the moral conscience enjoys must not be excessive; otherwise no one would dare criticize it, and it would too easily congeal into an immutable form. To make progress, individual originality must be able to express itself. In order that the originality of the idealist whose dreams transcend his century may find expression, it is necessary that the originality of the criminal, who is below the level of his time, shall also be possible. One does not occur without the other.

Nor is this all. Aside from this indirect utility, it happens that crime itself plays a useful role in this evolution. Crime implies not only that the way remains open to necessary changes but that in certain cases it directly prepares these changes. Where crime exists, collective sentiments are sufficiently flexible to take on a new form, and crime sometimes helps to determine the form they will take. How many times, indeed, it is only an anticipation of future morality – a step toward what will be! According to Athenian law, Socrates was a criminal, and his condemnation was no more than just. However, his crime, namely, the independence of his thought, rendered a service not only to humanity but to his country. It served to prepare a new morality and faith which the Athenians needed, since the traditions by which they had lived until then were no longer in harmony with the current conditions of life. Nor is the case of Socrates unique; it is reproduced periodically in history. It would never have been possible to establish the freedom of thought we now enjoy if the regulations prohibiting it had not been violated before being solemnly abrogated. At that time, however, the violation was a crime, since it was an offense against sentiments still very keen in the average conscience. And yet this crime was useful as a prelude to reforms which daily became more necessary. Liberal philosophy had as its precursors the heretics of all kinds who were justly punished by secular authorities during the entire course of the Middle Ages and until the eve of modern times.

From this point of view the fundamental facts of criminality present themselves to us in an entirely new light. Contrary to current ideas, the criminal no longer seems a totally unsociable being, a sort of parasitic element, a strange and unassimilable body, introduced into the midst of society. On the contrary, he plays a definite role in social life. Crime, for its part, must no longer be conceived as an evil that cannot be too much suppressed. There is no occasion for self-congratulation when the crime rate drops noticeably below the average level, for we may be certain that this apparent progress is associated with some social disorder. Thus, the number of assault cases never falls so low as in times of want. With the drop in the crime rate, and as a reaction to it, comes a revision, or the need of a revision in the theory of punishment. If, indeed, crime is a disease, its punishment is its remedy and cannot be otherwise conceived; thus, all the discussions it arouses bear on the point of determining what the punishment must be in order to fulfil this role of remedy. If crime is not pathological at all, the object of punishment cannot be to cure it, and its true function must be sought elsewhere.

[. . .]

8

Law and authority

Peter Kropotkin

If one studies the millions of laws that rule humanity, one can see easily that they are divisible into three main categories: protection of property, protection of government, protection of persons. And in analysing these three categories one comes to the same conclusion regarding each of them: *the uselessness and harmfulness of the law*.

As for the protection of property, the socialists know what that means. Laws regarding property are not fashioned to guarantee either individuals or society the fruits of their labour. They are made, on the contrary, to pilfer from the producer part of what he produces and to assure to the few whatever they have pilfered, either from the producers or from society as a whole. When the law established the right of Sir Such-and-Such over a house, for example, it established his right, not over a cabin that he might have built himself, nor over a house he might have erected with the help of a few friends; nobody would dispute his right if such had been the case. The law, on the contrary, established his rights over a mansion that *is not* the product of his labour, first because he has had it built by others, whom he has not paid the true value of their work, and next because his mansion represents a social value he could not produce on his own: the law establishes his rights over a portion of that which belongs to everybody and not to anyone in particular. The same house, built in the beautiful heart of Siberia, would not have the value it has in a large city. Its value derives, as we know, from the works of fifty generations who have built the city, adorned it, provided it with water and gas, with fine boulevards, universities, theatres and shops, with railways and roads radiating in all directions.

Thus in recognizing the rights of Sir Such-and-Such over a house in Paris, in London, in Rouen, the law appropriates to him – unjustly – a certain part of the products of the work of all humanity. And it is precisely because that appropriation is a crying injustice (all other forms of property have the same character) that it has needed a whole arsenal of laws and a whole army of soldiers, policemen and judges to sustain it, against the good sense and the feeling of justice that is inherent in humanity.

Thus the greater part of our laws – the civil codes of all countries – have no other object than to maintain this appropriation, this monopoly to the profit of a few

From *Words of a Rebel* (trans. G. Woodcock), pp. 159–64. (Montreal/New York: Black Rose Books, 1992. First published 1898.)

against the whole of humanity. Three-quarters of the cases judged by the tribunals are merely quarrels that have cropped up among monopolists; two robbers quarrelling over the booty. And a great part of our criminal laws have the same aim, since their object is to keep the worker in a position subordinate to the employer, to assure to one the exploitation of the other.

As to guaranteeing the producer the product of his work, there are not even any laws that provide it. That is so simple and so natural, so much in accordance with human customs and habits that the law has not even dreamed of it. Open brigandage, with arms in hand, no longer exists in our century; a worker need no longer dispute with another worker over the products of their toil; if there is some failure of understanding between them, they deal with it without having recourse to the law, by calling in a third party, and if there is anyone who insists on requiring from another person a part of what he has produced, it can only be the property-owner, coming to claim his lion's share. As to humanity in general, it respects everywhere the right of each person over what he has produced, without the need to have any special laws to cover it.

All these laws about property, which make up the great volumes of codes and are the delight of our lawyers, have no object but that of protecting the unjust appropriation of the work of humanity by certain monopolists, and thus have no reason to exist; and socialist revolutionaries are determined to make them vanish on the day of the revolution. We can, in fact and in full justice, make a great bonfire of *all* the laws that are related to the so-called 'rights of property', of all the property titles, of all the archives – in brief, of all that has reference to an institution which soon will be considered a blot on the history of humanity as humiliating as slavery and serfdom in past centuries.

What we have just said about the laws concerning property applies completely to the second category of laws – the laws that maintain the government – constitutional laws, in other words.

Once again there is a whole arsenal of laws, decrees, or ordinances, this time serving to protect the various forms of representative government – by delegation or usurpation – under which human societies struggle for existence. We know very well – the anarchists have often demonstrated it by their incessant criticism of the various forms of government – that the mission of *all* governments, monarchical, constitutional and republican, is to protect and maintain by force the privileges of the owning classes: aristocracy, priesthood and bourgeoisie. A good third of our laws, the 'fundamental' laws, laws on taxes, customs duties, on the organization of ministries and their chancelleries, on the army, the police, the church, etc. – and there are tens of thousands of them in every country – have no other end but to maintain, keep in repair and develop the governmental machine, which in its turn serves almost entirely to protect the privileges of these possessing classes. Analyse all these laws, observe them in action from day to day, and you will see that there is not a single one worth keeping, beginning with those that bound the communes hand and foot to the parson, the local merchant and the governmental boss, and ending with that famous constitution (the nineteenth or twentieth since 1789), which gives us a chamber of dunces and petty speculators ready for the dictatorship of any adventurer who comes along, for the rule of some crowned cabbage-head.

Briefly, regarding these laws there can be no doubt. Not only the anarchists, but also the more or less revolutionary middle class are in agreement on this: that the best use one can make of the laws concerning the organization of government is to burn them in a bonfire celebrating their end.

There remains the first category of laws, the most important, because most of the prejudices cluster around them; the laws regarding the protection of persons, the punishment and prevention of 'crimes'. If the law enjoys a certain consideration, it is because people believe this category of laws absolutely indispensable for the security of the individual in society. Laws have developed from the nucleus of customs that were useful for human societies and were exploited by the rulers to sanction their domination. The authority of the chiefs of the tribes, of the rich families of the communes, and of the kind, were supported by the function of judges which they exercised, and even to the present, when people talk of the need for government, it is its function of supreme judge that is implied. 'Without government, people would strangle each other', says the village wiseacre. 'The ultimate end of society is to give every accused person twelve honest jurors', said Edmund Burke.

But despite all the presuppositions that exist on this subject, it is high time the anarchists loudly declared that this category of the laws is as useless and harmful as the rest.

First of all, when we consider the so-called 'crimes', the attacks against the persons, it is well known that two-thirds or even three-quarters of them are inspired by the desire to lay hold of somebody's wealth. That immense category of so-called 'crimes and misdemeanours' would disappear on the day private property ceased to exist.

'But', we shall be told, 'there will still be the brutes who make attempts on the lives of citizens, who strike with the knife in every quarrel, who avenge the least offence by a murder, if there are not laws to restrain them and punishments to hold them back.' This is the refrain that has been sung to us ever since we expressed doubt of society's right to punish. Yet one fact has been clearly established: the severity of punishments in no way diminishes the number of crimes. You can hang, draw and quarter the murderers as much as you like, but the number of murders will not diminish. On the other hand, if you abolish the death penalty there will not be a single murder more. Statisticians and legists know that when the severity of the penal code is lessened there is never an increase in the number of attempts against the lives of citizens. On the other hand, when the crops are abundant, when bread is cheap and the weather is good, the number of murders decreases at once. It is proved by statistics that the number of crimes increases and declines in relation to the price of necessities and to good or bad weather. Not that all murders are inspired by hunger. Far from it; but when the harvests are good and necessities are affordably priced, people are happy and less wretched than usual, and they do not let themselves be led away by dark passions that tempt them to stick knives into the chests of their neighbours for futile reasons.

Besides, it is well known that fear of punishment has not halted a single murderer. Whoever is about to kill his neighbour for vengeance or poverty does not reflect a great deal on the consequences; there has never been a murderer who lacked the firm conviction that he would escape from prosecution. Let anyone think about this subject, let him analyse crimes and punishments, their motives and consequences, and if he knows how to reason without letting himself be influenced by preconceived ideas, he is bound to reach this conclusion:

'Without considering a society where people will receive a better education, where the development of all their faculties and the possibility of using them will give men and women so much pleasure that they would not risk it all by indulging in murder, without considering that future society, and taking into account only our present society, with the sad products of poverty we see everywhere in the low taverns of the cities, the number of murders would not increase in any way if one day it were decided that no punishment be inflicted on murderers; indeed it is very likely there would be a fall in the number of cases involving recidivists, brutalized in the prisons.'

We are told constantly of the benefits of the law and of the salutary effects of punishment. But has anyone ever tried to establish a balance between the benefits that are attributed to the law and its penalties, and the degrading effect of those penalties on humanity? One has merely to consider the accumulation of evil passions that are awakened among the spectators by the atrocious punishments inflicted publicly in our streets and squares. Who is it that has thus fostered and developed the instincts of cruelty among humanity (instincts unknown to the animals, man having become the most cruel animal on earth), if it is not the king, the judge and the priest, armed by the law, who had flesh torn away by strips, with burning pitch poured into the wounds, had limbs dislocated, bones broken, men sawn in two, so as to maintain their authority? You need merely consider the torrent of depravity let loose in human societies by spying and informing, encouraged by judges and paid for by the government in hard cash under the pretext of assisting the discovery of crimes. You need only to go into prisons and observe there what the man becomes who is deprived of liberty and thrust among other depraved beings permeated with all the corruption and vice that breed in our prisons today, to realize that the more they are 'reformed', the more detestable the prisons become, our modern and model penitentiaries being a hundred times more corrupting than the dungeons of the Middle Ages. Finally, you need only consider what corruption and deprivation of the mind is generated among humankind by these ideas of *obedience* (essence of the law), of punishment, of authority having the right to punish and judge apart from the urgings of conscience, by all the functions of executioners, jailers and informers – in brief by all that immense apparatus of law and authority. You have only to consider all that, and you will certainly be in agreement with us, when we say that law and its penalties are abominations that should cease to exist.

Meanwhile, people who are not ruled by police, and because of that are less imbued by authoritarian prejudices, have perfectly understood that someone called a 'criminal' is simply an unfortunate; that it is not a question of whipping or chaining him, or causing his death on the scaffold or in prison, but of succouring him by the most brotherly care, by treating him as an equal and taking him to live among honest people. And we hope the coming revolution will resound with this call:

'Burn the guillotines, demolish the prisons, drive away the judge, the policeman, the spy – an impure race if ever there was one – but treat as a brother him who has been led by passion to do ill to his kind; above all deprive the truly great criminals, those ignoble products of bourgeois idleness, of the possibility of parading their vices in seductive form, and you can be sure that we shall no longer have more than a very small number of crimes to point to in our society. Apart from idleness, what sustains crime is law and authority; the laws on property, the laws on government, the laws with their penalties and punishments. And Authority, which takes on itself to make these laws and apply them.

'No more laws! No more judges! Freedom, Brotherhood and the practice of Solidarity are the only effective bulwark we can raise to the anti-social instincts of a few among us.'

Part II

The problem of crime I: Causation

INTRODUCTION

Globally, the search for the causes of crime continues to form the bedrock of most criminological studies. The obsession with causation has also been critiqued by a variety of radical criminologies more concerned to reveal how crime and 'the criminal' are constructed through processes of law creation and enforcement (see Part III); and more recently has been dismissed as a fruitless and failed exercise which distracts attention away from the more pressing tasks of crime management, (see Parts IV and V). It is common for these criminologists to claim that studies of the aetiology of crime should be relegated to the status of history

However, this selection of readings should reveal that this is not necessarily the case. The selection has been governed by two main criteria. First, to illustrate the diverse schools of thought which make claim to the theorization of the causes of crime, and secondly, to establish that each of these schools has retained a strong contemporary presence. For this reason, rather than reprinting the classic statements of crime causation (such as Merton's 'anomie theory' or the Chicago School's notion of 'social disorganization' in the 1930s), we have chosen to focus upon a body of theoretical work which marks a reworking or critical development of earlier positions.

If Lombroso's work established a need to examine the biological bases of criminality, then the extract reproduced here from Mednick, Gabrielli and Hutchings represents its modern and more sophisticated version. Based on a detailed study of adoptees, their biological parents and adoptive parents, they make the claim that some genetic and biological factors are transmitted through the generations of some families and that these factors must be involved in the aetiology of at least some criminal behaviour. Eysenck's reiteration and reinforcement of his 1964 theory, that certain personality traits are likely to lead to a greater propensity towards anti-social behaviour, shares some of these concerns. However, biology alone, he argued, is an insufficient explanation. Eysenck's work is more concerned to reveal the impact of interrelationships between genetic factors and processes of socialization.

Whilst Mednick et al. and Eysenck are included here to illustrate the continuing influence of theories concerned with the individual basis of criminality, the following extracts are more concerned to explore the relevance of geo-graphical place and economic factors. Bottoms and Wiles suggest some ways in which micro (individual) and macro (social structure) levels of analysis might be combined (through the adoption of Giddens's structuration theory) in order to reach a more adequate understanding of the impact of space/time/sense of location on particular rates of crime.

Much public discussion of crime is more persuaded by the arguments of the American political scientist Charles Murray. He argues forcibly that rising crime rates are caused by the growth of an underclass – identified primarily by illegitimacy, family breakdown and welfare dependence. In his view the growth in crime is directly related to increasing numbers of barbaric young men who have grown up without the civilizing institution of marriage and without the moral awareness brought about through family responsibilities.

If Murray represents one strand of a contemporary conservative or 'right realist' criminology, the extract from Lea and Young represents a political response from some sections of the left. Advocating 'left realism', they argue that the key to the causes of crime is not absolute deprivation, or unemploy-ment, but relative deprivation. Crime occurs when there is an excess of expec-tations over opportunities for fulfilling them. The extract here from *What Is to Be Done about Law and Order?* explores how the Left can regain some of the political initiative on matters of law and order by adopting a middle ground which neither claims that crime is caused by abject poverty nor that it is a freely chosen activity on the part of the wicked. Rather it stems from economic and political discontent and an absence of economic and political opportunities.

In the next reading Hirschi and Gottfredson present and defend the conceptual utility of their theory of 'self control'. This represents a marked development of Hirschi's original version of control theory – the social bond perspective – which he traced back to Durkheim. Social control theories maintain that each individual is a potential law breaker and that contemporary societies create many criminal/deviant opportunities. The critical question becomes why do people choose to abide by the law? Hirschi's much tested original thesis argued that young people who engage in delinquency are free of intimate attachments, aspirations and moral beliefs that bind them to a law abiding existence. Young people are not forced into a delinquent way of life. They engage in delinquency because they are relatively free from the ties of the conventional social order. Hirschi and Gotttfredson's more psychologically oriented 'general theory of crime' identifies self-control rather than societal control as the root of criminality or conformity.

The extract from Katz's *Seductions and Repulsions of Crime* eschews all the reference to factors of individual or social structural causation in favour of examination of the situational inducements surrounding crime. This highly controversial criminological text explores (and exposes) what he defines as the unacknowledged 'seductive', 'sensually compelling' lived experience of crimin-ality – what does it mean, feel, sound, taste or look like to commit a crime is the question he poses. Critiqued by the Right for being overly concerned with the criminal's own point of view and by the Left for irresponsibly celebrating the thrill-seeking aspect of crime, Katz's argument is likely to remain influential in his insistence that all of us readily engage in activities which at other times and in other places we would unhesitatingly describe as being 'criminal'. Felson also departs from criminology's traditional focus on identifying the factors causing individuals to commit crime. He addresses the 'other side' of crime causation examining how society encourages or inhibits crime in the routine activities of everyday life. Routine activity theory is an opportunity theory in that it focuses on the convergence in space and time of the elements considered essential for a crime to occur: a motivated offender; a suitable target and the absence of a capable guardian against crime. The attractiveness of routine activity theory for policy makers is that like situational crime prevention it promises to reduce crime through common sense changes in the physical environment and patterns of everyday activity.

The final selections from Klein and Segal are designed to introduce the reader to an even more complex range of issues which are raised through interrogations of the relationship between crime and gender. Klein provides a thorough critique of many of the early criminologies not only for their relative neglect of the criminality of women but also for their assumptions about the inherent nature of women. Thus traditionally female crime has been analysed in terms of sexuality, biological drives, inferiority, deceit and mental instability. Above all, many of the concepts applied to male crime, such as those derived from economic and social determinism, are notably lacking in analyses of female crime. For example, economic offences such as shoplifting have for women been traditionally explained as outlets for sexual frustration. When Klein published her critique in 1973, feminist work on crime and criminality was in its infancy. As she notes in an afterword, published some twenty years after her original work, the field has subsequently burgeoned in a variety of directions (see also Part VI). The extract from Segal is but one of those directions. She explores the connections between crime (particularly violent crime) and masculinity. As most crime is committed by men and much more remains hidden in the home and domestic sphere, Segal argues (in contrast to some other feminist authors) that the wider causes of male behaviour must be located in societies which construct 'masculinity' in terms of heterosexual power. But neither 'violence' nor 'masculinity' are unitary phenomena. Rather masculinity is mediated through class, race and economic context to produce a situation in which the increased barbarism of public life is reflected back into an increased barbarism in private life. The issue then is not simply one of an essentialized masculinity.

Collectively these essays reveal that questions of aetiology remain fiercely debated. The issue remains, though, of how far any one theory is capable of providing a comprehensive explanation. It is more likely that *certain* theories will remain better placed to analyse *certain* behaviours and social events of which some may come to be defined as 'crime'. Numerous 'general theories' of crime causation continue to be advanced which seek to integrate many of the specific propositions raised in these individual chapters. But whatever is gained in generality is certainly lost in an unfettered multi-dimensional eclecticism. Given the widespread nature of crime, it may be that no specific motivational theory is required, or is indeed possible. Crime, as Durkheim (see Part I) argued, is as social fact. It may require no more or less an explanation than is required for any other everyday activity.

9

Genetic factors in the etiology of criminal behavior

Sarnoff A. Mednick, William F. Gabrielli Jr and Barry Hutchings

Human behavior patterns are generally ascribed to an interaction of life experiences and genetic predispositions, but the importance of genetic influences in shaping conduct has often been contested. This debate has been especially intense, and often emotional, in explaining criminal behavior (Sarbin and Miller, 1970). Reluctance to consider genetic factors in crime has had political overtones (Haller, 1968), but it may also reflect the fact that, until recently, the evidence for genetic influences consisted mainly of studies of twins, some of which were methodologically questionable.

Christiansen (1977a) reported on the criminality of a total population of 3,586 twin pairs from a well-defined area of Denmark. He found 52 per cent of the twins concordant for criminal behavior for (male–male) identical twin pairs and 22 per cent concordance for (male–male) fraternal twin pairs. This result suggests that identical twins inherit some biological characteristic (or characteristics) that increases their common risk of being registered for criminal behavior.

It has been pointed out, however, that identical twins are treated more alike than are fraternal twins (Christiansen, 1977b). Thus their greater similarity in criminal behavior may be partly related to their shared experience. This has produced a reluctance to accept in full the genetic implications of twin research. The study of adoptions better separates environmental and genetic effects; if convicted adoptees have a disproportionately high number of convicted biological fathers (given appropriate controls), this would suggest the influence of a genetic factor in criminal behavior. This conclusion is supported by the fact that almost none of the adoptees know their biological parents; adoptees often do not even realize they have been adopted.

Two US adoption studies have produced highly suggestive results. Crowe (1975) found an increased rate of criminality in 37 Iowan adoptees with criminal biological mothers. Cadoret (1978) reported on 246 Iowans adopted at birth. Antisocial

From *The Causes of Crime: New Biological Approaches* (eds S. Mednick, T. Moffit and S. Stack), pp. 74–91. (Cambridge: Cambridge University Press, 1987.)

Table 9.1 *Number of adoptions in five-year periods*

Years	Male	Female	Total
1924–8	578	1,051	1,629
1929–33	730	1,056	1,786
1934–8	832	1,092	1,924
1939–43	1,650	1,731	3,381
1944–7	2,890	2,782	5,672
(4 years)			
year uncertain	20	15	35
Total	6,700	7,727	14,427

behavior in these adoptees was significantly related to antisocial behavior in the biological parents. In a study of Swedish adoptees Bohman, Cloninger, Sigvardsson, and von Knorring (1982) found that criminal behavior in the biological parents was significantly related to criminal behavior in the adoptees. This relationship held only for property crimes.

The study to be described in this chapter was based on a register of all 14,427 non-familial adoptions in Denmark in the years 1924–47. This register was established at the Psykologisk Institut in Copenhagen by a group of American and Danish investigators (Kety et al., 1968). The register includes information on the adoptee and his or her adoptive and biological parents. We hypothesized that registered criminality in the biological parents would be associated with an increased risk of registered criminal behavior in the offspring.

PROCEDURES

Information on all non-familial adoptions in the Kingdom of Denmark between 1924 and 1947 ($n = 14,427$) was obtained from records at the Ministry of Justice. The distribution of adoptions by sex of adoptee for five-year periods appears in Table 9.1. Note the increase in adoptions with increasing population, especially during the war years, and the larger number of females adopted.

Criminality data

Court convictions were used as an index of criminal involvement. Minors (below 15 years of age) cannot receive court convictions. Court convictions information is maintained by the chief of the police district in which an individual is born. The court record (Strafferegister) contains information on the date of the conviction, the paragraphs of the law violated, and the sanction. To obtain access to these records it is necessary to know the place of birth. When subjects' conviction records could not be checked, it was usually because of a lack of information or ambiguity regarding their date and/or place of birth. The court record was obtained for all of the subjects for whom date and place of birth were available ($n = 65,516$).

Information was first recorded from the adoption files of the Ministry of Justice. In these files, birthplace was then available for the biological and adoptive parents

Table 9.2 *Conviction rates of completely identified members of adoptee families*

| Family member | Number identified | Number not identified | Number of criminal law court convictions | | | |
			None	One	Two	More than two
Male adoptee	6,129	571	0.841	0.088	0.029	0.040
Female adoptee	7,065	662	0.972	0.020	0.005	0.003
Adoptive father	13,918	509	0.938	0.046	0.008	0.008
Adoptive mother	14,267	160	0.981	0.015	0.002	0.002
Biological father	10,604	3,823	0.714	0.129	0.056	0.102
Biological mother	12,300	2,127	0.911	0.064	0.012	0.013

but not for the adoptees; birthplace for the adoptees was obtained from the Central Persons Register or the local population registers. The Central Persons Register was established in 1968; adoptees who died or emigrated before 1968 were thus excluded from the study. There were some difficulties in these searches. The criminal records of persons who have died or have reached the age of 80 are sometimes removed from the registers and archived in the Central Police Office in Copenhagen. Thus if an individual had a court conviction but had died before our search began, his or her record might have been transferred from the local police district to the Copenhagen Central Police Office. There the record would be maintained in a death register. In view of this, the entire population (adoptees and parents) was checked in the death register. If an adoptee had died or emigrated before the age of 30, the adoptee and parents were dropped from the study since the adoptee had not gone through the entire risk period for criminal conviction. A small section of Denmark in southern Jutland belonged to Germany until 1920. If an individual from this area was registered for criminality before 1920 but not *after* 1920, that individual's record was lost to this study.

For each individual we coded the following information: sex, date of birth, address, occupation, place of birth and size of the community into which the child was adopted. The subjects' occupations permitted us to code socioeconomic status (Svalastoga, 1959). For the adoptees we also coded marital status in 1976.

Not fully identified cases

It will be recalled that in order to check the court register it was necessary to have name, date and place of birth. A considerable number of cases were lost to this investigation for the following reasons. (a) There was no record of place and/or date of birth. (b) In Denmark the biological mother is required by law to name the biological father. In some few cases she refused, was unsure, or named more than one possible father. These cases were dropped from the population. (c) Among the adoptive parents, 397 were single women. This was because either the adoptive father died just before the formal adoption or the child was adopted by a single woman (not common in this era). (d) Because of additional difficulties involved in checking the criminal registers before 1910, individuals who were born before January 1, 1885, were excluded from the study.

In the case of exclusion of an *adoptee* for any of the above reasons the entire adoptive family was dropped. If a parent was excluded, the remaining subjects were retained for analysis. Table 9.2 presents the number of fully identified individuals in each of the subject categories.

Results

The data to be reported consist of convictions for violation of the Danish Criminal Code (Straffeloven). The levels of court convictions for each of the members of the adoption family are given in Table 9.2. The biological-father and male-adoptee conviction rates are considerably higher than the rates for the adoptive father. The rate for adoptive fathers is a bit below that (8 per cent) for men of this age group, in this time period (Hurwitz and Christiansen, 1971). Note also that most of the adoptive-father convictions are attributable to one-time offenders. The male adoptees and the biological fathers are more heavily recidivistic.

The rates of conviction for the women are considerably lower and there is considerably less recidivism than there is for men. The biological mothers and female adoptees have higher levels of court convictions than the adoptive mothers. The adoptive mothers are just below the population average for women of this age range and time period, 2.2 per cent. The individuals who gave up their children for adoption, and their biological offspring, show higher rates of court convictions than the general population and the adoptive parents.

In light of current adoption practices one might be surprised that adoptive parents with court convictions were permitted to adopt. It should be recalled, however, that many of these adoptions took place during the Great Depression and World War II. It was more difficult to find willing adoptive homes in these periods owing partly to the relative unavailability of adoptive parents and to the additional number of adoptees available. Adoptive parents were accepted if they had had a 5-year crime-free period before the adoption.

In most of the analyses that follow, we shall consider the relation between parents' criminal convictions and criminal convictions in the adoptees. If either mother or father (biological and/or adoptive) had received a criminal law conviction, the *parents* of that adoptee will be considered criminal. In view of the low level of convictions among the female adoptees, the analyses will concentrate on the criminal behavior of the male adoptees.

Types of crime

Of the adoptive parents, 5.50 per cent were convicted for property crimes; 1.05 per cent committed violent acts; and 0.54 per cent were convicted for sexual offenses. Of the biological parents, 28.12 per cent were responsible for property crimes; 6.51 per cent committed violent crimes; and 3.81 per cent committed sexual offenses. Individuals could be registered for more than one type of crime.

Table 9.3 *Cross-fostering analysis: percentage of adoptive sons convicted of criminal law offenses*

Have adoptive parents been convicted?	Have biological parents been convicted?	
	Yes	No
Yes	24.5 (of 143)	14.7 (of 204)
No	20.0 (of 1,226)	13.5 (of 2,492)

Note: Numbers in parentheses represent the total number for each cell.

Cross-fostering analysis

Because of the size of the population it is possible to segregate subgroups of adoptees who have combinations of convicted and non-convicted biological and adoptive parents. Table 9.3 presents the four groups in a design that is analogous to the cross-fostering paradigm used in behavior genetics. As can be seen in the lower-right-hand cell, if neither the biological nor adoptive parents are convicted, 13.5 per cent of their sons are convicted. If the adoptive parents are convicted and the biological parents are not convicted, this figure rises to only 14.7 per cent. Note that 20.0 per cent of the sons are convicted if the adoptive parents are *not* convicted and the biological parents are convicted. If *both* the biological and adoptive parents are convicted, we observe the highest level of conviction in the sons, 24.5 per cent. The comparison analogous to the cross-fostering paradigm favors a partial genetic etiology. We must caution, however, that simply knowing that an adoptive parent has been convicted of a crime does not tell us how criminogenic the adoptee's environment has been. (Recall the preponderance of one-time offenders in the adoptive parents and the adoptive agency's condition that the adoptive parents not have a conviction for the 5 years preceding the adoption.) On the other hand, at conception, the genetic influence of the biological father is already complete. Thus this analysis does not yield a fair comparison between environmental and genetic influences included in Table 9.3. However, this initial analysis does indicate that sons with a convicted biological parent have an elevated probability of being convicted. This suggests that some biological characteristic is transmitted from the criminal biological parent that increases the son's risk of obtaining a court conviction for a criminal law offense.

A log-linear analysis of the data in Table 9.3 is presented in Table 9.4. Adoptive-parent convictions are not associated with a significant increment in the son's level of convictions. The effect of the biological parents' convictions is marked. The model presented in Table 9.4 reveals that, considering only the *additive* effect of the biological parent and the adoptive parent, the improvement in the chi-square value leaves almost no room for improvement by an interaction effect.

The adoptive parents have a low frequency of court convictions. In order to simplify interpretation of the relations reported below we have excluded cases with adoptive-parent criminality. (Analyses completed that did include adoptive-parent criminality did not alter the nature of the findings to be reported.)

Table 9.4 *Log-linear analysis: influences of adoptive-parent and biological-parent convictions on male-adoptee convictions*

Model	Model			Improvement		
	χ^2	d.f.	p	χ^2	d.f.	p
Baseline (S, AB)	32.91	3	0.001			
Adoptive parent (SA, AB)	30.71	2	0.001	2.20	1	n.s.
Biological parent (SB, AB)	1.76	2	0.415	31.15	1	0.001
Combined influence (SB, SA, AB)	0.30	1	0.585	32.61	2	0.001
Biological parent given adoptive parent (SB/SA, AB)	–	–		28.95	1	0.001
Adoptive parent given biological parent (SA/SB, AB)	–	–		1.46	1	n.s.

Note: S denotes adoptee-son effect; A, adoptive-parent effect; B, biological-parent effect; n.s., not significant.

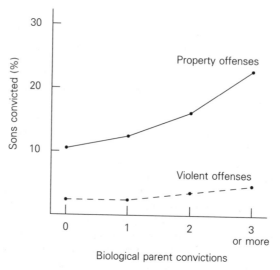

Figure 9.1 *Percentage of male adoptee property offenders and violent offenders by biological-parent convictions*

Figure 9.1 presents the relation between convictions in the sons and degree of recidivism in the biological parents. The relation is positive and relatively monotonic (with the scales utilized on the X and Y axes). Note also that the relation is highly significant for property crimes and not statistically significant for violent crimes.

The chronic offender

The chronic offender is rare but commits a markedly disproportionate number of criminal offenses. This extremely high rate of offending suggested that genetic predisposition may play an important role in these cases. We examined the relation between convictions of the chronic adoptee offender and his biological parents.

Table 9.5 *Proportion of chronic offenders, other offenders, and non-offenders among male adoptees as a function of convictions of biological parents*

Number of male-adoptee convictions	Number of biological-parent convictions			
	0	1	2	3 or more
Non-offenders (no convictions)	0.87	0.84	0.80	0.75
Other offenders (1 or 2 convictions)	0.10	0.12	0.15	0.17
Chronic offenders (3 or more convictions)	0.03	0.04	0.05	0.09
Number of adoptees	2,492	547	233	419

Note: Data do not include cases in which adoptive parents were convicted of criminal law violation.

In an important US birth cohort study (Wolfgang et al., 1972), the chronic offender was defined as one who had been arrested five or more times; these chronic offenders comprised 6 per cent of the males and had committed 52 per cent of the offenses. In our adoption cohort we recorded court convictions rather than arrest data. If we select as chronic offenders those with three or more court convictions, this includes 4.09 per cent of the male adoptees. This small group of recidivists accounts for 69.4 per cent of all the court convictions for all the male adoptees. This is a high concentration of crime in a very small fraction of the cohort.

Table 9.5 shows how the chronic offenders, the other offenders (one or two convictions), and the non-offenders are distributed as a function of level of crime in the biological parents. As can be seen, the proportion of chronic adoptee offenders increases as a function of level of recidivism in the biological parents.

Another way of expressing this concentration of crime is to point out that the chronic male adoptee offenders with biological parents with three or more offenses number only 37. Although they comprise only 1 per cent of the 3,691 male adoptees in Table 9.5, they are responsible for 30 per cent of the male adoptee convictions. We should also note that the mean number of convictions for the chronic adoptee offenders increases sharply as a function of biological parent recidivism. The biological parents with zero, one, two, or three or more convictions have male adoptees (i.e., male children who are subsequently adopted by others) averaging 0.30, 0.41, 0.48 and 0.70 convictions, respectively.

We have presented evidence that there is an association between biological parents' convictions and the convictions of their (subsequently) adopted sons. The relation seems stronger for chronic offenders. The sons of chronic offenders account for a disproportionate number of the convictions in the cohort.

Sibling analyses

There are a number of instances in which a biological mother and/or biological father contributed more than one child to this population. These offspring are, of course, full and half-siblings; they were sometimes placed in different adoptive homes. We would predict that the separated full siblings should show more concordance for criminal convictions than the separated half-siblings. Both of these groups should show more concordance than two randomly selected, unrelated, separately reared male adoptees.

Table 9.6 *Concordance for criminal law convictions in male siblings placed in separate adoptive homes*

Degree of genetic relation	Pairwise concordance (%)
Unrelated, raised apart	8.5
Half-siblings, raised apart	12.9
Full siblings, raised apart	20.0
Half-siblings and full siblings, raised apart, criminal father	30.8
Unrelated 'siblings' raised together in adoptive home	8.5

The probability of any one male adoptee being convicted is 0.159. The probability of drawing a pair of unrelated, separated male adoptees with at least one having a conviction is 0.293. The probability that both of the pair will have been convicted is 0.025. Thus pairwise concordance for unrelated separated male adoptees is 8.5 per cent. This can be seen as a baseline. There were 126 male–male half-sibling pairs placed in separate adoptive homes. Of these, 31 pairs had at least one member of the sibship convicted; of these 31 pairs, 4 pairs were concordant for convictions. This yields a concordance rate for half-siblings of 12.9 per cent. There were 40 male–male full-sibling pairs placed in different adoptive homes. Of these, 15 pairs had at least one member of the sibship convicted; of these 15 pairs, three pairs were concordant for convictions. This yields a concordance rate for full siblings of 20 per cent. These numbers are very small, but the results are in the predicted direction. As the degree of genetic relation increases, the level of concordance increases.

We also considered the level of concordance of the sibling pairs whose biological father was a criminal (had at least one conviction). Of 98 fathers with at least one pair of male–male, separated, adopted-away siblings, 45 had received at least one conviction. (It should be noted that this is a significantly higher rate of convictions (45.9 per cent) than the conviction rate (28.6 per cent) for the total population of biological fathers, $\psi^2(1) = 14.6$, $p < 0.01$.)

We combined full- and half-sibling pairs (because of the small number and because the siblings shared criminal biological fathers). Of the 45 sibling pairs, 13 had at least one member with a conviction; of these 13, four pairs were concordant for convictions. This yields a concordance rate of 30.8 per cent. Table 9.6 summarizes these sibling analyses. The pairwise concordance rates can be compared with the male–male rates for twins from a population twin study; Christiansen (1977a) reported 36 per cent pairwise concordance for identical twins and a 13 per cent rate for fraternal twins.

Although these numbers are very small, they represent all of the cases, as defined, in a total cohort of adoptions. The results suggest that a number of these separated, adopted siblings inherited some characteristic that predisposed both of them to being convicted for criminal behavior. As would be expected, in those instances in which the biological father was criminal, the effect was enhanced.

Specificity of a genetic relation

Earlier, we mentioned a study of a small sample of adoptees (Crowe, 1975). Crowe reported the impression that there was some similarity in the types of crime committed by the biological mother and the adoptee. This suggests specific genetic predispositions for different types of crime. In order to explore this possibility, we examined the rates of violent crimes in the adoptees as a function of violent crime in the biological parents. We completed similar analyses for property crimes. We also examined more specific types of crime (theft, fraud, assault, etc.) for similarity in the biological parent and the adoptee.

If the genetic predisposition was specific for type of crime, these 'specificity' analyses should have resulted in our observing a closer relation between adoptee and biological-parent levels of conviction for each of these types of crime. The best predictor of each type of adoptee crime, however, was number of biological-parent convictions rather than type of biological-parent offense. This suggests that the biological predisposition the adoptee inherits must be of a general nature, partly determining the degree of law abidance shown by the adoptee. It is also possible that the data of this study are too gross for the detection of a specificity relation. This may require careful coding of details of the criminal behavior. This was not possible in our study.

Sex differences

As can be seen in Table 9.2, convictions of females for criminal law violations are very infrequent. It might be speculated that those women who do exhibit a level of criminal behavior that prompts a court conviction must have a severe predisposition for such behavior. Criminal involvement of many men, on the other hand, may tend to be more socially or environmentally inspired. These statements suggest that convictions in the biological mother are more closely related to the adoptee's conviction(s) than criminal behavior in the biological father.

In every analysis we conducted, the relation between biological-mother conviction and adoptee conviction is significantly stronger than the relation between biological-father conviction and adoptee conviction. In comparison with the relation between biological-father and adoptee convictions, convictions of the biological mothers are more closely related to convictions of the daughters. This result is statistically significant, but the relatively low frequency of female convictions forces us to interpret these findings with caution.

Historical period

The period of these adoptions (1924–67) spans some important historical changes in Denmark, including a world war, the Great Depression, and industrialization. It is conceivable that the influence of genetic factors might be affected by these social upheavals. It is also possible that changes in level or type of crime during these years might influence the relations observed. Analyses conducted for the entire population were repeated for each of the 5-year periods. The results were virtually identical for all of the periods and virtually identical to the analyses of the total sample. The social changes during these years did not interact with the relation between biological-parent and adoptee crime.

Controlling genetic influence in examining environmental effects

In many social science investigations genetic characteristics are not considered. In some analyses this may contribute error; sometimes omission may lead to incomplete conclusions. For example, separation from a father is associated with an increased level of delinquency in a son. This has been interpreted as a result of failure of identification or lack of consistent discipline. As we can see from Table 9.2, some fathers who permit themselves to be separated from their child have a relatively high level of criminal convictions. The higher level of delinquency found for separated children might be partially due to a genetic transmission of criminogenic predispositional characteristics from antisocial fathers. If this genetic variance were partially accounted for, the environmental hypotheses could be more precisely tested. We utilized such partial genetic control to study an important criminological variable, social status. We separated the variance ascribable to 'genetic' social class and 'rearing' social class (Van Dusen et al., 1983). We examined adoptee convictions as a joint function of biological parents' social class and adoptive parents' social class. It is clear from inspection of Table 9.7 that male-adoptee convictions vary as a function of both genetic and environmental social class; log-linear analyses reveal that both effects are statistically significant. Although the genetic effect is of interest here, we emphasize that, to our knowledge, this is the first controlled demonstration that *environmental* aspects influence the social class–crime relation. This finding suggests that, regardless of genetic background, improved social conditions are likely to lead to a reduction in criminal behavior.

Table 9.7 is of interest in another regard. Careful inspection reveals a correlation between adoptive-parent socioeconomic status (SES) and biological-parent SES. This represents the attempt by the adoptive agency to match certain characteristics of the two sets of parents in order to increase the likelihood that the adoptee will fit into the adoptive home. In terms of the adoption research design, this correlation is undesirable because it reduces the independence of the genetic rearing and environmental influences on the adoptee. Since social class is not independent of convictions (Table 9.7), it is conceivable that the relation between biological-parent and adoptee convictions is, in part, mediated by social class. Inspection of Table 9.7 reveals, however, that this relation exists at each level of adoptive-parent social class. In addition we have conducted stepwise multiple regression analyses that varied the order of entry of biological-parent convictions and SES and adoptive-parent convictions and SES. These analyses indicate that, independent of SES, biological-parent convictions are significantly related to adoptee convictions.

METHODOLOGICAL ISSUES

Not fully identified subjects

If we are to generalize from the results of this study, it is useful to consider what biases might be introduced by the loss of subjects in specific analyses. Table 9.2 indicates the total number of subjects who could not be fully identified (name, birthday and birthplace). We should note that we know the name, occupation, birthdate and other facts concerning most of the lost subjects; in almost all cases a

Table 9.7 *Percentage of male adoptees with criminal convictions as a function of adoptive and biological parents' socioeconomic status*

Adoptive parents' SES	Biological parents' SES			
	High	Middle	Low	Total
High	9.30 (441)	11.52 (903)	12.98 (775)	11.58 (2,099)
Middle	13.44 (320)	15.29 (870)	16.86 (795)	15.62 (1,985)
Low	13.81 (210)	17.25 (568)	18.04 (787)	17.19 (1,565)
Total	11.64 (971)	14.31 (2,341)	16.00 (2,337)	14.55 (5,649)

Note: Numbers in parentheses represent total number for each cell.

subject could not be checked in the court conviction register because we were not certain of the subject's place of birth.

The information is relatively complete for the adoptive parents. In contrast, 26.5 per cent of the biological fathers and 14.7 per cent of the biological mothers are not fully identified. These differences probably reflect the relative importance of the adoptive and biological parents to the adoption agency. The agency's chief concern was with the placement and welfare of the adoptee. After the adoption, they had less reason to be concerned with the biological parents.

The most general characteristic of those not fully identified is that they tend *slightly* to come from areas outside Copenhagen. Perhaps the urban adoption offices followed more thorough recording procedures than did offices outside the city. The differences are very small. The sons of the biological fathers not fully identified have a rate of 10.3 per cent criminal law convictions; the identified biological fathers' sons have criminal law convictions in 11.4 per cent of cases. In cases in which the biological mother is not fully identified, slightly fewer of the sons have criminal law convictions (9.6 per cent). The adoptees who were not fully identified have biological mothers and biological fathers with slightly higher SES than those who were fully identified. Their rearing (adoptive) homes were of almost identical SES.

Our consideration of the characteristics of those not fully identified does not suggest that their inclusion would have altered the nature of the results presented above. Perhaps the most critical facts in this judgment are that the adopted-away sons of parents not fully identified have levels of criminal law convictions and rearing social status that are approximately the same as for the sons of those parents fully identified. The differences observed are small; it is difficult to formulate any manner in which the lost subjects might have an impact on the relations reported.

Transfer history

Most of these adoptions were the results of pregnancies of unwed women. The adoptive agency had a policy of taking newborns from their biological mothers and either immediately placing them in a previously arranged adoptive home (25.3 per cent of the adoptions) or placing them in an orphanage from which they were available for adoption. Of those placed in an orphanage, 50.6 per cent were placed with an adoptive family in the first year, 12.8 per cent were placed with an adoptive family in the second year, and 11.3 per cent were placed after the age of 2.

Within each of these age-of-transfer groups, analyses were conducted to ascertain whether the biological parents' convictions were related to male-adoptee conviction. Similar significant positive relations were observed at each transfer age. Age of transfer did not interact with genetic influence so as to alter significantly the relations observed with the full population. It should be noted that there was a statistically significant tendency for a high level of adoptee criminality to be associated with more time spent in an orphanage awaiting adoption. This effect was true for males only.

The operational definition of criminal behavior in this study included only court convictions for criminal law offenses. (We completed an analysis of police arrest data using a subsample of this adoption cohort and obtained very similar results; see Hutchings and Mednick, 1977.) Use of the conviction definition has some advantages. We are relatively certain that the individual actually committed the offense recorded. Court convictions imply a high threshold for inclusion; minor offenses are less likely to result in court conviction. There are also disadvantages. The subject's behavior goes through several screening points. Someone must make a complaint to the police, or the police must happen on the scene of the crime. The police must decide that a crime has been committed and apprehend the culprit. The prosecuting attorney must decide that the evidence is sufficient to warrant a court trial. The court must then find the culprit guilty. There are decision points all along the way that may result in the elimination of individuals who have actually committed offenses against the criminal code. Such individuals might then end up among our control subjects (assuming that they do not also commit offenses for which they are convicted). In this case they add error to the analyses. Data comparing self-reports of crimes and official records of crimes suggest, however, that whereas only a fraction of crimes committed by an individual are noted by the police, those who 'self-report' more crimes have more crimes recorded in the official registers. Those offenders who are not found in the official registers have typically committed very few and very minor offenses (Christie et al., 1965).

Labeling of the adoptee

The advantage of the adoption method is the good separation of genetic and rearing contributions to the adoptee's development. But the adoptions were not arranged as controlled experiments. The adoption agency's prime concern was the welfare of the adoptee and the adoptive parents. Prospective adoptive parents were routinely informed about the criminal convictions of the biological parents. This could result in the labeling of the adoptee; this in turn might affect the likelihood that the adoptee would commit criminal acts. Thus the convictions of the biological parents might have had an environmental impact on the adoptee via the reactions of the adoptive parents.

We examined one hypothesis related to this possibility. If the biological parents received a criminal conviction before the adoption, it is likely that the adoptive parents were so informed; if the biological parents' first conviction occurred after the adoption, the adoptive parents could not have been informed. Of the convicted biological parents, 37 per cent had received their first conviction before the adoption took place. In these cases, the adoptive parents were likely to have been informed of this criminal record. In 63 per cent of the cases the first conviction occurred after the adoption; in these cases the conviction information could *not* have been transmitted to the adoptive parents. For all convicted biological parents, the probability of a conviction in their adopted-away son was 15.9 per cent. In cases in which the biological parent was first convicted before adoption, 15.6 per cent of the male adoptees were convicted. In cases in which the biological parent was convicted after the adoption, 16.1 per cent of the male adoptees were convicted. In the case of female adoptees, these figures were 4 per cent and 4 per cent.

These analyses utilized convictions. In a previous analysis with a large subsample of this population a very similar result was obtained by studying the effect of timing of the initial arrest of the biological father (Hutchings and Mednick, 1977). Additional analyses by type or severity of crime revealed no effect of the adoptive parents' having been informed of the convictions of the biological parents. The fact that the adoptive parents had been informed of the biological parents' convictions did not alter the likelihood that the adoptive son would be convicted. This result should not be interpreted as suggesting that labeling (as defined) had no effect on the adoptees' lives. It did not, however, affect the probability that the adoptee would be convicted for a criminal act.

Denmark as a research site

This project was carried out in Denmark; on most crime-related social dimensions, Denmark must rank among the most homogeneous of the Western nations. This fact may have implications for the interpretation of this study. An environment with low variability permits better expression of existing genetic tendencies in individuals living in that environment. This factor probably magnifies the expression of any genetic influence. At the same time, however, the Danish population probably has less genetic variability than some Western nations; this, of course, would minimize the expression of genetic influence in research conducted in Denmark. It is very likely impossible to balance these two considerations quantitatively. We are reassured regarding the generality of our findings by similar results in adoption studies in Sweden and Iowa (Bohman et al., 1982; Cadoret, 1978; Crowe, 1975).

SUMMARY AND CONCLUSIONS

In a total population of adoptions, we noted a relation between biological-parent criminal convictions and criminal convictions in their adopted-away children. The relation is particularly strong for *chronic* adoptee and biological-parent offenders. There was no evidence that the type of biological-parent conviction was related to the type of adoptee conviction. A number of potentially confounding variables were considered; none of these proved sufficient to explain the genetic relation. We conclude that some factor is transmitted by convicted parents that increases the likelihood that their children will be convicted for criminal law offenses. This is especially true of chronic offenders. Because the transmitted factor must be biological, this implies that biological factors are involved in the etiology of at least some criminal behavior.

Biological factors and their interaction with social variables may make useful contributions to our understanding of the causes of criminal behavior.

REFERENCES

Bohman, M., Cloninger, C., Sigvardsson, S. and von Knorring, A.L. (1982) 'Predisposition to petty criminality in Swedish adoptees: genetic and environmental heterogeneity', *Archives of General Psychiatry*, 39(11): 1233–41.

Cadoret, R.J. (1978) 'Psychopathy in adopted away offspring of biological parents with antisocial behavior', *Archives of General Psychiatry*, 35: 176–84.

Christiansen, K.O. (1977a) 'A review of studies of criminality among twins', in S.A. Mednick and K.O. Christiansen (eds), *Biosocial Bases of Criminal Behavior*. New York: Gardner Press. pp. 45–88.

Christiansen, K.O. (1977b) 'A preliminary study of criminality among twins', in S.A. Mednick and K.O. Christiansen (eds), *Biosocial Bases of Criminal Behavior*. New York: Gardner Press. pp. 89–108.

Christie, N., Andenaes, J. and Skerbaekk, S. (1965) 'A study of self-reported crime', *Scandinavian Studies in Criminology*, 1: 86–116.

Crowe, R. (1975) 'Adoptive study of psychopathy: preliminary results from arrest records and psychiatric hospital records', in R. Fieve, D. Rosenthal and H. Brill (eds), *Genetic Research in Psychiatry*. Baltimore, MD: Johns Hopkins University Press.

Haller, M.H. (1968) 'Social science and genetics: a historical perspective', in D. Glass (ed.), *Genetics*. New York: Rockefeller University Press.

Hurwitz, S. and Christiansen, K.O. (1971) *Kriminologi*. Copenhagen: Glydendal.

Hutchings, B. and Mednick, S.A. (1977) 'Registered criminality in the adoptive and biological parents of registered male criminal adoptees', in S.A. Mednick and K.O. Christiansen (eds), *Biosocial Bases of Criminal Behavior*. New York: Gardner Press. pp. 127–42.

Kety, S.S., Rosenthal, D., Wender, P.H. and Schulsinger, F. (1968) 'The types and prevalence of mental illness in the biological adoptive families of adopted schizophrenics', in D. Rosenthal and S.S. Kety (eds), *The Transmission of Schizophrenia*, Oxford: Pergamon.

Sarbin, T.R. and Miller, J.E. (1970) 'Demonism revisited: the XYY chromosomal anomaly', *Issues in Criminology*, 5: 195–207.

Svalastoga, K. (1959), *Prestige, Class and Mobility*, Copenhagen: Gyldendal.

Van Dusen, K., Mednick, S.A., Gabrielli, W.F. and Hutchings, B. (1983) 'Social class and crime in an adoption cohort', *Journal of Criminal Law and Criminology*, 74(1): 249–69.

Wolfgang, M.E., Figlio, R.M. and Sellin, T. (1972) *Delinquency in a Birth Cohort*. Chicago: University of Chicago Press.

10

Personality theory and the problem of criminality

H.J. Eysenck

INTRODUCTION

In psychiatry generally, the diathesis–stress model is widely accepted; it postulates a *predisposition* to develop certain types of mental illness, such as neurosis or psychosis, which is activated by certain environmental stress factors. A similar conception can be applied to criminality; certain types of personality may be more prone to react with anti-social or criminal behaviour to environmental factors of one kind or another. To say this is not to accept the notion of 'crime as destiny', to quote Lange's famous monograph in which he showed that identical twins are much more alike with respect to criminal conduct than are fraternal twins. There is no predestination about the fact that heredity, mediated through personality, plays some part in predisposing some people to act in an anti-social manner. Environment is equally important, and, as we shall see, it is the interaction between the two which is perhaps the most crucial factor.

Much of the research in this field has been episodic and following the principles of benevolent eclecticism; in this chapter we will rather adopt the method of looking at a general theory of anti-social behaviour, which makes predictions as to the type of personality expected to indulge in such conduct, and summarize the evidence relating to the theory. Before turning to the evidence, it will therefore be necessary to present in brief outline the theory in question (Eysenck, 1960, 1977). The reason for singling out the theory is, in the first place, that it has attracted far more research than any other, and secondly, that it is the only one which has tried to link together genetic factors, a causal theory, and personality in one general theory.

STATEMENT OF THEORY

Briefly and concisely, the theory tries to explain the occurrence of socialized behaviour suggesting that anti-social behaviour, being obviously egocentric and

From *Applying Psychology to Imprisonment* (eds B. McGurk, D. Thornton and M. Williams), pp. 30–1; 34–46. (London: HMSO, 1987.)

orientated towards immediate gratification, needs no explanation. It is suggested that the socialization process is essentially mediated by Pavlovian conditioning, in the sense that anti-social behaviour will be punished by parents, teachers, peers etc., and that such punishment constitutes the *unconditioned stimulus* (US), where the contemplation or execution of such behaviour constitutes the conditioned stimulus. The pain/anxiety properties of the US transfer through conditioning to the CS [conditioned stimulus], and as a consequence the person will desist from committing anti-social acts, or even contemplating them, because of the painful CRs [conditioned responses] which inevitably follow. The theory is elaborated in Eysenck (1977), where supportive evidence will be found.

Individual differences in the speed and strength of formation of conditioned responses would, in terms of the theory, be fundamental in accounting for the observed relations between personality and criminality. As Eysenck (1967, 1980) has shown, there is considerable evidence to suggest that introverts form conditioned responses more quickly and more strongly than extraverts, and accordingly one would expect extraversion to be positively correlated with anti-social conduct. Emotional instability or neuroticism would be expected to multiply with the habits of socialized or anti-social conduct, according to Hull's general theory in which performance is a multiplicative function of habit and drive, with anxiety in this case acting as a drive (Eysenck, 1973). The third major dimension of personality, psychoticism, comes into the picture because of the well-documented relationship between crime and psychosis (Eysenck and Eysenck, 1976), and because the general personality traits subsumed under psychoticism appear clearly related to anti-social and non-conformist conduct. The precise nature of these three major dimensions of personality will be discussed later on in this chapter; here we will only look at one particular problem which is closely related to the general theory of conditioning as a basis for anti-social conduct.

The theory suggests that conditioning produces socialized behaviour, and that introverts will show more socialized behaviour because they condition more readily. The same theory would also imply, however, that if the socialization process were inverted, i.e. if parents, teachers, peers, etc. praised the child for anti-social conduct, and punished him for socialized behaviour, then introverts would be more likely to show anti-social behaviour. Raine and Venables (1981) have shown that this is indeed so; children who showed better conditioning in a laboratory situation than other children were remarkably socialized in their behaviour when brought up in a favourable type of environment, and remarkably anti-social in their behaviour when brought up in a non-favourable type of environment. This experiment shows more clearly than almost any other the inter-relationship between genetic factors on the one hand, and environmental ones on the other.
[. . .]

DIMENSIONS OF PERSONALITY

We will now turn to personality factors as more narrowly defined. Our discussion will begin with the three major dimensions of personality, which emerge from hundreds of correlational and factor analytic studies in many different countries. Royce and Powell (1983) have summarized and reanalysed these data, and confirm the theory developed by Eysenck and Eysenck (1976) that these three factors deal essentially with social interactions (extraversion–introversion), emotional reactions and anxieties (neuroticism), and aggressive and egocentric impulses and their control (psychoticism). Many different terms are of course used for these dimensions but Eysenck and Eysenck (1985) discuss the experimental literature which suggests the relevance of the terms proposed above.

The nature of these three major dimensions of personality can best be discerned from the data shown in Figures 10.1–10.3. These list the various traits, correlations between which have generated at the empirical level the three major dimensions of P, E and N. In this section we will simply look at descriptive studies involving the relationship between anti-social and criminal behaviour, on the one hand, and these major dimensions, and the traits relating thereto, on the other. [. . .] Here let us mainly stress that the personality traits and dimensions dealt with here have a strong genetic component [. . .]; this does not prove, but it does suggest that genetic factors may also play an important part in the genesis of anti-social and criminal behaviour.

Much of the early literature has been summarized by Passingham (1972), who found that while a number of studies supported Eysenck's hypothesis of a positive correlation between criminality and P, E and N, there were many exceptions, and occasional reversals. There are of course many reasons why results have not always been positive. Criminals are not a homogeneous group, and different investigators have studied different populations, specializing in different types of crime. Control groups have not always been carefully selected; some investigators, for instance, have used the usual students groups as controls, which is inadvisable. There has been a failure to control for dissimulation; there is evidence that high lie-scorers lower their neuroticism and psychoticism scores, and they seem to do the same for extraversion (McCue et al., 1976) [. . .] Some of the most negative reports contain evidence of high L scales, and are hence inadmissible. Other reasons refer to the incarceration of many delinquents; this would interfere with verbal responses on questionnaire items relating to sociability, and hence lead to an understatement of the delinquent's degree of extraversion. More important even than any of these reasons is probably the fact that many early investigations were done without any prior hypothesis being stated, and used questionnaires and other measures which bear only tangential relation to the Eysenck Questionnaires.

Eysenck (1977) lists many more recent investigations, most done from the point of view of testing the hypothesis linking criminality and P, E and N; these results are very much more positive. Some of the studies also strongly support the view that within the criminal fraternity different types of crimes are related to different personality patterns. Thus Eysenck, Rust and Eysenck (1977) studied five separate groups of criminals (conmen, i.e. confidence tricksters; criminals involved with crime against property; criminals specializing in violence; inadequate criminals, and a residual group, not specializing in one type of crime). Figure 10.4 shows the differential patterns of P, E and N of these various groups, with conmen for instance having a much lower P score than the other groups.

Mitchell et al. (1980) studied the difference between violent and non-violent delinquent behaviour and found that violence was more frequently associated with low trait anxiety than non-violent behaviour; their results agree with the Eysenck, Rust and Eysenck findings. Schwenkmezger (1983) subdivided his sample of delinquents into three major groups, corresponding to conmen, offences against property, and offences involving violence. As in the Eysenck, Rust and Eysenck study, conmen

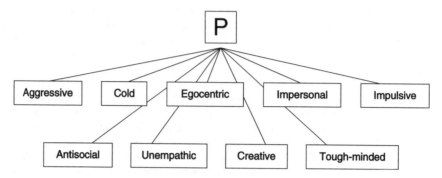

Figure 10.1   *Traits characterizing the psychoticism factor*

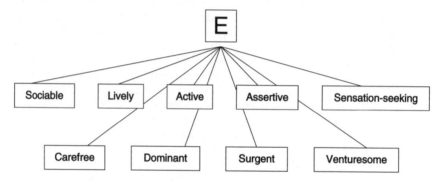

Figure 10.2   *Traits characterizing the extraversion factor*

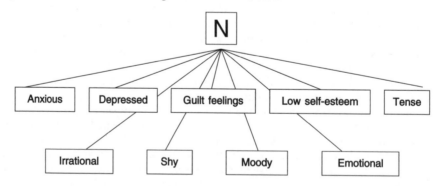

Figure 10.3   *Traits characterizing the neuroticism factor*

have much lower values on the various measures involved (impulsivity, risk taking, aggressiveness, dominance, and excitement) than the other two groups. Discriminant function analysis showed two significant functions, the first of which separates conmen from the other two groups. The second function involved mainly aggressive, dominant and risk taking behaviour, and has offences involving violence at one extreme.

The most recent study by Wardell and Yeudall (1980), specially concerned with this problem, used ten personality factors derived from an extensive psychological test battery administered to 201 patients on criminal wards at a mental hospital and showed many important differences between patients involved with different types of crime. Other recent studies supporting this view are by McGurk (1978), McGurk and McDougall (1981), McGurk and McEwan (1983), and McGurk, McEwan and Graham (1981). To this list might be added some studies cited by Eysenck (1977) showing that murderers (i.e. mainly the usual type of family murder) tend to be significantly introverted. Professional gunmen, on the other hand, are exceedingly extraverted, thus showing that even a single category (murder) may require subdivision in order to give comprehensible and replicable correlations with personality.

Rahman and Hussain (1984), studying female criminals in Bangladesh, found them to have much higher P and N scores than controls; those engaged in prostitution, fraud, kidnapping and possession of illegal arms also had high E scores. Murderers, on the other hand, were significantly introverted.

Holcomb et al. (1985) have shown how complex motivation and personality even within a single category of crime may be. They studied a sample of 80 male offenders charged with premeditated murder, and found that these could be divided into five personality types using MMPI scores. The results were cross validated using a second sample of 80 premeditated murders. A discriminant analysis resulted in a 96.25 correct classification of subjects from the second sample into the five types. Clinical data from a mental status interview schedule supported the external validity of these types. There were significant differences among the five types in hallucinations, disorientation, hostility, depression and paranoid thinking.

THE EYSENCK STUDIES

We may now turn to the work of the Eysencks in temporal order, as these were the major studies to try to obtain direct empirical evidence regarding the theory under discussion. In the first of these studies (Eysenck and Eysenck, 1970), 603 male prisoners were compared with a control group of over 1,000 males. Results supported strongly the hypothesis that prisoners would have higher P scores, moderately strongly the hypothesis that prisoners would have higher N scores, and rather more weakly the hypothesis that prisoners would have higher E scores. Similar results were found in a later study by Eysenck and Eysenck (1971), contrasting 518 criminals and 606 male trainee railmen. Significant differences were found on P and N, and on E the direction of the prediction was reversed, criminals having lower E scores than controls. In a later study of the personality of female prisoners (Eysenck and Eysenck, 1973) 264 female prisoners were found to be characterized by high P, high N and high E scores; for them therefore E agreed with the predicted direction.

In a study of personality and recidivism in Borstal boys (Eysenck and Eysenck, 1974), recidivists were insignificantly higher than non-recidivists on P and N, but significantly higher on E. In the last of this series of studies (Eysenck and Eysenck, 1977) over 2,000 male prisoners and over 2,400 male controls were given the Eysenck personality questionnaire, and then subdivided into age groups, ranging from 16 to 69 at the extremes. It was found that the lie-scale disclosed little dissimulation in either group. Scores on psychoticism, extraversion and neuroticism

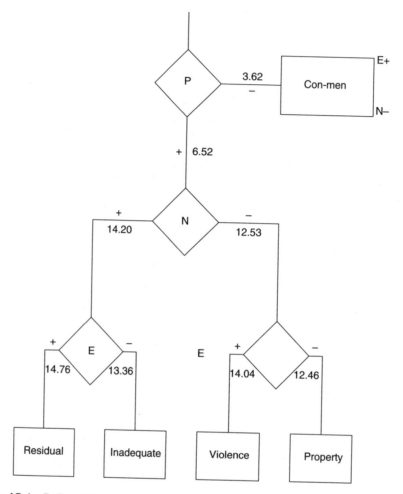

Figure 10.4   *P, E and N scores of different types of criminals (Eysenck et al., 1977)*

fell with age for both prisoners and controls. Prisoners had higher scores than controls, as predicted, on all three scales.

A replication of some of this work was carried out by Sanocki (1969) in Poland, using the short form of the Maudsley Personality Inventory on 84 Polish prisoners and 337 Polish controls, matched for age, education and social class. Criminals were found to be significantly more extraverted, and non-significantly more neurotic. Sanocki also found that different types of prisoners in his study differed significantly with respect to the inventory scores, adding another proof to the hypothesis of criminal heterogeneity. He also showed that a prisoner's behaviour in prison correlated with E, extraverts offending significantly more frequently against prison rules.

Two further points about the Eysenck studies may be of relevance. The first is that Eysenck and Eysenck (1971) constructed an empirical criminality scale by bringing together all those items which showed the greatest differentiation between criminals and normals; this will later on be referred to as the 'C' scale. The other point is made by Burgess (1972), who pointed out that Eysenck's theory implies that criminals and normals would differ on a combination of N and E, not necessarily on one or the other in separation; he was able to show that even in studies which failed to show significance for one or the other variable, the combination did show highly significant differences.

The 'C' scale was constructed for adults; similar scales have been proposed by Allsop and Feldman (1975), and by Saklofske, McKerracher and Eysenck (1978) for children. Like the adult scale they use selected items from the P, E and N scales. The scales have been found to be very useful in discriminating different groups of children. The data demonstrate clearly that delinquent boys have higher extraversion, psychoticism and neuroticism scores, and that the criminal propensity (C) scale discriminates even better between them and non-delinquent boys. Similar differences were also observed between well-behaved and badly behaved non-delinquent boys.

OTHER RECENT STUDIES

Barack and Widom (1978) studied American women awaiting trial. Compared to a heterogeneous control group, these women scored significantly higher on the neuroticism and psychoticism scales, and on Burgess's h scale ($h=E \times N$). Singh (1982) compared 100 Indian female delinquents with 100 female non-delinquents, matched in terms of socioeconomic status, age and urban versus rural place of residence; he found that delinquents had higher scores on extraversion and neuroticism than did non-delinquents. Smith and Smith (1977) looked at the psychoticism variable in relation to reconviction, and found a very highly significant correlation between psychoticism and reconviction. Their finding supported the results obtained by Saunders and Davies (1976), who administered the Jesness Inventory to samples of young male offenders, and concluded that:

> one can . . . see a picture of the continuing delinquent as being unsocialised, aggressive, anti-authority and unempathic. This appears to present a somewhat similar pattern of characteristics to that described by Eysenck as 'psychotic'.

Of particular interest are some results of a follow-up of an investigation carried out by West and Farrington (1973). (See also Farrington et al., 1982.) In the original study 411 boys, aged 8 to 9, attending six adjacent primary schools in a working class area of London, were given the Junior Maudsley Inventory at age 10 to 11, and again at age 14 to 15; they were also given the Eysenck Personality Inventory at age 16 to 17. The original data did not provide very strong support for the theory, but more interesting are new data relating to delinquency as a young adult, i.e. convictions in court for offences committed between a boy's 17th and 21st birthdays. Eighty-four boys were classified as juvenile delinquents, 94 as young adult delinquents, and 127 as delinquents at any age (up to 21). This study is particularly important because the delinquents were almost all non-institutionalized at the time of testing. (The following data were communicated privately by D.P. Farrington on 10 June 1976.)

Extraversion As regards juvenile delinquency, E scores were dichotomized into roughly equal halves, and 24 per cent of those with above average scores became juvenile delinquents, in comparison with 16 per cent of those with below average scores; so the lowest quarter of E scores at age 16 included significantly few juvenile delinquents – 12.6 per cent as opposed to 23.4 per cent. The tendency of above average E scorers at age 16 to become young adult delinquents was much clearer (30 per cent as opposed to 16 per cent). Farrington states that: 'Low E scores genuinely predicted a low likelihood of adult delinquency.' The major burden of these and other significant relationships was borne by the lowest quarter of E scorers; introverts were very unlikely to become delinquents.

Neuroticism There was little overall relationship between neuroticism and criminality except that those on the lowest quarter of N scorers at age 10 tended not to become adult delinquents (12 per cent as opposed to 25 per cent), and not to be delinquents at any age (17 per cent as opposed to 34 per cent). Quadrant analysis, of the kind suggested by Burgess (1972) shows that neurotic extraverts at age 16 included significantly more adult delinquents, and significantly more delinquents at any age, than the remainder.

The data, as Farrington points out, suggest that the personality theory might apply to adult delinquency rather than to juvenile delinquency. It is notable that the adult offences included proportionately more aggressive crimes, more damaging offences and more drug offences than the juvenile offences.

For reasons to be discussed presently, this seems an unlikely hypothesis; in school-boys for instance very clear-cut relationships between personality and anti-social behaviour often of a not very serious kind, have been found. These studies are mainly based on self-reports (Gibson, 1971), a type of study which furnishes the child with a list of minor and not-so-minor misdemeanours frequently committed by school children, and asks him or her anonymously to endorse those items which they have been guilty of. There are two studies which have related self-reported offending to the three major dimensions of personality (Allsop and Feldman, 1975, 1976). In addition, these studies used an outside criterion (teacher's ratings) in order to check on the validity of self ratings; results were very similar for both types of measures. The ratings of the teachers were concerned with school behaviour ('naughtiness'). Scores on the anti-social behaviour scale (ASB) were positively and significantly related to P, E and N in descending order of significance, and 'naughtiness' (Na) scores to P and N, although only the former achieved statistical significance. The P, E and N scores were then divided at the median points and the mean ASB and Na scores plotted for those high (i.e. above the median) on all 3, 2 only, one only, or none out of P, E and N. The results, which are quite striking, are shown in Figure 10.5. They clearly suggest the usefulness of combining personality scores when analysing self-report data. These data come from the study of secondary schoolgirls (Allsop and Feldman, 1975); a similar study, done on schoolboys, has obtained very similar results (Allsop and Feldman, 1976).

The differential relationship between personality and type of offence has also been studied using self-reports. Hindelang and Weis (1972), using cluster analysis, formed 26 offences self-reported by 245 Los Angeles middle class high-school males into seven groups, and then correlated the scores on each of the seven clusters with the four possible combinations of E and N. They expected a descending order of frequency of offending–EN, either En or eN, and en; this was obtained for 'general deviance' and 'traffic truancy' and partially obtained for two other clusters, concerning 'drug-taking' and 'malicious destruction', respectively. No difference between the combinations of E and N was found for theft and the second of two clusters concerning drugs. For the 'aggressive' clusters the En combination was the highest. These data again show the need to break down criminality into more homogeneous clusters, but of course the sample is a somewhat unusual one.

Allsop (1976) has reported one further study where he used 368 white boys between the ages of 13 and 16. Teachers were asked to rate the behaviour of the boys; on this basis they were divided into well and badly behaved. When these ratings were compared with the personality scale scores, the results indicated that:

> badly behaved boys predominate at the high level of P and at the low level of P where there is a combination of high E/high N scores; well-behaved boys predominate at the low level of P except where E and N are simultaneously high.

Using the ASB, he subdivided the total scale into ten sub-scales according to type of offence; this table sets out the correlations of P, E and N with each of the sub-scales as well as the total scale. It showed that all the correlations are positive, being highest with P and lowest with N.

Among non-incarcerated adolescents the pattern is much the same. R. Foggitt (1976) has studied a non-institutionalized sample of delinquent and non-delinquent adolescents. Factor analysis of the intercorrelations between the crimes and the personality scales of E and N showed that they were all positively intercorrelated and that a single general factor emerged from the analysis on which different crimes had loadings as follows. Truancy, 0.56; poor work history, 0.62; vagrancy, 0.71; attempted suicide, 0.56; frequency of violence, 0.74; destructiveness of violence, 0.72; heavy drinking, 0.45; excessive drugs, 0.52; theft, 0.71; fraud, 0.50; group-delinquency, 0.46; number of convictions, 0.59. For the personality variables the loadings were 0.44 for E and 0.42 for N.

Two interesting recent studies extend the scope of the work so far reviewed. Perez and Torrubia (1985) used Zuckerman's (1979) concept of sensation-seeking defined as the need for varied, novel and complex sensations and experiences, and willingness to take risks for the sake of such experiences. This scale, which is correlated with extraversion and defines one aspect of that dimension of personality (Eysenck and Eysenck, 1985) was measured in a Spanish translation of the scale published by Zuckerman, Eysenck and Eysenck (1978). Three hundred and forty-nine students were tested, using the sensation seeking scale as well as a 37-item Spanish version of a written self-report delinquency (SRD) scale. A correlation of 0.46 was obtained for the total of the sensation seeking scale, with the highest correlations going to the experience seeking (0.45) and disinhibition (0.43) scales. These are the values for males; for females they were 0.49 for the total scale, and 0.43 and 0.45 for the experience seeking and disinhibition scales. Correlations for the other two scales were smaller (in the neighbourhood of 0.20) but still significant.

Also using a self-report format, Rushton and Chrisjohn (1981) tested eight separate samples, obtaining significant positive correlations with extraversion, largely insignificant ones with neuroticism, and very positive and significant ones with psychoticism. Correlations with the lie scale were uniformly negative and mostly significant. Subjects of these experiments were high school and university students, totalling 410 in all. As the authors summarize their findings:

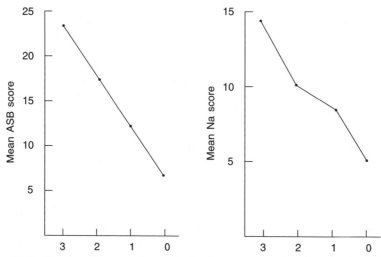

Figure 10.5 *Number of personality scales (P, E and N) on which subjects scored highly, as related to anti-social behaviour (ASB) score and naughtiness (Na) score (Allsop and Feldman, 1975)*

> The evidence showed clear support for a relationship between high delinquency scores and high scores on both extraversion and psychoticism. These relationships held up across diverse samples and different ways of analyzing the data. No support was found for a relationship between delinquency scores and the dimension of neuroticism. (1981: 11)

In another interesting study, Martin (1985) pointed out that:

> Attempts to verify Eysenck's theory of criminality have usually been concerned with the proportion by which delinquents differ from non-delinquents on the dimensions of extraversion, neuroticism and psychoticism. There are very few studies concerned with the proportion in which these dimensions are related to the acquisition of moral social rules, the real core of this theory. The current study examines the theory from a new approach, trying to show in what measures the value priorities of a group of 113 juvenile delinquents are related to the personality dimensions stated by Eysenck. (1985: 549)

It was found that extraversion and psychoticism showed the largest number of significant relationships. The youths who scored high and low on the E scale differed in six terminal values and six instrumental values out of a total of 36 values. Values concerned with morality, and those which imply an acceptance of the social norms, are considered the most important factors for the youths with low E scores.

Those who scored high on the psychoticism dimension consider the following values as the most important: 'An exciting life; pleasure; ability'; all these have clear personal significance. They gave less importance to values related to the social environment, such as 'world peace', 'equality' and 'social recognition'. As far as they go, these results are in good accord with the personality theory under discussion, and they also suggest a new approach to validating the theory.

Drug takers constitute a rather special sample of criminals, although the study just mentioned shows drug taking offences to be highly correlated with other types of criminality. Shanmugan (1979) compared 212 drug users and 222 non-drug users matched with respect to sex, age, educational qualification and socioeconomic status, and found that drug users were high on extraversion and neuroticism; stimulant-depressant drug users were found to be high on psychoticism as well as on the 'C' (criminal propensity) scale. Gossop (1978) studied the personality correlates of female drug addicts convicted of drug-related violent and other offences. Convicted subjects were more extraverted than non-convicted subjects. Another study, Gossop and Kristjansson (1977), investigated 50 drug takers and found that subjects convicted of non-drug offences scored higher on extraversion than subjects not convicted of such offences. Drug-dependent subjects altogether scored extremely highly on the 'C' (criminal propensity) scale. This reflects to some extent their high scores on the P and N dimensions.

SPECIFIC TRAITS AND CRIMINALITY

Before considering the large number of German-speaking studies using inventories derived from and similar to the Eysenck Questionnaires, it may be useful to consider quickly studies involving a number of specific traits which, as Figures 10.1–10.3 show, are involved in the three major dimensions of personality. Most work has been done on such factors as anxiety and depression, sensation-seeking, impulsiveness, impulse control, hostility and aggression, and lack of conformity. Typical and relatively recent studies only will be quoted; these usually have bibliographies referring to earlier studies.

Sensation or stimulation seeking has been studied by Farley and Sewell (1976) and Whitehill, De Myer-Gapin and Scott (1976), the former using a questionnaire, the latter a laboratory experimental technique. They found support for the hypothesis, which was formulated earlier by Quay (1965), that criminals would be sensation seekers. Robins (1972), can also be quoted in support.

Impulsiveness and lack of impulse control has frequently been suggested as a major component of criminality. Hormuth et al. (1977) using both questionnaires and experimental methods, were able to verify the prediction of less impulse control in delinquents with the former. The latter study also found positive results favouring the hypothesis. These data may be considered together with a related concept, namely that of risk-taking, which is often considered almost synonymous with impulsivity or lack of impulse control. A very thorough review of the literature is given by Lösel (1975), who found risk-taking more prominent among delinquents. The best available study on risk-taking, also giving a good summary of the literature, is by Schwenkmezger (1983); his conclusion is that results obtained by various investigators can best be interpreted in the sense that delinquent behaviour is favoured by impulsive, risky decision strategies, influenced more by hope of luck and chance than by realistic estimates of one's own abilities and possibilities.

Hostility and aggression are other traits frequently associated with criminality, and the Foulds scales (Foulds et al., 1960) have often been used as a measuring instrument. Data reported by Blackburn (1968, 1970), and Crawford (1977) suggest that positive relationships exist, with long-term prisoners generally having higher total hostility scores than normals, and violent offenders being more extra-punitive than non-violent offenders. Megargee's (1966) hypothesis contrasting over- and under-control would distinguish between extremely assaultive offenders (over-controlled) who would be expected to express less hostility than only moderately assaultive offenders. This theory was supported by Blackburn (1968) but not by Crawford (1977). Berman and Paisley (1984) compared juveniles convicted of assaultive offences with others convicted of other types of offences, and found that the former exhibited significantly higher psychoticism, extraversion and neuroticism scores; sensation seeking scores were also significantly lower for the non-assaultive group of property offenders.

A French Canadian group was studied by Coté and Leblanc (1982). Using the Jesness Inventory (Jesness, 1972) and the Eysenck Personality Inventory, they studied 825 adolescents from 14 to 19 years old, and correlated personality measures with self-reported indices of delinquency. They found the following traits very significantly correlated with delinquency; psychoticism (0.36), manifest aggressiveness (0.34), extraversion (0.32), bad social adjustment (0.32), alienation (0.25), repression (-0.25), and some traits showing even lower but still significant correlations.

The Jesness Inventory, just mentioned, consists of 155 items, scored on ten sub-scales (social maladjustment, value orientation, immaturity, alienation, autism, withdrawal, manifest aggression, social anxiety, repression and denial), and a predictive score, the Anti-social index. The relationships between the Eysenck and Jesness Personality Inventories have been explored by Smith (1974). Some of the observed correlations are quite high, e.g. between social maladjustment, autism, manifest aggression, withdrawal, on the one hand, and N and P, on the other. Social anxiety is negatively correlated with E, and highly positively with N. Saunders and Davies (1976) found evidence for the validity of the Jesness Inventory, as did Mott (1969). The scales most diagnostic appeared to be social maladjustment, value orientation, alienation, manifest aggression, and denial. In addition, Davies (1967) found some evidence in his follow-up studies for the validity of the autism, withdrawal and repression scales.

There are many studies using MMPI profiles, such as those of Davies and Sines (1971), and Beck and McIntyre (1977). The scales usually involved are the psychopathic deviate and hysteria scales, hypochondriasis, masculinity/femininity interest patterns, and mania; these suggest neurotic extraversion in the main. A more detailed account of work with the MMPI will be found in Dahlstrom and Dahlstrom (1980). As regards anxiety, a typical report is that by Lidhoo (1971), who studied 200 delinquent and 200 non-delinquent adolescents, matched for age, sex and socio-economic status; all the subjects were Indian. The main and highly significant differences observed were with respect to emotionality, with the delinquents more tense, more depressed, and more easily provoked, and sexual maladjustment.

With only one or two exceptions, all the studies so far considered have been published in English and relate to English and American populations. It may be useful to summarize the major findings before going on to the large body of German-speaking studies investigating the major theories here considered. Replication is the life-blood of science, and here we would seem to have an ideal opportunity to compare two sets of data, not just collected by different investigators, but collected in different countries and by means of different inventories, although the German inventory used in all these studies was explicitly based on the Eysenck Personality

Inventory. Thus we would here seem to have a cross-cultural replication, and if similar results are obtained, we could feel much more secure in regarding these conclusions as being firmly based.

The first conclusion which seems appropriate is that while the earlier studies summarized by Passingham were not theory centred, often used inappropriate questionnaires, and paid little attention to important methodological requirements, later studies summarized in Eysenck (1977), were methodologically much superior, and gave much more definitive and significant support to the personality theory in question. Studies carried out since then have maintained this improvement, and are nearly all equally positive in the outcome. Our first conclusion therefore must be that we now have good evidence for the implication of psychoticism, extraversion and neuroticism as predisposing factors in juvenile and adult criminality, and even in juvenile anti-social behaviour not amounting to legally criminal conduct. These correlations are based both on self-reported anti-social behaviour and criminal activity, and on legally defined criminality.

It would seem that different types of criminal activity may show differential relationships to personality, but too little has been done in that field to be very definitive to one's conclusions. Males and females seem to have similar personality patterns, as far as criminality is concerned, but little seems to have been done in making deliberate gender comparisons.

While P, E and N are related to criminality at all ages, there seem to be definite patterns suggesting that N is more important with older criminals, E with younger criminals. Why this should be so is not clear, but the data definitely tend in that direction. Possibly N, as a multiplicative drive variable, assumes greater importance with older people in whom habits have already been settled more clearly than is the case with younger persons. Another possibility is that the largely incarcerated adult samples cannot properly answer the social activity questions which make up a large part of the extraversion inventory. A study specifically directed to the solution of this problem would seem called for.

SUMMARY OF GERMAN STUDIES

A summary of 15 empirical German studies, using altogether 3,450 delinquents and a rather larger number of controls, has been reported by Steller and Hunze (1984). All these studies used the FPI (Freiburger Persönlichkeits Inventar) of Fahrenberg, Selg and Hampel (1978). In addition, Steller and Hunze report a study of their own, using a self-report device for the measurement of anti-social conduct. The FPI contains nine traits and three dimensional scales, the latter being extraversion, emotional ability or neuroticism, and masculinity. The nine trait scales relate to nervousness, aggressiveness, depression, excitability, sociability, stability, dominance, inhibition and openness. Typical of the general findings are those of the special study carried out by Steller and Hunze, where they found that delinquents showed higher scores on nervousness, depression, excitability, sociability, extraversion, and neuroticism. These results appeared separately on two alternative forms of the FPI.

In summarizing the results from all the other German studies, Steller and Hunze point out that for the trait scales there is a very clear picture. Delinquents are higher on depression, nervousness, excitability and aggression. Regarding the major dimensions, a great majority show excessive degrees of neuroticism, and to a lesser extent extraversion. Sociability, as a major trait involved in extraversion, was significantly elevated in 25 per cent of all the comparisons, with criminals being more sociable. If we can use aggressiveness as an important part of psychoticism, then it is clear that these results agree very well with those of the English-speaking samples.

German studies show a similar differentiation between older and younger subjects, as far as neuroticism and extraversion are concerned. For the younger groups, delinquents are characterized much more clearly by greater sociability, dominance and openness; extraversion is implicated in almost every comparison between young delinquents and non-delinquents. This agrees well with the English-speaking data.

The German data give evidence also for the fact that the different types of criminality may be related differentially to personality, but the data are not extensive enough to make any definitive summary possible. There is, however, an interesting summary of data relating personality to the duration of incarceration, suggesting an increase in emotional instability with incarceration. However, there is also evidence that prisoners on probation showed increases in emotional instability. Clearly a more detailed investigation of this question is in order, particularly as Bolton et al. (1976) report discrepant findings.

It is sometimes suggested that possibly the differences between criminals and non-criminals might be due to the process of incarceration itself. This is unlikely, because several of the studies discussed compared the anti-social and criminal activities of children and juveniles none of whom were incarcerated at any time. Even more relevant and impressive is work showing that long before anti-social acts are committed, children who later on commit them are already differentiated from those who do not. Consider as an example the work of Burt (1965) who reported on the follow-up of children originally studied over 30 years previously. Seven hundred and sixty-three children of whom 15 per cent and 18 per cent respectively later became habitual criminals or neurotics, were rated by the teachers for N and for E. Of those who later became habitual offenders, 63 per cent had been rated as high on N; 54 per cent had been rated as high on E, but only 3 per cent as high on introversion. Of those who later became neurotics, 59 per cent had been rated as high on N, 44 per cent had been rated as high on introversion, but only 1 per cent as high on E. Similar data are reported by Michael (1956), and more recently Taylor and Watt (1977) and Fakouri and Jerse (1976) have published data showing that prediction of future criminal behaviour is possible from early school records. Thus the future criminal, like the future neurotic, is already recognizable in the young child.

Several of the studies summarized by Steller and Hunze used self-reported delinquency, and found, very much as did the English-speaking studies, that very similar personality correlates were observed here as in the case of legally defined delinquency.

The authors conclude that:

in agreement with Eysenck's hypothesis and findings, it was found that in many samples emotional instability ('neuroticism') and high extraversion were found (in delinquents). The corresponding increases in the FPI dimensional scales were found most clearly in juvenile samples, but for grown-up delinquents were found in the FPI trait scales which represent major components of dimensional scales emotional instability and extraversion. (1984: 107)

We may thus conclude that this essay in replication has been eminently successful, in that identical findings are reported from the German literature as we have found to be representative of the English-speaking literature. There seems to be little doubt, therefore, that personality and anti-social and criminal behaviour are reasonably intimately correlated, and that these correlations can be found in cultures other than the Anglo-American. Eysenck (1977) has reported such confirmatory studies from widely different countries, including India, Hungary, Poland, and others, as well as the German and French-speaking samples mentioned in this chapter.

[. . .]

REFERENCES

Allsop, J.F. (1976) 'Investigations into the applicability of Eysenck's theory of criminality to the anti-social behaviour of schoolchildren'. Unpublished PhD thesis, University of London.

Allsop, J.F. and Feldman, M.P. (1975) 'Extraversion, neuroticism and psychoticism and anti-social behaviour in school girls', *Social Behaviour and Personality*, 2: 184–9.

Allsop, J.F. and Feldman, M.P. (1976) 'Item analyses of questionnaire measures of personality and anti-social behaviour in school girls', *British Journal of Criminology*, 16: 337–51.

Barack, L.I. and Widom, C.S. (1978) 'Eysenck's theory of criminality applied to women awaiting trial', *British Journal of Psychiatry*, 133: 452–6.

Beck, E.A. and McIntyre, C.S. (1977) 'MMPI patterns of shoplifters within a college population', *Psychological Reports*, 41: 1035–40.

Berman, T. and Paisley, T. (1984) 'Personality in assaultive and non-assaultive juvenile male offenders', *Psychological Reports*, 54: 527–30.

Blackburn, R. (1968) 'Personality in relation to extreme aggression in psychiatric offenders', *British Journal of Psychiatry*, 114: 821–8.

Blackburn, R. (1970) 'Personality types among abnormal homicides', Special Hospital Research, No. 1, London.

Bolton, N., Smith, F.V., Heskin, K.J. and Barister, P.A. (1976) 'Psychological correlates of long-term imprisonment', *British Journal of Criminology*, 16: 38–47.

Burgess, P.K. (1972) 'Eysenck's theory of criminality: a new approach', *British Journal of Criminology*, 12: 74–82.

Burt, C. (1965), 'Factorial studies of personality and their bearing in the work of the teacher', *British Journal of Educational Psychology*, 35: 308–28.

Coté, G. and Leblanc, M. (1982) 'Aspects de personalité et comportement delinquent', *Bulletin de Psychologique*, 36: 265–71.

Crawford, D.A. (1977) 'The HDHQ results of long-term prisoners: relationships with criminal and institutional behaviour', *British Journal of Social and Clinical Psychology*, 16: 391–4.

Dahlstrom, W.G. and Dahlstrom, L. (eds) (1980) *Basic Readings on the MMPI*. Minneapolis: University of Minnesota Press.

Davies, M.B. (1967) *The Use of the Jesness Inventory in a Sample of British Probationers*. London: HMSO.

Davies, K.R. and Sines, J.O. (1971) 'An anti-social behaviour pattern associated with a specific MMPI profile', *Journal of Consulting and Clinical Psychology*, 36: 229–34.

Eysenck, H.J. (1960) Symposium: 'The development of moral values in children. VII. The contribution of learning theory', *British Journal of Educational Psychology*, 30: 11–21.

Eysenck, H.J. (1967) *The Biological Basis of Personality*. Springfield, Ill.: C.C. Thomas.

Eysenck, H.J. (1970) *The Structures of Human Personality*, 3rd edn. London: Methuen.

Eysenck, H.J. (1973) 'Personality, learning and "anxiety"', in H.J. Eysenck (ed.), *Handbook of Abnormal Psychology*, 2nd edn. London: Pitman. pp. 390–419.

Eysenck, H.J. (1976) 'The biology of morality', in T. Lickona (ed.), *Moral Development and Behavior*. New York: Holt, Rinehart and Winston. pp. 108–23.

Eysenck, H.J. (1977) *Crime and Personality*, 3rd edn. London: Routledge and Kegan Paul.

Eysenck, H.J. (ed.) (1980) *A Model for Personality*. New York: Springer.

Eysenck, H.J. and Eysenck, M.W. (1985) *Personality and Individual Differences*. New York: Plenum.

Eysenck, H.J. and Eysenck, S.B.G. (1976) *Psychoticism as a Dimension of Personality*. London: Hodder and Stoughton.

Eysenck, H.J. and Eysenck, S.B.G. (1978) 'Psychopathy, personality and genetics', in R.D. Hare and D. Schalling (eds),*Psychopathic Behaviour*. London: John Wiley, pp. 197–223.

Eysenck, S.B.G. and Eysenck H.J. (1970) 'Crime and personality: an empirical study of the three-factor theory', *British Journal of Criminology*, 10: 225–39.

Eysenck, S.B.G. and Eysenck, H.J. (1971) 'A comparative study of criminals and matched controls on three dimensions of personality', *British Journal of Social and Clinical Psychology*', 10: 362–6.

Eysenck, S.B.G. and Eysenck, H.J. (1971) 'Crime and personality: item analysis of questionnaire responses', *British Journal of Criminology*, 11: 49–62.

Eysenck, S.B.G. and Eysenck, H.J. (1973) 'The personality of female prisoners', *British Journal of Psychiatry*, 122: 693–8.

Eysenck, S.B.G. and Eysenck, H.J. (1974) 'Personality and recidivism in Borstal boys', *British Journal of Criminology*, 14: 285–7.

Eysenck, S.B.G. and Eysenck, H.J. (1977) 'Personality differences between prisoners and controls', *Psychological Reports*, 40: 1023–8.

Eysenck, S.B.G., Rust, J. and Eysenck, H.J. (1977) 'Personality and the classification of adult offenders', *British Journal of Criminology*, 17: 169–79.

Fahrenberg, J.; Selg, H. and Hampel, R. (1978) *Das Freiburger Persönlichkeits–inventar*. Göttingen: Hogrefe.

Fakouri, E. and Jerse, F.W. (1976) 'Unobtrusive detection of potential juvenile delinquency', *Psychological Reports*, 39: 551–8.

Farley, F.H. and Sewell, T. (1976) 'Test of an arousal theory of delinquency', *Criminal Justice and Behaviour*, 3: 315–20.

Farrington, P.; Biron, L. and Leblanc, M. (1982) 'Personality and delinquency in London and Madrid', in J. Gunn and D.P. Farrington (eds), *Abnormal Offenders, Delinquency, and the Criminal Justice System*. New York: Wiley.

Foggitt, R. (1976) 'Personality and delinquency'. Unpublished PhD thesis, University of London.

Foulds, G.A., Caine, T.M. and Creasy, M.I. (1960) 'Aspects of extra- and intra-punitive expression in mental illness', *Journal of Mental Science*, 196: 599–610.

Gibson, H.B. (1971) 'The factorial structure of juvenile delinquency: a study of self-reported acts', *British Journal of Social and Clinical Psychology*, 10: 1–9.

Glueck, S. and Glueck, E. (1956) *Physique and Delinquency*. New York: Harper.

Gossop, M. (1978) 'Drug dependence, crime and personality among female addicts', *Drug and Alcohol Dependence*, 3: 359–64.

Gossop, M.R. and Kristjansson, I. (1977) 'Crime and personality', *British Journal of Criminology*, 17: 264–73.

Hindelang, M. and Weis, J.G. (1972) 'Personality and self-reported delinquency: an application of cluster analysis', *Criminology*, 10: 268–76.

Holcomb, W.R., Adam, N.A. and Ponder, H.N. (1985) 'The development and cross-validation upon MMPI typology of murderers', *Journal of Personality Assessment*, 49: 240–4.

Hormuth, S., Lamm, H., Michelitsch, I., Scheuermann, H., Trommsdorf, G. and Vogele, I. (1977) 'Impulskontrolle und einige Persönlichkeitscharakteristika bei delinquenten und nicht-delinquenten Jugendlichen', *Psychologische Beiträge*, 19: 340–59.

Jesness, C.F. (1972) *The Jesness Inventory: Manual*. Palo Alto, CA: Consulting Psychologist Press.

Lidhoo, M.L. (1971) 'An attempt to construct a psycho-diagnostic tool for the detection of potential delinquents among adolescents aged 14–19 years'. Unpublished PhD thesis, University of Panjab.

Lösel, F. (1975) *Handlungskontrolle und Jugend-delinquenz*. Stuttgart: Enke.

McCue, P., Booth, S. and Root, J. (1976) 'Do young prisoners under-state their extra-version on personality inventories?', *British Journal of Criminology*, 16: 282, 283.

McGurk, B.J. (1978) 'Personality types among "normal" homicides', *British Journal of Criminology*, 18: 146–61.

McGurk, B.J. and McDougall, C. (1981) 'A new approach to Eysenck's theory of criminality', *Personality and Individual Differences*, 2: 338–40.

McGurk, B.J. and McEwan, A.W. (1983) 'Personality types and recidivism among Borstal trainees', *Personality and Individual Differences*, 4: 165–70.

McGurk, B.J., McEwan, A.W. and Graham, F. (1981) 'Personality types and recidivism among young delinquents', *British Journal of Criminology*, 21: 159–65.

Martin, A.L. (1985) 'Values and personality: a survey of their relationship in the case of juvenile delinquency', *Personality and Individual Differences*, 4: 519–22.

Megargee, E.I. (1966) 'Undercontrolled and overcontrolled personality types in extreme anti-social aggression', *Psychological Monographs*, 80, Whole Number 611.

Michael, C.M. (1956) 'Follow-up studies of introverted children: IV. Relative incidence of criminal behaviour', *Journal of Criminal Law and Criminality*, 47, 414–22.

Mitchell, J., Rogers, R., Cavanaugh, J. and Wasyliw, O. (1980) 'The role of trait anxiety in violent and non-violent delinquent behavior', *American Journal of Forensic Psychiatry*.

Mott, J. (1969) *The Jesness Inventory: An Application to Approved School Boys*. London: HMSO.

Passingham, R.E. (1972) 'Crime and personality: a review of Eysenck's theory', in V.D.

Nebylitsyn and J.A. Gray (eds), *Biological Bases of Individual Behaviour*. London: Academic Press.

Perez, J. and Torrubia, R. (1985) 'Sensation seeking and anti-social behaviour in a student sample', *Personality and Individual Differences*, 6: 401–3.

Quay, H.C. (1965), 'Psychopathic personality as pathological stimulation-seeking', *American Journal of Psychiatry*, 122: 180–3.

Rahman, A. and Hussain, A. (1984) 'Personality and female criminals in Bangladesh', *Personality and Individual Differences*, 5: 473–4.

Raine, A. and Venables, P. (1981) 'Classical conditioning and socialization – a biosocial interaction', *Personality and Individual Differences*, 2: 273–83.

Robins, L.N. (1972) 'Follow-up studies of behaviour disorders in children', in H.C. Quay and J.S. Werry (eds), *Psychopathological Disorders of Childhood*. New York: Wiley.

Royce, J.P. and Powell, A. (1983) *Theory of Personality and Individual Differences: Factors, Systems and Processes*. Englewood Cliffs, NJ: Prentice-Hall.

Rushton, J.F. and Chrisjohn, R.D. (1981) 'Extraversion, neuroticism, psychoticism and self-reported delinquency: evidence from eight separate samples', *Personality and Individual Differences*, 2: 11–20.

Saklofske, D.H., McKerracher, D.W. and Eysenck, S.B.G. (1978) 'Eysenck's theory of criminality: a scale of criminal propensity as a measure of anti-social behaviour', *Psychological Reports*, 43: 683–6.

Sanocki, W. (1969) 'The use of Eysenck's inventory for testing young prisoners', *Przeglad Penitencjarny* (Warszawa), 7: 53–68.

Saunders, G.R. and Davies, M.B. (1976) 'The validity of the Jesness Inventory with British delinquents', *British Journal of Social and Clinical Psychology*, 15: 33–9.

Schwenkmezger, P. (1983) 'Risikoverhalten, Risikobereitschaft und Delinquenz: Theoretische Grundlagen und differentialdiagnostische Untersuchungen'. *Zeitschrift für Differentielle und Diagnostische Psychologie*, 4: 223–39.

Shanmugan, T.E. (1979) 'Personality factors underlying drug abuse among college students', *Psychological Studies*, 24–35.

Singh, A. (1982) 'A study of the personality and adjustments of female juvenile delinquents', *Child Psychiatry Quarterly*, 13: 52–9.

Smith, D.E. (1974) 'Relationships between the Eysenck and Jesness Personality Inventories', *British Journal of Criminology*, 14: 376–84.

Smith, D.E. and Smith, D.D. (1977) 'Eysenck's psychoticism scale and reconvictions', *British Journal of Criminology*, 17: 387–8.

Steller, M. and Hunze, D. (1984) 'Zur Selbstbeschreibung von Delinquenten im Freiburger Persönlichkeitsinventar (FPI) – Eine Sekundäranalyse empirischer Untersuchungen', *Zeitschrift für Differentielle und Diagnostische Psychologie*, 5: 87–110.

Taylor, T. and Watt, D.C. (1977) 'The relation of deviant symptoms and behaviour in a normal population to subsequent delinquency and maladjustment', *Psychological Medicine*, 7: 163–9.

Wardell, D. and Yeudall, L.T. (1980) 'A multidimensional approach to criminal disorders: the assessment of impulsivity and its relation to crime', *Advances in Behaviour Research and Therapy*, 2: 159–77.

West, D. and Farrington, D.P. (1973) *Who Becomes Delinquent?* London: Heinemann.

Whitehill, M., De Myer-Gapin, S. and Scott, T.J. (1976) 'Stimulation seeking in anti-social preadolescent children', *Journal of Abnormal Psychology*, 85: 101–4.

Zuckerman, M. (1979) *Sensation Seeking: Beyond the Optimal Level of Arousal.* Hillsdale: NJ: Erlbaum.

Zuckerman, M., Eysenck, S.B.G. and Eysenck, H.J. (1978) 'Sensation seeking in England and America: cross-cultural, age and sex comparisons', *Journal of Consulting and Clinical Psychology*, 1: 139–49.

11

Explanations of crime and place

Anthony E. Bottoms and Paul Wiles

The opportunity for two criminologists to reflect, in the company of geographers, upon some aspects of the spatial distribution of crime produces something of a dilemma. On the one hand we want to give full weight to and to welcome the very real contributions which geographers have recently made to this subject (e.g. in Britain alone, Davidson, 1981; Herbert, 1982; Smith, 1986); on the other hand, there seems little point in producing yet another substantive overview of what these writers, and their criminological and sociological colleagues, have discovered to date.

We have chosen, therefore, to write largely in a methodological vein, though with reference where appropriate to substantive findings. Our framework of approach is the intimate relationship of social relations and spatial structures found within the theory of 'structuration', a framework which has attracted considerable recent attention and critical debate among general human geographers and social theorists (e.g. Gregory and Urry, 1985), but which has so far been given little consideration in discussions of the spatial dimensions of crime and offending. We adopt this approach because structuration theory offers a model for explanation which brings together, in a coherent fashion, a number of elements which we have been developing in our own work on residential areas and crime; it offers, in our view, both a framework within which previous research can be synthesized, and a valuable stimulus for future research.

[. . .]

STATISTICAL DISTRIBUTIONS AND ETHNOGRAPHY: HISTORY AND PROBLEMATIC

The work of the pre-war Chicago researchers has justly remained important because they employed a wide variety of research methods, examining *inter alia* both the statistical data on offender distributions in the city (Shaw and McKay, 1942) and aspects of the ethnography of street life and crime (e.g. Cressey, 1932; Shaw, 1930).

From *Crime, Policing and Place: Essays in Environmental Criminology* (eds D.J. Evans, N.R. Fyfe and D.T. Herbert), pp. 11–35. (London: Routledge, 1992.)

They established that offender residence in Chicago was not randomly distributed across the city but was quite clearly patterned, with the highest offender rate areas located in an inner city zone close to the central business district, and then a diminution of the offender rate as one moved outwards towards the periphery of the city. In order to explain this distribution they utilized a theory of the growth of the city in terms of a historical process of urban development radiating outwards from the city's core. This theory seemed adequately to explain the distribution of land use they had found in Chicago, although it continued to be a matter of some debate as to how far the theory fitted other cities, and therefore whether it was a general theory. Their theory of urban development did not itself explain why offenders lived in some areas rather than others; however, from their ethnographic work the Chicagoans did develop an explanation of why and how offending occurred, based on the key concept of 'social disorganization'. Essentially their argument was that offending manifested itself in a lack of structurally located social bonds which encouraged legitimate and discouraged deviant behaviour. Such social disorganization was the result of new immigrant populations coming together and not having had the opportunity to develop a stable social structure with clear norms. Such populations were to be found in those areas of the city, immediately surrounding the inner core, which had been abandoned by more established groups and so offered the cheapest available housing for the new immigrants – the well-known 'interstitial areas' of the Chicago theory. The continuing process of immigration into Chicago meant that as immigrant groups developed more stable normative structures they moved out of the interstitial areas to be replaced, in their turn, by new immigrants. So the cycle was repeated, with new groups gradually developing from disorganization to more stable normative structures and at the same time moving their location gradually outward from the city's centre. In this way areas of the city continued to have patterned offender rates over time.

The Chicago theory of social disorganization has been very influential in the history of criminology. It appears to offer an answer to the problem of the relationship between studies of the areal statistical distribution of crime and offending, and studies of the ethnography of criminal behaviour. As a result much subsequent criminological research used the idea of social disorganization as a central concept. However, there are very real problems with the concept, and beginning with Whyte's (1943) classic *Street Corner Society*, it was subjected to a series of critiques. A number of writers pointed out that empirical studies of interstitial areas and/or deviant behaviour did not support the idea that illegal behaviour was always the result of 'disorganization' – rather, it might instead be the result of highly organized, but alternative sets of normative values. The fact that action is morally disapproved of does not mean that it is necessarily any less related to social organization (see e.g. Becker, 1963). The result, it was argued, was that the theory, like a number of other social theories of crime, was overdeterministic and therefore over-predictive of crime (Matza, 1964). Basically the concept of social disorganization was attacked as being at best a value judgement, and at worst empirically false.

Although the concept of social disorganization has been subject to so much criticism it has nevertheless lived on. For example, recent discussion in the United States has used the notion of an 'underclass', whose lack of a normative order is said to be demonstrated by the collapse of the (black) family, to explain the high crime rates of their cities' ghettos (for a discussion of how these ideas have been used in popular debate see e.g. *Chicago Tribune*, 1986). This renaissance of social disorganization is not entirely surprising since criminology has failed to develop any very satisfactory alternative concept to bridge the two levels of analysis. The alternative has all too often been simply to operate at just one level of analysis. Recent research in Britain has sometimes exemplified this approach. Janet Foster, in a study of crime on housing estates in south London, is most illuminating about the ethnography of crime but says little about the distribution of crime between or within estates (Foster, 1990). On the other hand, the analysis of the results of the British Crime Survey examined the distribution of crime across socially different types of areas (using the ACORN classifications) but said little about why these areas have such different crime rates or indeed whether the classification which was used captured socially similar areas within its categories (Mayhew et al., 1989). Of course, many problems of this kind may simply be due to the limitations of the particular research methods being used within a particular project, and in the end to the lack of the resources available to employ additional or alternative methods. However, the gap remains, and an adequate environmental criminology clearly needs a model of explanation which can link statistical analyses of the distribution of crime with ethnographic studies of criminal and social action.

STRUCTURATION THEORY

In order to explore what might be an adequate explanatory model for environmental criminology, we need first to explore the more general question of what an adequate explanatory model in social science might look like.

Social science has always had a problem with what form explanation ought to take, given that it is concerned with the activity of human beings. The twin dangers are that explanations either operate with models of human action which are so deterministic that they deny any role for human agency, or they are so voluntaristic and particularistic that they deny any real possibility of social science explanations at all. The history of social science could be written in terms of the various attempts to overcome this problem. Social science, like other human activities, has its fashions and at different times fashion has pushed researchers towards one or other of these extremes. The result has been that at different times explanations have been dominated by structural accounts, which have stressed the extent to which human behaviour is a product of the constraints imposed by social structures which are external to the individual (such as the economy), or alternatively by accounts of action, which have emphasized the extent to which human action is a consequence of the creative understanding of particular individuals, and their interaction with other actors. Both approaches have had the advantage of highlighting, often with great clarity, certain aspects of the human condition, but the disadvantage is that they remain partial.

Research in environmental criminology has been prone to just these difficulties. Explanations of where offences occur, or where offenders live, can all too easily assume that place or design acts as a deterministic and monocausal variable. Alternatively, they may assume that place can stand as an operational construct for other aspects of social structure, such as class, or employment status, or family structure; or that it is simply a sorting mechanism which brings together in one place those individuals who possess criminogenic attributes (generally of a genetic or psychological kind). These latter formulations use place as a second order explanation, parasitic on separate explanations of criminal behaviour, which simply accounts for the distribution of crime in geographical space. Alternatively again, structural explanations of this kind may combine the influence of place and the influence of class/employment/family structure, yet remain straightforwardly deterministic. All of these approaches can be criticized as giving insufficient weight to human agency (see for example the work of Sally Merry (1981) on the limitations of a purely design-orientated approach to crime).

A very different approach has been the 'appreciative' one, which has produced a rich harvest of qualitative studies giving a vivid picture of life in a particular area, or the life history of individuals. The difficulty with this approach is that it can ignore the fact that there is a spatial patterning of crime which is in need of explanation, and/or that there are structural aspects in the wider society which powerfully shape the day-to-day lives of individual actors. One researcher who recognized just these difficulties was Owen Gill (1977), who set out to write an appreciative ethnography of the lives of a group of boys from a 'problem council estate' in Merseyside, but found himself successively drawn into social structural issues (and in particular the local housing market) in order to make adequate sense of his ethnographic data.

Writing on social theory and the methodology of the social sciences is replete with warnings against the partiality of 'structural' and 'action-based' approaches, and numerous attempts have been made, with varying degrees of success, to provide a framework for explanation which overcomes the problem. A particularly interesting recent approach to the issue has been made by Anthony Giddens in his 'theory of structuration', the very term combining the connotations of structure and action within a single theory (Giddens, 1984). Giddens has argued not simply that explanations ought to be adequate at both these levels (as for example Max Weber did) but rather that it is a fundamental mistake to conceive of them as separate levels at all. Instead Giddens proposes that:

> The basic domain of study of the social sciences, according to the theory of structuration, is neither the experience of the individual actor, nor the existence of any form of societal totality, but social practices ordered across space and time. (1984: 2)

Space and time are central to Giddens's model of explanation, and so it is especially appropriate to consider this approach in developing theories of environmental criminology. As Giddens puts the matter:

> [Most] social scientists have failed to construct their thinking around the modes in which social systems are constituted across time–space. . . . investigation of this issue is one of the main tasks imposed by the 'problem of order' as conceptualized in the theory of structuration. It is not a particular type of 'area' of social science which can be pursued or discarded at will. *It is at the very heart of social theory, as interpreted through the notion of structuration, and should hence also be regarded as of very considerable importance for the conduct of empirical research in the social sciences.* (1984: 110, italics added)

We shall not attempt to summarize all Giddens's arguments but merely to indicate the most important elements for our purposes. These include the following:

1 Human subjects are knowledgeable agents, though this knowledgeability is bounded on the one hand by the unconscious, and on the other hand by unacknowledged conditions and/or unintended consequences of action.

2 Human subjects largely act within a domain of 'practical consciousness' which often cannot be expressed in terms such as 'motives' or 'reasons' but which 'consist of all the things which actors known tacitly about how to "go on" in the context of social life without being able to give them direct discursive expression' (Giddens, 1984: xxiii). This 'practical consciousness' must, however, be understood and made plain by the researcher in explanation.

3 Structuration theory seeks to escape from the traditional dualism in social theory between 'objectivism' and 'subjectivism'. Thus the theory accepts concepts of 'structure' and 'constraint', normally associated with 'objective' social science, but insists that they be understood only through the actions of knowledgeable agents; on the other hand it believes that 'subjectivist' social science has over-emphasized the degree to which everyday action is directly motivated.

4 Structures may act as constraints on individual action but they are also, and at the same time, the medium and outcome of the conduct they recursively organize – what Giddens refers to as the 'duality of structure'. Structures, therefore, do not exist outside of action, and they do not only constrain, but also enable social action.

5 'Routine' is a predominant form of agents' day-to-day activity: most daily practices are not directly motivated, and routinized practices are a prime expression of the 'duality of structure' in respect of the continuity of social life.

6 Structuration theory accepts and tries to elaborate Marx's famous dictum that human beings 'make history, but not in circumstances of their own choosing'. This is part of the duality of structure, and emphasizes that social change and social process, linked to the reflexivity of human action, is an intrinsic part of human social life, even though that social life also has considerable continuities.

Giddens insists that both action and structure exist only within the ongoing process of human existence, which is largely constituted in practical consciousness. Structures, for Giddens, are properties which both allow and result in a practical consciousness which is able to follow regular patterns over time/space. The same practical rules which guide the social action of individuals are at the same time the basis for the reproduction of social systems. Looked at in this way the 'structure' of place is not simply a constraint on action but instead is one part of the social system which informs the practical (and sometimes discursive) consciousness of social actors. Put more simply, if we want to understand the geography of crime we have to understand how place, over time, is part of the practical consciousness of social actors who engage in behaviour, including actions we define as criminal. The structure of place is central, but it is not external to human agency and must be understood as part of a historical process.

Giddens's theory, then, gives us a model of explanation which we can use to examine critically some recent environmental criminology. Place cannot be made epiphenomenal to the explanation of human activity (as some human geographers once, suicidally, seemed to want to suggest) because place, together with time, are intrinsic dimensions of human existence. In acting, agents have to come to terms with the intrinsicality of space/time – which [. . .] they frequently do through routines.

How they do so, whether they do so in different ways, and how modernity has extended the possible ways in which different actors operate in space/time are all interesting and empirical questions. All of us use our sense of 'locale' (for definition see note 1) to guide our everyday actions, and this is no less true in relation to crime. As Reiss put it, in mercifully straightforward terms,

> our sense of personal safety and potential victimisation by crime is shaped less by knowledge of specific criminals than it is by knowledge of dangerous and safe places and communities. (1986: 1)

To this one might add, first, that the general public's sense of safety relates not only to place but also to different times of day in place, and second, that the everyday life of offenders, as well as of victims and potential victims, is shaped in part by understandings of the nature of particular areas and, within them, of specific locations – and those understandings are undoubtedly important in shaping the geographical distribution of offending behaviour.

STRUCTURATION AND ENVIRONMENTAL CRIMINOLOGY

Let us now consider how structuration theory can help take forward the study of environmental criminology.

To assess this issue we shall examine a recent essay by Per-Olof Wikström (1990), written in an attempt to summarize the literature on crime, criminality and the urban structure as a background paper for a new and major empirical research project in Stockholm. Wikström's paper is both up-to-date and of high quality; it provides, therefore, a useful exemplar of the 'state of the art' in environmental criminology, and a way of testing whether the application of a structuration approach (which Wikström does not consider) might have something to offer to this field of study.

Like most environmental criminologists, Wikström draws a clear distinction between area offender rates and area offence rates [. . .] In summarizing the relationship between urban structure (especially housing) and area offender rates, Wikström postulates two main effects:

1 Housing and [offender-rate based] criminality are related because social groups with a greater propensity to crime are concentrated in certain types of housing. . . .
2 Housing can itself affect the resident's propensity to crime in that the local housing conditions are of importance both to the social life and the social control of the neighbourhood (the 'contextual' effect). This effect may be subdivided into
   (a) situational influence on propensity to offend; and
   (b) long-term influence on the development of the individual resident's personality and life-style, tending to reinforce a propensity to crime . . . (primarily applies to neighbourhood influences on children and young people). (1990: 17)

[. . .]

Turning to the relationship between urban structures and area offence rates, Wikström adopts an approach arising out of routine activities theory, and opportunity theory:

Inter-district variations in the use of urban land generate different activities more or less frequently *at different times of the week and day in different parts of the city*. Segregation and the spatial variation in the pursuit of various activities, each of which will be perceived as more or less attractive by different social groups, ensure that *the social make-up of residents and visitors at different times of day will show distinct inter-district variations*.

The type of activities being pursued and the social composition of the people in the district at any one time can be assumed to be related to

1 the availability of suitable criminal targets, the presence of motivated offenders and the presence of direct social control (capable guardians) [explanation of offence rates for instrumental crime];

2 the occurrence of encounters (environments) liable to provoke friction in the parochial and public orders [explanation of some expressive crime]. (1990: 23, italics added)

Wikström then offers a diagram (reproduced here as Figure 11.1) summarizing his approach to the explanation of offence rates.

These summary statements undoubtedly capture much of our present knowledge about the reasons for inter-area variation in offender rates and offence rates within cities.[2] They are a bold and interesting attempt at synthesis, though – as Wikström would, we think, be the first to agree – they incorporate within them both some points with solid support in empirical research, and others which in the present state of knowledge seem reasonable or even probable, but where the empirical support is much more slender.

From the perspective of structuration theory, two points stand out as interesting in Wikström's summaries. The first concerns the marked emphasis, in the offence rate summary, on the differential paths taken by different actors in space and time, linking with structuration theory's emphasis on space/time issues. The second and

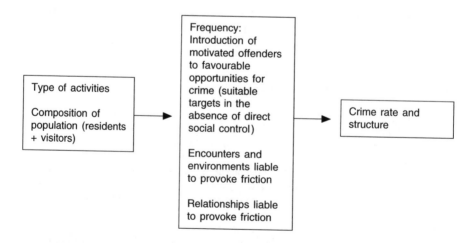

Figure 11.1 *Variation in crime (offence rate) and structure in the urban environment (after Wikström 1990)*

closely related point concerns the use of Cohen and Felson's routine activities theory (1979), emphasizing the extent to which offences either arise directly out of the routine (legal) activities of social actors, or how even a deliberately and consciously illegal activity (e.g. a planned burglary trip) may in practice be confined to areas or trunk roads already known to the offender(s) through their everyday lives (see Brantingham and Brantingham, 1981). Clearly, there is an intriguing link to be forged here between the centrality of *routines* in Giddens's structuration theory (itself an interesting innovation in general sociological theory) and the emerging importance of routine activities theory in environmental criminology.

But while one can see important points of contact between structuration theory and Wikström's approach, a structuration perspective also suggests some weaknesses in his otherwise excellent paper. Two such weaknesses seem particularly apparent, and it is worth elaborating these by way of constructive criticism.

First, Wikström's approach markedly understates the importance of social process. In his offender-rate based analysis, for example, it can be argued that insufficient attention is paid to the constantly changing nature of the local housing market, in particular districts (often linked to more macro-level economic changes, or alterations in government housing policies). In structuration theory, structures are always simultaneously both enabling and constraining, and therefore never static. Similarly, Wikström's diagram for considering offence rate variations (Figure 11.1) gives inadequate attention to the changes (as opposed to the continuities) in the use by social actors of different districts within the city, or (at a more micro-level as highlighted by Sherman et al., 1989) to the constantly evolving character of, for example, particular streets or particular bars in city centre locations.

Second, Wikström's approach arguably pays too little attention to the perceptions, routine activities and decisions of individual actors (as opposed to aggregate patterns of social activity). In so doing, he risks missing the important distinction, central to structuration theory, between the intended and unintended consequences of individual action. Yet unintended consequences of action can be of central importance in, for example, the operation of housing markets (itself central to Wikström's framework for understanding offender rate variations); or the evolution of particular micro-level locations towards or away from being 'hot spots' of crime.

A more detailed consideration of the issues of process and unintended consequences may therefore help in the development of a more adequate approach to environmental criminology.

UNINTENDED CONSEQUENCES OF ACTION AND PROCESSES OF CHANGE

An important aspect of Giddens's structuration theory is that the structures which result from human action are not just a result of the intended consequences of such actions. Indeed, Giddens's notion that human action largely follows 'routines' precisely emphasizes the inadequacy of a fully intentional model of human action. The result is that not only may the consequences of rationally calculated action be unforeseen by actors (or foreseen but unintended), but also human action may frequently not be guided by conscious intention at all. In sum, the structural results of a series of human actions may be quite different from what the actors may have foreseen or intended.

Giddens gives as an example a model of how racial segregation in a city might occur:

> A pattern of ethnic segregation might develop, without any of those involved intending this to happen, in the following way, which can be illustrated by analogy. Imagine a chessboard which has a set of 5-pence pieces and a set of 10-pence pieces. These are distributed randomly on the board, as individuals might be in an urban area. It is presumed that, while they feel no hostility towards the other group, the members of each group do not want to live in a neighbourhood where they are ethnically in a minority. On the chessboard each piece is moved around until it is in such a position that at least 50 per cent of the adjoining pieces are of the same type. The result is a pattern of extreme segregation. The 10-pence pieces end up as a sort of ghetto in the midst of the 5-pence pieces. The 'composition effect' is an outcome of an aggregate of acts – whether those of moving pieces on the board or those of agents in a housing market – each of which is intentionally carried out. But the eventual outcome is neither intended nor desired by anyone. It is, as it were, everyone's doing and no one's. (1984: 10)

It is interesting that Giddens introduces the concept of a 'market' into this example, since this concept is used by economists to signify the summation of the consequences of individual economic decisions, regardless of whether those consequences were intended or foreseen by the actors. Taub et al. (1984), in their study of the decline of neighbourhoods in Chicago in both racial and crime terms, use a similar market-based model to explain the actions of individual householders (as opposed to corporations etc). They argue that such individual residents, when faced with signs of neighbourhood decline, can take decisions only in terms of their own purposes and in the context of their (limited) understanding of what other residents will do. The result can be that, in a similar way to Giddens's example, while none of the residents have an interest in the neighbourhood declining, the unintended consequence of their individual decisions can be precisely that.

The idea of a 'market', of course, is a model developed to help understand the aggregate results of action from an economic point of view and although, as Taub et al. have shown, it can be usefully employed to help explain the processes by which neighbourhoods decline it is not in itself wholly adequate to explain why a neighbourhood's crime or offender-rate pattern changes. What seems to be needed, then, is a model of neighbourhood activity which helps us to understand how changing crime or offending behaviour can be the result of a summation of individual actions, and their intended, unintended and unforeseen consequences: in other words, we need a construct which will fulfil for criminology some of the functions which the market fulfils for economists.

Some time ago Albert Reiss suggested that changes in neighbourhood crime patterns could be thought of as analogous to communities having crime careers (Reiss, 1986). Reiss did not develop this idea of 'community crime careers' much further, but in our view it is extremely suggestive. The term 'community crime career' in effect encompasses the notion that a neighbourhood's crime pattern is the summation of the consequences, whether intended or not, of the way a multitude of actors interact (which itself is linked to their practical consciousness of locale) in an historical process. As such it can equally be applied to offender changes in or offence-rate crime patterns, or to the relationship between the two. [. . .]

Some help in developing this concept may perhaps be obtained by considering again the work of Taub et al. (1984), although the writing of these authors predates that of Reiss. When they constructed a general theory of neighbourhood change out of their research, Taub et al. argued that

> There are three types of social and ecological pressures that interactively determine the pattern of change in urban neighborhoods: (1) ecological facts; (2) corporate and institutional decisions; and (3) decisions of individual neighborhood residents. (1984: 182)

They pointed out that, traditionally, most urban theorists have concentrated on the 'ecological facts'[3] as the main explanatory variable as regards general social change in neighbourhoods, giving a strongly structural quality to such explanations. Such an emphasis, Taub and his colleagues believed,

> gives the wrong impression about the dynamics of neighborhood change. Individual residents and local corporate actors are, after all, the ones whose day-to-day decisions define the texture and quality of urban life. If ecological facts are overwhelming, it is because of the effect of these facts on the perceptions and actions of individual and corporate actors. In a neighborhood that goes up or down, it is ultimately the actions of these residents that make the outcomes real. (1984: 186)

Although their language is different these authors are essentially following the model of explanation proposed by Giddens in insisting that 'place' has to be considered always as it is constituted through human action. Their three-fold interactive model of ecological facts/individual decisions/corporate decisions also offers a valuable framework for analysis of area change,[4] even though the concept of 'ecological facts' needs some reinterpretation from the standpoint of structuration theory.[5]

Despite its merits, however, Taub et al.'s model is of limited value for present purposes because the analysis of individual and corporate actors' perceptions and decisions is applied only to the operations of the property market and its consequences. If we are to develop the notion of 'community crime career' more generally, then we need to extend this type of analysis to encompass all the structures which are relevant to the processes of change in offender and offence rates, as illustrated, for example, in Wikström's summaries. We return to this point, with examples, in the following section.

One other matter, of some importance for what we would regard as an adequate development of Taub et al.'s analysis, must be raised here. Even where actors appear to be operating in a market type situation, a model which focuses on their actions as motivated solely towards that market will have serious inadequacies. One only has to reflect momentarily on the reality of actors' behaviour in parts of the British housing market to see why this is so. Even after the changes of the 1980s a significant proportion of the British housing stock exists within a market of bureaucratic allocation, whose rules are very different from those of a price market. [. . .] In this sector actors need a very sophisticated understanding of the rules of the market in order adequately to foresee the consequences of their choices; yet there is some evidence to suggest that in some areas the allocation process is operated by the local authority in such a paternalistic way that actors do not even perceive that they have a choice. Even where actors do understand that they have a choice, and understand the rules of allocation, it does not necessarily follow that they will maximize the benefits available to them as the model of a rationally calculating market actor would suggest. In the 1980s replication stage of the Sheffield research tenants in a notorious high-rise block of flats had to be re-housed due to its impending demolition. Because of the rules of allocation in Sheffield, these 'clearance' tenants had priority in the allocation to vacant housing units in the local authority's stock, and they could therefore have secured transfers on to some of the most select council estates in the city. In fact few of them chose to do this even though advisers, ranging from community workers to police community constables, explained to them how to do so. Most of them instead chose to move to nearby (and by no means select) estates. The reason was because their bounded sense of location meant that they regarded the alternative select estates as inappropriate for them either in geographical terms (they did not 'belong' in a different sector of the city) or in class terms (the select estates were for the 'respectable'). Such a sense of locale is particularly powerful in Sheffield: one community constable, who was bemoaning the tenants' refusal to maximize the advantage available to them, was reminded by his colleague that he had himself declined a transfer to a different police division because he didn't feel at home in the area! However, a sense of location is merely one of the other aspects of structure which needs to be built in to the full development of a concept of community crime career, as should become clear from the final section of this chapter.

DEVELOPING THE COMMUNITY CRIME CAREER CONCEPT: OFFENDER AND OFFENCE RATE VARIATIONS RECONSIDERED

The concept of a community crime career is, of course, a concept embodying the idea of social change at a meso-level. Structuration theory, as we have seen, places considerable emphasis on social process and social change, holding indeed that such matters are intrinsic to social life as lived out by human agents acting reflexively. But Giddens (1984: ch. 5) also argues, correctly in our view, that given the premises of structuration theory no general theory of social change is possible:

> The reflexive nature of human social life subverts the explication of social change in terms of any simple and sovereign set of causal mechanisms. . . . To insist that social change be studied in 'world time' [i.e. examination of all social conjunctures in the light of reflexively monitored 'history'] is to emphasise the influence of varying forms of inter-societal system upon episodic transactions. If all social life is contingent, all social change is conjunctural. That is to say, it depends upon conjunctions of circumstances and events that may differ in nature according to variations of context, where context (as always) involves the reflexive monitoring by the agents involved of the conditions in which they 'make history'. (1984: 237, 245)

This does not mean, as Giddens goes on to emphasize (1984: 244f) that we cannot generalize at all about social change; it does mean, however, that there 'are no universal laws in the social sciences, and there will not be any' (1984: xxxii).

The implications of this for the concept of community crime careers are, first, that exact prediction of the precise course of such careers will be impossible, but secondly, that we should be able to analyse with some precision the general factors that may influence the development of such careers, in a probabilistic manner. At the present time our ability to specify these factors is rather rudimentary, but it should improve if more scholars develop empirical research specifically based upon the concept of community crime careers.

Let us take two particular examples, one focused upon an *offender-rate based* community crime career, and the other on an *offence-rate based* career. As to the former, Wikström's formulation (discussed earlier) carries considerable plausibility, provided that it is supplemented by an understanding of processes of social change and of the unintended consequences of choices made by individuals and corporate actors within the housing market, as previously discussed [. . .]. Wikström highlights the allocative functions of the housing market, and the contextual effect of housing allocations (itself divided into 'situational' and longer-term effects) as the explanation of changing offender rates. A way of elaborating the issues relevant to this approach, modifying an idea originally suggested by Wikström's colleague Peter Martens (1990: 66), is shown in Figure 11.2. In considering this diagram, it should be noted that in our view the housing market context (on the left of the diagram) has to be especially prioritized in the explanation, for the reason that it is the housing market which is responsible for the allocation of families and individuals to particular areas; but all the other matters shown in the diagram also come into play by way of contextual effects [. . .].

Figure 11.2 explicitly employs the terminology of 'macro', 'meso' and 'micro' processes. We use these terms for heuristic purposes only. We are aware that Giddens (1984: 139–44) eschews them and insists that such distinctions are merely interconnected aspects of how the social phenomenon being examined is located in space/time. Certainly Giddens is right to make this point, and we agree with him that structure is as relevant to micro-sociology as to macro-sociological issues, while no macro-sociological structure can be adequately understood aside from an understanding of the purposive decisions and routine activities of human agents, and their interaction with the constraining and enabling features of the social and material contexts within which that action takes place. Having said that, it remains in our view the case that a micro/meso/macro distinction has a clear heuristic value in environmental criminology, and that Figure 11.2 offers a possible way of conceptualizing it with regard to offender-rate variations in space and over time.

Turning now to offence-rate based community crime careers, Wikström's approach (see Figure 11.1) again offers a valuable starting-point, though once more needing supplementation from concepts of process and unintended consequences. It is, however, worth elaborating this approach a little by way of a specific example, that of city centre crime, in order to develop its potential.

City centres have few residents, but a disproportionate incidence of criminal incidents relative to their land use area (Baldwin and Bottoms, 1976). Thus the city centre is a paradigm case of a high offence area which is not a high offender area. In the daytime, the city centre is of course a hive of commercial and other activity; much of the daytime crime consists of shoplifting or auto-crime, but more personalized crime such as bag-snatching may also feature, considerably aided by the anonymity of the city centre crowd (Poyner, 1983; ch. 6). At night the city centre changes character in terms of both activities and its user population (the average age plummets as the centre is largely taken over by youths). Crimes of public violence

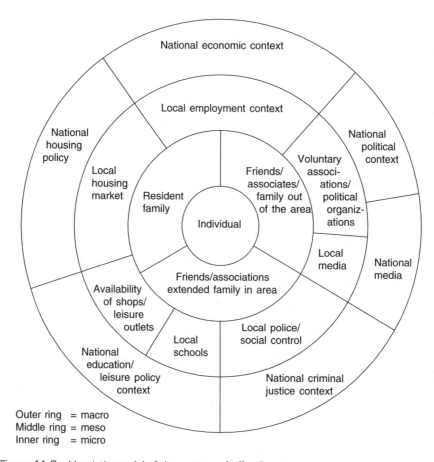

Figure 11.2 *Heuristic model of the context of offending*

and disorder occur disproportionately in city centres at night, often in or close to pubs, clubs or other places of entertainment: these crimes are highly focused upon Friday and Saturday evenings, with a special time focus on pub and club closing times (Hope, 1985; Ramsay, 1982; Wikström 1985). Such incidents are also highly localized, with a few locations providing a disproportionate share of the crimes (Hope, 1985; Sherman et al., 1989).

We immediately see here clear evidence of differential social activity in space/ time by different groups, even in an area which is open to all. Further detailed research would probably show age, class and/or sex segregation in specific locations within the city centre both by day and by night – and would almost certainly show some city centre users to be anxious about groups of youths hanging about (Phillips and Cochrane, 1988) or vagrant alcoholics (Ramsay, 1989). Owners of specific premises may seek to achieve a degree of social segregation by manipulating the sense of location (elaborate entrance portals to an exclusive hotel; interior design deliberately calculated to make a particular age group, class or sex feel at home);

others may seek to boost a sense of safety through the employment of private security companies (as, increasingly, in shopping malls with multiple retail outlets) or physical security devices (use of CCTV, and so on). There is clearly here a rich field of exploration in the patterning of use of the city centre, and, by those who do use it, in the patterning of the use of specific sites. Nor is any of this static. Perceptions of the desirability of a particular shop/café/bar can easily change over time, and individual decisions about custom can cumulatively have important long-term consequences. Add to this the fact that city centres themselves change over time, both in their land use and design (increasing use of pedestrianized streets, increasing development of multiple stores rather than small shops, and so on) and in their social use (the city centre in the evening in the early 1960s was much less predominantly a young person's domain), and we begin to see the complexity of the whole picture within which city centre crime must be understood. Wikström's model (Figure 11.1) is correct in so far as it goes, but needs a much greater understanding of the fluidity of social routines and practices before it can be fully adequate. [. . .]

These examples are no more than suggestive, and the concept of a community crime career clearly requires further elaboration. We hope, however, that the examples may help to bring alive some of the theoretical issues discussed in more abstract terms earlier in this chapter.

CONCLUSION

What we have tried to argue in this chapter is that a proper understanding of the spatial aspects of offences and offending is possible only if a model is employed which is capable of including the natural and built environment, the political, economic, social and cultural contexts and structures of areas and the actions of individuals and corporate bodies within areas, within a theory which accounts for the ongoing processes of interaction between them. We have used Giddens's structuration theory because we believe that it offers such a framework, and we have tried to show how the elements of this approach can illuminate current work within environmental criminology.

The task of developing a more adequate environmental criminology seems to us rather urgent at the present time, since for a variety of reasons the structures and understandings which underpin much existing scholarship are undergoing some rapid changes. [. . .] The tenure map of Britain is being redrawn, and this may well have significant consequences for the geography of crime. Perhaps more fundamental is the movement of the urban middle class into rural communities, and the consequential push of the less affluent rural young into the towns in search of affordable housing: the old rural/urban crime patterns will almost certainly be affected by this process. In the towns themselves, city centres are increasingly facing competition from large out-of-town shopping areas on the North American model, where rather different strategies of social control and segregation are being deployed. Industry and commerce, and even retailing, are also increasingly being segregated from residential areas and placed on industrial estates, technology parks, and so on. At the same time as the geography of Britain is being altered in these ways, so also technological innovations are constantly affecting the ability of social actors (both individuals and corporate bodies) to manipulate the constraints of both time and distance. If, as

Giddens suggests, our sense of location is a key aspect of our social existence and is a product of our experience and interaction within space/time then the sense of location of many modern Britons is likely to be significantly changed. If it is, then the appropriateness of place to life-style, including the criminal, and to life experiences, including victimization, will also change. It is therefore vital that we should possess an adequate model for understanding these processes and their criminological consequences. We can at any rate confidently predict that there will be no shortage of interesting research topics for future environmental criminologists.

NOTES

1 Sherman et al. define 'place' as 'a fixed physical environment that can be seen completely and simultaneously, at least on its surface, by one's naked eyes' (1989: 31). Our own usage in this chapter, not least in the title, is of course considerably broader than this. It should be added, however, that Sherman et al. are not blind to what they call the 'sociological concept of place', defined as 'the social organization of behaviour at a geographic place'. This point is developed and strengthened by Giddens (1984) in his concept of 'locales', which, he insists, 'are not just places but *settings* of interaction, the settings of interaction in turn being essential to specifying its *contextuality*' (pp. xxv, 118). Giddens's formal definition of a locale is as follows: 'a physical region involved as part of the setting of interaction, having definite boundaries which help concentrate interaction in one way or another' (1984: 375).

2 Even within its own terms, however, it can be argued that Wikström's formulation pays too little attention to the implications of spatial form and design for offence rate distribution (see Newman, 1972). Although we are stressing (following Giddens) that it is actors' conceptions of 'locale' which are critical (either in direct awareness or more usually in practical consciousness), nevertheless the physical nature of the environment must place some limits on what these conceptions can consist of.

3 'Ecological facts', according to Taub et al., 'define the social and economic context for a neighborhood' (1984: 182). The ecological facts of particular importance for neighbourhood decline are said to be:

1 the potential employment base for neighbourhood residents;
2 demographic pressures on the neighbourhood housing market;
3 the age and original quality of the housing stock;
4 external amenities such as attractive physical locations (hills, views, and so on).

4 Taub et al.'s distinction between corporate and individual actors is important because it recognizes that in a market situation corporate actors have greater power to influence outcomes, whether such corporate actors are commercial corporations, non-commercial organizations such as universities (the University of Chicago features strongly in one of Taub et al.'s area case studies) or individual actors who band together in a political or community organization in order to derive the benefits of corporate power. Of course, in markets the ultimate corporate actors are either those who hold a monopoly, or those who can use the legislative and administrative power of the state to redefine the nature of the market.

5 Some of the 'ecological facts' as defined by Taub et al. (e.g. the local employment base) are of course themselves part of the social structures which are constituted and reproduced in human action.

REFERENCES

Baldwin, J. and Bottoms, A.E. (1976) *The Urban Criminal*. London: Tavistock.

Becker, H.S. (1963) *Outsiders*. New York: Free Press.

Brantingham, P.L. and Brantingham, P.J. (1981) 'Notes on the geometry of crime', in P.J. Brantingham and P.L. Brantingham (eds), *Environmental Criminology*, Beverly Hills, CA: Sage.

Chicago Tribune (eds) (1986) *The American Millstone*. Chicago: Contemporary Books.

Cohen, L.E. and Felson, M. (1979) 'Social change and crime rate trends: a routine activities approach', *American Sociological Review*, 44: 588–608.

Cressey, P.G. (1932) *The Taxi-Dance Hall*. Chicago: University of Chicago Press.

Davidson, N. (1981) *Crime and Environment*. London: Croom Helm.

Foster, J. (1990) *Villains: Crime and Community in the Inner City*. London: Routledge.

Giddens, A. (1984) *The Constitution of Society*. Cambridge: Polity.

Gill, O. (1977) *Luke Street*. London: Macmillan.

Gregory, D. and Urry, J. (1985) *Social Relations and Spatial Structures*. London: Macmillan.

Herbert, D.T. (1982) *The Geography of Urban Crime*. London: Longman.

Hope, T. (1985) *Implementing Crime Prevention Measures*. Home Office Research Study 86. London: HMSO.

Martens, P.L. (1990) 'Family, neighbourhood and socialisation', in P.-O.H. Wikström (ed.), *Crime and Measures against Crime in the City*. Stockholm: National Council for Crime Prevention.

Matza, D. (1964) *Delinquency and Drift*. London: Wiley.

Mayhew, P., Elliott, D. and Dowds, L. (1989) *The 1988 British Crime Survey*. Home Office Research Study 111. London: HMSO.

Merry, S. (1981) 'Defensible space undefended: social factors in crime prevention through environmental design', *Urban Affairs Quarterly*,16: 397–422.

Newman, O. (1972) *Defensible Space*. New York: Macmillan.

Phillips, S. and Cochrane, R. (1988) *Crime and Nuisance in the Shopping Centre*. Crime Prevention Unit Paper 16. London: Home Office.

Poyner, B. (1983) *Design Against Crime: Beyond Defensible Space*. London: Butterworths.

Ramsay, M. (1982) *City Centre Crime*. Home Office Research and Planning Unit Paper 10. London: Home Office.

Ramsay, M. (1989) *Downtown Drinkers: the Perceptions and Fears of the Public in a City Centre*. Crime Prevention Unit Paper 19. London: Home Office.

Reiss, A.J. (1986) 'Why are communities important in understanding crime?', in A.J. Reiss and M. Tonry (eds), *Communities and Crime*. Chicago: University of Chicago Press.

Shaw, C.R. (1930) *The Jack Roller*. Chicago: University of Chicago Press.

Shaw, C.R. and McKay, H.D. (1942) *Juvenile Delinquency and Urban Areas*. Chicago: University of Chicago Press.

Sherman, L.W., Gartin, P.R. and Buerger, M.E. (1989) 'Hot spots of predatory crime: routine activities and the criminology of place', *Criminology*, 27: 27–55.

Smith, S.J. (1986) *Crime, Space and Society*. Cambridge: Cambridge University Press.

Taub, R., Taylor, D.G. and Dunham, J.D. (1984) *Paths of Neighborhood Change*. Chicago: University of Chicago Press.

Whyte, W.H. (1943) *Street Corner Society*. Chicago: University of Chicago Press.

Wikström, P.-O.H. (1985) *Everyday Violence in Contemporary Sweden*. Stockholm: National Council for Crime Prevention.

Wikström, P.-O.H. (1990) 'Delinquency and urban structure', in P.-O.H. Wikström (ed.), *Crime and Measures against Crime in the City*. Stockholm: National Council for Crime Prevention.

12

The underclass

Charles Murray

THE CONCEPT OF 'UNDERCLASS'

'Underclass' is an ugly word, with its whiff of Marx and the lumpenproletariat. Perhaps because it is ugly, 'underclass' as used in Britain tends to be sanitized, a sort of synonym for people who are not just poor, but especially poor. So let us get it straight from the outset: the 'underclass' does not refer to degree of poverty, but to a type of poverty.

It is not a new concept. I grew up knowing what the underclass was; we just didn't call it that in those days. In the small Iowa town where I lived, I was taught by my middle-class parents that there were two kinds of poor people. One class of poor people was never even called 'poor'. I came to understand that they simply lived with low incomes, as my own parents had done when they were young. Then there was another set of poor people, just a handful of them. These poor people didn't lack just money. They were defined by their behaviour. Their homes were littered and unkempt. The men in the family were unable to hold a job for more than a few weeks at a time. Drunkenness was common. The children grew up ill-schooled and ill-behaved and contributed a disproportionate share of the local juvenile delinquents.

British observers of the nineteenth century knew these people. To Henry Mayhew, whose articles in the *Morning Chronicle* in 1850 drew the Victorians' attention to poverty, they were the 'dishonest poor', a member of which was

> distinguished from the civilised man by his repugnance to regular and continuous labour – by his want of providence in laying up a store for the future – by his inability to perceive consequences ever so slightly removed from immediate apprehensions – by his passion for stupefying herbs and roots and, when possible, for intoxicating fermented liquors . . . .

Other popular labels were 'undeserving', 'unrespectable', 'depraved', 'debased', 'disreputable' or 'feckless' poor.

From *The Emerging Underclass*, pp. 1–23; 33–5. (London: Institute of Economic Affairs, 1990.)

As Britain entered the 1960s a century later, this distinction between honest and dishonest poor people had been softened. The second kind of poor person was no longer 'undeserving'; rather, he was the product of a 'culture of poverty'. But intellectuals as well as the man in the street continued to accept that poor people were not all alike. Most were doing their best under difficult circumstances; a small number were pretty much as Mayhew had described them. Then came the intellectual reformation that swept both the United States and Britain at about the same time, in the mid-1960s, and with it came a new way of looking at the poor. Henceforth, the poor were to be homogenized. The only difference between poor people and everyone else, we were told, was that the poor had less money. More importantly, the poor were all alike. There was no such thing as the ne'er-do-well poor person – he was the figment of the prejudices of a parochial middle class. Poor people, *all* poor people, were equally victims, and would be equally successful if only society gave them a fair shake.

The difference between the US and the UK

The difference between the Unites States and Britain was that the United States reached the future first. During the last half of the 1960s and throughout the 1970s something strange and frightening was happening among poor people in the United States. Poor communities that had consisted mostly of hardworking folks began deteriorating, sometimes falling apart altogether. Drugs, crime, illegitimacy, homelessness, drop-out from the job market, drop-out from school, casual violence – all the measures that were available to the social scientists showed large increases, focused in poor communities. As the 1980s began, the growing population of 'the other kind of poor people' could no longer be ignored, and a label for them came into use. In the US, we began to call them the underclass.

For a time, the intellectual conventional wisdom continued to hold that 'underclass' was just another pejorative attempt to label the poor. But the label had come into use because there was no longer any denying reality. What had once been a small fraction of the American poor had become a sizeable and worrisome population. An underclass existed, and none of the ordinary kinds of social policy solutions seemed able to stop its growth. One by one, the American social scientists who had initially rejected the concept of an underclass fell silent, then began to use it themselves.

By and large, British intellectuals still disdain the term. In 1987, the social historian John Macnicol summed up the prevailing view in the *Journal of Social Policy*, [vol. 16, no. 3, pp. 293–318] writing dismissively that underclass was nothing more than a refuted concept periodically resurrected by Conservatives 'who wish to constrain the redistributive potential of state welfare'. But there are beginning to be breaks in the ranks. Frank Field, the prominent Labour MP, has just published a book with 'underclass' in its subtitle. The newspapers, watching the United States and seeing shadows of its problems in Britain, have begun to use the term. As someone who has been analysing this phenomenon in the United States, I arrived in Britain earlier this year, a visitor from a plague area come to see whether the disease is spreading.

With all the reservations that a stranger must feel in passing judgement on an unfamiliar country, I will jump directly to the conclusion: Britain does have an underclass, still largely out of sight and still smaller than the one in the United States. But it is growing rapidly. Within the next decade, it will probably become as large (proportionately) as the United States' underclass. It could easily become larger.

I am not talking here about an unemployment problem that can be solved by more jobs, nor about a poverty problem that can be solved by higher benefits. Britain has a growing population of working-aged healthy people who live in a different world from other Britons, who are raising their children to live in it, and whose values are now contaminating the life of entire neighbourhoods – which is one of the most insidious aspects of the phenomenon, for neighbours who don't share those values cannot isolate themselves.

There are many ways to identify an underclass. I will concentrate on three phenomena that have turned out to be early-warning signals in the United States: illegitimacy, violent crime, and drop-out from the labour force. In each case I will be using the simplest of data, collected and published by Britain's Government Statistical Service. I begin with illegitimacy, which in my view is the best predictor of an underclass in the making.

ILLEGITIMACY AND THE UNDERCLASS

It is a proposition that angers many people. Why should it be a 'problem' that a woman has a child without a husband? Why isn't a single woman perfectly capable of raising a healthy, happy child, if only the state will provide a decent level of support so that she may do so? Why is raising a child without having married any more of a problem than raising a child after a divorce? The very word 'illegitimate' is intellectually illegitimate. Using it in a gathering of academics these days is a *faux pas*, causing pained silence.

I nonetheless focus on illegitimacy rather than on the more general phenomenon of one-parent families because, in a world where all social trends are ambiguous, illegitimacy is less ambiguous than other forms of single parenthood. It is a matter of degree. Of course some unmarried mothers are excellent mothers and some unmarried fathers are excellent fathers. Of course some divorced parents disappear from the children's lives altogether and some divorces have more destructive effects on the children than a failure to marry would have had. Being without two parents is generally worse for the child than having two parents, no matter how it happens. But illegitimacy is the purest form of being without two parents – legally, the child is without a father from day one; he is often without one practically as well. Further, illegitimacy bespeaks an attitude on the part of one or both parents that getting married is not an essential part of siring or giving birth to a child; this in itself distinguishes their mindset from that of people who do feel strongly that getting married is essential.

Call it what you will, illegitimacy has been sky-rocketing since 1979. I use 'sky-rocketing' advisedly. [. . .] From the end of the Second World War until 1960, Britain enjoyed a very low and even slightly declining illegitimacy ratio. From 1960 until 1978 the ratio increased, but remained modest by international standards – as late as 1979, Britain's illegitimacy ratio was only 10.6 per cent, one of the lowest rates in the industrialized West. Then, suddenly, during a period when fertility was steady, the illegitimacy ratio began to rise very rapidly – to 14.1 per cent by 1982, 18.9 per cent by 1985, and finally to 25.6 per cent by 1988. If present trends continue, Britain will pass the United States in this unhappy statistic in 1990.

The sharp rise is only half of the story. The other and equally important half is that illegitimate births are not scattered evenly among the British population. In this, press reports can be misleading. There is much publicity about the member of the royal family who has a child without a husband, or the socially prominent young career woman who deliberately decides to have a baby on her own, but these are comparatively rare events. The increase in illegitimate births is strikingly concentrated among the lowest social class.

Municipal Districts

This is especially easy to document in Britain, where one may fit together the Government Statistical Service's birth data on municipal districts with the detailed socioeconomic data from the general census. When one does so for 169 metropolitan districts and boroughs in England and Wales with data from both sources, the relationship between social class and illegitimacy is so obvious that the statistical tests become superfluous. Municipal districts with high concentrations of household heads in Class I (professional persons, by the classification used for many years by the Government Statistical Service) have illegitimacy ratios in the low teens (Wokingham was lowest as of 1987, with only nine of every 100 children born illegitimate) while municipalities like Nottingham and Southwark, with populations most heavily weighted with Class V household heads (unskilled labourers), have illegitimacy ratios of more than 40 per cent (the highest in 1987 was Lambeth, with 46 per cent).

The statistical tests confirm this relationship. The larger the proportion of people who work at unskilled jobs and the larger the proportion who are out of the labour force, the higher the illegitimacy ratio, in a quite specific and regular numeric relationship. The strength of the relationship may be illustrated this way: suppose you were limited to two items of information about a community – the percentage of people in Class V and the percentage of people who are 'economically inactive'. With just these two measures, you could predict the illegitimacy ratio, usually within just three percentage points of the true number. As a statistician might summarize it, these two measures of economic status 'explain 51 per cent of the variance' – an extremely strong relationship by the standards of the social sciences.

In short, the notion that illegitimate births are a general phenomenon, that young career women and girls from middle-class homes are doing it just as much as anyone else, is flatly at odds with the facts. There has been a *proportional* increase in illegitimate births among all communities, but the *prevalence* of illegitimate births is drastically higher among the lower-class communities than among the upper-class ones.

Neighbourhoods

The data I have just described are based on municipal districts. The picture gets worse when we move down to the level of the neighbourhood, though precise numbers are hard to come by. The proportion of illegitimate children in a specific poor neighbourhood can be in the vicinity not of 25 per cent, nor even of 40 per cent, but a hefty majority. And in this concentration of illegitimate births lies a generational catastrophe. Illegitimacy produces an underclass for one compelling practical reason having nothing to do with morality or the sanctity of marriage. Namely: communities need families. Communities need fathers.

This is not an argument that many intellectuals in Britain are ready to accept. I found that discussing the issue was like being in a time warp, hearing in 1989 the same rationalizations about illegitimacy that American experts used in the 1970s and early 1980s.

[. . .]

'Mainly a black problem'?

'It's mainly a black problem'. I heard this everywhere, from political clubs in Westminster to some quite sophisticated demographers in the statistical research offices. The statement is correct in this one, very limited sense: blacks born in the West Indies have much higher illegitimacy ratios – about 48 per cent of live births in the latest numbers – than all whites. But blacks constitute such a tiny proportion of the British population that their contribution to the overall illegitimacy ratio is minuscule. If there had been no blacks whatsoever in Britain (and I am including all blacks in Britain in this statement, not just those who were born abroad), the overall British illegitimacy ratio in 1988 would have dropped by about one percentage point, from 25 per cent to about 24 per cent. Blacks are not causing Britain's illegitimacy problem.

In passing, it is worth adding that the overall effect of ethnic minorities living in the UK is to *reduce* the size of the illegitimacy ratio. The Chinese, Indians, Pakistanis, Arabs and East Africans in Britain have illegitimacy ratios that are tiny compared with those of British whites.

'It's not as bad as it looks'

In the United States, the line used to be that blacks have extended families, with uncles and grandfathers compensating for the lack of a father. In Britain, the counterpart to this cheery optimism is that an increasing number of illegitimate births are jointly registered and that an increasing number of such children are born to people who live together at the time of birth. Both joint registration and living together are quickly called evidence of 'a stable relationship'.

The statements about joint registration and living together are factually correct. Of the 158,500 illegitimate births in England and Wales in 1987, 69 per cent were jointly registered. Of those who jointly registered the birth, 70 per cent gave the same address, suggesting some kind of continuing relationship. Both of these figures have increased – in 1961, for example, only 38 per cent of illegitimate births were jointly registered, suggesting that the nature of illegitimacy in the United Kingdom has changed dramatically.

You may make what you wish of such figures. In the United States, we have stopped talking blithely about the 'extended family' in black culture that would make everything okay. It hasn't. And as the years go on, the extended family argument becomes a cruel joke – for without marriage, grandfathers and uncles too become scarce. In Britain, is it justified to assume that jointly registering a birth, or living together at the time of the birth, means a relationship that is just as stable (or nearly as stable) as a marriage? I pose it as a question because I don't have the empirical answer. But neither did any of the people who kept repeating the joint-registration and living-together numbers so optimistically.

If we can be reasonably confident that the children of never-married women do considerably worse than their peers, it remains to explain why. Progress has been slow. Until recently in the United States, scholars were reluctant to concede that illegitimacy is a legitimate variable for study. Even as that situation changes, they remain slow to leave behind their equations and go out to talk with people who are trying to raise their children in neighbourhoods with high illegitimacy rates. This is how I make sense of the combination of quantitative studies, ethnographic studies and talking-to-folks journalism that bear on the question of illegitimacy, pulling in a few observations from my conversations in Britain.

Clichés about role models are true

It turns out that the clichés about role models are true. Children grow up making sense of the world around them in terms of their own experience. Little boys don't naturally grow up to be responsible fathers and husbands. They don't naturally grow up knowing how to get up every morning at the same time and go to work. They don't naturally grow up thinking that work is not just a way to make money, but a way to hold one's head high in the world. And most emphatically of all, little boys do not reach adolescence naturally wanting to refrain from sex, just as little girls don't become adolescents naturally wanting to refrain from having babies. In all these ways and many more, boys and girls grow into responsible parents and neighbours and workers because they are imitating the adults around them.

That's why single-parenthood is a problem for communities, and that's why illegitimacy is the most worrisome aspect of single-parenthood. Children tend to behave like the adults around them. A child with a mother and no father, living in a neighbourhood of mothers with no fathers, judges by what he sees. You can send in social workers and school teachers and clergy to tell a young male that when he grows up he should be a good father to his children, but he doesn't know what that means unless he's seen it. Fifteen years ago, there was hardly a poor neighbourhood in urban Britain where children did not still see plentiful examples of good fathers around them. Today, the balance has already shifted in many poor neighbourhoods. In a few years, the situation will be much worse, for this is a problem that nurtures itself.

Child-rearing in single-parent communities

Hardly any of this gets into the public dialogue. In the standard newspaper or television story on single-parenthood, the reporter tracks down a struggling single parent and reports her efforts to raise her children under difficult circumstances, ending with an indictment of a stingy social system that doesn't give her enough to get along. The ignored story is what it's like for the two-parent families trying to raise their children in neighbourhoods where they now represent the exception, not the rule. Some of the problems may seem trivial but must be painfully poignant to anyone who is a parent. Take, for example, the story told me by a father who lives in such a neighbourhood in Birkenhead, near Liverpool, about the time he went to his little girl's Christmas play at school. He was the only father there – hardly any of the other children had fathers – and his daughter, embarrassed because she was different, asked him not to come to the school anymore.

The lack of fathers is also associated with a level of physical unruliness that makes life difficult. The same Birkenhead father and his wife raised their first daughter as they were raised, to be polite and considerate – and she suffered for it. Put simply, her schoolmates weren't being raised to be polite and considerate – they weren't being 'raised' at all in some respects. We have only a small body of systematic research on child-rearing practices in contemporary low-income, single-parent communities; it's one of those unfashionable topics. But the unsystematic reports I heard in towns like Birkenhead and council estates like Easterhouse in Glasgow are consistent with the reports from inner-city Washington and New York: in communities without fathers, the kids tend to run wild. The fewer the fathers, the greater the tendency. 'Run wild' can mean such simple things as young children having no set bedtime. It can mean their being left alone in the house at night while mummy goes out. It can mean an 18-month-old toddler allowed to play in the street. And, as in the case of the couple trying to raise their children as they had been raised, it can mean children who are inordinately physical and aggressive in their relation-ships with other children. With their second child, the Birkenhead parents eased up on their requirements for civil behaviour, realizing that their children had to be able to defend themselves against threats that the parents hadn't faced when they were children. The third child is still an infant, and the mother has made a conscious decision. 'I won't knock the aggression out of her,' she said to me. Then she paused, and added angrily, 'It's *wrong* to have to decide that.'

The key to an underclass

I can hear the howls of objection already – lots of families raise children who have those kinds of problems, not just poor single parents. Of course. But this is why it is important to talk to parents who have lived in both kinds of communities. Ask them whether there is any difference in child-raising between a neighbourhood composed mostly of married couples and a neighbourhood composed mostly of single mothers. In Britain as in the United States – conduct the inquiries yourself – the overwhelming response is that the difference is large and palpable. The key to an underclass is not the individual instance but a situation in which a very large proportion of an entire community lacks fathers, and this is far more common in poor communities than in rich ones.

CRIME AND THE UNDERCLASS

Crime is the next place to look for an underclass, for several reasons. First and most obviously, the habitual criminal is the classic member of an underclass. He lives off mainstream society without participating in it. But habitual criminals are only part of the problem. Once again, the key issue in thinking about an underclass is how the community functions, and crime can devastate a community in two especially important ways. To the extent that the members of a community are victimized by crime, the community tends to become fragmented. To the extent that many people in a community engage in crime as a matter of course, all sorts of the socializing norms of the community change, from the kind of men that the younger boys choose as heroes to the standards of morality in general.

Consider first the official crime figures, reported annually for England by the Home Office. As in the case of illegitimacy, I took for granted before I began this exploration that England had much lower crimes rates than the United States. It therefore came as a shock to discover that England and Wales (which I will subsequently refer to as England) have a combined property crime rate apparently as high, and probably higher, than that of the United States. (I did not compare rates with Scotland and Northern Ireland, which are reported separately.) I say 'apparently' because Britain and the United States use somewhat different definitions of property crime. But burglaries, which are similarly defined in both countries, provide an example. In 1988, England had 1,623 reported burglaries per 100,000 population compared with 1,309 in the US. Adjusting for the transatlantic differences in definitions, England also appears to have had higher rates of motor vehicle theft than the United States. The rates for other kind of theft seem to have been roughly the same. I wasn't the only one who was surprised at these comparisons. I found that if you want to attract startled and incredulous attention in England, mention casually that England has a higher property crime rate than that notorious crime centre of the western world, the United States. No one will believe you.

Violent crime

The understandable reason why they don't believe you is that *violent* crime in England remains much lower than violent crime in the United States, and it is violent crime that engenders most anxiety and anger. In this regard, Britain still lags far behind the US. This is most conspicuously true for the most violent of all crimes, homicide. In all of 1988, England and Wales recorded just 624 homicides. The United States averaged that many every 11 days – 20,675 for the year.

That's the good news. The bad news is that the violent crime rate in England and Wales has been rising very rapidly. [. . .]

The size of the increase isn't as bad as it first looks, because England began with such a small initial rate (it's easy to double your money if you start with only a few pence – of which, more in a moment). Still, the rise is steep, and it became much steeper in about 1968. Compare the gradual increase from 1955 to 1968 with what happened subsequently. By 1988, England had 314 violent crimes reported per 100,000 people. The really bad news is that you have been experiencing this increase despite demographic trends that should have been working to your advantage. This point is important enough to explain at greater length.

The most frequent offenders, the ones who puff up the violent crime statistics, are males in the second half of their teens. As males get older, they tend to become more civilized. In both England and the United States, the number of males in this troublesome age group increased throughout the 1970s, and this fact was widely used as an explanation for increasing crime. But since the early 1980s, the size of the young male cohort has been decreasing in both countries. In the United Kingdom, for example, the number of males aged 15 to 19 hit its peak in 1982 and has subsequently decreased both as a percentage of the population and in raw numbers (by a little more than 11 per cent in both cases). Ergo, the violent crime rate 'should' have decreased as well. But it didn't. Despite the reduction in the number of males in the highest-offending age group after 1982, the violent crime rate in England from 1982 to 1988 rose by 43 per cent.

Here I must stop and briefly acknowledge a few of the many ways in which people will object that the official crime rates don't mean anything – but only briefly, because this way lies a statistical abyss.

The significance of official crime rates

One common objection is that the increase in the crime rate reflects economic growth (because there are more things to steal, especially cars and the things in them) rather than any real change in criminal behaviour. If so, one has to ask why England enjoyed a steady decline in crime through the last half of the nineteenth century, when economic growth was explosive. But, to avoid argument, let us acknowledge that economic growth does make interpreting the changes in the property crime rate tricky, and focus instead on violent crime, which is not so directly facilitated by economic growth.

Another common objection is that the increase in crime is a mirage. One version of this is that crime just seems to be higher because more crimes are being reported to the police than before (because of greater access to telephones, for example, or because of the greater prevalence of insurance). The brief answer here is that it works both ways. Rape and sexual assault are more likely to be reported now, because of changes in public attitudes and judicial procedures regarding those crimes. An anonymous purse-snatch is less likely to be reported, because the victim doesn't think it will do any good. The aggregate effect of a high crime rate can be to reduce reporting, and this is most true of poor neighbourhoods where attitudes toward the police are ambiguous.

The most outrageously spurious version of the 'crime isn't really getting worse' argument uses *rate* of increase rather than the *magnitude* of increase to make the case. The best example in Britain is the argument that public concern about muggings in the early 1970s was simply an effort to scapegoat young blacks, and resulted in a 'moral panic'. The sociologist Stuart Hall and his colleagues made this case at some length in a book entitled *Policing the Crisis* [London: Macmillan, 1978] in which, among other things, they blithely argued that because the rate of increase in violent crimes was decreasing, the public's concern was unwarranted. It is the familiar problem of low baselines. From 1950 to 1958, violent crime in England rose by 88 per cent (the crime rate began at 14 crimes per 100,000 persons and rose by 13). From 1980 to 1988 violent crime in England rose by only 60 per cent (it began at 196 crimes per 100,000 persons and rose by 118). In other words, by the logic of Hall and his colleagues, things are getting much better, because the rate of increase in the 1980s has been lower than it was during the comparable period of the 1950s. [. . .]

The intellectual conventional wisdom

The denial by intellectuals that crime really has been getting worse spills over into denial that poor communities are more violent places than affluent communities. To the people who live in poor communities, this doesn't make much sense. One man in a poor, high-crime community told me about his experience in an open university where he had decided to try to improve himself. He took a sociology course about poverty. The professor kept talking about this 'nice little world that the poor live in', the man remembered. The professor scoffed at the reactionary myth that poor communities are violent places. To the man who lived in such a community, it was 'bloody drivel'. A few weeks later, a class exercise called for the students to canvass a poor neighbourhood. The professor went along, but apparently he, too, suspected that some of his pronouncements were bloody drivel – he cautiously stayed in his car and declined to knock on doors himself. And that raises the most interesting question regarding the view that crime has not risen, or that crime is not especially a problem in lower-class communities: do any of the people who hold this view actually *believe* it, to the extent that they take no more precautions walking in a slum neighbourhood than they do in a middle-class suburb?

These comments will not still the battle over the numbers. But I will venture this prediction, once again drawn from the American experience. After a few more years, quietly and without anyone having to admit he had been wrong, the intellectual conventional wisdom in Britain as in the United States will undergo a gradual transition. After all the statistical artifacts are taken into account and argued over, it will be decided that England is indeed becoming a more dangerous place in which to live: that this unhappy process is not occurring everywhere, but disproportionately in particular types of neighbourhoods; and that those neighbourhoods turn out to be the ones in which an underclass is taking over. Reality will once again force theory to its knees.

UNEMPLOYMENT AND THE UNDERCLASS

If illegitimate births are the leading indicator of an underclass and violent crime a proxy measure of its development, the definitive proof that an underclass has arrived is that large numbers of young, healthy, low-income males choose not to take jobs. (The young idle rich are a separate problem.) The decrease in labour force participation is the most elusive of the trends in the growth of the British underclass.

The main barrier to understanding what's going on is the high unemployment of the 1980s. The official statistics distinguish between 'unemployed' and 'economically inactive', but Britain's unemployment figures (like those in the US) include an unknown but probably considerable number of people who manage to qualify for benefit even if in reality very few job opportunities would tempt them to work.

On the other side of the ledger, over a prolonged period of high unemployment the 'economically inactive' category includes men who would like to work but have given up. To make matters still more complicated, there is the 'black economy' to consider, in which people who are listed as 'economically inactive' are really working for cash, not reporting their income to the authorities. So we are looking through a glass darkly, and I have more questions than answers.

Economic inactivity and social class

The simple relationship of economic inactivity to social class is strong, just as it was for illegitimacy. According to the 1981 census data, the municipal districts with high proportions of household heads who are in Class V (unskilled labour) also tend to have the highest levels of 'economically inactive' persons of working age (statistically, the proportion of Class V households explains more than a third of the variance when inactivity because of retirement is taken into account).

This is another way of saying that you will find many more working-aged people who are neither working nor looking for work in the slums than in the suburbs. Some of these persons are undoubtedly discouraged workers, but two questions need to be asked and answered with far more data than are currently available – specifically, questions about lower-class young males.

Lower-class young males

First, after taking into account Britain's unemployment problems when the 1981 census was taken, were the levels of economic inactivity among young males consistent with the behaviour of their older brothers and fathers during earlier periods? Or were they dropping out more quickly and often than earlier cohorts of young men?

Second, Britain has for the past few years been conducting a natural experiment, with an economic boom in the south and high unemployment in the north. If lack of jobs is the problem, then presumably economic inactivity among lower-class healthy young males in the south has plummeted to insignificant levels. Has it?

The theme that I heard from a variety of people in Birkenhead and Easterhouse was that the youths who came of age in the late 1970s are in danger of being a lost generation. All of them did indeed ascribe the problem to the surge in unemployment at the end of the 1970s. 'They came out of school at the wrong time,' as one older resident of Easterhouse put it, and have never in their lives held a real job. They are now in their late twenties. As economic times improve, they are competing for the same entry-level jobs as people 10 years younger, and employers prefer to hire the youngsters. But it's more complicated than that, he added. 'They've lost the picture of what they're going to be doing.' When he was growing up, he could see himself in his father's job. Not these young men.

The generation gap

This generation gap was portrayed to me as being only a few years wide. A man from Birkenhead in his early thirties who had worked steadily from the time he left school until 1979, when he lost his job as an assembly-line worker, recalled how the humiliation and desperation to work remained even as his unemployment stretched from months into years. He – and the others in their thirties and forties and fifties – were the ones showing up at six in the morning when jobs were advertised. They were the ones who sought jobs even if they paid less than the benefit rate.

'The only income I wanted was enough to be free of the bloody benefit system,' he said. 'It was like a rope around my neck.' The phrase for being on benefit that some of them used, 'on the suck', says a great deal about how little they like their situation.

This attitude is no small asset to Britain. In some inner cities of the US, the slang for robbing someone is 'getting paid'. Compare that inversion of values with the values implied by 'on the suck'. Britain in 1989 has resources that make predicting the course of the underclass on the basis of the US experience very dicey.

But the same men who talk this way often have little in common with their sons and younger brothers. Talking to the boys in their late teens and early twenties about jobs, I heard nothing about the importance of work as a source of self-respect and no talk of just wanting enough income to be free of the benefit system. To make a decent living, a youth of 21 explained to me, you need £200 a week – after taxes. He would accept less if it was all he could get. But he conveyed clearly that he would feel exploited. As for the Government's employment training scheme, YTS, that's 'slave labour'. Why, another young man asked me indignantly, should he and his friends be deprived of their right to a full unemployment benefit just because they haven't reached 18 yet? It sounded strange to my ears – a 'right' to unemployment benefit for a school-age minor who's never held a job. But there is no question in any of their minds that that's exactly what the unemployment benefit is: a right, in every sense of the word. The boys did not mention what they considered to be their part of the bargain.

'I was brought up thinking work is something you are morally obliged to do,' as one older man put it. With the younger generation, he said, 'that culture isn't going to be there at all.' And there are anecdotes to go with these observations. For example, the contractors carrying out the extensive housing refurbishment now going on at Easterhouse are obliged to hire local youths for unskilled labour as part of a work-experience scheme. Thirty Easterhouse young men applied for a recent set of openings. Thirteen were accepted. Ten actually came to work the first day. By the end of the first week, only one was still showing up.

A generation gap by class

My hypothesis – the evidence is too fragmentary to call it more than that – is that Britain is experiencing a generation gap by class. Well-educated young people from affluent homes are working in larger proportions and working longer hours than ever. The attitudes and behaviour of the middle-aged working class haven't changed much. The change in stance toward the labour force is concentrated among lower-class young men in their teens and twenties. It is not a huge change. I am not suggesting that a third or a quarter or even a fifth of lower-class young people are indifferent to work. An underclass doesn't have to be huge to become a problem.

That problem is remarkably difficult to fix. It seems simple – just make decent-paying jobs available. But it doesn't work that way. In the States, we've tried nearly everything – training programmes, guaranteed jobs, special 'socialization' programmes that taught not only job skills but also 'work-readiness skills' such as getting to work on time, 'buddy' systems whereby an experienced older man tried to ease the trainee into the world of work. The results of these strategies, carefully evaluated against control groups, have consistently showed little effect at best, no effect most commonly, and occasionally negative effects.

If this seems too pessimistic for British youth, the Government or some private foundation may easily try this experiment: go down to the Bull Ring near Waterloo Bridge where one of London's largest cardboard cities is located. Pass over the young men who are alcoholics or drug addicts or mentally disturbed, selecting only those who seem clear-headed (there are many). Then offer them jobs at a generous wage for unskilled labour and see what happens. Add in a training component if you wish. Or, if you sympathize with their lack of interest in unskilled jobs, offer them more extensive training that would qualify them for skilled jobs. Carry out your promises to them, spend as much as you wish, and measure the results after 2 years against the experience of similar youths who received no such help. I am betting that you, too, will find 'no effect'. It is an irretrievable disaster for young men to grow up without being socialized into the world of work.

Work is at the centre of life

The reason why it is a disaster is not that these young men cause upright taxpayers to spend too much money supporting them. That is a nuisance. The disaster is to the young men themselves and the communities in which they live. Looking around the inner cities of the United States, a view which has been eloquently voiced in the past by people as disparate as Thomas Carlyle and Karl Marx seems increasingly validated by events: work is at the centre of life. By remaining out of the work force during the crucial formative years, young men aren't just losing a few years of job experience. They are missing out on the time in which they need to have been acquiring the skills and the networks of friends and experiences that enable them to establish a place for themselves – not only in the workplace, but a vantage point from which they can make sense of themselves and their lives.

Furthermore, when large numbers of young men don't work, the communities around them break down, just as they break down when large numbers of young unmarried women have babies. The two phenomena are intimately related. Just as work is more important than merely making a living, getting married and raising a family are more than a way to pass the time. Supporting a family is a central means for a man to prove to himself that he is a '*mensch*'. Men who do not support families find other ways to prove that they are men, which tend to take various destructive forms. As many have commented through the centuries, young males are essentially barbarians for whom marriage – meaning not just the wedding vows, but the act of taking responsibility for a wife and children – is an indispensable civilizing force. Young men who don't work don't make good marriage material. Often they don't get married at all; when they do, they haven't the ability to fill their traditional role. In either case, too many of them remain barbarians.
[. . .]

WHAT CAN BRITAIN LEARN FROM THE AMERICAN EXPERIENCE?

Britain is not the United States, and the most certain of predictions is that the British experience will play out differently from the US experience. At the close of this brief tour of several huge topics, I will be the first to acknowledge that I have skipped over complications and nuances and certainly missed all sorts of special British conditions of which I am ignorant. Still, so much has been the same so far. In both countries, the same humane impulses and the same intellectual fashions drove the reforms in social policy. The attempts to explain away the consequences have been similar, with British intellectuals in the 1980s saying the same things that American intellectuals were saying in the 1970s about how the problems aren't really as bad as they seem.

So if the United States has had so much more experience with a growing underclass, what can Britain learn from it? The sad answer is – not much. The central truth that the politicians in the United States are unwilling to face is our powerlessness to deal with an underclass once it exists. No matter how much money we spend on our cleverest social interventions, we don't know how to turn around the lives of teenagers who have grown up in an underclass culture. Providing educational opportunities or job opportunities doesn't do it. Training programmes don't reach the people who need them most. We don't know how to make up for the lack of good parents – day-care doesn't do it, foster homes don't work very well. Most of all, we don't know how to make up for the lack of a community that rewards responsibility and stigmatizes irresponsibility.

Let me emphasize the words: *we do not know how*. It's not money we lack, but the capability to social-engineer our way out of this situation. Unfortunately, the delusions persist that our social engineering simply hasn't been clever enough, and that we must strive to become more clever.

Authentic self-government is the key

The alternative I advocate is to have the central government stop trying to be clever and instead get out of the way, giving poor communities (and affluent communities, too) a massive dose of self-government, with vastly greater responsibility for the operation of the institutions that affect their lives – including the criminal justice, educational, housing and benefit systems in their localities. My premise is that it is unnatural for a neighbourhood to tolerate high levels of crime or illegitimacy or voluntary idleness among its youth: that, given the chance, poor communities as well as rich ones will run affairs so that such things happen infrequently. And when communities with different values run their affairs differently, I want to make it as easy as possible for people who share values to live together. If people in one neighbourhood think marriage is an outmoded institution, fine; let them run their neighbourhood as they see fit. But make it easy for the couple who thinks otherwise to move into a neighbourhood where two-parent families are valued. There are many ways that current levels of expenditure for public systems could be sustained (if that is thought to be necessary) but control over them decentralized. Money isn't the key. Authentic self-government is.

But this is a radical solution, and the explanation of why it might work took me 300 pages the last time I tried. In any case, no one in either the United States or Britain is seriously contemplating such steps. That leaves both countries with similar arsenals of social programmes which don't work very well, and the prospect of an underclass in both countries that not only continues but grows.

Oddly, this does not necessarily mean that the pressure for major reforms will increase. It is fairly easy to propitiate the consciences of the well-off and pacify rebellion among the poor with a combination of benefits and social programmes that at least employ large numbers of social service professionals. Such is the strategy that the United States has willy-nilly adopted. Even if the underclass is out there and still growing, it needn't bother the rest of us too much as long as it stays in its own part of town. Everybody's happy – or at least not so unhappy that more action has to be taken.

The bleak message

So, Britain, that's the bleak message. Not only do you have an underclass, not only is it growing, but, judging from the American experience, there's not much in either the Conservative or Labour agendas that has a chance of doing anything about it. A few years ago I wrote for an American audience that the real contest about social policy is not between people who want to cut budgets and people who want to help. Watching Britain replay our history, I can do no better than repeat the same conclusion. When meaningful reforms finally do occur, they will happen not because stingy people have won, but because generous people have stopped kidding themselves.

13

Relative deprivation

John Lea and Jock Young

[. . .]

Discontent is a product of *relative*, not *absolute*, deprivation. [. . .] Sheer poverty, for example, does not necessarily lead to a subculture of discontent; it may, just as easily, lead to quiescence and fatalism. Discontent occurs when comparisons between comparable groups are made which suggest that unnecessary injustices are occurring. If the distribution of wealth is seen as natural and just – however disparate it is – it will be accepted. An objective history of exploitation, or even a history of increased exploitation, does not explain disturbances. Exploitative cultures have existed for generations without friction: it is the perception of injustice – *relative deprivation* – which counts.

[. . .]

THE CAUSES OF CRIME

For orthodox criminology crime occurs because of a lack of conditioning into values: the criminal, whether because of evil (in the conventional model) or lack of parental training (in the welfare model), lacks the virtues which keep us all honest and upright. In left idealism, crime occurs not because of lack of values but simply because of lack of material goods: economic deprivation drives people into crime. In the conventional viewpoint on crime, the criminal is flawed; he or she lacks human values and cognition. In the radical interpretation of this, the very opposite is true. The criminal, not the honest person, has the superior consciousness: he or she has seen through the foolishness of the straight world. To be well conditioned is to be well deceived. The criminal then enters into a new world of value – a subculture, relieved in part of the mystifications of the conventional world.

We reject both these positions. The radical version smacks of theories of absolute deprivation; we would rather put at the centre of our theory notions of relative deprivation. And a major source of one's making comparisons – or indeed

From *What is to be Done about Law and Order?*, pp. 81; 95–101; 218–25. (Harmondsworth: Penguin, 1984.)

the feeling that one should, in the first place, 'naturally' compete and compare oneself with others – is capitalism itself.

We are taught that life is like a racetrack: that merit will find its own reward. This is the central way our system legitimates itself and motivates people to compete. But what a strange racetrack! In reality some people seem to start half-way along the track (the rich), while others are forced to run with a millstone around their necks (for example, women with both domestic and non-domestic employment), while others are not even allowed on to the track at all (the unemployed, the members of the most deprived ethnic groups). The values of an equal or meritocratic society which capitalism inculcates into people are constantly at loggerheads with the actual material inequalities in the world. And, contrary to the conservatives, it is the well-socialized person who is the most liable to crime. Crime is endemic to capitalism because it produces both egalitarian ideals and material shortages. It provides precisely the values which engender criticism of the material shortages which the radicals pinpoint.

A high crime rate occurs in precise conditions: where a group has learnt through its past that it is being dealt with invidiously; where it is possible for it easily to pick up the contradictions just referred to and where there is no political channel for these feelings of discontent to be realized. There must be economic and political discontent and there must be an absence of economic and political opportunities.

THE NATURE OF CRIME AND CRIMINAL VALUES

For conventional criminology, [. . .] crime is simply antisocial behaviour involving people who lack values. For left idealists it is the reverse: it is proto-revolutionary activity, primitive and individualistic, perhaps, but praiseworthy all the same. It involves, if it is a theft, a redistribution of income, or if it is part of youth culture, symbolic and stylistic awareness of, say, the loss of traditional working-class community or the repressive nature of the system. In either case it involves alternative values.

We would argue that both of these interpretations of crime are superficial. It is true that crime is antisocial – indeed the majority of working-class crime, far from being a prefigurative revolt, is directed against other members of the working class. But it is not antisocial because of lack of conventional values but precisely because of them. For the values of most working-class criminals are overwhelmingly conventional. They involve individualism, competition, desire for material goods and, often, machismo. Such crime could, without exaggeration, be characterized as the behaviour of those suitably motivated people who are too poor to have access to the Stock Exchange. Crime reflects the fact that our own worlds and our own lives are materially and ideologically riddled with the capitalist order within which we live. Street crime is an activity of marginals but its image is that of those right in the centre of convention and of concern. As Jeremy Seabrook puts it:

> What we cannot bear, rich and liberals alike, is to see our own image in actions that are ugly and more stark reflections of transactions in which we are all implicated in our social and economic relationships: the universal marketing, the superstitious faith in money, the instant profit, the rip-off, the easy money, the backhander, the quick fiddle, the

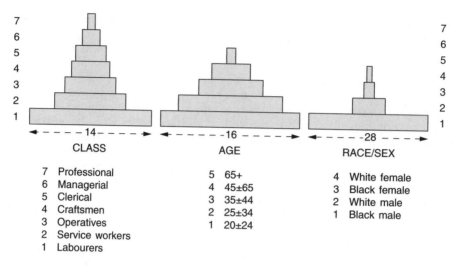

CLASS   AGE   RACE/SEX

CLASS	AGE	RACE/SEX
7 Professional	5 65+	4 White female
6 Managerial	4 45±65	3 Black female
5 Clerical	3 35±44	2 White male
4 Craftsmen	2 25±34	1 Black male
3 Operatives	1 20±24	
2 Service workers		
1 Labourers		

Figure 13.1 *Likelihood of going to prison*

comforting illusion that we can all get richer without hurting anyone, the way in which individual salvation through money has become a secularized and man-made substitute for divine grace. (1983: 64)

The radicals are correct when they see crime as a reaction to an unjust society. But they make a crucial mistake: they assume that the reaction to a just cause is necessarily a just one. On the contrary: it is often exactly the opposite. The reaction to poverty among poor whites, for example, may be to parade around waving Union Jacks: it may be the tawdry nationalism of the National Front. The reaction to relative deprivation may, as Paul Willis (1977) has so ably shown, be sexism, racism and anti-intellectualism. Crime is one form of egoistic response to deprivation. Its roots are in justice but its growth often perpetuates injustice.

THE NATURE OF THE CRIME STATISTICS

If we look at the official crime statistics in any Western capitalist country we see a remarkable similarity: the young are consistently seen to offend more than the old, the working class more than the middle class, black more than white, and men more than women. In Figure 13.1 we have constructed a series of Aztec pyramids each representing the likelihood of going to prison dependent on class, age, race and gender. We have used American statistics rather than British, as they are more complete. The British figures, particularly in terms of class and race, are kept much more closely guarded. The shape of these pyramids is, however, constant across cultures and there are close parallels; for example, one British study showed that the chances of going to prison by class were exactly the same as in America.

As can be seen, a labourer is 14 times more likely to go to prison than a professional; someone aged between 20 and 24 is 16 times more likely than a 65-

year-old; a black male is 28 times more likely than a white female. If one compounds these figures, of course, one achieves much higher ratios, the most extreme being the contrast between the chances of going to prison of an elderly, white professional woman compared to a young, black, lower-working-class man. This has some very dramatic results; for example, on an average day in the United States one in 450 Americans is in prison, but one black man in 26 between the ages of 25 and 34. Offenders, like victims, are sharply focused in terms of social category; in fact, the same social attributes which tend towards high victimization rates tend also towards high offender rates. [. . .] Serious crime, according to the official statistics, is a minority phenomenon within which certain social categories most marginal to society are vastly over-represented. The prisoner is thus on the fringe of the economy (unemployed or a casual labourer), has missed out on the educational system, and belongs to a minority group.

Now, these pyramids illustrate the major empirical problem for understanding crime. For conventional criminology it is scarcely a problem: the lower orders are much more likely to be badly socialized than the middle and upper echelons of society – hence the pyramid. For left idealists, however, this fact poses a considerable quandary. For, on the one hand, gross economic deprivation will surely lead to crime; but on the other, is it not true that the police pick on the poor, ignoring the crimes of the rich? Our response to this contradiction is simply to ask why either/or is a realistic analysis. There is no doubt that different social categories of people behave differently both in their degree of orderliness and criminality and that this relates to their position in the world; but there is also no doubt that the police react differently to different categories of people. If both these points are true, then the official statistics are a product of differences in the 'real' rates of crime between groups and differences in the police predisposition to arrest them. Thus the crime rate of old ladies is no doubt actually very low, but it probably appears *even* lower in the official statistics because of the police disinclination to suspect or arrest elderly persons. And as far as lower-working-class youths are concerned, the exact opposite is true: they commit more crimes and they are excessively harassed, the result being an augmented crime statistic. Moreover, different types of people commit different types of crimes. This point is put particularly well by Reiman. He writes:

> There is evidence suggesting that the particular pressure of poverty leads poor people to commit a higher proportion of the crimes that people fear (such as homicide, burglary, and assault) than their number in the population. There is no contradiction between this and the recognition that those who are well off commit many more crimes than is generally acknowledged both of the widely feared and of the sort not widely feared (such as 'white-collar' crimes). There is no contradiction here, because, as will be shown, the poor are arrested far more frequently than those who are well off when they have committed the same crimes – and the well-to-do are almost never arrested for white-collar crimes. Thus, if arrest records were brought in line with the real incidence of crime, it is likely that those who are well off would appear in the records far more than they do at present, even though the poor would still probably figure disproportionately in arrests for the crimes people fear. In addition to this . . . those who are well off commit acts that are not defined as crimes and yet that are as harmful or more so than the crimes people fear. Thus, if we had an accurate picture of who is really dangerous to society, there is reason to believe that those who are well off would receive still greater representation. (1979: 7–8)

In other words, (a) the pyramids we have constructed with regards to class and crime (and the same is true of race, gender and age) are quantitatively too dramatic: if middle-class people were equally subject to arrest and conviction the contrasts between each level could not be as steep. (b) Qualitatively, given the above provision, they are reasonably correct if one does *not* include white-collar crime and focuses, as Reiman outlines, on the 'normal' crimes which people fear. If people were arrested and imprisoned for white-collar crimes, then the pyramid would remain in shape but its gradient would be lessened even more. (c) To admit to a pyramid of crime by class is not, of course, to believe in a pyramid of impact. That is, the fact that lower-working-class males commit more crime than their upper-class counterparts does not mean that the overall impact of such crimes is necessarily greater. [. . .] it is probably less, although none of this suggests that we should concentrate on either one or the other, as criminologists, both radical and conventional, have done in the past. Both types of crime create considerable problems for the population.
[. . .]

Relative deprivation

Relative deprivation is the excess of expectations over opportunities. The importance of this concept is that it gets away from simplistic notions that try [to] relate discontent and collective violence to levels of absolute deprivation. The link between relative deprivation and political marginality is crucial for understanding riots and collective violence. Political marginality is unlikely to result in riot unless there is the added sense of frustration stemming from relative deprivation. A social group may be economically and politically marginalized, yet if it has no desire to participate in the structure of opportunities and social rights from which it is excluded, frustration need not occur. For the rioters of the eighteenth century the problem was not the failure to be included in a structure of opportunities stemming from industrial society, so much as the fact that an existing way of life was in the process of being destroyed by industrialization and its opportunity structure. In contemporary industrial societies social groups that have a high degree of economic and political marginality but a low sense of relative deprivation tend to be either deviant subcultures, particularly religious groups oriented to 'other-worldly pursuits', or first-generation immigrant communities. The latter, forced to take the worst jobs and the worst housing that industrial societies have to offer, may still, in the short term, be sheltered from a sense of relative deprivation by virtue of the fact that their standard of comparison is not so much the opportunity structure of the wider society from which they are excluded by racial discrimination or legal barriers, as the societies from which they recently emigrated by comparison with which living standards are higher.

Conversely, of course, a sense of relative deprivation can co-exist with the absence of economic or political marginality. This is the situation with regard to the majority of the organized working class in industrial societies faced with a marked inequality in the distribution of wealth and opportunities. Relative deprivation becomes the driving force of militant trade union and political struggles to increase living standards through the process of political negotiation and compromise. This distinction between relative deprivation combined with political integration and relative deprivation combined with political marginality enables us to understand some of the differences between the 1930s, with their relative absence of riots despite high levels of unemployment, and the present period. During the 1930s the experience of unemployment was not linked as closely as it is today with political marginality. Unemployment was concentrated in the older working-class communities centred in the basic industries of the north, iron and steel, shipbuilding, coal mining, etc. The experience of unemployment was often the collective experience of a whole community related to the slump of the industry around which the community lived and worked. This meant that the institutions of class politics – the trades councils, Labour Party and union branches – appeared to the unemployed as the natural weapons of struggle. The attempt to transfer these traditional methods of struggle *at* work into the arena of the struggle *for* work, such as in the construction of the National Unemployed Workers Movement, was an obvious course of action for the unemployed, most of whom had spent a period of their lives at work. Even the younger unemployed could be drawn into this through the general status and influence of labour-movement institutions in the cohesive working-class community.

The present period presents two contrasts to this. First, the working-class community, particularly in the inner-city areas throughout the country – not just in the older industrial areas – is far less cohesive. The fragmentation of employment between older, industrial employment in decline, newer state employment in the public services, and new small firms relying on cheap labour, combined with a greater cultural and ethnic diversity as older sections of the working class have moved out of the area or just ceased to exist and new immigrant communities have been established, has produced a much greater diversity of levels and types of labour-movement organization. It is not that organization has not emerged in the inner cities, but it no longer constitutes the cohesive and unifying force in the working-class community that it once did. Added to this is the massive growth in the number of young people who have never worked and therefore are not familiar with the organization and attitude of working-class politics. The isolation of youth from work and from class political organizations combines with the reduced hegemony of working-class institutions in the community, by comparison with the 1930s, to produce an acuteness of political marginality probably never previously experienced by any section of British society since industrialization.

But the burden of our argument here is that this acute political marginality is, for the young unemployed, combined with a greater sense of relative deprivation than in the 1930s. It is this volatile combination that underlies the rising street crime and collective violence that we see returning to our cities. This sharp growth of relative deprivation follows from quite fundamental changes, again by contrast with the 1930s, and even more with the nineteenth century, in the mechanisms determining the relationship between expectations and the opportunities for achieving them.

If we define relative deprivation as the excess of expectations over opportunities for fulfilling them, then it is easy to see a situation in which relative deprivation might be kept in check – one which undoubtedly corresponds to the vision of a stable society held by many belonging to what has come to be called the 'new right' in the Conservative Party, in which expectations and opportunities are generally determined by the same mechanism: the free competitive market. Where the competitive market exists not only as a mechanism for the allocation of society's resources but also as a 'moral force' in society, then expectations and opportunities will be brought into some sort of balance. People will not expect a higher income or standard of living than the sale of their particular skill or labour in the market brings, if it is generally considered that the standard of rewards obtaining from the competitive selling of labour or goods in the market is just. Also, in such a competitive society, if an individual does not achieve the same rewards as others from the sale of similar labour or goods, then that individual is likely to blame himself or herself on the grounds that this must be due to offering an inferior product for sale on the market.

Some politicians and academics would like to see this idealized world of *laissez-faire* present in society, in order to solve the problem of relative deprivation, but, to the extent that it actually functioned as a social force in industrial society, it did, and does, provide such a solution only for sections of the middle class. Under nineteenth and early twentieth century capitalism, the fact that the working-class community was insulated by both distance and communication from wealthier sections of society was a far more effective check on relative deprivation, especially coupled with the fact that remnants of pre-industrial religious and customary ways of thinking about society as an inevitable and justifiable hierarchy remained in the popular culture. As the working class became organized and the strength of trade unionism developed, the aims of working-class politics centred not so much around reaching the *same* standards of living as the employers and the ruling class as around the defence of existing working-class living standards, together with modest improvements.

What is even more important about the 1930s is that, despite the depths of the recession, militant discontent was never widespread. Wal Hannington, who led the National Unemployed Workers Movement, had to concede, despite the claims he made for the influence of his organization, that 'at no time has the standing membership approached even 10 per cent of the vast masses of the unemployed'. As Runciman notes:

> The Depression imposed severe and sometimes intolerable hardship on large sections of the working class and many non-manual workers also; but it did not heighten their feelings of relative deprivation in the way that both wars did. Particularly severe wage cuts were, as one would expect, resisted, notably in the textile industry. But the disposition to grin and bear it remained much more widespread than the disposition to storm the barricades. (1966: 64)

Particularly since the last war the growth of the Welfare State has combined with the mass media and mass secondary education to produce a steady growth in relative deprivation. The mass media have disseminated a standardized image of lifestyle particularly in the areas of popular culture and recreation which, for those unemployed and surviving through the dole queue, or only able to obtain employment at very low wages, has accentuated the sense of relative deprivation. The spread of mass state secondary education has had a similar effect, not so much by standardizing expectations of career patterns, living standards, etc., as by raising the minimum expectation. During the period of exceptional economic expansion of the 1950s and 1960s this posed no problems. But now the phenomenon of 'over-education' is beginning to appear. As Cloward and Ohlin (1960: 118–20) have pointed out, the excess of aspirations and opportunities can paradoxically lay the basis for social, racial and other forms of discrimination:

The democratic ideology of Equality of Opportunity creates constant pressure for formal criteria of evaluation that are universalistic rather than particularistic, achieved rather than ascribed – that is, for a structure of opportunities that are available to all on an open and competitive basis . . . However, the democratic society, like other types of society, is characterized by a limited supply of rewards and opportunities. Although many are eligible for success on the basis of formal criteria, relatively few can succeed, even in a rapidly expanding economy. It is therefore necessary to make choices on some basis or other among candidates who are equally eligible on formal grounds . . . In this situation, criteria based on race, religion, or class, that have been publicly repudiated in favour of achievement standards, are informally invoked to eliminate the surplus candidates. Thus the democratization of standards of evaluation tends to increase the competition for rewards and opportunities and hence the discrepancy between the formal and the actual criteria of selection for lower-class youngsters.

Finally, the Welfare State has had the same result. New concepts of need and minimum standards of living, coupled with a focus on the poorest sections of society have had the effect of raising the minimum expectation. The *Sunday Telegraph*, comparing the slump of the 1930s with that of today, grasped this well:

Though unemployment is similar in scale, social security benefits today are not far short of average living standards then. Today's problem, though, is just as acute since expectations, fostered by television and advertising, are high and the frustrations generated by our own slump are vast and dangerous. (*Sunday Telegraph*, 21 February 1982)

The consequence is that expectations have become governed by a set of mechanisms much more loosely, if at all, related to opportunities. The latter are still to a large extent determined by the market mechanism coupled, of course, with the massive growth of state intervention and investment, which itself has had an effect on relative deprivation. As it has become perceived that the state has taken responsibility for major components of the opportunity structure through careers and employment in state services, as well as the general responsibility undertaken by post-war governments, until recently, for maintaining the level of employment, so the discrepancy between expectations and opportunities, now growing as a result of economic recession and cutbacks in state spending, becomes blamed on the 'system' rather than on the individual.

Meanwhile, another quite important change was taking place, the consequences of which are now much clearer. While the tendency, as far as expectations were concerned, was for greater standardization and raising the minimum, the nature of post-war economic expansion was to create a working-class opportunity structure which was increasingly differentiated in terms of wage levels and working conditions. The decline of manufacturing employment in general and the rise of new highly paid white-collar and technical occupations, combined with new sectors of low pay in services (often combining low pay and unsocial hours) and small firms, has produced a more diverse set of opportunities at the same time as expectations have been becoming more standardized. In the short run the solution to this problem in most Western industrial societies was immigrant labour. [. . .] The passivity of the early, post-war, immigrant communities was based on a combination of a cultural orientation towards the homeland and an expected short stay in Britain. This meant that immigrant workers were prepared to accept working conditions which would not be accepted by native workers, such as low pay and flexible shift systems involving long periods of night work. In addition, the legal barriers of alien status and racial prejudice of the native British population generally excluded immigrants from better paid forms of employment.

This situation has been brought to a conclusion during the 1970s by the growth of a second generation of Britons of immigrant parentage. Going through the same education system (despite various forms of discrimination operating there), the children of immigrant families have grown up with the same spectrum of aspirations and expectations derived from the mass media and the education system as young people in general. Expectations and opportunities, then, have been moving in opposite directions, relative deprivation has been increasing, and, as the state has increasingly been seen as the determinant of opportunities, the resentment of unfulfilled expectations increasingly takes the form of resentment against the state and its manifestations, particularly those, like the police, who are encountered on a day-to-day basis by the young unemployed.

[. . .]

REFERENCES

Cloward, R. and Ohlin, L. (1960) *Delinquency and Opportunity*. New York: The Free Press.

Reiman, J. (1979) *The Rich Get Richer and the Poor Get Prison*. New York: Wiley.

Runciman, W.G. (1966) *Relative Deprivation and Social Justice*. London: Routledge and Kegan Paul.

Seabrook, J. (1983) 'The crime of poverty', *New Society*, 14 (April).

Willis, P. (1977) *Learning to Labour*. London: Saxon House.

14

The generality of deviance

Travis Hirschi & Michael R. Gottfredson

[. . .]

The theory [of self control] simply stated, is this: Criminal acts are a subset of acts in which the actor ignores the long-term negative consequences that flow from the act itself (e.g., the health consequences of drug use), from the social or familial environment (e.g., a spouse's reaction to infidelity), or from the state (e.g., the criminal justice response to robbery). All acts that share this feature, including criminal acts, are therefore likely to be engaged in by individuals unusually sensitive to immediate pleasure and insensitive to long-term consequences. The immediacy of the benefits of crime implies that they are obvious to the actor, that no special skill or learning is required. The property of individuals that explains variation in the likelihood of engaging in such acts we call 'self-control.' The evidence suggests to us that variation in self-control is established early in life, and that differences between individuals remain reasonably constant over the life course. It also suggests, consistent with the idea of self-control, that individuals will tend to engage in (or avoid) a wide variety of criminal and analogous behaviors—that they will not specialize in some to the exclusion of others, nor will they 'escalate' into more serious or skillful criminal behavior over time.

Both the stability of differences between individuals and the versatility of offenders can be derived from the fact that all such acts follow a predictable path over the life course, peaking in the middle to late teens, and then declining steadily throughout life. If children who offend by whining and pushing and shoving are the adults who offend by robbing and raping, it must be that whining and pushing and shoving are the theoretical equivalents of robbery and rape. If robbery and rape are theoretical equivalents, they should be engaged in by the same people. They *are* engaged in by the same people (putting the lie to the idea that each of them is peculiarly motivated). If deviant acts at different phases of the life course are engaged in differentially by the same individuals, the underlying trait must be extremely stable over time. If the same individuals tend to engage in serious and trivial acts, these acts must satisfy equivalent desires of the actor.

From *The Generality of Deviance*, pp. 1–23. (New Brunswick: Transaction Publishers, 1994.)

Evidence for a 'latent trait' that somehow causes deviant behavior thus comes from two primary sources. The first is the statistical association among diverse criminal, deviant, or reckless acts. Because these acts are behaviorally heterogeneous, because they occur in a variety of situations, and because they entail different sets of necessary conditions, it seems reasonable to suppose that what they have in common somehow resides in the person committing them. The second is the stability of differences between individuals over time. Because individuals relatively likely to commit criminal, deviant, or reckless acts at one point in time are also relatively likely to commit such acts at later points in time, it seems reasonable to ascribe these differences to a persistent underlying trait possessed in different degrees by those whose behavior is being compared.

The standards described are well-known as tests of internal consistency and test-retest reliability (or stability). When applied to measures of crime, they offer compelling evidence that a stable trait of personality underlies much criminal, deviant, and reckless behavior (Greenberg 1991; Rowe, Osgood, and Nicewander 1990; Osgood 1990; Osgood et al. 1988; Olweus 1979; Nagin and Farrington 1992).

If the evidence requires that we grant the existence of reliable differences among individuals in the tendency to commit deviant acts, the evidence it seems to us also requires that we conceptualize this 'latent trait' in particular ways. For example, we cannot make it conducive to specialization in some deviant acts rather than others, because that would be contrary to its generality (we cannot easily conceptualize it as 'internalization of norms,' because that would suggest the possibility of internalizing some norms and not others, an idea also contrary to the finding of generality); we cannot make it akin to aggressiveness, because that would be contrary to its often passive, furtive, or retreatist consequences; we cannot make it a positive force requiring for its satisfaction the commission of clearly criminal acts, because it is not conducive to persistence in a course of action but is instead conducive to momentary satisfaction of transient desires. Reasoning in this way, and from examination of the diverse acts produced by or consistent with this 'latent trait,' we concluded that it was best seen as *self-control*, the tendency to avoid acts whose long-term costs exceed their momentary advantages.

NATURAL SANCTIONS

This conception of the trait underlying criminal, deviant, and reckless behavior solves several problems. A persistent problem in this area is extinction, the tendency of responses created and maintained by sanctions to evaporate in the absence of continued reinforcement. How is self-control maintained when there are no obvious social or legal supports for it? It is not hard to find examples of people who continue to 'conform' during very long periods in which their behavior is not observed by other people or subject to the sanctions of the criminal law. In our view, self control is resistent to extinction because its ultimate sources are natural sanctions that by definition do not require continued input from others. Socialization, in this sense, may be seen as a process of educating individuals about the consequences of their behavior. Once they have such knowledge and the habit of acting on it, no further reinforcement is required. In fact in most areas natural sanctions so exceed in strength social or legal sanctions that the latter are not really necessary to explain the conformity of most people. The mystery is, rather, how some people can ignore or misapprehend the automatic consequences of their behavior, both positive and negative, and thus continue to act as though these consequences did not exist.

For example, opportunities to drink are virtually unlimited for all members of the population. Alcohol in one form or another is relatively cheap and is widely available. For many people, normative control is for all intents and purposes absent. They lead essentially private lives, or those around them do not really care about their consumption. The pleasures of alcohol are known and acknowledged by a large majority of the population. Yet self control predicts consumption of alcohol in both public and private settings over the life course. It must be that self-control is maintained by the natural consequences of behavior including but by no means limited to the reactions of others. Consistent with this argument, alcohol consumption also declines with age, suggesting that consumption is governed more by its physiological than by its social consequences.

Self control is highly efficient precisely because it is effective in a variety of settings, many of which lack social or legal surveillance, but few of which lack natural sanctions. People with self control do not risk accidents on lonely mountain roads even though no one is there to see them exceed the speed limit. They do not steal goods belonging to others despite countless opportunities to do so because such actions are inconsistent with prospects for success (prospects that do not allow a record of criminal behavior, but are otherwise independent of social or legal sanctions).

The idea of self control suggests that the origin of all sanctions or norms is to be found in natural sanctions, the rewards and punishments that follow automatically from particular acts or lines of behavior. Many natural sanctions are of course physical or physiological, affecting the health or well-being of the body – producing injury, disease, deterioration, or even death. Excessive use of drugs, interpersonal violence, promiscuous sexual behavior, and theft of all sorts can yield such consequences. As a result, normative and legal systems evolve to draw attention to these consequences (the difficulty we have in saying precisely what these systems are up to suggests that they have many sources and functions). The relation between natural and normative sanctions helps account for the universality of norms governing those behaviors with the most serious consequences, such as interpersonal violence and theft. At the same time, it helps explain society's ambiguous stance toward some norms and their enforcement, such as drug use and sexual promiscuity.

IMPLICATIONS OF SELF-CONTROL

Our conception of the trait underlying criminal, deviant, and reckless behavior is, we believe, consistent with

- research showing the importance of the family in delinquency causation (Glueck and Glueck 1950; Hirschi 1969; Loeber and Stouthamer-Loeber 1986);
- research showing the importance of opportunities to commit criminal acts (Cohen and Felson 1979);
- research showing a sharp decline in all kinds of criminal, deviant, and reckless behavior with age (Hirschi and Gottfredson 1983).

At the same time, this conceptualization of the trait underlying criminal, deviant, and reckless behavior is *in*consistent with

- the idea of a career criminal, an individual who makes a living from well-planned and executed crimes over an extended period of time, or who at least persists in a definite line of criminal activity;
- the idea of organized crime, or organized delinquent gangs engaged in long-term and highly profitable illegal activities, such as gambling, prostitution, and drug trafficking;
- the idea that the causes of 'adolescent delinquency' are different from the causes of 'adult crime' (see Trasler 1991:440);
- the idea that the causes of 'white-collar' crime are different from the causes of 'ordinary' crime;
- the idea that crime is learned, that it must be acquired from other people.

As might be expected from all this, the idea that low self-control underlies the bulk of criminal and deviant acts has not been greeted with enthusiasm by all segments of the criminological community. On the contrary, the theory has attracted a variety of criticisms. According to the critics, the theory

- is too general. It attempts to encompass too broad a range of deviant behavior. Instrumental and expressive crimes have different causes, as do white-collar and street crimes. Purposive criminal acts have little in common with accidents, bad habits, mental illnesses, or school truancy.
- is tautological. If criminal acts are defined as acts in which the long-term negative consequences for the actor outweigh the short-term gains, it is a matter of definition that those committing such acts tend to ignore or discount long-term consequences.
- is based on an erroneous conception of the relation between age and the various behaviors it attempts to explain, and ignores evidence that the causes of the onset of crime differ from the causes of persistence in and desistence from crime.
- ignores important distinctions between the incidence and prevalence of criminal or deviant behavior.
- fails to distinguish among classes of offenders who differ markedly in the level and variety of their deviant behavior.
- suggests erroneously that the penalties of the criminal justice system are ineffective in crime control. The theory also fails to anticipate important differences among offenders in their sensitivity to institutional experiences or sanctions.
- overstates the importance of self-control, regarding it as the sole cause of crime.
- ignores the fact that self-control is not the stable, general trait the theory claims it to be.

It is not a straightforward matter to respond to critiques of a theory. Such critiques have diverse origins. One ostensibly valid source of criticism is the research literature. But published research may be based on samples or data or interpretations of the theory that are inadequate or inappropriate, and response to research-based criticism therefore requires case-by-case examination of specific studies. Another presumably valid source of criticism is the compatibility between the theory and the rules described by experts in theory construction. But there is in fact considerable disagreement about the logical standards that one can legitimately employ in assessing the adequacy of a theory. Presumably, each theory has its own logic and its own basic assumptions. Adequate response to logic-based criticism would therefore require articulation of the philosophy of science underlying the theory and its competitors, a task that should not be undertaken lightly. Finally, there are the textbooks in a field. These books often provide extensive lists of criticisms of particular theories gathered from a variety of sources. But it is entirely possible that such generic lists of criticisms do more harm than good, suggesting as they do that everything is equally open to doubt, that all research and theory in the field is problematic, that the student is therefore free to believe anything he or she wishes to believe without fear of contradiction.

This is not to say, of course, that theories should be immune from criticism. In fact, in our view, the field suffers from lack of rigorous and persistent criticism of its theories, methods, and assumptions, and too readily accepts the view that all theories contain a grain of truth. (For a recent, excellent review of the field from a critical perspective, see Roshier 1989.) In our view, the primary test of a theory is its ability to organize the data in an area relative to the ability of alternative theories to organize the same data. We recognize that many scholars (e.g., Tittle 1991; Akers 1991) prefer to avoid drawing sharp distinctions between theories, or to presenting them in an oppositional mode. But in our view good criticism *must be comparative*, asking how one theory fares relative to its competitors. Our perspective places little value on lists of strengths and weaknesses of theories, and sees little benefit in uncritical 'integrations' of competing theories. It requires merely a willingness to abide by the dictates of logic and the results of competent research.

One problem with 'criticisms' of theories is that, absent a context of competing theories, they are hard to evaluate. Take the most damning criticism one can allege against a theory (after internal inconsistency): that it is false. The record is reasonably clear that even this criticism will have little impact on the viability of a theory in the absence of a competing theory that claims the same territory.

By the same token, the charge that a theory is 'too general' is hard to evaluate absent a context of competing theory. When specified in the statement 'robbery is not murder' (or, more telling, in the statement 'accidents are not crimes!') this criticism implies that these are such different events that they must have different explanations. But this is tantamount to a critique of the germ theory of disease that asserts that diphtheria is not whooping cough. The theory that diseases are caused by infectious agents is even more general than the germ theory. Is it 'too general' because it includes viruses as well as bacteria? Obviously, a general theory is not damaged by the charge of excess generality.

General theories do not assert that the concrete events or states they explain are identical. They assert only that they have something in common. They assert that robbery and murder have something in common that explains the fact that both are likely to be committed by the same people. It would be a legitimate criticism of such theory if the critic were able to show that people who commit robbery are not more likely than nonrobbers to commit murder, but that would only imply that the theory is wrong, not that it is 'too general.'

Even more curious is the charge that our theory is tautological (Akers 1991). In our view, the charge of tautology is in fact a compliment, an assertion that we followed the path of logic in producing an internally consistent result. Indeed, this is what we set out to do. We started with a conception of crime, and from it attempted to *derive* a conception of the offender. As a result, there should be strict definitional consistency between our image of the actor and our image of the act. What distinguishes our theory from many criminological theories is that we begin with the act, whereas they normally begin with the actor. Theories that start from the causes of crime—for example, economic deprivation—eventually define crime as a response to the causes they invoke. Thus, a theory that sees economic deprivation as the cause of crime will by definition see crime as an attempt to remedy economic deprivation, making the connection between cause and effect tautological.

What makes our theory *peculiarly* vulnerable to complaints about tautology is that we explicitly show the logical connections between our conception of the actor and the act, whereas many theorists leave this task to those interpreting or testing their theory, but again we are not impressed that we are unusual in this regard. One more example: Sutherland's theory of differential association says that offenders have peculiar skills and attitudes toward crime learned from their subcultures. Crime is thus a reflection of those skills and attitudes. In this theory too the connection between the image of the offender and the image of crime (both require particular skills and attitudes) is tautological.

In a comparative framework, the charge of tautology suggests that a theory that is nontautological would be preferable. But what would such a theory look like? It would advance definitions of crime and of criminals that are independent of one another (e.g., crime is a violation of the law; the criminal is a person denied access to legitimate opportunity). Several historically important theories cannot show an empirical connection between their definition of crime and their image of the offender, and must therefore be said to be false [. . .].

Those charging us with tautology do not see the issue in this light. Thus Akers says,

> it would appear to be tautological to explain the propensity to commit crime by low self-control. They are one and the same, and such assertions about them are true by definition. The assertion means that low self-control causes low self-control. Similarly, since no operational definition of self-control is given, we cannot know that a person has low self-control (stable propensity to commit crime) unless he or she commits crimes or analogous behavior. The statement that low self-control is a cause of crime, then, is also tautological. (1991:204)

It seems to us that here (and elsewhere) Akers's concept of self-control differs fundamentally from our own. We do not see self-control as the propensity to commit crime, or as the motivating force underlying criminal acts. Rather, we see self-control as the barrier than stands between the actor and the obvious momentary benefits crime provides. We explicitly propose that the link between self-control and crime is *not* deterministic, but probabilistic, affected by opportunities and other constraints. If so, the problem with our conception is more likely to be that it is nonfalsifiable than that it merely definitional.

Fortunately for the theory, Akers himself proposes that the problems he identifies can be resolved by operationalizing the concept of self-control. Thus, following the discussion above, he writes: 'To avoid the tautology problem, independent indicators of self-control are needed' (1991:204). The question then becomes, can independent indicators of self-control be identified. With respect to crime, we would propose such items as whining, pushing, and shoving (as a child); smoking and drinking and excessive television watching and accident frequency (as a teenager); difficulties in interpersonal relations, employment instability, automobile accidents, drinking, and smoking (as an adult). None of these acts or behaviors is a crime. They are logically independent of crime. Therefore the relation between them and crime is not a matter of definition, and the theory survives the charge that it is mere tautology and that it is nonfalsifiable.

Clearly, our theory cannot be at once nonfalsifiable, true by definition, and false. We know that many readers find that our description of crime rings true, that it corresponds on the whole to what they have seen and heard. Such readers will not understand that our conception is really radically different from the conceptions implicit in the theories that have dominated the field for many years. If they accuse us of being trite or true by definition, we cannot blame them—but we accept their inevitable conclusion that competing theories must be false.

The attractiveness of a theory that identifies commonalities among apparently disparate events is often counterbalanced by the feeling that too much has been sacrificed on the alter of generality. For theorists the problem is made worse by the modern tendency to divide the world into ever more narrow research problems ('homicide among the elderly female population'), each with its own cadre of experts, with the consequence that application of a general theory will be opposed by specialists in each subarea it was intended to subsume [. . .].

As stated, the theory applies to acts that provide immediate benefit at the risk of long-term cost to actors who find opportunities for such acts appealing. Because such acts are injurious to long-term individual and collective interests, they are universally resisted, at least at some level. Confusion arises from the obvious fact that groups vary in their reaction to such events, sometimes dealing with them harshly and formally in the criminal law, sometimes dealing with them as medical problems, sometimes as welfare problems, and sometimes appearing to ignore them altogether. From the point of view of the theory, such reactions are aspects of the long-term costs of the behavior, serving to reduce or intensify them, but never eliminating them altogether. To the extent that alterations in social costs affect the development of self control, they can be important in causing variation in the behaviors in question. Thus, for example, tobacco and alcohol use have natural consequences that to some degree limit their use, but variation in alcohol and tobacco use may also be traced to restrictions on availability and to differences in social and legal sanctions from one group to another. These differences do not negate the conclusion that tobacco and alcohol use fall within the purview of the theory; indeed they show that tobacco and alcohol are in the same class as such currently illegal substances an marijuana and cocaine.

A related source of confusion is the idea that some acts encompassed by the theory have not always been socially condemned, or may not be so condemned in the future. Thus, it is said, cigarette smoking was once actually fashionable, and it is possible to imagine a time when the use of marijuana will be promoted as socially and legally accepted behavior. Does the theory apply equally to both substances when they are legal and illegal? Indeed it does. The only requirement of the theory is that at all times those low in self-control are more likely to engage in the behavior than those high in self control. In fact, even when smoking was fashionable in the United States delinquents were much more likely than nondelinquents to smoke (Schoff 1915; Glueck and Glueck 1950; Hirschi 1969). We can therefore assume that when or if marijuana is legalized, the correlation between marijuana use and deviant behavior will remain at current levels.

These facts may suggest that self-control inhibits pursuit of immediate pleasure, whatever its long-term consequences—that is, the high self-control people have no fun even when it is free. We think this interpretation is probably incorrect. Knowledge that smoking has long-term harmful effects did not come into the world with the surgeon general's report in 1964. On the contrary, cigarettes were known as 'coffin nails' before the turn of the century. Similarly, it would be unlikely that the deleterious consequences of repeated marijuana use would escape the notice of those concerned with the long term.

The theory thus produces clear expectations about the generality of deviance and the versatility of offenders. [. . .]

REFERENCES

Akers, Ronald L. 1991. 'Self-Control as a General Theory of Crime.' *Journal of Quantitative Criminology* 7:201–11.

Cohen, Lawrence, and Marcus Felson. 1979. 'Social Change and Crime Rate Trends: A Routine Activity Approach.' *American Sociological Review* 44:588–608.

Glueck, Sheldon, and Eleanor Glueck. 1950. *Unraveling Juvenile Delinquency.* Cambridge, MA: Harvard University Press.

Greenberg, David. 1991. 'Modeling Criminal Careers.' *Criminology* 25:17–46.

Hirschi, Travis. 1969. *Causes of Delinquency.* Berkeley: University of California Press.

Hirschi, Travis, and Michael R. Gottfredson. 1983. 'Age and the Explanation of Crime.' *American Journal of Sociology* 89:552–84.

Loeber, Rolf, and Magda Stouthamer-Loeber. 1986. 'Family Factors as Correlates and Predictors of Juvenile Conduct Problems and Delinquency.' In *Crime and Justice: An Annual Review of Research*, vol. 7, ed. M. Tonry and N. Morris, 29–149. Chicago: University of Chicago Press.

Nagin, Daniel, and David Farrington. 1992. 'The Stability of Criminal Potential from Childhood to Adulthood.' *Criminology* 30:235–60.

Olweus, Dan. 1979. 'Stability of Aggressive Reaction Patterns in Males: A Review.' *Psychological Bulletin* 86:852–75.

Osgood, D. Wayne. 1990. 'Covariation and Adolescent Problem Behaviors.' Paper presented at the meetings of the American Society of Criminology, Baltimore, MD.

Osgood, D. Wayne, Lloyd Johnston, Patrick O'Malley, and Jerald Bachman. 1988. 'The Generality of Deviance in Late Adolescence and Early Adulthood.' *American Sociological Review* 53:81–93.

Roshier, Bob. 1989. *Controlling Crime: The Classical Perspective in Criminology.* Chicago: Lyceum Books.

Rowe, David, D. Wayne Osgood, and W. Alan Nicewander. 1990. 'A Latent Trait Approach to Unifying Criminal Careers.' *Criminology* 28:237–70.

Schoff, Hannah Kent. 1915. *The Wayward Child.* Indianapolis: Bobbs-Merrill.

Tittle, Charles R. 1991. Review of *A General Theory of Crime*, by Michael Gottfredson and Travis Hirschi. *American Journal of Sociology* 96:1609–1.

Trasler, Gordon. 1991. Review of *Explaining Criminal Behaviour: Interdisciplinary Approaches*, by Wouter Buikhuisen and Sarnoff A. Mednick. *Contemporary Psychology* 36:440–41.

15

The routine activity approach as a general crime theory

Marcus Felson

A *paradigm* is a fancy word for a general theory or framework that organizes a field of study (Kuhn 1962). Every science needs one to keep from going to pieces. Criminology lacks one. For example, a recent survey of criminologists found that no more than 17 percent agreed with any one general theory of crime (Ellis 1999). Indeed, criminologists dispersed their votes among 22 general theories. They did not even apply the same theories to serious and persistent offending that they applied to delinquency and minor offending. Some people will insist that criminology is a 'multiple-paradigm' field, but that violates the very idea of a paradigm as a single road map for scientific exploration.[1]

That does not mean that everyone in a discipline needs to agree on every matter, but nearly everyone must agree about the basic concepts and ideas organizing their field of study. Interestingly, criminologists do agree substantially about four basic crime correlations:

1. Family life discourages crime participation.
2. Males commit more crimes than do females.
3. Persons ages 12 to 25 years are disproportionate offenders.
4. As socioeconomic status rises, crime participation declines.

Criminologists disagree about which of these correlations to emphasize and how to put them together into a general theory. Adherents to each theory criticize the competition for neglecting one of the four correlations. A major problem faced by traditional crime theories is that all four of these correlations are overstated. Males commit relatively more crimes, but females are all too active in crime. Youths have no crime monopoly, and those who are older have extra employee theft opportunities. Crime occurs within families, and good parents can have bad kids. The income-crime correlation is not that strong. One never should hitch a paradigm to

From *Of Crime and Criminality* (ed. S.S. Simpson), pp. 205–216. (Thousand Oaks, Cal: Pine Forge Press, 2000.)

correlations as weak as these. This is why criminologists need a new general theory. What criteria should we use to develop it?

MAKING CRIME EXPLANATION COHERENT

Criminology already has plenty of facts and ideas. Our problem is to figure out which of these facts and ideas are central and which are peripheral. For example, it is tempting to exaggerate race differences in offending and to forget that nations lacking racial differences still have crime. The race issue, although very important for the operations of the criminal justice system, can become a distraction for studying the origins of crime itself.

Which facts and ideas should we use to forge a general science of crime? To make these difficult decisions, I suggest that we adopt from more successful sciences the following five standards of scientific coherence.

The 'touch-it' standard. Find highly tangible explanations at the outset. Take advantage of the physical world and our five senses to state the first principles in very down-to-earth terms. For example, Harvey figured out the human circulatory system by considering flows of blood among specific organs in a definite order, and Galileo dropped objects from the Tower of Pisa and watched when they hit the ground.

The 'near-and-far' standard. Find explanations that work as well at micro and macro levels, in different settings and eras, internationally, and for all types of crime (Brantingham and Brantingham 1984). A good explanation should help us to understand crime for the individual, neighborhood, town, city, metropolis, and nation as well as for the hour, day, week, month, year, decade, millennium, and epoch. For example, a physiologist can study submicroscopic and microscopic flows of blood as well as those visible with the naked eye. He or she can link capillaries to small blood vessels, to large vessels, to the largest vessel, the aorta. Labs can study blood flows by the second, minute, or hour. Good science is universal for all nations and ethnic groups. This point inspired Gottfredson and Hirschi (1990) to state their 'general theory of crime.' A general theory does not neglect variations among individual cases or localities; it merely puts these variations into a common framework.

The 'few-to-many' standard. Find a few scientific rules with many ramifications. If one's list of first principles gets too long or complex, then he or she is going to get lost. This is why Newton stated only three laws of thermodynamics. Darwin boiled about 1,000 pages of observations down to a single principle of natural selection. Scientists call this process 'Occam's razor,' cutting away at confusion and getting to the point on principles while elaborating on facts and derivations.

The 'exactly how' standard. Find clear *mechanisms*, that is, exactly *how* something leads to more or less crime (Pawson and Tilley 1997). Scientists want to know the direction in which blood flows, exactly what animals eat, how chlorophyll works, and how organisms live and die. Criminologists must find out exactly what burglars look for and how they break in. Even one's armchair speculations should say exactly how he or she *thinks* something happens. I would rather be precisely wrong than vaguely right.

The 'fit-the-facts' standard. Learn everything possible about specific crimes, their settings, their modus operandi, and how they are prevented. Make sure that the explanations are consistent with these facts (see, e.g., Clarke 1997). Modify the explanations as more facts come in. If explanations need to be contorted to fit the facts, then it is time for a new paradigm.

We can learn from the more successful sciences how to formulate a general theory for criminology. Fortunately, these five standards for coherent crime explanation apply to one extant general theory of crime: the routine activity approach to crime analysis.

THE ORIGINAL FORMULATION OF THE ROUTINE ACTIVITY APPROACH

The routine activity approach began by describing how a direct contact predatory offense occurred (Cohen and Felson 1979). Such an offense was predatory because it had, at a minimum, one offender and one target of crime. Direct physical contact between the offender and target also was required. The original formulation excluded threats from a distance, suicide, drug sales, and fights in which both participants were offenders. A direct contact predatory offense in the original formulation had three minimal elements:

- a likely offender;
- a suitable target; and
- the absence of a capable guardian against the offense.

During the era of its formulation, the routine activity approach differed greatly from other crime theories because it treated the offender as relatively less significant. The routine activity approach also defined the target of crime distinctly from the victim. The best guardian against a crime is neither a police officer nor a security guard. The best guardian is someone close such as a friend or relative. Guardianship against crime depends on someone's *absence*. Two presences (offender and target) and one absence (guardian) make the best crime setting. The convergence of these three conditions invites a criminal act to occur.

A suitable crime target might include a wallet, a purse, a car, or a human target for personal attack. A target's suitability for attack is determined by four criteria, summed up by the acronym VIVA:

- Value
- Inertia
- Visibility
- Access

The value of the target is defined from the offender's viewpoint, depending on what the offender wants. Find out what property someone might like to steal or vandalize or who an offender might prefer to attack or even kidnap. Usually, the offender would be discouraged if a target were high in inertia. For example, a heavy appliance is too difficult to carry out of a home, and a large or muscular person is difficult to outmuscle. Usually, an offender is drawn to a target more visible to him or her such as money flashed in a bar or someone who unwittingly invites an attack. The offender's access to a street or building renders its contents and people more subject to his or her illegal action.

The routine activity approach started with crime conditions right there. It considered how a criminal act occurs or fails to occur at specific times and places. Without the convergence of minimal elements for crime, a direct contact predatory criminal act would be virtually out of the question. Such immediate conditions are set in place from the routine activities of the surrounding community. The transportation system, the structure of work and household, and the technology and production of goods—in short, the everyday *macro*-level organization of the community and society—lead to *micro* convergences of conditions more or less favourable to crime.

Consider how a residential burglary occurs. A burglar tries to find a suitable household that is empty of guardians or within which the guardians are asleep or indisposed. The burglar seeks a place containing valuables easy to remove. Easy access and visibility draw the burglar further. The larger community structure offers the burglar crime opportunities by producing more lightweight but valuable goods and getting people out of their homes for work, school, or leisure. While they are out, the burglar goes in.

APPLYING THE FIVE STANDARDS OF COHERENT SCIENCE TO THE ROUTINE ACTIVITY APPROACH

The routine activities explanation for crime holds up quite well when tested against the five standards of scientific coherence. Following the *touch-it standard*, the routine activity approach is highly tangible, emphasizes the physical world, and considers physical convergences in its core requirements. Its image of the offender takes into account the offender's use of the five senses to carry out crime. Following the *near-and-far standard*, the routine activity approach works at both the micro and macro levels, in different settings and eras, internationally, and for different types of crime (Felson 2000). It shows how offenders, targets, and guardians move into and out of potential crime settings. The routine activity approach also uses a few clear and simple principles. Simplicity is not the same as simple-mindedness. Indeed, very diverse findings, difficult problems, and complex information can be absorbed within its few and simple principles. For example, the many features of home, neighborhood, and household activities could be summed up in one principle: the offender must find the target with nobody there to stop the offender from attacking it. Indeed, routine activity analysis brings forth many nuances of criminal acts, still maintaining coherence by deriving all this from a very few rules, in accordance with the *few-to-many standard*. It starts at a very simple level before it elaborates. If one gets lost, one can just go back to the few fundamentals to find his or her way once more.

The routine activity approach also seeks clear mechanisms, examining which features of daily life lead to more or less crime. Its adherence to the *exactly how standard* is well illustrated elsewhere (Felson 1998). For example, the old theories state vague and inexact hypotheses, for example, 'Social disorganization creates crime.' By contrast, the routine activity approach details mechanisms such as the following:

- Tough guys can seize local abandoned houses for their own illegal uses. For example, they can set up drug houses.
- Failed local businesses leave streets unsupervised and dangerous.

The routine activity approach also helps us to understand why some forms of 'social disorganization' do not give us more crime and might even produce less:

- Shabby paint on buildings might be ugly, but it probably does not itself contribute to more crime.
- Graffiti in subways probably does not lead to more robberies.
- Extreme deterioration of a neighborhood might cause vice crimes to decline by scaring away customers.

The *fit-the-facts standard* of scientific coherence is reflected in the growing convergence between the routine activity approach and several studies of crime specifics, settings, modus operandi, broken windows theory (Kelling and Coles 1996), and prevention. Relatively recent work is devoted to such convergences (Clarke and Felson 1993; Felson 1998; Felson and Clarke 1999).

Burglary offers us many cogent examples of how the routine activity approach follows all five standards of scientific coherence. A burglar follows the touch-it standard using his or her senses to determine crime opportunities and risks and to put criminal acts into motion. In accordance with the near-and-far standard, a burglar responds to specific and local crime opportunities while also benefiting from new transport systems that help the burglar get to additional crime settings. Specific routine factors assist the burglar (e.g., more lightweight goods, more cash in homes or businesses). The few-to-many standard also is very relevant; the burglar can consider a few aspects of his or her targets, such as VIVA (discussed earlier), to decide whether or not to break in. The burglar might seek easy access and lightweight things to carry away. These minimal elements have elaborate applications when considering what streets lead to a crime target, different types of buildings, the timing of commercial burglary versus residential burglary (weekend for the former and weekday for the latter), and variations among nations varying in how often households are left unsupervised. The exactly how standard demands that criminologists specify how the burglar gets there and chooses that building; what part of a building the burglar enters; where things are kept; lines of sight for guardians and offenders; and why the burglar overlooks other entries, buildings, or booty. For example, middle income areas with small backyards and easy sight lines tend to have low burglary rates; other middle income areas with both spouses working, high bushes, and large backyards tend to have high burglary rates. Finally, the specific settings and modus operandi of burglary and the details of its prevention become central for routine activity analysis of burglary. To study burglary in scientific terms, we have to consider who, what, where, when, and how. Because the routine activity approach does not try to divide the population into two groups—definite offenders and definite nonoffenders—this approach can more readily accommodate the details of crime research. This makes it easier to meet the fit-the-facts standard with the routine activity approach.

EXTENSIONS OF THE ROUTINE ACTIVITY APPROACH

During recent years, I have extended the routine activity approach well beyond direct contact predatory crimes (Felson 1998). Illegal drug sales depend on the physical convergences of buyers and sellers as well as the absence of those who would prevent these sales. Nonpredatory fights involve the convergence of antagonists with peacemakers absent and provokers present. Even suicides depend on absences of those who would prevent them. This approach now takes into account supervision of youths and offenders in general. The routine activity approach today goes far beyond its original statement. I always am surprised at those who describe the routine activity approach as it was 20 years ago, ignoring its life and growth. The extensions of this approach further demonstrate its adherence to the third standard of scientific coherence; it explores numerous ramifications derived from basic principles. [. . .]

CONCLUSION

Crime is complex, and criminology is difficult. Most theories have not been able to find their way through all this complexity or to find the elusive secret of individual disposition to commit crime. These theories failed because they tried to predict the unpredictable—what each individual is going to do next. It is much more promising to work with tangible processes and incidents. Five standards of scientific coherence provide us with the tools for progress. The routine activity approach uses these tools well and places the crime incident at the center of inquiry. Crime is a physical act, and we must not forget it.

NOTE

1 During a scientific revolution, two paradigms do battle for a brief period until the new one wins. Criminology today lives in a 'pre-paradigm state,' that is, theoretical chaos. Although many paradigms might exist over the total history of a science, they cannot live together simultaneously. Moreover, an old paradigm might have made good sense in its day given what was then known. But as new information comes along, so does a new and better paradigm. There is no turning back. For example, today's astronomers could not return to Ptolemy's image of the universe even if they wanted to. It just would not work.

REFERENCES

Brantingham, P.J. and P.L. Brantingham. 1984. *Patterns in Crime*. New York: Macmillan.
Clarke, R.V., ed. 1997. *Situational Crime Prevention: Successful Case Studies*. 2nd ed.
    New York: Harrow & Heston.

Clarke, R.V. and M. Felson. 1993. 'Introduction: Criminology, Routine Activity, and Rational Choice.' In *Routine Activity and Rational Choice: Advances in Criminological Theory*, vol. 5, edited by R.V. Clarke and M. Felson. New Brunswick, NJ: Transaction Books.

Cohen, L.E. and M. Felson. 1979. 'Social Change and Crime Rate Trends: A Routine Activity Approach.' *American Sociological Review* 4:588–608.

Ellis, Lee. 1999. 'Criminologists' Opinions About Causes and Theories of Crime and Delinquency.' *The Criminologist*, July/August, 1, 5.

Felson, M. 1998. *Crime and Everyday Life*. 2nd ed. Thousand Oaks, CA: Pine Forge.

Felson, M. 2000. 'The Routine Activity Approach: A Very Versatile Theory of Crime.' In *Explaining Crime and Criminals*, edited by R. Paternoster. Los Angeles: Roxbury.

Felson, M. and R.V. Clarke, 1999. *Opportunity Makes the Thief: Practical Theory for Crime Prevention*. Police Research Series, No. 98. London: Home Office, Policing and Reducing Crime Unit.

Gottfredson, M. and T. Hirschi. 1990. *A General Theory of Crime*. Stanford, CA: Stanford University Press.

Kelling, G.L. and C. Coles. 1996. *Fixing Broken Windows: Restoring Order and Reducing Crime in Our Communities*. New York: Free Press.

Kuhn, T.S. 1962. *The Structure of Scientific Revolutions*. Chicago: University of Chicago Press.

Pawson, R. and N. Tilley. 1997. *Realistic Evaluation*. Thousand Oaks, CA: Sage.

16

Seductions and repulsions of crime

Jack Katz

In 1835, in a small French village, Pierre Rivière killed half his family: his mother, a sister, and a brother. After his arrest, he wrote a lengthy explanation to the effect that he had killed his mother to protect his father from her ceaseless cruelties, which had frequently become public humiliations, and he had killed two siblings who were living with her because they had sided with her in the family quarrels, either actively or simply through sustained love. In addition, Rivière explained that by killing his young brother, whom he knew his father to love, he would turn his father against him, thus making less burdensome to his father Rivière's legally mandated death, which he expected would result from his crimes.[1] A team of scholars, led by Michel Foucault, traced the ensuing conflicts among the various 'discourses' engaged in by Rivière, the lawyers, doctors, the mayor, the priest, and the villagers, and they added their own.

Rivière wrote a carefully composed, emotionally compelling account of the background to his crime, recounting, as if reconstructing a contemporaneous journal, a long series of deceits and monetary exploitations by his mother against his father. But, although he entitled his account 'Particulars and Explanation of the Occurrence', in the sixty-seven pages his 'memoir' covers (in this translated reproduction), less than a sentence describes the 'particulars of the occurrence'. Rivière gave no specific significance to the aim or the force of the blows he struck with an axlike farm implement (he destroyed the vertebrae that had connected the head of his mother from her body, and he separated brain from skull, converting bone and muscle to mush); to the multiplicity of the blows, which extended far beyond what was necessary to accomplish death; to his mother's advanced state of pregnancy; or to details of the violence suffered by his brother and sister. Instead, he focused exclusively on the background of his family biography. Although Rivière's account was elaborately inculpating in substance, in style, it bespoke a sophisticated rationality, which in many eyes was exculpating. (Some even labeled it 'beautiful'.)

As an author, Pierre Rivière was primarily concerned with the moral power that the narrative could lend to his crime. By glossing over the homicidal event itself, he

From *Seductions of Crime: Moral and Sensual Attractions in Doing Evil*, pp. 310–24. (New York: Basic Books, 1988.)

continued the attack on his mother before a new, larger audience. The state and lay professional interpreters of his crime followed his lead, relying largely on facts he had acknowledged and discounting the situational details in favor of biographical, historical, and social ecological factors. As Foucault suggested, the very barbarity of the attack made it an act of resistance against the forms of civility. But after the fact, Rivière and many powerful groups in his society literally rationalized the event, locating it as the logical outcome of an ongoing family injustice, a form of madness or mental illness, or (in the comments offered later in the book by some of Foucault's colleagues) of the historical and class position of French peasants.[2]

In short, many of the interpreters sought to exploit too much from the murder to dwell on its gruesome lived reality. Rivière was motivated to construct an account that would make his viciously cruel, extremely messy act neatly reappear as a self-sacrificial, efficient blow for justice. The other commentators had general theoretical perspectives at stake: medical-psychological ideology, institutions of religious understanding, and politically significant interpretations (including the emergence of a school of thought around Foucault himself). On all sides, modern forms of civility would govern the posthumous experience of the crime.

Today, the contemporary incarnations of professional, legal-scientific, and civil interpretive spirits are both stronger and more petty than they were 150 years ago. The effective political spectrum for debate still features a Right and a Left, but most of the intellectual action is within a small and relatively tame segment on the left side of the scale. The length of the scale is much narrower than when the Church and tradition, and occasionally even anarchist voices, were powerful in the debate. Now various disciplines in the social sciences have a go at it, but they go at each other more than at 'lay' opinion, and what is at stake is less clearly the institutionalization of a field than the relative popularity of fads in research methodology.

[. . .] [T]he readily available, detailed meaning of common criminality has been systematically ruled out as ineligible for serious discussion in the conventions of modern sociological and political thought. Something important happened when it became obscenely sensational or damnably insensitive to track the lived experience of criminality in favor of imputing factors to the background of crime that are invisible in its situational manifestation. Somehow in the psychological and sociological disciplines, the lived mysticism and magic in the foreground of criminal experience became unseeable, while the abstractions hypothesized by 'empirical theory' as the determining background causes, especially those conveniently quantified by state agencies, became the stuff of 'scientific' thought and 'rigorous' method.

Whatever the historical causes for treating background factors as the theoretical core for the empirical study of crime, [. . .] it is not necessary to constitute the field back to front. We may begin with the foreground, attempting to discover common or homogeneous criminal projects and to test explanations of the necessary and sufficient steps through which people construct given forms of crime. If we take as our primary research commitment an exploration of the distinctive phenomena of crime, we may produce not just ad hoc bits of description or a collection of provocative anecdotes but a systematic empirical theory of crime – one that explains at the individual level the causal process of committing a crime and that accounts at the aggregate level for recurrently documented correlations with biographical and ecological background factors.

MORAL EMOTIONS AND CRIME

The closer one looks at crime, at least at the varieties examined here, the more vividly relevant become the moral emotions. Follow vandals and amateur shoplifters as they duck into alleys and dressing rooms and you will be moved by their delight in deviance; observe them under arrest and you may be stunned by their shame. Watch their strutting street display and you will be struck by the awesome fascination that symbols of evil hold for the young men who are linked in the groups we often call gangs. If we specify the opening moves in muggings and stickups, we describe an array of 'games' or tricks that turn victims into fools before their pockets are turned out. The careers of persistent robbers show us, not the increasingly precise calculations and hedged risks of 'professionals', but men for whom gambling and other vices are a way of life, who are 'wise' in the cynical sense of the term, and who take pride in a defiant reputation as 'bad'. And if we examine the lived sensuality behind events of cold-blooded 'senseless' murder, we are compelled to acknowledge the power that may still be created in the modern world through the sensualities of defilement, spiritual chaos, and the apprehension of vengeance.

Running across these experiences of criminality is a process juxtaposed in one manner or another against humiliation. In committing a righteous slaughter, the impassioned assailant takes humiliation and turns it into rage; through laying claim to a moral status of transcendent significance, he tries to burn humiliation up. The badass, with searing purposiveness, tries to scare humiliation off; as one ex-punk explained to me, after years of adolescent anxiety about the ugliness of his complexion and the stupidity of his every word, he found a wonderful calm in making 'them' anxious about *his* perceptions and understandings. Young vandals and shoplifters innovate games with the risks of humiliation, running along the edge of shame for its exciting reverberations. Fashioned as street elites, young men square off against the increasingly humiliating social restrictions of childhood by mythologizing differences with other groups of young men who might be their mirror image. Against the historical background of a collective insistence on the moral non-existence of their people, 'bad niggers' exploit ethnically unique possibilities for celebrating assertive conduct as 'bad'.

What does the moral fascination in the foreground of criminal experience imply for background factors, particularly poverty and social class? Is crime only the most visible peak of a mountain of shame suffered at the bottom of the social order? Is the vulnerability to humiliation skewed in its distribution through the social structure? To address these questions, we should examine the incidence and motivational qualities of what is usually called 'white-collar' crime. Perhaps we would find a greater level of involvement in criminality, even more closely linked to shameful motivations. But the study of white-collar crime has been largely a muckraking operation from the outside; despite isolated exceptions, we have no general empirical understanding of the incidence or internal feel of white-collar crime. This absence of data makes all the more remarkable the influence, within both academic and lay political thought on crime, of the assumption of materialist causation.

SENTIMENTAL MATERIALISM

But whatever the differential rates of deviant behavior in the several social strata, and we know from many sources that the official crime statistics uniformly showing higher rates

> in the lower strata are far from complete or reliable, it appears from our analysis that the greatest pressures toward deviation are exerted upon the lower strata.[3]

Just fifty years ago, Robert K. Merton published his 'Social Structure and Anomie', an article once counted as the single most frequently cited and reprinted paper in the history of American sociology.[4] Arguing against Freud and psychological analysis in general, Merton attributed deviance to a contradiction in the structure of modern society: 'Americans are bombarded on all sides' by the goal of monetary success, but the means or opportunities for achieving it are not as uniformly distributed. A generation later, Richard Cloward and Lloyd Ohlin, with a revised version of 'opportunity' theory, hit perhaps the pinnacle of academic and political success in the history of criminology, winning professional awards and finding their work adopted by the Kennedy administration as part of the intellectual foundations of what later became the War on Poverty.[5] After a hiatus during much of the Republican 1970s and 1980s, materialist theory – the Mertonian ideas now bolstered by rational-economic models of social action that had become academically attractive in the interim – is again promoting the lack of opportunity (unemployment, underemployment, and low 'opportunity cost') to explain crime.[6]

That this materialist perspective is twentieth century sentimentality about crime is indicated by its overwhelming inadequacy for grasping the experiential facts of crime. The 'model' or 'theory' is so persuasive that the observable facts really do not matter, as Merton put it: 'whatever the differential rates of deviant behavior in the several social strata . . . it appears from our analysis that the greatest pressures toward deviation are exerted upon the lower strata'.[7] Indeed, the Mertonian framework as originally presented, as elaborated in the 1960s, and as recently paralleled by the economist's perspective, should now be recognized as an institutionalized academic-political sensibility for systematically making literally unthinkable the contemporary horrors of deviance and for sustaining a quietist criminology.

Consider the many sensually explosive, diabolically creative, realities of crime that the materialist sentiment cannot appreciate. Where is the materialism in the experience of the *barrio* 'homeboy', the night before the first day of high school?

> Although I was not going to be alone, I still felt insecure . . . my mother, with an accentuated voice, ordered me to go to sleep. Nevertheless, my anxiety did not let my consciousness rest; instead, what I did was look in the mirror, and began practicing the traditional steps that would show my machismo. . . . Furthermore, I was nervously thinking about taking a weapon to the school grounds just to show Vatos from other barrios the answer of my holy clique. All kinds of evil thoughts were stirring in me.[8]

The problem for Merton and materialist theory is not simply with some youthful 'gang' activity. There is now strong evidence that a high proportion of those who go on to especially 'serious', 'heavy', 'career' involvements in criminality start in early adolescence, long before job opportunities could or, in a free social order, should become meaningful considerations.[9] Actually, when Albert Cohen pointed out, long ago, the '"versatility" and the "zest" with which some boys are observed to pursue their group-supported deviations', Merton was willing to concede that much of youth crime was beyond his theory of deviance.[10] It was enough if, as Cohen had offered in a conciliatory gesture, Merton's materialism applied to 'professional' or serious adult property criminals.

But if we look at persistent criminals, we see a life of action in which materialism is by no means the god. Instead, material goods are treated more like offerings to be burnt, quickly, lest retention become sacrilege. As suggested by 'dead presidents', a black street term for US cash, there is an aggressive attack on materialism as a potentially misleading, false deity. Robby Wideman seemed to have Merton in mind when he told his brother:

> Straight people don't understand. I mean, they think dudes is after the things straight people got. It ain't that at all. People in the life ain't looking for no home and grass in the yard and shit like that. We the show people. The glamour people. Come on the set with the finest car, the finest woman, the finest vines. Hear people talking about you. Hear the bar get quiet when you walk in the door. Throw down a yard and tell everybody drink up. . . . You make something out of nothing.[11]

The aspiration is not to what is advertised on television. Robby Wideman was not incapable of identifying what drove him; it was to be a star – something literally, distinctively transcendent. Street people are not inarticulate when they say that 'the endgame is to *get over*, to *get across*, to *make it*, to *step fast*'.[12] This language is only a 'poetic' indirect reference to aspirations for material status if we refuse to recognize that it directly captures the objective of transcendence.[13]

So, a lot of juvenile forms of violent crime and an important segment of serious adult crime do not fit the sentimentality of materialism. Neither does the central thrust that guides men and women to righteous slaughters, nor the project of primordial evil that makes 'senseless killings' compellingly sensible to their killers, nor the tactics and reverberations of sneaky thrills. None of these fits, in the Mertonian scheme, the actions of 'innovators' who accept the conventional aims but use deviant means. The aims are specifically unconventional: to go beyond the established moral definitions of the situation as it visibly obtains here and now. Nor can we categorize these deviants as 'retreatists' who reject conventional means and ends. For Merton, retreatists were a spiritually dead, socially isolated, lot of psychotics, drunkards, and vagrants; today's 'bag ladies' would fit that category. And, surely, these deviants are not 'rebels' with revolutionary ideas to implement new goals and means.

None of this argument denies the validity of the recurrent correlations between low socioeconomic status or relative lack of economic opportunity, on the one hand, and violent and personal property crime on the other. The issue is the causal significance of this background for deviance. A person's material background will not determine his intent to commit acquisitive crime, but a person, whether or not he is intent on acquisitive crime, is not likely to be unaware of his circumstances.

Instead of reading into ghetto poverty an unusually strong motivation to become deviant, we may understand the concentration of robbery among ghetto residents as being due to the fact that for people in economically more promising circumstances, it would literally make no sense – it would virtually be crazy – to commit robbery. Merton had no basis but the sentiments stirred by his theory to assume that crime, even materially acquisitive crime, was more common in the 'lower strata'. In part, the appeal of his theory was promoted by the obvious significance of material circumstance in the shaping of crime. We need fear only a few exceptions if we claim that lawyers will not stick up banks, 'frequent-flyer' executives will not kill their spouses in passionate rages, and physicians will not punch out their colleagues or that the unemployed will not embezzle, the indigent will not fix prices, and the politically powerless will not commit perjury in congressional testimony. But this is a different matter from claiming that crime or deviance is distributed in the social structure according to the relative lack of opportunity for material gain.

It is not inconsequential that major forms of contemporary criminality cannot simply be fit within the dominant sentimentality for understanding deviance. If it were recognized that changes in material circumstance affect the form more than the drive toward deviance, it would be more difficult to promote publicly financed programs to increase benefits or opportunities where they are most lacking. A revision of the theory of materialism that would limit it to the explanation of the quality, rather than the quantity, of deviance, would be much less palatable across the political spectrum. Such an analytic framework would not serve those on the Right who point to the social distribution of common crime, along with other pathologies, to discount the moral claims of lower-class minorities for governmental outlays. But neither would a comparative theory of the qualities of crime serve well the social-class sympathies that have often been promoted by the study of white-collar crime. For muckrakers, it has been important to depict the prevalence of elite deviance to weaken the moral basis of corporate political power; often they have argued that white-collar crime is every bit as 'real' and destructive a form of deviance as is street crime. But unless one agrees to reduce nonviolent crimes of deception to a less heinous status than violent personal crime, the comparative perspective will undercut traditional policies of social reform to aid the underprivileged. One has to promise more than a trade-off between street crime and administrative fraud to work up moral enthusiasm for job training programs.

More generally, from Marx through Durkheim and Freud to the contemporary sociological materialists, the hallmark of rhetorically successful theory has been its specification of the source of social evil.[14] Without the claim that background conditions breed the motivation to deviance, criminological theory would not serve the high priestly function of transforming diffuse anxiety about chaos into discrete problems that are confined to marginal segments of social life. Indeed, the research agenda implied by a theory that relates material conditions to the form or quality of deviance but not to its incidence or prevalence is profoundly disquieting.

REPULSIONS OF DEVIANCE

Whether their policy implications point toward increasing penalties to decrease crime or toward increasing legitimate opportunities or 'opportunity costs' to decrease crime, modern causal theories have obliterated a natural fascination to follow in detail the lived contours of crime. Perhaps the indecisive battle among competing determinist theories of crime is itself an important aspect of their persistent popularity, inside academia, in columnists' opinions, and in political speech. Methodological innovations, policy experiments, and the latest wave of governmental statistics continually stimulate the ongoing dialogue, with no side ever gaining a decisive advantage but all sharing in an ideological structure that blocks unsettling encounters with the human experience of crime.

What would follow if we stuck with the research tactic of defining the form of deviance to be explained from the inside and searching for explanations by examining how people construct the experience at issue and then, only as a secondary matter, turned to trace connections from the phenomenal foreground to the generational and social ecological background? We would have to acknowledge that just because blacks have been denied fair opportunity for so long, and so often,[15] the criminality of ghetto blacks can no longer be explained by a lack of opportunity. Just because the critique of American racial injustice has been right for so long, as criminological explanation it now is wrong. Even accepting the Mertonian analysis as initially valid, for how many generations can a community maintain a moral independence of means and ends, innovating deviance only to reach conventional goals? How does a people restrict its economic participation only to the stunted spiritual engagement permitted over centuries of racism? By what anthropological theory can one hold his real self somehow outside the cynical hustles he devises day by day, his soul, untouched by a constant pursuit of illicit action, waiting with confident innocence in some purgatory to emerge when a fair opportunity materializes? The realities of ghetto crime are literally too 'bad' to be confined to the role of 'innovative means' for conventional ends. This is not to deny that the history of racial injustice makes a morally convincing case for increasing opportunities for the ghetto poor. It is to say that materialist theories refuse to confront the spiritual challenge represented by contemporary crime.

The profundity of the embrace of deviance in the black ghetto and the tensions that will emerge among us if we discuss the lived details of these phenomena form one set of the contemporary horrors our positivist theories help us avoid facing. Another blindness they sustain is to the lack of any intellectual or political leadership to confront the massive bloodletting of mate against mate and brother against brother that continues to be a daily reality in the inner city. Each time the sentimentality of materialism is trotted out to cover the void of empirically grounded ideas, it seems more transparent and less inspiring; each time the exhortation to positivism carries a more desperate sentiment that it *has* to be right. And, finally, there is the incalculable chaos that would break out if the institutions of social science were to apply the methods of investigation used here to deviance all across the social order.

Theories of background causes lead naturally to a reliance on the state's definition of deviance, especially as assembled in official crime statistics, and they make case studies virtually irrelevant. But the state will never supply data describing white-collar crime that are comparable to the data describing street or common crime. Politically, morally, and logically, it can't.

The problem is due not to political bias in the narrow sense, but to the dialectical character of white-collar crime as a form of deviance that necessarily exists in a moral metaphysical suspense. To assess the incidence and consequences of common crimes like robbery, one can survey victims and count arrests in a research operation that may be conducted independently of the conviction of the offenders. But individual victims generally cannot authoritatively assert the existence of tax cheating, consumer fraud, insider trading, price fixing, and political corruption; when prosecutions of such crimes fail, not only can the defendants protest their personal innocence, but they can deny that *any* crime occurred. We are on especially shaky grounds for asserting with methodological confidence that white-collar crimes exist before the state fully certifies the allegation through a conviction.

On the one hand, then, white-collar crime can exist as a researchable social problem only if the state officially warrants the problem; on the other hand, white-collar crimes will *not* exist if the state gets too serious about them. The existence of prohibitions against white-collar crimes distinctively depends on the prohibitions not being enforced. The strength of public and political support for robbery and murder prosecutions is not weakened with increased enforcement. But if the official system for prosecuting tax cheating, pollution violations, and even immigration fraud becomes too vigorous, pressure will build to reduce the prohibitory reach of the underlying laws.[16] At the extreme, any group that becomes subject to massive state treatment as criminally deviant is either not an elite or is a class engaged in civil war.

Explanatory social research relies on the state's definition of deviance when it statistically manipulates the demographic and ecological variables quantified by the state, rather than documents in detail the experience and circumstances of the actual doings of deviance. So long as this reliance continues, we will be unable intellectually to constitute a field for the study of white-collar crime. Disparate, occasional studies of white-collar crime will continue to emerge from the margins of organization theory, from interests in equal justice that are sustained by the sociology of law, from studies of criminal justice agencies and of the professions, and from the atheoretical moral force generated by recurrent waves of scandal. But a reliance for explanation on background determinism has made twentieth century social theory fundamentally incapable of comprehending the causation of white-collar crime.

Consider how the traditional boundaries of the field of criminology would break down if we were to extend to white-collar crime the strategy taken in this work to explain common crime. [. . .] [I]n approaching criminal homicide, adolescent theft, gang delinquency and other forms of violent or personal property crime, we would begin, not with the state's official accounting of crime but by looking for lines of action, distinctive to occupants of high social position, that are homogeneously understood by the offenders themselves to enact a variety of deviance. We would quickly arrive at a broad field with vague boundaries between forms of conduct regarded by the offenders as criminal, civilly liable, professionally unethical, and publicly unseemly. Simultaneously, we would follow the logic of analytic induction and search for negative cases, which means that evidence would take the form of qualitative case studies.

Now, where would we get the data? With white-collar crime, we have a special problem in locating facts to demonstrate the lived experience of deviance. Despite their presumably superior capacity to write books and the healthy markets that await their publication efforts, we have virtually no 'how-I-did-it-and-how it-felt-doing-it' autobiographies by corrupted politicians, convicted tax frauds, and chief executive officers who have been deposed by scandals over insider trading. This absence of naturalistic, autobiographical, participant-observational data is itself an important clue to the distinctive emotional quality of white-collar crime. Stickup men, safe-crackers, fences, and drug dealers often wear the criminal label with pride, apparently relishing the opportunity to tell their criminal histories in colorful, intimate detail. But white-collar criminals, perhaps from shame or because the ties to those whom they would have to incriminate are so intimate a part of their own identities that they can *never* be broken, rarely publicly confess; when they do confess, they virtually never confess with the sustained attention to detail that characterizes, for example, almost any mugging related by an ordinary, semiliterate hustler like Henry Williamson.[17]

As a result, to obtain data, etiological theorists of white-collar crime would have to join forces with public and private investigators and with enemy constituencies of the elites under focus – hardly a promising tack for winning academic, much less governmental-institutional, support for developing a broad data base. Even more absurd is the suggestion that the researcher take up the data-generating task directly by working from readily accessible gossip and looking around one or another local corner. Depending on time and place, that might mean studying the chancellor's project to remodel his home; the law professor's marijuana smoking; the medical researcher's practice of putting his name on research papers, the data for which he has never seen; the alumni's means of supporting the football team; the professor's management of expenditures and accounting in research grants; the administrator's exploitation through real estate profiteering of inside information about the expansion of the university; the process of defaulting on student loans; and so on. By maintaining background determinism as the dominant framework for the study of crime, the social sciences leave the serious academic investigation of elite deviance to those proper intellectual folk, the ethical philosophers, who exploit qualitative case materials in the innocuous forms of delightful illustrations from literature, lively hypotheticals, and colorful histories documented by others. All who already have them retain their jobs and their sanity.

But is it so absurd to imagine a democratic society that would treat the arrogance, the public frauds, and the self-deceptions of its elites as a field that would be amenable to theoretically guided, empirical investigation? Is it obvious that institutionally supported social research on the etiology of deviance should seek causal drives more in the shame and impotence of poverty than in the hubris of affluence and power?

And we can go one step further. The fear of chaos that blocks a truly empirical study of crime is not just a repulsion for a disquieting process of investigation. There is also a substantive chaos – a crisis of meaning in collective identity – lurking more deeply behind the dogged appeal of traditions that intimidate the contemporary intellectual confrontation with the lived experience of deviance.

If we were to develop a comparative analysis of the crimes committed by ghetto residents and by occupants of high social positions, we would surely not be examining the identical qualities of experience. Where the ghetto resident may be proud of his reputation as a 'bad nigger' at home and on the streets, the governmental leader is likely to be ashamed, at least in some family and community settings, of a breach in his pristine image. Although the stickup man focuses on the simple requirements for instantly and unambiguously conveying to victims the criminal intentions of his actions, organization men will tacitly work out a concerted ignorance that provides each with 'deniability' while they arrange the most complex frauds.[18]

But considering the third causal condition that we have been tracing in the paths toward common crime – emotional processes that seduce people to deviance – it is much less clear that the quality of the dynamic differs by social position. Putting aside differences in the practical means that social position makes available and the different degrees and forms of moral stereotype and prejudice that are attached to social position, there may be a fundamental similarity in the dynamics that people create to seduce themselves toward deviance. Although the means differ, white middle-class youths may as self-destructively pursue spatial mobility, through reckless driving, as do ghetto youths in gang wars. The attractions of sneaky thrills may not disappear with age, but instead may migrate from shoplifting to adultery and embezzlement. And even the bump that the egocentric badass, strutting arrogantly outside his own neighborhood, arranges as an 'accident' compelling him to battle, is not without its analogies to the incidents that have been arranged by ethnocentric nations, provocatively sailing in foreign waters, to escalate wars.[19]

It would appear that, with respect to the moral-emotional dynamics of deviance, we have grounds to pursue a parallel across the social hierarchy. Consider two strong candidates for the status of most awful street and white-collar crimes: the killing of defenseless victims to sustain a career of robberies and the deception of democratic publics to support government-sponsored killings of defenseless foreigners. In both the street and the high-government cases, both the Left and the Right have their favored materialist-background explanations and accusations: poverty and lack of economic opportunity versus a liberal judiciary, 'handcuffed' police, and inadequate deterrents; the value to capitalists of maintaining power in foreign economic spheres versus the need to use military force against non-Russians to maintain a deterrent strength *vis-à-vis* the ever-menacing Soviet Union. For the most part, public discussion of both these lowly and exalted social problems proceeds as a ritualized exchange between two politically opposed materialist interpretations.

But in both forms of deviance the actors are engaged in a transcendent project to exploit the ultimate symbolic value of force to show that one 'means it'. Those who persist in stickups use violence when it is not justified on cost-benefit grounds because *not* to use violence would be to raise chaotic questions about their purpose in life. They understand that to limit their violence by materialist concerns would weaken them in conflicts with other hardmen and would raise a series of questions about their commitment to their careers that is more intimidating than is the prospect of prison. Just because materialist motivations do not control the drive toward doing stickups, the events are rife with foolish risks and fatal bungles.

It is a fair question whether the foreign exercises of Western governments in legally undeclared, surreptitiously instigated, and secretly aided military conflicts less often bungle into pathetic results – the shooting of innocent fishermen, the kidnapping of CIA chiefs, the mechanical surprises from helicopters and explosive devices, the failures to make 'operational' defenses against sea mines and air attacks, the lapses in security that allow massive military casualties from terrorist tactics, and the like. What is more remarkable still, is that utilitarian evaluations of success and failure do not dominate the public discussions of such interventions, any more than they dominate the career considerations of persistent robbers. In public debates, symbolic displays of national will, like the cultural style of the hardman, give cost-benefit analysis a cowardly overtone.

This is not to suggest that some collective machismo is behind the conspiratorial deceptions of domestic publics undertaken to support state killings of foreigners. (At the time of writing, the fresh examples are 'Contragate', the secret, illegal American government program for generating lies to promote the killing of Nicaraguans, and the French government's deceit over homicidal attacks on environmental activists.)[20] Postulated as a determining background factor, personality traits are no more convincing on the state level than on the individual street level. But in both arenas, the use of violence beyond its clear materialist justification is a powerful strategy for *constructing* purposiveness.

The case of Bernhard ('Bernie') Goetz provides us with a bridge between the street experience of the bad nigger and the collective moral perspective that state leaders may rely on in arranging their homicidal deceits. In 1984, Goetz, a white electrical engineer, shot four young 'bad' blacks in a New York City subway train. Acquitted (of all but the weapons charges) in 1987, Goetz became a hero for large segments of the public,[21] essentially because he manipulated to his advantage a detailed understanding of the doings of stickups.

First, Goetz identified a typical opening strategem in street robberies – the use of civility to move into a position of moral dominance. One of his victims approached him and said,

> 'How are you?' just, you know, 'How are you?' . . . that's a meaningless thing, but in certain circumstances that can be, that can be a real threat. You see, there's an implication there. . . .[22]

Next followed a 'request' for money, which Goetz (and one of the victims) recalled as, 'Give me five dollars', Goetz recalled:

> I looked at his eyes and I looked at his face . . . his eyes were shiny. He was enjoying himself . . . had this big smile on his face. You know at that point, you're in a bad situation. . . . I know in my mind they wanted to play with me . . . like a cat plays with a mouse. . . . I know my situation. I knew my situation.[23]

Next Goetz seized on this opening ambiguity, which he understood the blacks had created not simply to further their robbery or assault but to ridicule him, as a pause in which he could draw out his gun unopposed.[24] Goetz likewise turned the tightly enclosed space of the subway car to his advantage; now the impossibility of escape was a problem for them, not for him. Goetz was aware of the fantastic moral reversal he had effected: 'It was so crazy . . . because they had set a trap for me and only they were trapped. . . . I know this is disgusting to say – but it was so easy. I can't believe it'.

As in many stickups, Goetz's violence was, to a significant degree if not completely, gratuitous within the situational context of his shooting. Since his victims did not have guns, just showing his gun probably would have been enough. Instead, his five shots continued after the end of any personal threat that may have been present; before the last shot, which was aimed at the fourth, as yet uninjured victim, he announced, 'You seem to be all right; here's another.' After the fact, he recalled, 'My intention was to do anything I could to hurt them . . . to murder them, to hurt them, to make them suffer as much as possible.'[25]

Overall, Goetz demonstrated the rational irrationality of violence that characterizes hardened stickup men. Earlier, and independent of this scene, he had arranged to have hollowed-out ('dum-dum') bullets in his gun to enhance destructive consequence should he fire his weapon. Having been victimized in muggings twice before, he found that a readiness to instigate violence had become especially relevant to him for making sense of continuing to travel the streets and subways of New York City. Like the stickup man who routinely keeps a weapon close at hand so he might exploit a fortuitous circumstance, Goetz would not have carried a gun to the scene had he not had this larger, transsituational project.

Beyond practical danger, Goetz was intent on not suffering further humiliation – not simply the humiliations that muggers could inflict, but the humiliation of his own fear, of continuing in the world with the common, cowardly wish to believe that such things would not happen to him. A similar project guides the career of the criminal hardman, whose violence may go beyond what the resistance of a victim may require because he must not only get out of *this* situation but stay 'out there' and be ready to get into *the next*. An inquiry that is limited to the situational reasonableness of violence, which social scientists have often asked in relation to data on robberies in which the offenders harm the victims and that courts must ask of a defendant like Goetz, is, to a great degree, absurd. In both cases, the moral inquiry ignores the transcendent purpose of violent men. Put another way, whether violence was reasonably necessary to escape harm or capture in the situated interaction, the decision to *enter* the situation prepared for violence is not, in itself, a matter for reasonable calculations.

The celebrity that Goetz received was, in significant measure, a celebration by 'good people' of his transcendent meanness. This same spirit more often wreaks devastation through the instrumentality of national foreign policy. Indeed, if youth 'gangs' rely on military metaphors to organize their conflicts, the mobilization of military action in Western democracies also depends, through the chief executive's histrionics and the jingoism of the press, on fashioning international conflicts into dramaturgic lines of street-fighting tactics (showdowns and callings of bluff, ambushes and quick-draw contests, 'bumps' and the issuance of dares to cross lines that have been artificially drawn over international waters).[26] Surely, there are fundamental differences between the processes of using violence to manifest meanness on city streets and to dramatize resolute purposiveness in relations with foreign states. But we will not know just what the spiritual-emotional-moral differences are until we use a comprehensive theoretical approach to analyze and compare the varieties of criminal experience across the social order, including the uses of deceit by elites for conduct they experience as morally significant.

So it is appropriate to begin a study of the seductions of crime with cases of the use of torture by the American military to interrogate Vietnamese peasants and to close this phase of the study by suggesting that, in the late twentieth century, the great powers of the West find themselves in one dubious foreign, militarized situation after another – promoting wars they cannot win, achieving victories that bring them only the prize of emotional domestic support, and entering battles they would lose for winning – all because, at least in the immediate calculations, not to use violence would signal a loss of meaning in national history. Like the bad nigger who, refusing to be a 'chump' like others of his humbled class and ethnicity, draws innocent blood to construct a more self-respecting career that leads predictably to prison confinement, the Western democracies, still seduced by the colonial myth of omnipotence, must again and again strike down thousands so that when the inevitable retreat comes, it will lead over masses of corpses toward 'peace with honor'. Perhaps in the end, what we find so repulsive about studying the reality of crime – the reason we so insistently refuse to look closely at how street criminals destroy others and bungle their way into confinement to save their sense of purposive control over their lives – is the piercing reflection we catch when we steady our glance at those evil men.

NOTES

1 Michel Foucault (ed.), *I, Pierre Rivière, having slaughtered my mother, my sister, and my brother* . . . (New York, Pantheon Books, 1975), p. 106.

2 In the short essay he included in the volume, Foucault continued his pioneering emphasis on the unique phenomenon of power/knowledge. Some of his colleagues and students, however, were quick to impute causal force to class formations, the hypocrisies of the Enlightenment, the market economy, the contractual form, and so on. We learn of the situational facts essentially through the initial, brief reports of doctors who performed what we would today recognize as a coroner's investigation.

3 Robert K. Merton, 'Social structure and anomie', in his *Social Theory and Social Structure* (New York, Free Press, 1968), p. 198.

4 Stephen Cole, 'The growth of scientific knowledge', in Lewis A. Coser (ed.), *The Idea of Social Structure*, (New York, Harcourt Brace Jovanovich, 1975), p. 175.

5 Richard A. Cloward and Lloyd E. Ohlin, *Delinquency and Opportunity* (New York, Free Press, 1960).

6 Robert J. Sampson, 'Urban black violence: the effect of male joblessness and family disruption', *American Journal of Sociology* 93 (September, 1987) pp. 348–82; William Julius Wilson, *The Truly Disadvantaged: the Inner City, the Underclass, and Public Policy* (Chicago, University of Chicago Press, 1987); David Rauma and Richard A. Berk, 'Remuneration and recidivism: the long-term impact of unemployment compensation on ex-offenders', *Journal of Quantitative Criminology* 3 (March, 1987), pp. 3–27.

7 Merton, 'Social structure and anomie', p. 198.

8 Gus Frias, *Barrio Warriors: Homeboys of Peace* (n.p., Diaz Publications, 1982), p. 19.

9 Alfred Blumstein et al., *Criminal Careers and 'Career Criminals'* (Washington, DC, National Academy Press, 1986), 1, pp. 46–7; and Christy A. Visher, 'The Rand Inmate Survey: a reanalysis', in ibid., 2, 168. A recent theory sees adolescents as a social class defined – through legal requirements of school attendance, legal restrictions on employing youths, and laws excepting youths from minimum-wage rates – as having a common position in relation to the means of production. Attractive for their historical and theoretical color, these ideas account no more convincingly than do Merton's for vandalism, the use of dope, intergroup fighting, and the character of initial experiences in property theft as sneaky thrills. David F. Greenberg 'Delinquency and the Age Structure of Society', *Contemporary Crises*, 1 (April 1977), pp. 189–224.

10 Cohen, as quoted in Merton, 'Social structure and anomie', p. 232.

11 John Edgar Wideman, *Brothers and Keepers* (New York, Penguin Books, 1985), p. 131. Recently, the revelations of insider trading in securities markets have produced strikingly similar statements from high-level miscreants. When the take runs into millions of dollars and comes in faster than the criminals can spend it, it is difficult to explain crime with ideas of overly socialized materialistic aspirations. As the offenders themselves put it, at this level, money quickly becomes a way of keeping score.

12 Edith A. Folb, *Running Down Some Lines: the Language and Culture of Black Teenagers* (Cambridge, MA, Harvard University Press, 1980), p. 128 (emphasis in original).

13 Indeed, if we look at what is used to make materialism seductive in advertising, it is not clear that we find the American dream of shiny material success more than a version of 'street culture': soul-wrenching intonations of black music, whorish styles, fleeting images of men shooting craps in alleys and hustling in pool halls, torn shirts and motorcycles, and all the provocatively sensual evils of 'the night'. Judging from Madison Avenue, materialism may be less essential to the motivation to become deviant than an association with deviance is essential to the motivation to be acquisitive.

14 As Davis noted, 'Each classical social theorist shows how their fundamental factor

not only undermines the individual's integrity but also saps the society's vitality', See Murray Davis, '"That's Classic!" The Phenomenology and Rhetoric of Successful Social Theories', *Philosophy of Social Science* 16 (1986), p. 290.

15 And here the evidence continues to mount through increasingly sophisticated historical research that demonstrates the many episodes in which more-qualified Northern blacks were pushed aside when jobs were offered to less-qualified white immigrants. See Stanley Lieberson, *A Piece of the Pie* (Berkeley, CA, University of California Press, 1980). Roger Lane, *Roots of Violence in Black Philadelphia, 1860–1900* (Cambridge, MA, Harvard University Press, 1986), is a provocative argument that European ethnic groups who were new to the city in the nineteenth century (the Irish, then the Italians) initially had high rates of violent crime, sometimes higher than the rates for blacks, but the rates for white ethnics declined as these groups were incorporated into the industrial economy, while the rates for blacks, who were excluded from all but servile and dirty-work jobs by discriminatory preferences for less-qualified whites and by public segregation enforced by violence, continually rose.

16 Or when repeal would be too raw politically, the available alternative is to add constraints on the investigative-prosecutorial process. An obvious example from the 1980s is the move to abolish the office of special prosecutor. A less obvious example from the 1970s was built into the Tax Reform Act of 1976. For this and other examples that marked the closing of the Watergate era, see Jack Katz, 'The social movement against white-collar crime', in Egon Bittner and Sheldon Messinger (eds), *Criminology Review Yearbook* (Beverly Hills, CA, Sage, 1980), 2, pp. 161–84. An important appreciation of the distinctively negotiable character of enforcement efforts against white-collar crime in class-related partisan politics is found in Vilhelm Aubert, 'White collar crime and social structure', *American Journal of Sociology*, 58 (November, 1952), pp. 263–71.

17 See Henry Williamson, *Hustler! The Autobiography of a Thief*, ed. R. Lincoln Keiser (New York, Doubleday, 1965). In his encyclopedic study of bribery, Noonan found an admitted awareness of participating in bribery only in the diaries of Samuel Pepys. See John T. Noonan, Jr, *Bribes* (New York, Macmillan, 1984), p. xiv. In relation to differences in the quality of moral autobiographies written by authors of different social classes, we should consider the differential demands on writing talent. Much more interpersonal insight and attention to subtle interactional detail are required to trace the inside experience of white-collar crimes, given their elaborate diffusion of deceit over long careers and in complex social relations. The extraordinary biographies of Robert Moses and Lyndon Johnson by Robert Caro indicate the dimensions of the task. See Robert A. Caro, *The Power Broker: Robert Moses and the Fall of New York* (New York, Alfred A. Knopf, 1974); and *The Path to Power: the Years of Lyndon Johnson* (New York, Alfred A. Knopf, 1982). Talent aside, we should also consider that, for our deceitful elites, to bare all that was involved might entail unbearable self-disgust. It is notable that our social order is so constructed that it is virtually impossible emotionally for our elites truly to confess.

18 Jack Katz, 'Concerted ignorance: the social construction of cover-up', *Urban Life*, 8 (October, 1979), pp. 295–316; and Jack Katz, 'Cover-up and collective integrity', *Social Problems*, 25 (Fall, 1977), pp. 1–25.

19 See J.C. Goulden, *Truth Is the First Casualty: the Gulf of Tonkin Affair – Illusion and Reality* (Chicago, Rand McNally, 1969); and Anthony Austin, *The President's War* (Philadelphia, J.B. Lippincott, 1971).

20 John Dyson, *Sink the Rainbow! An Inquiry into the 'Greenpeace' Affair* (London, Gollancz, 1986); Leslie Cockburn, *Out of Control* (New York, Atlantic Monthly Press, 1987).

21 Ray Innis of the Congress on Racial Equality stated with regard to Goetz's attack, 'Some black men ought to have done it long before. . . . I wish it had been me'. And

Geoffrey Alpert, director of the University of Miami's Center for the Study of Law and Society, noted, 'It's something we'd all like to do. We'd all like to think we'd react the way he did'. And Patrick Buchanan, soon to be President Ronald Reagan's press chief, commented, 'The universal rejoicing in New York over the gunman's success is a sign of moral health'. See Lillian Rubin, *Quiet Rage: Bernie Goetz in a Time of Madness* (New York, Farrar, Straus and Giroux, 1986), pp. 10, 11, and 15, respectively.

22 Kirk Johnson, 'Goetz's account of shooting 4 men is given on tape to New York City jury', *New York Times*, April 30, 1987, p. 14, quotes a tape of Goetz's initial interview with the police.

23 Ibid.

24 There was some indecisive evidence that Goetz responded in kind, with an inverted morally aggressive, ambiguity. According to one victim, who recalled saying to Goetz, 'Mister, give me five dollars', Goetz responded with 'You all can have it'. Kirk Johnson, 'Goetz shooting victims say youths weren't threatening', *New York Times*, May 2, 1987, p. 31. Another version by the same victim, reported in Rubin, *Quiet Rage*, p. 7, had Goetz approached with, 'Hey man, you got five dollars for me and my friends to play video games?' and Goetz responding: 'Yeah, sure . . . I've got five dollars for each of you'. According to a paramedic, shortly after the shooting another victim commented that Goetz had preceded his attack with a threat: 'The guys I were with were hassling this guy for some money. He threatened us, then he shot us'. Kirk Johnson, 'A reporter's notebook', *New York Times*, June 15, 1987, p. B1.

25 Johnson, 'Goetz's account of shooting'.

26 And on blocking the public's encounter with the resulting corpses, injuries, and sorrows of relatives, even in popularly supported military conflicts. See Susan Greenberg, *Rejoice! Media Freedom and the Falklands* (London, Campaign for Press and Broadcasting Freedom, 1983), pp. 9–12; and Arthur Gavshon and Desmond Rice, *The Sinking of the Belgrano* (London, Secker and Warburg, 1984).

17

The etiology of female crime

Dorie Klein

INTRODUCTION

The criminality of women has long been a neglected subject area of criminology. Many explanations have been advanced for this, such as women's low official rate of crime and delinquency and the preponderance of male theorists in the field. Female criminality has often ended up as a footnote to works on men that purport to be works on criminality in general.

There has been, however, a small group of writings specifically concerned with women and crime. This paper will explore those works concerned with the etiology of female crime and delinquency, beginning with the turn-of-the-century writing of Lombroso and extending to the present. Writers selected to be included have been chosen either for their influence on the field, such as Lombroso, Thomas, Freud, Davis and Pollak, or because they are representative of the kinds of work being published, such as Konopka, Vedder and Somerville, and Cowie, Cowie and Slater. The emphasis is on the continuity between these works, because it is clear that, despite recognizable differences in analytical approaches and specific theories, the authors represent a tradition to a great extent. It is important to understand, therefore, the shared assumptions made by the writers that are used in laying the groundwork for their theories.

The writers see criminality as the result of *individual* characteristics that are only peripherally affected by economic, social and political forces. These characteristics are of a *physiological* or *psychological* nature and are uniformly based on implicit or explicit assumptions about the *inherent nature of women*. This nature is *universal*, rather than existing within a specific historical framework.

Since criminality is seen as an individual activity, rather than as a condition built into existing structures, the focus is on biological, psychological and social factors that would turn a woman toward criminal activity. To do this, the writers create two distinct classes of women: good women who are 'normal' non-criminals, and bad women who are criminals, thus taking a moral position that often

From *Issues in Criminology*, 1973, 8(2): 3–30.

masquerades as a scientific distinction. The writers, although they may be biological or social determinists to varying degrees, assume that individuals have *choices* between criminal and non-criminal activity. They see persons as atomistically moving about in a social and political vacuum; many writers use marketplace models for human interaction.

Although the theorists may differ on specific remedies for individual criminality, ranging from sterilization to psychoanalysis (but always stopping far short of social change), the basic thrust is toward *individual adjustment*, whether it be physical or mental, and the frequent model is rehabilitative therapy. Widespread environmental alterations are usually included as casual footnotes to specific plans for individual therapy. Most of the writers are concerned with *social harmony* and the welfare of the existing social structure rather than with the women involved or with women's position in general. None of the writers come from anything near a 'feminist' or 'radical' perspective.

In *The Female Offender*, originally published in 1903, Lombroso described female criminality as an inherent tendency produced in individuals that could be regarded as biological atavisms, similar to cranial and facial features, and one could expect a withering away of crime if the atavistic people were prohibited from breeding. At this time criminality was widely regarded as a physical ailment, like epilepsy. Today, Cowie, Cowie and Slater (1968) have identified physical traits in girls who have been classified as delinquent, and have concluded that certain traits, such as bigness, may lead to aggressiveness. This theme of physiological characteristics has been developed by a good number of writers in the last seventy years, such as the Gluecks (Glueck and Glueck, 1934). One sees at the present time a new surge of 'biological' theories of criminality; for example, a study involving 'violence-prone' women and menstrual cycles has recently been proposed at UCLA.[1]

Thomas, to a certain degree, and Freud extend the physiological explanation of criminality to propose a psychological theory. However, it is critical to understand that these psychological notions are based on assumptions of universal *physiological* traits of women, such as their reproductive instinct and passivity, that are seen as invariably producing certain psychological reactions. Women may be viewed as turning to crime as a *perversion of* or *rebellion against* their *natural feminine roles*. Whether their problems are biological, psychological or social-environmental, the point is always to return them to their roles. Thomas (1907, 1923), for example, points out that poverty might prevent a woman from marrying, whereby she would turn to prostitution as an alternative to carry on her feminine service role. In fact, Davis (1961) discusses prostitution as a parallel illegal institution to marriage. Pollak (1950) discusses how women extend their service roles into criminal activity due to inherent tendencies such as deceitfulness. Freud (1933, Jones, 1961) sees any kind of rebellion as the result of a failure to develop healthy feminine attitudes, such as narcissism, and Konopka (1966) and Vedder and Somerville (1970) apply Freudian thought to the problem of female delinquency.

The specific characteristics ascribed to women's nature and those critical to theories of female criminality are uniformly *sexual* in their nature. Sexuality is seen as the root of female behavior and the problem of crime. Women are defined as sexual beings, as sexual capital in many cases, physiologically, psychologically and socially. This definition *reflects* and *reinforces* the economic position of women as reproductive and domestic workers. It is mirrored in the laws themselves and in their enforcement, which penalize sexual deviations for women and may be more lenient with economic offenses committed by them, in contrast to the treatment given men. The theorists accept the sexual double standard inherent in the law, often noting that 'chivalry' protects women, and many of them build notions of the universality of *sex repression* into their explanations of women's position. Women are thus the sexual backbone of civilization.

In setting hegemonic standards of conduct for all women, the theorists define *femininity*, which they equate with healthy femaleness, in classist, racist and sexist terms, using their assumptions of women's nature, specifically their sexuality, to justify what is often in reality merely a defense of the existing order. Lombroso, Thomas and Freud consider the upper-class white woman to be the highest expression of femininity, although she is inferior to the upper-class white man. These standards are adopted by later writers in discussing femininity. To most theorists, women are inherently inferior to men at masculine tasks such as thought and production, and therefore it is logical that their sphere should be reproductive.

Specific characteristics are proposed to bolster this sexual ideology, expressed for example by Freud, such as passivity, emotionalism, narcissism and deceitfulness. In the discussions of criminality, certain theorists, such as Pollak, link female criminality to these traits. Others see criminality as an attempt away from femininity into masculinity, such as Lombroso, although the specifics are often confused. Contradictions can be clearly seen, which are explained by the dual nature of 'good' and 'bad' women and by the fact that this is a mythology attempting to explain real behavior. Many explanations of what are obviously economically motivated offenses, such as prostitution and shoplifting, are explained in sexual terms, such as prostitution being promiscuity, and shoplifting being 'kleptomania' caused by women's inexplicable mental cycles tied to menstruation. Different explanations have to be made for 'masculine' crimes, e.g., burglary, and for 'feminine' crimes, e.g., shoplifting. Although this distinction crops up consistently, the specifics differ wildly.

The problem is complicated by the lack of knowledge of the epidemiology of female crime, which allows such ideas as 'hidden crime', first expressed by Pollak (1950), to take root. The problem must be considered on two levels: women, having been confined to certain tasks and socialized in certain ways, are *in fact* more likely to commit crime related to their lives which are sexually oriented; yet even non-sexual offenses are *explained* in sexual terms by the theorists. The writers ignore the problems of poor and Third World women, concentrating on affluent white standards of femininity. The experiences of these overlooked women, who *in fact* constitute a good percentage of women caught up in the criminal justice system, negate the notions of sexually motivated crime. These women have real economic needs which are not being met, and in many cases engage in illegal activities as a viable economic alternative. Furthermore, chivalry has never been extended to them.

The writers largely ignore the problems of sexism, racism and class, thus their work is sexist, racist and classist in its implications. Their concern is adjustment of the woman to society, not social change. Hence, they represent a tradition in criminology and carry along a host of assumptions about women and humanity in general. It is important to explore these assumptions and traditions in depth in order to understand what kinds of myths have been propagated around women and crime. The discussions of each writer or writers will focus on these assumptions and their relevance to criminological theories. These assumptions of universal, biological/

psychological characteristics, of individual responsibility for crime, of the necessity for maintaining social harmony, and of the benevolence of the state link different theories along a continuum, transcending political labels and minor divergences. The road from Lombroso to the present is surprisingly straight.

LOMBROSO: 'THERE MUST BE SOME ANOMALY . . .'

Lombroso's work on female criminality (1920) is important to consider today despite the fact that his methodology and conclusions have long been successfully discredited. Later writings on female crime by Thomas, Davis, Pollak and others use more sophisticated methodologies and may proffer more palatable liberal theories. However, to varying degrees they rely on those sexual ideologies based on *implicit* assumptions about the physiological and psychological nature of women that are *explicit* in Lombroso's work. Reading the work helps to achieve a better understanding of what kinds of myths have been developed for women in general and for female crime and deviance in particular.

One specific notion of women offered by Lombroso is women's physiological immobility and psychological passivity, later elaborated by Thomas, Freud and other writers. Another ascribed characteristic is the Lombrosian notion of women's adaptability to surroundings and their capacity for survival as being superior to that of men. A third idea discussed by Lombroso is women's amorality: they are cold and calculating. This is developed by Thomas (1923), who describes women's manipulation of the male sex urge for ulterior purposes; by Freud (1933), who sees women as avenging their lack of penis on men; and by Pollak (1950), who depicts women as inherently deceitful.

When one looks at these specific traits, one sees contradictions. The myth of compassionate women clashes with their reputed coldness; their frailness belies their capacity to survive. One possible explanation for these contradictions is the duality of sexual ideology with regard to 'good' and 'bad' women.[2] Bad women are whores, driven by lust for money or for men, often essentially '*masculine*' in their orientation, and perhaps afflicted with a touch of penis envy. Good women are chaste, 'feminine', and usually not prone to criminal activity. But when they are, they commit crime in a most *ladylike* way such as poisoning. In more sophisticated theory, all women are seen as having a bit of both tendencies in them. Therefore, women can be compassionate *and* cold, frail *and* sturdy, pious *and* amoral, depending on which path they choose to follow. They are seen as rational (although they are irrational, too!), atomistic individuals making choices in a vacuum, prompted only by personal, physiological/psychological factors. These choices relate only to the *sexual* sphere. Women have no place in any other sphere. Men, on the other hand, are not held sexually accountable, although, as Thomas notes (1907), they are held responsible in *economic* matters. Men's sexual freedom is justified by the myth of masculine, irresistible sex urges. This myth, still worshipped today, is frequently offered as a rationalization for the existence of prostitution and the double standard. As Davis maintains, this necessitates the parallel existence of classes of 'good' and 'bad' women.

These dual moralities for the sexes are outgrowths of the economic, political and social *realities* for men and women. Women are primarily workers within the family, a critical institution of reproduction and socialization that services such basic needs as food and shelter. Laws and codes of behavior for women thus attempt to maintain the smooth functioning of women in that role, which requires that women act as a conservative force in the continuation of the nuclear family. Women's main tasks are sexual, and the law embodies sexual limitations for women, which do not exist for men, such as the prohibition of promiscuity for girls. This explains why theorists of female criminality are not only concerned with sexual violations by female offenders, but attempt to account for even *non-sexual* offenses, such as prostitution, in sexual terms, e.g., women enter prostitution for sex rather than for money. Such women are not only economic offenders but are sexual deviants, falling neatly into the category of 'bad' women.

The works of Lombroso, particularly *The Female Offender* (1920), are a foremost example of the biological explanation of crime. Lombroso deals with crime as an atavism, or survival of 'primitive' traits in individuals, particularly those of the female and non-white races. He theorizes that individuals develop differentially within sexual and racial limitations which differ hierarchically from the most highly developed, the white men, to the most primitive, the non-white women. Beginning with the assumption that criminals must be atavistic, he spends a good deal of time comparing the crania, moles, heights etc. of convicted criminals and prostitutes with those of normal women. Any trait that he finds to be more common in the 'criminal' group is pronounced an atavistic trait, such as moles, dark hair, etc., and women with a number of these telltale traits could be regarded as potentially criminal, since they are of the atavistic type. He specifically rejects the idea that some of these traits, for example obesity in prostitutes, could be the *result* of their activities rather than an indicator of their propensity to them. Many of the traits depicted as 'anomalies', such as darkness and shortness, are characteristic of certain racial groups, such as the Sicilians, who undoubtedly comprise an oppressed group within Italy and form a large part of the imprisoned population.

Lombroso traces an overall pattern of evolution in the human species that accounts for the uneven development of groups: the white and non-white races, males and females, adults and children. Women, children and non-whites share many traits in common. There are fewer variations in their mental capacities: 'even the female criminal is monotonous and uniform compared with her male companion, just as in general woman is inferior to man' (1920: 122), due to her being 'atavistically nearer to her origin than the male' (1920: 107). The notion of women's mediocrity, or limited range of mental possibilities, is a recurrent one in the writings of the twentieth century. Thomas and others note that women comprise 'fewer geniuses, fewer lunatics and fewer morons' (Thomas, 1907: 45); lacking the imagination to be at either end of the spectrum, they are conformist and dull . . . not due to social, political or economic constraints on their activities, but because of their innate physiological limitations as a sex. Lombroso attributes the lower female rate of criminality to their having fewer anomalies, which is one aspect of their closeness to the lower forms of less differentiated life.

Related characteristics of women are their passivity and conservatism. Lombroso admits that women's traditional sex roles in the family bind them to a more sedentary life. However, he insists that women's passivity can be directly traced to the 'immobility of the ovule compared with the zoosperm' (1920: 109), falling back on the sexual act in an interesting anticipation of Freud.

Women, like the lower races, have greater powers of endurance and resistance to mental and physical pain than men. Lombroso states: 'denizens of female prisons . . . have reached the age of 90, having lived within those walls since they were 29 without any grave injury to health' (1920: 125). Denying the humanity of women by denying their capability for suffering justifies exploitation of women's energies by arguing for their suitability to hardship. Lombroso remarks that 'a duchess can adapt herself to new surroundings and become a washerwoman much more easily than a man can transform himself under analogous conditions' (1920: 272). The theme of women's adaptability to physical and social surroundings, which are male initiated, male controlled, and often expressed by saying that women are actually the 'stronger' sex, is a persistent thread in writings on women.

Lombroso explains that because women are unable to feel pain, they are insensitive to the pain of others and lack moral refinement. His blunt denial of the age-old myth of women's compassion and sensitivity is modified, however, to take into account women's low crime rate:

> Women have many traits in common with children; that their moral sense is deficient; that they are revengeful, jealous . . . In ordinary cases these defects are neutralized by piety, maternity, want of passion, sexual coldness, weakness and an undeveloped intelligence. (1920: 151)

Although women lack the higher sensibilities of men, they are thus restrained from criminal activity in most cases by lack of intelligence and passion, qualities which *criminal* women possess as well as all *men*. Within this framework of biological limits of women's nature, the female offender is characterized as *masculine* whereas the normal woman is *feminine*. The anomalies of skull, physiognomy and brain capacity of female criminals, according to Lombroso, more closely approximate that of the man, normal or criminal, than they do those of the normal woman; the female offender often has a 'virile cranium' and considerable body hair. Masculinity in women is an anomaly itself, rather than a sign of development, however. A related notion is developed by Thomas, who notes that in 'civilized' nations the sexes are more physically different.

> What we look for most in the female is femininity, and when we find the opposite in her, we must conclude as a rule that there must be some anomaly . . . Virility was one of the special features of the savage woman . . . In the portraits of Red Indian and Negro beauties, whom it is difficult to recognize for women, so huge are their jaws and cheek-bones, so hard and coarse their features, and the same is often the case in their crania and brains. (1907: 112)

The more highly developed races would therefore have the most feminized women with the requisite passivity, lack of passion, etc. This is a *racist* and *classist* definition of femininity – just as are almost all theories of *femininity* and as, indeed, is the thing itself. The ideal of the lady can only exist in a society built on the exploitation of labor to maintain the woman of leisure who can *be* that ideal lady.

Finally, Lombroso notes women's lack of *property sense*, which contributes to their criminality.

In their eyes theft is . . . an audacity for which account compensation is due to the owner . . . as an individual rather than a social crime, just as it was regarded in the primitive periods of human evolution and is still regarded by many uncivilized nations. (1920: 217)

One may question this statement on several levels. Can it be assumed to have any validity at all, or is it false that women have a different sense of property than men? If it is valid to a degree, is it related to women's lack of property ownership and non-participation in the accumulation of capitalist wealth? Indeed, as Thomas (1907) points out, women are considered property themselves. At any rate, it is an interesting point in Lombroso's book that has only been touched on by later writers, and always in a manner supportive of the institution of private property.

THOMAS: 'THE STIMULATION SHE CRAVES'

The works of W.I. Thomas are critical in that they mark a transition from purely physiological explanations such as Lombroso's to more sophisticated theories that embrace physiological, psychological and social-structural factors. However, even the most sophisticated explanations of female crime rely on implicit assumptions about the *biological* nature of women. In Thomas's *Sex and Society* (1907) and *The Unadjusted Girl* (1923), there are important contradictions in the two approaches that are representative of the movements during that period between publication dates: a departure from biological Social-Darwinian theories to complex analyses of the interaction between society and the individual, i.e., societal repression and manipulation of the 'natural' wishes of persons.

In *Sex and Society* (1907), Thomas poses basic biological differences between the sexes as his starting point. Maleness is 'katabolic', the animal force which is destructive of energy and allows men the possibility of creative work through this outward flow. Femaleness is 'anabolic', analogous to a plant which stores energy, and is motionless and conservative. Here Thomas is offering his own version of the age-old male/female dichotomy expressed by Lombroso and elaborated on in Freud's paradigm, in the structural-functionalist 'instrumental-expressive' duality, and in other analyses of the status quo. According to Thomas, the dichotomy is most highly developed in the more civilized races, due to the greater differentiation of sex roles. This statement ignores the hard physical work done by poor *white* women at home and in the factories and offices in 'civilized' countries, and accepts a *ruling-class* definition of femininity.

The cause of women's relative decline in stature in more 'civilized' countries is a subject on which Thomas is ambivalent. At one point he attributes it to the lack of 'a superior fitness on the motor side' in women (1907: 94); at another point, he regards her loss of *sexual freedom* as critical, with the coming of monogamy and her confinement to sexual tasks such as wifehood and motherhood. He perceptively notes:

Women were still further degraded by the development of property and its control by man, together with the habit of treating her as a piece of property, whose value was enhanced if its purity was assured. (1907: 297)

However, Thomas's underlying assumptions in his explanations of the inferior status of women are *physiological* ones. He attributes to men high amounts of sexual energy, which lead them to pursue women for their sex, and he attributes to women maternal feelings devoid of sexuality, which lead *them* to exchange sex for domesticity. Thus monogamy, with chastity for women, is the *accommodation* of these basic urges, and women are domesticated while men assume leadership, in a true market exchange.

Why, then, does Thomas see problems in the position of women? It is because modern women are plagued by 'irregularity, pettiness, ill health and inserviceableness' (1907: 245). Change is required to maintain *social harmony*, apart from considerations of women's needs, and women must be educated to make them better wives, a theme reiterated throughout this century by 'liberals' on the subject. Correctly anticipating a threat, Thomas urges that change be made to stabilize the family, and warns that 'no civilization can remain the highest if another civilization adds to the intelligence of its men the intelligence of its women' (1907: 314). Thomas is motivated by considerations of social integration. Of course, one might question how women are to be able to contribute much if they are indeed anabolic. However, due to the transitional nature of Thomas's work, there are immense contradictions in his writing.

Many of Thomas's specific assertions about the nature of women are indistinguishable from Lombroso's; they both delineate a biological hierarchy along race and sex lines.

> Man has, in short, become more somatically specialized an animal than woman, and feels more keenly any disturbance of normal conditions with which he has not the same physiological surplus as woman with which to meet the disturbance . . . It is a logical fact, however, that the lower human races, the lower classes of society, women and children show something of the same quality in their superior tolerance of surgical disease. (1907: 36)

Like Lombroso, Thomas is crediting women with superior capabilities of survival because they are further down the scale in terms of evolution. It is significant that Thomas includes the lower classes in his observation; is he implying that the lower classes are in their position *because* of their natural unfitness, or perhaps that their *situation* renders them less sensitive to pain? At different times, Thomas implies both. Furthermore, he agrees with Lombroso that women are more nearly uniform than men, and says that they have a smaller percentage of 'genius, insanity and idiocy' (1907: 45) than men, as well as fewer creative outbursts of energy.

Dealing with female criminality in *Sex and Society* (1907), Thomas begins to address the issue of morality, which he closely links to legality from a standpoint of maintaining social order. He discriminates between male and female morality:

> Morality as applied to men has a larger element of the contractual, representing the adjustment of his activities to those of society at large, or more particularly to the activities of the male members of society; while the morality which we think of in connection with women shows less of the contractual and more of the personal, representing her adjustment to men, more particularly the adjustment of her person to men. (1907: 172)

Whereas Lombroso barely observes women's lack of participation in the institution of private property, Thomas's perception is more profound. He points out that women *are* property of men and that their conduct is subject to different codes.

> Morality, in the most general sense, represents the code under which activities are best carried on and is worked out in the school of experience. It is preeminently an adult and male system, and men are intelligent enough to realize that neither women nor children have passed through this school. It is on this account that man is merciless to woman from the standpoint of personal behavior, yet he exempts her from anything in the way of contractual morality, or views her defections in this regard with allowance and even with amusement. (1907: 234)

Disregarding his remarks about intelligence, one confronts the critical point about women with respect to the law: because they occupy a *marginal* position in the productive sphere of exchange commodities outside the home, they in turn occupy a marginal position in regard to 'contractual' law which regulates relations of property and production. The argument of differential treatment of men and women by the law is developed in later works by Pollak and others, who attribute it to the 'chivalry' of the system which is lenient to women committing offenses. As Thomas notes, however, women are simply not a serious *threat* to property, and are treated more 'leniently' because of this. Certain women do become threats by transcending (or by being denied) their traditional role, particularly many Third World women and political rebels, and they are *not* afforded chivalrous treatment! In fact, chivalry is reserved for the women who are least likely to ever come in contact with the criminal justice system: the ladies, or white middle-class women. In matters of *sexual* conduct, however, which embody the double standard, women are rigorously prosecuted by the law. As Thomas understands, this is the sphere in which women's functions *are* critical. Thus it is not a matter of 'chivalry' how one is handled, but of different forms and thrusts of social control applied to men and women. Men are engaged in productive tasks and their activities in this area *are* strictly curtailed.

In *The Unadjusted Girl* (1923), Thomas deals with female delinquency as a 'normal' response under certain social conditions, using assumptions about the nature of women which he leaves unarticulated in this work. Driven by basic 'wishes', an individual is controlled by society in her activities through institutional transmission of codes and mores. Depending on how they are manipulated, wishes can be made to serve social or antisocial ends. Thomas stresses the institutions that socialize, such as the family, giving people certain 'definitions of the situation'. He confidently – and defiantly – asserts:

> There is no individual energy, no unrest, no type of wish, which cannot be sublimated and made socially useful. From this standpoint, the problem is not the right of society to protect itself from the disorderly and antisocial person, but the right of the disorderly and antisocial person to be made orderly and socially valuable . . . The problem of society is to produce the right attitudes in its members. (1923: 232–3)

This is an important shift in perspective, from the traditional libertarian view of protecting society by punishing transgressors, to the *rehabilitative* and *preventive* perspective of crime control that seeks to control *minds* through socialization rather than to merely control behavior through punishment. The autonomy of the individual to choose is seen as the product of his environment which the state can alter. This is an important refutation of the Lombrosian biological perspective, which maintains that there are crime-prone individuals who must be locked up, sterilized or otherwise incapacitated. Today, one can see an amalgamation of the two perspectives in new theories of 'behavior control' that use tactics such as conditioning and brain surgery, combining biological and environmental viewpoints.[3]

Thomas proposes the manipulation of individuals through institutions to prevent antisocial attitudes, and maintains that there is no such person as the 'crime prone' individual. A hegemonic system of belief can be imposed by sublimating natural urges and by correcting the poor socialization of slum families. In this perspective, the *definition* of the situation rather than the situation *itself* is what should be changed; a situation is what someone *thinks* it is. The response to a criminal woman who is dissatisfied with her conventional sexual roles is to change not the roles, which would mean widespread social transformations, but to change her attitudes. This concept of civilization as repressive and the need to adjust is later refined by Freud.

Middle-class women, according to Thomas, commit little crime because they are socialized to sublimate their natural desires and to behave well, treasuring their chastity as an investment. The poor woman, however, 'is not immoral, because this implies a loss of morality, but amoral' (1923: 98). Poor women are not objectively driven to crime; they long for it. Delinquent girls are motivated by the desire for excitement or 'new experience', and forget the repressive urge of 'security'. However, these desires are well within Thomas's conception of *femininity*: delinquents are not rebelling against womanhood, as Lombroso suggests, but merely acting it out illegally. Davis and Pollak agree with this notion that delinquent women are not 'different' from non-delinquent women.

Thomas maintains that it is not sexual desire that motivates delinquent girls, for they are no more passionate than other women, but they are *manipulating* male desires for sex to achieve their own ulterior ends.

> The beginning of delinquency in girls is usually an impulse to get amusement, adventure, pretty clothes, favorable notice, distinction, freedom in the larger world . . . The girls have usually become 'wild' before the development of sexual desire, and their casual sex relations do not usually awaken sex feeling. Their sex is used as a condition of the realization of other wishes. It is their capital. (1923: 109)

Here Thomas is expanding on the myth of the manipulative woman, who is cold and scheming and vain. To him, good female sexual behavior is a protective measure – 'instinctive, of course' (1907: 241), whereas male behavior is uncontrollable as men are caught by helpless desires. This is the common Victorian notion of the woman as seductress which in turn perpetuates the myth of a lack of real sexuality to justify her responsibility for upholding sexual mores. Thomas uses a market analogy to female virtue: good women *keep* their bodies as capital to sell in matrimony for marriage and security, whereas bad women *trade* their bodies for excitement. One notes, of course, the familiar dichotomy. It is difficult, in this framework, to see how Thomas can make *any* moral distinctions, since morality seems to be merely good business sense. In fact, Thomas's yardstick is social harmony, necessitating *control*.

Thomas shows an insensitivity to real human relationships and needs. He also shows ignorance of economic hardships in his denial of economic factors in delinquency.

> An unattached woman has a tendency to become an adventuress not so much on economic as on psychological grounds. Life is rarely so hard that a young woman cannot earn her bread; but she cannot always live and have the stimulation she craves. (1907: 241)

This is an amazing statement in an era of mass starvation and illness! He rejects economic causes as a possibility at all, denying their importance in criminal activity with as much certainty as Lombroso, Freud, Davis, Pollak and most other writers.

FREUD: 'BEAUTY, CHARM AND SWEETNESS'

The Freudian theory of the position of women is grounded in explicit biological assumptions about their nature, expressed by the famous 'Anatomy is Destiny'. Built upon this foundation is a construction incorporating psychological and social-structural factors.

Freud himself sees women as anatomically inferior; they are destined to be wives and mothers, and this is admittedly an inferior destiny as befits the inferior sex. The root of this inferiority is that women's *sex organs* are inferior to those of men, a fact *universally* recognized by children in the Freudian scheme. The girl assumes that she has lost a penis as punishment, is traumatized, and grows up envious and revengeful. The boy also sees the girl as having lost a penis, fears a similar punishment himself, and dreads the girl's envy and vengeance. Feminine traits can be traced to the inferior genitals themselves, or to women's inferiority complex arising from their response to them: women are exhibitionistic, narcissistic, and attempt to compensate for their lack of a penis by being well dressed and physically beautiful. Women become mothers trying to replace the lost penis with a baby. Women are also masochistic, as Lombroso and Thomas have noted, because their *sexual* role is one of receptor, and their sexual pleasure consists of pain. This woman, Freud notes, is the *healthy* woman. In the familiar dichotomy, the men are aggressive and pain inflicting. Freud comments:

> The male pursues the female for the purposes of sexual union, seizes hold of her, and penetrates into her . . . by this you have precisely reduced the characteristic of masculinity to the factor of aggressiveness. (Millett, 1970: 189)

Freud, like Lombroso and Thomas, takes the notion of men's activity and women's inactivity and *reduces* it to the sexual level, seeing the sexual union itself through Victorian eyes: ladies don't move.

Women are also inferior in the sense that they are concerned with personal matters and have little social sense. Freud sees civilization as based on repression of the sex drive, where it is the duty of men to repress their strong instincts in order to get on with the worldly business of civilization. Women, on the other hand, have little sense of justice, and this is no doubt connected with the preponderance of envy in their mental life; for the demands of justice are a modification of envy; they lay down the conditions under which one is willing to part with it. We also say of women that their social interests are weaker than those of men and that their capacity for the sublimation of their instincts is less. (1933: 183)

Men are capable of sublimating their individual needs because they rationally perceive the Hobbesian conflict between those urges and social needs. Women are emotional and incapable of such an adjustment because of their innate inability to make such rational judgements. It is only fair then that they should have a marginal relation to production and property.

In this framework, the deviant woman is one who is attempting to be a *man*. She is aggressively rebellious, and her drive to accomplishment is the expression of her longing for a penis; this is a hopeless pursuit, of course, and she will only end up 'neurotic'. Thus the deviant woman should be treated and helped to *adjust* to her sex role. Here again, as in Thomas's writing, is the notion of individual accommodation that repudiates the possibility of social change.

In a Victorian fashion, Freud rationalizes women's oppression by glorifying their duties as wives and mothers:

> It is really a stillborn thought to send women into the struggle for existence exactly the same as men. If, for instance, I imagined my sweet gentle girl as a competitor, it would only end in my telling her, as I did seventeen months ago, that I am fond of her, and I implore her to withdraw from the strife into the calm, uncompetitive activity of my home . . . Nature has determined woman's destiny through beauty, charm and sweetness . . . in youth an adored darling, in mature years a loved wife. (Jones, 1961: 117–18)

In speaking of femininity, Freud, like his forebears, is speaking along racist and classist lines. Only upper- and middle-class women could possibly enjoy lives as sheltered darlings. Freud sets hegemonic standards of femininity for poor and Third World women.

It is important to understand Freudianism because it reduces categories of sexual ideology to explicit sexuality and makes these categories *scientific*. For the last fifty years, Freudianism has been a mainstay of sexist social theory. Kate Millett notes that Freud himself saw his work as stemming the tide of feminist revolution, which he constantly ridiculed:

> Coming as it did, at the peak of the sexual revolution, Freud's doctrine of penis envy is in fact a superbly timed accusation, enabling masculine sentiment to take the offensive again as it had not since the disappearance of overt misogyny when the pose of chivalry became fashionable. (Millett, 1970: 189)

Freudian notions of the repression of sexual instincts, the sexual passivity of women, and the sanctity of the nuclear family are conservative not only in their contemporary context, but in the context of their own time. Hitler writes:

> For her [woman's] world is her husband, her family, her children and her home . . . The man upholds the nation as the woman upholds the family. The equal rights of women

consist in the fact that in the realm of life determined for her by nature, she experience the high esteem that is her due. Woman and man represent quite different types of being. Reason is dominant in man . . . Feeling, in contrast, is much more stable than reason, and woman is the feeling, and therefore the stable, element. (Millett, 1970: 170)

One can mark the decline in the position of women after the 1920s through the use of various indices: by noting the progressively earlier age of marriage of women in the United States and the steady rise in the number of children born to them, culminating in the birth explosion of the late 1940s and 1950s; by looking at the relative decline in the number of women scholars; and by seeing the failure to liberate women in the Soviet Union and the rise of fascist sexual ideology. Freudianism has had an unparalleled influence in the United States (and came at a key point to help swing the tide against the women's movement) to facilitate the return of women during the depression and postwar years to the home, out of an economy which had no room for them. Freud affected such writers on female deviance as Davis, Pollak and Konopka, who turn to concepts of sexual maladjustment and neurosis to explain women's criminality. Healthy women would now be seen as masochistic, passive and sexually indifferent. Criminal women would be seen as *sexual* misfits. Most importantly, *psychological* factors would be used to explain criminal activity, and social, economic and political factors would be ignored. Explanations would seek to be *universal*, and historical possibilities of change would be refuted.

DAVIS: 'THE MOST CONVENIENT SEXUAL OUTLET FOR ARMIES . . .'

Kingsley Davis's work on prostitution (1961) is still considered a classical analysis on the subject with a structural-functionalist perspective. It employs assumptions about 'the organic nature of man' and woman, many of which can be traced to ideas proffered by Thomas and Freud.

Davis sees prostitution as a structural necessity whose roots lie in the *sexual* nature of men and women; for example, female humans, unlike primates, are sexually available year-round. He asserts that prostitution is *universal* in time and place, eliminating the possibilities of historical change and ignoring critical differences in the quality and quantity of prostitution in different societies. He maintains that there will always be a class of women who will be prostitutes, the familiar class of 'bad' women. The reason for the universality of prostitution is that sexual *repression*, a concept stressed by Thomas and Freud, is essential to the functioning of society. Once again there is the notion of sublimating 'natural' sex urges to the overall needs of society, namely social order. Davis notes that in our society sexuality is permitted only within the structure of the nuclear family, which is an institution of stability. He does not, however, analyse in depth the economic and social functions of the family, other than to say it is a bulwark of morality.

The norms of every society tend to harness and control the sexual appetite, and one of the ways of doing this is to link the sexual act to some stable or potentially stable social relationship . . . Men dominate women in economic, sexual and familial relationships and consider them to some extent as sexual property, to be prohibited to other males. They therefore find promiscuity on the part of women repugnant. (1961: 264)

Davis is linking the concept of prostitution to promiscuity, defining it as a *sexual crime*, and calling prostitutes sexual transgressors. Its origins, he claims, lie not in economic hardship, but in the marital restraints on sexuality. As long as men seek women, prostitutes will be in demand. One wonders why sex-seeking women have not created a class of male prostitutes.

Davis sees the only possibility of eliminating prostitution in the liberalization of sexual mores, although he is pessimistic about the likelihood of total elimination. In light of the contemporary American 'sexual revolution' of commercial sex, which has surely created more prostitutes and semi-prostitutes rather than eliminating the phenomenon, and in considering the revolution in China where, despite a 'puritanical' outlook on sexuality, prostitution has largely been eliminated through major economic and social change, the superficiality of Davis's approach becomes evident. Without dealing with root economic, social and political factors, one cannot analyse prostitution.

Davis shows Freudian pessimism about the nature of sexual repression:

> We can imagine a social system in which the motive for prostitution would be completely absent, but we cannot imagine that the system will ever come to pass. It would be a regime of absolute sexual freedom with intercourse practiced solely for pleasure by both parties. There would be no institutional control of sexual expression . . . All sexual desire would have to be mutually complementary . . . Since the basic causes of prostitution – the institutional control of sex, the unequal scale of attractiveness, and the presence of economic and social inequalities between classes and between males and females – are not likely to disappear, prostitution is not likely to disappear either. (1961: 286)

By talking about 'complementary desire', Davis is using a marketplace notion of sex: two attractive or unattractive people are drawn to each other and exchange sexual favors; people are placed on a scale of attractiveness and may be rejected by people above them on the scale; hence they (*men*) become frustrated and demand prostitutes. Women who become prostitutes do so for good pay *and* sexual pleasure. Thus one has a neat little system in which everyone benefits.

> Enabling a small number of women to take care of the needs of a large number of men, it is the most convenient sexual outlet for armies, for the legions of strangers, perverts and physically repulsive in our midst. (1961: 288)

Prostitution 'functions', therefore it must be good. Davis, like Thomas, is motivated by concerns of social order rather than by concerns of what the needs and desires of the women involved might be. He denies that the women involved are economically oppressed; they are on the streets through autonomous, *individual* choice.

> Some women physically enjoy the intercourse they sell. From a purely economic point of view, prostitution comes near the situation of getting something for nothing . . . Women's wages could scarcely be raised significantly without also raising men's. Men would then have more to spend on prostitution. (1961: 277)

It is important to understand that, given a *sexual* interpretation of what is an *economic* crime, and given a refusal to consider widespread change (even equalization of wages, hardly a revolutionary act), Davis's conclusion is the logical technocratic solution.

In this framework, the deviant women are merely adjusting to their feminine role in an illegitimate fashion, as Thomas has theorized. They are *not* attempting to be rebels or to be 'men', as Lombroso's and Freud's positions suggest. Although Davis sees the main difference between wives and prostitutes in a macrosocial sense as the difference merely between legal and illegal roles, in a personal sense he sees the women who *choose* prostitution as maladjusted and neurotic. However, given the universal necessity for prostitution, this analysis implies the necessity of having a perpetually ill and maladjusted class of women. Thus oppression is *built into* the system, and a healthy *system* makes for a sick *individual*. Here Davis is integrating Thomas's notions of social integration with Freudian perspectives on neurosis and maladjustment.

POLLAK: 'A DIFFERENT ATTITUDE TOWARD VERACITY'

Otto Pollak's *The Criminality of Women* (1950) has had an outstanding influence on the field of women and crime, being the major work on the subject in the postwar years. Pollak advances the theory of 'hidden' female crime to account for what he considers unreasonably low official rates for women.

A major reason for the existence of hidden crime, as he sees it, lies in the *nature* of women themselves. They are instigators rather than perpetrators of criminal activity. While Pollak admits that this role is partly a socially enforced one, he insists that women are inherently deceitful for *physiological* reasons.

> Man must achieve an erection in order to perform the sex act and will not be able to hide his failure. His lack of positive emotion in the sexual sphere must become overt to the partner, and pretense of sexual response is impossible for him, if it is lacking. Woman's body, however, permits such pretense to a certain degree and lack of orgasm does not prevent her ability to participate in the sex act. (1950: 10)

Pollak *reduces* women's nature to the *sex act*, as Freud has done, and finds women inherently more capable of manipulation, accustomed to being sly, passive and passionless. As Thomas suggests, women can use sex for ulterior purposes. Furthermore, Pollak suggests that women are innately deceitful on yet another level:

> Our sex mores force women to conceal every four weeks the period of menstruation . . .
> They thus make concealment and misrepresentation in the eyes of women socially required and must condition them to a different attitude toward veracity than men. (1950: 11)

Women's abilities at concealment thus allow them to successfully commit crimes in stealth.

Women are also vengeful. Menstruation, in the classic Freudian sense, seals their doomed hopes to become men and arouses women's desire for vengeance, especially during that time of the month. Thus Pollak offers new rationalizations to bolster old myths.

A second factor in hidden crime is the roles played by women which furnish them with opportunities as domestics, nurses, teachers and housewives to commit undetectable crimes. The *kinds* of crimes women commit reflect their nature: false accusation, for example, is an outgrowth of women's treachery, spite or fear and is a sign of neurosis; shoplifting can be traced in many cases to a special mental disease – kleptomania. Economic factors play a minor role; *sexual-psychological* factors account for female criminality. Crime in women is *personalized* and often accounted for by mental illness.

Pollak notes:

> Robbery and burglary . . . are considered specifically male offenses since they represent the pursuit of monetary gain by overt action . . . Those cases of female robbery which seem to express a tendency toward masculinization come from . . . [areas] where social conditions have favored the assumptions of male pursuits by women . . . The female offenders usually retain some trace of femininity, however, and even so glaring an example of masculinization as the 'Michigan Babes,' an all woman gang of robbers in Chicago, shows a typically feminine trait in the modus operandi. (1950: 29)

Pollak is defining crimes with economic motives that employ overt action as *masculine*, and defining as *feminine* those crimes for *sexual* activity, such as luring men as baits. Thus he is using circular reasoning by saying that feminine crime is feminine. To fit women into the scheme and justify the statistics, he must invent the notion of hidden crime.

It is important to recognize that, to some extent, women *do* adapt to their enforced sexual roles and may be more likely to instigate, to use sexual traps, and to conform to all the other feminine role expectations. However, it is not accidental that theorists label women as conforming even when they are *not*; for example, by inventing sexual motives for what are clearly crimes of economic necessity, or by invoking 'mental illness' such as kleptomania for shoplifting. It is difficult to separate the *theory* from the *reality*, since the reality of female crime is largely unknown. But it is not difficult to see that Pollak is using sexist terms and making sexist assumptions to advance theories of hidden female crime.

Pollak, then, sees criminal women as extending their sexual role, like Davis and Thomas, by using sexuality for ulterior purposes. He suggests that the condemnation of extramarital sex has 'delivered men who engage in such conduct as practically helpless victims' (1950: 152) into the hands of women blackmailers, overlooking completely the possibility of men blackmailing women, which would seem more likely, given the greater taboo on sex for women and their greater risks of being punished.

The final factor that Pollak advances as a root cause of hidden crime is that of 'chivalry' in the criminal justice system. Pollak uses Thomas's observation that women are differentially treated by the law, and carries it to a sweeping conclusion based on *cultural* analyses of men's feelings toward women.

> One of the outstanding concomitants of the existing inequality . . . is chivalry, and the general protective attitude of man toward woman . . . Men hate to accuse women and thus indirectly to send them to their punishment, police officers dislike to arrest them, district attorneys to prosecute them, judges and juries to find them guilty, and so on. (1950: 151)

Pollak rejects the possibility of an actual discrepancy between crime rates for men and women; therefore, he must look for factors to expand the scope of female crime. He assumes that there is chivalry in the criminal justice system that is extended to the women who come in contact with it. Yet the women involved are likely to be poor and Third World women or white middle-class women who have stepped *outside* the definitions of femininity to become hippies or political rebels, and chivalry is *not* likely to be extended to them. Chivalry is a racist and classist concept founded on the notion of women as 'ladies' which applies only to wealthy white women and ignores the double sexual standard. These 'ladies', however, are the least likely women to ever come in contact with the criminal justice system in the first place.[4]

THE LEGACY OF SEXISM

A major purpose in tracing the development and interaction of ideas pertaining to sexual ideology based on implicit assumptions of the inherent nature of women throughout the works of Lombroso, Thomas, Freud, Davis and Pollak, is to clarify their positions in relation to writers in the field today. One can see the influence their ideas still have by looking at a number of contemporary theorists on female criminality. Illuminating examples can be found in Gisela Konopka's *Adolescent Girl in Conflict* (1966), Vedder and Somerville's *The Delinquent Girl* (1970) and Cowie, Cowie and Slater's *Delinquency in Girls* (1968). The ideas in these minor works have direct roots in those already traced in this paper.

Konopka justifies her decision to study delinquency in girls rather than in boys by noting girls' *influence* on boys in gang fights and on future generations as mothers. This is the notion of women as instigators of men and influencers on children.

Konopka's main point is that delinquency in girls can be traced to a specific emotional response: loneliness.

> What I found in the girl in conflict was . . . loneliness accompanied by despair. Adolescent boys too often feel lonely and search for understanding and friends. Yet in general this does not seem to be the central core of their problems, not their most outspoken ache. While these girls also strive for independence, their need for dependence is unusually great. (1966: 40)

In this perspective, girls are driven to delinquency by an emotional problem – loneliness and dependency. There are *inherent* emotional differences between the sexes.

> Almost invariably her [the girl's] problems are deeply personalized. Whatever her offense – whether shoplifting, truancy or running away from home –it is usually accompanied by some disturbance or unfavorable behavior in the sexual area. (1966: 4)

Here is the familiar resurrection of female personalism, emotionalism, and above all, *sexuality* – characteristics already described by Lombroso, Thomas and Freud. Konopka maintains:

> The delinquent girl suffers, like many boys, from lack of success, lack of opportunity. But her drive to success is never separated from her need for people, for interpersonal involvement. (1966: 41)

Boys are 'instrumental' and become delinquent if they are deprived of the chance for creative success. However, girls are 'expressive' and happiest dealing with people as wives, mothers, teachers, nurses or psychologists. This perspective is drawn from the theory of delinquency as a result of blocked opportunity and from the instrumental/ expressive sexual dualism developed by structural-functionalists. Thus female delinquency must be dealt with on this *psychological* level, using therapy geared to their needs as future wives and mothers. They should be *adjusted* and given *opportunities* to be pretty, sociable women.

The important point is to understand how Konopka analyses the roots of girls' feelings. It is very possible that, given women's position, girls may be in fact more concerned with dependence and sociability. One's understanding of this, however, is based on an understanding of the historical position of women and the nature of their oppression. Konopka says:

> What are the reasons for this essential loneliness in girls? Some will be found in the nature of being an adolescent girl, in her biological make-up and her particular position in her culture and time. (1966: 41)

Coming from a Freudian perspective, Konopka's emphasis on female emotions as cause for delinquency, which ignores economic and social factors, is questionable. She employs assumptions about the *physiological* and *psychological* nature of women that very well may have led her to see only those feelings in the first place. For example, she cites menstruation as a significant event in a girl's development. Thus Konopka is rooted firmly in the tradition of Freud and, apart from sympathy, contributes little that is new to the field.[5]

Vedder and Somerville (1970) account for female delinquency in a manner similar to that of Konopka. They also feel the need to justify their attention to girls by remarking that (while female delinquency may not pose as much of a problem as that of boys) because women raise families and are critical agents of socialization, it is worth taking the time to study and control them. Vedder and Somerville also stress the dependence of girls on boys and the instigatory role girls play in boys' activities.

Like Freud and Konopka, the authors view delinquency as blocked access or maladjustment to the normal feminine role. In a blatant statement that ignores the economic and social factors that result from racism and poverty, they attribute the high rates of delinquency among black girls to their lack of 'healthy' feminine narcissism, *reducing* racism to a psychological problem in totally sexist and racist terms.

> The black girl is, in fact, the antithesis of the American beauty. However loved she may be by her mother, family and community, she has no real basis of female attractiveness on which to build a sound feminine narcissism . . . Perhaps the 'black is beautiful' movement will help the Negro girl to increase her femininity and personal satisfaction as a black woman. (1970: 159–60)

Again the focus is on a lack of *sexual* opportunities for women, i.e., the Black woman is not Miss America. *Economic* offenses such as shoplifting are explained as outlets for *sexual* frustration. Since healthy women conform, the individual delinquents should be helped to adjust; the emphasis is on the 'definition of the situation' rather than on the situation.

The answer lies in *therapy*, and racism and sexism become merely psychological problems.

> Special attention should be given to girls, taking into consideration their constitutional biological and psychological differences, and their social position in our male dominated culture. The female offender's goal, as any woman's, is a happy and successful marriage; therefore her self-image is dependent on the establishment of satisfactory relationships with the opposite sex. The double standard for sexual behavior on the part of the male and female must be recognized. (1970: 153)

Like Konopka, and to some extent drawing on Thomas, the authors see female delinquents as extending femininity in an illegitimate fashion rather than rebelling against it. The assumptions made about women's goals and needs, including *biological* assumptions, lock women into a system from which there is no escape, whereby any behavior will be sexually interpreted and dealt with.

The resurgence of biological or physiological explanations of criminality in general has been noteworthy in the last several years, exemplified by the XYY chromosome controversy and the interest in brain waves in 'violent' individuals.[6] In the case of women, biological explanations have *always* been prevalent; every writer has made assumptions about anatomy as destiny. Women are prey, in the literature, to cycles of reproduction, including menstruation, pregnancy, maternity and menopause; they experience emotional responses to these cycles that make them inclined to irrationality and potentially violent activity.

Cowie, Cowie and Slater (1968) propose a *chromosomal* explanation of female delinquency that hearkens back to the works of Lombroso and others such as Healy (Healy and Bronner, 1926), Edith Spaulding (1923) and the Gluecks (Glueck and Glueck, 1934). They write:

> The chromosomal difference between the sexes starts the individual on a divergent path, leading either in a masculine or feminine direction . . . It is possible that the methods of upbringing, differing somewhat for the two sexes, may play some part in increasing the angle of this divergence. (Cowie et al., 1968: 171)

This is the healthy, normal divergence for the sexes. The authors equate *masculinity* and *femininity* with *maleness* and *femaleness*, although contemporary feminists point out that the first categories are *social* and the latter ones *physical*.[7] What relationship exists between the two – how femaleness determines femininity – is dependent on the larger social structure. There is no question that a wide range of possibilities exist historically, and in a non-sexist society it is possible that 'masculinity' and 'femininity' would disappear, and that the sexes would differ only biologically, specifically by their sex organs. The authors, however, lack this understanding and assume an ahistorical sexist view of women, stressing the *universality* of femininity in the Freudian tradition, and of women's inferior role in the nuclear family.[8]

In this perspective, the female offender is *different* physiologically and psychologically from the 'normal' girl.

The authors conclude, in the tradition of Lombroso, that female delinquents are *masculine*. Examining girls for physical characteristics, they note:

> Markedly masculine traits in girl delinquents have been commented on . . . [as well as] the frequency of homosexual tendencies . . . Energy, aggressiveness, enterprise and the rebelliousness that drives the individual to break through conformist habits are thought of as being masculine . . . We can be sure that they have some physical basis. (1968: 172)

The authors see crime as a *rebellion* against sex roles rather than as a maladjusted expression of them. By defining rebellion as *masculine*, they are ascribing characteristics of masculinity to any female rebel. Like Lombroso, they spend time measuring heights, weights, and other *biological* features of female delinquents with other girls.

Crime defined as masculine seems to mean violent, overt crime, whereas 'ladylike' crime usually refers to sexual violations and shoplifting. Women are neatly categorized no matter *which* kind of crime they commit: if they are violent, they are 'masculine' and suffering from chromosomal deficiencies, penis envy, or atavisms. If they conform, they are manipulative, sexually maladjusted and promiscuous. The *economic* and *social* realities of crime – the fact that poor women commit crimes, and that most crimes for women are property offenses – are overlooked. Women's behavior must be *sexually* defined before it will be considered, for women count only in the sexual sphere. The theme of sexuality is a unifying thread in the various, often contradictory theories.

CONCLUSION

A good deal of the writing on women and crime being done at the present time is squarely in the tradition of the writers that have been discussed. The basic assumptions and technocratic concerns of these writers have produced work that is sexist, racist and classist; assumptions that have served to maintain a repressive ideology with its extensive apparatus of control. To do a new kind of research on women and crime – one that has feminist roots and a radical orientation – it is necessary to understand the assumptions made by the traditional writers and to break away from them. Work that focuses on human needs, rather than those of the state, will require new definitions of criminality, women, the individual and her/his relation to the state. It is beyond the scope of this paper to develop possible areas of study, but it is none the less imperative that this work be made a priority by women *and* men in the future.

NOTES

1 Quoted from the 1973 proposal for the Center for the Study and Reduction of Violence prepared by Dr Louis J. West, Director, Neuropsychiatric Institute, UCLA: 'The question of violence in females will be examined from the point of view that females are

more likely to commit acts of violence during the pre-menstrual and menstrual periods' (1973: 43).

2 I am indebted to Marion Goldman for introducing me to the notion of the dual morality based on assumptions of different sexuality for men and women.

3 For a discussion of the possibilities of psychosurgery in behavior modification for 'violence-prone' individuals, see Frank Ervin and Vernon Mark, *Violence and the Brain* (1970). For an eclectic view of this perspective on crime, see the proposal for the Center for the Study and Reduction of Violence (note 1).

4 The concept of hidden crime is reiterated in Reckless and Kay's report to the President's Commission on Law Enforcement and the Administration of Justice. They note:

> A large part of the infrequent officially acted upon involvement of women in crime can be traced to the masking effect of women's roles, effective practice on the part of women of deceit and indirection, their instigation of men to commit their crimes (the Lady Macbeth factor), and the unwillingness on the part of the public and law enforcement officials to hold women accountable for their deeds (the chivalry factor). (1967: 13)

5 Bertha Payak in 'Understanding the Female Offender' (1963) stresses that women offenders have poor self-concepts, feelings of insecurity and dependency, are emotionally selfish, and prey to irrationality during menstruation, pregnancy, and menopause (a good deal of their life!).

6 See Theodore R. Sarbin and Jeffrey E. Miller, 'Demonism revisited: the XYY chromosomal anomaly', *Issues in Criminology* 5(2), (1970).

7 Kate Millett notes that 'sex is biological, gender psychological and therefore cultural . . . if proper terms for sex are male and female, the corresponding terms for gender are masculine and feminine; these latter may be quite independent of biological sex' (1970: 30).

8 Zelditch (1960), a structural-functionalist, writes that the nuclear family is an inevitability and that within it, women, the 'expressive' sex, will inevitably be the domestics.

REFERENCES

Bishop, C. (1931) *Women and Crime*. London: Chatto and Windus.

Cowie, J., Cowie V. and Slater, E. (1968) *Delinquency in Girls*. London: Heinemann.

Davis, K. (1961) 'Prostitution', in R.K. Merton and R.A. Nisbet (eds), *Contemporary Social Problems*. New York: Harcourt Brace and Jovanovich. Originally published as 'The sociology of prostitution', *American Sociological Review*, 1937, 2(5).

Ervin, F. and Mark, V. (1970) *Violence and the Brain*. New York: Harper and Row.

Freud, S. (1933) *New Introductory Lectures on Psychoanalysis*. New York: W.W. Norton.

Glueck, E. and Glueck, S. (1934) *Four Hundred Delinquent Women*. New York: Alfred A. Knopf.

Healy, W. and Bronner, A. (1926) *Delinquents and Criminals: their Making and Unmaking*. New York: Macmillan and Company.

Jones, E. (1961) *The Life and Works of Sigmund Freud*. New York: Basic Books.

Konopka, G. (1966) *The Adolescent Girl in Conflict*. Englewood Cliffs, NJ: Prentice-Hall.

Lombroso, C. (1920) *The Female Offender* (trans.). New York: Appleton. Originally published in 1903.

Millett, K. (1970) *Sexual Politics*. New York: Doubleday.

Monahan, F. (1941) *Women in Crime*. New York: I. Washburn.

Payak, B. (1963) 'Understanding the female offender', *Federal Probation*, XXVII.

Pollak, O. (1950) *The Criminality of Women*. Philadelphia: University of Pennsylvania Press.

Reckless, W. and Kay, B. (1967) *The Female Offender*. Report to the President's Commission on Law Enforcement and the Administration of Justice. Washington, DC: U.S. Government Printing Office.

Sarbin, T.R. and Miller, J.E. (1970) 'Demonism revisited: the XYY chromosomal anomaly', *Issues in Criminology*, 5(2) (Summer).

Spaulding, E. (1923) *An Experimental Study of Psychopathic Delinquent Women*. New York: Rand McNally.

Thomas, W.I. (1907) *Sex and Society*. Boston: Little, Brown.

Thomas, W.I. (1923) *The Unadjusted Girl*. New York: Harper and Row.

Vedder, C. and Somerville, D. (1970) *The Delinquent Girl*. Springfield, Ill.: Charles C. Thomas.

West, J. (1973) *Proposal for the Center for the Study and Reduction of Violence*. Neuropsychiatric Institute, UCLA (10 April).

Zelditch, M. Jr (1960) 'Role Differentiation in the nuclear family: a comparative study', in N. Bell and E. Vogel (eds), *The Family*. Glencoe, Ill.: The Free Press.

AFTERWORD: TWENTY YEARS AGO . . . TODAY*

'The Etiology of Female Crime: a Review of the Literature', written two decades ago, ended in a call for 'a new kind of research on women and crime – one that has feminist roots and a radical orientation . . . that focuses on human needs, rather than those of the state, [and that] will require new definitions of criminality, women, the individual and her/his relation to the state.' At that time, in 1973, there was a new women's movement, paralleling other international and domestic liberation movements. It consisted of thousands of women forming groups, reading the few books or articles available, demonstrating, writing, and swapping pamphlets. At the School of Criminology at the University of California, Berkeley, where I was studying, there flourished a radical, oppositional criminology, determined to remake the field in the image of the movements of the time: prisoners' rights, community control of the police, and decriminalization of victimless offenses.

The presence of a critical mass of politically active women graduate students, at a time when few criminologists were female, allowed us to share and build on what little knowledge we had.[1] At that time there were no professional ethnographies of women law-breakers, no recent theoretical readings in criminology that centered on women or gender, no studies of female prisoners that did not focus on their homosexuality or 'affective' needs.

* From *The Criminal Justice System and Women* (eds B.R. Price and N.J. Sokoloff), pp. 47–53. (New York: McGraw-Hill, Inc., 1995.)

For a term paper, I decided to take what had been written on the causes of women's offenses and scrutinize it for its unexamined assumptions about women offenders.[2] Writing up what I found, I wondered naively, angrily, how, in our era and given the women's movement, such stereotypes about women could be taken seriously. The paper appeared in the special issue devoted to women by the School's journal (*Issues in Criminology*, 1973).

In the years since, the feminist critique of mainstream academic disciplines has exploded in volume and advanced light-years in depth, and interest in the issues of women, crime, victimization and justice has also grown. Today 'Etiology' may strike one as a long-ago first step, the passionate reaction of a beginner armed with the rhetoric of a young movement.

But have the concerns and hopes voiced in 'Etiology' been met, or vanished with time? I would suggest neither; rather, they have been expressed in numerous ways and in the process gone through sea-changes. In this Afterword, I will pose the challenge for feminist criminology in three areas which trace a common history to 'Etiology' and hold importance for the future: the scientific basis of theories, the gender and racial bias in science, and the definition of crime. The common thread of my discussion is a simple premise: It is time to move away from considering 'the feminist question in criminology' and toward exploring 'the criminology question in feminism' (see Bertrand, 1991, paraphrasing Harding). Specifically, how can feminist insights into gender, power and knowledge help us critically examine our understanding of crime, criminality, and victimization?

1. The debates over the scientific basis of theories of women's and men's behaviors have continued fiercely over two decades, although with new twists and turns around questions of biology and psychology.

Most recently, feminist philosophical and scientific critiques have argued that for many traditional European-identified thinkers, including Lombroso and his followers, femaleness was associated with biology or nature (e.g., primitive, irrational, nurturing), in contrast to male civilization. What is especially radical about these recent critiques is that they do not merely challenge the gender assignment of certain constructs, as earlier feminist work did (e.g., femaleness as a Lombrosian primitive). Rather, they question the very validity of these dichotomies: nature *versus* civilization, emotion *versus* reason, developed *versus* undeveloped world, female *versus* male (see Benhabib and Cornell, 1987; Nicholson, 1990; Sunstein, 1990).

The contemporary feminist argument is this: a quality that appears natural or biological must not be exclusively assigned to a gender; this very quality may be a historical ideological construction rather than an eternal objective truth. Woman herself is a constructed 'Other', in Simone de Beauvoir's classic phrase, who by definition exists only in contrast to man. This is much like the criminal, who cannot exist without the contrast of the law-abiding citizen. Women, like minority-group members, criminals, and other relatively less powerful 'Others', tend to be perceived in the dominant culture more one-dimensionally, more restrictively, than their opposites. Hence one finds the origins of the stereotyping of female offenders in traditional criminology, as discussed in 'Etiology'.

In contemporary criminology, on the other hand, there is now agreement that differences in women's and men's behaviors are social rather than natural, just as there is agreement that the sources of criminality are social rather than natural. Very few criminologists today argue that prostitution or shoplifting emerges out of women's nature or that violence is hormonal. More generally, few theories of criminality are based on nature. To this extent, criminology has moved away from overt biologism.[3] However, criminological work on women continues to focus on their experiences or qualities as they exist in comparison with those of men: in other words, the differences between the genders. Moreover, much work on women focuses uncritically on sexuality: first, as a natural, as opposed to a social, force, and second, as a female, rather than male, concern. Furthermore, in nearly all criminology, maleness remains the universal, femaleness the special case.

During the years, feminists have also wrestled with theoretical psychological perspectives on gender and sexuality, reexamining Freudianism with a far more sophisticated eye (certainly more so than mine in 1973!). One objective, among others, has been to understand how and why women and men are in fact made, as opposed to being born. The spotlight has been on such 'gender factories' as families, although much of the psychoanalytic theorization is limited in its relevance to affluent populations in modern Western societies.

Within feminist and critical criminology, there is much distrust of psychology as the discourse used in 'blaming the victim' and in the practices of social control. Within radical and critical feminism in general, there is similar distrust of psychological approaches to gender domination, such as those that put primacy on sex roles. Structurally oriented and Marxist-influenced feminisms have instead focused on large-scale institutional and cultural aspects of life, such as the division of paid and unpaid labor.

Yet today there is interest in exploring people's personal choices as well as their structural constraints: in other words, in deepening our understanding of the subjective relations between an individual and society. For example, there has been the intriguing and much-debated work of Carol Gilligan (1982) on differences in women's and men's views of morality. One question now being asked of any psychological theory of gender is not so much what is its specific content, but upon what scientific basis is it making psychological claims about gender differences? Is a psychological theory, for example, implicitly biological (e.g., resting on women's childbearing capacity), psychoanalytic, culturally bound (e.g., based on women's childrearing role), or structural?

Much mainstream criminology today, like the positivist correctionalism of the past, is psychological in orientation, focusing on the personal characteristics of known offenders and victims. Only recently has this criminology shown any likelihood of drawing upon feminist work, with recent attention paid to the possibilities of investigating why certain forms of criminality are disproportionately male behaviors.

In the 1970s and early 1980s, many feminist scholars in different fields, abandoning biology and psychology, searched for the social roots of women's oppression, which cuts across many eras and cultures. Most argued that whatever the causes of patriarchy, they were due to the structuring of gender rather than either to the biological fact of sexual difference or to differential psychological development alone.[4]

Some feminist scholars have recently called for abandoning the search for the primary universal social cause of sexism, not because the search has failed but because, they argue, there is no such thing. Rather, they argue, there are diverse, geographically specific, historically varying causes and fragmented standpoints inclusive of gender and other (ethnic, class, sexual) forces (Nicholson, 1990).

This brings us to the contemporary feminist argument I noted at the outset, which states, at its most extreme, that it is not just the dualism of femininity/masculinity that is socially constructed but femaleness/maleness itself. It is not the existence of two genders that generates sexism but the other way around; in other words, women and men are not just made, but made up. Not only is there no essential woman's nature, as traditionalists (and some feminists) have believed. And not only is there no universal female experience, as most feminists have heretofore argued, in their advocacy of sisterhood. That we divide humans into two genders is a social artifact, according to this radical new argument, and the way this division happens differs enormously across eras and societies.

This approach to the study of gender, and hence of sexism with all its institutional and ideological facets, parallels schools of thought that view many taken-for-granted concepts and problems as socially constructed rather than as naturally occurring or arising spontaneously in society. One particular example is race, and another is crime. What this approach suggests is not that real experiences around gender, race, or crime do not exist. It means that how we label and explain these experiences involves fluid choices rather than inevitabilities. There are no essences to such concepts as woman or man, black or white, criminal or victim, other than what we attach to them. What it means to be a woman or man, black or white, a criminal or victim changes dramatically with time and varies tremendously across cultures.

After acknowledging that something is socially constructed, there is still much to be done. Sexism, no more than racism or crime, cannot be 'deconstructed' away by academic analysis such as the aforementioned. We want to know how and, if possible, who and why, and, above all, what to do about it. This practical urgency will require the continuous generation of 'feminist roots and a radical orientation' for criminology as it considers specific victimizations and injustices.

2. A second, related aspect of the feminist critique concerns the question of whether science and expertise are fundamentally gendered and racially based.

Within criminology, the necessary first steps of this critique, including those begun in 'Etiology', were to challenge traditional assumptions about women, redirect the search for the causes of women's behaviors to their circumstances and experiences, and implicitly hold out the desirability of a fuller range of experiences and behaviors open to all, regardless of gender.

But the next steps were to explore whether science and philosophy are masculine in an even more profound sense than merely male-dominated and male-oriented. Only recently has feminism undertaken critiques of both science and law as gendered in method and philosophical base as well as in overt content (Benhabib and Cornell, 1987; Nicholson, 1990; Sunstein, 1990). In other words, the argument is that the fundamental premises of science and law are not neutral with respect to gender or with respect to cultural ethnicity. It has been difficult to see these biases because they are hidden in taken-for-granted ways of conceptualization, often nearly invisible.

One task, along with making visible and depathologizing femaleness in science and law, is to make visible and denormalize maleness. Unfortunately, criminology and criminal law have not yet been subjected to this level of critique, although recent efforts have been made (Daly and Chesney-Lind, 1988; Smart, 1989). As was true 20 years ago, criminology is implicitly about men, unless it is feminist – in which case it is only about women! And much of the latter is restricted to querying which traditional (masculinist) theories may pertain to women's behaviors!

An example of how criminology might conduct this critique of criminology as fundamentally gendered would be to use the problem of women not being taken seriously as victims and witnesses. Alongside the challenges to common negative images of women victims/witnesses (untrustworthy, provocative, complicit), we would analyse for its gendered content the normal or idealized positive image of the victim/witness (uninvolved with the victimizer, randomly chosen, harmed in public). One question would be, Is this an implicitly male victim/witness?

Another undone task is to constitute a feminist epistemology and methodology, and there has been much debate over what these might look like, if grounded in women's experiences. There has been little development of an explicitly feminist criminological methodology, although some recent studies of women offenders and victims attempt to involve them as subjects rather than examine them as objects. There is only a glimmer of understanding of exactly how women are made the objects of knowledge and power, of the unconscious male identification of the omniscient gaze of experts in criminology (see Benhabib and Cornell, 1987; Diamond and Quinby, 1988). To see the nexus of policing and correctional power, one must first transgress the traditional framework of criminology (Cain, 1989).

For those attempting to reorient their gaze from that of the controller to the standpoint of the dominated, the question changes from What should the discipline do with these people? to How can certain groups of people use the discipline?

One aspect of this shift must be the denormalizing and stepping outside of the dominant ethnic perspective. Race, unlike gender, has never been ignored in criminology, but this is not to say that mainstream criminology has sensitively or accurately addressed the deep and complex associations between criminalization and racism, or between violence and inequality.[5]

Critical criminology, from the days of 'Etiology' onward, certainly has perceived the enormous effects of race and class on criminal justice. A basic premise has been that correctionalism serves to shape and control the lives of the lower classes and people of color, incorporating different strategies: sometimes universalizing standards of the affluent, other times applying differential standards for the poor.

None the less, there has been little development of these issues within either the critical or feminist paradigms during the past 20 years. There has been scant in-depth examination of criminal justice in minority communities. Among feminists, there has been infrequent intellectual exchange between those concerned with criminalized women offenders, who emphasize the repressive and racist character of criminal justice, and those supporting victims of violence, who emphasize the protective and potentially reconciliatory aspects (Klein, 1988). Yet feminist criminology has the greatest potential of any discipline to make these connections (Bertrand, Daly and Klein, 1992). Women in minority communities often directly perceive criminal justice as neither simple protector nor mere oppressor but as the hydra-headed hybrid it is (Gordon, 1988; Klein, 1990). Feminist criminology would benefit from a reexamination of criminal justice from these women's view-point, thus addressing 'human needs, rather than those of the state'.

3. A third issue that feminist criminology must tackle is that of the definition of crime. As an applied field, criminology has tended to take its scope of study from government and policy rather than chart its own course. But to say merely that crime is anything that breaks the law, while self-evident, is tautological. Crime certainly has no natural or universal status. In fact, formerly criminalized activities are continually being legalized, such as abortion or (in Nevada) prostitution; and new crimes are continually being politically constructed, as in the case of recent laws on domestic violence (Klein, 1981). To take for granted the official definition of crime is to forgo both an analysis of the roots of law and the penal system and the possibility of developing alternative visions of justice.

Early radical criminologists of the 1970s, while not always explicitly challenging the official definition of crime in every discussion such as 'Etiology', rarely accepted it as given, arguing that it is steeped in racial and class and gender domination. Which activities are legal and which illegal and which laws are enforced are connected to the relative degrees of power of those involved. Many of us were very much aware of the necessity for disaggregating and transforming the suspect category crime (Schwendinger and Schwendinger, 1970). Yet even now this enterprise remains in the formative stages.

The feminist critique has the specific potential to contribute to what could be called the deconstruction of the taken-for-granted concept we call crime, through the prism of gender. Both law and order, on the one hand, and its opposite, criminality, on the other, are very much linked to complex constructions of power, including masculinity. But these possible connections are concealed by layers of rarely debated official morality.

In more practical terms, feminists have wrestled with whether to advocate the enhancement or the abolition of the criminal justice 'apparatus of control'. An example of the dilemma is the feminist debate over criminalizing violent or harmful pornography. Recently there have emerged tentative discussions about what feminist justice might look like (Gilligan, 1982; Daly, 1989; Sunstein, 1990; Bertrand et al., 1992). Despite many disagreements over the potential role of criminal justice, there is consensus that it should not resemble the existing cycles of partial punishment that characterize contemporary US criminal justice, 'partial' referring to the deeply rooted systemic biases (Rafter, 1985).

In conclusion, the current feminist debates relevant to criminology are those concerning defining crime and justice for women and men, gender and racial bias in science, and the validity of fundamental scientific concepts based on nature and dualism. Few of these debates have been concluded, few dilemmas resolved. Yet they have advanced our understanding to the point that today a proposed article titled 'Etiology of Female Crime' would probably be challenged. One would very likely be informed that the scientific concept of etiology is suspect, that the term 'female' must be deconstructed, and that the definition of crime itself should be reexamined.

NOTES

1 One important thing to note in assessing our accomplishments and limits is that most of us were European-American (as distinct from African-, Asian-, or Latino-American), although we did focus on racism as a fundamental issue for feminist criminology.

2 I was inspired to do this by the work then being engaged in by one of my professors, Herman Schwendinger (Schwendinger and Schwendinger, 1974).

3 Ironically, biologism is more influential in feminist theory than in contemporary criminology. Within the movement to end violence against women, influential works have drawn upon implicit assumptions about male biology (e.g., physical strength, sexual aggression) as explaining rape and other victimizations (Brownmiller, 1975; MacKinnon, 1989). Furthermore, feminist legal defenses for accused women have evolved around such controversial conceptualizations as the premenstrual syndrome.

4 Within mainstream criminology, and its ongoing search for the causes of crime, there has been little interest in this search for the roots of patriarchy. Unfortunately, gender issues have largely remained ignored, as in the days of 'Etiology'.

5 Instead, criminologists debate the accuracy and meaning of African-American, Latino, and Anglo/European rates of criminality in an exercise even longer and less productive than the debate over women's and men's rates.

REFERENCES

Benhabib, S. and Cornell, D. (eds) (1987) *Feminism as Critique: On the Politics of Gender*. Minneapolis: University of Minnesota.

Bertrand, M.-A. (1991) 'Advances in feminist epistemology of the social control of women'. Presented at the American Society of Criminology, San Francisco, November.

Bertrand, M.-A., Daly, K. and Klein, D. (eds) (1992) *Proceedings of the International Feminist Conference on Women, Law and Social Control*. Vancouver: International Centre for the Reform of Criminal Law and Criminal Justice Policy.

Brownmiller, S. (1975) *Against Our Will: Men, Women and Rape*. New York: Simon and Schuster.

Cain, M. (ed.) (1989) *Growing Up Good: Policing the Behaviour of Girls in Europe*. Newbury Park, CA: Sage.

Daly, K. (1989) 'New feminist definitions of justice', *Proceedings of the First Annual Women's Policy Research Conference*. Washington, DC: Institute for Women's Policy Research.

Daly, K. and Chesney-Lind, M. (1988) 'Feminism and criminology', *Justice Quarterly*, 5: 4.

Diamond, I. and Quinby, L. (eds) (1988) *Feminism and Foucault: Reflections on Resistance*. Boston, MA: Northeastern University Press.

Gilligan, C. (1982) *In a Different Voice: Psychological Theory and Women's Development*. Cambridge, MA: Harvard University Press.

Gordon, L. (1988) *Heroes of Their Own Lives: the Politics and History of Family Violence*. New York: Viking.

Klein, D. (1981) 'Violence against women: some considerations regarding its causes and its elimination', *Crime and Delinquency*, 27: 1.

Klein, D. (1988) 'Women and criminal justice in the Reagan era'. Presented at the Academy of Criminal Justice Sciences, San Francisco, April.

Klein, D. (1990) 'Losing (the war on) the war on crime', *Critical Criminologist*, 2: 4.

MacKinnon, C. (1989) *Towards a Feminist Theory of the State*. Cambridge, MA: Harvard University Press.

Nicholson, L. (ed.) (1990) *Feminism/Postmodernism*. New York: Routledge.

Rafter, N. (1985) *Partial Justice: Women in State Prisons, 1800–1935*. Boston, MA: Northeastern University Press.

Schwendinger, H. and Schwendinger, J. (1970) 'Defenders of order or guardians of human rights?' *Issues in Criminology*, 5: 2.

Schwendinger, H. and Schwendinger, J. (1974) *The Sociologists of the Chair*. New York: Basic Books.

Smart, C. (1989) *Feminism and the Power of Law*. New York: Routledge.

Sunstein, C. (ed.) (1990) *Feminism and Political Theory*. Chicago: University of Chicago Press.

18

Explaining male violence

Lynne Segal

'I have never been free of the fear of rape,' Susan Griffin declared in a memorable article in the radical Californian magazine *Ramparts* back in 1971, adding: 'I never asked why men raped; I simply thought it one of the many mysteries of human nature.'[1] Nearly two decades later – decades in which feminists have repeatedly asked the question, devoting books and articles to finding the answer – the puzzle of men's cruelty to women remains only just a little less mysterious. Griffin herself had an answer. In patriarchal culture, she argued, the basic elements of rape are present in all heterosexual relationships: 'If the professional rapist is to be separated from the average dominant heterosexual, it may be mainly a quantitative difference.'[2] Men in our culture are taught and encouraged to rape women as the symbolic expression of male power. Rape serves as 'a kind of terrorism' enabling men to control women and make them dependent: 'Rape is the quintessential act of our civilization.'[3]

Other feminists in those early days of women's liberation, including Kate Millett and Shulamith Firestone in the US, did not share Griffin's analysis that rape and male violence play such a central role in establishing and perpetuating male power.[4] Germaine Greer's popular feminism, urging women to become tough, hedonistic and autonomous, dismissed outright the significance of men's use of violence against women.[5] And in Britain, the early feminist texts (the classic books of Juliet Mitchell and Sheila Rowbotham, for example) assigned male violence little weight in their analysis of the way in which the sexual division of labour and its concordant ideologies produce men's power and women's subordination.[6] It was the publication of Susan Brownmiller's international bestseller *Against Our Will* in 1975 which was to prove a landmark in feminist thinking, in providing an analysis of male power which placed rape and male violence at the centre of the feminist problematic.[7]

Retrospectively, it is startling to realize that rape and men's violence towards women became a serious social and political issue only through feminist attention to them. There is no woman over 40 who cannot recall men's jokes trivializing rape as a violation which women secretly desire. This was true whatever the grouping of men, and however terrifying and violent the sexual assaults in the headline a mere twenty

From *Slow Motion: Changing Masculinities, Changing Men*, pp. 233–71. (London: Virago, 1990.)

or so years ago. There was much merriment, at that time, among male staff in the psychology department of Sydney University when I was a student over a rapist known as 'The Slasher', who climbed into women's bedrooms at dead of night raping and knifing women. The day the joking died was the day the headlines replaced 'the Slasher' stories with accounts of 'the Mutilator' – the deadly deeds of a man attacking *men's* genitals late at night in the Sydney parks.

There are still men today, pronouncing legal judgments, treating wounded women, writing psychological tracts, laughing with their peers, who downgrade women's suffering at the hands of men. The same cultural misogyny fuels their sentiments, but not the same casual ignorance, the same 'innocent' complicity with men's expressions of hatred and contempt for women. Today, they know they are doing it despite, and perhaps because of, the passionate protests and organized resistance of so many women against the many acts of male violence towards their sex. The first job of feminist analysis – and one which was performed with considerable success – was to expose the myths surrounding rape and male violence.

MYTHS OF RAPE: SEXIST AND ANTI-SEXIST

The first rape myth, swiftly exposed in feminist writing, was the idea that rape was a rare event in modern society, the product of some pathological sex-crazed maniac. Rape is a common event, often planned by the rapist, who usually has a wife or girlfriend, and attacks a woman he knows. The second rape myth concerns the assumption of men's desire to protect women from violence. Police, hospital and judicial treatment of rape victims were rapidly revealed to be frequently hostile to the assaulted woman, more protective of the 'rights' of the rapist (of his self-proclaimed 'misreading' of a woman's rejection as assent) than the rights of a woman – at any time, in any place – to say 'no' to sex. To take just one example from what is now a multitude of studies, Elizabeth Stanko's *Intimate Intrusions* (1985), based upon her research in Britain and the United States, describes the police and the courts as 'the second assailant' in so far as they have in practice so often made it hard for women to press charges against attackers or get convictions: 'Above all, the process of inquiry – from police to prosecutors to judges – is assaultive to women.'[8] Feminists emphasized that the prevalence of rape as a social practice exists precisely because of the myths surrounding it: because of the belief that women 'invite' or provoke attack, that men can be 'victims' of their own overpowering sex drive. Rape is a product, they argued, not of male libido, but rather of a culture which encourages men to see sexual activity as a way of 'conquering' women, and of a society which allows men to indulge in the sexual exploitation and physical abuse of women without, in many cases, fear of punishment.[9]

There are other rape myths, however, which dominant strands of feminist thinking have not demolished. Indeed, they have underwritten them. Susan Griffin, for example, states bluntly (and falsely): 'Men are not raped.'[10] And Brownmiller's popular elaboration of Griffin's analysis begins from certain basic definitions and premises about 'rape' which endorse at least some of the prevailing beliefs and myths surrounding it. She sees it as an 'accident of biology' that men can rape, and women cannot:

> When men discovered that they could rape, they proceeded to do it . . . Indeed one of the earliest forms of male bonding must have been the gang rape of one woman by a band of marauding men. This accomplished, rape became not only a male prerogative, but man's basic weapon of force against woman, the principal agent of his will and her fear.[11]

But what, apart from lack of inclination and possibly access to weapons, is to prevent a woman (or marauding gang of women) from buggering a man with bottle, fist or tongue, or from demanding orgasm through oral sex? These are, after all, among the most common forms of male sexual assault on women, and well within women's capacities should we so choose. (Feminists long ago rejected the misleading definition of 'rape' exclusively as forced penile penetration of the vagina.) I have little doubt that just a few women have precisely so chosen, as I seem to remember one or two men have alleged in courts in the US. After all – any woman could argue in her own defence should prosecution attend such rape – do men not fantasize about sexual assault by women? Against Brownmiller it seems clear to me that men's capacity to rape has very little to do with some men's *proclivity* to rape, and other men's tendency to condone it – any more than women's capacity to cook can explain why a few wives drop poison in their husband's supper, and other women have celebrated such deeds in song.[12] So why do men rape?

To men's biological capacity to rape, Brownmiller adds her conviction that men rape women as part of a conscious and collective, transhistorical and transcultural, political strategy to ensure women's subjection to them. Rapists are the 'shock troops' of patriarchy, necessary for male domination.[13] Some men may not rape, but only because their power over women is already secured by the rapists who have done their work for them: rape 'is nothing more or less than a conscious process of intimidation by which *all men* keep *all women* in a state of fear'.[14]

The force of Brownmiller's argument derives from her exposure of men's long-standing silence about violence against women, which in itself enables her to clarify many aspects of the history of rape. Although this very silence means we have little evidence of the historical incidence of rape, it seems unlikely that it was unknown in, say, late nineteenth-century Vienna. Yet Sigmund Freud, who not only developed the most complex and sophisticated psychology of human behaviour we possess, but based his life's work on theories of human sexuality and human aggression, failed to give even passing mention to rape – except in a philosophical aside illustrating differences between conscious and unconscious motivation.[15] Alfred Kinsey and the sex researchers at the Kinsey Institute, although interviewing tens of thousands of men and women in the late 1940s and early 1950s, dismissed the significance and horror of rape in women's lives, suggesting most 'rape' cases, as they referred to them, were the result of women attempting to conceal their sexual activity. They further claimed that only a small proportion of sexual advances made to young girls involved physical assault, and that when they did any consequent psychological damage could be attributed to 'cultural conditioning' rather than to anything intrinsic to the experience itself.[16] Like so many feminists in the years just before and since the publication of her book, Brownmiller exposed the routine and chilling under-reporting of rape, its extremely high incidence, the tendency of authorities and professionals (mostly male) to blame women who are raped for 'victim-precipitation' – that is, causing men's violence against them. The explanation of rape, Brownmiller – and all feminists – would now agree, cannot be sought in terms of isolated acts by individual rapists. It can only be seriously approached in terms of the wider social context of the power of men, and a general cultural contempt for women.

The weakness of Brownmiller's argument, however, is its sweeping general-ization in the face of evidence that the prevalence of rape in modern Western societies is neither historically nor cross-culturally universal. Peggy Reeves Sanday in her oft-cited anthropological work shows that the extent of rape in different societies varies considerably. She contrasts societies which are relatively 'rape-free', like West Sumatra, with those which are most 'rape-prone', like the United States. The former, in her description, are societies in which women are respected and influential members of their community, participating in public decision making, and where 'the relationship between the sexes tends to be symmetrical and equal'.[17] They are also societies with far lower levels of overall violence. Other anthropological studies of pre-industrial societies have reported little or no sexual violence. Margaret Mead's well-known study of the Arapesh American Indians, although now surrounded by controversy, reported a gentle, non-aggressive society and culture, free from sexual violence.[18] The accounts we possess of some African hunter–gatherer societies, like that of the Mbuti, report the same low incidence of violence, and no evidence of rape or sexual violence. Notwithstanding the methodological problems associated with such studies, they do seem to indicate that sexual violence against women (or men) corresponds closely to the general level of violence in a society.[19]

Somewhat less controversially, historical studies of Western societies also suggest wide variation in the incidence of rape. Roy Porter has carefully sifted historical data on British society. The writings of women in diaries and elsewhere provide no evidence of female fears of the menace of rape in pre-industrial England – despite the expression of a multitude of other fears.[20] Early feminists – from Mary Astell to Mary Wollstonecraft – decried the wrongs of women, yet did not mention rape. Those nineteenth-century feminists who wrote and campaigned against sexual abuses (child prostitution and the forcible medical examination of prostitutes) likewise fail to mention anxiety about rape. Porter concludes that rape, and women's fears of it, probably did not loom so large then as they do today. Contrary to Brownmiller's history of rape, it does not seem that rape was the principal agent used to subordinate women in this period. The historical reality of men's oppression and exploitation of women in British society is not in doubt. But what Porter suggests is that men had little need to employ the threat of rape to maintain their dominance: 'Men no more cherished the threat of the rapist in the wings to maintain their authority over women than property owners encouraged thieves to justify the apparatus of law and order.'[21]

A study of eighteenth-century Massachusetts by Barbara Lindemann comes to similar conclusions.[22] Only one rape per decade reached the high court before 1729, and the *recorded* rape level remained consistently low throughout the century, averaging one every two years. Neither wars, the presence of high concentrations of bored and lonely American and British troops, nor economic crises and rootless destitution affected recorded rape levels. Lindemann considers, more fully than Porter, the possibilities of unreported rape and, more significantly still, the narrow definition of rape – defined by law and custom to refer exclusively to a woman who resisted a man who had no rights of sexual access to her. One reason so few rape cases occurred, she suggests, was because sexual assaults committed by upper- and middle-class men on servants would not be perceived as rapes, even by the women victims. They were a form of men's sexual assertion of authority for which neither wives nor servants would have legal redress. Notwithstanding these factors, however, Lindemann nevertheless argues that 'The conclusion is inescapable that the number of rape prosecutions was so much smaller in eighteenth-century Massachusetts than it is today because many fewer rapes were committed in proportion to the population.'[23] She attributes this to the cultural condemnation and frequent punishment of extra-marital sexual activity by men and women alike, and to the belief that women were as interested in sex as men: 'The rape prototype of female enticement, coy female resistance, and ultimate male conquest was not built into the pattern of normal sexual relations.'[24] This was a culture which, while securely patriarchal, discouraged rape, and a community which offered fewer opportunities for its perpetration.

Other studies highlight historical contrasts in men's expression of sexual violence. Writing of the high incidence of husband–wife violence in working-class lives in London between 1870 and 1914, when many wives 'did not hesitate to beat up their husbands' (though it was the former who would more likely be injured in violent rows), Ellen Ross links such violence to the upheavals of domestic life and men's power in the home caused, in particular, by male unemployment and chronic family poverty.[25] This overt physical antagonism between men and women was usually over money; men's failure or inability to provide for wife and children inducing women to challenge their domestic authority. And yet despite this violence, and despite men's belief in the 'right' of husbands to beat up wives, Ross suggests that London's pub culture in the generations before the First World War was 'less poisonously misogynous' than it would later become: 'Sexuality was not yet the domestic and social battleground it had become by the mid-twentieth century or the locus of the belligerent assertion of male power.'[26]

Even in contemporary Western societies the prevalence of rape, and its threat, seem to vary greatly: the United States, for example, has not twice, but over seventeen times the rate of reported rapes as Britain, (34.5 forcible rapes per 100,000 of population in 1979 compared to 2 per 100,000 in the United Kingdom in 1981).[27] Rather than being the indispensable weapon used by men to ensure the subordination of women, might not rape be the deformed behaviour of men accompanying the destabilization of gender relations, and the consequent contradictions and insecurities of male gender identities, now at their peak in modern America? It may be, as Porter wryly observes, an anachronism 'to assume that all the world has been America'.[28] Although it may be a possibility, of course, and a disastrous one – not only for women – that all the world could become North America!

In terms of developing a sexual politics against rape and male violence, it hardly seems helpful to refuse to distinguish, in the manner of Brownmiller and so many subsequent Western feminists, between men who rape and men who don't. Although not without its justifications, it is a politics of the profoundest pessimism. Feminists' increasing despair at the ever-mounting evidence of men's sexual violence against women is captured by Brownmiller when she says: 'Never one to acknowledge my vulnerability, I found myself forced by my sisters in feminism to look it squarely in the eye.'[29] It was the new visibility of the extent and the horror of rape, especially for feminists engaged in aiding its victims to cope with the trauma, which created the rising levels of feminist fear and anger. 'All men are potential rapists', became the disturbing slogan of many a feminist activist in the late 1970s and 1980s. The rapist is 'the man next door', whoever he might be; he is the man in our beds, the father of our children, the man who 'pays the rent'.[30] 'It was almost as if,' Ann Snitow comments, 'by naming the sexual crimes, by ending female denial, we frightened ourselves more than anyone else.'[31]

Is any man a potential rapist? The simple answer, I believe, is 'no' – in so far as the word 'potential' has any practical significance. Is any woman a potential victim? In theory, yes; in practice, the risk we face is far greater for some women than for others. Both these statements, however, are not just controversial but explosive in feminist discourse. They need the most careful study.

They are explosive because what feminist analysis has so far been unwilling to explore is why *some* men become rapists and use violence against women, and *some* men do not. The reasons feminists have been unwilling to make such distinctions are important. First, it is seen as a reversion to an individual, rather than a social, treatment of the problem of rape. (Although it seems to me that no human problems, however apparently 'individual', from cancer to catatonic schizophrenia, can ever be adequately understood isolated from their social context.) Secondly, it is seen as facilitating victim-blaming – if we can differentiate between men, then it can be suggested that some women are more likely to choose violent rather than non-violent men – a form of explanation insidiously popular amongst male (and a few female) professionals and social scientists. Finally, it is seen as letting men off the hook, for all men are certainly a part of the climate and culture of misogyny which permits violence against women to occur with so very little protest or protection from men, (though a handful of men, now growing in number, have always protested – from John Stuart Mill to pro-feminist men today).

[. . .] [F]eminists are right to proclaim that the cause of violent crimes against women cannot be located *simply* in pathological individuals, brutal families, or the stresses and humiliations of poverty and racism (alongside the violent sub-cultures) of many rapists, batterers and murderers. But, contrary to many feminist claims currently being made, these factors are also crucial in understanding *which* men are most likely to resort to sexual violence or violence against women and children, what *type* of violence they are most likely to display, and which women are most likely to be its targets. The wider causes of men's violence must be located in societies which construct 'masculinity' in terms of the assertion of heterosexual power (in its polarized difference from 'femininity'), and which continue to see sex as sinful, while locating the object of sexuality in women, and the subject of sexual desire in men. But this does not mean that any man could be Peter Sutcliffe, even when, like his younger peers on the Leeds football grounds, they may delight in taunting police with chants of 'You'll never catch the Ripper' and '11–0' (referring to what was then the number of Sutcliffe's victims).[32]

Peter Sutcliffe was nicknamed 'the Yorkshire Ripper'. In her analysis of the hundred years of 'Ripper' stories and iconography since the original Jack the Ripper murdered and mutilated five prostitute women in London in 1888, Judith Walkowitz points to the crucial role of the popular press in establishing the Ripper as a media hero, and amplifying the threat of male violence to women. The message of the Ripper mythology, as Walkowitz sees it, was to establish the cities as a dangerous place for women, and to sanction the covert expression of male antagonism toward women, as well as to buttress male authority over them. But feminists, Walkowitz agues, need to probe behind Ripper mythology to uncover the complex reality it masks:

> By flattening history into myth, the Ripper story has rendered all men suspect, vastly increasing female anxieties, and obscuring the distinct material conditions that generate sexual antagonism and male violence . . . In the 'real' world, neither male violence nor female victimization has single-root causes or effects. Only our cultural nightmares and media fantasies construct life this way.[33]

Women are right to see our society as riddled with the cultural expression of contempt for them as the subordinate sex – a contempt by no means confined to pornography. The continuum of men's violence is real in the very particular sense that it is experienced by women as such, in a world where we are everywhere threatened by petty acts of violence or at least of sexual intrusiveness. Overall, women are less at risk from men's violence in public than are other men. But women feel more vulnerable. They feel more vulnerable because, as Elizabeth Stanko illustrates from her research, and women know from everyday experience, if we include all the forms of intimidation women suffer at men's hands – the smacking of lips, muttering of obscenities, kerb crawling, grabbing of breasts and so on – women are subject to a kind of constant intimidation.[34] When a flasher jumps out at a woman, or a voyeur lurks at our window, he is usually not a rapist or killer. But he just might be. His actions certainly serve to make the world feel unsafe for women, particularly when we are likely to have read fairly recently of some serious sex attack – always given greater media prominence than men's attacks on men.

There is a continuum of men's violence in so far as the effects of the variety of men's intrusive acts all contribute to women's experience of lack of safety. What is not convincing, however, is some feminists' insistence that all men really are similar in terms of the individual threat they pose for women. We need to get to grips with the paradox that while women are mainly afraid of men whom they do not know, those women who are physically attacked are generally assaulted by men they do know.

As feminists, however, we can agree that a society which equates masculinity with assertiveness, sexual and otherwise, is one which encourages and condones men's violence against women. People with power have usually been allowed to express anger at, and often use force against, the less powerful with relative impunity. It is surely true that a central aspect of men's use of violence against women lies in social assumptions of men's right to dominate women and expect servicing from them. This has allowed men to express anger and use physical force to get what they want, and get away with it – at least in the domestic sphere.

[. . .]

IS VIOLENCE MASCULINE?

One reason it has been so easy to ignore women's relationship to violence is that terms like 'power', 'force', 'aggression' – so seemingly direct and obvious – are not the simplest to define. Feminism begins from an awareness that relations between men and women have, in all known places and times, occurred in a context in which there has been an apparently inextricable connection between gender and power – though it has assumed different forms and obtained to differing degrees. Feminists writing on men and violence have always tended to see this power as an exclusively uni-directional, top-down process. Viewed in this way, women's participation in maintaining or undermining men's ability to control them according to their own needs, is obscured. But this is not how power has been theorized in more traditional sociological literature or, indeed, more sophisticated feminist analysis. Power relations imply a process whereby those with power can organize those who are less powerful according to their own ends. Yet this, according to sociologists like Anthony Giddens, does not necessarily – indeed, does not 'normally' – take the form of any straightforward process of control through threat, force or violence. Rather, the exercise of power involves the deployment of resources and skills to which some people have easier access, the use of force being exceptional.[35] And despite this differential access to resources, power relations, as Kathy Davis argues, are always reciprocal, involving some degree of autonomy and dependence in each direction:

> Power is never a simple matter of 'have's' and 'have-not's'. Such a conception can only lead to an over-estimation of the power of the powerful, closing our eyes to the chinks in the armour of the powerful as well as the myriad ways that the less powerful have to exercise control over their lives, even in situations where stable, institutionalised power relations are in operation.[36]

[. . .] [I]n the area of personal life it has been women's traditional lack of any access to independent economic resources within the institution of marriage which has been pivotal to the normal functioning of domestic arrangements to suit men's needs. That institution is now changing, and the most significant common characteristic of women who are battered today is not their gender as such, but their lack of resources to escape marriages which are violent.[37] That domestic violence is not some fatality inscribed in male–female relationship is apparent if we look at the different types of family forms which have generated violence. In *Naming the Violence: Speaking Out About Lesbian Battery*, various women in the United States write of their experience of violence from other women. 'We were so clear about violence as a feature of heterosexual relationships', Barbara Hart announces with dismay, that it was hard to accept that 'women were beating and terrorizing other women'.[38] These women report daily episodes of violence which had become almost a ritual in some lesbian bars in the US. Moreover, as with heterosexual violence, other lesbians 'shunned the victim', and the battered lesbian tended to blame herself.[39] In addition to psychological and emotional abuse, these battered lesbians reported physical assault with guns, knives and other weapons, experiences of rape, sex on demand, forced sex with others and involuntary prostitution – as well as economic dependence through their partners' control over income and assets.

Most of the dynamics of lesbian battering seem similar to heterosexual abuse – in particular, the tendency of women to remain in an abusive relationship because they feel sorry for the abuser: 'I still feel sorry for her . . . She came from a home situation where she was the victim of what ranged from severe neglect to severe violence,' writes Donna Cecere of her experience of lesbian battering;[40] 'I had returned once again because . . . she said she had changed . . . when she held me I felt loved . . . In those years love was a scarcity and myself hardly lovable,' explains Cedar Gentlewind;[41] 'On a subconscious level I felt I got what I deserved . . . Our social life was limited to gay bars where physical violence was also the norm,' writes Breeze.[42] The majority of the lesbian abusers and victims in these accounts are working-class lesbians, many from ethnic minorities, often already victims of family violence, as well as of the violence and racism which surrounded them.

That women, like men, are affected by the general levels of violence in their immediate social world is illustrated by the dramatic increase in young women's involvement in crimes of violence over the last fifteen years – an increase which, comparatively, exceeds that of men. As Anne Campbell[43] argues in criticism of much feminist rhetoric, virtually all our ideas of 'femininity' are derived from the middle-class 'lady': 'To be pampered, egotistical, passive, nurturant, care-taking requires a certain level of economic security.'[44] Surveying a sample of 251 16-year-old schoolgirls from working-class areas of London, Liverpool and Oxford, Campbell found that 89 per cent of them had engaged in at least one physical fight. These girls were mostly negative in their attitudes towards fighting, but did not see it as 'unfeminine'. The Borstal girls whom Campbell interviewed, on the other hand, mostly felt positive about fighting, regarding it as a good way of releasing anger and perhaps settling disputes.[45] As with young male delinquents, most of them had been systematically encouraged to fight by their parents: 'In the subcultures from which these girls come . . . interpersonal violence emerges as the vicious expression of hatred and resentment and is bound up more with establishing and maintaining a tough reputation than with settling disputes.'[46] Campbell is critical of a feminism which can see women only as the victims of men, rather than of a whole economic system: 'Without more radical change in the *status quo*, we shall succeed only in liberating women into poverty, alienation, despair and crime – along with the men who are there already.'[47]

Somewhat analogously, in his study of soccer hooliganism David Robins asks, 'What were the girls doing while the boys were putting the boot in on the terraces?' Many, he says, were up there with them. There are more boys than girls, but the girls do join in the fighting and encourage the boys to fight. Where girls' gangs do exist, they not only emulate but may try to outdo the boys: 'We go to fight,' the 'Leeds Angels' told Robins. 'At Norwich and Ipswich, there's sometimes more lasses than boys . . . When Man. United played Norwich . . . there were forty arrests and must have been thirty lasses got arrested.'[48] It is obvious that in our society physical violence and aggression are still predominantly seen as masculine, and acted out by men. Working-class images of masculinity in terms of physical hardness have been analysed, by Tolson and others, as bound up with the requirements of manual labour and earning a wage.[49] This image persists. But with nearly 50 per cent of young people in Britain leaving school for the dole, enjoying little hope and not much self-esteem, Robins argues, 'working-class youth is being forced into a position of wildness and irresponsibility'.[50] And while they may lack the symbolic trappings of power which unite the boys in their sexist jibes, and rarely be afforded the same freedom of action and choice as men, young women, Robins believes, are learning that they can give as good as they get.[51]

Nevertheless, even if aggressiveness is not exclusively masculine, there is no doubt that the media and the public at large display their greatest anxiety in connection with violence from men – mostly from young, working-class men in the form of vandalism, gang fighting and football hooliganism. Football hooliganism is now a prominent cause of social concern, feeding the appeal of the law-and-order politics of the right. Some researchers, like Peter Marsh, Elizabeth Rosser and Rom Harre, have stressed that the degree of serious violence, as distinct from ritual violence, on and around the football terraces is exaggerated by the media.[52] But the extent of young men's violence is not merely a media creation; nor is its association with lower working-class men merely middle-class phobia. Sociological studies of football hooliganism like that of Eric Dunning and his co-workers conclusively demonstrate men in football gangs are overwhelmingly from the lower levels of the working class.[53]

We need to ask why a type of working-class aggressive masculinity seems such a perennial feature of the social environment, a feature which feeds today's feminist imagination in its equation of violence as male. Dunning stresses the inevitable homogeneity, circumscribed horizons and narrow neighbourhood loyalty of men who, at best, will find work in low-paid, insecure and monotonous jobs at the bottom of all authority and status hierarchies. Moreover, in jobs sex-typed as male, and with home lives which remain strongly male-dominated (the equivalent jobs for women of this class, if any, being even less well-paid, lower in status and more insecure) the lower working class tends to produce sharper sex-role distinctions than other classes. Just as there is a Black underclass, so too a white underclass exists, in which the men are the most likely of all men to adopt aggressive masculine styles and values whereby status is imparted to males who display loyalty and bravery in confrontation with 'outsiders':

> Apart from the 'street smartness' and the ability and willingness to fight of [these] adolescent and adult males, they have few power resources. This combination of narrowness of experience and relative lack of power tends to lead them to experience unfamiliar territories and people as potentially threatening. Usually it is only in the company of people with whom they are familiar and who are like themselves that it is possible for them to feel a relatively high degree of social assurance . . . Being part of a group augments their sense of power. It also provides an opportunity to hit back at the established order and a context in which they can 'get their own back' by taking the lid off . . . For a short illusory moment, the outsiders are the masters; the downtrodden come out on top.[54]

The aggressive masculine style which lower working-class men are more likely to value and adopt is not exclusive to them, of course. It is part of the fantasy life, if not the lived reality, of the majority of men enthralled by images of masculinity which equate it with power and violence (where would Clint Eastwood be without his gun?). However, [. . .] there is no simple, direct transmission from men's shared collective fantasies to individual action. Many social mediators – from school, jobs, friends, family, religion and politics – affect the way fantasies may, or may not, be channelled into any active expression, and determine what form, if any, they take. It is the sharp and frustrating conflict between the lives of lower working-class men and the image of masculinity as power, which informs the adoption and, for some, the enactment, of a more aggressive masculinity. There was a time, it seems to me, when feminists would not so readily have lost sight of the significance of class oppression for the sake of identifying a universal male beastliness. But that was in the early 1970s, when they were more actively a part of a left politics and culture which was itself more aware than it has since become of the alienation and exploitation of class relations.

It is true that women can be, and some women are, as aggressive and violent in their behaviour as men. It is equally true, however, that from an early age most women are made aware of obstacles to, and restrictions upon, the expression of their own desires – if only in terms of the expectations of those around them. More importantly, they are sensitized to greater social condemnation of female aggressiveness – shouting, fighting, swearing, and so on. Men, by contrast, in sport and elsewhere, are more likely to engage in at least the rituals of aggressive display, and to enjoy greater social tolerance for many forms of aggressiveness.[55] But I think we should be aware that women's greater suppression of their own aggressiveness is not necessarily healthy. Women's attempts to disown and repress their feelings of frustration and aggression almost certainly result in them turning such aggressive feelings against themselves, or their children. This would account for women's greater vulnerability to depression (twice as high as that for men), or expression of their own pain in emotional abuse of children.[56] It can also lead, as Janet Sayers, Jean Temperley and other clinicians have commented, to women projecting their aggressiveness and violence onto others, or onto the world in general, as in paranoia and agoraphobia.[57] [. . .] Jane Temperley suggests from her work with women patients that we need to consider whether women's perception of, preoccupation with, and (as she sees it), attempts to provoke, men's violence towards them may not be overlaid by women's projection onto men of their own frustration and aggression; thereby permitting women to retain for themselves a monopoly of moral righteousness and virtue.[58]

Some feminists, as well as therapists like Temperley, have seen in women's image of the all-pervasive, all-threatening nature of male sexuality a projection of women's own aggression and frustrated power. The political journalist and feminist Sarah Benton, for example, suggests that because it is less legitimate for women to be aggressive and powerful, and because women are so much less accustomed to taking responsibility for the state of the world, 'We project all power, all aggression onto men.'[59] Moreover, she detects in this projection, women's denial of sexuality itself. It is a denial bound up with women's difficulties, in sexist culture, in accepting and expressing their own sexuality; in particular, acknowledging that female sexuality can be violent, cruel and 'perverse', as well as masochistic, yielding and submissive. 'The barrier to that acceptance and expression,' she concludes, 'is more to do with our difficulty in getting, exercising and accepting power in the world at large than any specific sexual threat from men.'[60] The fact that women are the main readers of true-crime magazines, which provide salacious case histories of the most violent, often sexual, murders,[61] and that it is women who appear in large numbers at the trials of sex-murderers, where they feel entitled to display extremes of punitive moral aggression, verbal and even physical violence, would seem to lend credence to such interpretations.

However, the extent of some men's violence (and many men's viciousness) towards women, the tendency of those with power either to ignore, or to blame women for, its occurrence, and the general context of men's greater power and control over women, all dictate that we must proceed very carefully – more carefully, at any rate, than Temperley and most psychoanalytic commentators have done – in assigning weight to arguments which suggest that women may have an investment in feeling victimized. There is no doubt that many women's entrapment in dependency and powerlessness makes it hard for them to envisage any positive alternative to suppressing their own anger and aggression, while suffering, however resentfully, aggression from men. At the same time, it is equally necessary for us to be aware of the need to understand what happens to women's aggression, and for us to abandon the dominant conservative and, more recently, popular feminist attachment to ideal-ized views of women as inherently less aggressive than men (the former regarding the connection as biological, the latter, more often as cultural).

Some of our perception of the social and cultural linkages between 'masculinity' and violence derives from the fact that most of the socially approved uses of force and violence are the jobs of men – the police, army, prison officers and other agencies of 'defence' or correction. It is men, rarely women, who are officially trained to use violence in our society. Yet, as David Morgan has sug-gested, it is possible in this context to reverse the assumed causal links between 'masculinity' and 'violence'. It could be that it is men's socially determined, systematic involvement in various forms of violence which constructs our notions of 'masculinity' as indissolubly linked with 'violence'.[62] The idea that what is at stake here is state violence in the hands of men (rather than, as many feminists believe, male violence in the hands of the state) is supported by reports of women's use of force and violence when they are placed in jobs analogous to men's. For example, women prison officers were found in the late nineteenth century to enforce especially severe physical and corporal punishments on their female charges for any infraction of rules, by comparison with those meted out to male prisoners and, to this day, women prisoners are more consistently punished and put on report by their female warders than are men.[63] Similar tales of women's zealous use of force, including conventionally defined acts of violence, appear in many accounts of women's behaviour when in positions of power. I have written elsewhere of the importance, often repressed or denied, of women's relationship to war and military enterprises – both as passionate supporters of war or in active military engagement themselves.[64] Nevertheless, it is apparent that some men's far more formal training in the use of violence is something which can, and from the evidence of women who are battered, frequently does, spill over into these men's greater resort to violence in their personal relations with women. It also provides opportunities for men to be particularly vicious to women (and men) in the performance of their public 'duties'.

Black feminists have been especially clear on the importance of distinguishing state violence from male violence. Kum-Kum Bhavnani, for example, rejects the idea that violence is 'essentially masculine'.[65] Such a belief denies Black people's knowledge of white women's past-and-present involvement in violence against them – both directly and indirectly, in the support and maintenance of racism. And it denies the reality of the violent resistance from women and men which state violence brings forth, not only in the streets of South Africa, but in the street-uprisings in Britain. The idea prevalent in white feminism that women 'have a peaceful past', Bhavnani argues, is offensive to Black women. (It is also, she points out, offensive to white working-class women, who have resisted, sometimes violently, attacks on their class; and to the many other women who have fought against violent and oppressive conditions; not to mention its erasure from the history of the British Suffragettes.) 'Non-violence' and 'peace', she suggests, 'end up being meaningless terms unless given tactical accuracy and political definition.'[66] Bell Hooks also writes of learning to oppose war from the persistent anti-war stance of her grandfather, and of so many other southern Black males who despised militarism: 'Their attitudes showed us that all men do not glory in war, that all men who fight in wars do not necessarily believe that wars are just, that men are not inherently capable of killing.'[67] The sex-role division of labour, she adds, does not necessarily mean that women think differently from men about violence and about war, or, if empowered to do so, would behave differently from men.

'Violence', it seems clear, cannot simply be equated with 'masculinity'. Neither are unitary phenomena.[68] There are many different types of violence, some legitimated (from sport and beating children to policing and warfare), and some not (from corporal punishment in state schools to rape and murder). It is easier to understand and attempt to change men's engagement in these practices if we see them as operating relatively autonomously from each other. Fear of violent attack from men is the number one fear of women in both the United States and Britain today. But if we want to get to the heart of this fear, and the escalating rates of violence in modern society, we shall have to include, but also progress beyond, an analysis simply in terms of gender.

There are links between the prevalence of violence in our society and men's endeavours to affirm 'masculinity'. And these links may even be reinforced, as the assumption of men's dominance over women – part of the traditional definition of 'masculinity' – continues to crumble. Some men, increasingly less sure of such dominance, may resort more to violence in their attempt to shore up a sense of masculine identity. Others, however, may not. Some, indeed, may turn towards new ways of being men, even to support for the struggle to put an end to men's use of violence against women. For it should be remembered that some men have always worked in organizations committed to non-violence – even when this has provoked the harshest ridicule and punishment, including loss of life. At the same time, there are links between the prevalence of violence in our society and forces which are not those of gender: forces, indeed, which have impacted as strongly on certain groups of men as on certain groups of women. There are close and frightening links between sexual assaults on women and the steep rise in crimes of violence generally – the primary targets of which remain other men.

These links derive from the creation of a permanent underclass in many Western X societies – an underclass built around dependency, self-destruction, crimes against property and crimes against people. Twenty years ago Martin Luther King was shot dead for his vision of a more equal society in the United States. Today, that society is less equal than it was then: the number of Black men leaving college is dropping, the life expectancy of Black men is decreasing, and economic segregation of Blacks and other ethnic minorities into the worst schools, worst neighbourhoods, worst housing (if they are lucky), is increasing.[69] Drugs, crime and violence are the desperate and bitter legacy of the withdrawal of federal funds for welfare provision at local and national levels throughout the United States, in combination with the smashing of the trade union movement and the restructuring of labour which has destroyed many traditional working-class jobs and communities. With welfare all but eliminated, homelessness, joblessness, and hopelessness are now escalating in the US. Comparing the contrasting appeals of Martin Luther King for peaceful Black protest thirty years ago, with Malcolm X's justification of violent protest a decade later, Black film-maker Spike Lee announces today:

Things are leaning more towards Malcolm than King. I think black people are getting tired of being on the receiving end of police shotguns and nightsticks.[70]

Who or what, then, do we identify as the epitome of 'violence', 'abuse' and 'aggression' in that society? Those who are brutalized within an underworld of fear and exploitation? Or those who may never directly engage in acts of violence or physical force, but orchestrate the degradation and brutalization of others? The entrenchment of poverty and inequality in the world's richest nation has occurred precisely to enable the US to spend ever-greater sums on 'defence', and to conduct aggressive interventions in Central America, the Caribbean and the Middle East.

The USA shows the way, and through the International Monetary Fund (IMF) and other such agencies attempts to force the American Way on the rest of the world. If feminists are seriously to confront the problem of sexual violence, we shall have to realize that what we are up against is something far worse, something far more destructive, than the power of any man, or group of men – something worse even than the mythic qualities of Dworkin's atomic phallus. However old-fashioned it may sound in these 'post-political' days, what we are confronting here is the barbarism of private life reflecting back the increased barbarism of public life, as contemporary capitalism continues to chisel out its hierarchies along the familiar grooves of class, race and gender.

NOTES

1 Susan Griffin, Reprint from 'Rape: the All-American Crime', *Ramparts*, September (1971), pp. 26–35.

2 Ibid.

3 Ibid., p. 35.

4 Shulamith Firestone, *The Dialectic of Sex* (London, Paladin; 1971); Kate Millett, *Sexual Politics* (London, Abacus, 1972).

5 Germaine Greer, *The Female Eunuch*, (London, MacGibbon and Kee, 1970).

6 Sheila Rowbotham, *Women's Consciousness, Man's World* (Harmondsworth, Penguin, 1973); Juliet Mitchell, *Woman's Estate* (Harmondsworth, Penguin, 1971).

7 Susan Brownmiller, *Against Our Will: Men, Women and Rape* (Harmondsworth, Penguin, 1976).

8 Elizabeth Stanko, *Intimate Intrusions: Women's Experience of Male Violence*, (London, Routledge and Kegan Paul, 1985).

9 For example, see Rape Crisis Centre, *First Annual Report* (London, Rape Counselling and Research Project, 1977).

10 Griffin, 'Rape', p. 22.

11 Brownmiller, *Against Our Will*, p. 14.

12 For example, as portrayed in the British film, *Distant Voices, Still Lives*, Terrence Davies, 1988.

13 Brownmiller, *Against Our Will*, p. 209.

14 Ibid., p. 15.

15 See John Forrester, 'Rape, seduction and psychoanalysis' in Tomaselli, S. and Porter, R. (eds), *Rape* (Oxford, Basil Blackwell, 1985), p. 62.

16 See Alfred Kinsey et al., *Sexual Behaviour in the Human Female*, (Philadelphia, W.B. Saunders, 1953), p. 410, pp. 116–22.

17 Peggy Reeves Sanday, 'Rape and the silencing of the feminine', in Tomaselli and Porter, *Rape*, p. 85.

18 Margaret Mead, *Sex and Temperament in Three Primitive Societies* (London, Routledge and Kegan Paul, 1985).

19 For these and other examples see Julia Schwendinger and Herman Schwendinger, *Rape and Inequality* (London, Sage, 1983).

20 Roy Porter, 'Rape – does it have a historical meaning?', in Tomaselli and Porter, *Rape*.

21 Ibid., p. 223.

22 Barbara Lindemann, '"To ravish and carnally know": rape in eighteenth-century Massachusetts', *Signs*, Autumn, vol. 10 (1984), 1.

23 Ibid., p. 72.

24 Ibid., p. 81.

25 Ellen Ross, '"Fierce questions and taunts": married life in working-class London, 1870–1914', *Feminist Studies*, 8, 2 (Fall) (1982).

26 Ibid., p. 596.

27 Figures quoted in Donald West, 'The victim's contribution to sexual offences' in June Hopkins (ed.), *Perspectives on Rape and Sexual Assault* (London, Harper and Row, 1984), p. 2. See also Jennifer Temkin, *Rape and the Legal Process* (London, Sweet and Maxwell, 1987), p. 9.

28 Porter, 'Rape', p. 223.

29 Brownmiller, *Against Our Will*, p. 9.

30 Ruth Hall et al., *The Rapist Who Pays the Rent: Evidence Submitted by Women Against Rape, Britain to the Criminal Law Revision Committee* (Bristol, Falling Wall Press, 1981); Ruth Hall, *Ask Any Woman: a London Inquiry into Rape and Sexual Assault* (Bristol, Falling Wall Press, 1985).

31 Ann Snitow, 'Retrenchment vs transformation: the politics of the anti-pornography movement', in Kate Ellis et al., *Caught Looking* (New York, Caught Looking Inc., 1985).

32 Quoted in David Robins, *We Hate Humans* (Harmondsworth, Penguin, 1984).

33 Judith Walkovitz, 'Jack the Ripper and the myth of male violence', in *Feminist Studies*, 8, 3 (Fall) (1982), p. 570.

34 A recent survey by Granada Television found that nearly 70 per cent of women said they either would not go out alone after dark or would go out only if absolutely necessary: 34 per cent of these women had been sworn at in the street, 18 per cent had experienced unwelcome physical contact and 17 per cent had been flashed at. (World In Action, Granada TV 9.1.89.)

35 Anthony Giddens, *The Constitution of Society* (Cambridge, Polity, 1984), p. 175.

36 Kathy Davis, 'The Janus-Face of power: some theoretical considerations involved in the study of gender and power'. Paper presented at the symposium, *The Gender of Power* (Leiden, 1987).

37 J. Pahl, *Private Violence and Public Policy* (London, Routledge and Kegan Paul, 1985).

38 Barbara Hart, in Kerry Lobel (ed.), *Naming the Violence: Speaking Out About Lesbian Battery* (Washington: Seal Press, 1986), p. 9.

39 Ibid., p. 11.

40 In ibid., p. 24.

41 Ibid., p. 46.

42 Ibid., p. 52.

43 Anne Campbell, *Girl Delinquents* (Oxford, Basil Blackwell, 1981), p. 133.

44 Ibid., p. 150.

45 Ibid., p. 181.

46 Ibid., p. 196.

47 Ibid., p. 237.

48 Robins, *We Hate Humans*, p. 95.

49 Andrew Tolson, *The Limits of Masculinity* (London, Tavistock, 1977).

50 Robins, *We Hate Humans*, p. 153.

51 Ibid., p. 152.

52 Peter Marsh, Elizabeth Rosser and Rom Harre, *The Rules of Disorder* (London, Routledge and Kegan Paul, 1978).

53 Eric Dunning, Patrick Murphy and John Williams, *The Roots of Football Hooliganism: an Historical and Sociological Study* (London, Routledge, 1988), p. 187.

54 Ibid., p. 206.

55 Marsh et al., *Rules of Disorder*.

56 See Janet Sayers, *Sexual Contradictions: Psychology, Psychoanalysis, and Feminism* (London, Tavistock, 1986), p. 142.

57 Ibid., p. 157; Jane Temperley, 'Our Own Worst Enemies: Unconscious Factors in Female Disadvantage', *Free Associations*, Pilot Issue (1984).

58 Temperley, ibid.

59 Sarah Benton, (unpub.), 'Notes on sex and violence'.

60 Ibid.

61 D. Cameron and E. Frazer, *The Lust to Kill* (Cambridge, Polity, 1987).

62 David Morgan (unpub.), Research Proposals for a Study of Masculinity and Violence.

63 Russell Dobash, R. Emerson Dobash, Sue Gutteridge, *The Imprisonment of Women* (Oxford, Basil Blackwell, 1986), p. 86, p. 147.

64 Lynn Segal, *Is the Future Female?* (London, Virago, 1987), ch. 5.

65 Kum-Kum Bhavnani, 'Turning the World Upside Down' in *Charting the Journey* (London, Sheba, 1987), p. 264.

66 Ibid., p. 268.

67 Bell Hooks, 'Feminism and militarism: a comment', in Hooks, *Talking Back: Thinking Feminist – Thinking Black* (London, Sage, 1989).

68 Morgan, Masculinity and Violence.

69 Martin Walker, *The Guardian*, 16 January 1989.

70 Spike Lee talks to Steve Goldman, 'Heat of the Moment', *Weekend Guardian*, 24–5 June, 1989, p. 15.

Part III

The problem of crime II: Criminalization

INTRODUCTION

This selection of readings has been chosen to reflect the parameters of a *radical/critical criminology* which first emerged in the 1960s in the USA and the UK. Although the readings reveal the disparate nature of such an enterprise, they all mark a reappraisal of the purpose and function of criminology, in particular by taking to task positivism's obsession with scientifically establishing the causes of crime. Here the key concern is with definitional questions – why have certain behaviours and situations come to be defined as criminal? – rather than with questions of individual motivation. Collectively, they illustrate how the central problematic of criminology is not simply one of crime causation, but of accounting for particular processes of criminalization.

The publication of Taylor, Walton and Young's *The New Criminology* in 1973 has long been taken as the starting-point of a radical criminology in Britain. The text remains influential because it provides a sweeping critique of the hitherto unchallenged sovereignty of traditional criminology in which psychologists, psychiatrists and forensic scientists dominated. Rather than focusing on the elusive search for the individual causes of crime, Taylor, Walton and Young sought to illustrate how 'crime' was socially constructed through the power and capacity of state institutions to define and confer criminality on others. This intellectual shift set out to reject notions of 'crime as behaviour' and to promote a more critical conception of 'crime as a political process'. In tandem, the aim was to transform criminology from a science of social control and into a struggle for social justice.

The *New Criminology* did not, however, emerge in a social and intellectual vacuum. Its impact lay as much in its attempt to synthesize several different existing theoretical perspectives, as it did in the desire to establish a new criminological agenda. In particular it maintained links with interactionism (and questions of meaning and authenticity), labelling (and questions of power and social control) and Marxism (and questions of class relations and political economy).

This part thus opens with readings from the American criminologists Matza and Sykes, Becker and Chambliss who have provided classic expressions of these three important theoretical precursors. Matza and Syke's contribution not only provides a critique of positivism and its tendency to dehumanize delinquent behaviours, but also contends that most delinquent values are not particularly different from those held by the mainstream. Their work forces us to appreciate the ways in which young people themselves view and justify their actions. Becker's work also adopts a position of anti-positivism by arguing that definitions of crime and deviance will remain forever problematic because deviance only arises through the imposition of social judgements on the behaviour of others. Deviance can never be an absolutely known fact, because it is constructed through a series of transactions between rule makers and rule violators. Deviance only occurs when a particular social group is able to make its own rules and enforce their application onto others. The proposition that the causes of deviance lie in processes of law creation and social control effectively stood the premises of mainstream criminology on their head. While labelling opened the way for analyses of how deviance was defined and processed, a Marxist-based analysis furthered that the relations between definer and defined are not simply subjective encounters. Control agencies have an institutional location and function within particular structures of power. Chambliss contends that processes of criminalization depend not simply on relations of power, but on power derived from particular class and economic positions: thus the propositions that acts are defined as criminal because it is in the interests of a ruling class to define them as such and that criminal law, in the main, is designed to protect ruling class interests.

In these ways the study of crime was effectively politicized as part of a more comprehensive sociology of the state and political economy, in which questions of political and social control took precedence over behavioural and correctional issues. Criminology's horizons were expanded, whereby the key problematic was no longer to simply account for individual criminal acts, but to reach a critical understanding of the social order and the power to criminalize.

The radical agenda established by Taylor, Walton and Young subsequently burgeoned in a number of directions. The reading from Box illustrates how 'common sense' assumptions about crime can be effectively challenged once we acknowledge the widespread nature of personal and property crime engaged in by corporate officials, manufacturers, governments and governmental control agencies. The prevalence of a restricted image of 'the crime problem' in public and political discourse, he argues, is but another way in which the social control of the underprivileged and the powerless is maintained.

Hall's contribution is to account for the origins and impact of an increasingly authoritarian – law and order – society in Britain in the 1970s. Here he finds the signifier of 'crime' to play a crucial role not only in legitimating greater powers for law enforcement agencies, but in justifying the diminution of civil, welfare and labour rights and the development of disciplinary forms of regulation in all walks of life. The end result, he envisaged, would be the further criminalization of protest movements and deviant lifestyles.

Scraton and Chadwick set out the parameters for a critical criminology in the 1990s. Acknowledging earlier tendencies to reduce all crime to the materialism of capitalist economies, they argue that the true complexity of processes of power, the marginalization of particular groups and criminalization can only be grasped by remaining alive to the impact of, and interplay between, the three primary determining contexts of production, reproduction and neo-colonialism. As such, a critical analysis of crime and criminal justice must be grounded in analyses of patriarchy and racism as well as class and economic production.

Hall's analysis is reflected in an important body of literature that details how in many societies 'crime' has become a racialized discourse. At certain moments, 'race' coalesces with other key signifiers of crime such as 'the inner city', 'the underclass', 'immigration' etc. We have included a seminal article by Angela Y. Davis that examines the consequences of US government policy shifting from social welfare to crime control mode. She argues that the utilization of mass incarceration to make problem groups 'disappear' has become 'big business'. What Davis defines as a 'prison industrial complex' relies on racialized assumptions of criminality, racialized fear of crime and racist criminal justice practices. She also points to the role that the corporatization of crime control now plays within the US economy. For Davis the only progressive course of action is to mobilize public opinion behind a radical abolitionist project.

The selection from Hulsman takes critical criminology in yet another direction. Again noting that notions of crime depend crucially on formulations of criminal law, he argues that the concept of crime should be abandoned once and for all. The development of a radical and critical understanding of crime, criminalization and criminal justice is continually hampered by the continual return to a state-constructed category as its key empirical referent. Rather he suggests the development of alternative conceptual tools – 'troubles', 'problems' – which can be recognized and responded to without recourse to the formal, narrow and inflexible processes of criminal justice.

The final reading is Jock Young's clarion call for a 'left realist' criminology that is imaginative, sophisticated and above all policy relevant. The essential requirement for radical criminology is to a reorient itself to take crime seriously by addressing the problem of conventional criminality and generating effective crime control policies. To make 'realism' a fundamental marker, Young rejects virtually every aspect of radical criminology's idealist imaginary.

19

Techniques of neutralization

Gresham M. Sykes and David Matza

In attempting to uncover the roots of juvenile delinquency, the social scientist has long since ceased to search for devils in the mind or stigma of the body. It is now largely agreed that delinquent behavior, like most social behavior, is learned and that it is learned in the process of social interaction.

The classic statement of this position is found in Sutherland's theory of differential association, which asserts that criminal or delinquent behavior involves the learning of (a) techniques of committing crimes and (b) motives, drives, rationalizations, and attitudes favorable to the violation of law.[1] Unfortunately, the specific content of what is learned – as opposed to the process by which it is learned – has received relatively little attention in either theory or research. Perhaps the single strongest school of thought on the nature of this content has centered on the idea of a delinquent subculture. The basic characteristic of the delinquent subculture, it is argued, is a system of values that represents an inversion of the values held by respectable, law-abiding society. The world of the delinquent is the world of the law-abiding turned upside down and its norms constitute a countervailing force directed against the conforming social order. Cohen[2] sees the process of developing a delinquent subculture as a matter of building, maintaining, and reinforcing a code for behavior which exists by opposition, which stands in point by point contradiction to dominant values, particularly those of the middle class. Cohen's portrayal of delinquency is executed with a good deal of sophistication, and he carefully avoids overly simple explanations such as those based on the principle of 'follow the leader' or easy generalizations about 'emotional disturbances'. Furthermore, he does not accept the delinquent sub-culture as something given, but instead systematically examines the function of delinquent values as a viable solution to the lower-class, male child's problems in the area of social status. Yet in spite of its virtues, this image of juvenile delinquency as a form of behavior based on competing or countervailing values and norms appears to suffer from a number of serious defects. It is the nature of these defects and a possible alternative or modified explanation for a large portion of juvenile delinquency with which this paper is concerned.

From 'Techniques of neutralization: a theory of delinquency', *American Sociological Review*, 1957, 22: 664–70.

The difficulties in viewing delinquent behavior as springing from a set of deviant values and norms – as arising, that is to say, from a situation in which the delinquent defines his delinquency as 'right' – are both empirical and theoretical. In the first place, if there existed in fact a delinquent subculture such that the delinquent viewed his illegal behavior as morally correct, we could reasonably suppose that he would exhibit no feelings of guilt or shame at detection or confinement. Instead, the major reaction would tend in the direction of indignation or a sense of martyrdom.[3] It is true that some delinquents do react in the latter fashion, although the sense of martyrdom often seems to be based on the fact that others 'get away with it' and indignation appears to be directed against the chance events or lack of skill that led to apprehension. More important, however, is the fact that there is a good deal of evidence suggesting that many delinquents *do* experience a sense of guilt or shame, and its outward expression is not to be dismissed as a purely manipulative gesture to appease those in authority. Much of this evidence is, to be sure, of a clinical nature or in the form of impressionistic judgements of those who must deal first hand with the youthful offender. Assigning a weight to such evidence calls for caution, but it cannot be ignored if we are to avoid the gross stereotype of the juvenile delinquent as a hardened gangster in miniature.

In the second place, observers have noted that the juvenile delinquent frequently accords admiration and respect to law-abiding persons. The 'really honest' person is often revered, and if the delinquent is sometimes overly keen to detect hypocrisy in those who conform, unquestioned probity is likely to win his approval. A fierce attachment to a humble, pious mother or a forgiving, upright priest (the former, according to many observers, is often encountered in both juvenile delinquents and adult criminals) might be dismissed as rank sentimentality, but at least it is clear that the delinquent does not necessarily regard those who abide by the legal rules as immoral. In a similar vein, it can be noted that the juvenile delinquent may exhibit great resentment if illegal behavior is imputed to 'significant others' in his immediate social environment or to heroes in the world of sport and entertainment. In other words, if the delinquent does hold to a set of values and norms that stand in complete opposition to those of respectable society, his norm-holding is of a peculiar sort. While supposedly thoroughly committed to the deviant system of the delinquent subculture, he would appear to recognize the moral validity of the dominant normative system in many instances.[4]

In the third place, there is much evidence that juvenile delinquents often draw a sharp line between those who can be victimized and those who cannot. Certain social groups are not to be viewed as 'fair game' in the performance of supposedly approved delinquent acts while others warrant a variety of attacks. In general, the potentiality for victimization would seem to be a function of the social distance between the juvenile delinquent and others and thus we find implicit maxims in the world of the delinquent such as 'don't steal from friends' or 'don't commit vandalism against a church of your own faith'.[5] This is all rather obvious, but the implications have not received sufficient attention. The fact that supposedly valued behavior tends to be directed against disvalued social groups hints that the 'wrongfulness' of such delinquent behavior is more widely recognized by delinquents than the literature has indicated. When the pool of victims is limited by consideration of kinship, friendship, ethnic group, social class, age, sex, etc., we have reason to suspect that the virtue of delinquency is far from unquestioned.

In the fourth place, it is doubtful if many juvenile delinquents are totally immune from the demands for conformity made by the dominant social order. There is a strong likelihood that the family of the delinquent will agree with respectable society that delinquency is wrong, even though the family may be engaged in a variety of illegal activities. That is, the parental posture conducive to delinquency is not apt to be a positive prodding. Whatever may be the influence of parental example, what might be called the 'Fagin' pattern of socialization into delinquency is probably rare. Furthermore, as Redl has indicated, the idea that certain neighborhoods are completely delinquent, offering the child a model for delinquent behavior without reservations, is simply not supported by the data.[6]

The fact that a child is punished by parents, school officials, and agencies of the legal system for his delinquency may, as a number of observers have cynically noted, suggest to the child that he should be more careful not to get caught. There is an equal or greater probability, however, that the child will internalize the demands for conformity. This is not to say that demands for conformity cannot be counteracted. In fact, as we shall see shortly, an understanding of how internal and external demands for conformity are neutralized may be crucial for understanding delinquent behavior. But it is to say that a complete denial of the validity of demands for conformity and the substitution of a new normative system is improbable, in light of the child's or adolescent's dependency on adults and encirclement by adults inherent in his status in the social structure. No matter how deeply enmeshed in patterns of delinquency he may be and no matter how much this involvement may outweigh his associations with the law-abiding, he cannot escape the condemnation of his deviance. Somehow the demands for conformity must be met and answered; they cannot be ignored as part of an alien system of values and norms.

In short, the theoretical viewpoint that sees juvenile delinquency as a form of behavior based on the values and norms of a deviant subculture in precisely the same way as law-abiding behavior is based on the values and norms of the larger society is open to serious doubt. The fact that the world of the delinquent is embedded in the larger world of those who conform cannot be overlooked nor can the delinquent be equated with an adult thoroughly socialized into an alternative way of life. Instead, the juvenile delinquent would appear to be at least partially committed to the dominant social order in that he frequently exhibits guilt or shame when he violates its proscriptions, accords approval to certain conforming figures, and distinguishes between appropriate and inappropriate targets for his deviance. It is to an explanation for the apparently paradoxical fact of his delinquency that we now turn.

As Morris Cohen once said, one of the most fascinating problems about human behavior is why men violate the laws which they believe. This is the problem that confronts us when we attempt to explain why delinquency occurs despite a greater or lesser commitment to the usages of conformity. A basic clue is offered by the fact that social rules or norms calling for valued behavior seldom if ever take the form of categorical imperatives. Rather, values or norms appear as *qualified* guides for action, limited in their applicability in terms of time, place, persons, and social circumstances. The moral injunction against killing, for example, does not apply to the enemy during combat in time of war, although a captured enemy comes once again under the prohibition. Similarly, the taking and distributing of scarce goods in a time of acute social need is felt by many to be right, although under other circumstances private property is held inviolable. The normative system of a society, then, is marked by what Williams has termed *flexibility*; it does not consist of a body of rules held to be binding under all conditions.[7]

This flexibility is, in fact, an integral part of the criminal law in that measures for 'defenses to crimes' are provided in pleas such as nonage, necessity, insanity, drunkenness, compulsion, self-defense, and so on. The individual can avoid moral culpability for his criminal action – and thus avoid the negative sanctions of society – if he can prove that criminal intent was lacking. *It is our argument that much delinquency is based on what is essentially an unrecognized extension of defenses to crimes, in the form of justifications for deviance that are seen as valid by the delinquent but not by the legal system or society at large.*

These justifications are commonly described as rationalizations. They are viewed as following deviant behavior and as protecting the individual from self-blame and the blame of others after the act. But there is also reason to believe that they precede deviant behavior and make deviant behavior possible. It is this possibility that Sutherland mentioned only in passing and that other writers have failed to exploit from the viewpoint of sociological theory. Disapproval flowing from internalized norms and conforming others in the social environment is neutralized, turned back, or deflected in advance. Social controls that serve to check or inhibit deviant motivational patterns are rendered inoperative, and the individual is freed to engage in delinquency without serious damage to his self image. In this sense, the delinquent both has his cake and eats it too, for he remains committed to the dominant normative system and yet so qualifies its imperatives that violations are 'acceptable' if not 'right'. Thus the delinquent represents not a radical opposition to law-abiding society but something more like an apologetic failure, often more sinned against than sinning in his own eyes. We call these justifications of deviant behavior techniques of neutralization; and we believe these techniques make up a crucial component of Sutherland's 'definitions favorable to the violation of law'. It is by learning these techniques that the juvenile becomes delinquent, rather than by learning moral imperatives, values or attitudes standing in direct contradiction to those of the dominant society. In analyzing these techniques, we have found it convenient to divide them into five major types.

The denial of responsibility In so far as the delinquent can define himself as lacking responsibility for his deviant actions, the disapproval of self or others is sharply reduced in effectiveness as a restraining influence. As Justice Holmes has said, even a dog distinguishes between being stumbled over and being kicked, and modern society is no less careful to draw a line between injuries that are unintentional, i.e., where responsibility is lacking, and those that are intentional. As a technique of neutralization, however, the denial of responsibility extends much further than the claim that deviant acts are an 'accident' or some similar negation of personal accountability. It may also be asserted that delinquent acts are due to forces outside of the individual and beyond his control such as unloving parents, bad companions, or a slum neighborhood. In effect, the delinquent approaches a 'billiard ball' conception of himself in which he sees himself as helplessly propelled into new situations. From a psychodynamic viewpoint, this orientation toward one's own actions may represent a profound alienation from self, but it is important to stress the fact that interpretations of responsibility are cultural constructs and not merely idiosyncratic beliefs. The similarity between this mode of justifying illegal behavior assumed by the delinquent and the implications of a 'sociological' frame of reference or a 'humane' jurisprudence is readily apparent.[8] It is not the validity of this orientation that concerns us here, but its function of deflecting blame attached to violations of social norms and its relative independence of a particular personality structure.[9] By learning to view himself as more acted upon than acting, the delinquent prepares the way for deviance from the dominant normative system without the necessity of a frontal assault on the norms themselves.

The denial of injury A second major technique of neutralization centers on the injury or harm involved in the delinquent act. The criminal law has long made a distinction between crimes which are *mala in se* and *mala prohibita* – that is between acts that are wrong in themselves and acts that are illegal but not immoral – and the delinquent can make the same kind of distinction in evaluating the wrongfulness of his behavior. For the delinquent, however, wrongfulness may turn on the question of whether or not anyone has clearly been hurt by his deviance, and this matter is open to a variety of interpretations. Vandalism, for example, may be defined by the delinquent simply as 'mischief' – after all, it may be claimed, the persons whose property has been destroyed can well afford it. Similarly, auto theft may be viewed as 'borrowing', and gang fighting may be seen as a private quarrel, an agreed upon duel between two willing parties, and thus of no concern to the community at large. We are not suggesting that this technique of neutralization, labelled the denial of injury, involves an explicit dialectic. Rather, we are arguing that the delinquent frequently, and in a hazy fashion, feels that his behavior does not really cause any great harm despite the fact that it runs counter to law. Just as the link between the individual and his acts may be broken by the denial of responsibility, so may the link between acts and their consequences be broken by the denial of injury. Since society sometimes agrees with the delinquent, e.g., in matters such as truancy, 'pranks', and so on, it merely reaffirms the idea that the delinquent's neutralization of social controls by means of qualifying the norms is an extension of common practice rather than a gesture of complete opposition.

The denial of the victim Even if the delinquent accepts the responsibility for his deviant actions and is willing to admit that his deviant actions involve an injury or hurt, the moral indignation of self and others may be neutralized by an insistence that the injury is not wrong in light of the circumstances. The injury, it may be claimed, is not really an injury; rather, it is a form of rightful retaliation or punishment. By a subtle alchemy the delinquent moves himself into the position of an avenger and the victim is transformed into a wrong-doer. Assaults on homosexuals or suspected homosexuals, attacks on members of minority groups who are said to have gotten 'out of place', vandalism as revenge on an unfair teacher or school official, thefts from a 'crooked' store owner – all may be hurts inflicted on a transgressor, in the eyes of the delinquent. As Orwell has pointed out, the type of criminal admired by the general public has probably changed over the course of years and Raffles no longer serves as a hero;[10] but Robin Hood, and his latter day derivatives such as the tough detective seeking justice outside the law, still capture the popular imagination, and the delinquent may view his acts as part of a similar role.

To deny the existence of the victim, then, by transforming him into a person deserving injury is an extreme form of a phenomenon we have mentioned before, namely, the delinquent's recognition of appropriate and inappropriate targets for his delinquent acts. In addition, however, the existence of the victim may be denied for the delinquent, in a somewhat different sense, by the circumstances of the delinquent act itself. In so far as the victim is physically absent, unknown or a vague abstraction (as is often the case in delinquent acts committed against property), the awareness of the victim's existence is weakened. Internalized norms and anticipations of the reactions of others must somehow be activated, if they are to serve as guides for behavior; and it is possible that a diminished awareness of the victim plays an important part in determining whether or not this process is set in motion.

The condemnation of the condemners A fourth technique of neutralization would appear to involve a condemnation of the condemners or, as McCorkle and Korn have phrased it, a rejection of the rejectors.[11] The delinquent shifts the focus of attention from his own deviant acts to the motives of his violations. His condemners, he may claim, are hypocrites, deviants in disguise, or impelled by personal spite. This orientation toward the conforming world may be of particular importance when it hardens into a bitter cynicism directed against those assigned the task of enforcing or expressing the norms of the dominant society. Police, it may be said, are corrupt, stupid and brutal. Teachers always show favoritism and parents always 'take it out' on their children. By a slight extension, the rewards of conformity – such as material success – become a matter of pull or luck, thus decreasing still further the stature of those who stand on the side of the law-abiding. The validity of this jaundiced viewpoint is not so important as its function in turning back or deflecting the negative sanctions attached to violations of the norms. The delinquent, in effect, has changed the subject of the conversation in the dialogue between his own deviant impulses and the reactions of others; and by attacking others, the wrongfulness of his own behavior is more easily repressed or lost to view.

The appeal to higher loyalties Fifth, and last, internal and external social controls may be neutralized by sacrificing the demands of the larger society for the demands of the smaller social groups to which the delinquent belongs such as the sibling pair, the gang, or the friendship clique. It is important to note that the delinquent does not necessarily repudiate the imperatives of the dominant normative system, despite his failure to follow them. Rather, the delinquent may see himself as caught up in a dilemma that must be resolved, unfortunately, at the cost of violating the law. One aspect of this situation has been studied by Stouffer and Toby in their research on the conflict between particularistic and universalistic demands, between the claims of friendship and general social obligations, and their results suggest that 'it is possible to classify people according to a predisposition to select one or the other horn of a dilemma in role conflict'.[12] For our purposes, however, the most important point is that deviation from certain norms may occur not because the norms are rejected but because other norms, held to be more pressing or involving a higher loyalty, are accorded precedence. Indeed, it is the fact that both sets of norms are believed in that gives meaning to our concepts of dilemma and role conflict.

The conflict between the claims of friendship and the claims of law, or a similar dilemma, has of course long been recognized by the social scientist (and the novelist) as a common human problem. If the juvenile delinquent frequently resolves his dilemma by insisting that he must 'always help a buddy' or 'never squeal on a friend', even when it throws him into serious difficulties with the dominant social order, his choice remains familiar to the supposedly law-abiding. The delinquent is unusual, perhaps, in the extent to which he is able to see the fact that he acts in behalf of the smaller social groups to which he belongs as a justification for violations of society's norms, but it is a matter of degree rather than of kind.

'I didn't mean it.' 'I didn't really hurt anybody.' 'They had it coming to them.' 'Everybody's picking on me.' 'I didn't do it for myself.' These slogans or their variants, we hypothesize, prepare the juvenile for delinquent acts. These 'definitions of the situation' represent tangential or glancing blows at the dominant normative system rather than the creation of an opposing ideology; and they are extensions of patterns of thought prevalent in society rather than something created *de novo*.

Techniques of neutralization may not be powerful enough to fully shield the individual from the force of his own internalized values and the reactions of conforming others, for as we have pointed out, juvenile delinquents often appear to suffer from feelings of guilt and shame when called into account for their deviant behavior. And some delinquents may be so isolated from the world of conformity that techniques of neutralization need not be called into play. None the less, we would argue that techniques of neutralization are critical in lessening the effectiveness of social controls and that they lie behind a large share of delinquent behavior. Empirical research in this area is scattered and fragmentary at the present time, but the work of Redl,[13] Cressey,[14] and others has supplied a body of significant data that has done much to clarify the theoretical issues and enlarge the fund of supporting evidence. Two lines of investigation seem to be critical at this stage. First, there is need for more knowledge concerning the differential distribution of techniques of neutralization, as operative patterns of thought, by age, sex, social class, ethnic groups, etc. On a priori grounds it might be assumed that these justifications for deviance will be more readily seized by segments of society for whom a discrepancy between common social ideals and social practice is most apparent. It is also possible however, that the habit of 'bending' the dominant normative system – if not 'breaking' it – cuts across our cruder social categories and is to be traced primarily to patterns of social interaction within the familial circle. Secondly, there is a need for a greater understanding of the internal structure of techniques of neutralization, as a system of beliefs and attitudes, and its relationship to various types of delinquent behavior. Certain techniques of neutralization would appear to be better adapted to particular deviant acts than to others, as we have suggested, for example, in the case of offenses against property and the denial of the victim. But the issue remains far from clear and stands in need of more information.

In any case, techniques of neutralization appear to offer a promising line of research in enlarging and systematizing the theoretical grasp of juvenile delinquency. As more information is uncovered concerning techniques of neutralization, their origins, and their consequences, both juvenile delinquency in particular, and deviation from normative systems in general may be illuminated.

NOTES

1 E.H. Sutherland, *Principles of Criminology*, revised by D.R. Cressey (Chicago, Lippincott, 1955), pp. 77–80.

2 Albert, K. Cohen, *Delinquent Boys* (Glencoe, Ill., The Free Press, 1955).

3 This form of reaction among the adherents of a deviant subculture who fully believe in the 'rightfulness' of their behavior and who are captured and punished by the

agencies of the dominant social order can be illustrated, perhaps, by groups such as Jehovah's Witnesses, early Christian sects, nationalist movements in colonial areas, and conscientious objectors during World Wars I and II.

4 As Weber has pointed out, a thief may recognize the legitimacy of legal rules without accepting their moral validity. Cf. Max Weber, *The Theory of Social and Economic Organization* (translated by A.M. Henderson and Talcott Parsons) (New York, Oxford University Press, 1947), p. 125. We are arguing here, however, that the juvenile delinquent frequently recognizes *both* the legitimacy of the dominant social order and its moral 'rightness'.

5 Thrasher's account of the 'Itschkies' – a juvenile gang composed of Jewish boys – and the immunity from 'rolling' enjoyed by Jewish drunkards is a good illustration. Cf. F. Thrasher, *The Gang* (Chicago, The University of Chicago Press, 1947), p. 315.

6 Cf. Solomon Kobrin, 'The conflict of values in delinquency areas', *American Sociological Review*, 16 (October, 1951), pp. 653–61.

7 Cf. Robin Williams Jr, *American Society* (New York, Knopf, 1951), p. 28.

8 A number of observers have wryly noted that many delinquents seem to show a surprising awareness of sociological and psychological explanations for their behavior and are quick to point out the causal role of their poor environment.

9 It is possible, of course, that certain personality structures can accept some techniques of neutralization more readily than others, but this question remains largely unexplored.

10 George Orwell, *Dickens, Dali, and Others* (New York, Revnal, 1946).

11 Lloyd W. McCorkle and Richard Korn, 'Resocialization within walls', *Annals of the American Academy of Political and Social Science, 293* (May, 1954), pp. 88–98.

12 See Samuel A. Stouffer and Jackson Toby, 'Role conflict and personality', in T. Parsons and E.A. Shils (eds), *Toward a General Theory of Action* (Cambridge, MA, Harvard University Press, 1951), p. 494.

13 See Fritz Redl and David Wineman, *Children Who Hate* (Glencoe, Ill., The Free Press, 1956).

14 See D.R. Cressey, *Other People's Money* (Glencoe, Ill., The Free Press, 1953).

20

Outsiders

Howard Becker

All social groups make rules and attempt, at some times and under some circumstances, to enforce them. Social rules define situations and the kinds of behavior appropriate to them, specifying some actions as 'right' and forbidding others as 'wrong'. When a rule is enforced, the person who is supposed to have broken it may be seen as a special kind of person, one who cannot be trusted to live by the rules agreed on by the group. He is regarded as an *outsider*.

But the person who is thus labeled an outsider may have a different view of the matter. He may not accept the rule by which he is being judged and may not regard those who judge him as either competent or legitimately entitled to do so. Hence, a second meaning of the term emerges: the rule-breaker may feel his judges are *outsiders*.

In what follows, I will try to clarify the situation and process pointed to by this double-barrelled term: the situations of rule-breaking and rule-enforcement and the processes by which some people come to break rules and others to enforce them.

Some preliminary distinctions are in order. Rules may be of a great many kinds. They may be formally enacted into law, and in this case the police power of the state may be used in enforcing them. In other cases, they represent informal agreements, newly arrived at or encrusted with the sanction of age and tradition; rules of this kind are enforced by informal sanctions of various kinds.

Similarly, whether a rule has the force of law or tradition or is simply the result of consensus, it may be the task of some specialized body, such as the police or the committee on ethics of a professional association, to enforce it; enforcement, on the other hand, may be everyone's job or, at least, the job of everyone in the group to which the rule is meant to apply.

Many rules are not enforced and are not, in any except the most formal sense, the kind of rules with which I am concerned. Blue laws, which remain on the statute books though they have not been enforced for a hundred years, are examples. (It is important to remember, however, that an unenforced law may be reactivated for various reasons and regain all its original force, as recently occurred with respect

From *Outsiders: Studies in the Sociology of Deviance*, pp. 1–18. (New York: Free Press, 1963.)

to the laws governing the opening of commercial establishments on Sunday in Missouri.) Informal rules may similarly die from lack of enforcement. I shall mainly be concerned with what we can call the actual operating rules of groups, those kept alive through attempts at enforcement.

Finally, just how far 'outside' one is, in either of the senses I have mentioned, varies from case to case. We think of the person who commits a traffic violation or gets a little too drunk at a party as being, after all, not very different from the rest of us and treat his infraction tolerantly. We regard the thief as less like us and punish him severely. Crimes such as murder, rape, or treason lead us to view the violator as a true outsider.

In the same way, some rule-breakers do not think they have been unjustly judged. The traffic violator usually subscribes to the very rules he has broken. Alcoholics are often ambivalent, sometimes feeling that those who judge them do not understand them and at other times agreeing that compulsive drinking is a bad thing. At the extreme, some deviants (homosexuals and drug addicts are good examples) develop full-blown ideologies explaining why they are right and why those who disapprove of and punish them are wrong.

DEFINITIONS OF DEVIANCE

The outsider – the deviant from group rules – has been the subject of much speculation, theorizing and scientific study. What laymen want to know about deviants is: why do they do it? How can we account for their rule-breaking? What is there about them that leads them to do forbidden things? Scientific research has tried to find answers to these questions. In doing so it has accepted the common-sense premise that there is something inherently deviant (qualitatively distinct) about acts that break (or seem to break) social rules. It has also accepted the common-sense assumption that the deviant act occurs because some characteristic of the person who commits it makes it necessary or inevitable that he should. Scientists do not ordinarily question the label 'deviant' when it is applied to particular acts or people but rather take it as given. In so doing, they accept the values of the group making the judgment.

It is easily observable that different groups judge different things to be deviant. This should alert us to the possibility that the person making the judgment of deviance, the process by which that judgment is arrived at, and the situation in which it is made may all be intimately involved in the phenomenon of deviance. To the degree that the common-sense view of deviance and the scientific theories that begin with its premises assume that acts that break rules are inherently deviant and thus take for granted the situations and processes of judgment, they may leave out an important variable. If scientists ignore the variable character of the process of judgment, they may by that omission limit the kinds of theories that can be developed and the kind of understanding that can be achieved.[1]

Our first problem, then, is to construct a definition of deviance. Before doing this, let us consider some of the definitions scientists now use, seeing what is left out if we take them as a point of departure for the study of outsiders.

The simplest view of deviance is essentially statistical, defining as deviant anything that varies too widely from the average. When a statistician analyses the results of an agricultural experiment, he describes the stalk of corn that is exceptionally tall and the stalk that is exceptionally short as deviations from the mean or average. Similarly, one can describe anything that differs from what is most common as a deviation. In this view, to be left-handed or redheaded is deviant, because most people are right-handed and brunette.

So stated, the statistical view seems simple-minded, even trivial. Yet it simplifies the problem by doing away with many questions of value that ordinarily arise in discussions of the nature of deviance. In assessing any particular case, all one need do is calculate the distance of the behavior involved from the average. But it is too simple a solution. Hunting with such a definition, we return with a mixed bag – people who are excessively fat or thin, murderers, redheads, homosexuals and traffic violators. The mixture contains some ordinarily thought of as deviants and others who have broken no rule at all. The statistical definition of deviance, in short, is too far removed from the concern with rule-breaking which prompts scientific study of outsiders.

A less simple but much more common view of deviance identifies it as something essentially pathological, revealing the presence of a 'disease'. This view rests, obviously, on a medical analogy. The human organism, when it is working efficiently and experiencing no discomfort, is said to be 'healthy'. When it does not work efficiently, a disease is present. The organ or function that has become deranged is said to be pathological. Of course, there is little disagreement about what constitutes a healthy state of the organism. But there is much less agreement when one uses the notion of pathology analogically, to describe kinds of behavior that are regarded as deviant. For people do not agree on what constitutes healthy behavior. It is difficult to find a definition that will satisfy even such a select and limited group as psychiatrists; it is impossible to find one that people generally accept as they accept criteria of health for the organism.[2]

Sometimes people mean the analogy more strictly, because they think of deviance as the product of mental disease. The behavior of a homosexual or drug addict is regarded as the symptom of a mental disease just as the diabetic's difficulty in getting bruises to heal is regarded as a symptom of his disease. But mental disease resembles physical disease only in metaphor:

> Starting with such things as syphilis, tuberculosis, typhoid fever, and carcinomas and fractures, we have created the class 'illness'. At first, this class was composed of only a few items, all of which shared the common feature of reference to a state of disordered structure or function of the human body as a physiochemical machine. As time went on, additional items were added to this class. They were not added, however, because they were newly discovered bodily disorders. The physician's attention had been deflected from this criterion and had become focused instead on disability and suffering as new criteria for selection. Thus, at first slowly, such things as hysteria, hypochondriasis, obsessive-compulsive neurosis, and depression were added to the category of illness. Then, with increasing zeal, physicians and especially psychiatrists began to call 'illness' (that is, of course, 'mental illness') anything and everything in which they could detect any sign of malfunctioning, based on no matter what norm. Hence, agoraphobia is illness because one should not be afraid of open spaces. Homosexuality is illness because heterosexuality is the social norm. Divorce is illness because it signals failure of marriage. Crime, art, undesired political leadership, participation in social affairs, or withdrawal from such participation – all these and many more have been said to be signs of mental illness.[3]

The medical metaphor limits what we can see much as the statistical view does. It accepts the lay judgment of something as deviant and, by use of analogy, locates its source within the individual, thus preventing us from seeing the judgment itself as a crucial part of the phenomenon.

Some sociologists also use a model of deviance based essentially on the medical notions of health and disease. They look at a society, or some part of a society, and ask whether there are any processes going on in it that tend to reduce its stability, thus lessening its chance of survival. They label such processes deviant or identify them as symptoms of social disorganization. They discriminate between those features of society which promote stability (and thus are 'functional') and those which disrupt stability (and thus are 'dysfunctional'). Such a view has the great virtue of pointing to areas of possible trouble in a society of which people may not be aware.[4]

But it is harder in practice than it appears to be in theory to specify what is functional and what dysfunctional for a society or social group. The question of what the purpose or goal (function) of a group is and, consequently, what things will help or hinder the achievement of that purpose, is very often a political question. Factions within the group disagree and maneuver to have their own definition of the group's function accepted. The function of the group or organization, then, is decided in political conflict, not given in the nature of the organization. If this is true, then it is likewise true that the questions of what rules are to be enforced, what behavior regarded as deviant, and which people labeled as outsiders must also be regarded as political.[5] The functional view of deviance, by ignoring the political aspects of the phenomenon, limits our understanding.

Another sociological view is more relativistic. It identifies deviance as the failure to obey group rules. Once we have described the rules a group enforces on its members, we can say with some precision whether or not a person has violated them and is thus, on this view, deviant.

This view is closest to my own, but it fails to give sufficient weight to the ambiguities that arise in deciding which rules are to be taken as the yardstick against which behavior is measured and judged deviant. A society has many groups, each with its own set of rules, and people belong to many groups simultaneously. A person may break the rules of one group by the very act of abiding by the rules of another group. Is he, then, deviant? Proponents of this definition may object that while ambiguity may arise with respect to the rules peculiar to one or another group in society, there are some rules that are very generally agreed to by everyone, in which case the difficulty does not arise. This, of course, is a question of fact, to be settled by empirical research. I doubt there are many such areas of consensus and think it wiser to use a definition that allows us to deal with both ambiguous and unambiguous situations.

DEVIANCE AND THE RESPONSES OF OTHERS

The sociological view I have just discussed defines deviance as the infraction of some agreed-upon rule. It then goes on to ask who breaks rules, and to search for the factors in their personalities and life situations that might account for the infractions. This assumes that those who have broken a rule constitute a homogeneous category, because they have committed the same deviant act.

Such an assumption seems to me to ignore the central fact about deviance: it is created by society. I do not mean this in the way it is ordinarily understood, in which the causes of deviance are located in the social situation of the deviant or in 'social factors' which prompt his action. I mean, rather, that *social groups create deviance by making the rules whose infraction constitutes deviance*, and by applying those rules to particular people and labeling them as outsiders. From this point of view, deviance is *not* a quality of the act the person commits, but rather a consequence of the application by others of rules and sanctions to an 'offender'. The deviant is one to whom that label has successfully been applied; deviant behavior is behavior that people so label.[6]

Since deviance is, among other things, a consequence of the responses of others to a person's act, students of deviance cannot assume that they are dealing with a homogeneous category when they study people who have been labeled deviant. That is, they cannot assume that these people have actually committed a deviant act or broken some rule, because the process of labeling may not be infallible; some people may be labeled deviant who in fact have not broken a rule. Furthermore, they cannot assume that the category of those labeled deviant will contain all those who actually have broken a rule, for many offenders may escape apprehension and thus fail to be included in the population of 'deviants' they study. In so far as the category lacks homogeneity and fails to include all the cases that belong in it, one cannot reasonably expect to find common factors of personality or life situation that will account for the supposed deviance.

What, then, do people who have been labeled deviant have in common? At the least, they share the label and the experience of being labeled as outsiders. I will begin my analysis with this basic similarity and view deviance as the product of a transaction that takes place between some social group and one who is viewed by that group as a rule-breaker. I will be less concerned with the personal and social characteristics of deviants than with the process by which they come to be thought of as outsiders and their reactions to that judgment.

Malinowski discovered the usefulness of this view for understanding the nature of deviance many years ago, in his study of the Trobriand Islands:

> One day an outbreak of wailing and a great commotion told me that a death had occurred somewhere in the neighborhood. I was informed that Kima'i, a young lad of my acquaintance, of sixteen or so, had fallen from a coco-nut palm and killed himself. . . . I found that another youth had been severely wounded by some mysterious coincidence. And at the funeral there was obviously a general feeling of hostility between the village where the boy died and t!at into which his body was carried for burial.
>
> Only much later was I able to discover the real meaning of these events. The boy had committed suicide. The truth was that he had broken the rules of exogamy, the partner in his crime being his maternal cousin, the daughter of his mother's sister. This had been known and generally disapproved of but nothing was done until the girl's discarded lover, who had wanted to marry her and who felt personally injured, took the initiative. This rival threatened first to use black magic against the guilty youth, but this had not much effect. Then one evening he insulted the culprit in public – accusing him in the hearing of the whole community of incest and hurling at him certain expressions intolerable to a native.
>
> For this there was only one remedy; only one means of escape remained to the unfortunate youth. Next morning he put on festive attire and ornamentation, climbed a

coco-nut palm and addressed the community, speaking from among the palm leaves and bidding them farewell. He explained the reasons for his desperate deed and also launched forth a veiled accusation against the man who had driven him to his death, upon which it became the duty of his clansmen to avenge him. Then he wailed aloud, as is the custom, jumped from a palm some sixty feet high and was killed on the spot. There followed a fight within the village in which the rival was wounded; and the quarrel was repeated during the funeral. . . .

If you were to inquire into the matter among the Trobrianders, you would find . . . that the natives show horror at the idea of violating the rules of exogamy and that they believe that sores, disease and even death might follow clan incest. This is the ideal of native law, and in moral matters it is easy and pleasant strictly to adhere to the ideal – when judging the conduct of others or expressing an opinion about conduct in general.

When it comes to the application of morality and ideals to real life, however, things take on a different complexion. In the case described it was obvious that the facts would not tally with the ideal of conduct. Public opinion was neither outraged by the knowledge of the crime to any extent, nor did it react directly – it had to be mobilized by a public statement of the crime and by insults being hurled at the culprit by an interested party. Even then he had to carry out the punishment himself. . . . Probing further into the matter and collecting concrete information, I found that the breach of exogamy – as regards intercourse and not marriage – is by no means a rare occurrence, and public opinion is lenient, though decidedly hypocritical. If the affair is carried on *sub rosa* with a certain amount of decorum, and if no one in particular stirs up trouble – 'public opinion' will gossip, but not demand any harsh punishment. If, on the contrary, scandal breaks out – everyone turns against the guilty pair and by ostracism and insults one or the other may be driven to suicide.[7]

Whether an act is deviant, then, depends on how other people react to it. You can commit clan incest and suffer from no more than gossip as long as no one makes a public accusation; but you will be driven to your death if the accusation is made. The point is that the response of other people has to be regarded as problematic. Just because one has committed an infraction of a rule does not mean that others will respond as though this had happened. (Conversely, just because one has not violated a rule does not mean that he may not be treated, in some circumstances, as though he had.)

The degree to which other people will respond to a given act as deviant varies greatly. Several kinds of variation seem worth noting. First of all, there is variation over time. A person believed to have committed a given 'deviant' act may at one time be responded to much more leniently than he would be at some other time. The occurrence of 'drives' against various kinds of deviance illustrates this clearly. At various times, enforcement officials may decide to make an all-out attack on some particular kind of deviance, such as gambling, drug addiction, or homosexuality. It is obviously much more dangerous to engage in one of these activities when a drive is on than at any other time. (In a very interesting study of crime news in Colorado newspapers, Davis found that the amount of crime reported in Colorado newspapers showed very little association with actual changes in the amount of crime taking place in Colorado. And, further, that people's estimate of how much increase there had been in crime in Colorado was associated with the increase in the amount of crime news but not with any increase in the amount of crime.)[8]

The degree to which an act will be treated as deviant depends also on who commits the act and who feels he has been harmed by it. Rules tend to be applied more to some persons than others. Studies of juvenile delinquency make the point clearly. Boys from middle-class areas do not get as far in the legal process when they are apprehended as do boys from slum areas. The middle-class boy is less likely, when picked up by the police, to be taken to the station; less likely when taken to the station to be booked; and it is extremely unlikely that he will be convicted and sentenced.[9] This variation occurs even though the original infraction of the rule is the same in the two cases. Similarly, the law is differentially applied to Negroes and whites. It is well known that a Negro believed to have attacked a white woman is much more likely to be punished than a white man who commits the same offense; it is only slightly less well known that a Negro who murders another Negro is much less likely to be punished than a white man who commits murder.[10] This, of course, is one of the main points of Sutherland's analysis of white-collar crime: crimes committed by corporations are almost always prosecuted as civil cases, but the same crime committed by an individual is ordinarily treated as a criminal offense.[11]

Some rules are enforced only when they result in certain consequences. The unmarried mother furnishes a clear example. Vincent[12] points out that illicit sexual relations seldom result in severe punishment or social censure for the offenders. If, however, a girl becomes pregnant as a result of such activities the reaction of others is likely to be severe. (The illicit pregnancy is also an interesting example of the differential enforcement of rules on different categories of people. Vincent notes that unmarried fathers escape the severe censure visited on the mother.)

Why repeat these commonplace observations? Because, taken together, they support the proposition that deviance is not a simple quality, present in some kinds of behavior and absent in others. Rather, it is the product of a process which involves responses of other people to the behavior. The same behavior may be an infraction of the rules at one time and not at another; may be an infraction when committed by one person, but not when committed by another; some rules are broken with impunity, others are not. In short, whether a given act is deviant or not depends in part on the nature of the act (that is, whether or not it violates some rule) and in part on what other people do about it.

Some people may object that this is merely a terminological quibble, that one can, after all, define terms any way he wants to and that if some people want to speak of rule-breaking behavior as deviant without reference to the reactions of others they are free to do so. This, of course, is true. Yet it might be worthwhile to refer to such behavior as *rule-breaking behavior* and reserve the term *deviant* for those labeled as deviant by some segment of society. I do not insist that this usage be followed. But it should be clear that in so far as a scientist uses 'deviant' to refer to any rule-breaking behavior and takes as his subject of study only those who have been *labeled* deviant, he will be hampered by the disparities between the two categories.

If we take as the object of our attention behavior which comes to be labeled as deviant, we must recognize that we cannot know whether a given act will be categorized as deviant until the response of others has occurred. Deviance is not a quality that lies in behavior itself, but in the interaction between the person who commits an act and those who respond to it.

WHOSE RULES?

I have been using the term 'outsiders' to refer to those people who are judged by others to be deviant and thus to stand outside the circle of 'normal' members of the group. But the term contains a second meaning, whose analysis leads to another important set of sociological problems: 'outsiders', from the point of view of the person who is labeled deviant, may be the people who make the rules he had been found guilty of breaking.

Social rules are the creation of specific social groups. Modern societies are not simple organizations in which everyone agrees on what the rules are and how they are to be applied in specific situations. They are, instead, highly differentiated along social class lines, ethnic lines, occupational lines, and cultural lines. These groups need not and, in fact, often do not share the same rules. The problems they face in dealing with their environment, the history and traditions they carry with them, all lead to the evolution of different sets of rules. In so far as the rules of various groups conflict and contradict one another, there will be disagreement about the kind of behavior that is proper in any given situation.

Italian immigrants who went on making wine for themselves and their friends during Prohibition were acting properly by Italian immigrant standards, but were breaking the law of their new country (as, of course, were many of their Old American neighbors). Medical patients who shop around for a doctor may, from the perspective of their own group, be doing what is necessary to protect their health by making sure they get what seems to them the best possible doctor; but, from the perspective of the physician, what they do is wrong because it breaks down the trust the patient ought to put in his physician. The lower-class delinquent who fights for his 'turf' is only doing what he considers necessary and right, but teachers, social workers, and police see it differently.

While it may be argued that many or most rules are generally agreed to by all members of a society, empirical research on a given rule generally reveals variation in people's attitudes. Formal rules, enforced by some specially constituted group, may differ from those actually thought appropriate by most people.[13] Factions in a group may disagree on what I have called actual operating rules. Most important for the study of behavior ordinarily labeled deviant, the perspectives of the people who engage in the behavior are likely to be quite different from those of the people who condemn it. In this latter situation, a person may feel that he is being judged according to rules he has had no hand in making and does not accept, rules forced on him by outsiders.

To what extent and under what circumstances do people attempt to force their rules on others who do not subscribe to them? Let us distinguish two cases. In the first, only those who are actually members of the group have any interest in making and enforcing certain rules. If an orthodox Jew disobeys the laws of kashruth only other orthodox Jews will regard this as a transgression; Christians or non-orthodox Jews will not consider this deviance and would have no interest in interfering. In the second case, members of a group consider it important to their welfare that members of certain other groups obey certain rules. Thus, people consider it extremely important that those who practice the healing arts abide by certain rules; this is the reason the state licenses physicians, nurses, and others, and forbids anyone who is not licensed to engage in healing activities.

To the extent that a group tries to impose its rules on other groups in the society, we are presented with a second question: Who can, in fact, force others to accept their rules and what are the causes of their success? This is, of course, a question of political and economic power. [. . .] [P]eople are in fact always *forcing* their rules on others, applying them more or less against the will and without the consent of those others. By and large, for example, rules are made for young people by their elders. Though the youth of this country exert a powerful influence culturally – the mass media of communication are tailored to their interests, for instance – many important kinds of rules are made for our youth by adults. Rules regarding school attendance and sex behavior are not drawn up with regard to the problems of adolescence. Rather, adolescents find themselves surrounded by rules about these matters which have been made by older and more settled people. It is considered legitimate to do this, for youngsters are considered neither wise enough nor responsible enough to make proper rules for themselves.

In the same way, it is true in many respects that men make the rules for women in our society (though in America this is changing rapidly). Negroes find themselves subject to rules made for them by whites. The foreign-born and those otherwise ethnically peculiar often have their rules made for them by the Protestant Anglo-Saxon minority. The middle class makes rules the lower class must obey – in the schools, the courts, and elsewhere.

Differences in the ability to make rules and apply them to other people are essentially power differentials (either legal or extralegal). Those groups whose social position gives them weapons and power are best able to enforce their rules. Distinctions of age, sex, ethnicity, and class are all related to differences in power, which accounts for differences in the degree to which groups so distinguished can make rules for others.

In addition to recognizing that deviance is created by the responses of people to particular kinds of behavior, by the labeling of that behavior as deviant, we must also keep in mind that the rules created and maintained by such labeling are not universally agreed to. Instead, they are the object of conflict and disagreement, part of the political process of society.

NOTES

1 Cf. Donald R. Cressey, 'Criminological research and the definition of crimes', *American Journal of Sociology*, LVI (May, 1951), pp. 546–51.

2 See the discussion in C. Wright Mills, 'The professional ideology of social pathologists', *American Journal of Sociology*, XLIX (September, 1942), pp. 165–80.

3 Thomas Szasz, *The Myth of Mental Illness* (New York, Paul B. Hoeber, 1961), pp. 44–5; see also Erving Goffman, 'The medical model and mental hospitalization', in *Asylums: Essays on the Social Situation of Mental Patients and Other Inmates* (Garden City, NY, Anchor Books, 1961), pp. 321–86.

4 See Robert K. Merton, 'Social problems and sociological theory', in Robert K. Merton and Robert A. Nisbet (eds), *Contemporary Social Problems* (New York, Harcourt, Brace and World, 1961), pp. 697–737; and Talcott Parsons, *The Social System* (New York, The Free Press of Glencoe, 1951), pp. 249–325.

5 Howard Brotz similarly identifies the question of what phenomena are 'functional'

or 'dysfunctional' as a political one in 'Functionalism and dynamic analysis', *European Journal of Sociology*, II (1961), pp. 170–9.

6 The most important earlier statements of this view can be found in Frank Tannenbaum, *Crime and the Community* (New York, McGraw-Hill, 1951), and E.M. Lemert, *Social Pathology* (New York, McGraw-Hill, 1951). A recent article stating a position very similar to mine is John Kitsuse, 'Societal reaction to deviance: problems of theory and method', *Social Problems*, 9 (Winter, 1962), pp. 247–56.

7 Bronislaw Malinowski, *Crime and Custom in Savage Society* (New York, Humanities Press, 1926), pp. 77–80. Reprinted by permission of Humanities Press and Routledge and Kegan Paul Ltd.

8 F. James Davis, 'Crime news in Colorado newspapers', *American Journal of Sociology*, LVII (January, 1952), pp. 325–30.

9 See Albert K. Cohen and James F. Short Jr, 'Juvenile delinquency', in Merton and Nisbet, *Contemporary Social Problems*, p. 87.

10 See Harold Garfinkel, 'Research notes on inter- and intra-racial homicides', *Social Forces*, 27 (May, 1949), pp. 369–81.

11 Edwin H. Sutherland, 'White Collar Criminality', *American Sociological Review*, V (February, 1940), pp. 1–12.

12 Clark Vincent, *Unmarried Mothers* (New York: The Free Press of Glencoe, 1961), pp. 3–5.

13 Arnold M. Rose and Arthur E. Prell, 'Does the punishment fit the crime? – a study in social valuation', *American Journal of Sociology*, LXI (November, 1955), pp. 247–59.

21

Toward a political economy of crime

William J. Chambliss

In attempting to develop a Marxist theory of crime and criminal law we are handicapped by the fact that Marx did not devote himself very systematically to such a task. There are none the less several places in his analysis of capitalism where Marx did direct his attention to criminality and law.[1] Furthermore, the logic of the Marxian theory makes it possible to extrapolate from the theory to an analysis of crime and criminal law in ways that are extremely useful. Thus, in what follows I will be focusing on the implications of the Marxist paradigm as well as relying heavily on those Marxist writings that directly addressed these issues.

As with the general Marxist theory, the starting-point for the understanding of society is the realization that the most fundamental feature of people's lives is their relationship to the mode of production. The mode of production consists of both the means of production (the technological processes) and the relationship of different classes to the means of production – whether they own them or work for those who do. Since ultimately, the only source of an economic surplus is that amount of goods which is produced beyond what the worker consumes, then the distinction between those who own and those who work for others is crucial to understanding the control of the surplus in the society.

All of this is of course elementary Marxism and was only briefly summarized here to get us started.

We must then speak of historical periods according to the mode of production which characterizes them. The most fundamental distinction would be between those societies where the means of production are owned privately, and societies where the means of production are not. Obviously there are many possible variations on these two ideal types: societies where the means of production are owned by the state (for example, the Soviet Union) as contrasted with societies where the means of production are controlled by small groups of workers (for example, Yugoslavia), or where the means of production are owned by collective units of workers, farmers, peasants and other strata (China, for example). Each of these different modes of production would of course lead to quite different social relations and therefore to different forms of crime and criminal law.

From *Theory and Society*, 1975, 2: 149–70.

Capitalist societies, where the means of production are in private hands and where there inevitably develops a division between the class that rules (the owners of the means of production) and the class that is ruled (those who work for the ruling class), create substantial amounts of crime, often of the most violent sort, as a result of the contradictions that are inherent in the structure of social relations that emanate from the capitalist system.

The first contradiction is that the capitalist enterprise depends upon creating in the mass of the workers a desire for the consumption of products produced by the system. These products need not contribute to the well-being of the people, nor do they have to represent commodities of any intrinsic value; none the less, for the system to expand and be viable, it is essential that the bulk of the population be oriented to consuming what is produced. However, in order to produce the commodities that are the basis for the accumulation of capital and the maintenance of the ruling class, it is also necessary to get people to work at tedious, alienating and unrewarding tasks. One way to achieve this, of course, is to make the accumulation of commodities dependent on work. Moreover, since the system depends as it does on the desire to possess and consume commodities far beyond what is necessary for survival, there must be an added incentive to perform the dull meaningless tasks that are required to keep the productive process expanding. This is accomplished by keeping a proportion of the labor force impoverished or nearly so.[2] If those who are employed become obstreperous and refuse to perform the tasks required by the productive system, then there is a reserve labor force waiting to take their job. And hanging over the heads of the workers is always the possibility of becoming impoverished should they refuse to do their job.

Thus, at the outset the structure of capitalism creates both the desire to consume and – for a large mass of people – an inability to earn the money necessary to purchase the items they have been taught to want.

A second fundamental contradiction derives from the fact that the division of a society into a ruling class that owns the means of production and a subservient class that works for wages *inevitably* leads to conflict between the two classes. As those conflicts are manifest in rebellions and riots among the proletariat, the state, acting in the interests of the owners of the means of production will pass laws designed to control, through the application of state sanctioned force, those acts of the proletariat which threaten the interests of the bourgeoisie. In this way, then, acts come to be defined as criminal.

It follows that as capitalism develops and conflicts between social classes continue or become more frequent or more violent (as a result, for example, of increasing proletarianization), more and more acts will be defined as criminal.

The criminal law is thus *not* a reflection of custom (as other theorists have argued), but is a set of rules laid down by the state in the interests of the ruling class, and resulting from the conflicts that inhere in class structured societies; criminal behavior is, then, the inevitable expression of class conflict resulting from the inherently exploitative nature of the economic relations. What makes the behavior of some criminal is the coercive power of the state to enforce the will of the ruling class; criminal behavior results from the struggle between classes whereby those who are the subservient classes individually express their alienation from established social relations. Criminal behavior is a product of the economic and political system, and in a capitalist society has as one of its principal consequences the advancement of technology, use of surplus labor and generally the maintenance of the established relationship between the social classes. Marx says, somewhat facetiously, in response to the functionalism of bourgeois sociologists:

> crime takes a part of the superfluous population off the labor market and thus reduces competition among the laborers – up to a certain point preventing wages from falling below the minimum – the struggle against crime absorbs another part of this population. Thus the criminal comes in as one of those natural 'counterweights' which bring about a correct balance and open up a whole perspective of 'useful' occupation . . . the criminal . . . produces the whole of the police and of criminal justice, constables, judges, hangmen, juries, etc.; and all these different lines of business, which form equally many categories of the social division of labor, develop different capacities of the human spirit, create new needs and new ways of satisfying them. Torture alone has given rise to the most ingenious mechanical inventions, and employed many honorable craftsmen in the production of its instruments.[3]

Paradigms, as we are all well aware, do much more than supply us with specific causal explanations. They provide us with a whole set of glasses through which we view the world. Most importantly, they lead us to emphasize certain features of the world and to ignore or at least de-emphasize others.

The following propositions highlight the most important implications of a Marxian paradigm of crime and criminal law.[4]

A On the content and operation of criminal law

1 Acts are defined as criminal because it is in the interests of the ruling class to so define them.
2 Members of the ruling class will be able to violate the laws with impunity while members of the subject classes will be punished.
3 As capitalist societies industrialize and the gap between the bourgeoisie and the proletariat widens, penal law will expand in an effort to coerce the proletariat into submission.

B On the consequences of crime for society

1 Crime reduces surplus labor by creating employment not only for the criminals but for law enforcers, locksmiths, welfare workers, professors of criminology and a horde of people who live off the fact that crime exists.
2 Crime diverts the lower classes' attention from the exploitation they experience, and directs it toward other members of their own class rather than towards the capitalist class or the economic system.
3 Crime is a reality which exists only as it is created by those in the society whose interests are served by its presence.

C On the etiology of criminal behavior

1 Criminal and non-criminal behavior stem from people acting rationally in ways that are compatible with their class position. Crime is a reaction to the life conditions of a person's social class.
2 Crime varies from society to society depending on the political and economic structures of society.
3 Socialist societies should have much lower rates of crime because the less intense class struggle should reduce the forces leading to and the functions of crime.

[. . .]

ON THE CONTENT AND OPERATION OF THE CRIMINAL LAW

The conventional, non-Marxian interpretation of how criminal law comes into being sees the criminal law as a reflection of widely held beliefs which permeate all 'healthy consciences' in the society. This view has been clearly articulated by Jerome Hall:

> The moral judgements represented in the criminal law can be defended on the basis of their derivation from a long historical experience, through open discussion . . . the process of legislation, viewed broadly to include participation and discussion by the electorate as well as that of the legislature proper, provides additional assurance that the legal valuations are soundly established . . . .[5]

THE MARXIAN THEORY OF CRIMINAL LAW

There is little evidence to support the view that the criminal law is a body of rules which reflect strongly held moral dictates of the society.[6] Occasionally we find a study on the creation of criminal law which traces legal innovations to the 'moral indignation' of a particular social class.[7] It is significant, however, that the circumstances described are quite different from the situation where laws emerge from community consensus. Rather, the research points up the rule by a small minority which occupies a particular class position and shares a viewpoint and a set of social experiences which brings them together as an active and effective force of social change. For example, Joseph Gusfield's astute analysis of the emergence of prohibition in the United States illustrates how these laws were brought about through the political efforts of a downwardly mobile segment of America's middle class. By effort and some good luck this class was able to impose its will on the majority of the population through rather dramatic changes in the law.[8] Svend Ranulf's more general study of *Moral Indignation and Middle Class Psychology* shows similar results, especially when it is remembered that the lower middle class, whose emergence Ranulf sees as the social force behind legal efforts to legislate morality, was a decided *minority* of the population. In no reasonable way can these inquiries be taken as support for the idea that criminal laws represent *community* sentiments.

By contrast, there is considerable evidence showing the critically important role played by the interests of the ruling class as a major force in the creation of criminal laws. Jerome Hall's analysis of the emergence of the laws of theft and Chambliss's study of vagrancy laws both point up the salience of the economic interests of the ruling class as the fountainhead of legal changes.[9] A more recent analysis of the legislative process behind the creation of laws attempting to control the distribution of amphetamine drugs has also shown how the owners of the means of production (in this case, the large pharmaceutical companies) are involved in writing and lobbying for laws which affect their profits.[10]

The surface appearance of legal innovations often hides the real forces behind legislation. Gabriel Kolko's studies of the creation of laws controlling the meat packing and railroad industries in the United States have shown how the largest corporations in these industries were actively involved in a campaign for federal control of the industries, as this control would mean increased profits for the large manufacturers and industrialists.[11]

Research on criminal law legislation has also shown the substantial role played by state bureaucracies in the legislative process.[12] In some areas of criminal law it seems that the law enforcement agencies are almost solely responsible for the shape and content of the laws. As a matter of fact, drug laws are best understood as laws passed as a result of efforts of law enforcement agencies which managed to create whatever consensus there is. Other inquiries point up the role of conflicting interests between organized groups of moral entrepreneurs, bureaucrats and businessmen.[13]

In all of these studies there is substantial support for the Marxian theory. The single most important force behind criminal law creation is doubtless the economic interest and political power of those social classes which either (1) own or control the resources of the society, or (2) occupy positions of authority in the state bureaucracies. It is also the case that conflicts generated by the class structure of a society act as an important force for legal innovation. These conflicts may manifest themselves in an incensed group of moral entrepreneurs (such as Gusfield's lower middle class, or the efforts of groups such as the ACLU, NAACP or Policemen's Benevolent Society) who manage to persuade courts or legislatures to create new laws.[14] Or the conflict may manifest itself in open riots, rebellions or revolutions which force new criminal law legislation.

There is, then, evidence that the Marxian theory with its emphasis on the role of the ruling classes in creating criminal laws and social class conflict and as the moving force behind legal changes is quite compatible with research findings on this subject. [. . .]

THE ETIOLOGY OF CRIMINAL BEHAVIOR

It is obviously fruitless to join the debate over whether or not contemporary theories of criminal etiology are adequate to the task. The advocates of 'family background', 'differential association', 'cultural deprivation', 'opportunity theory', and a host of other 'theories' have debated the relative merits of their explanations *ad infinitum* (one might even say *ad nauseam*).

[. . .] Everyone commits crime. And many, many people whether they are poor, rich or middling are involved in a way of life that is criminal; and furthermore, no one, not even the professional thief or racketeer or corrupt politician commits *crime all the time*. To be sure, it may be politically useful to say that people become criminal through association with 'criminal behavior patterns', and thereby remove the tendency to look at criminals as pathological. But such a view has little scientific value, since it asks the wrong questions. It asks for a psychological cause of what is by its very nature a socio-political event. Criminality is simply *not* something that people have or don't have; crime is not something some people do and others don't. Crime is a matter of who can pin the label on whom, and underlying this socio-political process is the structure of social relations determined by the political economy.

[. . .]

The argument that criminal acts, that is, acts which are a violation of criminal law, are more often committed by members of the lower classes is not tenable. Criminal acts are widely distributed throughout the social classes in capitalist societies. The rich, the ruling, the poor, the powerless and the working classes *all* engage in criminal activities on a regular basis. It is in the enforcement of the law that the lower classes are subject to the effects of ruling class domination over the legal system, and which results in the appearance of a concentration of criminal acts among the lower classes in the official records. In actual practice, however, class differences in rates of criminal activity are probably negligible. What difference there is would be a difference in the type of criminal act, not in the prevalence of criminality.

The argument that the control of the state by the ruling class would lead to a lower propensity for crime among the ruling classes fails to recognize two fundamental facts. First is the fact that many acts committed by lower classes and which it is in the interests of the ruling class to control (e.g., crimes of violence, bribery of public officials, and crimes of personal choice, such as drug use, alcoholism, driving while intoxicated, homosexuality, etc.) are just as likely – or at least very likely – to be as widespread among the upper classes as the lower classes. Thus, it is crucial that the ruling class be able to control the discretion of the law enforcement agencies in ways that provide them with immunity; for example, having a legal system encumbered with procedural rules which only the wealthy can afford to implement and which, if implemented, nearly guarantees immunity from prosecution, not to mention more direct control through bribes, coercion and the use of political influence.

The Marxian paradigm must also account for the fact that the law will also reflect conflict between members of the ruling class (or between members of the ruling class and the upper class 'power elites' who manage the bureaucracies). So, for example, laws restricting the formation of trusts, misrepresentation in advertising, the necessity for obtaining licenses to engage in business practices are all laws which generally serve to reduce competition among the ruling classes and to concentrate capital in a few hands. However, the laws also apply universally, and therefore apply to the ruling class as well. Thus, when they break these laws they are committing criminal acts. Again, the enforcement practices obviate the effectiveness of the laws, and guarantee that the ruling class will rarely feel the sting of the laws, but their violation remains a fact with which we must reckon.

[. . .]

SUMMARY AND CONCLUSION

As Gouldner and Fredrichs have recently pointed out, social science generally, and sociology in particular is in the throes of a 'paradigm revolution'.[15] Predictably, criminology is both a reflection of and a force behind this revolution.

The emerging paradigm in criminology is one which emphasizes social conflict – particularly conflicts of social class interests and values. The paradigm which is being replaced is one where the primary emphasis was on consensus, and within which 'deviance' or 'crime' was viewed as an aberration shared by some minority. This group had failed to be properly socialized or adequately integrated into society or, more generally, had suffered from 'social disorganization'.

The shift in paradigm means more than simply a shift from explaining the same facts with new causal models. It means that we stretch our conceptual framework and look to different facets of social experience. Specifically, instead of resorting inevitably to the 'normative system', to 'culture' or to socio-psychological experiences of individuals, we look instead to the social relations created by the political and economic structure. Rather than treating 'society' as a full-blown reality (reifying it into an entity with its own life), we seek to understand the present as a reflection of the economic and political history that has created the social relations which dominate the moment we have selected to study.

The shift means that crime becomes a rational response of some social classes to the realities of their lives. The state becomes an instrument of the ruling class enforcing laws here but not there, according to the realities of political power and economic conditions.

There is much to be gained from this re-focusing of criminological and sociological inquiry. However, if the paradigmatic revolution is to be more than a mere fad, we must be able to show that the new paradigm is in fact superior to its predecessor. In this paper I have tried to develop the theoretical implications of a Marxian model of crime and criminal law [. . .] The general conclusion is that the Marxian paradigm provides a long neglected but fruitful approach to the study of crime and criminal law.

NOTES

1 Primary source materials for Marx's analysis of crime and criminal law are: *Capital*, v.1 (London, Lawrence and Wishart, 1970), pp. 231–98, 450–503, 556–7, 574, 674–8, 718–25, 734–41; *The Cologne Communist Trial* (London, Lawrence and Wishart, 1971); *The German Ideology (1845–6)* (London, Lawrence and Wishart, 1965), pp. 342–79; *Theories of Surplus Value*, v. 1, pp. 375–6; 'The state and the law', in T.B. Bottomore and Maximilien Rubel (eds), *Karl Marx: Selected Writings in Sociology and Social Philosophy* (New York, McGraw-Hill, 1965), pp. 215–31.

2 In the United Sates the proportion of the population living in poverty is between 15 and 30 per cent of the labor force.

3 Marx, *Theories of Surplus Value*, pp. 375–6.

4 For an excellent statement of differences in 'order and conflict' theories, see John Horton, 'Order and conflict approaches to the study of social problems', *American Journal of Sociology*, May (1966); see also Gerhard Lenski, *Power and Privilege* (New York, McGraw-Hill, 1966); William J. Chambliss, *Sociological Readings in the Conflict Perspective* (Reading, MA, Addison-Wesley, 1973).

5 Jerome Hall, *General Principles of Criminal Law* (Indianapolis, Bobbs-Merrill, 1947), pp. 356–7.

6 For a more thorough analysis of this issue, see William J. Chambliss 'The state, the

law and the definition of behavior as criminal or delinquent, in Daniel Glaser (ed.), *Handbook of Criminology* (Chicago, Rand McNally, 1974), ch. 1, pp. 7–43.

7 Svend Ranulf, *The Jealousy of the Gods*, vols 1 and 2 (London, Williams and Northgate, 1932) and *Moral Indignation and Middle Class Psychology* (Copenhagen, Levin and Monkagord, 1938); Joseph Gusfield, *Symbolic Crusade: Status Politics and the American Temperance Movement* (Urbana, Ill., University of Illinois Press, 1963).

8 Gusfield, *Symbolic Crusade*; see also Andrew Sinclair *Era of Excess: A Social History of the Prohibition Movement* (New York, Harper and Row, 1964).

9 Jerome Hall, *Theft, Law and Society* (Indianapolis: Bobbs-Merill and Co., 1952); William J. Chambliss, 'A sociological analysis of the law of vagrancy', *Social Problems*, Summer (1964), pp. 67–77.

10 James M. Graham, 'Profits at all costs: amphetamine profits on Capitol Hill', *Transaction*, January (1972), pp. 14–23.

11 Gabriel Kolko, *Railroads and Regulations* (Princeton, NJ, Princeton University Press, 1965) and *The Triumph of Conservatism* (New York, The Free Press of Glencoe, 1963).

12 Alfred R. Lindesmith, *The Addict and the Law* (Bloomington, Ind., Indiana University Press, 1965); Edwin M. Lemert, *Social Action and Legal Change: Revolution Within the Juvenile Court* (Chicago, Aldine, 1964); Troy Duster, *The Legislation of Morality: Law, Drugs and Moral Judgement* (New York, The Free Press, 1970).

13 Pamela A. Roby, 'Politics and criminal law: revision of the New York State Penal Law on Prostitution', *Social Problems*, Summer (1969), pp. 83–109.

14 William J. Chambliss and Robert B. Seidman, *Law, Order and Power* (Reading, MA, Addison-Wesley, 1971).

15 Alvin W. Gouldner, *The Coming Crisis in Western Sociology* (New York, Basic Books, 1970); Robert W. Frederichs, *A Sociology of Sociology* (New York, The Free Press, 1970). For a more general discussion of paradigm revolution in science, see Thomas S. Kuhn, *The Structure of Scientific Revolutions*, 2nd edn (Chicago, University of Chicago Press, 1970).

22

The new criminology

Ian Taylor, Paul Walton and Jock Young

[. . .]

The *formal* requirements of [a fully social theory of deviance] are concerned with the scope of the theory. It must be able to cover, and sustain, the connections between:

1 THE WIDER ORIGINS OF THE DEVIANT ACT

The theory must be able, in other words, to place the act in terms of its wider structural origins. These 'structural' considerations will involve recognition of the intermediate structural questions that have traditionally been the domain of sociological criminology (e.g. ecological areas,[1] subcultural location,[2] distribution of opportunities for theft) (cf. Armstrong and Wilson, 1973) but it would place these against the overall social context of inequalities of power, wealth and authority in the developed industrial society. Similarly, there would be consideration of the questions traditionally dealt with by psychologists concerned with the structures conducive to individual breakdown, that is with an individual's exclusion from 'normal' interaction (Hepworth, 1971, 1972). But, again, there would be an attempt, as in the later work of the anti-psychiatry school, to place these psychological concerns (e.g. with the schizophrenic nature of the bourgeois nuclear family) in the context of a society in which families are just one part of an interrelating but contradictory structural whole. The move would be away from the view of man as an atomistic individual, cut off within families or other specific subcultural situations, insulated from the pressures of existence under the prevailing social conditions.

The wider origins of the deviant act could only be understood, we would argue, in terms of the rapidly changing economic and political contingencies of advanced industrial society. At this level, the formal requirement is really for what might be called *a political economy of crime*.

From *The New Criminology*, pp. 268–82. (London: Routledge, 1973.)

2 IMMEDIATE ORIGINS OF THE DEVIANT ACT

It is, of course, the case, however, that men do not experience the constraints of a society in an undifferentiated fashion. Just as subcultural theorists, operating in the anthropological tradition, have argued that the subcultural notion is useful to explain the different kinds of ways in which men resolve the problems posed by the demands of a dominant culture (Downes, 1966: ch. 1), so we would argue that an adequately social theory of deviance must be able to explain the different events, experiences or structural developments that precipitate the deviant act. The theory must explain the different ways in which structural demands are interpreted, reacted against, or used by men at different levels in the social structure, in such a way that an essentially deviant choice is made. The formal requirement, at this level, that is, is for a *social psychology of crime*: a social psychology which, unlike that which is implicit in the work of the social reaction theorists, recognizes that men may *consciously* choose the deviant road, as the one solution to the problems posed by existence in a contradictory society (cf. Hepworth, 1971, 1972; L. Taylor, 1972).

3 THE ACTUAL ACT

Men may choose to engage in particular solutions to their problems, without being able to carry them out. An adequate social theory of deviance would need to be able to explain the relationship between beliefs and action, between the optimum 'rationality' that men have chosen and the behaviours they actually carry through. A working-class adolescent, for example, confronted with blockage of opportunity, with problems of status frustration, alienated from the kind of existence offered out to him in contemporary society, may want to engage in hedonistic activities (e.g. finding immediate pleasure through the use of alcohol, drugs, or in extensive sexual activities) or he may choose to kick back at a rejecting society (e.g. through acts of vandalism). He may also attempt to assert some degree of control over, for example, the pace at which he is asked to work (cf. L. Taylor and Walton, 1971) or the ways in which his leisure time interests are controlled (cf. S. Cohen, 1972a; I. Taylor, 1971a, 1971b). But he may find that these options themselves are not easily achieved. Cloward and Ohlin have argued that adolescent 'drop-outs' in the United States, failures in the legitimate society, can also experience 'double-failure' in being rejected in delinquent subcultures themselves. Deviant individuals can find that they are rejected by other deviants (as 'uncool', physically inadequate or unattractive, or generally undesirable). Whilst we would argue that there is always a relationship between individual choice (a set of beliefs) and action it is not necessarily a simple one: an adolescent boy could choose the hedonistic, the rejective or the assertive options without there being any chance of sustaining them. Adjustments of some kind would then be necessitated. The formal requirement at this level then is for an explanation of the ways in which the actual acts of men are explicable in terms of the rationality of choice or the constraints on choice at the point of precipitation into action. The formal requirement, here, is for an account of real *social dynamics* surrounding the actual acts.

4 IMMEDIATE ORIGINS OF SOCIAL REACTION

Just as the deviant act itself may be precipitated by the reactions of others (e.g. as a result of an adolescent's attempt to win acceptance as 'cool' or 'tough' in a sub-culture of delinquency, or from a businessman's attempt to show ability as a sharp practitioner) so the subsequent definition of the act is the product of close personal relationships. A certain behaviour may encourage a member of the actor's family or peer group to refer that actor to a doctor, to a child guidance clinic, or to a psychiatrist (because that behaviour is seen to be odd). Or another behaviour may result in the individual being reported to the police by people outside the individual's immediate family circle or friendship group (because he has been acting suspiciously, or actually been seen committing an illegal act). In both instances, there is a degree of choice on the part of the social audience: it may be thought that the behaviour *is* odd, but that it is preferable to keep it in the family; or it may be thought that although the individual *has* been acting suspiciously or has been behaving illegally, it would be too troublesome to involve the police.

Even when the formal agencies of social control themselves – in particular, the police, but also the various agencies of the 'Welfare State' – directly apprehend the individual in the course of his law-breaking (which is relatively rare), a degree of choice is exercised by the agent in his reaction to the deviant. The complex mix of classical liberalism (emphasizing, for example, 'police discretion' and the role of the local constable as a part-time social worker) and the lay theories of criminality (emphasizing what a real criminal, hooligan, junkie, or 'villain' actually looks like)[3] contributes to the moral climate and lays down the boundaries within which informal social reaction to deviance is likely to occur.

The requirement at this level is for an explanation of the immediate reaction of the social audience in terms of the range of choices available to that audience. The requirement, in other words, is for a *social psychology of social reaction*: an account of the contingencies and the conditions which are crucial to the decision to act against the deviant.

5 WIDER ORIGINS OF DEVIANT REACTION

In the same way that the choices available to the deviant himself are a product of his structural location, primarily, and, secondarily, his *individual* attributes (his accept-ability to significant others – both those involved in legitimate activity and those who are engaged in rule-breaking activity of one kind or another), so the social psy-chology of social reaction (and the lay theories of deviance behind it) is explicable only in terms of the position and the attributes of those who instigate the reaction against the deviant. It is obviously the case that members of a law-breaker's immediate family group are far less likely to react against his activity than those who are strangers to him.[4] But it is also the case that the 'lay' theories of criminality and deviance adhered to by strangers will vary enormously: social work ideology (with its positivistic stress on reform) is continually at odds with the more classically punitive ideologies of correctional institutions and their controllers; police ideology is sometimes at odds with the philosophies of courtroom practice (in particular, the adjudicatory powers of the non-professional jury);[5] and even amongst those without formal positions in the structure of social control (the 'public') the lay theories found to be acceptable will vary across the contours of social class, ethnic group and age (Simmons and Chambers, 1965).

The predominant tendencies in criminological treatments of the wider origins of deviant reaction, so far as they have been dealt with at all, have been to see these as located in occupational groups and their particular needs (Box, Dickson), in a rather ambiguously defined set of pluralistic interests (Quinney, Lemert), in authority–subject relationships within 'imperatively-coordinated associations' (Turk), or in simple superordinate–subordinate political relationships (Becker). All of these treatments of the sources of reactions against the deviant are, of course, implicit political sociologies of the state; and [. . .] few criminologists have really grappled in an effective way with the debates about social structure in the traditions of grand social theory. In particular, few criminologists have been able to deal with the ways in which the political initiatives that give rise to (or abolish) legislation, that define sanctionable behaviour in society or ensure the enforcement of that legislation, are intimately bound up with the structure of the *political economy* of the state. Sutherland's treatment of white-collar crime, for example, was informed hardly at all by an examination of the ways in which white-collar infractions were (and are) functional to industrial-capitalist societies at points in their development: rather it was concerned with illuminating what he saw to be the inequitable use of law in controlling behaviour in defiance of formally defined rules of conduct (cf. Pearce, 1973). The fact that the political sociologies of crime in criminology remain implicit and ambiguous is some indication of the extent to which criminology has moved away from the concerns of the classical social thinkers. [. . .] [I]t was impossible for Durkheim to conceive of crime and deviance without his conceiving also of a certain set of productive social arrangements overarched by a certain collective conscience (a forced division of labour being associated with 'functional rebellion' as well as with the 'skewed deviant' adaptation). [. . .] [F]or him it was impossible to talk of the dimunition of crime without talking politically of the abolition of the forced division of labour, the abolition of inherited wealth, and the setting up of occupational associations in tune with (politically enforceable) social arrangements based on a biological meritocracy. [. . .] Marx's political sociology of crime was also inextricably bound up with a political critique and a clear-headed analysis of existing social arrangements. For him, crime was expression of men's situation of constraint within alienating social arrangements – and in part an indication of a struggle to overcome them. The fact that criminal action was no political answer in itself to those situations was explained in terms of the political and social possibilities of the *Lumpenproletariat* as a parasitical agency on the organized working class itself. [. . .] [F]or the time being, it is sufficient to mention them not only as evidence of the *dilution of theory* in twentieth century investigations of crime but also as an indictment of the *depoliticization* of the issues involved in the classical discussions in social theory on crime, accomplished and applauded by those who carry out work in the field of contemporary 'applied' criminology.

For the moment it is sufficient to assert that one of the important formal requirements of a fully social theory of deviance, that is almost totally absent in existing literature, is an effective model of the political and economic imperatives that underpin on the one hand the 'lay ideologies' and on the other the 'crusades' and initiatives that emerge periodically either to control the amount and level of deviance (cf. Manson and Palmer, 1973) or else (as in the cases of prohibition, certain homosexual activity, and, most recently, certain 'crimes without victims') to remove certain behaviours from the category of 'illegal' behaviours. We are lacking a *political economy of social reaction.*

6 THE OUTCOME OF THE SOCIAL REACTION ON DEVIANTS' FURTHER ACTION

One of the most telling contributions of the social reaction theorists to an understanding of deviance was their emphasis on the need to understand deviant action as being, in part, an attempt to come to terms by the rule-breaker with the reaction against his initial infraction. [. . .] [O]ne of the superficial strengths of the social reaction perspective was its ability to see the actor as using the reaction against him in a variety of ways (that is, in exercising choice). This [was] an advance on the deterministic view of the impact of sanctions on further behaviour in positivistic views of 'reform', 'rehabilitation', and, most particularly, 'conditioning'. We argue, however, that the notion of secondary deviation was undialectical; that is, that it could have the same status as an explanation of what the social reaction theorists separate out as primary deviation, and that, in reality, it might be impossible to distinguish between the causes of primary and secondary deviation.

A fully social theory of deviance – premised on the notion of man as consciously involved (however inarticulately) in deviant choices – would require us to see the reaction he evolves to rejection or stigmatization (or, for that matter, sanction in the form of institutionalization) as being bound up with the conscious choices that precipitated the initial infraction. It would require us to reject the view which is paramount in Lemert's discussion of secondary deviation (1967: 51), namely that 'most people drift into deviance by specific actions rather than by formed choices of social roles and statuses' and that, because of this, they unintentionally, unwittingly and (implicitly) rather tragically enter what Lemert terms a 'staging area set up for an ideological struggle between the deviant seeking to normalize his actions and thoughts, and agencies seeking the opposite (1967: 44). Actually, Lemert [. . .] is not able to show that the problems faced by the deviant are always the result of his being apprehended and reacted against (either formally or informally) in this rather straightforward sense. He writes at one point (1967: 48) that:

> Becoming an admitted homosexual ('coming out') may endanger one's livelihood or professional career, but it also absolves the individual from failure to assume the heavy responsibilities of marriage and parenthood, and it is a ready way of fending off painful involvements in heterosexual affairs.

In other words, the act of breaking through what Gouldner has termed the normalized repression of everyday routine expectations, consciously and wittingly, does not always require precipitation in the form of social reaction. It only requires one to know one's enemy and to know how to deal with the stigmatization and exclusion that may then result. Just as a homosexual preparing to 'come out' may take a long time to prepare his revelation (and thus be consciously prepared for the reaction against him), so any deviant can be understood as having some degree of consciousness of what to expect in the event of apprehension and reaction. A fully social explanation of the outcome of social reaction to the further actions of the apprehended deviant, therefore, would be one in which the deviant actor is always endowed with some degree of consciousness about the likelihood and consequences of reaction against him, and in which his subsequent decisions are developed from that initial degree of consciousness.[6] All those writers who see deviants as 'naive' must now realize that they are dealing with a minority of deviants, even in situations where the degree or extent of social reaction is unexpected (because, for example, of a moral panic amongst the powerful about a particular kind of offence, or because a campaign of control has been instigated against it – as in the case of the white adolescents who received unexpectedly heavy sentences for their role during the Notting Hill race riots in 1959), it would still be important to have a social explanation of the ways in which the deviants responded to their sentences with a degree of consciousness about 'the law' which they had developed before they had had a formal contact with it.

In a fully social theory, then, the consciousness conventionally allowed deviants in the secondary deviation situation would be seen as explicable – at least in part – in terms of the actors' consciousness of the world in general.

7 THE NATURE OF THE DEVIANT PROCESS AS A WHOLE

The formal requirements of a fully social theory are formal in the sense that they refer to the *scope* of the theoretical analysis. In the real world of social action, these analytical distinctions merge, connect and often appear to be indistinguishable. We have already indicted social reaction theory, which is in many ways the most sophisticated rejection of the simpler forms of positivism (concentrating as they do on the pathologies of the individual actor), as onesidedly deterministic: in seeing the deviant's problems and consciousness simply as a response to apprehension and the application of social control. Positivistic explanations stand accused of being unable to approach an explanation not only of the *political economy* of crime (the background to criminal action) but also of what we have called the *political economy*, the *social psychology* and the *social dynamics* of social reaction to deviance. And most of the classical and earlier biological psychological positivists [. . .] are unable to offer out even a satisfactorily social explanation of the relationship between the individual and society: the individual in these accounts appears by and large as an isolated atom unaffected by the ebb and flow of social arrangements, social change, and contradictions in what is, after all, a society of social arrangements built around the capitalist mode of production.

The central requirement of a fully social theory of deviance, however, is that these formal requirements must not be treated simply as essential factors all of which need to be present (in invariant fashion) if the theory is to be social. Rather it is that these formal requirements must all appear in the theory, as they do in the real world, in a complex, dialectical relationship to one another. Georg Lukács's criticism of Solzhenitsyn's early work is instructive here, if only because it is so well applicable to the work of Goffman, Garfinkel, Becker, Lemert and other thinkers who have been concerned with the impact that 'social control' (whether institutional or otherwise) has on its victims. Writing of Solzhenitsyn's early work on the prison camp (which

Lukács correctly takes as a metaphor intended to apply to the whole society), Lukács (1971) observed that:

> Solzhenitsyn's development . . . of [his] technique from his first story not only, of necessity, increases the number of prisoners whose life is shown . . . it also demands that the initiators and organisers of this internment of large masses of people must also be depicted on a wider basis and more concretely. . . . Only thus does the 'place of action' receive its concrete socially determined significance. . . . In the last resort it is a social fact that the internment camp confronts both its victims and its organisers spontaneously and irresistibly with its provocative basic questions . . .

[. . .]

The great merit of Solzhenitsyn, using the skills and the techniques of the novelist, is that he is able, in a way that many formal models in existing social theory are not, to encompass the substance of man in his many manifestations. Man is both determined by the fact of his imprisonment, and also determining, in the sense that he creates (and is able to struggle against) his own imprisonment. Some men (the guards) have interests (up to a point) in the maintenance of imprisonment; others (the inmates, their relatives and sympathizers) do not. There is, in Solzhenitsyn's 'prison', a sense of the contingencies and sequences that may lead some men to imprison others: a view of the social and political origins of repression and the segregation of deviants. There is some conception too of the real political, material and symbolic imperatives that lie at the back of such sequences and processes. And, finally, there is an implicit prescription in Solzhenitsyn, a *politics* for which he is now experiencing exclusion and segregation himself, a politics which implies that man is able consciously to abolish the imprisonment that he consciously created.

It may well be, as Lukács's criticism implies, that these substantive features of Solzhenitsyn's writings are not held together and continuously, in an ongoing dialectic of resistance and control. Nevertheless, Solzhenitsyn's attempts to achieve this fare well by comparison with many sociological excursions into the area. The substantive history of twentieth century criminology is, by and large, the history of the empirical emasculation of theories (like those of Marx and Durkheim) which attempted to deal with the whole society, and a history therefore of the depoliticization of criminological issues.

THE NEW CRIMINOLOGY

The conditions of our time are forcing a reappraisal of this compartmentalization of issues and problems. It is not just that the traditional focus of applied criminology on the socially deprived working-class adolescent is being thrown into doubt by the criminalization of vast numbers of middle-class youth (for 'offences' of a hedonistic or specifically oppositional nature) (S. Cohen, 1971c; I. Taylor, 1971d). Neither is it only that the crisis of our institutions has deepened to the point where the 'master institutions' of the state, and of the political economy, are unable to disguise their own inability to adhere to their own rules and regulations (cf. Kennedy, 1970; Pearce, 1973). It is largely that the total interconnectedness of these problems and others is being revealed.

A criminology which is to be adequate to an understanding of these developments, and which will be able to bring politics back into the discussion of what were previously technical issues, will need to deal with the society as a totality. This 'new' criminology will in fact be an *old* criminology, in that it will face the same problems that were faced by the classical social theorists. Marx saw the problem with his usual clarity when he began to develop his critique of the origins of German idealism:

> The first work which I undertook for a solution to the doubts which assailed me was a critical review of the Hegelian philosophy of right, a work the introduction to which appeared in 1844 in the *Deutsch-Französische Jahrbücher* published in Paris. My investigations led to the result that legal relations as well as forms of state are to be grasped neither from themselves nor from the so-called general development of the human mind, but rather have their roots in the material conditions of life, the sum total of which Hegel, following the example of Englishmen and Frenchmen of the eighteenth century, combines under the name 'civil society', that however the anatomy of civil society is to be sought in political economy. (1951: 328–9)

We have argued here for a political economy of criminal action, and of the reaction it excites, and for a politically informed social psychology of these ongoing social dynamics. We have, in other words, laid claim to have constructed the formal elements of a theory that would be adequate to move criminology out of its own imprisonment in artificially segregated specifics. We have attempted to bring the parts together again in order to form the whole.

Implicitly, we have rejected that contemporary trend which may claim for itself the mantle of a new criminology, or a new deviance theory, and which presumably claims to find a solution to our present discontents largely in the search for the sources of individual meaning. Ethnomethodology, however, is a historical creature too: its pedigree goes back to the phenomenological contemplations that were so prominent in an earlier period of uncertainty and doubt: the collapse of European social democracy and the rise of fascism. Phenomenology looks at the prison camp and searches for the *meaning* of the 'prison' rather than for its alternative; and it searches for the meaning in terms of individual definitions rather than in terms of a political explanation of the necessity to imprison.

Indeed, one of the recurring criticisms we have [. . .] of many theorists [. . .] is the way in which they place men apart from society. The view of man in society is sometimes *additive* (in the sense that environmental 'factors' are seen as having a more or less significant impact on some fundamental fact of human nature – as in Eysenck); sometimes it is *discontinuous* (in that there is a recognition of interplay between man and social influences, but an interplay which is curtailed by men's differential ability to be socialized – as in Durkheim – or in the appropriateness of certain social patterns for different men in different periods – as in Durkheim and in Merton), and when there is a fusion of man and society, it is only in terms of man's given biological or psychological pathologies (which, for example, force him to gravitate into delinquent areas, as in Shaw and Mackay and the early ecologists). Phenomenology and ethnomethodology make the break between man and society by reifying experience and meaning, as specifics in their own right, which we cannot take (for granted) to be socially determined in any currently identifiable manner.

Increasingly, it is becoming clear that the contemplation and suspension involved in these (and other) traditions are not enough. There is a crisis not just in social theory and social thought (Gouldner, 1971) but in the society itself. The new criminology must therefore be a normative theory: it must hold out the possibilities of a resolution to the fundamental questions, and a social resolution.

It is this normative imperative that separates out the European schools of criminology from the eclecticism and reformism in professional American sociology (cf. Nicolaus, 1969)[7]. The domination of orthodox positivism over European criminology has been most clearly challenged recently by the emergence of a social welfare-oriented criminology in Scandinavia, centring particularly around the Institute of Criminology and Criminal Law at the University of Oslo, and by the beginnings of a politically informed 'structuralism' in the formation of the National Deviancy Conference in Britain.

The new Scandinavian criminology, which has been several years in the making (N. Christie, 1965, 1968, 1971; Mathiesen, 1965, 1972) has been fundamentally concerned with the description and explanation of the forms assumed, as the titles of their publications imply, by the 'aspects of social control in welfare states'. Working in relatively underpopulated societies, and in the urban centres where the major bureaucracies of the city and the university were constantly meeting up and inter-penetrating, the Scandinavian criminologist originally took on a role and an ideology not unlike that of the early Chicago ecologists – or indeed the role of the cautious rebel as advocated by Merton. That is, they acted as agitators of public opinion *and* advisers to governments on questions of prison administration, the reform of juvenile training schools, preventive programmes and the like. The result of this inter-penetration was not so much the alleviation of social problems or of social control as it was the co-optation of the new criminologists. The new criminology has now split, on friendly terms, into two distinct tendencies: on the one hand, the poetic social democratic, and the other, the direct action revolutionary.

The first tendency is described by Nils Christie (1971):

> We have not made clear that our role as criminologists is not first and foremost to be received as useful problem-solvers, *but as problem-raisers*. Let us turn our weakness into strength by admitting – and enjoying – that our situation has a great resemblance to that of artists and men of letters. We are working on a culture of deviance and social control. . . . Changing times create new situations and bring us to new crossroads. Together with other cultural workers – because these fields are central to all observers of society – but equipped with our special training in scientific method and theory, it is our obligation as well as pleasure to penetrate these problems. Together with other cultural workers, we will probably have to keep a constant fight going against being absorbed, tamed, and made responsible, and thereby completely socialized into society – as it is.

For Thomas Mathiesen and others, however, the limitations of the original social welfare approach to social control did not dissolve simply into the problem of avoiding personal co-option. For him, the problem, even in the relatively benign atmosphere of Scandinavia, was action; to change society 'as it is': not simply to describe 'The Defences of the Weak' but to organize them. The normative prescription of the new Scandinavian criminology led to the formation of the KRUM, a trade union for inmates of Scandinavian prisons, and a union which was able [in 1971] to co-ordinate a prison strike across three national boundaries and across several prison walls (Mathiesen, 1972).

Something of the same dilemma faces the normative criminology of the kind being developed in Britain (cf. S. Cohen, 1971a; Rock, 1973; Rock and McIntosh, 1973; I. Taylor, 1971d) and advocated via an immanent critique of other explanations of crime, deviance and dissent. [. . .] The retreat from theory is over, and the politicization of crime and criminology is imminent. Close reading of the classical social theorists reveals a basic agreement; the abolition of crime *is* possible under certain social arrangements. Even Durkheim, with his notion of human nature as a fixed biological given, was able to allow for the substantial diminution of crime under conditions of a free division of labour, untrammelled by the inequalities of inherited wealth and the entrenchment of interests of power and authority (by those who were not deserving of it).

It should be clear that a criminology which is not normatively committed to the abolition of inequalities of wealth and power, and in particular of inequalities in property and life-chances, is inevitably bound to fall into correctionalism. And all correctionalism is irreducibly bound up with the identification of deviance with pathology. A fully social theory of deviance must, by its nature, break entirely with correctionalism (even with social reform of the kind advocated by the Chicagoans, the Mertonians and the romantic wing of Scandinavian criminology) precisely because [. . .] the causes of crime must be intimately bound up with the form assumed by the social arrangements of the time. Crime is ever and always that behaviour seen to be problematic within the framework of those social arrangements: for crime to be abolished, then, those social arrangements themselves must also be subject to fundamental social change.

It has often been argued, rather misleadingly, that for Durkheim *crime* was a normal social fact (that it was thus a fundamental feature of human ontology). For us, as for Marx and for other new criminologists, *deviance* is normal – in the sense that men are now consciously involved (in the prisons that are contemporary society and in the real prisons) in asserting their human diversity. The task is not merely to 'penetrate' these problems, not merely to question the stereotypes, or to act as carriers of 'alternative phenomenological realities'. The task is to create a society in which the facts of human diversity, whether personal, organic or social, are not subject to the power to criminalize.

NOTES

1 A highly suggestive attempt to wed the concerns of ecological analysis with the wider context of power, authority and political domination is made by Gail Armstrong and Mary Wilson (1973).

2 The largely uncharted history of youth subcultures in Britain since the war is at last being attempted against the background of some kind of structural analysis. (Cf. P. Cohen, 1972; S. Cohen, 1971a, 1972a 1972b; Rock and Cohen, 1970; Willis, 1972.)

3 The notion of 'lay theories of criminality' is taken up by Box (1971: 180–1) in a discussion of the particular 'theories' informing the everyday exercise of police discretion. He writes:

In order to cope with the chaos of an infinite number of suspects, the police develop theories on the causes of crime and the nature of the criminal. These theories are refractions of professional theories, past and present, which have been transmitted, like rumours, from the writings of 'experts' through the mass media and into the heads of the lay public, including policemen, who then mould and slightly recast them to fit in with their occupational experiences, and to facilitate occupational performances.

One of the central features of lay theories, as adopted by the police and the magistracy in particular, is what one of the present authors has termed their 'absolutist' view of society. In this version of 'theory', deviants are divided into the real – committed, pathological – types (e.g. the drug-pusher, or, as in Yablonsky, the disturbed sociopath who wins positions of authority in working-class fighting gangs and in the middle-class communes of hippies) on the one hand, and the misled innocents on the other (the immature and stupid youth who buys –under pressure – from the ruthless pusher; or the ordinary street-kid who follows a gang leader because he has no healthy youth club leader as an alternative focus of identification). Cf. the discussion of the ways in which policemen encourage the drug-user to accept this distinction in exchange for sympathetic treatment in court, in Young (1971a: 188–9).

4 This is evidenced, most significantly, in the low rate of reportability of certain kinds of sexual offences (e.g. forcible rape) – a large proportion of which (contrary to media representation) occur within family groups or amongst relatively close acquaintances (cf. for example, Menachem Amir, 1967, 1971).

5 From time to time, of course, attempts are made by one interest group to win other groups to its own version of lay theory. At the time of writing, for example, proposals are being mooted by the Criminal Law Revision Committee (under pressure from the Police Federation, the press and others) to the Home Secretary in the United Kingdom, to withdraw certain safeguards traditionally accorded defendants. The net effect of these proposals (centring around the withdrawal of the right to remain silent, the placing of the accused in the witness-box and the admissibility of forcibly obtained confessions) would be that the lay theory of the non-professional juries would be replaced as the decisive courtroom reality by the lay theory adhered to by the police (cf. Michael Zander, *Guardian*, 7 April 1972).

6 It is worth noting that studies of prison subcultures are moving precisely in this direction. Where many writers have adopted a view of inmates as relatively passive and malleable creatures of institutional regime, capable at most of what Goffman terms 'secondary adjustment' in the face of the mortification of imprisonment, there has been a tendency in recent literature towards an examination of 'what the inmates bring with them'. This tendency has been most noticeable in studies of adult prisons, and in a sense is an inevitable consequence of the rise of the prison movement in the United States (especially amongst blacks and especially in California), the inmate unions in Scandinavia, some acts of resistance in British maximum security prisons and the formation of the Preservation of Rights of Prisoners. Cf. L. Taylor and S. Cohen (1972); and also, in a less detailed and empirical fashion, John Irwin and Donald Cressey (1962). Less dramatic evidence of the connections between the consciousness of *juvenile* delinquents prior to apprehension and their 'adjustments' in juvenile institutions is presented in an unpublished paper 'Theories of action in juvenile correctional institutions', by Ian Taylor (1971c).

7 The eclecticism of American criminology and deviancy theory is probably explic-able partly in terms of a critique of American social thought in general, of the kind that Gouldner is currently engaged in. For the time being we can characterize the two central themes in American criminology as reformism and millenarianism, both of which have in common a theoretical naïveté and a normative incongruity. Criminal lawyers like Sanford Kadish and 'radical' sociologists like Howard Becker can both identify the 'care-taking

institutions' as 'overcriminalizing' American youth and American deviants in general, and argue for change at the attitude level amongst the guardians of public order (Becker, 1967, 1972; Kadish, 1968). The more radical wing can respond to the politicization of deviance and the rise of a prison movement amongst the black *Lumpenproletariat* by polemics which pass for theory, calling for the removal of a legal system which is unjust in its choice of victims (Quinney, 1972). The continuing crisis of American institutions, and the continuing polarization of social forces within the society, may result in a clarification of criminological politics, and a revival of theory to accompany it. As yet, these possibilities exemplify themselves only in an embryonic sociology of law (Chambliss and Siedman, 1971) and in a return to social history (Quinney, 1970; Weis, 1971) – both of these tendencies basing themselves on an ambiguous middle-range 'theory' of interest group conflict. They are open to all the limitations of the new conflict theorists in general.

REFERENCES

Amir, M. (1967) 'Patterns of forcible rape', in M.B. Clinard and R. Quinney (eds), *Criminal Behavior Systems*.New York: Holt, Rinehart and Winston.

Amir, M. (1971) *Patterns in Forcible Rape*. Chicago: University of Chicago Press.

Armstrong, G. and Wilson, M. (1973) 'City politics and deviancy amplification', in L. Taylor and I. Taylor (eds), *Politics and Deviance*. Harmondsworth: Penguin (for the National Deviancy Conference).

Becker, H.S. (1967) 'Whose side are we on?', *Social Problems*, 14(3): 239–47.

Becker, H.S. (1971) *Sociological Work*. London: Allen Lane.

Becker, H.S. (1972) 'Labelling theory revisited', in P. Rock and M. McIntosh, (eds) *Deviance and Social Control*. London: Tavistock.

Box, S. (1971) *Deviance, Reality and Society*. London: Holt, Rienhart and Winston.

Chambliss, W.J. and Siedman, R.B. (1971) *Law, Order and Power*. Reading, MA: Addison-Wesley.

Christie, N. et al. (1965, 1968, 1971) *Scandinavian Studies in Criminology*. London: Tavistock; Oslo: Universitetsforlaget (3 vols).

Christie, N. (1971) 'Scandinavian criminology facing the 1970's', in N. Christie et al. (1971), pp. 121–49.

Cohen, P. (1972) 'Subcultural conflict and working class community', in *Working Papers in Cultural Studies* (2) (Centre for Contemporary Cultural Studies, University of Birmingham). pp. 5–52.

Cohen, S. (ed.) (1971a) *Images of Deviance*. Harmondsworth: Penguin (for the National Deviancy Conference).

Cohen, S. (1971b) 'Directions for research on adolescent group violence and vandalism', *British Journal of Criminology*, 11(4): 319–40.

Cohen, S. (1971c) 'Protest, unrest and delinquency: convergences in labels or behaviour?'. Paper given to the International Symposium on Youth Unrest, Tel-Aviv, 25–27 October.

Cohen, S. (1972a) *Moral Panics and Folk Devils*. London: MacGibbon and Kee.

Cohen, S. (1972b) 'Breaking out, smashing up, and the social context of aspiration', in B. Riven (ed.), *Youth at the Beginning of the Seventies*. London: Martin Robertson.

Downes, D. (1966) *The Delinquent Solution*. London: Routledge and Kegan Paul.

Gouldner, A.W. (1971) *The Coming Crisis of Western Sociology*. London: Heinemann Educational (New York: Basic Books, 1970).

Hepworth, M. (1971) 'Deviants in disguise: blackmail and social acceptance', in S. Cohen (ed.), *Images of Deviance*. Harmondsworth: Penguin. pp. 192–218.

Hepworth, M. (1972) 'Missing persons', in P. Rock and M. McIntosh (eds), *Deviance and Social Control*. London: Tavistock.

Irwin, J. and Cressey, D. (1962) 'Thieves, convicts and the inmate culture', *Social Problems*, 10(2): 142–55.

Jackson, G. (1970) *Soledad Brother*. Harmondsworth: Penguin.

Kadish, S. (1968) 'The crisis of overcriminalization', *American Criminal Law Quarterly*, 7: 17.

Kennedy, M. (1970) 'Beyond incrimination: some neglected facets in the theory of punishment', *Catalyst*, 5 (Summer): 1–37.

Lemert, E.M. (1967) *Human Deviance, Social Problems and Social Control*. New York: Prentice-Hall.

Lukács, G. (1971) *Solzhenitsyn*. London: Merlin Press.

Manson, I. and Palmer, J. (1973) *The Dirty Old Man on the Last Tube: the Social Response to Pornography*. London: Davis-Poynter.

Marx, K. (1951) Preface to *A Contribution to the Critique of Political Economy*, in *Marx–Engels Selected Works*, vol. 1. Moscow: Foreign Languages Publishing House.

Mathiesen, T. (1965) *The Defences of the Weak: a Study of a Norwegian Correctional Institution*. London: Tavistock.

Mathiesen, T. (1972) *Beyond the Boundaries of Organizations*. California: Glendessary Press.

Nicolaus, M. (1969) 'The professional organization of sociology: a view from below', *Antioch Review*, Fall, pp. 375–87.

Pearce, F. (1973) 'Crime, corporations and the American social order', in L. Taylor and I. Taylor, (eds) *Politics and Deviance*. Harmondsworth: Penguin (for the National Deviancy Conference).

Quinney, R. (1970) *The Social Reality of Crime*. Boston: Little Brown and Co.

Quinney, R. (1972) 'The ideology of law: notes for a radical alternative to legal oppression', *Issues in Criminology*, 7(1): 1–36.

Rock, P. (1973) *A Sociology of Deviance*. London: Hutchinson.

Rock, P. and Cohen, S. (1970) 'The Teddy Boys', in V. Bogdanor and R. Skidelsky (eds), *The Age of Affluence 1951–1964*. London, Macmillan. pp. 288–320.

Rock, P. and McIntosh, M. (eds) (1973) *Deviance and Social Control*. London: Tavistock (for the British Sociological Association).

Simmons, J.L. and Chambers, H. (1965) 'Public stereotypes of deviants', *Social Problems*, 13: 223–32.

Taylor, I. (1971a) 'Soccer consciousness and soccer hooliganism', in S. Cohen (ed.), *Images of Deviance*. Harmondsworth: Penguin. pp. 134–64.

Taylor, I. (1971b) '"Football mad" – a speculative sociology of soccer hooliganism' in Eric Dunning (ed.), *The Sociology of Sport: a Selection of Readings*. London: Cass.

Taylor, I. (1971c) 'Theories of action in juvenile correctional institutions'. Unpublished paper given to the First Anglo-Scandinavian Seminar in Criminology, Norway, September 1971.

Taylor, I. (1971d) 'The new criminology in an age of doubt', *New Edinburgh Review*, 15 (November): 14–17.

Taylor, L. (1972) 'The significance and interpretation of replies to motivational questions: the case of sex offenders', *Sociology*, 6(1): 23–40.

Taylor, L. and Cohen, S. (1972) *Psychological Survival: the Experience of Long-Term Imprisonment*. Harmondsworth: Penguin.

Taylor, L. and Walton, P. (1971) 'Industrial sabotage: motives and meanings', in S. Cohen (ed.), *Images of Deviance*. Harmondsworth: Penguin.

Weis, J.G. (1971) 'Dialogue with David Matza', *Issues in Criminology*, 6(1): 33–53.

Willis, P. (1972) 'The motorbike within a subcultural group', *Working Papers in Cultural Studies*, 2 (Centre for Contemporary Cultural Studies, University of Birmingham).

Young, J. (1971a) *The Drugtakers: the Social Meaning of Drug Use*. London: MacGibbon and Kee/Paladin.

Young, J. (1971b) 'The role of the police as amplifiers of deviancy, negotiators of reality and translators of fantasy: some consequences of our present system of drug control as seen in Notting Hill', in S. Cohen (ed.), *Images of Deviance*. Harmondsworth: Penguin. pp. 27–61.

23

Crime, power and ideological mystification

Steven Box

Murder! Rape! Robbery! Assault! Wounding! Theft! Burglary! Arson! Vandalism! These form the substance of the annual official criminal statistics on indictable offences (or the Crime Index offences in America). Aggregated, they constitute the major part of 'our' crime problem. Or at least, we are told so daily by politicians, police, judges and journalists who speak to us through the media of newspapers and television. And most of us listen. We don't want to be murdered, raped, robbed, assaulted, or criminally victimized in any other way. Reassured that our political leaders are both aware of the problem's growing dimensions and receptive to our rising anxieties, we wait in optimistic but realistic anticipation for crime to be at least effectively reduced. But apart from the number of police rapidly increasing, their technological and quasi-military capacities shamelessly strengthened, their discretionary powers of apprehension, interrogation, detention and arrest liberally extended, and new prisons built or old ones extensively refurbished (all with money the government claims the country has not got to maintain existing standards of education, health, unemployment welfare, and social services), nothing much justifies the optimism.

The number of recorded serious crimes marches forever upward. During the decade 1970–80, serious crimes recorded by the police increased for nearly every category: violence against the person rose by 136 per cent, burglary by 44 per cent, robbery by 138 per cent, theft and handling by 54 per cent and fraud and forgery by 18 per cent. These increases were not merely artefacts of an increased population available to commit serious crimes. For even when the changing population size is controlled statistically, crimes continue to rise. Thus in 1950, there were 1,094 per 100,000 population. This rose to 1,742 by 1960, then to 3,221 by 1970, and reached 5,119 by 1980. From 1980 to 1981 they rose a further 10 per cent, to reach an all-time record. Ironically, as 'our' crime problem gets worse, the demand for even more 'law and order' policies increases, even though these are blatantly having no effect on the level of serious crimes. At least not on the level recorded by the police.

The result, so we are told, is that the 'fear of crime' has now been elevated into a national problem. Techniques for avoiding victimization have become a serious

From *Power, Crime and Mystification*, pp. 1–15. (London: Tavistock, 1983.)

preoccupation: more locks on doors and windows, fewer visits after dark to family, friends, and places of entertainment, avoidance of underground and empty train carriages, mace sprays or personal alarm sirens held nervously in coat pockets, a growing unwillingness to be neighbourly or engage in local collective enterprises, furtive suspicious glances at any stranger, and attempts to avoid any encounter except with the most trusted and close friends.

Who are these 'villains' driving us into a state of national agoraphobia? We are told a fairly accurate and terrifying glimpse can be obtained of 'our' Public Enemies by examining the convicted and imprisoned population. For every 100 persons convicted of these serious crimes, 85 are male. Amongst this convicted male population, those aged less than 30 years, and particularly those aged between 15 and 21 years are over-represented. Similarly, the educational non-achievers are over-represented – at the other end of the educational achievement ladder there appear to be hardly any criminals, since only 0.05 per cent of people received into prison have obtained a university degree. The unemployed are currently only (*sic*) 14 per cent of the available labour force, but they constitute approximately 40 per cent of those convicted. Only 4 per cent of the general population are black, but nearly one-third of the convicted and imprisoned population are black. Urban dwellers, particularly inner-city residents, are over-represented. Thus the typical people criminally victimizing and forcing us to fear each other and fracture our sense of 'community' are young uneducated males, who are often unemployed, live in a working-class impoverished neighbourhood, and frequently belong to an ethnic minority. These villains deserve, so 'law and order' campaigners tell us ceaselessly in their strident moral rhetoric, either short, sharp, shock treatment, including death by hanging or castration by chemotherapy – 'off with their goolies' – or long, endless, self-destroying stretches as non-paying guests in crumbling, insanitary, overcrowded prisons constructed for the redemption of lost Christian souls by our Victorian ancestors. If only these ideas were pursued vigorously and with a vengeance morally justified by the offender's wickedness, then 'our' society would be relatively crime-free and tranquil. So 'law and order' campaigners tell us.

It is tempting to call all this hype – but that would be extreme! 'Conventional' crimes do have victims whose suffering is real; steps should be taken to understand and control these crimes so that fewer and fewer people are victimized. A radical criminology which appears to deny this will be seen as callous and rightly rejected. Furthermore, those crimes so carefully recorded and graphed in official criminal statistics *are* more likely to be committed by young males, living in poor neighbourhoods and so on. A radical criminology which appears to deny this will be seen as naive and rightly rejected. Finally, there are very good grounds for believing that the rising crime wave is real – material conditions for large sections of the community have deteriorated markedly. A radical criminology which remained insensitive of this would be guilty of forgetting its theoretical roots and rightly rejected. So the official portrait of crime and criminals is not entirely without merit or truth.

None the less, before galloping off down the 'law and order' campaign trail, it might be prudent to consider whether murder, rape, robbery, assault, and other crimes focused on by state officials, politicians, the media, and the criminal justice system do constitute the major part of our real crime problem. Maybe they are only *a* crime problem and not *the* crime problem. Maybe what is stuffed into our consciousness as *the* crime problem is in fact an illusion, a trick to deflect our attention away from other, even more serious crimes and victimizing behaviours, which objectively cause the vast bulk of avoidable death, injury and deprivation.

At the same time, it might be prudent to compare persons who commit other serious but under-emphasized crimes and victimizing behaviours with those who are officially portrayed as 'our' criminal enemies. For if the former, compared to the latter, are indeed quite different types of people, then maybe we should stop looking to our political authorities and criminal justice system for protection from those beneath us in impoverished urban neighbourhoods. Instead maybe we should look up accusingly at our political and judicial 'superiors' for being or for protecting the 'real' culprits.

If we do this, we might also cast a jaundiced eye at the view that serious criminals are 'pathological'. This has been the favourite explanatory imagery of mainstream positivistic criminology. It was, however, an explanation that only remained plausible if crimes were indeed committed by a minority of individuals living in conditions of relative deprivation. For whilst this was true it was obvious, at least to the conservative mind, that 'something must be wrong with them'. However, if we look up rather than down the stratification hierarchy and see serious crimes being committed by the people who are respectable, well-educated, wealthy and socially privileged then the imagery of pathology seems harder to accept. If these upper- and middle-class criminals are also pathological, then what hope is there for any of us! Wanting to avoid this pessimistic conclusion, we might instead entertain the idea that these powerful persons commit crimes for 'rational' – albeit disreputable – motives which emerge under conditions that render conformity a relatively unrewarding activity. Having rescued the powerful from 'abnormality' we might do the same for the powerless. Maybe they too are rational rather than irrational, morally disreputable rather than organically abnormal, overwhelmed by adversity rather than by wickedness.

If these are the lessons of prudence, then standing back from the official portrait of crime and criminals and looking at it critically might be a very beneficial move towards getting our heads straight.

However, there is an agonizing choice to make between at least two pairs of spectacles we might wear to take this critical look. We could wear the liberal 'scientific' pair, as did many young trendy academics during the 1960s and early 1970s when the stars of interactionism and phenomenology were in the ascendant. Or we might wear the radical 'reflexive' pair, whose lenses have been recently polished to a fine smoothness by those same trendy academics who have now entered a middle-age period of intellectual enlightenment! These spectacles do provide quite different views on the official portrait of crime and criminals.

LIBERAL 'SCIENTISM': PARTIALLY BLIND JUSTICE

One way of getting a clear perspective on those crimes and criminals causing us most harm, injury and deprivation is to excavate unreported, unrecorded and non-prosecuted crimes. This can be achieved by sifting evidence from numerous self-reported crime studies and criminal victimization surveys. This is undoubtedly an important exercise for it leads us to reconsider the *validity* of official criminal statistics and the more extreme pronouncements made directly and uncritically from them.

What lessons are there to be learnt from the results of these surveys? First, there is much more serious crime being committed than the official police records indicate. The emerging consensus is that one serious crime in three (excluding burglary and car theft) is reported to the police. This knowledge can and does add fuel to the alarmist 'law and order' fire: 'it's even worse than we imagined!' Second, although the official portrait of criminals is not untrue, it is inaccurate. It is more like a distorting mirror; you immediately recognize yourself, but not quite in a flattering shape and form familiar to you. Thus self-report data indicate that serious crimes are disproportionately committed by the young uneducated males amongst whom the unemployed and ethnically oppressed are over-represented, but the contribution they make is less than the official data implies. There are, it appears, more serious crimes being committed by white, respectable, well-educated, slightly older males and females than we are led to believe (Box, 1981a: 56–93).

To the liberal 'scientific' mind, there are two problems here of 'slippage', one more slight than the other. Too many people fail to report crimes because they consider the police inefficient; we need to restore police efficiency in order to increase the reportage rate and hence obtain a better, more reliable gauge of crime. The second, more important slippage, is that the administration of criminal justice is fine in principle, but is failing slightly in practice. The police pursue policies of *differential deployment* (for example, swamping certain parts of London where the West Indian population is prominent) and *'methodological suspicion'* (that is, routinely suspecting only a limited proportion of the population, particularly those with criminal records or known criminal associates). Coupled with these practices are *plea-bargaining* (negotiating a guilty plea in return for being charged with a less serious offence) and *'judicious' judicial decisions* (which take as much notice of who you are as they do of what you have apparently done). In other words, the police, magistrates, judges, and other court officials have too much discretion. The result is too much 'street-justice', 'charge-dealing', 'plea-bargaining' and 'disparate sentencing'. In these judicial negotiations and compromises, the wealthy, privileged and powerful are better able to secure favourable outcomes than their less powerful counterparts (Box, 1981a: 157–207). This slippage between ideal and practice reveals a slightly disturbing picture. The process of law enforcement, in its broadest possible interpretation, operates in such a way as to *conceal* crimes of the powerful against the powerless, but to *reveal* and *exaggerate* crimes of the powerless against 'everyone'.

Furthermore, because a substantial section of this criminalized population is stigmatized and discriminated against, particularly in the field of employment, its reproduction is secured; many of them, out of resentment, injustice, or desperation, turn to more persistent and even more serious forms of crime. This vicious circle increases the over-representation of the powerless in the highly publicized 'hardened' criminal prisoner population.

The outcome of these processes is that the official portrait of crime and criminals is highly selective, serving to conceal crimes of the powerful and hence shore up their interests, particularly the need to be legitimated through maintaining the appearance of respectability. At the same time, crimes of the powerless are revealed and exaggerated, and this serves the interests of the powerful because it legitimizes their control agencies, such as the police and prison service, being strengthened materially, technologically and legally, so that their ability to survey, harass, deter, both specifically and generally, actual and potential resisters to political authority is enhanced.

To the liberal 'scientific' mind, a solution of this second and more important slippage would involve a strict limitation on police and judicial discretion and less stigmatization either by decriminalizing some behaviours, or imposing less incarceration (Schur, 1973). The adoption of these policies would narrow the 'official' differential in criminal behaviour between the disreputable poor and the respectable middle class so that it approximated more closely the actual differences in criminal behaviour – at least criminal behaviour as defined by the state.

RADICAL 'REFLEXIVENESS': ARTFUL CRIMINAL DEFINITIONS

Although an enormous amount of carefully buried crime can be unearthed by this liberal 'scientific' excavation work, we will still be denied an adequate view of those whose crimes and victimizing behaviours cause us most harm, injury and deprivation.

Through radical 'reflexive' spectacles, all this excavation work occurs so late in the process of constructing crime and criminals that it never gets to the foundations. Those committed to self-report and victimization surveys do not start off asking the most important question of all: 'what is serious crime?' Instead they take serious crime as a pre- and state-defined phenomenon. But by the time crime categories or definitions have been established, the most important foundation stone of 'our crime problem' has been well and truly buried in cement, beyond the reach of any liberal 'scientific' shovel.

Aware that liberal 'scientists' arrive too late on the scene, radicals resolve to get up earlier in the morning. Instead of merely examining how the law enforcement process in its broadest sense constructs a false image of serious crime and its perpetrators, they suggest we should consider the *social construction of criminal law categories*. This involves not only reflecting on why certain types of behaviours are defined as criminal in some historical periods and not others, but also why a particular criminal law comes to incorporate from relatively homogeneous behaviour patterns only a portion and excludes the remainder, even though each and every instance of this behaviour causes avoidable harm, injury, or deprivation.

Some sociologists have pondered these issues and come to the conclusion that *criminal law categories are ideological constructs* (Sumner, 1976). Rather than being a fair reflection of those behaviours objectively causing us collectively the most avoidable suffering, criminal law categories are artful, creative constructs designed to criminalize only some victimizing behaviours, usually those more frequently committed by the relatively powerless, and to exclude others, usually those frequently committed by the powerful against subordinates.

Numerous researchers (Chambliss 1964; Duster 1970; Graham 1972; Gunningham 1974; Hall 1952; Haskins 1960; Hay 1975; Hopkins 1978; McCaghy and Denisoff 1973; Platt 1969; Thompson 1975) have produced evidence consistent with the view that criminal law categories are ideological reflections of the interests of particular powerful groups. As such, criminal law categories are resources, tools, instruments, designed and then used to criminalize, demoralize, incapacitate, fracture and sometimes eliminate those problem populations perceived by the powerful to be potentially or actually threatening the existing distribution of power, wealth and privilege. They constitute one, and only one way by which social control over subordinate, but 'resisting', populations is exercised. For once behaviour more typically engaged in by subordinate populations has been incorporated into criminal law, then legally sanctioned punishments can be 'justifiably' imposed.

In a society such as ours, populations more likely to be controlled in part through criminalization,

> tend to share a number of social characteristics but most important among these is the fact that their behaviour, personal qualities, and/or position threaten the social relationships of production. . . . In other words, populations become generally eligible for management as deviant when they disturb, hinder, or call into question . . . capitalist modes of appropriating the product of human labour . . . the social conditions under which capitalist production takes place . . . patterns of distribution and consumption . . . the process of socialization for productive and non-productive roles . . . and . . . the ideology which supports the functioning of capitalist society. (Spitzer, 1975: 642)

However, this argument needs qualification. It does not maintain that all criminal laws directly express the interests of one particular group, such as the ruling class. Clearly some legislation reflects temporary victories of one interest or allied interest groups over others, and none of these may necessarily be identical or coincide with the interests of the ruling class. Yet the above argument does not demand or predict that every criminal law directly represents the interests of the ruling class. It recognizes that some laws are passed purely as symbolic victories which the dominant class grants to inferior interest groups, basically to keep them quiet; once passed, they need never be efficiently or systematically enforced. It also recognizes that occasionally the ruling class is forced into a tactical retreat by organized subordinate groups, and the resulting shifts in criminal law enshrine a broader spectrum of interests. But these victories are short lived. Powerful groups have ways and means of clawing back the spoils of tactical defeats. In the last instance, definitions of crime reflect the interests of those groups who comprise the ruling class. This is not to assume that these interests are homogeneous and without serious contradictions (Chambliss, 1981). Indeed, it is just the space between these contradictions that subordinate groups fill with their demands for legal change.

It might be objected that even though *some* criminal laws are in the interests of the dominant class and that others which are obviously not in these interests are ineffectively enforced, thus making them dead-letter laws, it still remains true that laws proscribing those types of victimizing behaviours of which we are all too aware and which set the nerve-ends of neo-classical/conservative criminologists, such as Wilson (1975) and Morgan (1978) tingling with fear and loathing, *are in all our interests*. None of us wants to be murdered, raped, or robbed; none of us wants our property stolen, smashed, or destroyed, none of us wants our bodies punched, kicked, bitten, or tortured. In that sense, criminal laws against murder, rape, arson, robbery, theft and assault are in all our interests, since in principle we all benefit equally from and are protected by their existence. Without them life would be 'nasty, poor, solitary, brutish, and short'.

This is all true, but it is not all the truth. For some groups of people benefit more than others from these laws. It is not that they are less likely to be murdered, raped, robbed or assaulted – although the best scientific evidence based on victimization surveys shows this to be true (Hindelang et al., 1978) – but that in the criminal law, definitions of murder, rape, robbery, assault, theft and other serious crimes are so constructed as to exclude many similar, and in important respects, identical acts, and these are just the acts likely to be committed more frequently by powerful individuals.

Thus the criminal law defines only some types of avoidable killing as murder: it excludes, for example, deaths resulting from acts of negligence, such as employers' failure to maintain safe working conditions in factories and mines (Swartz, 1975); or deaths resulting from an organization's reluctance to maintain appropriate safety standards (Erickson, 1976); or deaths that result from governmental agencies' giving environmental health risks a low priority (Liazos, 1972); or deaths resulting from drug manufacturers' failure to conduct adequate research on new chemical compounds before embarking on aggressive marketing campaigns (Silverman and Lee, 1974); or deaths from a dangerous drug that was approved by health authorities on the strength of a bribe from a pharmaceutical company (Braithwaite and Geis, 1981); or deaths resulting from car manufacturers refusing to recall and repair thousands of known defective vehicles because they calculate that the costs of meeting civil damages will be less (Swigert and Farrell, 1981); and in most jurisdictions deaths resulting from drunken or reckless people driving cars with total indifference to the potential cost in terms of human lives are also excluded.

The list of avoidable killings not legally construed as murder even in principle could go on and on. But the point should be clear. We are encouraged to see murder as a particular act involving a very limited range of stereotypical actors, instruments, situations and motives. Other types of avoidable killing are either defined as a less serious crime than murder, or as matters more appropriate for administrative or civil proceedings, or as events beyond the justifiable boundaries of state interference. In all instances, the perpetrators of these avoidable 'killings' deserve, so we are told, less harsh community responses than would be made to those committing legally defined murder. The majority of people accept this because the state, by excluding these killings from the murder category, has signified its intention that we should not treat them as capital offenders. As the state can muster a galaxy of skilled machiavellian orators to defend its definitions, and has, beyond these velvet tongues, the iron fist of police and military physical violence, it is able to persuade most people easily and convincingly.

It may be just a strange coincidence, as Vonnegut often suggests, that the social characteristics of those persons more likely to commit these types of avoidable killings differ considerably from those possessed by individuals more likely to commit killings legally construed in principle as murder. That the former are more likely to be relatively more powerful, wealthy and privileged than the latter could be one of nature's accidents. But is it likely?

The criminal law sees only some types of property deprivation as robbery or theft; it excludes, for example, the separation of consumers and part of their money that follows manufacturers' malpractices or advertisers' misrepresentations; it excludes shareholders losing their money because managers behaved in ways which they thought would be to the advantage of shareholders even though the only tangible benefits accrued to the managers (Hopkins, 1980b); it excludes the *extra* tax citizens, in this or other countries, have to pay because: (i) corporations and the very wealthy are able to employ financial experts at discovering legal loopholes through which money can be safely transported to tax havens; (ii) Defence Department officials have been bribed to order more expensive weaponry systems or missiles in 'excess' of those 'needed'; (iii) multinational drug companies charge our National Health Services prices which are estimated to be at least £50 million in excess of alternative supplies. If an employee's hand slips into the governor's pocket and removes any spare cash, that is theft; if the governor puts his hand into employees' pockets and takes their spare cash, i.e. reduces wages, even below the legal minimum, that is the labour market operating reasonably. To end the list prematurely and clarify the point, the law of theft includes, in the words of that anonymous poet particularly loved by teachers of 'A' level economic history, 'the man or woman who steals the goose from off the common, but leaves the greater villain loose who steals the common from the goose'.

The criminal law includes only one type of non-consensual sexual act as rape, namely the insertion of penis in vagina by force or threatened force; it excludes sexual intercourse between husband and wife, no matter how much the latter is beaten by the former to exercise his 'conjugal right'; it excludes most sexual acts achieved by fraud, deceit, or misrepresentation – thus a man may pose as a psychiatrist and prescribe sexual intercourse as therapy to a 'gullible female', because he knows the law will regard this as acceptable seduction rather than rape; it excludes men who use economic, organizational, or social power rather than actual or threatened force to overcome an unwilling but subordinate, and therefore vulnerable female; it excludes the forced insertion of any other instrument, no matter how sharp or dangerous. Thus out of a whole range of 'sexual' acts where the balance of consent versus coercion is at least ambiguous, the criminal law draws a line demarcating those where physical force is used or threatened from those where any other kind of power is utilized to overcome a female's resistance. The outcome is that men who have few resources other than physical ones are more likely to commit legally defined rape, whilst those men who possess a whole range of resources from economic patronage to cultural charm are likely to be viewed by the law as 'real men' practising their primeval arts – and that is something the majesty of the law should leave alone!

The criminal law defines only some types of violence as criminal assault; it excludes verbal assaults that can, and sometimes do, break a person's spirit; it excludes forms of assault whose injuries become apparent years later, such as those resulting from working in a polluted factory environment where the health risk was known to the employer but concealed from the employee (Swartz, 1975); it excludes 'compulsory' drug-therapy or electric-shock treatment given to 'mentally disturbed' patients or prisoners who are denied the civilized rights to refuse such beneficial medical help (Mitford, 1977; Szasz, 1970, 1977a, 1977b); it excludes chemotherapy prescribed to control 'naughty' schoolboys, but includes physically hitting teachers (Box, 1981b; Schrag and Divoky, 1981).

The criminal law includes and reflects our proper stance against 'murderous' acts of terrorism conducted by people who are usually exploited or oppressed by forces of occupation. But it had no relevance, and its guardians remained mute ten years ago, when bombs, with the United States' and allied governments' blessing, fell like rain on women and children in Cambodia (Shawcross, 1979), or when the same governments aid and support other political/military regimes exercising mass terror and partial genocide against a subjugated people (Chomsky and Herman, 1979a, 1979b). The criminal law, in other words, condemns the importation of murderous terrorist acts usually against powerful individuals or strategic institutions, but goes all quiet when governments export or support avoidable acts of killing usually against the underdeveloped countries' poor. Of course there are exceptions – the Russian 'invasion' of Afghanistan was a violation of international law and a crime against humanity. It may well have been, but what about Western governments' involvement in Vietnam, Laos, Cambodia, Chile, El Salvador, Nicaragua, Suez, and Northern Ireland? Shouldn't they at least be discussed within the same context of international law and crimes against humanity? And if not, why not?

Thus criminal laws against murder, rape, robbery and assault do protect us all, but they do not protect us all equally. They do not protect the less powerful from being killed, sexually exploited, deprived of what little property they possess, or physically and psychologically damaged through the greed, apathy, negligence, indifference and the unaccountability of the relatively more powerful.

Of course, what constitutes murder, rape, robbery, assault and other forms of serious crime varies over historical periods and between cultural groups, as the changes and contradictions *within* and *between* powerful interest groups, and the shifting alliances of the less powerful bring about slight and not-so-slight tilts of society's power axis (Chambliss, 1981). But it is not justifiable to conclude from this that criminal law reflects a value-consensus or even results from the state's neutral refereeing among competing interest groups. It is, however, plausible to view criminal laws as the outcomes of clashes between groups with structurally generated conflicting interests, and to argue that the legislators' intention, or if that is too conspiratorial, then the law's latent function, is to provide the powerful with a resource to reduce further the ability of some groups to resist domination. Needless to stress the point, it is a resource eagerly used to punish and deter actual and potential resisters and thereby help protect the established social order.

NOTHING BUT MYSTIFICATION

Unfortunately for those committed to the radical 'reflexive' view, there is nothing but mystification. Most people accept the 'official' view. They are very aware and sensitized to muggers, football hooligans, street vandals, housebreakers, thieves, terrorists and scroungers. But few are aware and sensitized to crimes committed by *corporate top and middle management* against stockholders, employees, consumers and the general public. Similarly there is only a fog, when it comes to crimes committed by *governments* (Douglas and Johnson, 1977), particularly when these victimize Third World countries (Shawcross, 1979) or become genocidal (Brown, 1971; Horowitz, 1977), or by *governmental control agencies* such as the police when they assault or use deadly force unwarrantedly against the public or suspected persons, or prison officers (Coggan and Walker, 1982; Thomas and Pooley, 1980), or special prison hospital staff when they brutalize and torture persons in their protective custody.

Few people are aware how men, who on the whole are more socially, economically, politically and physically powerful than women, use these resources frequently to *batter* wives and cohabitees (Dobash and Dobash, 1981), *sexually harass* their female (usually subordinate) co-workers, or *assault/rape* any woman who happens to be in the way. But we are very aware of female shoplifters and prostitutes, and those poor female adolescents who are 'beyond parental control' and in 'need of care and protection', even though this is a gross misrepresentation of female crime and though the relative absence of serious female crime contradicts the orthodox view that crime and powerlessness go hand in hand.

Few people become aware of crimes of the powerful or how serious these are, because their attention is glued to the highly publicized social characteristics of the convicted and imprisoned population. It is not directed to the records, files and occasional publications of those quasi-judicial organizations (such as the Factory Inspectorate in the UK or the Federal Drug Administration in the US) monitoring and regulating corporate and governmental crimes. Because of this, people make the attractive and easy deduction that those behind bars constitute our most serious criminals. As this captive audience is primarily young males amongst whom the unemployed and ethnic minorities are over-represented, it is believed that they, and those like them, constitute our 'public enemies'. Had the results of self-report/victimization surveys and the investigations of quasi-judicial agencies been publicized as much as 'official criminal statistics', and had the radical jaundiced and cynical view of criminal definitions been widely publicized, then the mystification produced by focusing exclusively on the characteristics of the prison population would not be so easily achieved. Instead, there would be a greater awareness of how the social construction of criminal definitions and the criminal justice system operate to bring about this misleading image of serious criminals.

Definitions of serious crime are essentially ideological constructs. They do not refer to those behaviours which objectively and *avoidably* cause us the most harm, injury and suffering. Instead they refer to only a sub-section of these behaviours, a sub-section which is more likely to be committed by young, poorly educated males who are often unemployed, live in working-class impoverished neighbourhoods, and frequently belong to an ethnic minority. Crime and criminalization are therefore *social control strategies*. They:

1 render underprivileged and powerless people more likely to be arrested, convicted and sentenced to prison, even though the amount of personal damage and injury they cause may be less than the more powerful and privileged cause;
2 create the illusion that the 'dangerous' class is primarily located at the bottom of various hierarchies by which we 'measure' each other, such as occupational prestige, income level, housing market location, educational achievement, racial attributes – in this illusion it fuses relative poverty and criminal propensities and sees them both as effects of moral inferiority, thus rendering the 'dangerous' class deserving of both poverty and punishment;
3 render invisible the vast amount of avoidable harm, injury and deprivation imposed on the ordinary population by the state, transnational and other cor-porations, and thereby remove the effects of these 'crimes' from the causal nexus for explaining 'conventional crimes' committed by ordinary people. The conditions of life for the powerless created by the powerful are simply ignored by those who explain crime as a manifestation of individual pathology or local neighbourhood friendship and cultural patterns – yet in many respects the unrecognized victimization of the powerless by the powerful constitutes a part of those conditions under which the powerless choose to commit crimes;

4 elevate the criminal justice into a 'community service' – it is presented as being above politics and dispensing 'justice for all' irrespective of class, race, sex, or religion – this further legitimates the state and those whose interests it wittingly, or otherwise, furthers;

5 make ordinary people even more dependent upon the state for protection against 'lawlessness' and the rising tidal wave of crime, even though it is the state and its agents who are often directly and indirectly victimizing ordinary people.

Not only does the state with the help and reinforcement of its control agencies, criminologists and the media conceptualize a particular and partial ideological version of serious crime and who commits it, but it does so by concealing and hence mystifying its own propensity for violence and serious crimes on a much larger scale. Matza captured this sad ironic 'truth' when he wrote:

> in its avid concern for public order and safety, implemented through police force and penal policy, the state is vindicated. By pursuing evil and producing the *appearance* of good, the state reveals its abiding method – the perpetuation of its good name in the face of its own propensity for violence, conquest, and destruction. Guarded by a collective representation in which theft and violence reside in a dangerous class, morally elevated by its correctional quest, the state achieves the legitimacy of its pacific intention and the acceptance of legality – even when it goes to war and massively perpetuates activities it has allegedly banned from the world. But that, the reader may say, is a different matter altogether. So says the state – and that is the final point of the collective representation [i.e. ideological construction – author]. (Matza, 1969: 196)

For too long too many people have been socialized to see crime and criminals through the eyes of the state. There is nothing left, as Matza points out, but mystification. This is clearly revealed in the brick wall of indignation which flattens any suggestion that the crime problem defined by the state is not the only crime problem, or that criminals are not only those processed by the state. There is more to crime and criminals than the state reveals. But most people cannot see it.

REFERENCES

Box, S. (1981a) *Deviance, Reality and Society*, 2nd edn. London: Holt, Rinehart and Winston.

Box, S. (1981b) 'Where have all the naughty children gone?', in National Deviancy Symposium, *Permissiveness and Control*, London: Macmillan.

Braithwaite, J. and Geis, G. (1981) 'On theory and action for corporate crime control'. Unpublished paper.

Brown, D. (1971) *Bury My Heart at Wounded Knee*. New York: Holt, Rinehart and Winston.

Chambliss, W.J. (1964) 'A sociological analysis of the law of vagrancy', *Social Problems*, 12: 46–67.

Chambliss, W.J. (1978) *On The Take: From Petty Crooks to Presidents*. Indiana: Indiana University Press.

Chambliss, W.J. (1981) 'The criminalization of conduct', in H.L. Ross (ed.), *Law and Deviance*. London: Sage.

Chomsky, N. and Herman, E.S. (1979a) *The Washington Connection and Third World Fascism*. Nottingham: Spokesman.

Chomsky, N. and Herman, E.S. (1979b) *After the Cataclysm*. Nottingham: Spokesman.

Coggan, G. and Walker, M. (1982) *Frightened For My Life: An Account of Deaths in British Prisons*. London: Fontana.

Dobash, R.E. and Dobash, R. (1981) *Violence Against Wives*. London: Open Books.

Douglas, J.D. and Johnson, J.M. (eds) (1977) *Official Deviance*. New York: Lippincott.

Duster, T. (1970) *The Legislation of Morality*. New York: Free Press.

Erickson, K.T. (1976) *Everything in its Path*. New York: Simon and Schuster.

Graham, J.M. (1972) 'Amphetamine politics on Capitol Hill', *Society*, 9: 14–23.

Gunningham, N. (1974) *Pollution, Social Interest and the Law*. London: Martin Robertson.

Hall, J. (1952) *Theft, Law and Society*, rev. edn. Indianapolis: Bobbs–Merrill.

Haskins, G. (1960) *Law and Authority in Early Massachusetts*. New York: Macmillan.

Hay, D. (1975) 'Property, authority and criminal law', in D. Hay et al., *Albion's Fatal Tree*. London: Allen Lane.

Hindelang, M.J., Gottfredson, M. and Garofalo, L. (1978) *Victims of Personal Crimes*. Cambridge, MA: Ballinger.

Hopkins, A. (1978) *Crime, Law and Business*. Canberra: Australian Institute of Criminology.

Hopkins, A. (1980a) 'Controlling corporate deviance', *Criminology*, 18: 198–214.

Hopkins, A. (1980b) 'Crimes against capitalism – an Australian case', *Contemporary Crises*, 4: 421–32.

Horowitz, I.L. (1977) *Genocide: State-Power and Mass Murder*, end edn. New Jersey: Transaction Books.

Liazos, A. (1972) 'The poverty of the sociology of deviance: nuts, sluts and perverts', *Social Problems*, 20: 103–20.

Matza, D. (1969) *Becoming Deviant*, Englewood Cliffs, NJ: Prentice-Hall.

Mitford, J. (1977) *The American Prison Business*. London: Penguin.

Morgan, P. (1978) *Delinquent Fantasies*. London: Temple Smith.

McCaghy, C.H. and Denisoff, R.S. (1973) 'Pirates and politics', in R.S. Denisoff and C.H. McCaghy (eds), *Deviance, Conflict and Criminality*. Chicago: Rand-McNally.

Platt, A. (1969) *The Child Savers*. Chicago: Chicago University Press.

Schrag, P. and Divoky, D. (1981) *The Myth of the Hyperactive Child*. Harmondsworth: Penguin.

Schur, E.M. (1973) *Radical Non-Intervention*. Englewood Cliffs, NJ: Spectrum.

Shawcross, W. (1979) *Side Show: Kissinger, Nixon and the Destruction of Cambodia*. London: Andre Deutsch.

Silverman, M. and Lee, P.R. (1974) *Pills, Profits and Politics*. Berkeley, CA: University of California Press.

Smith, D.C. (1974) '*We're Not Mad, We're Angry*'. Vancouver: Women's Press.

Spitzer, S. (1975) 'Towards a Marxian theory of crime', *Social Problems*, 22: 368–401.

Sumner, C. (1976) Marxism and deviance theory, in P. Wiles (ed.), *Crime and Delinquency in Britain*, vol. 2. London: Martin Robertson.

Swartz, J. (1975) 'Silent killers at work', *Crime and Social Justice*, 3: 15–20.

Swigert, V. and Farrell, R. (1976) *Murder, Inequality and the Law*. Lexington, MA: Heath.

Swigert, V. and Farrell, R. (1981) 'Corporate homicide: definitional processes in the creation of deviance', *Law and Society Review*, 15: 161–82.

Szasz, T. (1970) *Ideology and Insanity*. New York: Anchor.

Szasz, T. (1977a) *Psychiatric Slavery*. New York: Free Press.

Szasz, T. (1977b) *The Theology of Medicine*. Oxford: Oxford University Press.

Thomas, J.E. and Pooley, R. (1980) *The Exploding Prison*. London: Junction Books.

Thompson, E.P. (1975) *Whigs and Hunters*. London: Allen Lane.

Wilson, J.Q. (1975) *Thinking About Crime*. New York: Basic Books.

24

Race and criminalization: Black Americans and the punishment industry

Angela Y. Davis

[. . .]

When the structural character of racism is ignored in discussions about crime and the rising population of incarcerated people, the racial imbalance in jails and prisons is treated as a contingency, at best as a product of the 'culture of poverty,' and at worst as proof of an assumed black monopoly on criminality. The high proportion of black people in the criminal justice system is thus normalized and neither the state nor the general public is required to talk about and act on the meaning of that racial imbalance. Thus Republican and Democratic elected officials alike have successfully called for laws mandating life sentences for three-time 'criminals,' without having to answer for the racial implications of these laws. By relying on the alleged 'race-blindness' of such laws, black people are surreptitiously constructed as racial subjects, thus manipulated, exploited, and abused, while the structural persistence of racism—albeit in changed forms—in social and economic institutions, and in the national culture as a whole, is adamantly denied.

Crime is thus one of the masquerades behind which 'race,' with all its menacing ideological complexity, mobilizes old public fears *and* creates new ones. The current anticrime debate takes place within a reified mathematical realm—a strategy reminiscent of Malthus's notion of the geometrical increase in population and the arithmetical increase in food source, thus the inevitability of poverty and the means of suppressing it: war, disease, famine, and natural disasters. As a matter of fact, the persisting neo-Malthusian approach to population control, which, instead of seeking to solve those pressing social problems that result in real pain and suffering in people's lives, calls for the elimination of those suffering lives—finds strong resonances in the public discussion about expurgating the 'nation' of crime. These discussions include arguments deployed by those who are leading the call for more prisons and employ statistics in the same fetishistic and misleading way as Malthus did more than two

From *The House that Race Built.* (ed. W. Lubiano), pp. 264–278. (New York, Vintage Books, 1998.)

centuries ago. Take for example James Wooten's comments in the *Heritage Foundation State Backgrounder*:

> If the 55% of the estimated 800,000 current state and federal prisoners who are violent offenders were subject to serving 85% of their sentence, and assuming that those violent offenders would have committed 10 violent crimes a year while on the street, then the number of crimes prevented each year by truth in sentencing would be 4,000,000. That would be over 2/3 of the 6,000,000 violent crimes reported.[1]

In *Reader's Digest*, Senior Editor Eugene H. Methvin writes:

> If we again double the present federal and state prison population—to somewhere between 1 million and 1.5 million and leave our city and county jail population at the present 400,000, we will break the back of America's 30 year crime wave.[2]

The real human beings—a vastly disproportionate number of whom are black and Latino/a men and women—designated by these numbers in a seemingly race-neutral way are deemed fetishistically exchangeable with the crimes they have or will allegedly commit. The real impact of imprisonment on their lives never need be examined. The inevitable part played by the punishment industry in the reproduction of crime never need be discussed. The dangerous and indeed fascistic trend toward progressively greater numbers of hidden, incarcerated human populations is itself rendered invisible. All that matters is the elimination of crime—and you get rid of crime by getting rid of people who, according to the prevailing racial common sense, are the most likely people to whom criminal acts will be attributed. Never mind that if this strategy is seriously and consistently pursued, the majority of young black men and fast-growing proportion of young black women will spend a good portion of their lives behind walls and bars in order to serve as a reminder that the state is aggressively confronting its enemy.[3]

While I do not want to locate a response to these arguments on the same level of mathematical abstraction and fetishism I have been problematizing, it is helpful, I think, to consider how many people are presently incarcerated or whose lives are subject to the direct surveillance of the criminal justice system. There are already approximately 1 million people in state and federal prisons in the United States, not counting the 500,000 in city and county jails or the 600,000 on parole or the 3 million people on probation or the 60,000 young people in juvenile facilities. Which is to say that there are presently over 5.1 million people either incarcerated, on parole, or on probation. Many of those presently on probation or parole would be behind bars under the conditions of the recently passed crime bill. According to the Sentencing Project, even before the passage of the crime bill, black people were 7.8 times more likely to be imprisoned that whites.[4] The Sentencing Project's most recent report[5] indicates that 32.2 percent of young black men and 12.3 percent of young Latino men between the ages of twenty and twenty-nine are either in prison, in jail, or on probation or parole. This is in comparison with 6.7 percent of young white men. A total of 827,440 young African-American males are under the supervision of the criminal justice system, at a cost of $6 billion per year. A major strength of the 1995 report, as compared to its predecessor, is its acknowledgement that the racialized impact of the criminal justice system is also gendered and that the relatively smaller number of African-American women drawn into the system should not relieve us of the responsibility of understanding the encounter of gender and race in arrest and incarceration practices. Moreover, the increases in women's contact with the criminal justice system have been even more dramatic than those of men.

> The 78% increase in criminal justice control rates for black women was more than double the increase for black men and for white women, and more than nine times the increase for white men. . . . Although research on women of color in the criminal justice system is limited, existing data and research suggest that it is the combination of race and sex effects that is at the root of the trends which appear in our data. For example, while the number of blacks and Hispanics in prison is growing at an alarming rate, the rate of increase for women is even greater. Between 1980 and 1992 the female prison population increased 276%, compared to 163% for men. Unlike men of color, women of color thus belong to two groups that are experiencing particular dramatic growth in their contact with the criminal justice system.[6]

It has been estimated that by the year 2000 the number of people imprisoned will surpass 4 million, a grossly disproportionate number of whom will be black people, and that the cost will be over $40 billion a year,[7] a figure that is reminiscent of the way the military budget devoured—and continues to devour—the country's resources. This out-of-control punishment industry is an extremely effective criminalization industry, for the racial imbalance in incarcerated populations is not recognized as evidence of structural racism, but rather is invoked as a consequence of the assumed criminality of black people. In other words, the criminalization process works so well precisely because of the hidden logic of racism. Racist logic is deeply entrenched in the nation's material and psychic structures. It is something with which we are all very familiar. The logic, in fact, can persist, even when direct allusions to 'race' are removed.

Even those communities that are most deeply injured by this racist logic have learned how to rely upon it, particularly when open allusions to race are not necessary. Thus, in the absence of broad, radical grassroots movements in poor black communities so devastated by new forms of youth-perpetrated violence, the ideological options are extremely sparse. Often there are no other ways to express collective rage and despair but to demand that police sweep the community clean of crack and Uzis, and of the people who use and sell drugs and wield weapons. Ironically, Carol Moseley-Braun, the first black woman senator in our nation's history, was an enthusiastic sponsor of the Senate Anticrime Bill, whose passage in November 1993 paved the way for the August 25, 1994, passage of the bill by the House. Or perhaps there is little irony here. It may be precisely because there is a Carol Moseley-Braun in the Senate and a Clarence Thomas in the Supreme Court— and concomitant class differentiations and other factors responsible for far more heterogeneity in black communities than at any other time in this country's history— that implicit consent to antiblack racist logic (not to speak of racism toward other groups) becomes far more widespread among black people. Wahneema Lubiano's explorations of the complexities of state domination as it operates within and through the subjectivities of those who are the targets of this domination facilitates an understanding of this dilemma.[8]

Borrowing the title of Cornel West's recent work, race *matters*. Moreover, it matters in ways that are far more threatening and simultaneously less discernible than those to which we have grown accustomed. Race matters inform, more than ever, the ideological and material structures of U.S. society. And, as the current discourses on crime, welfare, and immigration reveal, race, gender, and class matter enormously in the continuing elaboration of public policy and its impact on the real lives of human beings.

And how does race matter? Fear has always been an integral component of racism. The ideological reproduction of a fear of black people, whether economically or sexually grounded, is rapidly gravitating toward and being grounded in a fear of crime. A question to be raised in this context is whether and how the increasing fear of crime—this ideologically produced fear of crime—serves to render racism simultaneously more invisible and more virulent. Perhaps one way to approach an answer to this question is to consider how this fear of crime effectively summons black people to imagine black people as the enemy. How many black people present at this conference have successfully extricated ourselves from the ideological power of the figure of the young black male as criminal—or at least seriously confronted it? The lack of a significant black presence in the rather feeble opposition to the 'three strikes, you're out' bills, which have been proposed and/or passed in forty states already, evidences the disarming effect of this ideology.

California is one of the states that has passed the 'three strikes, you're out' bill. Immediately after the passage of that bill, Governor Pete Wilson began to argue for a 'two strikes, you're out' bill. Three, he said, is too many. Soon we will hear calls for 'one strike, you're out.' Following this mathematical regression, we can imagine that at some point the hard-core anticrime advocates will be arguing that to stop the crime wave, we can't wait until even one crime is committed. Their slogan will be: 'Get them before the first strike!' And because certain populations have already been criminalized, there will be those who say, 'We know who the real criminals are—let's get them before they have a chance to act out their criminality.'

The fear of crime has attained a status that bears a sinister similarity to the fear of communism as it came to restructure social perceptions during the fifties and sixties. The figure of the 'criminal'—the racialized figure of the criminal—has come to represent the most menacing enemy of 'American society.' Virtually anything is acceptable—torture, brutality, vast expenditures of public funds—as long as it is done in the name of public safety. Racism has always found an easy route from its embeddedness in social structures to the psyches of collectives and individuals precisely because it mobilizes deep fears. While explicit, old-style racism may be increasingly socially unacceptable—precisely as a result of antiracist movements over the last forty years—this does not mean that U.S. society has been purged of racism. In fact, racism is more deeply embedded in socioeconomic structures, and the vast populations of incarcerated people of color is dramatic evidence of the way racism systematically structures economic relations. At the same time, this structural racism is rarely recognized as 'racism.' What we have come to recognize as open, explicit racism has in many ways begun to be replaced by a secluded, camouflaged kind of racism, whose influence on people's daily lives is as pervasive and systematic as the explicit forms of racism associated with the era of the struggle for civil rights.

The ideological space for the proliferations of this racialized fear of crime has been opened by the transformations in international politics created by the fall of the European socialist countries. Communism is no longer the quintessential enemy against which the nation imagines its identity. This space is now inhabited by ideological constructions of crime, drugs, immigration, and welfare. Of course, the enemy within is far more dangerous than the enemy without, and a black enemy within is the most dangerous of all.

Because of the tendency to view it as an abstract site into which all manner of undesirables are deposited, the prison is the perfect site for the simultaneous production and concealment of racism. The abstract character of the public perception of prisons militates against an engagement with the real issues afflicting the communities from which prisoners are drawn in such disproportionate numbers. This is the ideological work that the prison performs—it relieves us of the responsibility of seriously engaging with the problems of late capitalism, of transnational capitalism. The naturalization of black people as criminals thus also erects ideological barriers to an understanding of the connections between late-twentieth-century structural racism and the globalization of capital.

The vast expansion of the power of capitalist corporations over the lives of people of color and poor people in general has been accompanied by a waning anticapitalist consciousness. As capital moves with ease across national borders, legitimized by recent trade agreements such as NAFTA and GATT, corporations are allowed to close shop in the United States and transfer manufacturing operations to nations providing cheap labor pools. In fleeing organized labor in the U.S. to avoid paying higher wages and benefits, they leave entire communities in shambles, consigning huge numbers of people to joblessness, leaving them prey to the drug trade, destroying the economic base of these communities, thus affecting the education system, social welfare—and turning the people who live in those communities into perfect candidates for prison. At the same time, they create an economic demand for prisons, which stimulates the economy, providing jobs in the correctional industry for people who often come from the very populations that are criminalized by this process. It is a horrifying and self-reproducing cycle.

Ironically, prisons themselves are becoming a source of cheap labor that attracts corporate capitalism—as yet on a relatively small scale—in a way that parallels the attraction unorganized labor in Third World countries exerts. A statement by Michael Lamar Powell, a prisoner in Capshaw, Alabama, dramatically reveals this new development:

> I cannot go on strike, nor can I unionize. I am not covered by workers' compensation of the Fair Labor Standards Act. I agree to work late-night and weekend shifts. I do just what I am told, no matter what it is. I am hired and fired at will, and I am not even paid minimum wage: I earn one dollar a month. I cannot even voice grievances or complaints, except at the risk of incurring arbitrary discipline or some covert retaliation.
>
> You need not worry about NAFTA and your jobs going to Mexico and other Third World countries. I will have at least five percent of your jobs by the end of this decade.
>
> I am called prison labor. I am The New American Worker.[9]

This 'new American worker' will be drawn from the ranks of a racialized population whose historical superexploitation—from the era of slavery to the present—has been legitimized by racism. At the same time, the expansion of convict labor is accompanied in some states by the old paraphernalia of ankle chains that symbolically links convict labor with slave labor. At least three states—Alabama, Florida, and Arizona—have reinstituted the chain gang. Moreover, as Michael Powell so incisively reveals, there is a new dimension to the racism inherent in this process, which structurally links the superexploitation of prison labor to the globalization of capital.

In California, whose prison system is the largest in the country and one of the largest in the world, the passage of an inmate labor initiative in 1990 has presented businesses seeking cheap labor with opportunities uncannily similar to those in Third World countries. As of June 1994, a range of companies were employing prison labor in nine California prisons. Under the auspices of the Joint Venture Program, work now being performed on prison grounds includes computerized telephone messaging, dental apparatus assembly, computer data entry, plastic parts fabrication, electronic component manufacturing at the Central California Women's facility at Chowchilla, security glass manufacturing, swine production, oak furniture manufacturing, and the production of stainless steel tanks and equipment. In a California Corrections Department brochure designed to promote the program, it is described as 'an innovative public-private partnership that makes good business sense.'[10] According to the owner of Tower Communications, whom the brochure quotes,

> The operation is cost effective, dependable and trouble free. . . . Tower Communications has successfully operated a message center utilizing inmates on the grounds of a California state prison. If you're in business leader planning expansion, considering relocation because of a deficient labor pool, starting a new enterprise, look into the benefits of using inmate labor.

The employer benefits listed by the brochure include

> federal and state tax incentives; no benefit package (retirement pay, vacation pay, sick leave, medical benefits); long term lease agreements at far below market value costs; discount rates on Workers Compensation; build a consistent, qualified work force; on call labor pool (no car breakdowns, no babysitting problems); option of hiring job-ready ex-offenders and minimizing costs; becoming a partner in public safety.

There is a major, yet invisible, racial supposition in such claims about the profitability of a convict labor force. The acceptability of the superexploitation of convict labor is largely based on the historical conjuncture of racism and incarceration practices. The already disproportionately black convict labor force will become increasingly black if the racially imbalanced incarceration practices continue.

The complicated yet unacknowledged structural presence of racism in the U.S. punishment industry also includes the fact that the punishment industry which sequesters ever-larger sectors of the black population attracts vast amounts of capital. Ideologically, as I have argued, the racialized fear of crime has begun to succeed the fear of communism. This corresponds to a structural tendency for capital that previously flowed toward the military industry to now move toward the punishment industry. The ease with which suggestions are made for prison construction costing in the multibillions of dollars is reminiscent of the military buildup: economic mobilization to defeat communism has turned into economic mobilization to defeat crime. The ideological construction of crime is thus complemented and bolstered by the material construction of jails and prisons. The more jails and prisons are constructed, the greater the fear of crime, and the greater the fear of crime, the stronger the cry for more jails and prisons, ad infinitum.

The law enforcement industry bears remarkable parallels to the military industry (just as there are anti-Communist resonances in the anti-crime campaign). This connection between the military industry and the punishment industry is revealed in a *Wall Street Journal* article entitled "Making Crime Pay: The Cold War of the '90s":

> Parts of the defense establishment are cashing in, too, scenting a logical new line of business to help them offset military cutbacks. Westinghouse Electric Corp., Minnesota Mining and Manufacturing Co., GDE Systems (a division of the old General Dynamics) and Alliant Techsystems Inc., for instance, are pushing crime-fighting equipment and have created special divisions to retool their defense technology for America's streets.

According to the article, a conference sponsored by the National Institute of Justice, the research arm of the Justice Department, was organized around the theme 'Law Enforcement Technology in the 21st Century.' The secretary of defense was a major presenter at this conference, which explored topics like 'the role of the defense industry, particularly for dual use and conversion':

> Hot topics: defense-industry technology that could lower the level of violence involved in crime fighting. Sandia National Laboratories, for instance, is experimenting with a dense foam that can be sprayed at suspects, temporarily blinding and deafening them under breathable bubbles. Stinger Corporation is working on 'smart guns,' which will fire only for the owner, and retractable spiked barrier strips to unfurl in front of fleeing vehicles. Westinghouse is promoting the 'smart car,' in which mini-computers could be linked up with big mainframes at the police department, allowing for speedy booking of prisoners, as well as quick exchanges of information.[11]

Again, race provides a silent justification for the technological expansion of law enforcement, which, in turn, intensifies racist arrest and incarceration practices. This skyrocketing punishment industry, whose growth is silently but powerfully sustained by the persistence of racism, creates an economic demand for more jails and prisons and thus for similarly spiraling criminalization practices, which, in turn fuels the fear of crime.

Most debates addressing the crisis resulting from overcrowding in prisons and jails focus on male institutions. Meanwhile, women's institutions and jail space for women are proportionately proliferating at an even more astounding rate than men's. If race is largely an absent factor in the discussions about crime and punishment, gender seems not even to merit a place carved out by its absence. Historically, the imprisonment of women has served to criminalize women in a way that is more complicated than is the case with men. This female criminalization process has had more to do with the marking of certain groups of women as undomesticated and hypersexual, as women who refuse to embrace the nuclear family as paradigm. The current liberal-conservative discourse around welfare criminalizes black single mothers, who are represented as deficient, manless, drug-using breeders of children, and as reproducers of an attendant culture of poverty. The women who does drugs is criminalized both because she is a drug user and because, as a consequence, she cannot be a good mother. In some states, pregnant women are being imprisoned for using crack because of possible damage to the fetus.

According to the U.S. Department of Justice, women are far more likely than men to be imprisoned for a drug conviction.[12] However, if women wish to receive treatment for their drug problems, often their only option, if they cannot pay for a drug program, is to be arrested and sentenced to a drug program via the criminal justice system. Yet when U.S. Surgeon General Joycelyn Elders alluded to the importance of opening discussion on the decriminalization of drugs, the Clinton administration immediately disassociated itself from her remarks. Decriminalization of drugs would greatly reduce the numbers of incarcerated women, for the 278 percent increase in the numbers of black women in state and federal prisons (as compared to the 186 percent increase in the numbers of black men) can be largely attributed to the phenomenal rise in drug-related and specifically crack-related imprisonment. According to the Sentencing Project's 1995 report, the increase amounted to 828 percent.[13]

Official refusals to even consider decriminalization of drugs as a possible strategy that might begin to reverse present incarceration practices further bolsters the ideological staying power of the prison. In his well-known study of the history of the prison and its related technologies of discipline, Michel Foucault pointed out that an evolving contradiction is at the very heart of the historical project of imprisonment.

> For a century and a half, the prison has always been offered as its own remedy: . . . the realization of the corrective project as the only method of overcoming the impossibility of implementing it.[14]

As I have attempted to argue, within the U.S. historical context, racism plays a pivotal role in sustaining this contradiction. In fact, Foucault's theory regarding the prison's tendency to serve as its own enduring justification becomes even more compelling if the role of race is also acknowledged. Moreover, moving beyond the parameters of what I consider the double impasse implied by his theory—the discursive impasse his theory discovers and that of the theory itself—I want to conclude by suggesting the possibility of radical race-conscious strategies designed to disrupt the stranglehold of criminalization and incarceration practices.

In the course of a recent collaborative research project with U.C. Santa Barbara sociologist Kum-Kum Bhavnani, in which we interviewed thirty-five women at the San Francisco County Jail, the complex ways in which race and gender help to produce a punishment industry that reproduces the very problems it purports to solve became dramatically apparent. Our interviews focused on the women's ideas about imprisonment and how they themselves imagine alternatives to incarceration. Their various critiques of the prison system and of the existing 'alternatives,' all of which are tied to reimprisonment as a last resort, led us to reflect more deeply about the importance of retrieving, retheorizing, and reactivating the radical abolitionist strategy first proposed in connection with the prison-reform movements of the sixties and seventies.

We are presently attempting to theorize women's imprisonment in ways that allow us to formulate a radical abolitionist strategy departing from, but not restricted in its conclusions to, women's jails and prisons. Our goal is to formulate alternatives to incarceration that substantively reflect the voices and agency of a variety of imprisoned women. We wish to open up channels for their involvement in the current debates around alternatives to incarceration, while not denying our own role as mediators and interpreters and our own political positioning in these debates. We also want to distinguish our explorations of alternatives from the spate of 'alternative punishments' or what are now called 'intermediate sanctions' presently being proposed and/or implemented by and through state and local correctional systems.

This is a long-range project that has three dimensions: academic research, public policy, and community organizing. In other words, for this project to be successful, it must build bridges between academic work, legislative and other policy interventions, and grassroots campaigns calling, for example, for the decriminalization of drugs and prostitution—and for the reversal of the present proliferation of jails and prisons.

Raising the possibility of abolishing jails and prisons as the institutionalized and normalized means of addressing social problems in an era of migrating corporations, unemployment and homelessness, and collapsing public services, from health care to education, can hopefully help to interrupt the current law-and-order discourse that has such a grip on the collective imagination, facilitated as it is by deep and hidden influences of racism. This late-twentieth-century 'abolitionism,' with its nineteenth-century resonances, may also lead to a historical recontextualization of the practice of imprisonment. With the passage of the Thirteenth Amendment, slavery was abolished for all except convicts—and in a sense the exclusion from citizenship accomplished by the slave system has persisted within the U.S. prison system. Only three states allow prisoners to vote, and approximately 4 million people are denied the right to vote because of their present or past incarceration. A radical strategy to abolish jails and prisons as the normal way of dealing with the social problems of late capitalism is not a strategy for abstract abolition. It is designed to force a rethinking of the increasingly repressive role of the state during this era of late capitalism and to carve out a space for resistance.

NOTES

1 Charles S. Clark, 'Prison Overcrowding,' *Congressional Quarterly Researcher* 4, no. 5 (Feb. 4, 1994): 97–119.

2 Ibid.

3 Marc Mauer, 'Young Black Men and the Criminal Justice System: A Growing National Problem,' Washington, D.C.: The Sentencing Project, February 1990.

4 Alexander Cockburn, *Philadelphia Inquirer*, August 29, 1994.

5 Marc Mauer and Tracy Huling, 'Young Black Americans and the Criminal Justice System: Five Years Later,' Washington, D.C.: The Sentencing Project, October 1995.

6 Ibid., 18.

7 *See* Cockburn.

8 *See* Lubiano's essay . . . as well as 'Black Ladies, Welfare Queens, and State Minstrels: Ideological War by Narrative Means,' in *Race-ing Justice, En-gendering Power: Essays on Anita Hill, Clarence Thomas, and the Construction of Social Reality*, ed. Toni Morrison (New York: Pantheon, 1992), 323–63.

9 Unpublished essay, 'Modern Slavery American Style,' 1995.

10 I wish to acknowledge Julie Brown, who acquired this brochure from the

California Department of Correction in the course of researching the role of convict labor.

11 *Wall Street Journal*, May 12, 1994.

12 Lawrence Rence, A. Greenfield, Stephanie Minor-Harper, *Women in Prison* (Washington, D.C.: U.S. Dept. of Justice, Office of Justice Programs, Bureau of Statistics, 1991).

13 Mauer and Huling, 'Young Black Americans,' 19.

14 Michel Foucault, *Discipline and Punish: The Birth of the Prison*, trans. Alan Sheridan (New York: Vintage, 1979), 395.

25

The theoretical and political priorities of critical criminology

Phil Scraton and Kathryn Chadwick

[. . .]

ESTABLISHING A FRAMEWORK FOR CRITICAL ANALYSIS

> We should admit that power produces knowledge (and not *simply* by encouraging it because it serves power or applying it because it is useful); that power and knowledge *directly* imply one another; that there is no power relation without the correlative constitution of a field of knowledge, or any knowledge that does not presuppose and constitute at the same time power relations. (Foucault, 1977: 27–8, emphases added)

Gouldner's (1969, 1973) devastating indictment of Western sociology established that the 'domain assumptions' of academic disciplines and their pre-eminent theoretical perspectives had been influenced massively by those powerful vested interests who commissioned research. Academic research was identified as essential to the management of advanced capitalism's inherent contradictions and conflicts. For Foucault, however, power is not unidimensional nor is it restricted to those formal relations of dominance in the economic or political spheres. As Sim (1990: 9) remarks, power is 'dispersed through the body of society' and exercised through the processes of 'discipline, surveillance, individualization and normalization'. Crucially the power–knowledge axis permeates all formal or official discourses, their language, logic, forms of definition and classification, measurement techniques and empiricism as essential elements in the technology of discipline and the process of normalization. 'Professionals', as key interventionists in societal relations and in the political management of social arrangements, pursue a 'logic and language of control' revealing a daunting 'power to classify' with clear consequences for the reproduction of 'bodies' of knowledge and for the maintenance of dominant power relations (Cohen, 1985: 196).

From *The Politics of Crime Control* (eds K. Stenson and D. Cowell), pp. 166–85. (London: Sage, 1991.)

Foucault's work demonstrates that the challenges to mainstream theoretical traditions have adopted the agendas of those traditions, taking their premises as legitimate points of departure. While starting with 'knowledge-as-it-stands', that which is 'known', a radical alternative must also contextualize knowledge – its derivation, consolidation and recognition – within dominant structural relations. Undoubtedly professionals, be they employed in the caring agencies, the military, the criminal justice system or private industry, operate on the basis of professional training and work experience enjoying discretionary powers in accord with their rank and status. Yet whatever the quality and implications of decisions formulated and administered at the interpersonal level of 'agency', their recognition and legitimacy are rooted in the determining contexts of 'structure' and their manifestation in the professional ideologies of control and political management (Giddens, 1979, 1984).

The dynamics and visibility of power, however, are not always so obvious. For, 'power may be at its most alarming, and quite often at its most horrifying, when applied as a sanction of force' but it is 'typically at its most intense and durable when running through the repetition of institutionalized practices' (Giddens, 1987: 9). As power is mediated through the operational practices of institutions their daily routines become regularized, even predictable. It is important to establish that the routine world of 'agency', of interpersonal relations, is neither spontaneous nor random. Personal reputations and collective identities are ascribed and become managed via official discourses, themselves derived within the dominant social relations of production, reproduction and neocolonialism. For these represent the primary determining contexts which require and reproduce appropriate relations of power and knowledge.

The structural contradictions of advanced capitalist patriarchies require political management. While grassroots resistance has remained a persistent feature in Western social democracies their great achievement has been to contain opposition through relying on 'consensus' rather than 'coercion'. Relations of domination and exploitation, both material and physical, have become redefined and broadly accepted as the justifiable pursuit of competing interests. The smooth and successful operation of power in this context is dependent on social arrangements, forms of political management and cultural traditions which together contribute towards hegemony (Gramsci, 1971). Dissent and disorder are regulated by social forces and cultural transmission rather than by physical coercion. To challenge orthodoxy, to question the established order or to raise doubts concerning formal authority are not perceived as acts of progression towards worthwhile change but are presented in official discourses as acts of subversion which undermine shared identities and common interests.

While 'power', 'regulation' or 'control' can be identified in personal action and social reaction as part and parcel of the daily routine of *agency*, critical analysis seeks to bring to the fore *structural* relations, involving the economy, the state and ideology, in explaining the significance of the power–knowledge axis and relating it to the processes by which dominant ideas gain political legitimacy. Discrimination on the basis of class, gender, sexuality and perceived ethnicity clearly operates at the level of attitude, on the street, in the home, at the workplace or at social venues. Once institutionalized, however, classism, sexism, heterosexism and racism become systematic and structured. They become the taken-for-granted social histories and contemporary priorities which constitute state institutions, informing policies and underwriting practices, and which provide legitimacy to interpersonal discrimination. Through the process of institutionalization, relations of dominance and subjugation achieve structural significance. Critical analysis of crime and the criminal justice process must be grounded in these theoretical imperatives.

CLASS ANALYSIS AND THE DETERMINING CONTEXT OF PRODUCTION

Much of the post-war optimism over capital reconstruction and economic growth was derived in the 'Butskellite' compromises which married Keynesian principles concerning state management of the economy to a protected programme of capital investment and development in the private sector (Gamble, 1981; Taylor-Gooby, 1982). This programme was made possible through the initiation of effective, albeit often illusory, programmes of state welfare and social justice. Through initiatives in public housing, access to health care and medicine, new educational priorities and state benefits the popular assumption, also embodied in academic accounts of welfarism, was that benevolent reformism and its commitment to social justice had broken the hold of the free enterprise economy and its market forces over the social well-being of the nation. The era of 'welfare capitalism' had arrived, led by entrepreneurs of conscience who claimed 'people before profit'.

A cursory glance, however, at the relationship between the public and private sectors which emerged during this period reveals the grand illusion through a series of ambiguities and contradictions. In all sections of public service and ownership – schooling, housing, health and medicine – a strong and privileged private sector, bolstered by the inheritance of wealth, was maintained. Property ownership continued to become more centralized and concentrated within fewer hands. The expansion of state interventionism, local and central, ensured that the state became the largest employer and also the primary customer of private capital. Those industries which came under 'state ownership' were those essential to the reconstruction and consolidation of private manufacturing capital yet those deemed to be the least profitable or in need of the most reinvestment: coal, roads, railways, steel, communications, etc. The optimistic portrayal of this new pluralist society – based on equality of opportunity and access, on cradle-to-grave welfarism – disguised the structural contradictions inherent within the social arrangements and relations of the new dawn of economic expansionism.

Friend and Metcalfe (1981) graphically illustrate the divisions, well-established and noted during the depression of the 1920s and 1930s, of regional decline. Although unemployment in the 1950s remained relatively low so too did wages, job security, working conditions and living standards (Nightingale, 1980). The growth in immigration during the 1950s provided further evidence of this apparent expansionism. What was never made clear, however, was that throughout this period emigration exceeded immigration and that many immigrants, particularly from black Commonwealth countries and from Ireland, were fed directly into the worst jobs with the lowest pay and the fewest prospects (Cashmore, 1989; Hall et al., 1978; Miles, 1982; Sivanandan, 1983).

The 'attack on poverty' meant the virtual end of widespread destitution and starvation and there were major advances in housing, health care, schooling and the general 'quality of life' – but the divisions remained. Capital reconstruction, despite the veneer of state interventionism in the management of the economy, meant capital accumulation and this, in turn, delivered the further centralization and concentration of capital. National monopolies became multinational conglomerates and, despite the institution of tiers of executive management as the 'controllers' of industry, ownership – and *effective* control – of industry became even more focused.

Parsons (1951) proclaimed the success of 'integration' of diverse elements within the social system, and Lipset (1960) announced that the fundamental conflicts of early capitalism had been resolved. The argument was that through the decomposition of capital and labour and the 'end of ideology' (Bell, 1960) more affluent and secure workers had taken on the characteristics, lifestyle and ambitions of the middle-class white-collar workers – the consolidation of contemporary industrial societies as essentially classless (Dahrendorf, 1959). This gave academic legitimacy to the dubious claim that the period of economic reconstruction was also one of significant political reconstruction. Class conflict represented a politics of the past matched by class analysis as a theoretical endeavour of the past. In its rush to bury Marxism and to proclaim the arrival of a new, meritocratic form of industrialism, structural functionalism replaced class analysis with stratification theory. Effectively this work failed to recognize that the post-war reconstruction of capital brought with it the reconstruction of class relations including the consolidation of the new professional and managerial class forms, in both the private and public domain, and their internal hierarchies. It also produced new hierarchies of labour within the transitional working class. These were complex developments, particularly as the dynamics of intra-class location encompassed divisions around gender, ethnicity and region as new contexts of class fragmentation.

The broadsides fired by stratification theorists and 'grand theorists' such as Parsons led to the reappraisal of Marxist analysis. Ten years after Dahrendorf's requiem for Marxism, Miliband (1969) and Quinney (1970) published their influential analyses of the advanced capitalist state. There followed a decade of important commentary on the state which picked up and developed the complexities of Miliband's central thesis that those who have occupied the key positions of state power for generations have been drawn from a different class position than those to whom the state administers, and that the legitimacy for that power is found within the dominant political–economic relations and not in the body politic. It proposed that in its mediation of existing class relations and conflict the state, through the rule of law, intervenes to protect, maintain and reproduce the very contradictions which it sets out to mediate (Thompson, 1975). Class rule, claimed Therborn (1978: 132), 'is exercised through state power . . . through the interventions or policies of the state'.

Braverman (1974: 110) noted that the complexity of the class structure of advanced capitalism lay in the fact that 'almost all of the population has been transformed into employees of capital' through 'the purchase and sale of labor power'. For Braverman, as with Thompson, the historical relations of production have given rise to class formations within modes of production, each set of relations bearing the birthmarks of the previous mode. Given that productive relations create shared positions within the process of production it is logical to conclude that the social relations of production are structurally determined. Thus, while class represents a social process reflected in the concrete world of 'human relationships', it represents also a *structural location* within capitalist modes of production. It is precisely because class relations are in process, historically determined yet *responsive* to human relationships, that specific class locations shift as capitalism develops, refines and reconstructs through its stages of accumulation. Any interpretation of the political economy demands the theorization of class relations, for these relations are part of the essential foundations of contemporary social policy, of welfare programmes, of family relations, of culture and subculture of 'community' and of government.

The reaffirmation of class analysis produced important work on class location (Carchedi, 1977; Hunt, 1977; Miliband, 1977; Poulantzas, 1973, 1975; Wright, 1976, 1978) in which the process by which classes were conceptualized and class location established was explored. Braverman and Wright each indicated that class boundaries are located in terms of the economic demands of capital while emphasizing the structural significance of ideological and political criteria. As Poulantzas argued, the divisions which arise out of supervisory or managerial functions occur at the political level. Functionaries of capital, be they in the factory, the state or the police, occupy ambiguous and contradictory class locations. Classes, however, remain 'in motion', they organize and disorganize, they extend and retract their capacities and they are fixed permanently in struggle. The fundamental criteria for the location of classes are economic, however, and this has been clearly evident in the 1980s as the free market economy has expanded but not required a comparable expansion of labour, and substantial numbers of workers have been forced into the relative surplus population.

Marginality, and the process of marginalization, is an important concept in the structural analysis of contemporary class location, class fragmentation and Wright's discussion of contradictory class locations. Implicit in this analysis is the premise that during periods of economic recession part of the total workforce is used as the disposable surplus of wage-labour essential to the reconstruction of capital. During the 1980s while international companies enjoyed unprecedented profits and those with secure incomes took part in a decade of unchecked consumerism, approximately one-third of the population sat, marginalized, on or below the poverty line (Walker and Walker, 1987). While the private sector in housing, education, health care and transport flourished, the National Health Service, state schools, council housing and public transport offered a reduced service staffed by disillusioned workers.

Set within the context of the structural location of class the concept of marginality is both rigorous and significant. Marginality is manifested not only in terms of economic relations but also in terms of the subsequent political and ideological responses to those relations. Just as certain groups occupy 'contradictory class locations' so groups are pushed beyond the marginal locations of the relative surplus population. A range of identifiable groups and individuals, while relying on the capitalist mode of production and social democracy to provide them with an economic opportunity structure, live outside the 'legitimate' social relations of production. Marx (1961: 644) identified those condemned to 'pauperism', 'the hospital of the active labour army . . .' as the 'demoralized and ragged'. They constituted the 'dangerous classes' because their conditions were seen as the breeding ground of dissension and a real threat to civil order and social stability.

The link – unemployment, destitution, crime – has provided an important starting-point for research which has developed the 'surplus population' thesis and its relevance in explaining not only certain categories of crime but also the process of criminalization of certain groups of people. While the 'immiseration thesis' cannot explain fully 'all' crimes it has demonstrated that the broader structural contexts of production and distribution, of poverty and unemployment, are significant in the involvement of people in 'crime' but also in the processes which define, adjust, enforce and administer the criminal law. The policy of targeting identifiable and vulnerable groups through heavy or saturation policing, for example, often precipitates a quasi-political resistance from marginal groups. While street crime might arise out of social, political and economic conditions it is not a progressive 'political' expression. Not only is it unlikely to stimulate long-term solutions to structural problems but inevitably it carries negative consequences. It divides the working class, nourishes racism, popularizes 'law and order' campaigns, victimizes the poor, consolidates the threat of violence towards women and increases the vulnerability of poor neighbourhoods. Consequently street crime, burglary and assault are often intra-class, and exacerbate problems and sharpen contradictions. Clearly poverty and long-term unemployment increase the propensity of the poor to commit 'survival' crime (Box, 1987; Franey, 1983) but this process of immiseration has divisive and threatening consequences as well as the potential for sharpening political consciousness and action.

Criminalization, the application of the criminal label to an identifiable social category, is dependent on *how* certain acts are labelled and on *who* has the power to label, and is directly limited to the political economy of marginalization. The power to criminalize is not derived necessarily in consensus politics but it carries with it the ideologies associated with marginalization and it is within these portrayals that certain actions are named, contained and regulated. This is a powerful process because it mobilizes popular approval and legitimacy in support of powerful interests within the state. As Hillyard's (1987) discussion of Northern Ireland illustrates clearly, public support is more likely to be achieved for state intervention against 'criminal' acts than for the repression or suppression of a 'political' cause. Further, even where no purposeful political intention is involved, the process of criminalization can divert attention from the social or political dynamics of a movement and specify its 'criminal' potential. If black youth is portrayed exclusively as 'muggers' (Hall et al., 1978) there will be less tolerance of organized campaigns which emphasize that they have legitimate political and economic grievances (Gilroy, 1987a). The marginalization of women who campaign for rights or for peace and the questioning of their sexuality is a further example of the process by which meaningful and informed political action can be undermined, de-legitimized and criminalized (Chadwick and Little, 1987; Young, 1990). Fundamental to the criminalization thesis is the proposition that while political motives are downplayed, the degree of *violence* involved is emphasized. In industrial relations, for example, it is the violence of the pickets which is pinpointed (Beynon, 1985; Fine and Millar, 1985; Scraton and Thomas, 1985), rather than the importance, for the success of a strike, of preventing supplies getting through to a factory. The preoccupation with the 'violence' of political opposition makes it easier to mobilize popular support for measures of containment.

In many of these examples, 'criminalization' is a process which has been employed to underpin the repressive or control functions of the state. This compounds further the difficult distinction between 'normal' and 'social' crime, since criminalization fuses the categories. The problem remains that even when violence is only used tactically it is double-edged. It breaks the assumed agreement to pursue conflicts by 'democratic', 'parliamentary' means which is the basis of the social contract and the legitimacy of the liberal-democratic state. The state is then certain to react, by fair means or foul (Poulantzas, 1975). Consequently it becomes difficult to disentangle those instances in which criminalization is part of the maintenance of social order, and where it is not. Theoretically, however, it highlights a significant function of the law in the ideological containment of class conflict. Married to the process of marginalization, through which identifiable groups systematically and structurally become peripheral to the core relations of the political economy, criminalization offers a strong analytical construct. Taken together these theses provide the foundations to critical analyses of the state, the rule of law and social conflict in advanced capitalist society.

RACISM, CRIME AND THE POLITICS OF NEO-COLONIALISM

> . . . if you were to ask a taxi driver, hotel clerk or news vendor in London they would explain the increase in violent crime, especially robbery, by the presence of West Indians.
> (Wilson, 1977: 69)

This statement, made by one of the leading New Right criminologists in the USA, directly attributes the escalation of street crime – and other 'predatory' crime – to the behaviour of a clearly identifiable group. It consolidated the media-hyped imagery of the 1970s which first named 'mugging' and then located it within the actions of black Afro-Caribbean youth. What this confirmed, according to Gilroy (1987b: 108), was a generally held assumption that 'undesired immigrants' are infected by a 'culture of criminality and inbred inability to cope with that highest achievement of civilization – the rule of law'. That these views are prevalent in popular culture, the media coverage of 'hard news' and political commentaries is sufficient evidence of the breadth and depth of racism in Britain, but it is their institutionalization as all-pervasive (Gordon, 1983) which transforms imagery into ideology. The ideological construction of the race–crime–black criminality debate has been an essential condition upon which the differential policing and discriminatory punishment afforded to specific neighbourhoods has been based.

Following the serious disturbances in Toxteth, Liverpool, during the summer of 1981 the then Chief Constable of Merseyside Kenneth Oxford justified the well-established principle of heavy policing of Liverpool's black population by direct references to immigration. Immigrants, from as early as 1335, had contributed to the 'turbulent character of the Liverpool populace': 'Each of these new communities brought with them associated problems, disputes and tensions, which on occasion spilled over into outbreaks of violence' (Oxford, 1981: 4). On this basis Oxford defended differential policing and discriminatory practices and discounted allegations of racial harassment or violence. These views, combining traditional criminological theories of individual pathology with those of social pathology, create a 'neat dovetail of genetic characteristics and environmentalism' (Scraton, 1982: 35). They are commonly held throughout the criminal justice process (Gordon, 1983), and inform the decisions and actions of powerful definers throughout all institutions of the British state. While evidence of this was overwhelming in the police-commissioned Policy Studies Institute study of police–community relations in London (PSI, 1983), Scarman (1981) denied the existence of 'institutionalized racism' either in the police or in other state agencies.

Essential to understanding the process of institutionalized racism, however, is the proposition that:

> marginalization is not a 'condition' suddenly inflicted on the Afro-Caribbean or Asian community simply by a downturn in the economy. It is written into the statutory definitions of immigration law and reflected in the political management of identities throughout state practices. (Sim et al., 1987: 44)

In constructing an analysis of the social relations of neocolonialism as a determining context, clearly the connection has to be made with class and the relations of production. Advanced capitalism persistently has required relations based on national domination as well as the provision of a ready supply of cheap materials, fuel and labour power. Central to this is the historical development of class fragmentation, particularly the use and abuse of immigrant or migrant labour as 'reserve armies'. Ironically named 'guest workers', the exploitation of cheap labour from the colonies has been a key feature in the construction of European and US labour forces throughout the twentieth century. Sivanandan's (1982) work, as with the excellent Institute of Race Relations' journal *Race and Class*, has done much to remind critical theorists that the connection between 'race' and labour power has formed an essential basis for the consolidation of multinational capitalism. Certainly the relationship between immigrant/ migrant labour and the 'core' working class has created a complex dynamic in the interpretation of class locations. With the political and ideological criteria referred to earlier clearly evident in the politics of racism, black workers, like their late nineteenth century Irish equivalents, have been allocated the least desirable, most insecure and poorest paid work. Their marginalization (some authors argue that they constitute an underclass) is primarily economic and the political and ideological struggles around this process have certainly contributed to the fractionalizing of the working class (Miles, 1982). As Sivanandan suggests, the process of economic marginalization, manifest at all material levels, has brought with it organized resistance and spontaneous rebellion. In his 'reversal' of the orthodoxy Gilroy (1987a) is not as far away from this position as it first seems when he emphasizes the reciprocity of race and class as determining contexts. His concern is to free racism of its subservience to classism, that racism is simply reduced to its function for capital. Racism *can be* and often is implicated in intra-class struggle but it has become central in establishing rational explanations, in the minds as well as the hearts of working class white communities, for diminishing circumstances. Racism, in that sense, is part of British hegemonic consciousness – it carries convincing explanations, it offers plausible accounts and its *logic* must not be underestimated (Cashmore, 1987).

What has become clear during the 1980s, however, is the simple proposition that the differential policing and targeting of particular communities has not only led to rebellion (Scraton, 1987) but has also completed the process of marginalization. While it is incorrect to homogenize groups under the ascribed labels of 'black', 'brown', 'people of colour', this is precisely what racism does and organized resistance has emerged. Yet these are the very groups that remain targeted and, as with the earlier discussion on class, the process of criminalization has been hand-in-glove with that of marginalization. Even if identifiable groups have a greater propensity to commit crimes than other comparable groups, and there is no evidence to suggest that 'black crime' is any more prevalent than 'crime' in other communities, that does not explain the ferocity with which the criminal justice process has reacted to the black people with which it deals.

A House of Lords debate in March 1989 on violent crime brought claims by Conservative peers that 61 per cent of all street robbery was committed by black people. It was alleged that in London boroughs where only 14 per cent of the population were black 72 per cent of rapes were committed by black men. This brought renewed calls to identify the racial background of offenders. Given that further crime surveys in Britain have found that 49 per cent of people 'feared' personal attack on the streets it is clear that the renewed campaign directed towards connecting race and crime has encouraged people to fear young blacks on the streets.

Black defendants are more likely to go to prison earlier, for longer periods and their social workers' reports are more likely to be ignored by the courts, than in the case of comparable offences committed by whites. Afro-Caribbean youths are given custodial sentences more readily and are remanded in custody, despite fewer convictions, than whites. In 1987 83.8 per cent of the male and 72.7 per cent of the women's prison population was classified as 'white'. The increase in black and 'ethnic' imprisonment has been rising by 1 per cent per year since the mid-1980s. In all offence categories black people are sentenced for longer periods, have fewer previous convictions and less serious charges. While the number of young people in black/ethnic groups is approximately 4.3 per cent of the population in most detention or remand centres they number 20–30 per cent of those incarcerated.

The main conclusion to be drawn from the above material is that the reassurances given by the Home Office, by government inquiries and by the liberal commentaries of academics – that racism in the criminal justice process is an issue of the attitudinal approach of individuals and not an institutional problem – are false. It is clear that in terms of access, recruitment, training and development the criminal justice institutions and their professions have failed to deal with their well-established traditions of discrimination. Further, it is clear that racism is endemic in the policies, priorities and practices of the criminal justice institutions.

The shift from labour-intensive production and the uneven distribution of the effects of economic crisis in Britain have contributed significantly to the imposition of long-term, structural unemployment. The inevitable consequences of the economic, political and ideological location of black communities is that they are overrepresented in this surplus population.

> As with the late nineteenth century constructions of moral degeneracy and social contagion, black people have found themselves on the wrong end of the rough–respectable and nondeserving–deserving continua. This series of factors have created the preconditions in which black communities can be identified as the new 'dangerous classes'. (Sim et al., 1987)

THE FEMINIST CRITIQUES AND THE DETERMINING CONTEXT OF PATRIARCHY

> Women appear in a sociology predicated on the universe occupied by men . . . its
> methods, conceptual schemes and theories [have] been based on and built up within the
> male social universe. (Smith, 1973: 7)

Patriarchy, as the systematic domination of women by men both in the public and
private spheres, embodies more than material and physical processes of power. It
legitimates its rule, its politics, its universalism through knowledge forms based on
'themes, assumptions, metaphors and images' (Smith, 1975: 354) which underpin
academic discourse, as self-evident truths. One such truth is fundamental, that is the
defining and differentiating of women with reference to men: 'He is the Subject, He is
the Absolute . . . She is the Other' (de Beauvoir, 1972: 16). What academic discourse
has assumed is the 'fixed and inevitable destiny' of women as daughters, wives,
mothers, mistresses and servicers to their menfolk whose consolidation of power
rests on the cultural–legal regulation of paternity (O'Brien, 1981).

Undoubtedly patriarchies develop distinctive and unique characteristics which
produce complex institutional forms and social arrangements (Segal, 1987) but the
subordination of women is both universal and structural (Connell, 1987; Morgan,
1986). The marginalization of women within patriarchies takes a variety of political
and economic forms: the unwaged and unrecognized domestic mode of production
(Delphy, 1984); the 'control of women's labour power' (Hartmann, 1979: 14) and
the all-pervasiveness of masculine values and processes in paid work (Cockburn,
1986; Walby, 1986); the threat and reality of physical violence (Kelly, 1988; Stanko,
1985). While the caveat of 'false universalism' (Eisenstein, 1984: 141) has recognized
the diversity of women's experiences, needs and desires, the project of the feminist
critiques of patriarchy has been the deconstruction of the power–knowledge axis
within advanced capitalist societies.

While the standpoints and priorities of feminist analyses remain distinctive,
particularly in the debates around the relationship between advanced capitalist
relations and patriarchal relations, the critiques have been successful and progressive
in challenging 'the assumptions which historically have normalized and subordinated
political relations based on perceived natural constructs of gender and sexuality . . .
assumptions etched deep in the institutional fabric of the political economy which
form part of the national consciousness and which become central to the profession-
alisation of knowledge' (Scraton, 1990: 15). In terms of the earlier discussion of
power these assumptions not only underwrite, even encourage, the institutionalized
sexism and heterosexism of state institutions but also form part of the daily, hourly
round of interpersonal relations which deny women access to social space, silence
their voices, violate their bodies and denigrate their resistance.

While state institutions 'coercively and authoritatively constitute the social order
in the interest of men as a gender' (Mackinnon, 1983: 44) and advanced capitalism
has been eminently successful in its assimilation of quite diverse forms of patriarchies,
academic knowledge has provided both the legitimacy and justification for the
determining contexts of gender and sexuality (Harding, 1986; Smith, 1988; Sydie,
1987). Within criminology, as Carol Smart first noted in 1976, the 'wider moral,
political economic and sexual spheres which influence women's status and position in
society' [have] been neglected or seen as irrelevant to the priority of studying men and

crime (Smart, 1976: 185). More recent feminist research and publication has posed 'fundamental questions about the adequacy' of criminological analyses which [have] taken for granted the 'exclusion of women' (Gelsthorpe and Morris, 1990: 7). The substantive debates have prioritized: the relationship between patriarchy, the rule of law and the underpinnings of theoretical criminology (Smart, 1989); the universality of violence against women and the persistent reluctance of the state to intervene (Kelly and Radford, 1987); women's incarceration in prisons (Carlen, 1983) and in mental institutions (Showalter, 1987); family law and its 'role in enforcing women's position in society' (Bottomley, 1985: 184).

In addition to this work there has been further critical research into women and crime (Carlen, 1988; Carlen and Worrall, 1987; Heidensohn, 1985). Hilary Allen's (1987: 1) work, for example, confirmed previous research in showing that women are 'twice as likely as a man to be dealt with by psychiatric rather than penal means'. Further, the trend – first reported in 1988 – of a sharp increase in the imprisonment of women, more readily and for longer sentences, has consolidated as courts have become more severe on women offenders. This trend applies also to women with dependent children. In June 1988, 58 per cent of women taken into custody had committed offences involving theft, handling stolen property or fraud. Twenty-five per cent of women prisoners admitted were black. The average sentence increased by 36 per cent on 1987. Of the 1,765 women in prison over half had dependent children and most were convicted of non-violent crimes.

What this range of work has achieved has been to locate these issues within the material base of patriarchy demonstrating the diversity of women's oppression and the dynamics of male dominance. This includes 'women's access to production' and 'control over biological reproduction' but also through 'control of women's sexuality through a particular form of heterosexuality' (Mahony, 1985: 70). For 'male identity' and 'male sexuality' are 'crucial to the maintenance of male power' (Mahony, 1985). The determining context of patriarchal relations is based on the material and physical power appropriated by – but also ascribed to – men, and this is supported by a 'hegemonic form of masculinity in the society as a whole' with women 'oriented to accommodating the interests and desires of men' (Connell, 1987: 183). While women fight back individually and collectively, 'emphasized femininity' internalizes the ideology of servicing and use-value, and feeds the politics of dependency. It is within this process that gender divisions and ascribed sexualities become legitimated as 'natural' and, therefore, inevitable.

As with Connell's work, Brittan (1989) and Segal (1990) have explored the importance of hegemonic masculinity or masculinism in its subordination not only of women's sexuality, but also other male sexualities. As Mort (1987) observes, it is the historical processing of medico-legal discourses concerning 'dangerous sexualities' which has rendered alternative expressions of sexuality unacceptable, abnormal and unnatural. The broad consensus around what Rich (1977) labelled 'compulsory heterosexuality' has had a major impact on legislation but also has lessened significantly official responses to crimes against lesbians and gay men. Once again, the duality of marginalization is clear: the criminalization of the 'outcrop' (prostitutes not clients, homosexuals not harassers etc.), and the reluctance to regulate or act against the oppressors.

Clearly all women are controlled by the public and private realities and fears inherent within male power relations but when they assert their rights, contest their oppression or organize against the discriminatory practices of the law, they become the threat. These are the women, already economically marginalized by the dependency relations of advanced capitalist patriarchy, who are further marginalized by their politics of opposition. Ultimately, as Chadwick and Little (1987) show, they are criminalized. The feminist critiques of criminology, both old and new, have demonstrated that critical criminology must have at its core the marginalization and criminalization of women, women's experiences of the criminal justice process and relationship of women to crime. They provide not only an essential contribution to critical analysis but also to the realization of a critical methodology which interprets the interpersonal experiences of women within the broader structural relations of advanced capitalist patriarchy.

CONCLUSION

What this discussion has pursued is the central argument that critical criminology recognizes the reciprocity inherent in the relationship between *structure* and *agency* but also that structural relations embody the primary determining contexts of production, reproduction and neocolonialism. In order to understand the dynamics of life in advanced capitalist societies and the institutionalization of ideological relations within the state and other key agencies it is important to take account of the historical, political and economic contexts of classism, sexism, heterosexism and racism. These categories do not form hierarchies of oppression, they are neither absolute nor are they totally determining, but they do carry with them the weight and legitimacy of official discourse. They reflect and succour the power–knowledge axis both in popular culture and in academic endeavour.

While the state, as a series of often contradictory relations, negotiates with oppositional forces and develops administrative and professional strategies/alliances to deal with political struggle, its essential objective is the maintenance of the established order. The politics of liberal democracy demands room for manoeuvre, some discretionary possibilities and occasional progressive reform but the state's legacy is essentially conservative. It is that of containment, caution and political management. As Sim et al. (1987: 62) state:

> Advanced capitalism, with the added complexity of managerial relations and class fractions, is served and serviced but rarely confronted by the state's institutions whose members share its ends, if not always its means, in a common ideology. It is at this level that the function of institutions, exemplified by the rule of law, tutors and guides the broad membership of society.

The above discussion demonstrates the basis upon which class fragmentation occurs and how those economically marginalized are exposed to the processes of criminalization. Additionally the post-colonial exploitation of migrant and immigrant labour has served capitalism and has led to a form of immiseration connected directly to racism. Finally, patriarchy has been functional for capital both in the public and private spheres. The interpretation and analysis of these primary determining contexts, however, cannot be limited to economic imperatives. Patriarchy and neo-colonialism are also political forms which give rise to opposition and challenge. Yet, at the ideological level, their construction as oppressive social and political orders is justified and reinforced. The criminal justice process and the rule of law assist in the management of structural contradictions and the process of criminalization is central to such management. While maintaining the face of consent, via negotiation, the tacit understanding is that coercion remains the legitimate and sole prerogative of the liberal democratic state. Liberalism and authoritarianism do not form distinctive regimes or administrations within the context of democracy, they constitute a well-established spectrum of legitimate state rule and its use of legal censures.

REFERENCES

Allen, H. (1987) *Justice Unbalanced: Gender, Psychiatry and Judicial Decisions*. Milton Keynes: Open University Press.

Bell, D. (1960) *The End of Ideology*. New York: Free Press.

Beynon, H. (1985) *Digging Deeper: Issues in the Miners' Strike*. London: Verso.

Bottomley, A. (1985) 'What is happening to family law? A feminist critique of conciliation', in J. Brophy and C. Smart (eds), *Women in Law*. London: Routledge and Kegan Paul.

Box, S. (1987) *Recession, Crime and Punishment*. London: Macmillan.

Braverman, H. (1974) *Labor and Monopoly Capital*. New York: Monthly Review Press.

Brittan, A. (1989) *Masculinity and Power*. Cambridge: Polity.

Carchedi, G. (1977) *On the Economic Identification of Social Classes*. London: Routledge and Kegan Paul.

Carlen, P. (1983) *Women's Imprisonment*. London: Routledge and Kegan Paul.

Carlen, P. (1988) *Women, Crime and Poverty*. Milton Keynes: Open University Press.

Carlen, P. and Worrall, A. (1987) *Gender, Crime and Justice*. Milton Keynes: Open University Press.

Cashmore, E.E. (1987) *The Logic of Racism*. London: Allen and Unwin.

Cashmore, E.E. (1989) *United Kingdom? Class, Race and Gender since the War*. London: Unwin Hyman.

Chadwick, K. and Little, C. (1987) 'The criminalisation of women', in P. Scraton (ed.), *Law, Order and the Authoritarian State*. Milton Keynes: Open University Press.

Cockburn, C. (1986) *Machineries of Dominance*. London: Pluto.

Cohen, S. (1985) *Visions of Social Control*. Cambridge: Polity.

Connell, R.W. (1987) *Gender and Power*. Cambridge: Polity.

Dahrendorf, R. (1959) *Class and Class Conflict in Industrial Society*. Stanford, CA: Stanford University Press.

de Beauvoir, S. (1972) *The Second Sex*. Harmondsworth: Penguin.

Delphy, C. (1984) *Close to Home: a Materialist Analysis of Women's Oppression*. London: Hutchinson.

Eisenstein, H. (1984) *Contemporary Feminist Thought*. London: Counterpoint.

Fine, B. and Millar, R. (eds) (1985) *Policing the Miners' Strike*. London: Lawrence and Wishart.

Foucault, M. (1977) *Discipline and Punish: the Birth of the Prison*. London: Allen Lane.

Franey, R. (1983) *Poor Law*. London: CHAR/NCCL.

Friend, A. and Metcalfe, A. (1981) *Slump City: the Politics of Mass Unemployment*. London: Pluto Press.

Gamble, A. (1981) *Britain in Decline*. London: Papermac.

Gelsthorpe, L. and Morris, A. (eds) (1990) *Feminist Perspectives in Criminology*. Milton Keynes: Open University Press.

Giddens, A. (1979) *Central Problems in Social Theory*. London: Macmillan.

Giddens, A. (1984) *The Constitution of Society*. Cambridge: Polity.

Giddens, A. (1987) *The Nation-State and Violence*. Cambridge: Polity.

Gilroy, P. (1987a) *There Ain't No Black in the Union Jack*. London: Hutchinson.

Gilroy, P. (1987b) 'The myth of black criminality', in P. Scraton (ed.), *Law, Order and the Authoritarian State*. Milton Keynes: Open University Press.

Gordon, P. (1983) *White Law*. London: Pluto Press.

Gouldner, A.W. (1969) *The Coming Crisis in Western Sociology*. London: Heinemann.

Gouldner, A.W. (1973) 'Foreword' in I. Taylor, P. Walton and J. Young, *The New Criminology*. London: Routledge and Kegan Paul.

Gramsci, A. (1971) *Selections from the Prison Notebooks*. London: Lawrence and Wishart.

Hall, S., Critcher, C., Jefferson, T., Clarke, J. and Roberts, B. (1978) *Policing the Crisis*. London: Macmillan.

Harding, S. (1986) *The Science Question in Feminism*. Milton Keynes: Open University Press.

Hartmann, H. (1979) 'The unhappy marriage of Marxism and feminism: towards a progressive union', *Capital and Class*, 8.

Heidensohn, F. (1985) *Women and Crime*. London: Macmillan.

Hillyard, P. (1987) 'The normalization of special powers: from Northern Ireland to Britain', in P. Scraton (ed.), *Law, Order and the Authoritarian State*. Milton Keynes: Open University Press.

Hunt, A. (ed.) (1977) *Class and Class Structure*. London: Lawrence and Wishart.

Kelly, L. (1988) *Surviving Sexual Violence*. Cambridge: Polity.

Kelly, L. and Radford, J. (1987) 'The problem of men: feminist perspectives on sexual violence', in P. Scraton (ed.), *Law, Order and the Authoritarian State*. Milton Keynes: Open University Press.

Lipset, S. (1960) *Political Man*. New York: Doubleday.

Mackinnon, C.A. (1983) 'Feminism, Marxism, method and the state: toward feminist jurisprudence', *Signs*, 8(4): 635–58.

Mahony, P. (1985) *Schools for the Boys? Co-education Reassessed*. London: Hutchinson.

Marx, K. (1961) *Capital*, vols I–III. London: Lawrence and Wishart.

Miles, R. (1982) *Racism and Migrant Labour*. London: Routledge and Kegan Paul.

Miliband, R. (1969) *The State in Capitalist Society*. London: Weidenfeld and Nicolson.

Miliband, R. (1977) *Class and Politics*. London: Macmillan.

Morgan, R. (ed.) (1986) *Sisterhood is Global*. Harmondsworth: Penguin.

Mort, F. (1987) *Dangerous Sexualities*. London: Routledge and Kegan Paul.

Nightingale, M. (1980) *Merseyside in Crisis*. Liverpool: Merseyside Socialist Research Group.

O'Brien, M. (1981) *The Politics of Reproduction*. London: Routledge and Kegan Paul.

Oxford, K. (1981) *Report of the Police Committee on Merseyside Disorders* (Evidence to the Scarman Inquiry) [K. Oxford, Chief Constable]. Liverpool: Merseyside Police.

Parsons, T. (1951) *The Social System*. London: Routledge and Kegan Paul.

Poulantzas, N. (1973) 'On social classes', *New Left Review*, 78: 27–55.

Poulantzas, N. (1975) *Political Power and Social Classes*. London: New Left Books.

PSI Report (1983) *Police and People in London*, vols I–IV. London: Policy Studies Institute.

Quinney, R. (1970) *The Social Reality of Crime*. Boston: Little Brown.

Rich, A. (1977) *Of Woman Born: Motherhood as Experience and Institution*. London: Virago.

Scarman, Lord (1981) *The Scarman Report: the Brixton Disorders 10–12 April 1981*. Cmnd 8427. London: HMSO.

Scraton, P. (1982) 'Policing and institutionalised racism on Merseyside', in D. Cowell, T.Jones and J. Young (eds), *Policing the Riots*. London: Junction Books.

Scraton, P. (1987) 'Unreasonable force: policing, punishment and marginalisation', in P. Scraton (ed.), *Law, Order and the Authoritarian State*. Milton Keynes: Open University Press.

Scraton, P. (1990) 'Scientific knowledge or masculine discourses? Challenging patriarchy in criminology', in L. Gelsthorpe and A. Morris (eds), *Feminist Perspectives in Criminology*. Milton Keynes: Open University Press.

Scraton, P. and Thomas, P. (1985) *The State v. The People: Lessons from the Coal Dispute (Journal of Law and Society*, special issue). Oxford: Basil Blackwell.

Segal, L. (1987) *Is the Future Female? Troubled Thoughts on Contemporary Feminism*. London: Virago.

Segal, L. (1990) *Slow Motion: Changing Masculinities, Changing Men*. London: Virago.

Showalter, E. (1987) *The Female Malady. Women, Madness and English Culture, 1830–1980*. London: Virago.

Sim, J. (1990) *Medical Power in Prisons: the Prison Medical Service in England 1774–1989*. Milton Keynes: Open University Press.

Sim, J., Scraton, P. and Gordon, P. (1987) 'Crime, the state and critical analysis: an introduction', in P. Scraton (ed.), *Law, Order and the Authoritarian State*. Milton Keynes: Open University Press.

Sivanandan, A. (1982) 'From resistance to rebellion', *Race and Class*, special issue, XXIII.

Sivanandan, A. (1983) *A Different Hunger*. London: Pluto Press.

Smart, C. (1976) *Women, Crime and Criminology*. London: Routledge and Kegan Paul.

Smart, C. (1989) *Feminism and the Power of Law*. London: Routledge.

Smith, D. (1973) 'Women's perspective as a radical critique of sociology', *Sociological Inquiry*, 44.

Smith, (1975) 'An analysis of the ideological structures and how women are excluded', *Canadian Journal of Sociology and Anthropology*, 12(4).

Smith, D. (1988) *The Everyday World as Problematic: a Feminist Sociology*. Milton Keynes: Open University Press.

Stanko, E. (1985) *Intimate Intrusions*. London: Routledge and Kegan Paul.

Sydie, R. (1987) *Natural Women, Cultured Men: a Feminist Perspective on Sociological Theory*. Milton Keynes: Open University Press.

Taylor–Gooby, P. (1982) *The Welfare State from the Second World War to the 1980s*. D355 Social Policy and Social Welfare. Milton Keynes: Open University Press.

Therborn, G. (1978) *What Does the Ruling Class Do When It Rules?* London: New Left Books.

Thompson, E.P. (1975) *Whigs and Hunters: the Origin of the Black Act*. London: Allen Lane.

Walby, S. (1986) *Patriarchy at Work*. Cambridge: Polity.

Walker, A. and Walker, C. (eds) (1987) *The Growing Divide: a Social Audit 1979–1987*. London: CPAG.

Wilson, J.Q. (1977) 'Crime and punishment in England', in R.E. Tyrrell Jr (ed.), *The Future that Doesn't Work: Social Democracy's Failures in Britain*. New York: Doubleday.

Wright, E.O. (1976) 'Class boundaries in advanced capitalist societies;, *New Left Review*, 98: 3–41.

Wright, E.O. (1978) *Class, Crisis and the State*. London: New Left Books.

Young, A. (1990) *Femininity in Dissent*. London: Routledge.

26

Critical criminology and the concept of crime

Louk H.C. Hulsman

ARE CRIMINAL EVENTS EXCEPTIONAL? PROBLEMATIZING THE NORMAL OUTLOOK ON CRIME

[. . .]

People who are involved in 'criminal' events do not appear in themselves to form a special category of people. Those who are officially recorded as 'criminal' constitute only a small part of those involved in events that legally are considered to require criminalization. Among them young men from the most disadvantaged sections of the population are heavily over-represented.

Within the concept of criminality a broad range of situations are linked together. Most of these, however, have separate properties and no common denominator: violence within the family, violence in an anonymous context in the streets, breaking into private dwellings, completely divergent ways of illegal receiving of goods, different types of conduct in traffic, pollution of the environment, some forms of political activities. Neither in the motivation of those who are involved in such events, nor in the nature of the consequences or in the possibilities of dealing with them (be it in a preventive sense, or in the sense of the control of the conflict) is there any common structure to be discovered. All [that] these events have in common is that the CJS [criminal justice system] is authorized to take action against them. Some of these events cause considerable suffering to those involved, quite often affecting both perpetrator and victim. Consider for example traffic accidents and violence within the family. The vast majority of the events which are dealt with within the CJS in the sphere of crime, however, would not score particularly high on an imaginary scale of personal hardship. Matrimonial difficulties, difficulties between parents and children, serious difficulties at work and housing problems will, as a rule, be experienced as more serious both as to degree and duration. If we compare 'criminal events' with other events, there is – on the level of those directly involved – nothing which distinguishes those 'criminal' events intrinsically from other difficult

From *Contemporary Crises*, 1986, 10(1): 63–80.

or unpleasant situations. Nor are they singled out as a rule by those directly involved themselves to be dealt with in a way differing radically from the way other events are dealt with. Last, not least, some of these events are considered by those directly involved (and sometimes also by 'observers') as positive and harmless.

It is therefore not surprising that a considerable proportion of the events which would be defined as serious crime within the context of the CJS remain completely outside that system. They are settled within the social context in which they take place (the family, the trade union, the professional association, the circle of friends, the workplace, the neighbourhood) in a similar way as other non-criminal trouble.

All this means that there is no 'ontological reality' of crime.

CRITICAL CRIMINOLOGY AND THE CONCEPT OF CRIME: WHAT HAS BEEN PROBLEMATIZED AND WHAT NOT?

Critical criminology has naturally problematized and criticized many of the 'normal' notions about crime [. . .]. The contribution to this form of 'debunking' varies according to the different perspectives of the stream of critical criminology involved. In a certain period, Marxist criminology predominantly took the stand that 'crime' was a product of the capitalistic system, and that crime would disappear if a new society took birth. In this perspective the disappearance of 'crime' was seen as a disappearance of the 'problematic situations' which are supposed to trigger the criminalization processes. Disappearance of crime was not seen as 'the disappearance of criminalization processes *as an answer* to problematic situations'. In a later stage, critical criminology problematized the class-biased and 'irrational' aspects of the processes of primary and secondary criminalization. In those endeavours the 'functionality' as well as the 'legal equality principle', which are so often invoked as legitimation of processes of primary criminalization, were de-mystified. On the basis of such a de-mystification, critical criminology has argued for partial decriminalization, a more restrictive policy with respect to recourse to criminal law, radical non-intervention with respect to certain crimes and certain criminals. It has pointed to the far more weighty crimes of the powerful and asked for a change in criminal justice activities from the weak and the working class towards 'white-collar crime'. It has pictured the war against crime as a sidetrack from the class struggle, at best an illusion invented to sell news, at worst an attempt to make the poor scapegoats. With very few exceptions, however, the concept of crime as such, the ontological reality of crime, has not been challenged.

[. . .]

WHAT DOES IT MEAN WHEN WE DO NOT PROBLEMATIZE (AND REJECT) THE CONCEPT OF CRIME?

When we do not problematize (and reject) the concept of crime it means that we are stuck in a catascopic view on society in which our informational base (as well the 'facts' as their 'interpretational frame') depends mainly on the institutional framework of criminal justice. It means therefore that we do not take effectively into account the critical analyses of this institutional framework by 'critical criminology'.

[. . .] [C]ritical criminology has to abandon a catascopic view on social reality, based on the definitional activities of the system which is the subject of its study, and has instead to take an anascopic stance towards social reality. This makes it necessary to abandon as a tool in the conceptual frame of criminology the notion of 'crime'. Crime has no ontological reality. Crime is not the *object* but the *product* of criminal policy. Criminalization is one of the many ways to construct social reality. In other words, when someone (person or organization) wants to criminalize, this implies that he:

1 deems a certain 'occurrence' or 'situation' as undesirable;
2 attributes that undesirable occurrence to an individual;
3 approaches this particular kind of individual behaviour with a specific style of social control: the style of punishment;
4 applies a very particular style of punishment which is developed in a particular (legal) professional context and which is based on a 'scholastic' (last-judgement) perspective on the world. In this sense the style of punishment used in criminal justice differs profoundly from the styles of punishment in other social contexts;
5 wants to work in a special organizational setting – criminal justice. This organizational setting is characterized by a very developed division of labour, a lack of accountability for the process as a whole and a lack of influence of those directly involved in the 'criminalized' event on the outcome of the process.

[. . .]

DEVELOPING AN ANASCOPIC VIEW

Defining and dealing with trouble outside a formal context

[. . .]

The meanings which those directly involved (and observers) bestow upon situations influence how they will deal with them. Laura Nader (1980) distinguishes the following procedures people use in dealing with trouble:

- *Lumping it*. The issue or problem that gave rise to a disagreement is simply ignored and the relationship with the person who is part of the disagreement is continued.
- *Avoidance or exit*. This option entails withdrawing from a situation or curtailing or terminating a relationship by leaving.
- *Coercion*. This involves unilateral action.
- *Negotiation*. The two principal parties are the decision makers, and the settlement of the matter is one to which both parties agree, without the aid of a third party. They do not seek a solution in terms of rules, but try to create the rules by which they can organize their relationship with one another.
- *Mediation*. Mediation, in contrast, involves a third party who intervenes in a dispute to aid the principals in reaching an agreement.
- Other procedural modes that are used in attempts to handle trouble are *arbitration* and *adjudication*. In *arbitration* both principals consent to the intervention

of a third party whose judgement they must agree to accept beforehand. When we speak about *adjudication* we refer to the presence of a third party who has the authority to intervene in a dispute whether or not the principals wish it.

The list of ways of dealing with trouble which Nader gives is by no means exhaustive. People can address themselves for help to different professional or non-professional settings. They may engage in a 'ritual of reordering' which does not involve the other person earlier implied in the problematic situation (Pfohl, 1981).

People may also engage in collective action to bring about a structural change in the situations which cause them trouble (Abel, 1982).

Which of these many courses of action will an involved person choose?

The meaning which a directly involved person bestows upon a situation will influence [. . .] his course of action. That course of action will also be influenced by the degree to which different strategies to deal with trouble are available and accessible for him; in other words, the degree to which he has a real possibility of choice. This degree of choice is largely influenced by his place in the network of power which shapes his environment and by his practical possibilities to change the 'tribes' of which he is a part for other ones.

Formal and informal ways of defining trouble and dealing with it compared

The process of bestowing meaning on what is going on in life is flexible in face to face relations in so far as those involved in this process feel relatively 'free' towards each other as equal human beings. In other words, if they feel not constrained by the requirements of organizational or professional roles, and [if] they are not caught in a power relation which prevents some of the parties [from fully taking part] in this process. This flexibility has many advantages. It increases the possibilities to reach by negotiation a common meaning of problematic situations. It provides also possibilities for learning. Experience can teach people that the application of a certain frame of interpretation and a certain focus does not lead very far in certain sectors of life.

This flexibility is often lacking when situations are defined and dealt with in a highly formalized context. The more such a context is specialized, the more the freedom of definition – and thus of reaction – is limited by a high degree of division of labour or by a high degree of professionalization. In such a case it depends on the type of institution which has – fortuitously – taken the case up which definition and which answer will be given. It is improbable that a definition and a reaction provided for in such a context [will correspond] with the definition and reactions of [those directly] involved.

There are, however, important differences in the degree of flexibility which formal institutions involved in a problematic situation show. In many countries we find a high degree of flexibility in parts of the police organization, e.g. the neighbourhood police. The same may be true of the first echelons of the health and social work system. Of all formalized control systems the criminal justice system seems the most inflexible. The organizational context (high division of labour) and the internal logic of its specific frame of interpretation (peculiar style of punishment in which a gravity scale modelled according to the 'last judgement' plays an over-riding role) both contribute to this inflexibility. Another factor in the particularly alienating effect of criminal justice involvement in problematic situations is its extremely narrow focus: only very specific events modelled in accordance with a legal incrimination may be taken into account and these may only be considered as they were supposed to be [at] a certain moment in time. The dynamic side of constructing reality [is lacking] completely in this particular system. Thus the construction of reality as it is pursued in criminal justice will practically never coincide with the dynamics of the construction of reality of [those directly] involved. In criminal justice one is generally deciding on a reality which exists only within the system and seldom finds a counterpart in the outside world.

[. . .]

CONCLUSION

What would be the task of a critical criminology which has abandoned, according to the view developed above, 'crime' as a conceptual tool? The main tasks of such a critical criminology can be summarized as follows:

1   Continue to describe, explain and demystify the activities of criminal justice and its adverse social effects. This activity should, however, be more directed than up till now to the defining activities of this system. To do that, it would be necessary to compare in concrete fields of human life the activities of criminal justice (and their social effects) with those of other formal control systems (legal ones, like the civil justice system, and non-legal ones, like the medical and social work systems). The activities of those formal control systems with respect to a certain area of life should be at the same time compared with informal ways of dealing with such an area of life. In such a task, critical criminology can be stimulated by the developments in (legal) anthropology and in a more general way by sociology in an interpretative paradigm. This implies abandoning 'behaviour' and deviance as a starting-point for analysis and adopting instead a situation-oriented approach, micro and macro.

2   Illustrate – but only as a way of example without pretending to be a 'science of problematic situations' – how in a specific field problematic situations could be addressed at different levels of the societal organization without having recourse to criminal justice.

3   Study strategies [on] how to abolish criminal justice; in other words, how to liberate organizations like the police and the courts [from] a system of reference which turns them away [from] the variety of life and the needs of those directly involved.

4   One of these strategies ought to be to contribute to the development of another overall language in which questions related to criminal justice and to public problems which generate claims to criminalization can be discussed without the bias (Cohen, 1985) of the present 'control babble'.

REFERENCES

Abel, R. (ed.) (1982) *The Politics of Informal Justice*. New York: Academic Press.
Cohen, S. (1985) *Visions of Social Control*. Cambridge: Polity.
Nader, L. (ed.) (1980) *No Access to Law: Alternatives to the American Judicial System*. New York: Academic Press.
Pfohl, S.J. (1981) 'Labelling criminals', in H.L. Ross (ed.), *Law and Deviance*, Beverly Hills, CA: Sage.

27

The need for a radical realism

Jock Young

[. . .]

A silent revolution has occurred in conventional criminology in the United States and in Great Britain. The demise of positivism and social democratic ways of reforming crime has been rapid. A few perceptive commentators have noted the sea-change in the orthodox centre of criminology but the extent of the paradigm shift has been scarcely analysed, or its likely impact understood.

The first sighting of realignment in Western criminology was in a perceptive article written in 1977 by Tony Platt and Paul Takagi entitled 'Intellectuals for law and order' (Platt and Takagi, 1981). They grouped together writers such as Ernest van den Haag, James Q. Wilson and Norval Morris and noted how they represented the demise of 'liberal', social democratic ways of understanding crime and prisons in the United States. 'Intellectuals for law and order are not a criminological fad', they write, but 'a decisive influence in criminology' (Platt and Takagi, 1981: 54). Developing this line of argument, Donald Cressey writes:

> The tragedy is in the tendency of modern criminologists to drop the search for causes and to join the politicians rather than develop better ideas about why crime flourishes, for example, these criminologists Wilson, and van den Haag, Ehrlich, Fogel, Morris and Hawkins – and hundreds of others – seem satisfied with a technological criminology whose main concern is for showing policy-makers how to repress criminals and criminal justice work more efficiently, [and he adds:] If more and more criminologists respond – and they seem to be doing so – criminology will eventually have only 'handcuffs 1a' orientation. (Cressey, 1978)

There is an unfortunate tendency to conflate these various thinkers together as if they were politically similar. But van den Haag is very much a traditional conservative whereas Morris is a 'J.S. Mill' type of liberal and Wilson differs explicitly from both of them. Such a confusion makes it difficult to understand the particular purchase which writers such as James Q. Wilson in the United States and Ron Clarke

From *Confronting Crime* (eds R. Matthews and J. Young), pp. 9–30. (London: Sage, 1986.)

in Britain have had on the new administrative criminology and their ability to mobilize writers of various positions in support for a broad policy. The basis of this is what all these writers have in common, namely:

1   An antagonism to the notion of crime being determined by social circumstances – 'the smothering of sociological criminology' as Cressey puts it.
2   A lack of interest in aetiology. As Platt and Takagi note: '[they] are basically uninterested in the causes of crime. For them, it's a side issue, a distraction and a waste of their valuable time' (Platt and Takagi, 1981: 45). The historic research programme of criminology into causes and the possibilities of rehabilitation is thus abandoned.
3   A belief in human choice in the criminal act.
4   An advocacy of deterrence.

The key figure in this shift is James Q. Wilson in his role as a theoretician, as author of the bestselling book *Thinking About Crime* and as an adviser to the Reagan administration. His central problem and starting-point is the aetiological crisis of social democratic positivist theory and practice:

> If in 1960 one had been asked what steps society might take to prevent a sharp increase in the crime rate, one might well have answered that crime could best be curtailed by reducing poverty, increasing educational attainment, eliminating dilapidated housing, encouraging community organization, and providing troubled or delinquent youth with counseling services . . . .
>
> Early in the decade of the 1960s, this country began the longest sustained period of prosperity since World War II, much of it fueled, as we later realized, by a semi-war economy. A great array of programs aimed at the young, the poor, and the deprived were mounted. Though these efforts were not made primarily out of a desire to reduce crime, they were wholly consistent with – indeed, in their aggregate money levels, wildly exceeded – the policy prescription that a thoughtful citizen worried about crime would have offered at the beginning of the decade.
>
> Crime soared. It did not just increase a little; it rose at a faster rate and to higher levels than at any time since the 1930s and, in some categories, to higher levels than any experienced in this century.
>
> It all began in about 1963. That was the year, to over-dramatize a bit, that a decade began to fall apart. (Wilson, 1975: 3–4)

What then can be done about crime? Wilson does not rule out that crime may be caused by psychological factors or by the breakdown of family structure. But he argues that there is little that public policy can do in this region. He adamantly rules out the option of reducing crime by improving social conditions. In terms of this interpretation of the aetiological crises – the amelioration of social conditions has resulted in an exponential rise in crime rather than its decline. Thus reform on any level is discarded and with it the notion that the reduction of crime can be achieved by an increase in social justice. But there are other factors that policy can manipulate and it is to these that Wilson turns his attention.

Although the poor commit crime more than the rich, he notes that only a small minority of the poor ever commit crimes. People obviously, then, have a choice in the matter; furthermore, these moral choices can be affected by the circumstances decreed by governments. And here he focuses in on the jugular of liberal thinking about crime and punishment:

> If objective conditions are used to explain crime, spokesmen who use poverty as an explanation of crime should, by the force of their own logic, be prepared to consider the capacity of society to deter crime by raising the risks of crime. But they rarely do. Indeed, those who use poverty as an explanation are largely among the ranks of those who vehemently deny that crime can be deterred. (Wilson, 1975: xiv. See also Van den Haag, 1975: 84–90).

The goal of social policy must be to build up effective deterrents to crime. The problem is not to be solved, he argues, by the conservative measures of draconian punishments but rather by an increase of police effectiveness; the certainty of punishment, not its severity, is his key to government action. Thus Wilson differentiates his view from both conservatives and 'liberal'/social democrats. He advocates punishment but punishment which is appropriate and effective. He sees the informal controls of community as eventually more important than the formal, but that in areas where community has broken down and there is a high incidence of crime, formal control through policing can regenerate the natural regulative functions of the community (the influential Wilson–Kelling hypothesis, see Wilson and Kelling, 1982).

This intellectual current is immensely influential on policy-making in the United States. Thus, the working party set up in the United States in the early years of the Reagan administration under the chairmanship of Wilson gave a low priority, amongst other things, to 'the aetiology of delinquency and a high rating to work in the area of the effects of community cohesiveness and policing for controlling crime' (see Trasler, 1984; Wilson, 1982).

A similar 'social control' theory of crime has been dominant in Britain at the Home Office Research Unit in the recent period particularly influenced by their major theoretician Ron Clarke (see Clarke, 1980). Here, as with Wilson, causal theories of crime came under caution as unproven or impractical (Clarke calls them disposition theories). Situational factors, however, are eminently manipulable. The focus should, therefore, be on making the opportunities for crime more difficult through target hardening, reducing the opportunities for crime and increasing the risks of being caught. This represents a major shift in emphasis against the dispositional bias in almost all previous criminologies.

This move to administrative criminology (or varieties of 'control theory' as Downes and Rock, 1982, would have it) represents the re-emergence of neo-classicist theory on a grand scale. The classicist theory of Beccaria and Bentham had many defects, among them a uniform notion of the impact of the various deterrent devices legislated to control crime (see Rutter and Giller, 1983: 261–2). By introducing concepts of differential risk and opportunity as variables which can be varied by policy-makers and police on a territorial basis, they add a considerable refinement to this model of control. [. . .]

LEFT IDEALISM: THE LOSS OF A CRIMINOLOGY

I have detailed elsewhere the fundamental characteristics of left idealism (Lea and Young, 1984; Young, 1979). Suffice it to say that the tenets of left idealism are simple and familiar to all of us. Crime is seen to occur amongst working-class people as an inevitable result of their poverty, the criminal sees through the inequitable nature of present day society and crime itself is an attempt – however clumsily and ill-thought out – to redress this balance. There is little need to have complex explanations for working-class crime. Its causes are obvious and to blame the poor for their criminality is to blame the victim, to point moral accusations at those whose very actions are a result of their being social casualties. In contrast, the real crime on which we should focus is that of the ruling class: the police, the corporations and the state agencies. This causes real problems for the mass of people, unlike working-class crime which is seen as minor, involving petty theft and occasional violence, of little impact to the working-class community. If the causes of working-class crime are obviously poverty, the causes of upper-class crime are equally obvious: the natural cupidity and power-seeking of the powerful as they enact out the dictates of capital. Criminal law in this context is a direct expression of the ruling class; it is concerned with the protection of their property and the consolidation of their political power. The 'real' function of policing is political rather than the control of crime *per se*; it is social order rather than crime control which is the *raison d'être* of the police.

[. . .]

THE CONVERGENCE BETWEEN LEFT IDEALISM AND ADMINISTRATIVE CRIMINOLOGY

I have noted that the anomaly which traditional positivist criminology confronted was what I have termed the aetiological crisis; that is, a rapidly rising crime rate despite the increase in all the circumstances which were supposed to decrease crime. This was coupled by a crisis in rehabilitation – the palpable failure of the prison system despite decades of penal 'reform'. With the passing of the 1960s the new administrative criminology concluded that, given that affluence itself had led to crime, it was social control which was the only variable worth focusing upon. On the other hand, left idealism forgot about the affluent period altogether and found the correlation between crime and the recession too obvious to merit a discussion of aetiology. If administrative criminology side-stepped the aetiological crisis, left idealism conveniently forgot about it. Both, from their own political perspective, saw social control as the major focus of the study, both were remarkably unsophisticated in their analysis of control within the wider society – and anyway were attempting the impossible, to explain the crime control whilst ignoring the causes of crime itself - the other half of the equation.

In a way, such a convergence suggests a stasis in criminological theory. And, of course, this is precisely what has occurred over the past ten years. But, as I have tried to indicate, theory is very much influenced by changes in empirical data and in social and political developments. And it is in this direction, particularly in the phenomenal rise of criminal victimization studies, that we must look for the motor forces which begin to force criminology back to theory.

The empirical anomalies arising from both radical and conventional victimology were a major spur to the formation of realist criminology. Paradoxically, findings which nestled so easily with administrative criminology caused conceptual abrasions with left idealism. Thus, as the crisis of aetiology waned, the problem of the victim became predominant.

THE NATURE OF LEFT REALISM

> The basic defect of pathology and of its romantic opposite is that both yield concepts that are untrue to the phenomenon and which thus fail to illuminate it. Pathology reckons without the patent tenability and durability of deviant enterprise, and without the subjective capacity of man to create novelty and manage diversity. Romance, as always, obscures the seamier and more mundane aspects of the world. It obscures the stress that may underlie resilience. (Matza, 1969: 44)

The central tenet of left realism is to reflect the reality of crime, that is in its origins, its nature and its impact. This involves a rejection of tendencies to romanticize crime or to pathologize it, to analyse solely from the point of view of the administration of crime or the criminal actor, to underestimate crime or to exaggerate it. And our understanding of methodology, our interpretation of the statistics, our notions of aetiology follow from this. Most importantly, it is realism which informs our notion of practice: in answering what can be done about the problems of crime and social control.

It is with this in mind that I have mapped out the fundamental principles of left realism

[. . .]

> It is unrealistic to suggest that the problem of crime like mugging is merely the problem of mis-categorization and concomitant moral panics. If we choose to embrace this liberal position, we leave the political arena open to conservative campaigns for law and order – for, however exaggerated and distorted the arguments conservatives may marshal, the reality of crime in the streets *can be* the reality of human suffering and personal disaster. (Young, 1975: 89)

To be realistic about crime as a problem is not an easy task. We are caught between two currents, one which would grotesquely exaggerate the problems of crime, another covering a wide swathe of political opinion that may seriously underestimate the extent of the problem. Crime is a staple of news in the Western mass media and police fiction a major genre of television drama. We have detailed elsewhere the structured distortion of images of crime, victimization and policing which occur in the mass media (see Cohen and Young, 1981). It is a commonplace of criminological research that most violence is between acquaintances and is intra-class and intra-racial. Yet the media abound with images of the dangerous stranger. On television we see folk monsters who are psychopathic killers or serial murderers yet offenders who even remotely fit these caricatures are extremely rare. The police are portrayed as engaged in an extremely scientific investigative policy with high clear-up rates and exciting denouements although the criminologist knows that this is far from the humdrum nature of reality. Furthermore, it grossly conceals the true relationship between police and public in the process of detection, namely that there is an extremely high degree of dependence of the police on public reporting and witnessing of crime.

The nature of crime, of victimization and of policing is thus systematically distorted in the mass media. And it is undoubtedly true that such a barrage of misinformation has its effect – although perhaps scarcely in such a one-to-one way that is sometimes suggested. For example, a typical category of violence in Britain is a man battering his wife. But this is rarely represented in the mass media – instead we have numerous examples of professional criminals engaged in violent crime – a quantitatively minor problem when compared to domestic violence. So presumably the husband can watch criminal violence on television and not see himself there. His offence does not exist as a category of media censure. People watching depictions of burglary presumably get an impression of threats of violence, sophisticated adult criminals and scenes of desecrated homes. But this is of course not at all the normal burglary – which is typically amateurish and carried out by an adolescent boy. When people come home to find their house broken into there is no one there and their fantasies about the dangerous intruder are left to run riot. Sometimes the consequences of such fantastic images of criminals are tragic. For example, people buy large guard dogs to protect themselves. Yet the one most likely to commit violence is the man of the house against his wife, and there are many more relatives – usually children – killed and injured by dogs than by burglars!

In the recent period there has been an alliance between liberals (often involved in the new administrative criminology) and left idealists which evokes the very mirror image of the mass media. The chance of being criminally injured, however slightly, the British Crime Survey tells us, is once in a hundred years (Hough and Mayhew, 1983) and such a Home Office view is readily echoed by left idealists who inform us that crime is, by and large, a minor problem and indeed the fear of crime is more of a problem than crime itself. Thus, they would argue, undue fear of crime provides popular support for conservative law and order campaigns and allows the build-up of further police powers whose repressive aim is political dissent rather than crime. For radicals to enter into the discourse of law and order is further to legitimize it. Furthermore, such a stance maintains that fear of crime has not only ideological consequences, it has material effects on the community itself. For to give credence to the fear of crime is to divide the community – to encourage racism, fester splits between the 'respectable' and 'non-respectable' working class and between youths and adults. More subtly, by emptying the streets particularly at night, it actually breaks down the system of informal controls which usually discourage crime.

Realism must navigate between these two poles; it must neither succumb to hysteria nor relapse into a critical denial of the severity of crime as a problem. It must be fiercely sceptical of official statistics and control institutions without taking the posture of a blanket rejection of all figures or, indeed, the very possibility of reform.

Realism necessitates an accurate victimology. It must counterpoise this against those liberal and idealist criminologies, on the one side, which play down victimization or even bluntly state that the 'real' victim is the offender and, on the other, those conservatives who celebrate moral panic and see violence and robbery as ubiquitous on our streets.

To do this involves mapping out who is at risk and what precise effect crime has on their lives. This moves beyond the invocation of the global risk rates of the average citizen. All too often this serves to conceal the actual severity of crime amongst significant sections of the population whilst providing a fake statistical backdrop for the discussion of 'irrational' fears.

A radical victimology notes two key elements of criminal victimization. First, that crime is focused both geographically and socially on the most vulnerable sections of the community. Secondly, that the impact of victimization is a product of risk rate and vulnerability. Average risk rates across a city ignore such a focusing and imply that equal crimes impact equally. As it is, the most vulnerable are not only more affected by crime, they also have the highest risk rates.

Realism must also trace accurately the relationship between victim and offender. Crime is not an activity of latter day Robin Hoods – the vast majority of working-class crime is directed within the working class. It is intra-class *not* inter-class in its nature. Similarly, despite the mass media predilection for focusing on inter-racial crime it is overwhelmingly intra-racial. Crimes of violence, for example, are by and large one poor person hitting another poor person – and in almost half of these instances it is a man hitting his wife or lover.

This is not to deny the impact of crimes of the powerful or indeed of the social problems created by capitalism which are perfectly legal. Rather, left realism notes that the working class is a victim of crime from all directions. It notes that the more vulnerable a person is economically and socially the more likely it is that *both* working-class and white-collar crime will occur against them; that one sort of crime tends to compound another, as does one social problem another. Furthermore, it notes that crime is a potent symbol of the antisocial nature of capitalism and is the most immediate way in which people experience other problems, such as unemployment or competitive individualism.

Realism starts from problems as people experience them. It takes seriously the complaints of women [with regard to] the dangers of being in public places at night, it takes note of the fears of the elderly with regard to burglary, it acknowledges the widespread occurrence of domestic violence and racist attacks. It does not ignore the fears of the vulnerable nor recontextualize them out of existence by putting them into a perspective which abounds with abstractions such as the 'average citizen' bereft of class or gender. It is only too aware of the systematic concealment and ignorance of crimes against the least powerful. Yet it does not take these fears at face value – it pinpoints their rational kernel but it is also aware of the forces towards irrationality.

Realism is not empiricism. Crime and deviance are prime sites of moral anxiety and tension in a society which is fraught with real inequalities and injustices. Criminals can quite easily become folk devils onto which are projected such feelings of unfairness. But there is a rational core to the fear of crime just as there is a rational core to the anxieties which distort it. Realism argues with popular consciousness in its attempts to separate out reality from fantasy. But it does not deny that crime is a problem. Indeed, if there were no rational core the media would have no power of leverage to the public consciousness. Crime becomes a metaphor but it is a metaphor rooted in reality.

When one examines anxiety about crime, one often finds a great deal more rationality than is commonly accorded to the public. Thus, frequently a glaring discrepancy has been claimed between the high fear of crime of women and their low risk rates. Recent research, particularly by feminist victimologists, has shown that this is often a mere artefact of a low reporting of sexual attacks to interviewers – a position reversed when sympathetic women are used in the survey team (see Hall, 1985; Hanmer and Saunders, 1984; Russell, 1982). Similarly, it is often suggested that fear of crime is somehow a petit bourgeois or upper middle-class phenomenon despite the lower risk rates of the more wealthy. Yet the Merseyside Crime Survey, for example, showed a close correspondence between risk rate and the prioritization of crime as a problem, with the working class having far higher risk rates *and* estimation of the importance of crime as a problem. Indeed, they saw crime as the second problem after unemployment whereas in the middle-class suburbs only 13 per cent of people rated crime as a major problem (see Kinsey et al., 1986). Similarly, Richard Sparks and his colleagues found that working-class people and blacks rated property crimes more seriously than middle-class people and whites (Sparks et al., 1977). Those affected by crime and those most vulnerable are the most concerned about crime.

Of course, there is a fantastic element in the conception of crime. The images of the identity of the criminal and his mode of operation are, as we have seen, highly distorted. And undoubtedly *fear displacement* occurs, where real anxieties about one type of crime are projected on another, as does *tunnel vision*, where only certain sorts of crime are feared, but the evidence for a substantial infrastructure of rationality is considerable.

The emergence of a left realist position in crime has occurred in the last five years. This has involved criminologists in Britain, Canada, the United States and Australia. In particular, the Crime and Justice Collective in California have devoted a large amount of space in their journal for a far-ranging discussion on the need for a left-wing programme on crime control (see e.g., *Crime and Social Justice*, Summer, 1981). There have been also violent denunciations, as the English journalist Martin Kettle put it:

> For their pains the [realists] have been denounced with extraordinary ferocity from the left, sometimes in an almost paranoid manner. To take crime seriously, to take fear of crime seriously and, worst of all, to take police reform seriously, is seen by the fundamentalists as the ultimate betrayal and deviation. (Kettle, 1984: 367)

This, apart, the basis of a widespread support for a realist position has already been made. What remains now is the task of creating a realist *criminology*. For although the left idealist denial of crime is increasingly being rejected, the tasks of radical criminology still remain. That is, to create an adequate explanation of crime, victimization and the reaction of the state. And this is all the more important given that the new administrative criminology has abdicated all such responsibility and indeed shares some convergence with left idealism.

[. . .]

CONCLUSION

This article has argued for the need for a systematic programme within radical criminology which should have theoretical, research and policy components. We must develop a realist theory which adequately encompasses the scope of the criminal act. That is, it must deal with both macro- and micro-levels, with the causes of criminal action and social reaction, and with the triangular inter-relationship between offender, victim and the state. It must learn from past theory, take up again the debates between the three strands of criminological theory and attempt to bring them together within a radical rubric. It must stand for theory in a time when criminology has all but abandoned theory. It must rescue the action of causality whilst stressing both the specificity of generalization and the existence of human choice and value in any equation of criminality.

On a research level we must develop theoretically grounded empirical work against the current of atheoretical empiricism. The expansion of radical victimology in the area of victimization surveys is paramount but concern should also be made with regard to developments in qualitative research and ethnography (see West, 1984). The development of sophisticated statistical analysis (see for example Box and Hale, 1986; Greenberg, 1984; Melossi, 1985) should not be anathema to the radical criminologist nor should quantitative and qualitative work be seen as alternatives from which the radical must obviously choose. Both methods, as long as they are based in theory, complement and enrich each other.

In terms of practical policy we must combat impossibilism: whether it is the impossibility of reform, the ineluctable nature of a rising crime rate or the inevitable failure of rehabilitation. It is time for us to *compete* in policy terms, to get out of the ghetto of impossibilism. Orthodox criminology with its inability to question the political and its abandonment of aetiology is hopelessly unable to generate workable policies. All commentators are united about the inevitability of a rising crime rate. Left idealists think it cannot be halted because without a profound social transformation nothing can be done; the new administrative criminologists have given up the ghost of doing anything but the most superficial containment job. Let us state quite categorically that the major task of radical criminology is to seek a solution to the problem of crime and that of a socialist policy is substantially to reduce the crime rate. And the same is true of rehabilitation. Left idealists think that it is at best a con-trick, indeed argue that unapologetic punishment would at least be less mystifying to the offender. The new administrative criminologists seek to construct a system of punishment and surveillance which discards rehabilitation and replaces it with a social behaviourism worthy of the management of white rats in laboratory cages. They both deny the moral nature of crime, that choice is always made in varying determining circumstances and that the denial of responsibility fundamentally mis-understands the reality of the criminal act. As socialists it is important to stress that most working class crime is intra-class, that mugging, wife battering, burglary and child abuse are actions which cannot be morally absolved in the flux of determinacy. The offender should be ashamed, he/she should feel morally responsible within the limits of circumstance and rehabilitation is truly *impossible* without this moral dimension.

Crime is of importance politically because unchecked it divides the working class community and is materially and morally the basis of disorganization: the loss of political control. It is also a potential unifier – a realistic issue, *amongst others*, for recreating community.

Bertram Gross, in a perceptive article originally published in the American magazine *The Nation*, wrote: 'on crime, more than on most matters, the left seems bereft of ideas' (Gross, 1982: 51). He is completely correct, of course, in terms of there being a lack of any developed strategy amongst socialists for dealing with crime. I have tried to show, however, that it was the prevalence – though often implicit and frequently ill-thought [out] – of left idealist ideas which, in fact, directly resulted in the neglect of crime. There is now a growing consensus amongst radical criminologists that crime really is a problem for the working class, women, ethnic minorities: for all the most vulnerable members of capitalist societies, and that something must be done about it. But to recognize the reality of crime as a problem is only the first stage of the business. A fully blown theory of crime must relate to the contradictory reality of the phenomenon as must any strategy for combating it. And it must analyse how working class attitudes to crime are not merely the result of false ideas derived from the mass media and such like but have a rational basis in one moment of a contradictory and wrongly contextualized reality.

In a recent diatribe against radical criminology Carl Klockars remarked: 'Imagination is one thing, criminology another' (Klockars, 1980: 93). It is true that recent criminology has been characterized by a chronic lack of imagination – although I scarcely think that this was what Klockars lamented by his disparaging remark. Many of us were attracted to the discipline because of its theoretical verve, because of the centrality of the study of disorder to understanding society, because of the flair of its practitioners and the tremendous human interest of the subject. Indeed many of the major debates in the social sciences in the 1960s and 1970s focused quite naturally around deviance and social control. And this is as it should be – as it has been throughout history both in social science and in literature – both in mass media and the arts. What is needed now is an intellectual and political imagination which can comprehend the way in which we learn about order through the investigation of disorder. The paradox of the textbook in orthodox criminology is that it takes that which is of great human interest and transmits it into the dullest of 'facts'. I challenge anyone to read one of the conventional journals from cover to cover without having a desperate wish to fall asleep. Research grants come and research grants go and people are gainfully employed but crime remains, indeed it grows and nothing they do seems able to do anything about it. But is it so surprising that such a grotesquely eviscerated discipline should be so ineffective? For the one-dimensional discourse that constitutes orthodox criminology does not even know its own name. It is often unaware of the sociological and philosophical assumptions behind it. James Q. Wilson, for example, has become one of the most influential and significant of the new administrative criminologists. Yet his work and its proposals have scarcely been examined outside of the most perfunctory empiricist discussions. The discipline is redolent with a scientism which does not realize that its relationship with its object of study is more metaphysical than realistic, an apolitical recital of facts, more facts and even more facts [and] then does not want to acknowledge that it is profoundly political, a paradigm that sees its salvation in the latest statistical innovation rather than in any ability to engage with the actual reality of the world. It is ironic that it is precisely in orthodox criminology, where practitioners and researchers are extremely politically constrained, that they write as if crime and criminology were little to do with politics. Radical criminology, by stressing the political nature of crime and social censure, and the philosophical and social underpinnings of the various criminologies is able immediately to take such problems aboard. The key virtue of realist criminology is the central weakness of its administrative opponent.

We are privileged to work in one of the most central, exciting and enigmatic fields of study. It is the very staple of the mass media, a major focus of much day to day public gossip, speculation and debate. And this is as it should be. But during the past decade the subject has been eviscerated, talk of theory, causality and justice has all but disappeared and what is central to human concern has been relegated to the margins. It is time for us to go back to the drawing boards, time to regain our acquaintanceship with theory, to dispel amnesia about the past and adequately comprehend the present. This is the central task of left realist criminology: we will need more than a modicum of imagination and scientific ability to achieve it.

REFERENCES

Box, S. and Hale, C. (1986) 'Unemployment, crime and imprisonment, and the enduring problem of prison overcrowding', in R. Matthews and J. Young (eds), *Confronting Crime*. London: Sage.

Clarke, R. (1980) 'Situational crime prevention: theory and practice', *British Journal of Criminology*, 20(2): 136–47.

Cohen, S. and Young, J. (1981) *The Manufacture of News*, rev. edn. London: Constable/Beverly Hills, CA: Sage.

Cressey, D. (1978) 'Criminological theory, social science, and the repression of crime', *Criminology*, 16: 171–91.

Downes, D. and Rock, P. (1982) *Understanding Deviance*. Oxford: Clarendon Press.

Greenberg, D.F. (1984) 'Age and crime: in search of sociology'. Mimeo.

Gross, B. (1982) 'Some anticrime proposals for Progressives', *Crime and Social Justice*, Summer, 51–4.

Hall, R.E. (1985) *Ask Any Woman – a London Enquiry into Rape and Sexual Assault*. Bristol: Falling Wall Press.

Hanmer, J. and Saunders, S. (1984) *Well-Founded Fears: a Community Study of Violence to Women*. London: Hutchinson.

Hough, M. and Mayhew, P. (1983) *The British Crime Survey: First Report*. London: Home Office Research and Planning Unit.

Kettle, M. (1984) 'The police and the Left', *New Society*, 70(1146): 366–7.

Kinsey, R., Lea, J. and Young, J. (1986) *Losing the Fight Against Crime*. Oxford: Blackwell.

Klockars, C. (1980) 'The contemporary crisis of Marxist criminology', in J. Incardi (ed.), *Radical Criminology: the Coming Crisis*, Beverly Hills, CA: Sage.

Lea, J. and Young, J. (1984) *What is to be Done About Law and Order?* Harmondsworth: Penguin.

Matza, D. (1969) *Becoming Deviant*. Englewood Cliffs, NJ: Prentice Hall.

Melossi, D. (1985) 'Punishment and social action', in S.C. McNall (ed.), *Current Perspectives in Social Theory*. Greenwich, CT: JAI Press.

Platt, T. and Takagi, P. (1981) 'Intellectuals for law and order: a critique of the New Realists', in T. Platt and P. Takagi (eds), *Crime and Social Justice*. London: Macmillan.

Russell, D. (1982) *Rape in Marriage*. New York: Macmillan.

Rutter, M. and Giller, H. (1983) *Juvenile Delinquency*. Harmondsworth: Penguin Books.

Sparks, R., Genn, H. and Dodd, D. (1977) *Surveying Victims: a Study of the Measurement of Criminal Victimisation*. Chichester: Wiley.

Trasler, G. (1984) *Crime and Criminal Justice Research in the United States*, Home Office Research Bulletin, 18, HMSO.

Van den Haag, E. (1975) *Punishing Criminals*. New York: Basic Books.

West, G. (1984) 'Phenomenon and form', in L. Barton and S. Walker (eds), *Educational Research and Social Crisis*. London: Croom Helm.

Wilson, J.Q. (1975) *Thinking About Crime*. New York: Vintage.

Wilson, J.Q. (1982) *Report and Recommendations of the Ad Hoc Committee on the Future of Criminal Justice Research*. Washington, DC: National Institute of Justice.

Wilson, J.Q. and Kelling, G. (1982) 'Broken Windows', *The Atlantic Monthly*, March, pp. 29–38.

Young, J. (1975) 'Working class criminology', in I. Taylor, P. Walton and J. Young (eds), *Critical Criminology*. London: Routledge and Kegan Paul.

Young, J. (1979) 'Left idealism, reformism and beyond: from New Criminology to Marxism', in B. Fine et al. (eds), *Capitalism and the Rule of Law: From Deviancy Theory to Marxism*. London: Hutchinson.

Part IV

Crime control I: Criminal justice and crime prevention

INTRODUCTION

In 1974 Robert Martinson declared that '[w]ith few and isolated exceptions, the rehabilitative efforts that have been reported so far have had no appreciable effect on recidivism' ('What works? Questions and answers about penal reform', *The Public Interest*, no.35, p.25). This 'nothing works' statement heralded the final death knell for those who believed that modern post-war Western societies had the capacity to rehabilitate and/or treat offenders and reduce recidivism. As the readings in this section indicate, it also sparked off a wide-ranging, high profile post-rehabilitation debate about whether and how crime could be controlled/prevented effectively.

James Q. Wilson argues that we need to forget theorizing about the causes of crime and concentrate on the realities and pragmatics of crime and criminality. He stresses that a significant and meaningful reduction can be achieved by recognizing that crime is a quasi-economic endeavour whose occurrence can be made to vary with the costs imposed upon it. By imposing prison sentences swiftly and without exception, society can remove from circulation the most frequently convicted and most active criminals for a significant portion of their criminal careers. The knowledge of swift processing and near certain incarceration, he argues, could, in addition to incapacitating convicted criminals, also intimidate potential offenders. Thus society could, if it chose to, control crime to some degree by recognizing that punishment is a worthy objective of the criminal justice system and by raising the stakes considerably. In the course of the 1990s this perspective coined the populist soundbite 'prison works'.

Andrew von Hirsch proposes what he and the members of the Committee for the Study of Incarceration view as a politically feasible alternative to the populist 'lock 'em up' approach of Wilson. 'Just and commensurate deserts' or retributivism stressed that punishment rather than rehabilitation or treatment is important because it implies blame and the severity of the punishment symbolizes the degree of blame. Once we have acknowledged that certain forms of action and behaviour are wrong and ought to be punished, we can set reasonable limits on the extent of the punishment and retribution. The severity of the punishment should be proportionate to the gravity of the offence. Stringent punishments should be limited to crimes that inflict serious harm and indicate considerable culpability on the part of the offender. As the magnitude of the crime diminishes so should the nature of the punishment. This theory attempts to centre the question 'What is fair and just?' rather than 'What works?' In doing so, it is not interested in speculating on the motives of offenders or in attempting to socially engineer lower crime rates.

In the next reading, Francis T. Cullen and K.E.Gilbert mount a spirited defence of the rehabilitative ideal against both Wilson and 'just deserts'. They argue that liberals and those on the Left should not abandon rehabilitation because it: imposes positive obligations on the state to have regard for the welfare of offenders; can act as a bulwark against the punitive law and order demands of the Right; has considerable support within the criminal justice system; and is essentially humanitarian, compassionate and optimistic in orientation.

Ron Clarke offers another highly pragmatic vision of what effective crime control would entail. If we view crime as being the consequence of immediate choices and decisions by offenders about risks and rewards then a whole series of possibilities for preventing crime situationally present themselves. He argues that it is perfectly possible to reduce substantially the physical opportunities for offending and to increase the chances of a given offender being caught in the act. Despite being initially berated for its rational choice suppositions about human nature and anti-theoretical stance, this approach enjoys remarkable political popularity. Like routine activities theory it carries the positive message that a multitude of crimes can be effectively designed out and eradicated and that all of us can take active collective and individual steps to protect ourselves and our property from the criminal.

Betsy Stanko provides a feminist critique of crime prevention strategies that attempt to assuage women's fear of crime by suggesting that women adopt individually managed precautionary strategies to minimize risky encounters with dangerous male strangers. Stanko argues that taking women's fear of crime seriously will require a reconsideration of conventional crime prevention and fear reduction strategies.

Elliot Currie presents us with a left realist social crime prevention programme. For him the transition to a market-based society has had a devastating impact on key areas of social, economic and cultural life. The result is spiralling crime rates, social fragmentation and individual alienation. Currie stresses that effective crime control requires confronting the roots of the problem. To tackle economic and social inequalities we need pro-active state coordinated labour market policies and comprehensive welfare strategies which are based on the notion of inclusive citizenship. We also need as a matter of urgency to develop a package of very specific child and family interventions, youth-oriented policies and imaginative drug regulation programmes.

Willem De Haan argues beyond the other approaches by stating that responding positively and constructively requires abandoning the notion of 'crime'. We need to talk and think about diverse troubles, conflicts, harms, damage, conflicting interests, unfortunate events and accidents. We also

need to break with the crime control = punishment = imprisonment nexus. It is only then that we will be in a position to construct rational, innovative and constructive redress-based mechanisms for resolving conflicts, settling disputes and preventing social negativity. De Haan does not under-estimate the problems that such a radical imaginary will encounter but he argues forcefully that the other proposals have manifestly failed to deliver long-term crime control and should be in fact viewed as part of the problem rather than as part of the solution.

The Australian criminologist John Braithwaite presents the case for a genuine alternative to carceral and coercive methods of social control: 'Reintegrative shaming'. By this he means dealing with offenders in ways in which embody the expression of community and familial disapproval, but also incorporate a process of re-acceptance. Rather than stigmatizing offenders and excluding them from society, this restorative justice approach aims to bring them back into society and thus to enhance social solidarity.

Our final reading is the internationally acclaimed 'Broken windows' thesis of Wilson and Kelling. Although originally published in 1982 it did not really impact upon criminal justice debates until the 1990s when it was repackaged by the NYPD as 'zero tolerance' or 'quality of life' policing and marketed globally as the future of law enforcement. Wilson and Kelling's central thesis is that small signs of disorder in a neighbourhood, like broken windows or graffiti, can encourage more serious forms of criminality by giving the symbolic impression that nobody cares. The 'Broken windows' thesis declares that civility and order are baseline components of society and it both requires and mandates the police to restore and maintain neighbourhood order and civility through proactive, confident street policing.

28

On deterrence

James Q. Wilson

The average citizen hardly needs to be persuaded of the view that crime will be more frequently committed if, other things being equal, crime becomes more profitable compared to other ways of spending one's time. Accordingly, the average citizen thinks it obvious that one major reason why crime has gone up is that people have discovered it is easier to get away with it; by the same token, the average citizen thinks a good way to reduce crime is to make the consequences of crime to the would-be offender more costly (by making penalties swifter, more certain, or more severe), or to make the value of alternatives to crime more attractive (by increasing the availability and pay of legitimate jobs), or both. Such opinions spring naturally to mind among persons who notice, as a fact of everyday life, that people take their hands off hot stoves, shop around to find the best buy, smack their children to teach them not to run out into a busy street, and change jobs when the opportunity arises to earn more money for the same amount of effort.

These citizens may be surprised to learn that social scientists who study crime are deeply divided over the correctness of such views. To some scholars, especially economists, the popular view is also the scientifically correct one – becoming a criminal can be explained in much the same way we explain becoming a carpenter or buying a car. To other scholars, especially sociologists, the popular view is wrong – crime rates do not go up because people discover they can get away with it and will not come down just because society decides to get tough on criminals.

The debate over the effect on crime rates of changing the costs and benefits of crime is usually referred to as a debate over deterrence – a debate, that is, over the efficacy (and perhaps even the propriety) of trying to prevent crime by making would-be offenders more fearful of committing crime. But that is something of a misnomer, because the theory of human nature on which is erected the idea of deterrence (the theory that people respond to the penalties associated with crime) is also the theory of human nature that supports the idea that people will take jobs in preference to crime if the jobs are more attractive. In both cases, we are saying that would-be offenders are reasonably rational and respond to their perception of the

From *Thinking About Crime*, pp. 117–23; 142–4. (New York: Basic Books, 1983. Second Revised Edition. First published 1975.)

costs and benefits attached to alternative courses of action. When we use the word 'deterrence', we are calling attention only to the cost side of the equation. There is no word in common scientific usage to call attention to the benefit side of the equation; perhaps 'inducement' might serve. To a psychologist, deterring persons from committing crimes or inducing persons to engage in non-criminal activities are but special cases of using 'reinforcements' (or rewards) to alter behavior.

The reason there is a debate among scholars about deterrence is that the socially imposed consequences of committing a crime, unlike the market consequences of shopping around for the best price, are characterized by delay, uncertainty, and ignorance. In addition, some scholars contend that a large fraction of crime is committed by persons who are so impulsive, irrational, or abnormal that even if there were no delay, uncertainty, or ignorance attached to the consequences of criminality, we would still have a lot of crime.

Imagine a young man walking down the street at night with nothing on his mind but a desire for good times and high living. Suddenly he sees a little old lady standing alone on a dark corner stuffing the proceeds of her recently cashed social security check into her purse. There is nobody else in view. If the boy steals the purse, he gets the money immediately. That is a powerful incentive, and it is available immediately and without doubt. The costs of taking it are uncertain; the odds are at least fourteen to one that the police will not catch a given robber, and even if he is caught the odds are very good that he will not go to prison, unless he has a long record. On the average, no more than three felonies out of 100 result in the imprisonment of the offender. In addition to this uncertainty, whatever penalty may come his way will come only after a long delay; in some jurisdictions, it might take a year or more to complete the court disposition of the offender, assuming he is caught in the first place. Moreover, this young man may, in his ignorance of how the world works, think the odds in his favor are even greater and that the delay will be even longer.

Compounding the problems of delay and uncertainty is the fact that society cannot feasibly reduce the uncertainty attached to the chances of being arrested by more than a modest amount and though it can to some degree increase the probability and severity of a prison sentence for those who are caught, it cannot do so drastically by, for example, summarily executing all convicted robbers or even by sending all robbers to 20-year prison terms. Some scholars add a further complication: the young man may be incapable of assessing the risks of crime. How, they ask, is he to know his chances of being caught and punished? And even if he does know, is he perhaps 'driven' by uncontrollable impulses to snatch purses whatever the risks?

As if all this were not bad enough, the principal method by which scholars have attempted to measure the effect on crime of differences in the probability and severity of punishment has involved using data about aggregates of people (entire cities, counties, states, and even nations) rather than about individuals. In a typical study, of which there have been several dozen, the rate at which, say, robbery is committed in each state is 'explained' by means of a statistical procedure in which the analyst takes into account both the socioeconomic features of each state that might affect the supply of robbers (for example, the percentage of persons with low incomes, the unemployment rate, or the population density of the big cities) and the operation of the criminal justice system of each state as it attempts to cope with robbery (for example, the probability of being caught and imprisoned for a given robbery and the length of the average prison term for robbery). Most such studies find, after controlling for socioeconomic differences among the states, that the higher the probability of being imprisoned, the lower the robbery rate. Isaac Ehrlich, an economist, produced the best known of such analyses using data on crime in the United States in 1940, 1950, and 1960. To simplify a complex analysis, he found, after controlling for such factors as the income level and age distribution of the population, that the higher the probability of imprisonment for those convicted of robbery, the lower the robbery rate. Thus, differences in the certainty of punishment seem to make a difference in the level of crime. At the same time, Ehrlich did not find that the severity of punishment (the average time served in prison for robbery) had, independently of certainty, an effect on robbery rates in two of the three time periods (1940 and 1960).[1]

But there are some problems associated with studying the effect of sanctions on crime rates using aggregate data of this sort. One is that many of the most important factors are not known with any accuracy. For example, we are dependent on police reports for our measure of the robbery rate, and these undoubtedly vary in accuracy from place to place. If all police departments were inaccurate to the same degree, this would not be important; unfortunately, some departments are probably much less accurate than others, and this variable error can introduce a serious bias into the statistical estimates of the effect of the criminal justice system.

Moreover, if one omits from the equation some factor that affects the crime rate, then the estimated effect of the factors that are in the equation may be in error because some of the causal power belonging to the omitted factor will be falsely attributed to the included factors. For example, suppose we want to find out whether differences in the number of policemen on patrol among American cities are associated with differences in the rate at which robberies take place in those cities. If we fail to include in our equation a measure of the population density of the city, we may wrongly conclude that the more police there are on the streets, the *higher* the robbery rate and thus give support to the absurd policy proposition that the way to reduce robberies is to fire police officers. Since robberies are more likely to occur in larger, densely settled cities (which also tend to have a higher proportion of police), it would be a grave error to omit such measures of population from the equation. Since we are not certain what causes crime, we always run the risk of inadvertently omitting a key factor from our efforts to see if deterrence works.

Even if we manage to overcome these problems, a final difficulty lies in wait. The observed fact (and it has been observed many times) that states in which the probability of going to prison for robbery is low are also states which have high rates of robbery can be interpreted in one of two ways. It can mean *either* that the higher robbery rates are the results of the lower imprisonment rates (and thus evidence that deterrence works) *or* that the lower imprisonment rates are caused by the higher robbery rates. To see how the latter might be true, imagine a state that is experiencing, for some reason, a rapidly rising robbery rate. It arrests, convicts, and imprisons more and more robbers as more and more robberies are committed, but it cannot quite keep up. The robberies are increasing so fast that they 'swamp' the criminal justice system; prosecutors and judges respond by letting more robbers off without a prison sentence, or perhaps without even a trial, in order to keep the system from becoming hopelessly clogged. As a result, the proportion of arrested robbers who go to prison goes down while the robbery rate goes up. In this case, we ought to conclude, not that prison deters robbers, but that high robbery rates 'deter' prosecutors and judges.

The best analysis of these problems in statistical studies of deterrence is to be found in a report of the Panel on Research on Deterrent and Incapacitative Effects, set up by the National Research Council (an arm of the National Academy of Sciences). That panel, chaired by Alfred Blumstein of Carnegie-Mellon University, concluded that the available statistical evidence (as of 1978) did not warrant reaching any strong conclusions about the deterrent effect of existing differences among states or cities in the probability of punishment. The panel (of which I was a member) noted that 'the evidence certainly favors a proposition supporting deterrence more than it favors one asserting that deterrence is absent' but urged 'scientific caution' in interpreting this evidence.[2]

Subsequently, other criticisms of deterrence research, generally along the same lines as those of the panel, were published by Colin Loftin[3] and by Stephen S. Brier and Stephen E. Feinberg.[4]

Some commentators believe that these criticisms have proved that 'deterrence doesn't work' and thus the decks have now been cleared to get on with the task of investing in those programs, such as job creation and income maintenance, that *will* have an effect on crime. Such a conclusion is, to put it mildly, a bit premature.

REHABILITATING DETERRENCE

People are governed in their daily lives by rewards and penalties of every sort. We shop for bargain prices, praise our children for good behavior and scold them for bad, expect lower interest rates to stimulate home building and fear that higher ones will depress it, and conduct ourselves in public in ways that lead our friends and neighbors to form good opinions of us. To assert that 'deterrence doesn't work' is tantamount to either denying the plainest facts of everyday life or claiming that would-be criminals are utterly different from the rest of us. They may well be different to some degree – they most likely have a weaker conscience, worry less about their reputation in polite society, and find it harder to postpone gratifying their urges – but these differences of degree do not make them indifferent to the risks and gains of crime. If they were truly indifferent, they would scarcely be able to function at all, for their willingness to take risks would be offset by their indifference to loot. Their lives would consist of little more than the erratic display of animal instincts and fleeting impulses.

The question before us is whether feasible changes in the deferred and uncertain penalties of crime [. . .] will affect crime rates in ways that can be detected by the data and statistical methods at our disposal. Though the unreliability of crime data and the limitations of statistical analysis are real enough and are accurately portrayed by the Panel of the National Research Council, there are remedies and rejoinders that, on balance, strengthen the case for the claim that not only does deterrence work (the panel never denied that), it probably works in ways that can be measured, even in the aggregate.

The errors in official statistics about crime rates have been addressed by employing other measures of crime, in particular reports gathered by Census Bureau interviewers from citizens who have been victims of crime. While these victim surveys have problems of their own (such as the forgetfulness of citizens), they are not the same problems as those that affect police reports of crime. Thus, if we obtain essentially the same findings about the effect of sanctions on crime from studies that use victim data as we do from studies using police data, our confidence in these findings is strengthened. Studies of this sort have been done by Itzhak Goldberg at Stanford and by Barbara Boland and myself, and the results are quite consistent with those from research based on police reports.[5] As sanctions become more likely, crime becomes less common.

There is a danger that important factors will be omitted from any statistical study of crime in ways that bias the results, but this problem is no greater in studies of penalties than it is in studies of unemployment rates, voting behavior, or any of a hundred other socially significant topics. Since we can never know with certainty everything that may affect crime (or unemployment, or voting), we must base our conclusions not on any single piece of research, but on the general thrust of a variety of studies analyzing many different causal factors. The Panel of the National Research Council took exactly this position. While noting that 'there is the possibility that as yet unknown and so untested' factors may be affecting crime, 'this is not a sufficient basis for dismissing' the common finding that crime goes up as sanctions become less certain because 'many of the analyses have included some of the more obvious possible third causes and they still find negative associations between sanctions and crimes.'[6]

It is possible that rising crime rates 'swamp' the criminal justice system so that a negative statistical association between, say, rates of theft and the chances of going to prison for theft may mean not that a decline in imprisonment is causing theft to increase, but rather that a rise in theft is causing imprisonment to become less likely. This might occur particularly with respect to less serious crimes, such as shoplifting or petty larceny; indeed, the proportion of prisoners who are shoplifters or petty thieves has gone down over the last two decades. But it is hard to imagine that the criminal justice system would respond to an increase in murder or armed robbery by letting some murderers or armed robbers off with no punishment. There is no evidence that convicted murderers are any less likely to go to prison today than they were 20 years ago. Moreover, the apparent deterrent effect of prison on serious crimes, such as murder and robbery, was apparently as great in 1940 or 1950, when these crimes were much less common, as it is today, suggesting that swamping has not occurred.[7]

The best studies of deterrence that manage to overcome many of these problems provide evidence that deterrence works. Alfred Blumstein and Daniel Nagin studied the relationship between draft evasion and the penalties imposed for evading the draft. After controlling for the socioeconomic characteristics of the states, they found that the higher the probability of conviction for draft evasion, the lower the evasion rates. This is an especially strong finding because it is largely immune to some of the problems of other research. Draft evasion is more accurately measured than street crime, hence errors arising from poor data are not a problem. And draft evasion cases did not swamp the federal courts in which they were tried, in part because such cases (like murder in state courts) make up only a small fraction of the courts' workload (7 per cent in the case of draft evasion) and in part because the attorney general had instructed federal prosecutors to give high priority to these cases. Blumstein and Nagin concluded that draft evasion is deterrable.[8]

Another way of testing whether deterrence works is to look, not at differences among states at one point in time, but at changes in the nation as a whole over a long period of time. Historical data on the criminal justice system in America is so spotty that such research is difficult to do here, but it is not at all difficult in England where the data are excellent. Kenneth I. Wolpin analyzed changes in crime rates and in various parts of the criminal justice system (the chances of being arrested, convicted, and punished) for the period 1894 to 1967, and concluded that changes in the probability of being punished seemed to cause changes in the crime rate. He offers reasons for believing that this causal connection cannot be explained away by the argument that the criminal justice system was being swamped.[9]

Given what we are trying to measure – changes in the behavior of a small number of hard-to-observe persons who are responding to delayed and uncertain penalties – we will never be entirely sure that our statistical manipulations have proved that deterrence works. What is impressive is that so many (but not all) studies using such different methods come to similar conclusions. [. . .]

The relationship between crime on the one hand and the rewards and penalties at the disposal of society on the other is complicated. It is not complicated, however, in the way some people imagine. It is not the case (except for a tiny handful of pathological personalities) that criminals are so unlike the rest of us as to be indifferent to the costs and benefits of the opportunities open to them. Nor is it the case that criminals have no opportunities. [. . .]

It is better to think of both people and social controls as arrayed on a con- tinuum. People differ by degrees in the extent to which they are governed by internal restraints on criminal behavior and in the stake they have in conformity;[10] they also differ by degrees in the extent to which they can find, hold, and benefit from a job. Similarly, sanctions and opportunities are changeable only within modest limits. We want to find out to what extent feasible changes in the certainty, swiftness, or severity of penalties will make a difference in the behavior of those 'at the margin' – those, that is, who are neither so innocent nor so depraved as to be prepared to ignore small changes (which are, in fact, the only feasible changes) in the prospects of punishment. By the same token, we want to know what feasible (and again, inevitably small) changes in the availability of jobs will affect those at the margin of the labor market – those, that is, who are neither so eager for a good job or so contemptuous of 'jerks' who take 'straight jobs' as to ignore modest changes in job opportunities. I am aware of no evidence supporting the conventional liberal view that while the number of persons who will be affected by changing penalties is very small, the number who will be affected by increasing jobs is very large; nor am I aware of any evidence supporting the conventional conservative view, which is the opposite of this.

I believe that the weight of the evidence – aggregate statistical analyses, evalu- ations of experiments and quasi-experiments, and studies of individual behavior – supports the view that the rate of crime is influenced by its costs. This influence is greater – or easier to observe – for some crimes and persons than for others. It is possible to lower the crime rate by increasing the certainty of sanctions, but inducing the criminal justice system to make those changes is difficult, especially if committing the offense confers substantial benefits on the perpetrator, if apprehending and punishing the offender does not provide substantial rewards to members of the criminal justice system, or if the crime itself lacks the strong moral condemnation of society. In theory, the rate of crime should also be sensitive to the benefits of non-crime – for example, the value and availability of jobs – but thus far efforts to show that relationship have led to inconclusive results.[11] Moreover, the nature of the connection between crime and legitimate opportunities is complex: unemployment (and prosperity!) can cause crime, crime can cause unemployment (but probably not prosperity), and both crime and unemployment may be caused by common third factors. Economic factors probably have the greatest influence on the behavior of low-rate, novice offenders and the least on high-rate, experienced ones. Despite the uncertainty that attaches to the connection between the economy and crime, I believe the wisest course of action for society is to try simultaneously to increase both the benefits of non-crime and the costs of crime, all the while bearing in mind that no feasible changes in either part of the equation are likely to produce big changes in crime rates.

Some may grant my argument that it makes sense to continue to try to make those marginal gains that are possible by simultaneously changing in desirable directions both the costs of crime and benefits of non-crime, but they may still feel that it is better to spend more heavily on one side or the other of the cost-benefit equation. I have attended numerous scholarly gatherings where I have heard learned persons subject to the most searching scrutiny any evidence purporting to show the deterrent effect of sanctions but accept with scarcely a blink the theory that crime is caused by a 'lack of opportunities.'[12] Perhaps what they mean is that since the evidence on both propositions is equivocal, then it does less harm to believe in – and invest in – the 'benign' (that is, job-creation) program. If so, they are surely wrong. If we try to make the penalties for crime swifter and more certain, and it should turn out that deterrence does not work, then all we have done is increase the risks facing persons who commit a crime. If we fail to increase the certainty and swiftness of penalties, and it should turn out that deterrence *does* work, then we have needlessly increased the risk of innocent persons being victimized.

[. . .]

NOTES

1 Isaac Ehrlich, 'Participation in illegitimate activities: a theoretical and empirical investigation', *Journal of Political Economy*, 81 (1973), pp. 521–65.

2 Alfred Blumstein, Jacqueline Cohen and Daniel Nagin (eds.), *Deterrence and Incapacitation: Estimating the Effects of Criminal Sanctions on Crime Rates* (National Academy of Sciences, Washington, DC, 1978). Isaac Ehrlich responds to this report and its criticisms of his work in Ehrlich and Mark Randall, 'Fear of deterrence', *Journal of Legal Studies*, 6 (1977), pp. 293–316.

3 Colin Loftin, 'Alternative estimates of the impact of certainty and severity of punishment on levels of homicide in American states', in Stephen E. Feinberg and Albert J. Reiss (eds), *Indicators of Crime and Criminal Justice: Quantitative Studies*, report number NCJ-62349 of the Bureau of Justice Statistics (US Department of Justice, Washington, DC, 1980), pp. 75–81.

4 Stephen S. Brier and Stephen E. Feinberg, 'Recent econometric modeling of crime and punishment: support for the deterrence hypothesis?' in Feinberg and Reiss, *Indicators of Crime and Criminal Justice*, pp. 82–97.

5 Itzhak Goldberg, 'A note on using victimization rates to test deterrence', Technical Report CERDCR-5-78, Center for Econometric Studies of the Justice System, Stanford University (December 1978); James Q. Wilson and Barbara Boland, 'Crime', in William Gorham and Nathan Glazer (eds), *The Urban Predicament* (Urban Institute, Washington, DC, 1976).

6 Blumstein et al., *Deterrence and Incapacitation*, p. 23.

7 Isaac Ehrlich and Mark Randall, 'Fear of deterrence', *Journal of Legal Studies*, 6 (1977), pp. 304–7.

8 Alfred Blumstein and Daniel Nagin, 'The deterrent effect of legal sanctions on draft evasion', *Stanford Law Review*, 28 (1977), pp. 241–75.

9 Kenneth I. Wolpin, 'An economic analysis of crime and punishment in England and Wales, 1894–1967', *Journal of Political Economy*, 86 (1978), pp. 815–40.

10 The concept of a 'stake in the conformity' is from Jackson Toby, 'Social disorganization and stake in conformity', *Journal of Criminal Law and Criminology*, 48 (1957), pp. 12–17.

11 Cf. Richard B. Freeman, 'Crime and unemployment' in James Q. Wilson (ed.), *Crime and Public Policy* (Institute for Contemporary Studies, San Francisco, 1983), ch. 6.

12 An egregious example of the double standard at work is Charles Silberman, *Criminal Violence, Criminal Justice* (Random House, New York, 1978), wherein the studies on deterrence are closely criticized (pp. 182–95) in a way that leads the author to conclude that 'more punishment is not the answer' (p. 197) but 'community development programs' are found (on the basis of virtually no data whatsoever) to lead to 'community regeneration' and a virtual absence of criminal violence (pp. 430–66).

29

Giving criminals their just deserts

Andrew von Hirsch

The limits on state power over the individual have yet to be charted in the field of criminal sentencing. The state now has virtually untrammeled authority to sentence a convicted criminal for any purpose and with any degree of severity. It is incumbent upon civil libertarians to suggest, in the interest of fairness to those being sentenced, what the constraints on the state's sentencing power should be.

Attitudes about the criminal sentence have changed. Until recently the ideal of treatment dominated: The sentence was supposed to rehabilitate, and sentencing judges and parole boards were supposed to have wide discretion so they could tailor the sentence to the offender's needs. This notion still had sufficient vitality to prompt David J. Rothman to warn of its dangers in his thoughtful article, 'De-carcerating Prisoners and Patients', in the Fall 1973 issue of *Civil Liberties Review*. Is it rational or fair, he asked, to sentence for treatment without good reason to expect that the therapy will work? Might not the rehabilitative ideology give a misleading aura of beneficence to the harsh realities of punishing people – and thus legitimize more intervention in offenders' lives with fewer constraints on official behavior? Since that article was published, there has been a marked decline of faith in rehabilitation.

Although penal reformers have urged the treatment of offenders for over a century, it was not until the 1940s and 1950s that experimental programs were widely tried and evaluated. The results were disappointing: Offenders placed in correctional treatment programs usually returned to crime about as often as those who did not participate. Thus, for example, a survey by Robert Martinson and his collaborators of most of the major experimental programs between 1945 and 1967 concludes that 'with few and isolated exceptions, the rehabilitative efforts that have been reported so far have had no appreciable effect on recidivism'.

Since spring 1974, when Martinson published the conclusions of his survey, the thesis that treatment seldom works has become familiar in professional circles, has been mentioned in newspaper articles, and has been noted in several presidential speeches. Now it is the advocates of treatment who are on the defensive – who insist, almost plaintively, that the failure of many treatment programs in the past does not necessarily mean that all treatments are doomed to fail. As doubts about the

From *Civil Liberties Review*, 1976, No. 3, pp. 23–35.

effectiveness of treatment grow, traditional faith in the rehabilitative sentence – the sentence especially designed to meet the offender's need for correctional therapy – is declining, and may already be moribund.

What has persisted, however, is the idea that the sentence should primarily be a crime control technique. This assumption underlay the rehabilitative sentence: the offender would be less likely to offend again if consigned to the proper treatment. Now, when rehabilitation seemingly has failed, interest has shifted to other sentencing approaches that supposedly will do the crime control job more effectively.

A renewed faith in incapacitation is symptomatic of this continuing search for the sentence that best prevents crime. If offenders cannot be cured of their criminal tendencies, it is argued, they can at least be isolated – placed behind bars where they cannot prey on those outside. Simple restraint replaces therapy, and restraint works: prisons may have few other merits, but they surely can protect the community against offense-prone persons – at least during the period of confinement. As former Attorney General William B. Saxbe put it in a 1974 speech to a convention of police chiefs: 'Too many dangerous convicted offenders are placed back in society . . . and that simply must stop.'

Those less conservative than Saxbe have also been attracted to this approach. The National Council on Crime and Delinquency, a vocal critic of American prisons, issued a policy statement that 'prisons are destructive to prisoners and to those charged with holding them', and that the only offenders who should be sentenced to prison are those 'who, if not confined, would be a serious danger to the public'. The prison sanction, in other words, should be a means of restraining those who would harm others if released. The recent National Advisory Commission on crime likewise urged that the prison sentence be used chiefly to isolate the dangerous recidivist. The theory has been embraced even by those who see themselves as radical critics of today's criminal justice system.

[. . .]

Gary Wills, in an article in the *New York Review of Books*, denounced prisons as 'human sewers' and declared that their supposed justifications – rehabilitation, deterrence, or retribution – have no merit whatever. Conclusion: abolish the prison, right? Wrong. A letter from a prisoner in a subsequent issue of the *New York Review* asked Wills what he proposed to do with 'people who go about chronically molesting children, or continually stealing and burglarizing'. Wills replied: 'once we properly identify the chronic molester he should be removed from society. . . . There is an irreducible minimum of people who present an active danger to society whenever they are released into it. They should be sequestered, in places which have no other aim *except* sequestration.' In plain English, dangerous offenders should be locked up.

Confining the 'dangerous' has its undeniable attractions: low-risk offenders can be decarcerated, and use of the prison can be limited to those who present high risks of returning to crime. But there are hazards. One is the difficulty of distinguishing the dangerous individuals from the non-dangerous. As Leonard Orland pointed out in 'Can we establish the rule of law in prisons?' (*Civil Liberties Review*, Fall 1975), 'our ability to predict *future* criminal behavior is very limited; it may be nonexistent'. When forecasting serious crimes, there is a strong tendency to over-predict; most of those identified as risks will be 'false positives' – persons mistakenly predicted to offend.

Class bias is another problem. If the sole aim of the sentence is to prevent recurrences, its severity will depend on the offender's status. When a public official or corporation executive commits a heinous crime in office, he can be prevented from doing it again simply by depriving him of his position of power. By contrast, the poor person who commits a grave offense has no position of power to lose, and he is sent to prison to keep him from offending again. Finally, there is the potential for escalation. When the sentence is viewed as a means for isolating dangerous convicts, sentencers will be criticized every time they release someone who subsequently commits a crime, and will respond by steadily widening the net – by opting for confinement whenever there is any doubt whether the individual will stay within the law. They will, in other words, adopt the maxim of California's Attorney General Evelle Younger: 'I'd rather run the risk of keeping the wrong man [in prison] a little longer than let the wrong man out too soon.'

Harvard's James Q. Wilson suggests a more sophisticated approach to incapacitating criminals in his thoughtful and widely read book *Thinking About Crime* (whose influence, incidentally, is manifest in President Ford's and Senator Edward Kennedy's proposals for mandatory minimum sentences). Wilson starts with the hypothesis that most serious crimes are committed by a relatively small number of repeaters who, because of the large number of crimes they perpetrate, sooner or later are caught and convicted. Current sentencing policy imposes long prison terms on a few of these individuals, but allows most of them to be released on probation and thus to return to crime if they so choose. (In Los Angeles County, Wilson notes, the proportion of convicted robbers with major prior records who were sent to prison in 1970 was only 27 per cent.)

If prison sentences – even of modest length – were invariably imposed in such cases, the incapacitative payoff would be substantial, Wilson suggests. One would be taking out of circulation most of those responsible for serious crimes, at least for a portion of their criminal careers. (There would be no need to try to predict which individual convicts are dangerous; instead, there would simply be a rule that conviction for certain crimes results in a stated period of imprisonment.) The crime control benefits from such a strategy, he claims, would be very large. 'Were we to devote [our] resources to a strategy [that is] well within our abilities – namely, to incapacitating a larger fraction of the convicted serious robbers,' he says, 'then not only is a 20 per cent reduction [in robbery] possible, but even larger ones are conceivable.'

Wilson's proposals certainly sound appealing: moderate sentences, less disparity (because judges would have less discretion), and huge payoffs in community protection – with 20 per cent fewer robberies. But Wilson does not ask the uncomfortable question: What if the promised crime-control benefits do not materialize? The history of sentencing reform has been characterized by high hopes for reducing crime followed by disappointment. In the 1820s, long sentences to penitentiaries offering inmates 'moral therapy' were supposed to cut the crime rate. They did not. In the 1900s, probation for treatable offenders and lengthy sentences for dangerous ones were supposed to do the job. They did not. In the 1960s, fewer prison sentences and more sentences to treatment in the community were supposed to succeed. They did not. Now Wilson claims that imprisoning a larger proportion of those convicted will do the crime control job where previous strategies failed. But can one really be so sure?

To sustain his claim, Wilson has to assume that relatively few 'habitual criminals' are responsible not only for the crimes for which they are convicted, but also for the bulk of the unsolved crimes as well. While this is a plausible assumption, it is no more than that: the evidence on who is responsible for crimes committed with impunity is, for obvious reasons, sketchy at best. (Wilson cites calculations by Reuel Shinnar of the CCNY School of Engineering that purport to show a large reduction in the crime rate if every person convicted of a serious crime is imprisoned for a stated period. Shinnar's calculations, however, are no more accurate than the postulates he makes about who commits the unsolved crimes. He himself admits that his estimates would be seriously awry if much of unsolved crime were committed either by occasional criminals or by skilled professionals who never are convicted for a serious crime. The estimates would also be in error if such crimes as robbery were economically attractive enough so that the removal of some robbers from circulation would result in newly recruited robbers taking their places.) Were these assumptions mistaken, the incapacitative payoff from Wilson's sentencing strategy could be much smaller than he expects.

One must therefore be prepared for the possibility of disappointing results. As David Rothman has wisely counselled, strategies for sentencing reform should be based on a failure model – of what is minimally acceptable even if the hoped-for crime control benefits do not materialize. Wilson's plan is the archetypal success model, and that is its weakness. Despite the formidable record of past failures and the speculative nature of his own estimates, Wilson does not seriously ask: 'and what if the scheme led to only 1 per cent fewer robberies, or none fewer?'

That question leads to others that are worrisome. For example, how much extra suffering is inflicted in the interest of a crime control strategy that may fail? Wilson's proposals, if implemented, could mean imprisoning many more people than are confined today. Such persons will lose their liberty on the supposition that their loss will protect the rights of others, the potential victims of crime. But to the extent that Wilson's plan fails, that supposition will have been wrong. We will have added to offenders' suffering without gaining the promised protection of the rights of others, scarcely a morally satisfactory outcome. Granted, we are speaking of persons who have already been convicted of crimes. But if such persons are sent to prison when – but for Wilson's incapacitative theories – they would have received lighter punishments, the moral difficulty persists. (Wilson might reply that his program is experimental, that it should be tried and if it does not work we can still go back to incarcerating fewer people. But the question remains: how much added suffering would there be while this experiment was being carried out? An experiment can be ethically unacceptable if it exacts too great a human toll.)

This problem of inflicting unnecessary suffering is highlighted by Wilson's comments about new prison construction. Disagreeing with many reformers who have urged a moratorium on new prisons, Wilson calls for building more facilities to house those whom he would incapacitate. Imagine, then, the following scenario. To accommodate Wilson's sentencing scheme, new prisons go up. Then, contrary to expectation, the promised reduction in the crime rate does not occur. What are we left with? The same old high crime rate, but more prisons with more beds to fill. Experience suggests that once the facilities are built, the pressures to keep them full of inmates are hard to resist. Wilson's experiment, in short, is apt to be irreversible, whether or not it succeeds in reducing crime.

Another danger is the possibility of escalation of sentences. Wilson assumes that prison terms of moderate length, if invariably imposed on those who have been convicted, will interfere sufficiently with most offenders' criminal careers to diminish crime rates. But suppose his 'modest' sentences do not work? Does not his incapacitative rationale point, then, to much longer sentences? After all, the only sure way to prevent criminally inclined persons from offending again is to hold them until they 'burn out' – until aging has depleted their criminal propensities. Wilson argues that the longer sentences are, the more reluctant sentencers will be to impose them. But if those in charge of the sentencing system take his incapacitative aims seriously, and if experience convinces them that shorter sentences are not enough to do the job, that reluctance may disappear. The possibility of escalation raises the issue [of what] *moral* limits [there should] be on the use of very long prison terms to incapacitate, even if such sentences were effective in reducing crime.

Where Wilson goes wrong, I think, is in his underlying assumption: his preoccupation with crime control to the near exclusion of considerations of justice. It has commonly been supposed – and Wilson continues in this tradition – that justice has largely been satisfied once an offender has been tried and convicted with due process. Thereafter, the focus has been almost exclusively on crime prevention – on which sentencing strategies (rehabilitation or incapacitation? long sentences or short?) serve public safety best. Seldom is the word justice found in the sentencing literature.

The emphasis, I am convinced, should be precisely the reverse: primacy should be given to considerations of justice in sentencing. A system of criminal justice can be tolerable in a free society only if we are determined to make it what its name implies: a system of justice, not a social engineering project. In punishing the convicted, the consequences to the individual are too harsh to permit us to act as if we were merely totting up costs and benefits, seeking the maximum efficiency in preventing crime. Concededly, no sentencing system operating in a society as fraught with inequalities as ours can come close to being truly just. But after conviction as before, justice should not be merely a euphemism for law enforcement; it should be an ideal which we should at least try to approximate.

In the [early 1970s] I was involved in an effort to think through a sentencing scheme grounded mainly on ideas about justice. It was undertaken by the Committee for the Study of Incarceration,[1] an interdisciplinary group which included law professors, sociologists, a psychoanalyst, a criminologist, and (atypically for an inquiry about sentencing) a historian and a philosopher. Instead of continuing the debate about what 'works', we decided at the outset to focus on the question: What is the just sentence?

Suppose one begins with a general definition of justice – (Aristotle's) – that like cases should be treated alike and unlike cases should be treated proportionate to their differences. One must then ask what kind of likeness is relevant for purposes of justice. (Is it, for example, the equally deserving or the equally needy who should be treated alike?) That is a hard question when there are no clues: there is nothing about wealth, for example, that suggests on its face whether it should be distributed according to merit or need. In the case of punishments, rewards and grades, however, the answer should be more obvious. Justice requires that they be distributed according to their recipients' deserts, because they *purport* to be deserved.

Academic grades illustrate this point. Suppose a student writes a poor exam paper. Suppose he needs an A to get into law school. Why not give him the grade he needs? The answer is, of course, that an A symbolizes a superior performance; that the student's performance, in fact, was poor; and hence that he simply does not deserve the A, whatever his needs. Desert is the only fair criterion, because that is precisely what a grade connotes. The same is true of punishment. It treats the person as though he deserves the pain inflicted – and does so because of its symbolism, its implicit moral condemnation of the offender. Punishment is not merely disagreeable (so are taxes and conscription); it implies that the person acted wrongfully and is blameworthy for having done so. Where standards of what constitutes criminal behavior are concerned, this point is a familiar one. It was made two decades ago by the late Henry M. Hart of Harvard Law School in his defense of the criminal law's requirements of culpable intent. Since punishment characteristically ascribes blame, he argued, violations should not be punished unless the offender was at fault (i.e., acted intentionally, or negligently). Accidental violations should not be punished because they are not blameworthy.

What is usually overlooked, however, is that the same argument holds after conviction, when sentence is imposed. By then, it has been decided that the offender deserves punishment, but the question of how much he deserves remains. The severity of the punishment connotes the degree of blame: the sterner the penalty, the greater the implicit reproof. Sending someone away to prison for years implies that he is more to be condemned than does jailing him for a few months or putting him on probation. In deciding severity, therefore, the crime must be sufficiently serious to merit the blame.

This means that sentences should, as a matter of justice, be decided according to a principle of *commensurate deserts*. The severity of punishment should comport with the seriousness of the crime. Stringent punishments should be limited to crimes that are serious; as the gravity of the crime diminishes, so should the severity of the punishment. When this principle is not observed, the degree of blame becomes inappropriate. If an offender convicted of a lesser crime is punished severely, the moral obloquy which so drastic a penalty carries will attach to him – and unjustly so, given the not-so-very-wrongful character of his offense. Conversely, giving a mild punishment to someone convicted of a serious crime understates the blame – and thus depreciates the importance of the values at stake. [. . .]

Once it is accepted as a requirement of justice, the commensurate-deserts principle should determine the sentencing structure. The seriousness of the offender's crime – not his need for treatment, his dangerousness, or the deterrence of others – ought to be decisive. Penalties must be scaled in accordance with the gravity of the offense, and departures from the deserved sentence should be impermissible – even if they had some crime-control usefulness.

A sentencing system based on this conception of justice would have the following principal features.

- The degree of likelihood that the offender might return to crime would be irrelevant to the choice of sentence. Even if crime forecasting techniques could be improved, an offender simply doesn't deserve to have his punishment increased on the basis of what he may do rather than on the basis of what he has done.
- Indeterminacy of sentence would be abolished. Since the seriousness of the crime (the only proper basis for the sentence, in our theory) is known at the time of verdict, there would be no need to delay the decision on sentence length to see

how well the offender is adjusting. Prisoners would no longer be kept in agonizing suspense for years, waiting for the parole board to make up its mind about discharge.

- Sentencing discretion would be sharply reduced (and hence today's problem of vast disparities among sentences alleviated). The wide leeway which sentencers now enjoy was sustained by the traditional assumption that the sentence was a means for altering the offender's behavior and had to be especially fashioned to his needs. When this assumption is given up, the basis for such broad discretion crumbles. In order for the sentence to be deserved, there must be standards governing how severely offenders should be punished for different crimes. (Otherwise, sentences will not be consistent; one judge could treat an offense as serious and punish accordingly, while another judge, having a different set of values, could treat the same infraction as minor.) The Incarceration Committee's report thus proposes a system of standardized penalties. For each gradation in seriousness of criminal behavior, a definite penalty – the 'presumptive sentence' – would be set. Offenders convicted of crimes of that degree of gravity would normally receive that specific sentence – except when there were unusual circumstances of mitigation or aggravation.
- Imprisonment would be limited to serious offenses. The commensurate-deserts principle allows severe punishments only for serious crimes. Imprisonment is necessarily a severe penalty. (Even if prison conditions are improved, the loss of liberty itself is a great deprivation.) Prison thus should be the sanction only for crimes, which cause or risk grievous harm – such as assault, armed robbery, and rape – and not for most non-violent larcenies of personal belongings. Even for serious crimes, moreover, the length of imprisonment ought to be stringently rationed, given the painfulness of the prison sanction. The Incarceration Committee's report recommends that most prison sentences be kept below three years. (Bear in mind that we are speaking of actual time in prison, not of a purported sentence that can later by cut back by a parole board.)
- Penalties less severe than imprisonment would be for the non-serious offences which constitute the bulk of the criminal justice system's caseload. These milder penalties would not be rehabilitative measures but, simply and explicitly, less severe punishments. Warnings, limited deprivations of leisure time (and perhaps fines) would be used in lieu of imprisonment. Probation would be phased out because of its discretionary and treatment-oriented features.

There is potential for disagreement, of course, about which crimes are serious. Yet assessments of seriousness – of how harmful the conduct is, and how culpable the offender – at least are moral judgments akin to those we make in everyday life. It should be easier (or certainly no harder) to make such judgments than to surmise on slight evidence how a given sentencing policy will affect crime rates. Moreover, the extent of disagreement on questions of seriousness should not be exaggerated. Beginning [. . .] with the work of the criminologists Thorsten Sellin and Marvin Wolfgang at the University of Pennsylvania, several studies have measured popular perceptions of the gravity of crimes and found a surprising degree of consensus. When asked to rank common acts of theft, fraud and violence on a scale according to their degree of heinousness, people from widely different walks of life tend to make similar ratings.

In this highly compressed description, I have skipped several of the harder (and more interesting) issues. Why should punishment exist at all? (Why shouldn't we, instead, adopt a wholly different kind of social control mechanism?) How can a just deserts model for sentencing be defended in a society that is not itself just? Is one permitted, in a desert-based system, to take an offender's earlier crimes into account? We try to wrestle with these questions in the Incarceration Committee's report.

In sketching this sentencing scheme, I have considered only the requirements of justice. But the system could have some collateral usefulness in controlling crime, even if it is not fashioned with crime control specifically in mind. While sentences would be much shorter, they would be more certain: Anyone convicted of a sufficiently serious crime would face some time in prison – and increasing the certainty of a substantial punishment may be useful as a deterrent. There also could be some incapacitative benefit. Since all offenders convicted of serious crimes would be imprisoned, those who were inclined to offend again would be restrained, at least temporarily. But we would always bear in mind that these benefits might fail to materialize. Perhaps there will not be a sufficiently large increase in certainty of punishment – because too many of those who commit serious crimes do not get caught, or too many of those caught avoid conviction or succeed in bargaining the charges down. But even with such disappointed hopes (even, in fact, if the scheme proves to have no greater efficiency than today's system), it is still defensible because it is a fairer system. Offenders' punishments would more closely approximate what they deserve, and equally blameworthy individuals would receive more nearly similar sentences. Because the scheme is grounded chiefly on equity, a failure in its crime control effectiveness (always a risk to any criminal justice strategy) would not be so devastating as it would be to a scheme such as Wilson's, which relies almost exclusively on the promise that it will work.

A desert-based scheme can serve, moreover, as a baseline – a norm for judging sentencing systems that have been devised with crime control more immediately in mind. Let us suppose that a penologist wants to build an 'efficient' sentencing system and, for the sake of crime-control efficacy, proposes sentences which diverge from those that are deserved. Is it enough for him to show that his system is likely to work? Certainly not, for our desert-based system may work also. Perhaps his system is capable of reducing serious crime by, say, 5 per cent – but our system of deserved sentences might, conceivably, also affect the crime rate by a similar percentage. In that event, his system should be rejected out of hand, for it sacrifices justice while having little or no greater impact on crime than a more just system would. The burden thus falls on him to show not merely how his system will discourage crime, but how it will do so more effectively than a desert-based system would – and that would be no easy matter to establish. Even if this burden were met, a moral decision would have to be made: whether the added crime-control benefits warranted the sacrifice of equity involved. The greater the departure from just (that is, deserved) sentences, the stronger the moral argument for rejecting the proposal, notwithstanding its expected usefulness in curbing crime.

To illustrate this point, let us look once more at Wilson's proposals. Where serious offenses are concerned, his recommended sentences are not dissimilar to the ones we suggest, despite his different rationale. Wilson proposes that anyone convicted of a major offense such as armed robbery (especially when it is a second or third conviction) be sentenced to prison, but that long sentences be avoided. He promises a dramatic (20 per cent or more) reduction in robberies as the result of such a policy. As we have seen, one well might be skeptical that this result will occur. But even if there were no measurable reduction in the robbery rate, Wilson's recommendation could still be defended – but on our grounds of desert: armed robbery is serious, and serious crimes deserve severe punishments.

The conclusion differs, however, with less serious offenses. Wilson proposes that these more venial infractions (unless 'manifestly trivial') be punished by a 'deprivation of liberty' for a few days, weeks, or months. He allows that the deprivation might be something less than full-time imprisonment (confinement only at night, for example, leaving the offender free to go to work during the day), but states that the choice between full and partial restraint should depend on the need to 'protect society'. This leaves open the possibility that lesser offenders could suffer full-time imprisonment if (as is often the case) they seemed likely to return to crime if released. Here, the moral objection is evident: crimes such as shoplifting, passing bad checks, and the like are not serious enough to deserve the harsh sanction of imprisonment.

As this aspect of Wilson's scheme departs from the requirements of justice, one would have to ask, what reason is there to believe that such stiff penalties for lesser offenses would be appreciably more effective than the more modest sanctions of a desert-based system? And even if they were more effective, is the crime-control payoff really worth the sacrifice of fairness? To the second question, my answer would clearly be no, given my philosophical assumption that primacy ought to be accorded the ends of justice. But the answer might still be no, even were one a little readier to compromise ideals of fairness for the sake of crime control – since the suggested severer than just penalties are for crimes which, being less serious, pose no terrible threat to the community's safety.

It may seem strange that the Incarceration Committee's liberal professors and activists, when faced with the choice between rehabilitation and desert, chose desert. Why go back to so ancient a notion? Why not continue to focus on what works best, and leave what is deserved to casuists and theologians? Unfashionable as the idea of desert has been, we found it essential to justice in sentencing. It is crucial to the question that civil libertarians ought to be asking: What are the ethical limits on making convicted individuals suffer for the sake of preventing crime? The point was aptly stated ninety years ago by F.H. Wines, one of the few prison reformers of that age to question the then dominant ideal of rehabilitation, when he said: 'Of the retribution theory, it may at least be said that if it is an assertion of the right to inflict all the pain which a particular criminal act may merit, it is the denial of the right to inflict on any human being any needless and unmerited pain'.

NOTES

1 See A. von Hirsch, *Doing Justice: the Choice of Punishments*. Report of the Committee for the Study of Incarceration (New York, Hill and Wang, 1976).

30

The value of rehabilitation

Francis T. Cullen and Karen E. Gilbert

[. . .] [P]reoccupation with the misuses and limitations of treatment programs has perhaps blinded many current-day liberals to the important benefits that have been or can be derived from popular belief in the notion that offenders should be saved and not simply punished. In this respect, the persistence of a strong rehabilitative ideology can be seen to function as a valuable resource for those seeking to move toward the liberal goal of introducing greater benevolence into the criminal justice system. Alternatively, we can begin to question whether the reform movement sponsored by the Left will not be undermined should liberal faith in rehabilitation reach a complete demise. In this context, four major reasons are offered below for why we believe that liberals should reaffirm and not reject the correctional ideology of rehabilitation.

1 *Rehabilitation is the only justification of criminal sanctioning that obligates the state to care for an offender's needs or welfare.* Admittedly, rehabilitation promises a payoff to society in the form of offenders transformed into law-abiding, productive citizens who no longer desire to victimize the public. Yet treatment ideology also conveys the strong message that this utilitarian outcome can only be achieved if society is willing to punish its captives humanely and to compensate offenders for the social disadvantages that have constrained them to undertake a life in crime. In contrast, the three competing justifications of criminal sanctioning – deterrence, incapacitation and retribution (or just deserts) – contain not even the pretence that the state has an obligation to do good for its charges. The only responsibility of the state is to inflict the pains that accompany the deprivation of liberty or of material resources (e.g., fines); whatever utility such practices engender flows only to society and not to its captives. Thus, deterrence aims to protect the social order by making offenders suffer sufficiently to dissuade them as well as onlookers entertaining similar criminal notions from venturing outside the law on future occasions. Incapacitation also seeks to preserve the social order but through a surer means; by caging criminals – 'locking 'em up and throwing away the keys' – inmates will no longer be at liberty

From *Reaffirming Rehabilitation*, pp. 247–63. (Cincinnati, OH: Anderson, 1982.)

to prey on law-abiding members of society. The philosophy of retribution, on the other hand, manifests a disinterest in questions of crime control, instead justifying punishment on the grounds that it presumably provides society and crime victims with the psychic satisfaction that justice has been accomplished by harming offenders in doses commensurate with the harms their transgressions have caused. [. . .]

These considerations lead us to ask whether it is strategically wise for liberals wishing to mitigate existing inhumanities in the criminal justice system to forsake the only prevailing correctional ideology that is expressly benevolent toward offenders. It is difficult to imagine that reform efforts will be more humanizing if liberals willingly accept the premise that the state has no responsibility to do good, only to inflict pain. Notably, Gaylin and Rothman, proponents of the justice model, recognized the dangers of such a choice when they remarked that 'in giving up the rehabilitative model, we abandon not just our innocence but perhaps more. The concept of deserts is intellectual and moralistic; in its devotion to principle, it turns back on such compromising considerations as generosity and charity, compassion and love'.[1] They may have shown even greater hesitation in rejecting rehabilitation and affirming just deserts had they had an opportunity to dwell on the more recent insights of radical thinkers Herman and Julia Schwendinger:

> Nevertheless, whatever the expressed qualifications, the justice model now also justifies objectively retrogressive outcomes because of its insistence that social policies give priority to punishment rather than rehabilitation. Punishment, as we have seen, is classically associated with deprivation of living standards. Rehabilitation, on the other hand, has served as the master symbol in bourgeois ideology that legitimated innumerable reformist struggles against this deprivation. By discrediting rehabilitation as a basic principle of penal practice, the justice modelers have undermined their own support for better standards of living in penal institutions.[2]

Now it might be objected by liberal critics of rehabilitation that favoring desert as the rationale for criminal sanctioning does not mean adopting an uncaring orientation toward the welfare of offenders. The reform agenda of the justice model not only suggests that punishment be fitted to the crime and not the criminal, but also that those sent to prison be accorded an array of rights that will humanize their existence. The rehabilitative ideal, it is countered, justifies the benevolent treatment of the incarcerated but only as a means to achieving another end – the transformation of the criminal into the conforming. In contrast, the justice perspective argues for humanity as an end in and of itself, something that should not in any way be made to seem conditional on accomplishing the difficult task of changing the deep-seated criminogenic inclinations of offenders. As such, liberals should not rely on state enforced rehabilitation to somehow lessen the rigors of imprisonment, but instead should campaign to win legal rights for convicts that directly bind the state to provide its captives with decent living conditions. [. . .]

It is not with ease that those of us on the political Left can stop short of completely and publically embracing the concept that 'humanity for humanity's sake' is sufficient reason for combating the brutalizing effects of prison life. This value-stance is, after all, fundamental to the logic that informs liberal policies on criminal justice issues. In this light, it should be clear that we applaud attempts to earn inmates human rights [. . .] and urge their continuance. However, we must stand firm against efforts to promote the position that the justice model with its emphasis on rights should replace the rehabilitative ideal with its emphasis on caring as the major avenue of liberal reform. [. . .] [S]upport for the principles of just deserts and determinacy has only exacerbated the plight of offenders both before and after their incarceration. But there are additional dangers to undertaking a reform program that abandons rehabilitation and seeks *exclusively* to broaden prisoner rights. Most importantly, the realities of the day furnish little optimism that such a campaign would enjoy success. [. . .]

Further, the promise of the rights perspective is based on the shaky assumption that more benevolence will occur if the relationship of the state to its deviants is fully adversarial and purged of its paternalistic dimensions. Instead of the government being entrusted to reform its charges through care, now offenders will have the comfort of being equipped with a new weapon – 'rights' – that will serve them well in their battle against the state for a humane and justly administered correctional system. Yet this imagery contains only surface appeal. As David Rothman has warned, 'an adversarial model, setting interest off against interest, does seem to run the clear risk of creating a kind of ultimate shoot-out in which, by definition, the powerless lose and the powerful win. How absurd to push for confrontation when all the advantages are on the other side'.[3]
[. . .]

Moreover, the rights perspective is a two-edged sword. While rights ideally bind the state to abide by standards insuring a certain level of due process protection and acceptable penal living conditions, rights also establish the limits of the good that the state can be expected or obligated to provide. A rehabilitative ideology, in contrast, constantly pricks the conscience of the state with its assertion that the useful and moral goal of offender reformation can only be effected in a truly humane environment. Should treatment ideology be stripped away by liberal activists and the ascendancy of the rights model secured, it would thus create a situation in which criminal justice officials would remain largely immune from criticism as long as they 'gave inmates their rights' – however few they may be at the time. [. . .]

Even more perversely, the very extension of new rights can also be utilized to legitimate the profound neglect of the welfare of those under state control. The tragic handling of mental patients [. . .] is instructive in this regard. As it became apparent that many in our asylums were being either unlawfully abused or deprived of their liberty, the 'mentally ill' won the right to be released to or remain in the community if it could be proven that they were of no danger to themselves or others. [. . .] Yet, what has been the actual result of this 'right' to avoid state enforced therapy? It brought forth not a new era in the humane treatment of the troubled but a new era of state neglect. Instead of brutalizing people within institutional structures, the state now permits the personally disturbed to be brutalized on the streets of our cities.
[. . .]

2 The ideology of rehabilitation provides an important rationale for opposing the conservatives' assumption that increased repression will reduce crime. Those embracing the conservatives' call for 'law and order' place immense faith in the premise that tough rather than humane justice is the answer to society's crime problem. In the political Right's view, unlawful acts occur only when individuals have calculated that they are advantageous, and thus the public's victimization will only subside if criminal choices are made more costly. This can be best accomplished by sending more offenders away to prison for more extended and uncomfortable stays. Indeed, the very existence of high crime rates is *prima facie* evidence that greater repression is required to insure that lawlessness in our nation no longer pays.

Liberals have traditionally attacked this logic on the grounds that repressive tactics do not touch upon the real social roots of crime and hence rarely succeed in even marginally reducing criminal involvement. Campaigns to heighten the harshness of existing criminal penalties – already notable for their severity – will only serve to fuel the problem of burgeoning prison populations and result in a further deterioration of penal living standards. The strategy of 'getting tough' thus promises to have substantial costs, both in terms of the money wasted on the excessive use of incarceration and in terms of the inhumanity it shamefully introduces.

It is clear that proponents of the justice model share these intense liberal concerns over the appealing but illusory claims of those preaching law and order. However, their opposition to repressive crime control policies encounters difficulties because core assumptions of the justice model converge closely with those found in the paradigm for crime control espoused by conservatives. Both perspectives, for instance, argue that (1) offenders are responsible beings who freely choose to engage in crime; (2) regardless of the social injustices that may have prompted an individual to breach the law, the nature of the crime and not the nature of the circumstances surrounding a crime should regulate the severity of the sanction meted out; and (3) the punishment of offenders is deserved – that is, the state's infliction of pain for pain's sake is a positive good to be encouraged and not a likely evil to be discouraged. Admittedly, those wishing to 'do justice' would contend that current sanctions are too harsh and that prison conditions should be made less rigorous. But having already agreed with conservatives that punishing criminals is the fully legitimate purpose of the criminal justice system, they are left with little basis on which to challenge the logic or moral justification of proposals to get tough. Instead, their opposition to such measures is reduced to a debate with conservatives over the exact amount of deprivation of liberty and of living conditions during incarceration that each criminal act 'justly deserves'. [. . .]

In contrast, the ideology of rehabilitation disputes every facet of the conclusion that the constant escalation of punishment will mitigate the spectre of crime. To say that offenders are in need of rehabilitation is to reject the conservatives' notion that individuals, regardless of their position in the social order – whether black or white, rich or poor – exercise equal freedom in deciding whether to commit a crime. Instead, it is to reason that social and personal circumstances often constrain, if not compel, people to violate the law; and unless efforts are made to enable offenders to escape these criminogenic constraints, little relief in the crime rate can be anticipated. Policies that insist on ignoring these realities by assuming a vengeful posture toward offenders promise to succeed only in fostering hardships that will, if anything, deepen the resentment that many inmates find difficult to suppress upon their release back into society [. . .]

A rehabilitative stance thus allows us to begin to speak about, in Karl Menninger's words, not the 'punishment of crime' but the 'crime of punishment'.[4] The conservatives' plea for repression is exposed as a 'crime' because it both needlessly dehumanizes society's captives and falsely deceives the public that strict crime control measures will afford citizens greater safety. Drawing on the logic of the

Positivist School of criminology while casting aside the classical image of the law-breaker, the concept of rehabilitation reveals that fundamental changes in offenders will not be realized as long as inflicting deprivation remains the legitimate goal of our system of criminal 'injustice'. [. . .] [A] treatment ideology prompts us first to appreciate the troubles and disadvantages that drive many into crime and then to reach out and assist offenders to deal with the conditions and needs that have moved them to break the law. The demand is made, in short, that caring rather than hurting be the guiding principle of the correctional process. Moreover, in sensitizing us to the fact that much of the illegality that plagues society is intimately linked to existing social inequalities and injustices, rehabilitative ideology makes clear that a true solution to the crime problem ultimately rests in the support of reform programs that will bring about a more equitable distribution of resources through a broad structural transformation of the social order. This is in notable contrast to the philosophy of just deserts that assumes full individual responsibility, focuses on the culpability of the single perpetrator, and therefore 'acquits the existing social order of any charge of injustice'.[5]

It is apparent, then, that the ideology of rehabilitation is fully oppositional to the conservatives' agenda for the repression of crime. Importantly, it thus furnishes liberals seeking to effect criminal justice reform with a coherent framework with which to argue that benevolence and not brutality should inform society's attempts to control crime. Sharing no assumptions with the Right's paradigm of law and order, it does not, as in the case of the justice model, easily give legitimacy to either repressive punishment policies or the neglect of offender well-being. Instead, it remains a distinctly liberal ideology that can be utilized as a resource in the Left's quest to illustrate the futility of policies that increase pain but accomplish little else.

3 Rehabilitation still receives considerable support as a major goal of the correctional system. With prison populations exploding and punitive legislation being passed across the nation, it is of little surprise to find opinion polls indicating a hardening of public attitudes toward crime control [. . .] In this light, it can be imagined that public opinion would constitute a serious and perhaps insurmountable obstacle to any proposals advocating the treatment rather than the mere punishment of offenders. The viability of liberal reform strategies aimed at reaffirming rehabilitation would thus seem questionable at best.

But this is not the case. While the average citizen clearly wants criminals to be severely sanctioned – in particular, sent to prison for longer stays – survey research consistently reveals that the American public also believes that offenders should be rehabilitated. [. . .]

[E]xisting survey data suggest that rehabilitation persists as a prevailing ideology within the arena of criminal justice. This does not mean that treatment programs in our prisons are flourishing and remain unthreatened by the pragmatics and punitiveness of our day. But it is to assert that the rehabilitative ideal and the benevolent potential it holds are deeply anchored within our correctional and broader cultural heritage. That is, rehabilitation constitutes an ongoing rationale that is accepted by or 'makes sense to' the electorate as well as to criminal justice interest groups and policy-makers. Consequently, it provides reformers with a valuable vocabulary with which to justify changes in policy and practice aimed at mitigating the harshness of criminal sanctions – such as the diversion of offenders into the community for 'treatment' or the humanization of the prison to develop a more effective 'therapeutic environment'. Unlike direct appeals for inmate rights to humane and just living conditions that can be quickly dismissed as the mere coddling of the dangerous ('Why should we care about their rights when they certainly didn't care about the rights of their innocent victims?'), liberal reforms undertaken in the name of rehabilitation have the advantage of resonating with accepted ideology and hence of retaining an air of legitimacy. [. . .] If the public is not willing to pay now to facilitate the betterment of those held in captivity, it can be made clear to them that they will be forced to pay in more bothersome, if not tragic, ways at a later date.

Our message here is simple but, in light of the advent of the justice model, telling in its implications: for liberals to argue vehemently against the ideology of rehabilitation – to say that treatment cannot work because the rehabilitative ideal is inherently flawed – is to undermine the potency of one of the few resources that can be mobilized in the Left's pursuit of less repression in the administration of criminal punishments.

4 Rehabilitation has historically been an important motive underlying reform efforts that have increased the humanity of the correctional system. Liberal critics have supplied ample evidence to confirm their suspicions that state enforced therapy has too frequently encouraged the unconscionable exploitation of society's captives. Their chilling accounts of the inhumanities completed under the guise of 'treatment' call forth the compelling conclusion that far greater benevolence would grace the criminal justice system had notions of rehabilitation never taken hold.

However, while the damages permitted by the corruption of the rehabilitative ideal should neither be denied nor casually swept aside, it would be misleading to idealize the 'curious' but brutal punishments of 'bygone days' and to ignore that reforms undertaken in the name of rehabilitation have been a crucial humanizing influence in the darker regions of the sanctioning process. [. . .] It is instructive as well to contemplate fully the thoughtful observations of Graeme Newman:

> Yet it would seem that to throw out the whole idea of good intentions, because most of the time they do not reach the lofty heights they were supposed to achieve, may be to throw out many other values that have often accompanied them: human values, the wish, at least, to treat people humanely. Some argue that we do not need the medical [rehabilitative model] as an 'excuse' to treat offenders humanely, that we ought to do it for the sake of being humane in and of itself. But this argument, although admirably principled, does not recognize the great cultural difficulties (largely unconscious) that we have had, and continue to have, in acting humanely to those who are society's outcasts. Surely this is the lesson of history. It is only a couple of hundred years since we gave up mutilating, disemboweling, and chopping up criminals, and we still cannot make up our minds whether to stop killing them. It would seem to me, therefore, that while the medical [rehabilitative] model has its own drawbacks, it has brought along with it a useful baggage of humane values that might never have entered the darkness of criminal justice otherwise.[6]

Those who have traditionally sought to treat offenders have also sought to lessen the discomforts convicts are made to suffer. In part, this occurs, as Allen has remarked, because 'the objectives both of fundamental decency in the prisons and the rehabilitation of prisoners . . . appears to require the same measures'.[7] Yet the studies of Torsten Eriksson suggest that it is the case as well that those endeavoring to pioneer 'the more effective treatment of criminals' have commonly been united in their 'indomitable will to help their erring brother'. They stand out as 'beacons in the history of mankind, the part that deals with compassion with one's fellow man'.[8] In this context, we can again question the wisdom of liberal attempts to unmask the rehabilitative ideal as at best a 'noble lie' and at worst an inevitably coercive fraud. For in discrediting rehabilitation, liberal critics may succeed in deterring a generation of potential reformers from attempting to do good in the correctional system by teaching that it is a futile enterprise to show care for offenders by offering to help these people lead less destructive lives. And should rehabilitation be forfeited as the prevailing liberal ideology, what will remain as the medium through which benevolent sentiments will be expressed and instituted into meaningful policy? Will the medium be a justice model that is rooted in despair and not optimism, that embraces punishment and not betterment, that disdains inmate needs and disadvantages in favor of a concern for sterile and limited legal rights, and whose guiding principle of reform is to have the state do less for its captives rather than more? Or will, as we fear, this vacuum remain unfilled and the liberal camp be left without an ideology that possesses the vitality – as has rehabilitation over the past 150 years – to serve as a rallying cry for or motive force behind reforms that will engender lasting humanizing changes?

NOTES

1 Willard Gaylin and David J. Rothman, 'Introduction' in Andrew von Hirsch, *Doing Justice: the Choice of Punishments* (New York, Hill and Wang, 1976), p. xxxix.

2 Herman and Julia Schwendinger, 'The new idealism and penal living standards', in Tony Platt and Paul Takagi (eds), *Punishment and Penal Discipline: Essays on the Prison and the Prisoners' Movement* (Berkeley, CA., Crime and Social Justice Associates, 1980), p. 187.

3 David J. Rothman, 'The state as parent: social policy in the Progressive era', in Willard Gaylin, Ira Glasser, Steven Marcus, and David Rothman (eds), *Doing Good: the Limits of Benevolence* (New York, Pantheon, 1978), p. 94.

4 Karl Menninger, *The Crime of Punishment* (New York, Penguin Books, 1966).

5 Jeffrey H. Reiman, *The Rich Get Richer and the Poor Get Prison: Ideology, Class and Criminal Justice* (New York, John Wiley, 1979), p. 144.

6 Graeme Newman, 'Book Review of *Conscience and Convenience: the Asylum and its Alternatives in Progressive America, David J. Rothman*', *Crime and Delinquency*, 27 (July 1981), p. 426.

7 Francis A. Allen, *The Decline of the Rehabilitative Ideal: Penal Policy and Social Purpose* (New Haven, CT, Yale University Press, 1981), p. 81.

8 Torsten Eriksson, *The Reformers: an Historical Survey of Pioneer Experiments in the Treatment of Criminals* (New York, Elsevier, 1976), p. 252.

31

'Situational' crime prevention: Theory and practice

Ronald V.G. Clarke

Conventional wisdom holds that crime prevention needs to be based on a thorough understanding of the causes of crime. Though it may be conceded that preventive measures (such as humps in the road to stop speeding) can sometimes be found without invoking sophisticated causal theory, 'physical' measures which reduce opportunities for crime are often thought to be of limited value. They are said merely to suppress the impulse to offend which will then manifest itself on some other occasion and perhaps in even more harmful form. Much more effective are seen to be 'social' measures (such as the revitalization of communities, the creation of job opportunities for unemployed youth, and the provision of sports and leisure facilities), since these attempt to remove the root motivational causes of offending. These ideas about prevention are not necessarily shared by the man-in-the-street or even by policemen and magistrates, but they have prevailed among academics, administrators and others who contribute to the formulation of criminal policy. They are also consistent with a preoccupation of criminological theory with criminal 'dispositions' (cf. Gibbons, 1971; Jeffery, 1971; Ohlin, 1970) and the purpose of this paper is to argue that an alternative theoretical emphasis on choices and decisions made by the offender leads to a broader and perhaps more realistic approach to crime prevention.

'DISPOSITIONAL' THEORIES AND THEIR PREVENTIVE IMPLICATIONS

With some exceptions noted below, criminological theories have been little concerned with the situational determinants of crime. Instead, the main object of these theories (whether biological, psychological, or sociological in orientation) has been to show how some people are born with, or come to acquire, a 'disposition' to behave in a consistently criminal manner. This 'dispositional' bias of theory has been identified as a defining characteristic of 'positivist' criminology, but it is also to be

From *British Journal of Criminology*, 1980, 20(2): 136–47.

found in 'interactionist' or deviancy theories of crime developed in response to the perceived inadequacies of positivism. Perhaps the best-known tenet of at least the early interactionist theories, which arises out of a concern with the social definition of deviance and the role of law enforcement agencies, is that people who are 'labelled' as criminal are thereby prone to continue in delinquent conduct (see especially Becker, 1962). In fact, as Tizard (1976) and Ross (1977) have pointed out, a dispositional bias is prevalent throughout the social sciences.

The more extreme forms of dispositional theory have moulded thought about crime prevention in two unfortunate ways. First, they have paid little attention to the phenomenological differences between crimes of different kinds, which has meant that preventive measures have been insufficiently tailored to different kinds of offence and of offender; secondly they have tended to reinforce the view of crime as being largely the work of a small number of criminally disposed individuals. But many criminologists are now increasingly agreed that a 'theory of crime' would be almost as crude as a general 'theory of disease'. Many now also believe, on the evidence of self-report studies (see Hood and Sparks, 1970), that the bulk of crime – vandalism, auto-crime, shoplifting, theft by employees – is committed by people who would not ordinarily be thought of as criminal at all.

Nevertheless, the dispositional bias remains and renders criminological theory unproductive in terms of the preventive measures which it generates. People are led to propose methods of preventive intervention precisely where it is most difficult to achieve any effects, i.e. in relation to the psychological events or the social and economic conditions that are supposed to generate criminal dispositions. As James Q. Wilson (1975) has argued, there seem to be no acceptable ways of modifying temperament and other biological variables, and it is difficult to know what can be done to make parents more inclined to love their children or exercise consistent discipline. Eradicating poverty may be no real solution either, in that crime rates have continued to rise since the war despite great improvements in economic conditions. And even if it were possible to provide people with the kinds of jobs and leisure facilities they might want, there is still no guarantee that crime would drop; few crimes require much time or effort, and work and leisure in themselves provide a whole range of criminal opportunities. As for violent crime, there would have to be a much clearer link between this and media portrayals of violence before those who cater to popular taste would be persuaded to change their material. Finally, given public attitudes to offending, which, judging by some opinion surveys, can be quite punitive, there may not be a great deal of additional scope for policies of diversion and decriminalization which are favoured by those who fear the consequences of 'labelling'.

These difficulties are primarily practical, but they also reflect the uncertainties and inconsistencies of treating distant psychological events and social processes as the 'causes' of crime. Given that each event is in turn caused by others, at what point in the infinitely regressive chain should one stop in the search for effective points of intervention? This is an especially pertinent question in that it is invariably found that the majority of individuals exposed to this or that criminogenic influence do not develop into persistent criminals. Moreover, 'dispositions' change so that most 'official' delinquents cease to come to the attention of the police in their late 'teens or early twenties (presumably because their lives change in ways incompatible with their earlier pursuits, cf. Trasler, 1979). Finally, it is worth pointing out that even the most persistently criminal people are probably law-abiding for most of their potentially available time, and this behaviour, too, must equally have been 'caused' by the events and experiences of their past. Some of the above theoretical difficulties could be avoided by conceiving of crime not in dispositional terms, but as being the outcome of immediate choices and decisions made by the offender. This would also have the effect of throwing a different light on preventive options.

An obvious problem is that some impulsive offences, and those committed under the influence of alcohol or strong emotion, may not easily be seen as the result of choices or decisions. Another difficulty is that the notion of 'choice' seems to fit uncomfortably with the fact that criminal behaviour is to some extent predictable from knowledge of a person's history. This difficulty is not properly resolved by the 'soft' determinism of Matza (1964) under which people retain some freedom of action albeit within a range of options constrained by their history and environment. A better formulation would seem to be that recently expounded by Glaser (1977): 'both free will and determinism are socially derived linguistic representations of reality' brought into play for different explanatory purposes at different levels of analysis and they may usefully co-exist in the scientific enterprise.

Whatever the resolution of these difficulties – and this is not the place to discuss them more fully – commonsense as well as the evidence of ethnographic studies of delinquency (e.g. Parker, 1974) strongly suggest that people are usually aware of consciously choosing to commit offences. This does not mean that they are fully aware of all the reasons for their behaviour nor that their own account would necessarily satisfy a criminologically sophisticated observer, who might require information at least about: (i) the offender's motives; (ii) his mood; (iii) his moral judgements concerning the act in question and the 'techniques of moral neutralization' open to him (cf. Matza, 1964); (iv) the extent of his criminal knowledge and his perception of criminal opportunities; (v) his assessment of the risks of being caught as well as the likely consequences; and finally, as well as of a different order, (vi) whether he has been drinking. These separate components of subjective state and thought processes which play a part in the decision to commit a crime will be influenced by immediate situational variables and by highly specific features of the individual's history and present life circumstances in ways that are so varied and countervailing as to render unproductive the notion of a generalized behavioural disposition to offend. Moreover, as will be argued below, the specificity of the influences upon different criminal behaviours gives much less credence to the 'displacement' hypothesis; the idea that reducing opportunities merely results in crime being displaced to some other time or place has been the major argument against situational crime prevention.

In so far as an individual's social and physical environments remain relatively constant and his decisions are much influenced by past experience, this scheme gives ample scope to account not only for occasional offending but also for recidivism; people acquire a repertoire of different responses to meet particular situations and if the circumstances are right they are likely to repeat those responses that have previously been rewarding. The scheme also provides a much richer source of hypotheses than 'dispositional' views of crime for the sex differences in rates of offending: for example, shoplifting may be a 'female' crime simply because women are greater users of shops (Mayhew, 1977). In view of the complexity of the behaviours in question, a further advantage (Atkinson, 1974) is that the scheme gives some accommodation to the variables thought to be important in most existing theories of crime, including those centred on dispositions. It is perhaps closest to a social learning theory of behaviour (Bandura, 1973; Mischel, 1968) though it owes something to the sociological model of crime proposed by the 'new criminologists' (Taylor et al., 1973). There are three features, however, which are particularly worth drawing out for the sake of the ensuing discussion about crime prevention: first, explanation is focused more directly on the criminal event; second, the need to develop explanations for separate categories of crime is made explicit; and, third, the individual's current circumstances and the immediate features of the setting are given considerably more explanatory significance than in 'dispositional' theories.

PREVENTIVE IMPLICATIONS OF A 'CHOICE' MODEL

In fact, just as an understanding of past influences on behaviour may have little preventive pay-off, so too there may be limited benefits in according greater explanatory importance to the individual's current life circumstances. For example, the instrumental attractions of delinquency may always be greater for certain groups of individuals such as young males living in inner-city areas. And nothing can be done about a vast range of misfortunes which continually befall people and which may raise the probability of their behaving criminally while depressed or angry.

Some practicable options for prevention do arise, however, from the greater emphasis upon situational features, especially from the direct and immediate relationship between these and criminal behaviour. By studying the spatial and temporal distribution of specific offences and relating these to measurable aspects of the situation, criminologists have recently begun to concern themselves much more closely with the possibilities of manipulating criminogenic situations in the interests of prevention. To date studies have been undertaken of residential burglary (Brantingham and Brantingham, 1975; Reppetto, 1974; Scarr, 1973; Waller and Okihiro, 1978) shoplifting (Walsh, 1978) and some forms of vandalism (Clarke, 1978; Ley and Cybrinwsky, 1974) and it is easy to foresee an expansion of research along these lines. Since offenders' perceptions of the risks and rewards attaching to different forms of crime cannot safely be inferred from studies of the distribution of offences, there might be additional preventive benefits if research of this kind were more frequently complemented by interviews with offenders (cf. Tuck, 1979; Walker, 1979).

The suggestions for prevention arising out of the 'situational' research that has been done can be conveniently divided into measures which (i) reduce the physical opportunities for offending or (ii) increase the chances of an offender being caught. These categories are discussed separately below though there is some overlap between them; for example, better locks which take longer to overcome also increase the risks of being caught. The division also leaves out some other 'situational' crime prevention measures such as housing allocation policies which avoid high concentrations of children in certain estates or which place families in accommodation that makes it easier for parents to supervise their children's play and leisure activities. Both these measures make it less likely that children will become involved in vandalism and other offences (cf. Wilson, 1978).

REDUCING PHYSICAL OPPORTUNITIES FOR CRIME AND THE PROBLEM OF DISPLACEMENT

Variations in physical opportunities for crime have sometimes been invoked to explain differences in crime rates within particular cities (e.g. Boggs, 1965; Baldwin and Bottoms, 1975) or temporal variations in crime; for example, Wilkins (1964) and Gould and his associates (Gould, 1969; Mansfield et al., 1974) have related levels of car theft to variations in the number of vehicles on the road. But these studies have not generally provided practicable preventive ideas – for example, the number of cars on the road cannot be reduced simply to prevent their theft – and it is only recently that there has been a concerted effort on the part of criminologists to find viable ways of blocking the opportunities for particular crimes.

The potential for controlling behaviour by manipulating opportunities is illustrated vividly by a study of suicide in Birmingham (Hassal and Trethowan, 1972). This showed that a marked drop in the rates of suicide between 1962 and 1970 was the result of a reduction in the poisonous content of the gas supplied to householders for cooking and heating, so that it became much more difficult for people to kill themselves by turning on the gas taps. Like many kinds of crime, suicide is generally regarded as being dictated by strong internal motivation and the fact that its incidence was greatly reduced by a simple (though unintentional) reduction in the opportunities to commit it suggests that it may be possible to achieve similar reductions in crime by 'physical' means. Though suicide by other methods did not increase in Birmingham, the study also leads to direct consideration of the fundamental theoretical problem of 'displacement' which, as Reppetto (1976) has pointed out, can occur in four different ways: time, place, method and type of offence. In other words, does reducing opportunities or increasing the risks result merely in the offender choosing his moment more carefully or in seeking some other, perhaps more harmful method of gaining his ends? Or, alternatively, will he shift his attention to a similar but unprotected target, for example, another house, car or shop? Or, finally, will he turn instead to some other form of crime?

For those who see crime as the outcome of criminal disposition, the answers to these questions would tend to be in the affirmative ('bad will out') but under the alternative view of crime represented above matters are less straightforward. Answers would depend on the nature of the crime, the offender's strength of motivation, knowledge of alternatives, willingness to entertain them, and so forth. In the case of opportunistic crimes (i.e. ones apparently elicited by their very ease of accomplishment such as some forms of shoplifting or vandalism) it would seem that the probability of offending could be reduced markedly by making it more difficult to act. For crimes such as bank robbery, however, which often seem to be the province of those who make a living from crime, reducing opportunities may be less effective. (This may be less true of increasing the risks of being caught except that for many offences the risks may be so low at present that any increase would have to be very marked.) Providing effective protection for a particular bank would almost certainly displace the attention of potential robbers to others, and if all banks were given increased protection many robbers would no doubt consider alternative means of gaining their ends. It is by no means implausible, however, that others – for example, those who do not have the ability to develop more sophisticated methods or who may not be willing to use more violence – may accept their reduced circumstances and may even take legitimate employment.

It is the bulk of offences, however, which are neither 'opportunistic' nor 'professional' that pose the greatest theoretical dilemmas. These offences include many burglaries and instances of auto-crime where the offender, who may merely supplement his normal income through the proceeds of crime, has gone out with the deliberate intention of committing the offence and has sought out the opportunity to do so. The difficulty posed for measures which reduce opportunity is one of the vast number of potential targets combined with the generally low overall level of security. Within easy reach of every house with a burglar alarm, or car with an anti-theft device, are many others without such protection.

In some cases, however, it may be possible to protect a whole class of property, as the Post Office did when they virtually eliminated theft from telephone kiosks by replacing the vulnerable aluminium coin-boxes with much stronger steel ones (cf. Mayhew et al., 1976). A further example is provided by the [UK] law which requires all motor-cyclists to wear crash helmets. This measure was introduced to save lives, but it has also had the unintended effect of reducing thefts of motor-cycles (Mayhew et al., 1976). This is because people are unlikely to take someone else's motorbike on the spur of the moment unless they happen to have a crash helmet with them – otherwise they could easily be spotted by the police. But perhaps the best example comes from West Germany where, in 1963, steering column locks were made compulsory on *all* cars, old and new, with a consequent reduction of more than 60 per cent in levels of taking and driving away (Mayhew et al., 1976). (When steering column locks were introduced in this country in 1971 it was only to new cars and, although these are now at much less risk of being taken, overall levels of car-taking have not yet diminished because the risk to older cars had increased as a result of displacement.)

Instances where criminal opportunities can be reduced for a whole class of property are comparatively few, but this need not always be a fatal difficulty. There must be geographical and temporal limits to displacement so that a town or city may be able to protect itself from some crime without displacing it elsewhere. The less determined the offender, the easier this will be; a simple example is provided by Decker's (1972) evidence that the use of 'slugs' in parking-meters in a New York district was greatly reduced by replacing the meters with ones which incorporated a slug-rejector device and in which the last coin inserted was visible in a plastic window. For most drivers there would be little advantage in parking their cars in some other district just because they could continue to use slugs there.

The question of whether, when stopped from committing a particular offence, people would turn instead to some other quite different form of crime is much more difficult to settle empirically, but many of the same points about motivation, knowledge of alternatives and so forth still apply. Common-sense also suggests, for example, that few of those Germans prevented by steering column locks from taking cars to get home at night are likely to have turned instead to hijacking taxis or to mugging passers-by for the money to get home. More likely, they may have decided that next time they would make sure of catching the last bus home or that it was time to save up for their own car.

INCREASING THE RISKS OF BEING CAUGHT

In practice, increasing the chances of being caught usually means attempting to raise the chances of an offender being seen by someone who is likely to take action. The police are the most obvious group likely to intervene effectively, but studies of the effectiveness of this aspect of their deterrent role are not especially encouraging (Clarke and Hough, 1980; Kelling et al., 1974; Manning, 1977). The reason seems to be that, when set against the vast number of opportunities for offending represented by the activities of a huge population of citizens for the 24 hours of the day, crime is a relatively rare event. The police cannot be everywhere at once and, moreover, much crime takes place in private. Nor is much to be expected from the general public (Mayhew et al., 1979). People in their daily round rarely see crime in progress; if they do they are likely to place some innocent interpretation on what they see; they may be afraid to intervene or they may feel the victims would resent interference; and they may encounter practical difficulties in summoning the police or other help in time. They are much more likely to take effective action to protect their own homes or immediate neighbourhood, but they are often away from these for substantial periods of the day and, moreover, the risks of crime in residential settings, at least in many areas of this country, are not so great as to encourage much vigilance. For instance, assuming that about 50 per cent of burglaries are reported to the police (cf. Home Office, 1979), a house in this country will on average be burgled once every 30 years. Even so, there is evidence (Department of the Environment, 1977; Wilson, 1978) that 'defensible space' designs on housing estates confer some protection from vandalism, if not as much as might have been expected from the results of Newman's (1973) research into crime on public housing projects in the United States (cf. Clarke,1979; Mayhew, 1979).

A recent Home Office Research report (Mayhew et al., 1979) has argued, however, that there is probably a good deal of unrealized potential for making more deliberate use of the surveillance role of employees who come into regular and frequent contact with the public in a semi-official capacity. Research in the United States (Newman, 1973; Reppetto, 1974) and Canada (Waller and Okihiro, 1978) has shown that apartment blocks with doormen are less vulnerable to burglary, while research in [the UK] has shown that vandalism is much less of a problem on buses with conductors (Mayhew et al., 1976) and on estates with resident caretakers (Department of the Environment, 1977). There is also evidence (in Post Office Records) that public telephones in places such as pubs or launderettes, which are given some supervision by staff, suffer almost no vandalism in comparison with those in kiosks; that car parks with attendants in control have lower rates of auto-crime (*The Sunday Times*, 9 April 1978); that football hooliganism on trains has been reduced by a variety of measures including permission for club stewards to travel free of charge; and that shoplifting is discouraged by the presence of assistants who are there to serve the customers (Walsh, 1978). Not everybody employed in a service capacity would be suited or willing to take on additional security duties, but much of their deterrent role may result simply from their being around. Employing more of them, for greater parts of the day, may therefore be all that is needed in most cases. In other cases, it may be necessary to employ people more suited to a surveillance role, train them better to carry it out, or even provide them with surveillance aids. Providing the staff at four London Underground stations with closed circuit television has been shown in a recent Home Office Research Unit study (Mayhew et al., 1979) to have substantially reduced theft and robbery offences at those stations.

SOME OBJECTIONS

Apart from the theoretical and practical difficulties of the approach advocated in this paper, it is in apparent conflict with the 'nothing works' school of criminological thought as given recent expression by Wolfgang (1977): 'the weight of empirical evidence indicates that no current preventative, deterrent, or rehabilitative intervention scheme has the desired effect of reducing crime'. But perhaps a panacea is being sought when all it may be possible to achieve is a reduction in particular forms of crime as a result of specific and sometimes localized measures. Examples of such reductions are given above and, while most of these relate to rather commonplace offences of theft and vandalism, there is no reason why similar measures cannot be successfully applied to other quite different forms of crime. It has been argued by many people (Rhodes, 1977, provides an example) that reducing the availability of hand-guns through gun-control legislation would reduce crimes of violence in the United States and elsewhere. Speeding and drunken driving could probably be reduced by fitting motor vehicles with devices which are now at an experimental stage (Ekblom, 1979). And there is no doubt (Wilkinson, 1977) that the rigorous passenger and baggage screening measures introduced at airports, particularly in the United States, have greatly reduced the incidence of airline hijackings. There are many crimes, however, when the offender is either so determined or so emotionally aroused that they seem to be beyond the scope of this approach. A further constraint will be costs: many shops, for example, which could reduce shoplifting by giving up self-service methods and employing more assistants or even store detectives, have calculated that this would not be worth the expense either in direct costs or in a reduction of turnover. Morally dubious as this policy might at first sight appear, these shops may simply have learned a lesson of more general application, i.e. a certain level of crime may be the inevitable consequence of practices and institutions which we cherish or find convenient and the 'cost' of reducing crime below this level may be unacceptable.

The gradualist approach to crime prevention advocated here might also attract criticism from some social reformers, as well as some deviancy theorists, for being unduly conservative. The former group, imbued with dispositional theory, would see the only effective way of dealing with crime as being to attack its roots through the reduction of inequalities of wealth, class and education – a solution which, as indicated above, has numerous practical and theoretical difficulties. The latter group would criticize the approach, not for its lack of effectiveness but – on the grounds that there is insufficient consensus in society about what behaviour should be treated as crime – for helping to preserve an undesirable status quo. Incremental change, however, may be the most realistic way of achieving consensus as well as a more equitable society. Most criminologists would probably also agree that it would be better for the burden of crime reduction to be gradually shifted away from the criminal justice system, which may be inherently selective and punitive in its operation, to preventive measures whose social costs may be more equitably distributed among all members of society. The danger to be guarded against would be that the attention of offenders might be displaced away from those who can afford to purchase protection to those who cannot. This probably happens already to some extent and perhaps the best way of dealing with the problem would be through codes of security which would be binding on car manufacturers, builders, local transport operators and so forth. Another danger is that those who have purchased protection might become less willing to see additional public expenditure on the law enforcement and criminal justice services – and this is a problem that might only be dealt with through political leadership and public education.

Many members of the general public might also find it objectionable that crime was being stopped, not by punishing wrong-doers, but by inconveniencing the law-abiding. The fact that opportunity-reducing and risk-increasing measures are too readily identified with their more unattractive aspects (barbed wire, heavy padlocks, guard-dogs and private security forces) adds fuel to the fire. And in some of their more sophisticated forms (closed circuit television surveillance and electronic intruder alarms) they provoke fears, on the one hand, of 'big brother' forms of state control and, on the other, of a 'fortress society' in which citizens in perpetual fear of their fellows scuttle from one fortified environment to another.

Expressing these anxieties has a value in checking potential abuses of power, and questioning the means of dealing with crime can also help to keep the problem of crime in perspective. But it should also be said that the kind of measures discussed above need not always be obtrusive (except where it is important to maximize their deterrent effects) and need not in any material way infringe individual liberties or the quality of life. Steel cash compartments in telephone kiosks are indistinguishable from aluminium ones, and vandal-resistant polycarbonate looks just like glass. Steering column locks are automatically brought into operation on removing the ignition key, and many people are quite unaware that their cars are fitted with them. 'Defensible space' designs in housing estates have the additional advantage of promoting feelings of neighbourliness and safety, though perhaps too little attention has been paid to some of their less desirable effects such as possible encroachments on privacy as a result of overlooking. And having more bus conductors, housing estate caretakers, swimming bath attendants and shop assistants means that people benefit from improved services – even if they have to pay for them either directly or through the rates.

Finally, the idea that crime might be most effectively prevented by reducing opportunities and increasing the risks is seen by many as, at best, representing an over-simplified mechanistic view of human behaviour and, at worst, a 'slur on human nature' (cf. Radzinowicz and King, 1977). (When the contents of *Crime as Opportunity* (Mayhew et al., 1976) were reported in the press in advance of publication an irate psychiatrist wrote to the Home Secretary demanding that he should suppress the publication of such manifest nonsense.) As shown above, however, it is entirely compatible with a view of criminal behaviour as predominantly rational and autonomous and as being capable of adjusting and responding to adverse consequences, anticipated or experienced. And as for being a pessimistic view of human behaviour, it might indeed be better if greater compliance with the law could come about simply as a result of people's free moral choice. But apart from being perilously close to the rather unhelpful dispositional view of crime, it is difficult to see this happening. We may therefore be left for the present with the approach advocated [here], time-consuming, laborious and limited as it may be.

SUMMARY

It is argued that the 'dispositional' bias of most current criminological theory has resulted in 'social' crime prevention measures being given undue prominence and 'situational' measures being devalued. An alternative theoretical emphasis on decisions and choices made by the offender (which in turn allows more weight to the circumstances of offending) results in more support for a situational approach to prevention. Examples of the effectiveness of such an approach are provided and some of the criticisms that have been made of it on social and ethical grounds are discussed.

REFERENCES

Atkinson, M. (1974) 'Versions of deviance', Extended review in *Sociological Review*, 22: 616–24.

Baldwin, J. and Bottoms, A.E. (1975) *The Urban Criminal*. London: Tavistock.

Bandura, A. (1973) *Aggression: a Social Learning Analysis*. London: Prentice Hall.

Becker, H.S. (1962) *Outsiders: Studies in the Sociology of Deviance*. Glencoe, Ill.: The Free Press.

Boggs, S.L. (1965) 'Urban crime patterns', *American Sociological Review*, 30: 899–908.

Brantingham, P.J. and Brantingham, P.L. (1975) 'The spatial patterning of burglary', *Howard Journal of Penology and Crime Prevention*, 14: 11–24.

Clarke, R.V.G. (ed.) (1978) *Tackling Vandalism*. Home Office Research Study No. 47. London: HMSO.

Clarke, R.V.G. (1979) 'Defensible space and vandalism: the lessons from some recent British research', *Stadtebau und Kriminalamt (Urban planning and Crime)*. Papers of an international symposium, Bundeskriminalamt, Federal Republic of Germany, December, 1978.

Clarke, R.V.G. and Hough, J.M. (eds) (1980) *The Effectiveness of Policing*. Farnborough, Hants: Gower.

Decker, J.F. (1972) 'Curbside deterrence: an analysis of the effect of a slug-rejector device, coin view window and warning labels on slug usage in New York City parking meters', *Criminology*, August, pp. 127–42.

Department of the Environment (1977) *Housing Management and Design*. (Lambeth Inner Area Study). IAS/IA/18. London: Department of the Environment.

Ekblom, P. (1979) 'A crime-free car?', *Research Bulletin No. 7*. Home Office Research Unit. London: Home Office.

Gibbons, D.C. (1971) 'Observations on the study of crime causation', *American Journal of Sociology*, 77: 262–78.

Glaser, D. (1977) 'The compatibility of free will and determinism in criminology: comments on an alleged problem', *Journal of Criminal Law and Criminology* 67: 486–90.

Gould, L.C. (1969) 'The changing structure of property crime in an affluent society', *Social Forces*, 48: 50–9.

Hassal, C. and Trethowan, W.H. (1972) 'Suicide in Birmingham', *British Medical Journal*, 1: 717–18.

Home Office (1979) *Criminal Statistics: England and Wales 1978*. London: HMSO.

Hood, R. and Sparks, R. (1970) *Key Issues in Criminology*. London: Weidenfeld and Nicolson.

Jeffery, C.R. (1971) *Crime Prevention Through Environmental Design*. Beverly Hills, CA: Sage.

Kelling, G.L., Pate, T., Dieckman, D. and Brown C.E. (1974) *The Kansas City Preventive Patrol Experiment*. Washington, DC: Police Foundation.

Ley, D. and Cybrinwsky, R. (1974) 'The spatial ecology of stripped cars', *Environment and Behaviour*, 6: 53–67.

Manning, P. (1977) *Police Work: the Social Organisation of Policing*. London: Massachusetts Institute of Technology Press.

Mansfield, R., Gould, L.C. and Namenwirth, J.Z. (1974) 'A socioeconomic model for the prediction of societal rates of property theft'. *Social Forces*, 52: 462–72.

Matza, D. (1964) *Delinquency and Drift*. New York: John Wiley and Sons.

Mayhew, P. (1977) 'Crime in a man's world', *New Society*, 16 June.

Mayhew, P. (1979) 'Defensible space: the current status of a crime prevention theory', *The Howard Journal of Penology and Crime Prevention*, 18: 150–9.

Mayhew, P., Clarke, R.V.G., Sturman, A. and Hough, J.M. (1976) *Crime as Opportunity*. Home Office Research Study No. 34. London: HMSO.

Mayhew, P., Clarke, R.V.G., Burrows, J.N., Hough, J.M. and Winchester, S.W.C. (1979) *Crime in Public View*. Home Office Research Study No. 49. London: HMSO.

Mischel, W. (1968) *Personality and Assessment*. New York: John Wiley and Sons.

Newman, O. (1973) *Defensible Space: People and Design in the Violent City*. London: Architectural Press.

Ohlin, L.E. (1970) *A Situational Approach to Delinquency Prevention*. Youth Development and Delinquency Prevention Administration. US Department of Health, Education and Welfare.

Parker, H. (1974) *View from the Boys*. Newton Abbot: David and Charles.

Radzinowicz, L. and King, J. (1977) *The Growth of Crime*. London: Hamish Hamilton.

Reppetto, T.A. (1974) *Residential Crime*. Cambridge, MA: Ballinger.

Reppetto, T.A. (1976) 'Crime prevention and the displacement phenomenon', *Crime and Delinquency*, April, 166–77.

Rhodes, R.P. (1977) *The Insoluble Problems of Crime*. New York: John Wiley and Sons.

Ross, L. (1977) 'The intuitive psychologist and his shortcomings: distortions in the attribution process', in L. Berkowitz (ed.), *Advances in Experimental Social Psychology*, Vol. 10. New York: Academic Press.

Scarr, H.A. (1973) *Patterns of Burglary*. US Department of Justice, Washington DC: Government Printing Office.

Taylor, I., Walton, P. and Young, J. (1973) *The New Criminology*. London: Routledge and Kegan Paul.

Tizard, J. (1976) 'Psychology and social policy', *Bulletin of the British Psychological Society*, 29: 225–33.

Trasler, G.B. (1979) 'Delinquency, recidivism, and desistance', *British Journal of Criminology*, 19: 314–22.

Tuck, M. (1979) 'Consumer behaviour theory and the criminal justice system: towards a new strategy of research', *Journal of the Market Research Society*, 21: 44–58.

Walker, N.D. (1979) 'The efficacy and morality of deterrents', *Criminal Law Review*, March, 129–44.

Waller, I. and Okihiro, N. (1978) *Burglary: the Victim and the Public.* Toronto: University of Toronto Press.

Walsh, D.P. (1978) *Shoplifting: Controlling a Major Crime.* London: Macmillan.

Wilkins, L.T. (1964) *Social Deviance.* London: Tavistock.

Wilkinson, P. (1977) *Terrorism and the Liberal State.* London: Macmillan.

Wilson, J.Q. (1975) *Thinking About Crime.* New York: Basic Books.

Wilson, S. (1978) 'Vandalism and "defensible space" on London housing estates', in R.V.G. Clarke, (ed.), *Tackling Vandalism.* Home Office Research Study No. 47. London: HMSO.

Wolfgang, M.E. (1977) 'Real and perceived changes in crime', in S.F. Landau and L. Sebba, (eds), *Criminology in Perspective.* Lexington, MA: Lexington Books.

32

Social crime prevention strategies in a market society

Elliott Currie

[. . .]

All societies make some use of market mechanisms to allocate goods and services. And most of us would acknowledge that the exact determination of what the market does better in this regard and what is best accomplished by other means is often an empirical question. The best balance of private and public is not easy to weigh, and it shifts over time as social needs and technological capacities change. But 'market society', as I will use the term, is a different animal altogether. By market society I mean a society in which the pursuit of private gain increasingly becomes the organizing principle for all areas of social life, not simply a mechanism which we use to accomplish certain circumscribed economic ends. The balance between private and public shifts dramatically, so that the public retreats to a minuscule and disempowered part of social and economic life and the idea of common purposes and common responsibility steadily withers as an important social value.

In market society all other principles of social organization become subordinated to the over-reaching one of private gain. Alternative sources of livelihood, of social support and of cultural value, even of personal identity, become increasingly eroded or obliterated. As a result, individuals, families and communities are more and more dependent on what we somewhat misleadingly call the 'free' market to provide for their human needs, not only material needs but also cultural, symbolic and psychic needs. I say 'somewhat misleadingly' because, as critics have often pointed out, this sort of society – as it is increasingly found in the US, for example – isn't really adequately characterized by the notion of the 'free' market. Economic and social power and the expanded life-chances and opportunities that go with them are not 'free' in the classical Adam Smithian sense of being equally accessible to all who demonstrate sufficient merit, skill and enterprise. Instead, some groups have increasingly been able to protect themselves against the judgement of the economic market

From *International Developments in Crime and Social Policy*, NACRO Crime and Social Policy, pp. 107–20. (London: NACRO, 1991.)

and from the need to perform efficiently at all, while others are subjected to the market's mercies at an ever-accelerating pace.

Now, as I'm using the term, 'market society' is an abstraction, an 'ideal type', and it doesn't, yet, exist anywhere in a pure form. But it has approximations in the real world, both developed and developing, and the United States again has proceeded farther down the road towards market society than any other advanced industrial nation. The UK has, of course, made very considerable efforts in that direction over the past 12 years, but there's still a long way to go before arriving at the evolution of market society we've 'attained'. But something like a broad drift towards market society is increasingly apparent in many other countries across the world. And that's troubling for a variety of reasons but, for our purposes here, specifically because market societies are extraordinarily fertile ground for the growth of crime. I stress again that market society is not the same as the mere existence of a market *economy*. The idea that a serious crime problem is an inevitable accompaniment of a vibrant economy or a free political order is both wrong and pernicious. It is, however, a predictable accompaniment of the growth of market *society*. Why?

Well, let me offer you five propositions about market society's impact on several overlapping areas of social, economic and cultural life which in turn strongly influence the shape and dimensions of the crime problem. (That close overlap is, in fact, what makes the concept of market society helpful in understanding the nature of crime in the industrial societies today. It helps, among other things, to explain why some factors taken individually – say, the unemployment rate, or levels of poverty – may not always fit so well as explanations of crime, an issue much seized upon by some of our conservative colleagues. Looking at the role of these factors through the more holistic perspective offered by the idea of 'market society' helps us understand why poverty, for example, is much more salient for understanding crime in some kinds of societies, at some points in their development, than in others.)
[. . .]

LINKS BETWEEN MARKET SOCIETY AND CRIME

First mechanism

Market society promotes crime by increasing inequality and concentrated economic deprivation.   In the US the rise in violent crime has – not at all unexpectedly from the standpoint of several different lines of criminological theory – gone hand-in-hand with the sharpest rise of economic inequality in our postwar history, the attainment of the widest gap in incomes since we began gathering statistics after the Second World War. In turn, that rising economic inequality in the US can be traced to several related trends.

One is the deterioration of the labour market, both private and public. Throughout the economy, vast numbers of 'middle-level' jobs, especially but not exclusively in blue-collar industry, have disappeared to be replaced by a significant rise in extremely well-rewarded jobs at the top, and a much larger increase in poor jobs, including unstable and part-time ones, at the bottom. This downward shift has been especially destructive to the prospects of younger people. According to data from the US Senate Budget Committee, more than four-fifths of the net new jobs available to young men under 35 during the 1980s paid poverty-level wages or below. In the course of that decade there was a net loss of 1.6 million middle-level jobs available to men of that age group.

This shift in the labour market is not, of course, a matter of the mysterious workings of fate or even of politically neutral changes in technology or demography. It has been driven by deliberate social policy in several ways:

- through the continuing flight of capital and jobs to low-wage havens both in parts of the US itself and, increasingly, overseas, especially to Asia and the Caribbean;
- through the lowering of the real value of the minimum wage, which ensures that new job creation has been overwhelmingly concentrated in poverty-level, low productivity jobs;
- and relatedly, by a more or less conscious policy of achieving profits and staying afloat in the face of international economic competition primarily by lowering wages rather than by increasing the productivity of the workforce and the efficiency of management, what some writers in the US call the deliberate 'dumbing-down' of the labour force.

All of this has resulted in a growing tendency toward what has been called an 'hourglass' income distribution. This tendency is compounded by two other important thrusts of the market-driven social policy of the past fifteen years: the erosion of income support benefits for low-income people and the unemployed, and a pattern of systematically regressive taxation [. . .]

The result of these compounded distributional policies has been to raise the top to unprecedented pinnacles of wealth and of personal consumption, while dropping the poor into a far deeper and more abysmal hole than they were in before, which was already the deepest among advanced industrial societies.

Today we not only have about six million more poor Americans than we did in 1979, but they are much poorer both relative to the affluent and, often, in absolute terms. As the job structure has narrowed and income support shrivelled, it is now far more difficult, as surveys have discovered, for them to get *out*, at least through legitimate means, a fact which is not lost on the urban poor, especially the young.

We are now in real danger of creating something like an economic apartheid and it is by no means just a problem of the so-called, hard-core urban 'underclass', but of an increasingly threatened and declining bottom third of the American population.

Nor are these general trends confined to the US. [. . .] The trend towards growing inequality is increasingly international in scope and international in its consequences. And it is deeply implicated in the pattern of crime.

Second mechanism

Market society promotes crime by weakening the capacity of local communities for 'informal' support, mutual provision and socialization and supervision of the young. This is closely related to the first link: it is, in part, a function of the declining economic security and rising deprivation in low income communities, as well as the rapid movement of capital and accordingly of opportunities for stable work which are hallmarks of the advance of market society.

Under the sustained impact of market forces, communities suffer not only from the long-term loss of stable livelihoods, but also from the excessive geographic mobility that results from that loss. The process is by no means confined to the US; it is central to the experience of many countries and especially many in the developing world and those on the periphery of European prosperity. It is compounded, in the US, by the crisis in housing for low-income people as market forces drive up the cost of shelter at the same time that they drive down wages. The loss of stability of shelter, in turn, helps destroy the basis of local social cohesion.

Communities suffering these compounded stresses begin to exhibit the phenomenon some researchers call 'drain': as the ability of families to support themselves and care for their children drops below a certain critical point, they can no longer sustain those informal networks of social support and help that can otherwise be a buffer against the impact of the economic grinding of the market. If you're having tough times you can't lean on your neighbours or your cousins, even if they still live in the same community, because they're having tough times too; and there are therefore decreasing resources, both emotional and material, to offer to anyone else.

Third mechanism

Market society promotes crime by stressing and fragmenting the family. Again, this is deeply enmeshed with the first and second mechanisms. The growing economic deprivation and community fragmentation characteristic of market society put enormous pressures on family life, and it is partly through these pressures that the growth of market society generates crime.

These connections are many and complex: let me just mention two of them for now, again using the American experience as an example.

First, the long-term economic marginalization of entire communities which characterizes market society tends to inhibit the formation of stable families in the first place – as the sociologist William J. Wilson has powerfully argued for the US case – by diminishing the 'pool' of marriageable men who are seen as capable of achieving a legitimate livelihood that can support a family. The result is to encourage single parenthood and its associated poverty.

But unemployment itself is only one way in which the deterioration of the labour market has affected families. The flip side is overwork in inadequate jobs. Because so much of the employment recently created pays poverty-level wages, great numbers of families, especially young families, can only stay afloat by drastically increasing their hours of work, often taking on two or even three jobs. This is an increasingly common phenomenon in low-income communities in the US and one I've encountered over and over again in working with delinquent kids. [. . .] This has given us a generation of parents, especially young parents and single parents, who have virtually no leisure time and who are (a) constantly stressed to breaking point and (b) absent from the home and the community for most of the time.

It is important not to only blame parents for this. But the results are very real and very troubling. The socializing and nurturing capacities of many families have been seriously compromised and children in America are too often thrown back on their own resources and their own peer groups for guidance, support and supervision.

Again, these mechanisms overlap. The pressure of market forces on community stability aggravates the strains on families. Once upon a time, families facing adverse economic conditions could look to other families in the community for help; parents burdened by overwork could look to informal networks of relatives and friends to help care for children. As market society advances, families are increasingly severed from these informal connections and forced to struggle against the uncertainties and deprivations of the market economy alone. The resulting 'social impoverishment' fuses with economic deprivation and insecurity to produce overwhelming stresses, domestic violence and child abuse. [. . .]

These adverse impacts on families are all the more severe because of the *fourth* link between market society and crime.

Fourth mechanism

Market society promotes crime by withdrawing public provision of basic services for those it has already stripped of livelihoods, economic security and 'informal' communal support. Once again, this process has been most advanced in the US among industrial societies. But we are not alone. Before the advent of the Reagan Administration, the US already stood lowest among several industrial countries in the rate at which public benefits brought families and children out of poverty. We became much more miserly during the 1980s when, for example, our income benefits lifted one in five families out of poverty in 1979; the figure is less than one in nine today, and falling.

Beyond public income support there have been substantial cuts in those public services which could prevent or repair some of the damages inflicted by the compound impacts of economic deprivation, family stress and community breakdown. That process has accelerated enormously in the current fiscal crisis of the 1990s, leading to huge cuts in the kind of preventative health and mental health care that might help intervene with some of the children most 'at risk' of delinquency and drug abuse; a tragic shortfall of effective intervention for families at high risk of child abuse; and a continuing inability to develop nurturing and accessible child care for low-income families whipsawed by low wages and overwork.

All these impacts also must be understood in the light of the fifth link between market society and crime.

Fifth mechanism

Market society promotes crime by magnifying a culture of Darwinian competition for status and dwindling resources and by urging a level of consumption that it cannot fulfil for everyone through legitimate channels. I won't dwell on this now: it's been a recurrent theme in criminological theory. My own favourite exposition of this point is that of the great Dutch criminologist Willem Bonger.

Bonger believed that, 'To make prosperity and culture as general as possible' was the 'best preventive against crime'. But he stressed that he meant 'prosperity, not luxury': for 'There is not a weaker spot to be found in the social development of our times than the ever-growing and ever-intensifying covetousness, which, in its turn, is the result of powerful social forces.' Bonger wrote in the early 1930s; . . . what he would see today in the US and in many parts of the world would surely blow his mind.

A full-blown market culture promotes crime in several ways: by holding out standards of economic status and consumption which increasing numbers of people cannot legitimately meet, and more subtly, by weakening other values more supportive of the intrinsic worth of human life and well-being and of the value of what we might call 'craft', the value of creative work, of productive contribution, of a job well done.

One of the most chilling features of much violent street crime in America today, and also in some developing countries, is how directly it expresses the logic of immediate gratification in the pursuit of consumer goods, or of instant status and recognition. Some of our delinquents will cheerfully acknowledge that they blew someone away for their running shoes or because they made the mistake of looking at them disrespectfully on the street. People who study crime, perhaps especially from a 'progressive' perspective, sometimes shy away from looking hard at these less tangible 'moral' aspects. In the US we are certainly witnessing a kind of demoralization that must be acknowledged and confronted if we wish to understand crime today. [. . .] The point is not simply to bemoan the ascendancy of those values among some of the urban young, but to recognize that they are, as Bonger said, the 'result of powerful social forces', a direct and unmediated reflection of the inner logic of market society, part of the total package that we must be prepared to accept if we accept that package at all.

There are other links as well between the growth of market society, market culture and crime. A full analysis of those connections would need to consider, for example, the impact on crime of the specifically psychological distortions of market society, its tendency to produce personalities less and less capable of relating to others except as consumer items or as trophies in a quest for recognition among one's peers. And we need also to consider the long-term political impacts of market society that are related to crime, in particular its tendency to weaken and erode the alternative political means by which those who are victimized by destructive social and economic policies might express their frustration and their desperation in transformative rather than predatory ways. And, finally, the ways of market society also magnify the opportunities for white-collar crime and may simultaneously minimize the seriousness of the governmental response to it.

It is not, then, simply by increasing one or another specific social ill that market policies stimulate crime: it's when you put them together that the effects emerge in full force. But that is precisely what market society does. The growth of market society is a multifaceted process which is at its core destructive of the economic, social and cultural requisites of social peace and personal security.

KEY STRATEGIES

To me these developments point directly to some key strategies that ought to be essential parts of our approach to social crime prevention in the 1990s and in the next century. I will only point to three 'macro' and, briefly, three 'micro' strategies which I believe are especially critical in the face of these global transformations.

The three 'macro' policies are central because they directly attack the growing inequality in the emerging market society. There is much we can do by way of crime prevention without them but we will most certainly be swimming upstream.

First, and I believe central to much else, genuinely social crime prevention strategy requires a supportive labour market policy – what in Scandinavia is called an 'active' labour market policy which seeks to provide all citizens with both the competence and skills to participate in the necessary work of the larger society *and* concrete opportunities to put those skills to work. This necessarily involves a substantial role for the public sector – a deliberate and unapologetic use of public resources not merely to train the labour force for hoped-for jobs in the private sector, but also to create dignified public and non-profit jobs in areas of pressing social need.

One of the most wistfully myopic economic ideas of our time is the belief that an adequate supply of such good, stable jobs, of the kind that can provide a sense of membership in a productive community and the livelihood to support a family in dignity and security, will flow automatically from the normal operation of the private market if we just leave that market alone. Our American pundits, in particular, are much given to expressing confidence that the massive levels of unemployment and subemployment in the US, in the Third World and, increasingly, in some countries of Eastern Europe are simply 'transitional', and they will go away once the market has been left alone long enough to work its magic. The trouble is, of course, that we've already been waiting for generations for that transition to be over in Harlem and Appalachia and Detroit, not to mention San Paulo and San Juan.

Now don't get me wrong. The idea that the private market unaided will provide dignified and meaningful employment for all is a delightful and soothing idea. I too would like to believe it because it would make life, and social policy, a great deal easier. The hard reality is that the long-term tendency of the unaided market is to sharply divide societies into those who have and those who do not have access to stable and rewarding work. The lesson of both historical experience and careful research is abundantly clear. Those countries that have managed to maintain full and dignified human resources are those that have taken on a deliberate, active national commitment to full employment and comprehensive training, usually including the strategic use of public sector employment. The countries that have recently done the worst in this regard, including the US and the UK, have on the contrary worked to dismantle much of the public employment and training system they once had. That strategy flies in the face of everything we know about human resources and economic productivity: it is foolish, self-defeating, counterproductive, and expensive.

Exactly what such an active labour market policy should look like will vary in different countries. Some, of course, including Sweden and, in its' own way, Japan, have already committed themselves to remarkably effective full employment strategies. In the US, it translates into the crying need for a national commitment to publicly supported, community-oriented job creation, especially in the provision of those critical needs of the social and physical infrastructure that have been sorely neglected or systematically attacked for many years. With that kind of strategy we will kill several birds with one stone. We rebuild that eroded social and material infrastructure in health care, housing, community amenities and we also create an economic base that can serve as the catalyst for overall economic development in communities that the private market has essentially abandoned. And we also provide a whole spectrum of new and genuinely challenging opportunities for respected work and community contribution for young people now lured by the very genuine challenges of high-risk delinquency and the drug culture.

Secondly, a long-term approach to social crime prevention also requires a concerted, unapologetic strategy to reduce extremes of social and economic inequality by upgrading earnings and public benefits and services for low-income people both in and out of the paid labour force. This is complementary to an active labour market policy and is precisely the opposite of what many governments have lately been doing in the name of freeing the 'free market'.

I've suggested that one of the links between market society and crime lies in the stripping away of public services and supports which is today routinely justified in the name of a supposedly beneficial privatization of public functions. But the long-term result, which we see increasingly in the US, is that we are now perilously close to creating two distinct classes of citizenship. On one side are those who by virtue of their connection with the stable part of the labour force can afford what are increasingly private, and increasingly expensive, fundamentals of social life, from health care to housing to education. Those essentials are today more often tied to high-wage employment and are frequently part of the fruits of the 'semi-private welfare state' that has grown up to serve the well-employed. But on the other side are those who are condemned to scramble after the shrinking and increasingly inadequate vestiges of public provision for these needs.

In place of that trend toward two classes of citizenship, we need to counterpose what might be thought of as a post-industrial version of the 'basic needs' strategy often advocated for developing countries. We need to insist that it is society's *first* responsibility, not its last and most expendable, to ensure equal access to those institutions which allow for competent, healthy and respected citizenship: and that means an unshakeable national-level commitment to public health care for all, quality public education and the guarantee of dignified shelter as well as adequate and non-demeaning income benefits for those out of the paid labour force. This, of course, requires the existence of an active labour market policy, because without a productive and an employed labour force you cannot support universally accessible, high-quality public services or generous social benefits.

Meanwhile, for those in that paid labour force, we need likewise to reverse the dramatic present trend toward earnings inequality, especially the growth of what the Senate Budget Committee study in the US calls 'wage impoverishment' at the lower end of the scale. This means a commitment to steadily rising minimum wages. But beyond establishing a minimum floor on earnings, we also need to move in the long run toward what the Scandinavians call a 'solidaristic' wage policy, one that is explicitly aimed at reducing earnings inequality throughout the workforce.

This strategy should explicitly include an effort to reduce the gaps in the earnings of men and women. We have not yet talked much about gender issues, but we should. The low earnings of women are deeply implicated in crime in a variety of complex ways of which only the most obvious is the way they encourage violence against women in the home. As long as women's capacity for self-support is compromised by poor wages – and meagre benefits – then they are especially vulnerable to being trapped in abusive and violent relationships with men, as are their children. Increasing women's economic independence would go a very long way toward reducing the massive tragedy of family violence especially in countries like the US and many in the developing world where violence against women and children is very high and women's overall economic condition is very low. Not to mention the benefits of making greater resources available for poor children, great numbers of whom are growing up in families maintained by women.

Measures like these, designed to reduce inequality and promote competent citizenship, have been systematically attacked by conservative governments around the world on the grounds that they interfere with the market and thereby hinder economic efficiency. Yet nothing could be farther from reality. Again, the lessons of both research and experience are crystal clear. Healthy, well-educated, competent and self-confident citizens are what makes an economy work. The state of the United States economy, today, I'm afraid, is a tragic demonstration of what happens when that lesson is ignored.

Thirdly, we should work internationally toward an active, supportive child and family policy, one that firmly and unapologetically puts the needs of families and children for adequate furtherance, time and income above the private pursuit of material gain.

The two strategies I've already suggested – an active labour market policy and a concerted attack on the widening inequalities of wages and benefits – are in themselves two of the most important elements of that kind of supportive family policy.

But more is needed as well. In particular, we need strategies to reduce the sharp and in many countries growing conflicts between family and work. That means (1) freeing up time from work for parents to be with their children through generous family and parental leave policies and (2) putting in place a high-quality accessible child care system for working families.

In the US, both of these have been fought tooth and nail by the private business community. Here we are far behind some European countries like Sweden or France. In the US, our stunningly timid legislative effort to provide six weeks of unpaid parental leave at the birth of a child has been successfully resisted for years by the business community and its political allies. Once again, that resistance has been justified, fantastically, in the name of economic efficiency. But the reality is that our failure to develop policies to reduce the intolerable work-related stresses of families amounts to a massive, covert subsidy to private business in that it requires the rest of us to pay in the long run for the consequences of the resulting economic strains on families; consequences including child abuse, delinquency, mental illness and a mushrooming expenditure for the remedial programmes to contain them.

The long-range vision behind all three proposals and others is to progressively replace what I've called 'market society' with what I'll call a 'sustaining' society.

That kind of vision calls for creative programmes on the 'micro' level as well, on the close-in level of working directly with individuals and families who've been made most vulnerable by the massive changes now reshaping our societies. For now, I'll only mention briefly three kinds of interventions that I think, on the evidence, must be among the most urgent in a truly effective strategy of social crime prevention: (a) comprehensive child and family support programmes; (b) a youth intervention strategy that focuses on the expansion of tangible opportunities; and (c) a 'user-friendly' approach to drug abuse prevention and treatment.

First, [we need] a comprehensive 'package' of child and family interventions that emphasizes (1) the prevention of child abuse, (2) the provision of early childhood education and (3) of a wide range of supports for parents in coping with the real-world stresses in their communities. [. . .] Let me focus on child abuse and neglect prevention for a moment. In the US, and I think in many other countries as well, there's been a tendency for the people who deal with child abuse and neglect to be different from, and unconnected with, those who deal with crime policy. Child abuse thus becomes somebody else's problem, and it is not, at least where I come from, taken very seriously, certainly not as an integral part of a strategy of social crime prevention. But that's a mistake. Where serious violent crime is concerned, I'm increasingly convinced of the critical role of abusive, neglectful, harshly punitive childhood experiences. Our experience in the US does not suggest a simple pro-grammatic response that can be replicated in cookie-cutter fashion, but it does point to successful programmes that show promise. One is hands-on work with high-risk parents from pre-natal period, following them up from birth with counselling on child-rearing methods, home visits, and help with day care, health care and trans-portation. Another is comprehensive family support programmes of a kind now springing up across the US, that offer high-risk families the tangible help they need to take better care of their children: better knowledge about child-rearing, support groups of other parents in similar conditions, and help in securing the necessities – health care for themselves and their children, housing, income support. These are best delivered in a comprehensive setting that is community-based and culturally sensitive.

Secondly, we need a comprehensive youth intervention strategy. Again, many of the disruptive changes now affecting societies across the world are having their most profound and alienating effect on young people. I'm convinced that the single most important part of a youth strategy is the active labour market policy I spoke of already, for without it we are frankly condemning vast numbers of young men and women around the world to a bleak and uncertain life on the periphery of purposive society. But we also need more specific interventions to work with the young at highest risk. But here, perhaps even more than in other areas of social policy, it is terribly important to separate wheat from chaff and there is a great deal of chaff in the world of youth policy, certainly in the US. There is some tendency to see any youth programme that isn't prison as a worthy endeavour and to tout programmes that are poorly evaluated and theoretically weak as saviours of inner-city youth or, at best, to over-promise on the capacity of very minor interventions to make a big difference in the lives of kids who face very real and profound deprivations.

I believe the accumulating evidence strongly suggests that the youth-oriented strategies that work best are those which actually provide changed lives, that offer new and expanded possibilities for young people where few existed before. I think that what our programme experience in the US shows most clearly is that if you simply try to offer social services of various kinds to youth without changing their probable futures, without genuinely altering their realistic trajectory in life, then you are probably not going to make much of a difference. You are not going to wean many kids away from drug and alcohol abuse, away from the distinct and very powerful appeal of some kinds of delinquency, away from the comradeship and satisfaction that they can find in gangs.

But much of our debate on youth policy, such as it is, in the US today is stuck on the level at best of what I'd call a 'service' strategy of the kind we have recurrently tried, without much success, at various periods since the nineteenth century. In turn, this strategy is typically based on what I've called a 'deficiency' model of delin-quency. In a nutshell, the deficiency model assumes that the problem is some lack or deficit within the young person which needs fixing, or filling; we then design some service to patch it. But two years of intensive interviewing of delinquent kids has convinced me that for most American delinquents, extreme cases aside, far more critical than any such internal deficits is the rapidly shrinking opportunity for them to make legitimate use of the strengths and capacities they already have – a problem greatly exacerbated by the 'dumbing-down' of the economy I spoke of earlier. Quite simply, the kids often have far more skill than the increasingly constricted labour markets allow them to use in legitimate ways; delinquency allows them to *be* more than the straight world can.

To me, this suggests the usefulness of what I'd call an 'opportunity model' of intervention in place of the 'deficiency model' and that is supported by my reading of what works best in the youth programmes we've tried in the US – serious and intensive skills training programmes, such as the Job Corps, which actually provide usable formal skills; or the equally tangible opportunities by a programme like Eugene Lang's 'I Have a Dream', which guarantees college tuition for disadvantaged kids who stay in school. These have among the most consistently encouraging evaluations, and I think that's no accident.

Thirdly, similar considerations apply to a third area of priority, what I'd call 'user-friendly' drug and alcohol assistance. Today in the US, where of course the drug-crime problem is worst, the debate about drugs is now mainly between those who continue to push for more incarceration and harsher penalties for drug users and dealers, versus those who push for more conventional 'treatment'. But I don't think *either* path is the right one.

Like our approach to delinquency, our drug intervention strategies are often rooted in a model which is almost schizophrenically divorced from what the evidence tells us about the causes of the problem. In the US, the model typically underlying drug treatment efforts is some version of an individual medical or psychiatric model. Yet the accumulating research tells us over and over again that mass drug abuse of the kind that is now endemic in many American (and some British) communities is driven less by any identifiable pharmacological or psychological needs than by the systematic, long-term blockage of opportunities and the often overwhelmingly stressful and depriving conditions of life in communities suffering from multiple economic and social deprivation. This is a syndrome that is deepening with the advance of market society, here in Britain as in the US. [. . .]

We need to rethink treatment as well as expand it. Our current models of treatment tend to assume that addiction is a medical condition, rather like a broken leg or a kidney infection; it is not. People don't catch it and then want to come in and fix it. We're learning that addiction has less to do with the physical properties of the drugs themselves than with the barriers to alternative ways of achieving gratification, status, structure and esteem. The lesson too little heeded is that interventions should be tailored accordingly; they should be oriented more closely to the social context of addiction; should help abusers move away successfully from the drug cultures in which they're enmeshed; open realistic opportunities for stable employment, and offer help with starting and maintaining strong relationships and family ties which the research increasingly tells us is key to successfully moving away from drugs.

In turn, this means making drug programmes more 'user-friendly', in particular addressing the specific needs of groups who are now, at least in the US, largely left out or alienated by conventional treatment including teenagers, women and some minority groups. Much of our conventional treatment in the US is actually user-hostile to those critically important potential clients. It is shaped by what are essentially middle-class, male, adult and psychological models and assumptions, often relying on invasive group therapies based on a kind of 'encounter' model that appeals at best to a sliver of the drug-abusing population, which is why the great majority of that population is not in treatment. We especially need youth-supportive drug programmes that are capable of attracting the young rather than alienating them. Ideally, these ought to be part of a broader commitment to community-based, comprehensive adolescent health-care services that also engage problems of risk-taking behaviour, violence and sexually transmitted disease. Similarly, many treatment programmes for women will not even take pregnant women, much less address the crucial real-world issues many addicted women present; issues of child care, housing, poor employment and relationships with abusive men. These are just three specific directions but there are many more.

[. . .]

What all this means is that real social crime prevention, like the prevention of other social ills, is now more than ever dependent on our capacity to build more effective movements for social action and social change. These movements should challenge effectively those forces dimming the life chances of vast numbers of people in the developed and developing worlds. Building organisations should be committed to the long-range effort to replace a society based increasingly on the least inspiring of human values with one based on the principles of social solidarity and contributive justice.

[. . .]

33

Abolitionism and crime control

Willem De Haan

An abolitionist perspective on crime control might seem like a contradiction in terms not unlike a peace research approach to waging a war. Abolitionism is based on the moral conviction that social life should not and, in fact, cannot be regulated effectively by criminal law and that, therefore, the role of the criminal justice system should be drastically reduced while other ways of dealing with problematic situations, behaviours and events are being developed and put into practice. Abolitionists regard crime primarily as the result of the social order and are convinced that punishment is not the appropriate reaction. Instead a minimum of coercion and interference with the personal lives of those involved and a maximum amount of care and service for all members of society is advocated.

 The term 'abolitionism' stands for a social movement, a theoretical perspective and a political strategy. As a social movement committed to the abolition of the prison or even the entire penal system, abolitionism originated in campaigns for prisoners' rights and penal reform. Subsequently, it developed into a critical theory and praxis concerning crime, punishment and penal reform. As a theoretical perspective, abolitionism takes on the two-fold task of providing a radical critique of the criminal justice system while showing that there are other, more rational ways of dealing with crime. As a political strategy, abolitionism is based on an analysis of penal reform and restricted to negative reforms, such as abolishing parts of the prison system, rather than providing concrete alternatives.

[. . .] [T]he abolitionist perspective will be discussed along the lines of this distinction. First, we will deal with abolitionism as a penal reform movement, then as a theoretical perspective on crime and punishment and, more specifically, the prison. Next, a conceptualization of the notions of crime and punishment will be offered in the form of the concept of redress. At the same time, strategies for penal reform will be examined. Finally, the implications of the abolitionist perspective for crime control will be discussed. In conclusion, it will be argued that what is needed is a wide variety of social responses rather than a uniform state reaction to the problem of crime. In policy terms it is claimed that social policy instead of crime policy is

From *The Politics of Crime Control* (eds K. Stenson and D. Cowell), pp. 203–17. (London: Sage, 1991.)

needed in dealing with the social problems and conflicts that are currently singled out as the problem of crime.

ABOLITIONISM AS A SOCIAL MOVEMENT

Abolitionism emerged as an anti-prison movement when, at the end of the 1960s, a destructuring impulse took hold of thinking about the social control of deviance and crime among other areas (Cohen, 1985). In Western Europe, anti-prison groups aiming at prison abolition were founded in Sweden and Denmark (1967) Finland and Norway (1968), Great Britain (1970), France (1970), and the Netherlands (1971). Their main objective was to soften the suffering which society inflicts on its prisoners. This implied a change in general thinking concerning punishment, humanization of the various forms of imprisonment in the short run and, in the long run, the replacement of the prison system by more adequate and up-to-date measures of crime control.

It has been suggested that abolitionism typically emerged in small countries or countries with little crime and 'would never have been "invented" in a country like the United States of America with its enormous crime rate, violence, and criminal justice apparatus' (Scheerer, 1986: 18). However, in Canada and the United States family members of (ex-)convicts, church groups and individuals were also engaged in prisoners' support work and actively struggling for prison reform. More specifically, these prison abolitionists in the United States considered their struggle for abolition of prisons to be a historical mission, a continuation and fulfilment of the struggle against slavery waged by their forebears. Imprisonment is seen as a form of blasphemy, as morally objectionable and indefensible and, therefore, to be abolished (Morris, 1976: 11). To this aim, a long-term strategy in the form of a three-step 'attrition model' is proposed, consisting of a total freeze on the planning and building of prisons, excarceration of certain categories of lawbreakers by diverting them from the prison system and decarceration, or the release of as many inmates as possible.

Originating in prison reform movements in the 1960s and 1970s in both Western Europe and North America, abolitionism developed as a new paradigm in (critical) criminology and as an alternative approach to crime control. As academic involvement increased and abolitionism became a theoretical perspective, its focus widened from the prison system to the penal system, thereby engaging in critical analyses of penal discourse and, in particular, the concepts of crime and punishment, penal practices, and the penal or criminal justice system.

ABOLITIONISM AS A THEORETICAL PERSPECTIVE

As a theoretical perspective abolitionism has a negative and a positive side. Negatively, abolitionism is deeply rooted in a criticism of the criminal justice system and its 'prison solution' to the problem of crime. Positively, on the basis of this criticism an alternative approach to crime and punishment is offered both in theory and in practice. Thus, the abolitionist approach is essentially reflexive and (de)constructivist. We will first take a look at the negative side of abolitionism which will be followed by a brief exposé of its positive side.

From the abolitionist point of view, the criminal justice system's claim to protect people from being victimized by preventing and controlling crime, seems grossly exaggerated. Moreover, the notion of controlling crime by penal intervention is ethically problematic as people are used for the purpose of 'deterrence', by demonstrating power and domination. Punishment is seen as a self-reproducing form of violence. The penal practice of blaming people for their supposed intentions (for being bad and then punishing and degrading them accordingly) is dangerous because the social conditions for recidivism are thus reproduced. Morally degrading and segregating people is especially risky when the logic of exclusion is reinforced along the lines of differences in sex, race, class, culture or religion.

For the abolitionist, current crime policies are irrational in their assumptions that: crime is caused by individuals who for some reason go wrong; that crime is a problem for the state and its criminal justice system to control; and that criminal law and punishment or treatment of individual wrongdoers are appropriate means of crime control (Steinert, 1986). Crime control is based on the fallacy of taking *pars pro toto* or, as Wilkins (1984) has put it, crime control policy is typically made by reference to the dramatic incident, thereby assuming that all that is necessary is to get the micro-model right in order for the macro-model to follow without further ado. According to Wilkins, we must consider not only the specific criminal act but also the environment in which it is embedded. It could be added that the same argument holds for punishment and, more specifically, for imprisonment as an alleged solution to the problem of crime.

ABOLITIONISM ABOUT PRISON

For abolitionists, the United States is a prime example of a country suffering from the consequences of a punitive obsession. In the course of a 'get tough' policy of crime control, increasing numbers of people are being sent to prison for longer periods of time. As a result, the prison population in the United States has increased dramatically from roughly 350,000 in the 1970s to 850,000 at the end of the 1980s. Almost 80 per cent of the recent increase in prison admissions is accounted for by drugs offenders. By September 1988 about 44 per cent of all federal prisoners were incarcerated for drug law violations. According to the 1989 National Council of Crime and Delinquency Prison Population Forecast the impact of the 'war on drugs' will be yet another increase of the prison population 1989–1994 by over 68 per cent to a total of 1,133,000 prisoners among whom people of colour will remain strongly over-represented. With an incarceration rate of 440 prisoners per 100,000 population, the United States will more than consolidate its top rank position in the world. Even with its incarceration rate increasing from about 30 in 1980 to about 50 in the mid-1990s, the Netherlands will remain at the bottom end of the scale. At the same time, the crime problem in the Netherlands can hardly be considered worse than in the United States.

As in the United States, 'street crime' is also considered a major social problem in the Netherlands. In fact, the first International Crime Survey (van Dijk et al., 1990) showed that overall victimization rates 1983–1988 in the United States and the Netherlands were higher than in any other country in the survey. However, there were considerable differences both in the seriousness of the crime problem and the effectiveness of its control. Whereas overall victimization rates in the Netherlands and the United States were similarly high, in the Dutch case this was strongly influenced by the extraordinarily high prevalence of bicycle theft, whereas victim- ization rates for homicide, robbery and (sexual) assault were particularly high in the United States.

If anything, this proves that the relationship between crime and crime control by imprisonment is much more complex than proponents of the prison solution seem to assume. In terms of protection the 'get tough' approach to crime control has little to offer, and the 'war on drugs' can never be won but has serious repercussions.

Taken together, the prison system is counter-productive, difficult to control, and itself a major social problem. Therefore, abolitionists have given up entirely on the idea that the criminal justice system has anything to offer in terms of protection. They are also pessimistic about the criminal law's potential for conflict resolution. It is felt that the present penal system is making things worse, not better.

In the course of the 'war against drugs' which is currently being waged in the United States and many other countries around the world, the use of ethically problematic techniques for apprehending suspects is being condoned if not required. As a result various forms of organizational complicity undermine the already waning legitimacy of the criminal justice system even further. According to Roshier (1989), the 'war against drugs' must be seen as a forced attempt to reach efficiency in the field of law enforcement or, at least, the appearance of it by using purely technical or even military means of surveillance and policing. It is the criminal justice system that defines, selects, documents and disposes of crime. As a result, legal definitions of suspicion, criminal offence etc., are being stretched. Thus, the criminal justice system itself increasingly specifies both the nature of the crime problem and what is to be done about it (Roshier, 1989: 128).

Thus, the criminal justice system is part of the crime problem rather than its solution. Not only does it fail to work in terms of its own stated goals and not only are the negative consequences of the infliction of suffering by the state threatening to get out of hand but, more importantly, it is based on a fundamentally flawed way of understanding. Therefore, there is no point in trying to make the criminal justice system more effective or more just. The abolitionist critique of the criminal justice system and its approach to crime control may be summarized by saying that if this is the solution, what is the problem? Or, put differently, crime as a social problem and object of social analysis needs to be rethought.

ABOLITIONISM ABOUT 'CRIME'

The current approach to crime control, the definition of crime and the justification of punishment is 'systemic', that is, based on an instrumentalist point of view and confined within the limits of the criminal justice system. From an abolitionist point of view, these issues require a fundamental reconceptualization in a broader social context. This is where the alternative, positive side of abolitionism starts from. Abolitionists argue that there is no such thing as 'crime'. In fact, 'the very form of criminal law, with its conception of "crime" (not just the contents of what is at a given time and place defined into that category, but the category itself) and the ideas on what is to be done about it, are historical "inventions"' (Steinert, 1986: 26).

'Crime' is a social construction, to be analysed as a myth of everyday life (Hess, 1986). As a myth, crime serves to maintain political power relations and lends legitimacy to the expansion of the crime control apparatus and the intensification of surveillance and control. It justifies inequality and relative deprivation. Public attention is distracted from more serious problems and injustices. Thus, the bigger the social problems are, the greater the need for the crime myth (Hess, 1986: 24–5).

However, not only should the concept of crime be discarded (Hulsman, 1986), but we need to get rid of the theories of crime as well. As Quensel (1987) has pointed out, theories about 'crime' acquire their plausibility largely by virtue of their building on and, at the same time, reinforcing an already-present 'deep structure'. One element of this 'deep structure' is the notion that 'crime' is inherently dangerous and wicked; another is that crime control is a 'value-inspired' call for action against that evil (p. 129).

Abolitionists argue that the crucial problem is not explaining but rather understanding crime as a social event. Thus, what we need is not a better theory of crime, but a more powerful critique of crime. This is not to deny that there are all sorts of unfortunate events, more or less serious troubles or conflicts which can result in suffering, harm, or damage to a greater or lesser degree. These troubles are to be taken seriously, of course, but not as 'crimes' and, in any case, they should not be dealt with by means of criminal law. When we fully appreciate the complexity of a 'crime' as a socially constructed phenomenon any simplified reaction to crime in the form of punishment becomes problematic.

Spector (1981) has argued that when a person offends, disturbs, or injures other people, various forms of social disapproval exist to remedy the situation. The matter may be treated as a disease, a sin, or, indeed, as a crime. However, other responses are also feasible, like considering the case as a private conflict between the offender and the victim or defining the situation in an administrative way and responding, for example by denial of a licence, permit, benefit or compensation. Our images, language, categories, knowledge, beliefs and fears of troublemakers are subject to constant changes. Nevertheless, crime continues to occupy a central place in our thinking about troublesome people (1981: 154). Spector suggests that, perhaps, 'we pay too much attention to crime because the disciplines that study trouble and disapprove – sociology and criminology – were born precisely in the era when crime was at its zenith' (Quensel, 1987; Spector, 1981).

The concept of 'crime' figures prominently in common sense and has definite effects on it. By focusing public attention on a definite class of events, these 'crimes' can then be almost automatically seen as meriting punitive control. 'Punishment' is thereby regarded as the obvious and proper reaction to 'crime'.

ABOLITIONISM ABOUT PUNISHMENT

Abolitionists do not share the current belief in the criminal law's capacity for crime control. They radically deny the utility of punishment and claim that there can be no valid justification for it, particularly since other options are available for law enforcement. They discard criminal justice as an absurd idea. It is ridiculous to claim that one pain can or, indeed, ought to be compensated by another state-inflicted one. According to them, the 'prison solution' affects the moral quality of life in society at large. Therefore, the criminal justice perspective needs to be replaced by an orientation towards all avoidance of harm and pain (Steinert, 1986: 25). Christie (1982), particularly, has attacked the traditional justifications for punishment. He criticizes deterrence theory for its sloppy definitions of concepts, its immunity to challenge, and for the fact that it gives the routine process of punishment a false legitimacy in an epoch where the infliction of pain might otherwise have appeared problematic. The neo-classicism of the justice model is also criticized: punishment is justified and objectified, the criminal is blamed, the victim is ignored, a broad conception of justice is lacking, and a 'hidden message' is transmitted which denies legitimacy to a whole series of alternatives which should, in fact, be taken into consideration. However, Christie not only criticizes the 'supposed justifications' for punishment, but also claims a decidedly moral position with regard to punishment, which is the intentional infliction of pain which he calls 'moral rigorism'. He deliberately co-opts the terms 'moralism' and 'rigorism' associated primarily with protagonists of 'law and order' and more severe penal sanctions. His 'rigorist' position, however, is that there is no reason to believe that the recent level of pain infliction is the right or natural one and that there is no other defensible position than to strive for a reduction of man-inflicted pain on earth. Since punishment is defined as pain, limiting pain means an automatic reduction of punishment.

More recently, Christie and Mathiesen have both suggested that the expansion of the prison system involves general ethical and political questions such as what could be the effects of all the punishments taken together? What would constitute an acceptable level of punishment in society? What would be the right prison population within a country? How should we treat fellow human beings? And, last but not least, how do we want to meet the crime problem (Christie, 1986; Mathiesen, 1986)?

However, in common-sense and legal discourse alike, 'crime' and 'punishment' continue to be seen 'as independent species – without reference to their sameness or how continuity of both depends on the character of dominating institutions' (Kennedy, 1974: 107). It should be kept in mind, however, that crime comprises but one of several kinds of all norm violations, that punishment is but one of many kinds of reprisals against such violations, that criteria for separating them refer to phenomena external to actual behaviours classed by legal procedure as crime versus punishment, and that even within the criminal law itself, the criteria by which crime is identified procedurally apply with equal validity to punishment (Kennedy, 1974: 108).

Criminology needs to rid itself of those theories of punishment which assume there are universal qualities in forms of punishment or assume a straightforward connection between crime and punishment. Given the perseverance of this conventional notion of 'punishment' as essentially a 'good' against an 'evil', any effort at changing common-sense notions of 'crime' and 'crime control' requires a reconceptualization of both concepts: 'crime' and 'punishment'.

REDRESS

We need to concern ourselves with the interrelationship and combined effects of crime and punishment. Crime and punishment are closely related with 'social negativity' (Baratta, 1986), destructive developments within contemporary society, in particular, as they affect its already most vulnerable members. In order to formulate a convincing politics of penal reform, crime and punishment should not be seen as action and reaction, but as spiralling cycles of harm (Pepinsky, 1986).

Elsewhere, I have introduced the concept of 'redress' as an alternative to both the concepts of 'punishment' and 'crime' (de Haan, 1990). This seemingly 'obsolete' concept carries an elaborate set of different meanings. The *Concise Oxford Dictionary* offers a wide variety of meanings for 'redress': for instance, to put right or in good order again, to remedy or remove trouble of any kind, to set right, repair, rectify something suffered or complained of like a wrong, to correct, amend, reform or do away with a bad or faulty state of things, to repair an action, to atone a misdeed or offence, to save, deliver from misery, to restore or bring back a person to a proper state, to happiness or prosperity, to the right course, to set a person right by obtaining or (more rarely) giving satisfaction or compensation for the wrong or loss sustained, teaching, instructing and redressing the erroneous by reason (Sixth Edition, 1976: 937).

To claim redress is merely to assert that an undesirable event has taken place and that something needs to be done about it. It carries no implications concerning what sort of reaction would be appropriate; nor does it define reflexively the nature of the initial event. Since claiming redress invites an open discussion about how an unfortunate event should be viewed and what the appropriate response ought to be, it can be viewed as a rational response par excellence. It puts forth the claim for a procedure rather than for a specific result. Punitive claims already implied in defining an event as a 'crime' are opened up to rational debate. Thus, to advocate 'redress' is to call for 'real dialogue' (Christie, 1982). Christie has suggested that social systems be constructed in ways that 'crimes' are more easily seen as expressions of conflicting interests, thereby becoming a starting-point for a 'real dialogue' (1982: 11).

The conceptual innovation suggested here offers a perspective for a politics of redress, aimed at the construction and implementation of procedures along the lines of an ethic of practical discourse. As we have seen, the handling of normative conflicts by rational discourse presupposes other procedures than the present criminal ones. In order to increase chances for participation for those involved, procedures based on the rules and preconditions of rational discourse would, therefore, need to be established outside the realm of criminal law; that is in civil law or even in the life world itself. Instead of the panacea which the criminal justice system pretends to provide for problems of crime control, abolitionism seeks to remedy social problems, conflicts, or troubles within the context of the real world, taking seriously the experiences of those directly involved and taking into account too the diversity which is inherent [in] the social world. The aim of a politics of redress would be to 'arrange it so that the conflict settling mechanisms themselves, through their organization reflect the type of society we should like to see reflected and help this type of society come into being' (Christie, 1982: 113). Social problems or conflicts might be absorbed in order to use them as valuable aids to the social integration of real life and the prevention of social harm.

Abolitionism assumes that social problems or conflicts are unavoidable as they are inherent to social life as such. Therefore, they will have to be dealt with in one way or another. Rather than delegating them to professional specialists, however, they should be dealt with under conditions of mutuality and solidarity. These very conditions will have to be created by social and political action.

The urgent question that remains, of course, is how this might be done. To begin with, no single solution to the problem should be expected. Taking into account the diversity of relevant social phenomena requires the development of a wide variety of forms of social regulation which are not located in or defined by the state but operate (semi-)autonomously as alternative, progressive and emancipatory forms of dispute settlement and conflict resolution.

In reaction to the deeply felt dissatisfaction with the present penal system and, more generally, with the legal system, we see an increasing interest in 'autonomous' forms of conflict resolution and dispute settlement. Other 'styles of social control' (Black, 1976: 4–5) are seen as attractive, promising to provide the parties involved with more chances for participation in settling a dispute or problem. The aim is compensation rather than retaliation; reconciliation rather than blame allocation. To this end, the criminal justice system needs to be decentralized and neighbourhood courts established as a complement or substitute.

The development of alternative procedures for conflict resolution and dispute settlement faces some rather ticklish questions which have proved intractable in current debates, questions concerning voluntarism versus determinism, 'account-ability', 'responsibility' and 'guilt', that is, the moral evaluation of behaviour, the fair allocation of blame and the proper dissemination of consequences. Emphasis on participatory processes of definition or the contextuality of conflicts may be wel-come, but it can also lead to problematic outcomes. Among the wide variety of reactions the notion of redress entails there might be sanctions which need to be subjected to legal principles and restraints. For these reasons, legal form is still required to ensure fairness. Just as we need sociological imagination to ensure an open discussion, we need legal imagination to be able to put an end to potentially endless debates as well as allow for the possibility of appeal.

However, by allowing for more complexity in the interpretation of social behaviour, social situations and events, the simplistic image of human beings and their activities currently employed in criminal law and reproduced in criminal justice could be avoided. Through contextualization, the dichotomized character of criminal justice (Christie, 1986: 96) could be replaced with a continuum. Participants would be urged to confront and grapple with complexities around notions of human 'agency', 'intentionality', 'responsibility' and 'guilt' rather than reducing them to manageable proportions by applying the binary logic of criminal law. By dropping the simplistic dichotomies of the criminal law and allowing for differential meanings, justice might finally be done to the complexity of human actions and social events. Such a discourse would feature a concept of 'social responsibility' allowing for interpretations which primarily blame social systems rather than individuals (Christie, 1986: 97).

ABOLITIONISM AS A POLITICAL STRATEGY

Initially, a political strategy had been developed on the bases of the experiences of prison reform groups in their political struggle for penal and social reform. This 'politics of abolition' (Mathiesen, 1974, 1986) consistently refuses to offer 'positive' alternatives or solutions. It restricts itself to advancing open-ended, 'unfinished', 'negative' reforms, such as abolishing parts of the prison system. This requires that they be conceptualized in terms alien to current criminal justice discourse.

More recently, positive alternatives to punishment are also being considered. Various proposals have been made by abolitionists and others to decentralize or even completely dismantle the present penal system in order to create forms of 'informal justice' as an addition to or replacement of the present criminal justice system.

Their implementation also raises many questions, however, concerning allegations about widening the net of social control and, at the same time, thinning the mesh, extending and blurring the boundaries between formal penal intervention and other, informal forms of social control, thereby masking the coercive character of alternative interventions (Abel, 1982: Cohen, 1985).

Fundamental reform of the penal system requires not only imaginative alternatives but, at the same time, a radical change in the power structure. Thus a 'politics of abolition' aims at a negative strategy for changing the politics of punishment by abolishing not only the criminal justice system but also the repressive capitalist system part by part or step by step (Mathiesen, 1986).

A fundamental reform of the penal system presupposes not only a radical change of the existing power structure but also of the dominant culture. However, currently there is no appropriate social agency for any radical reform of the politics of punishment. There seems no immediate social basis upon which a progressive, let alone an abolitionist, strategy of crime control might be spontaneously constructed (Matthews, 1987: 389). Abolitionists tend to refer to the re-emergence of the subcultures of the new social movements with their own infrastructure of interaction and communication and their new ethics of solidarity, social responsibility, and care (Steinert, 1986: 28–9; see also Christie, 1982: 75–80). As Harris argues, the inadequacy of virtually all existing reform proposals lies in the failure to step outside the traditional and dominant ways of framing the issues. To explore alternative visions of justice we need to consider 'philosophies, paradigms, or models that transcend not only conventional criminological and political lines, but also natural and cultural boundaries and other limiting habits of the mind' (Harris, 1987: 11). According to Harris a wide range of visions of a better world and a better future offer a rich resource for a fundamental rethinking of our approach to crime and justice. The new social movements, in particular the women's movement, have pointed out fundamental weaknesses or biases in criminology's background assumptions, conceptual frameworks, methodology and tacit morality (Gelsthorpe and Morris, 1990). However, the relationship between abolitionism and, for example, feminism is not without stress (van Swaaningen, 1989).

ABOLITIONISM ON CRIME CONTROL

Abolitionism argues for a structural approach to the prevention of 'social negativity', or redressing problematic situations by taking social problems, conflicts and troubles seriously but not as 'crime'. Therefore, abolitionism argues for social policy rather than crime control policy. Examples of this structural approach would be dealing with drug problems in terms of mental health, with violence in terms of social pathology, and with property crime in terms of economy.

Abolitionism calls for decriminalization, depenalization, destigmatization, decentralization and deprofessionalization, as well as the establishment of other, informal, participatory, (semi-)autonomous ways of dealing with social problems.

Problematic events may just as well be defined as social troubles, problems or conflicts due to negligence or caused by 'accident' rather than by purpose or criminal intent. What is needed is a wide variety of possible responses without a priori assuming criminal intent and responsibility.

As we have seen, prison abolition, let alone penal abolition, requires an imaginative rethinking of possible ways of handling problematic situations as social problems, conflicts, troubles, accidents etc., as well as reconceptualizing punishment and developing new ways of managing 'deviance' on the basis of, at least partial, suspension of the logic of guilt and punishment. Without fixation on individual guilt, responsibility and punishment, 'crimes' would appear as 'conflicts', 'accidents' or 'problematic events' to be dealt with in a more reasonable and caring way by using forms of conflict management which are not exclusively geared towards individuals and confined to the limitations of criminal law in the books as well as in action (Steinert, 1986: 30). Therefore, abolitionists focus instead on extra-legal, autonomous ways for dealing with social problems and conflicts involving offences. The abolitionist challenge to abolish the present prison system now is to construct more participatory, popular or socialist forms of penality (Garland and Young, 1983).

This way of looking at crime and crime control is, of course, controversial. The abolitionist perspective is sometimes criticized for being naive and idealistic. In practice, however, the abolitionist approach turns out to be realistic in that social problems and conflicts are seen as inherent to social life. Since it is illusory that the criminal justice system can protect us effectively against such unfortunate events, it seems more reasonable to deal with troubles pragmatically rather than by approaching them in terms of guilt and punishment. Effectively to prevent and control unacceptable situations and behaviours requires a variety of social responses, one and only one of which is the criminal justice system. Its interventions are more of symbolic importance than of practical value. With some social, technical and organizational imagination 'crime' could be coped with in ways much more caring for those immediately involved. A variety of procedures could be established and institutionalized where social problems or conflicts, problematic events or behaviours could be dealt with through negotiation, mediation, arbitration, at intermediate levels. For dealing with the most common or garden varieties of crime, which is in any case the vast bulk of all recorded criminality, criminal prosecutions are simply redundant.

Certainly for those who are most directly concerned there is little or no benefit. Also in such cases as state or corporate crime where a full abolitionist agenda of dispute settlement – like the criminal justice approach – has profound limitations, it does make sense to look for more workable alternatives to the criminal justice system's mechanisms of apprehension, judgment and punishment. Most of these problems could be dealt with by means of economic, administrative, environmental, health or labour law, rather than by criminal law. Even in cases where a person has become an unacceptable burden to his or her relatives or community, imprisonment could be avoided. Agreements might be reached or orders might be given about temporary or permanent limitations in access to certain people, places or situations. The problems of the really bad and the really mad remain. In these relatively few cases and by way of last resort it might be unavoidable to deprive someone of their liberty, at least for the time being. This exceptional decision should be simply in order to incapacitate and be carried out in a humane way, that is as a morally problematic decision in a dilemma. However, even in these cases it would make sense to look for more just and humane alternatives based on mutual aid, good neighbourliness and real community rather than continue to rely on the solutions of bureaucracies, professionals and the centralized state. Criticism of the inhumanity and irrationality of the prison solution is as valid today as it was twenty or seventy years ago. Therefore, Cohen suggests that three interrelated strategies be followed: first, cultivating an experimental and inductive attitude to the actual historical record of alternatives, innovations and experiments; secondly, being sensitive, not just to failures, co-options and con-tricks, but to success stories – the criterion for success should be, and can be nothing other than, an approximation to preferred values; and thirdly, escaping the clutches of criminology (radical or realistic) by expanding the subject of social control way beyond the scope of the criminal justice system (for example, to systems of informal justice, utopian communes and experiments in self-help) (Cohen, 1988: 131).

In countries with an elaborate welfare system like the Scandinavian countries or the Netherlands, these strategies may seem more reasonable given that their crime problem is less dramatic and, traditionally, their crime control policy is already more cautious. In the context of a relatively mild penal climate with a pragmatic and reductionist penal policy already being implemented, even penal abolition may seem realistic as a long-term goal. However, in those countries where prison populations are enormous and penal institutions are simply 'warehousing' people in order to incapacitate them from reoffending, prison abolition is more acute. When in the early 1970s several commissions and task forces concluded that the American prison system is beyond reform and, therefore, other ways of dealing with criminal offenders need to be developed, the prison population was about one-third of the current one. These criticisms hold true even more under the present conditions of overcrowding in the prisons. Prisons are places where a lot more harm is done than is necessary or legitimate. Moreover, these institutions contribute to a further brutalization of social conditions. Even in the United States where average prison sentences are much longer than for example in the Netherlands, 99 per cent of the prison population will sooner or later hit the streets again. Therefore, there is a definite need not only for prison reform but also for penal reform. Current crime control policy boils down to doing more of the same. In the long run, however, the resulting spiral of harm needs to be reversed in a downward direction. This can only be achieved by doing more rather than less, albeit not more of the same but more of what generally might be called care.

REFERENCES

Abel, R. (ed.) (1982) *The Politics of Informal Justice*, vols 1 and 2. New York: Academic Press.

Baratta, A. (1986) 'Soziale Probleme und Konstruktion der Kriminalität', *Kriminologisches Journal*, 1: 200–18.

Black, D. (1976) *The Behavior of Law*. New York: Academic Press.

Christie, N. (1982) *Limits to Pain*. Oxford: Martin Robertson.

Christie, N. (1986) 'Images of man in modern penal law', *Contemporary Crises*, 10: 95–106.

Cohen, S. (1985) *Visions of Social Control. Crime, Punishment and Classification.* Cambridge: Polity Press.

Cohen, S. (1988) *Against Criminology.* New York: Transaction Books.

Dijk, J. van, Mayhew, P. and Killias, M. (1990) *Experiences of Crime across the World. Key Findings from the 1989 International Crime Survey.* Boston: Kluwer.

Garland, D. and Young, P. (1983) 'Towards a social analysis of penality', in D. Garland and P. Young (eds), *The Power to Punish. Contemporary Penality and Social Analysis.* London: Heinemann, pp. 1–36.

Gelsthorpe, L. and Morris, A. (eds) (1990) *Feminist Perspectives in Criminology.* Milton Keynes: Open University Press.

Haan, W. de (1990) *The Politics of Redress. Crime, Punishment and Penal Abolition.* London: Unwin Hyman.

Harris, K. (1987) 'Moving into the new millennium: toward a feminist vision of justice', *The Prison Journal*, 67: 27–38.

Hess, H. (1986) 'Kriminalität als Alltagsmythos. Ein Plädoyer dafür, Kriminologie als Ideologiekritik zu betreiben', *Kriminologisches Journal*, 18(1): 22–44.

Hulsman, L. (1986) 'Critical criminology and the concept of crime', *Contemporary Crises*, 10: 63–80.

Kennedy, M. (1974) 'Beyond incrimination', in C. Reasons (ed.), *The Criminologist and the Criminal.* Pacific Palisades: Goodyear. pp. 106–35.

Mathiesen, T. (1974) 'The politics of abolition. Essays', in *Political Action Theory.* London: Martin Robertson.

Mathiesen, T. (1986) 'The politics of abolition', *Contemporary Crises*, 10: 81–94.

Matthews, R. (1987) 'Taking realist criminology seriously', *Contemporary Crises*, 11: 371–401.

Morris, M. (ed.) (1976) *Instead of Prisons: a Handbook for Abolitionists.* Syracuse, NY: Prison Research Action Project.

Pepinsky, H. (1986) 'A sociology of justice', *Annual Review for Sociology*, 12: 93–108.

Quensel, S. (1987) 'Let's abolish theories of crime', in J. Blad, H. van Mastrigt and N. Uitdriks (eds), *The Criminal Justice System as a Social Problem: an Abolitionist Perspective.* Rotterdam: Mededelingen can het Juridisch Instituut van de Erasmus Universiteit. pp. 123–32.

Roshier, B. (1989) *Controlling Crime. The Classical Perspective in Criminology.* Milton Keynes: Open University Press.

Scheerer, S. (1986) 'Towards abolitionism', *Contemporary Crises*, 10: 5–20.

Spector, M. (1981) 'Beyond crime: seven methods to control troublesome rascals', in H. Ross (ed.), *Law and Deviance.* Beverly Hills, CA: Sage, pp. 127–57.

Steinert, H. (1986) 'Beyond crime and punishment', *Contemporary Crises*, 10: 21–39.

Swaaningen, R. van (1989) 'Feminism and abolitionism as critiques of criminology', *International Journal of the Sociology of Law*, 17: 287–306.

Wilkins, L. (1984) *Consumerist Criminology.* London: Heinemann.

34

Reintegrative shaming

John Braithwaite

[. . .]

It would seem that sanctions imposed by relatives, friends or a personally relevant collectivity have more effect on criminal behavior than sanctions imposed by a remote legal authority. I will argue that this is because repute in the eyes of close acquaintances matters more to people than the opinions or actions of criminal justice officials. As Blau (1964: 20) points out: 'a person who is attracted to others is interested in proving himself attractive to them, for his ability to associate with them and reap the benefits expected from the association is contingent on their finding him an attractive associate and thus wanting to interact with him'.

A British Government Social Survey asked youths to rank what they saw as the most important consequences of arrest. While only 10 per cent said 'the punishment I might get' was the most important consequence of arrest, 55 per cent said either 'What my family' or 'my girlfriend' would think about it. Another 12 per cent ranked 'the publicity or shame of having to appear in court' as the most serious consequence of arrest, and this was ranked as a more serious consequence on average than 'the punishment I might get' (Zimring and Hawkins, 1973: 192). There is clearly a need for more empirical work to ascertain whether the following conclusion is too sweeping, but Tittle would seem to speak for the current state of this literature when he says:

> social control as a general process seems to be rooted almost completely in informal sanctioning. Perceptions of formal sanction probabilities or severities do not appear to have much of an effect, and those effects that are evident turn out to be dependent upon perceptions of informal sanctions. (Tittle, 1980: 214)

Only a small proportion of the informal sanctions which prevent crime are coupled with formal sanctions, so this literature in a sense understates the importance of informal sanctions. These studies are also by no means tests of the theory of reintegrative shaming [. . .] but they certainly suggest that we are looking in the

From *Crime, Shame and Reintegration*, pp. 69–83. (Cambridge: Cambridge University Press, 1989.)

right place for an explanation of crime. To quote Tittle (1980: 198) again, they suggest that 'to the extent that individuals are deterred from deviance by fear, the fear that is relevant is most likely to be that their deviance will evoke some respect or status loss among acquaintances or in the community as a whole'. In the rational weighting of the costs and benefits of crime, loss of respect weighs more heavily for most of us than formal punishment. Yet in learning theory terms this rational weighing results from the operant conditioning part of learning. There is also the much more important effect of consciences which may be classically conditioned by shame [. . .].

A related reading of the deterrence literature is that it shows it is not the formal punitive features of social control that matter, but rather its informal moralizing features. The surprising findings of a classic field experiment by Schwartz and Orleans (1967) has fostered such a reading. Taxpayers were interviewed during the month prior to the filing of income tax returns, with one randomly selected group exposed to an interview stressing the penalties for income tax evasion, the other to an interview stressing the moral reasons for tax compliance. Whereas the moral appeal led to a significant increase in the actual tax paid, the deterrent threat was associated with no significant increase in tax paid compared to a control group.

BEYOND DETERRENCE, BEYOND OPERANT CONDITIONING: CONSCIENCE AND SHAMING

Jackson Toby (1964: 333) suggests that deterrence is irrelevant 'to the bulk of the population who have introjected the moral norms of society'. People comply with the law most of the time not through fear of punishment, or even fear of shaming, but because criminal behavior is simply abhorrent to them. Most serious crimes are unthinkable to most people; these people engage in no rational weighing of the costs and benefits of crime before deciding whether to comply with the law. Shaming, we will argue, is critical to understanding why most serious crime is unthinkable to most of us.

The unthinkableness of crime is a manifestation of our conscience or superego, whatever we want to call it depending on our psychological theoretical preferences. [. . .] We will leave it to the psychologists to debate how much the acquisition and generalization of conscience is a conditioning or a cognitive process. The point is that conscience is acquired.

For adolescents and adults, conscience is a much more powerful weapon to control misbehavior than punishment. In the wider society, it is no longer logistically possible, as it is in the nursery, for arrangements to be made for punishment to hang over the heads of persons whenever temptation to break the rules is put in their path. Happily, conscience more than compensates for absence of formal control. For a well-socialized individual, conscience delivers an anxiety response to punish each and every involvement in crime – a more systematic punishment than haphazard enforcement by the police. Unlike any punishment handed down by the courts, the anxiety response happens without delay, indeed punishment by anxiety precedes the rewards obtained from the crime, while any punishment by law will follow long after the reward. For most of us, punishment by our own conscience is therefore a much more potent threat than punishment by the criminal justice system.

Shaming is critical as the societal process that underwrites the family process of building consciences in children. Just as the insurance company cannot do business without the underwriter, the family could not develop young consciences in the cultural vacuum which would be left without societal practices of shaming. Shaming is an important child-rearing practice in itself; it is an extremely valuable tool in the hands of a responsible loving parent. However, as children's morality develops, as socialization moves from building responsiveness to external controls to responsiveness to internal controls, direct forms of shaming become less important than induction: appealing to the child's affection or respect for others, appealing to the child's own standards of right and wrong. [. . .]

However, the external controls must still be there in the background. If the maturation of conscience proceeds as it should, direct forms of shaming, and even more so punishment, are resorted to less and less. But there are times when conscience fails all of us, and we need a refresher course in the consequences of a compromised conscience. In this backstop role, shaming has a great advantage over formal punishment. Shaming is more pregnant with symbolic content than punishment. Punishment is a denial of confidence in the morality of the offender by reducing norm compliance to a crude cost–benefit calculation; shaming can be a reaffirmation of the morality of the offender by expressing personal disappointment that the offender should do something so out of character, and, if the shaming is reintegrative, by expressing personal satisfaction in seeing the character of the offender restored. Punishment erects barriers between the offender and punisher through transforming the relationship into one of power assertion and injury; shaming produces a greater interconnectedness between the parties, albeit a painful one, an interconnectedness which can produce the repulsion of stigmatization or the establishment of a potentially more positive relationship following reintegration. Punishment is often shameful and shaming usually punishes. But whereas punishment gets its symbolic content only from its denunciatory association with shaming, shaming is pure symbolic content.

Nevertheless, just as shaming is needed when conscience fails, punishment is needed when offenders are beyond being shamed. Unfortunately, however, the shameless, the remorseless, those who are beyond conditioning by shame are also likely to be those beyond conditioning by punishment – that is, psychopaths (consider, for example, the work of Mednick on conditionability and psychopathy – which would seem equally relevant to conditioning by fear of shame or fear of formal punishment (Mednick and Christiansen, 1977; Wilson and Herrnstein, 1985: 198–204)). The evidence is that punishment is a very ineffective ultimate backstop with people who have developed beyond the control techniques which were effective when they were infants. This is the problem with behavior modification (based on either rewards or punishment) for rehabilitating offenders. Offenders will play the game by reverting to pre-adolescent responsiveness to reward–cost social control because this is the way they can make their life most comfortable. But when they leave the institution they will return to behaving like the adults they are in an adult world in which punishment contingencies for indulging deviant conduct are remote.

The conscience-building effects of shaming that give it superiority over control strategies based simply on changing the rewards and costs of crime are enhanced by the participatory nature of shaming. Whereas an actual punishment will only be administered by one person or a limited number of criminal justice officials, the shaming associated with punishment may involve almost all of the members of a community. Thus, in the following passage, when Znaniecki refers to 'punishment', he really means the denunciation or shaming associated with the punishment:

> Regardless of whether punishment really does deter future violation of the law or not, it seems to significantly reinforce agreement and solidarity among those who actively or vicariously participate in meting it out . . . Opposing the misdemeanours of other people increases the conformity of those administering the punishment, thus leading to the maintenance of the systems in which they participate. (Znaniecki, 1971: 604)

Participation in expressions of abhorrence toward the criminal acts of others is part of what makes crime an abhorrent choice for us ourselves to make. [. . .]

When we shame ourselves, that is when we feel pangs of conscience, we take the role of the other, treating ourselves as an object worthy of shame (Mead, 1934; Shott, 1979). We learn to do this by participating with others in shaming criminals and evil-doers. Internal control is a social product of external control. Self-regulation can displace social control by an external agent only when control has been internalized through the prior existence of external control in the culture.

Cultures like that of Japan, which shame reintegratively, follow shaming ceremonies with ceremonies of repentance and reacceptance. The nice advantage such cultures get in conscience building is two ceremonies instead of one, but, more critically, confirmation of the moral order from two very different quarters – both from those affronted and from him who caused the affront. The moral order derives a very special kind of credibility when even he who has breached it openly comes out and affirms the evil of the breach.

This is achieved by what Goffman (1971: 113) calls disassociation:

> An apology is a gesture through which an individual splits himself into two parts, the part that is guilty of an offense and the part that disassociates itself from the delict and affirms a belief in the offended rule.

In cultures like that of Japan which practise disassociation, the vilification of the self that misbehaved by the repentant self can be much more savage than would be safe with vilification by other persons: 'he can overstate or overplay the case against himself, thereby giving others the task of cutting the self-derogation short' (Goffman, 1971: 113).

[. . .]

In summary then, shame operates at two levels to effect social control. First, it deters criminal behavior because social approval of significant others is something we do not like to lose. Second, and more importantly, both shaming and repentance build consciences which internally deter criminal behavior even in the absence of any external shaming associated with an offense. Shaming brings into existence two very different kinds of punishers – social disapproval and pangs of conscience.

[. . .] Community-wide shaming is necessary because most crimes are not experienced within the average household. Children need to learn about the evil of murder, rape, car theft and environmental pollution offenses through condemnation of the local butcher or the far away image on the television screen. But the shaming of the local offender known personally to children in the neighborhood is especially important, because the wrongdoing and the shaming are so vivid as to leave a lasting impression.

Much shaming in the socialization of children is of course vicarious, through stories. Because they are not so vivid as real-life incidents of shaming, they are not so powerful. Yet they are necessary because so many types of misbehavior will not occur in the family or the neighborhood. A culture without stories for children in which morals are clearly drawn and evil deeds clearly identified would be a culture which failed the moral development of its children. Because human beings are story-telling animals, they get much of their identity from answers to the question 'Of what stories do I find myself a part?' 'Deprive children of stories and you leave them unscripted, anxious stutterers in their actions as in their words' (MacIntyre, 1984: 138).

Essentially, societal processes of shaming do three things:

1 They give content to a day-to-day socialization of children which occurs mainly through induction. As we have just seen, shaming supplies the morals which build consciences. The evil of acts beyond the immediate experience of children is more effectively communicated by shaming than by pure reasoning.
2 Societal incidents of shaming remind parents of the wide range of evils about which they must moralize with their children. Parents do not have to keep a checklist of crimes, a curriculum of sins, to discuss with their offspring. In a society where shaming is important, societal incidents of shaming will trigger vicarious shaming within the family so that the criminal code is eventually more or less automatically covered. Thus, the child will one day observe condemnation of someone who has committed rape, and will ask a parent or other older person about the basis of this wrongdoing, or will piece the story together from a series of such incidents. Of course societies which shame only half-heartedly run a risk that the full curriculum of crimes will not be covered. Both this point and the last one could be summarized in another way by saying that public shaming puts pressure on parents, teachers and neighbors to ensure that they engage in private shaming which is sufficiently systematic.
3 Societal shaming in considerable measure takes over from parental socialization once children move away from the influence of the family and the school. Put another way, shaming generalizes beyond childhood principles learnt during the early years of life.
    This third principle is about the 'criminal law as a moral eye-opener' as Andenaes (1974: 116–17) calls it. As a child, I may have learnt the principle that killing is wrong, but when I leave the familiar surroundings of the family to work in the unfamiliar environment of a nuclear power plant, I am taught by a nuclear safety regulatory system that to breach certain safety laws can cost lives, and so persons who breach them are treated with a comparable level of shame. The principle that illegal killing is shameful is generalized. To the extent that genuine shame is not directed against those who defy the safety rules, however, I am liable to take them much less seriously. Unfortunately, societal shaming processes often do fail to generalize to organizational crime.

Recent years in some Western societies have seen more effective shaming directed at certain kinds of offenses – drunk driving, occupational health and safety and environmental offenses, and political corruption. [. . .] This shaming has for many adults integrated new categories of wrongdoing (for which they had not been socialized as children) into the moral frameworks pre-existing from their childhood.

While most citizens are aware of the content of most criminal laws, knowledge of what the law requires of citizens in detail can be enhanced by cases of public shaming. Through shaming directed at new legal frontiers, feminists in many countries have clarified for citizens just what sexual harassment, rape within marriage, and employment discrimination mean. Social change is increasingly rapid, particularly in the face of burgeoning technologies which require new moralities of nuclear, environmental and consumer safety, responsible use of new technologies of information exchange and electronic funds transfer, ethical exploitation of new institutions such as futures exchanges, and so on. Shaming is thus particularly vital in sustaining a contemporarily relevant legal and moral order.

[. . .]

THE PROBLEM OF DISCONTINUITY IN SOCIALIZATION PRACTICES

The most fundamental problem of socialization in modern societies is that as children mature in the family we gradually wean them from control by punishment to shaming and reasoned appeals to internal controls. The transition from family to school involves a partial reversion back to greater reliance on formal punishment for social control. The further transition to social control on the streets, at discos and pubs by the police is an almost total reversion to the punishment model. A discontinuity with the developmental pattern set in the family is established by the other major socializing institutions for adolescents – the school and the police.

[. . .] Japanese society handles this discontinuity much better than Western societies by having a criminal justice system (and a school system) much more orientated to catalysing internal controls than ours. Japanese police, prosecutors and courts rely heavily on guilt-induction and shaming as alternatives to punishment. If appeals to shame produce expressions of guilt, repentance and a will to seek reunification and forgiveness from loved ones (and/or the victim), this is regarded as the best result by all actors in the drama of criminal justice. The Japanese phenomena of neighborhood police, reintegrative shaming at work and school as alternatives to formal punishment processes, have two effects. First, they put social control back into the hands of significant others, where it can be most effective. Second, they soften some of the discontinuity between the increasing trust to inner controls of family life and the shock of a reversion to external control in the wide world. Just as the evidence shows that aggression and delinquency is the reaction to excessive use of punishment and power assertion as the control strategy within the family, we might expect rebellion against a demeaning punitiveness on the street to be all the more acute when families have eschewed authoritarianism in favor of authoritativeness.

[. . .]

In short, societies which replace much of their punitive social control with shaming and reintegrative appeals to the better nature of people will be societies with less crime. These societies will do better at easing the crushing discontinuity between the shift away from punitive control in home life and the inevitable reversion to heavier reliance on punitive control in the wider society.

[. . .]

REFERENCES

Andenaes, J. (1974) *Punishment and Deterrence*. Ann Arbor: University of Michigan Press.

Blau, P.M. (1964) *Exchange and Power in Social Life*. New York: Wiley.

Goffman, E. (1971) *Relations in Public*. New York: Basic Books.

MacIntyre, A. (1984) 'The virtues, the unity of a human life and the concept of a tradition', in M. Sandel (ed.), *Liberalism and Its Critics*. Oxford: Basil Blackwell.

Mead, G.H. (1934) *Mind, Self and Society*. Chicago: University of Chicago Press.

Mednick, S. and Christiansen, K.O. (1977) *Biosocial Bases of Criminal Behavior*. New York: Gardner Press.

Schwartz, R.D. and Orleans, S. (1967) 'On legal sanctions', *University of Chicago Law Review*, 34: 274–300.

Shott, S. (1979) 'Emotion and social life: a symbolic interactionist's analysis', *American Journal of Sociology*, 84: 1317–34.

Tittle, C.R. (1980) *Sanctions and Social Deviance*. New York: Praeger.

Toby, J. (1964) 'Is punishment necessary?' *Journal of Criminal Law, Criminology and Political Science*, 55: 332–7.

Wilson, J.Q. and Herrnstein, R. (1985) *Crime and Human Nature*. New York: Simon and Schuster.

Zimring, F.E. and Hawkins, G.J. (1973) *Deterrence: the Legal Threat in Crime Control*. Chicago: University of Chicago Press.

Znaniecki, F. (1971) *Nauki o Kulturze*. Warsaw: PWN.

35

Broken windows: The police and neighborhood safety

James Q. Wilson and George L. Kelling

In the mid-1970s, the state of New Jersey announced a 'Safe and Clean Neighborhoods Program,' designed to improve the quality of community life in twenty-eight cities. As part of that program, the state provided money to help cities take police officers out of their patrol cars and assign them to walking beats. The governor and other state officials were enthusiastic about using foot patrol as a way of cutting crime, but many police chiefs were skeptical. Foot patrol in their eyes, had been pretty much discredited. It reduced the mobility of the police, who thus had difficulty responding to citizen calls for services, and it weakened headquarters control over patrol officers.

Many police officers also disliked foot patrol, but for different reasons: it was hard work, it kept them outside on cold, rainy nights, and it reduced their chances for making a 'good pinch.' In some departments, assigning officers to foot patrol had been used as a form of punishment. And academic experts on policing doubted that foot patrol would have any impact on crime rates; it was, in the opinion of most, little more than a sop to public opinion. But since the state was paying for it, the local authorities were willing to go along.

Five years after the program started, the Police Foundation, in Washington, D.C., published an evaluation of the foot-patrol project. Based on its analysis of a carefully controlled experiment carried out chiefly in Newark, the foundation concluded, to the surprise of hardly anyone, that foot patrol had not reduced crime rates. But residents of the foot-patrolled neighborhoods seemed to feel more secure than persons in other areas, tended to believe that crime had been reduced, and seemed to take fewer steps to protect themselves from crime (staying at home with the doors locked, for example). Moreover, citizens in the foot-patrol areas had a more favourable opinion of the police than did those living elsewhere. And officers walking beats had higher morale, greater job satisfaction, and a more favorable attitude toward citizens in their neighborhoods than did officers assigned to patrol cars.

From *The Atlantic Monthly*, March, 1982, pp. 29–38.

These findings may be taken as evidence that the skeptics were right—foot patrol has no effect on crime; it merely fools the citizens into thinking that they are safer. But in our view, and in the view of the authors of the Police Foundation study (of whom Kelling was one), the citizens of Newark were not fooled at all. They knew what the foot-patrol officers were doing, they knew it was different from what motorized officers do, and they knew that having officers walk beats did in fact make their neighborhoods safer.

But how can a neighborhood be 'safer' when the crime rate has not gone down—in fact, may have gone up? Finding the answer requires first that we understand what most often frightens people in public places. Many citizens, of course, are primarily frightened by crime, especially crime involving a sudden, violent attack by a stranger. This risk is very real, in Newark as in many large cities. But we tend to overlook or forget another source of fear—the fear of being bothered by disorderly people. Not violent people, nor, necessarily, criminals, but disreputable or obstreperous or unpredictable people: panhandlers, drunks, addicts, rowdy teenagers, prostitutes, loiterers, and mentally disturbed.

What foot-patrol officers did was to elevate, to the extent they could, the level of public order in these neighborhoods. Though the neighborhoods were predominantly black and the foot patrolmen were mostly white, this 'order-maintenance' function of the police was performed to the general satisfaction of both parties.

One of us (Kelling) spent many hours walking with Newark foot-patrol officers to see how they defined 'order' and what they did to maintain it. One beat was typical: a busy but dilapidated area in the heart of Newark, with many abandoned buildings, marginal shops (several of which prominently displayed knives and straight-edged razors in their windows), one large department store, and, most important, a train station and several major but stops. Though the area was run-down, its streets were filled with people, because it was a major transportation center. The good order of this area was important not only to those who lived and worked there but also to many others, who had to move through it on their way home, to supermarkets, or to factories.

The people on the street were primarily black; the officer who walked the street was white. The people were made up of 'regulars' and 'strangers.' Regulars included both 'decent folk' and some drunks and derelicts who were always there but who 'knew their place.' Strangers were, well, strangers, and viewed suspiciously, some-times apprehensively. The officer—call him Kelly—knew who the regulars were, and they knew him. As he saw his job, he was to keep an eye on strangers, and make certain that the disreputable regulars observed some informal but widely understood rules. Drunks and addicts could sit on the stoops, but could not lie down. People could drink on side streets, but not at the main intersection. Bottles had to be in paper bags. Talking to, bothering, or begging from people waiting at the bus stop was strictly forbidden. If a dispute erupted between a businessman and a customer, the businessman was assumed to be right, especially if the customer was a stranger. If a stranger loitered, Kelly would ask him if he had any means of support and what his business was; if he gave unsatisfactory answers, he was sent on his way. Persons who broke the informal rules, especially those who bothered people waiting at bus stops, were arrested for vagrancy. Noisy teenagers were told to keep quiet.

These rules were defined and enforced in collaboration with the 'regulars' on the street. Another neighborhood might have different rules, but these, everybody understood, were the rules for *this* neighborhood. If someone violated them, the regulars not only turned to Kelly for help but also ridiculed the violator. Sometimes what Kelly did could be described as 'enforcing the law,' but just as often it involved taking informal or extralegal steps to help protect what the neighborhood had decided was the appropriate level of public order. Some of the things he did probably would not withstand a legal challenge.

A determined skeptic might acknowledge that a skilled foot-patrol officer can maintain order but still insist that this sort of 'order' has little to do with the real sources of community fear—that is, with violent crime. To a degree, that is true. But two things must be borne in mind. First, outside observers should not assume that they know how much of the anxiety now endemic in many big-city neighborhoods stems from a fear of 'real' crime and how much from a sense that the street is disorderly, a source of distasteful, worrisome encounters. The people of Newark, to judge from their behavior and their remarks to interviewers, apparently assign a high value to public order, and feel relieved and reassured when the police help them maintain that order.

Second, at the community level, disorder and crime are usually inextricably linked, in a kind of developmental sequence. Social psychologists and police officers tend to agree that if a window in a building is broken *and is left unrepaired*, all the rest of the windows will soon be broken. This is as true in nice neighborhoods as in run-down ones. Window-breaking does not necessarily occur on a large scale because some areas are inhabited by determined window-breakers whereas others are populated by window-lovers; rather, one unrepaired broken window is a signal that no one cares, and so breaking more windows costs nothing. (It has always been fun.)

Philip Zimbardo, a Stanford psychologist, reported in 1969 on some experiments testing the broken-window theory. He arranged to have an automobile without license plates parked with its hood up on a street in the Bronx and a comparable automobile on a street in Palo Alto, California. The car in the Bronx was attacked by 'vandals' within ten minutes of its 'abandonment.' The first to arrive were a family—father, mother, and young son—who removed the radiator and battery. Within twenty-four hours, virtually everything of value had been removed. Then random destruction began—windows were smashed, parts torn off, upholstery ripped. Children began to use the car as a playground. Most of the adult 'vandals' were well-dressed, apparently clean-cut whites. The car in Palo Alto sat untouched for more than a week. Then Zimbardo smashed part of it with a sledgehammer. Soon, passersby were joining in. Within a few hours, the car had been turned upside down and utterly destroyed. Again, the 'vandals' appeared to be primarily respectable whites.

Untended property becomes fair game for people out for fun or plunder, and even for people who ordinarily would not dream of doing such things and who probably consider themselves law-abiding. Because of the nature of community life in the Bronx—its anonymity, the frequency with which cars are abandoned and things are stolen or broken, the past experience of 'no one caring'—vandalism begins much more quickly than it does in staid Palo Alto, where people have come to believe that private possessions are cared for, and that mischievous behavior is costly. But vandalism can occur anywhere once communal barriers—the sense of mutual regard and the obligations of civility—are lowered by actions that seen to signal that 'no one cares.'

We suggest that 'untended' behavior also leads to the breakdown of community controls. A stable neighborhood of families who care for their homes, mind each other's children, and confidently frown on unwanted intruders can change, in a few years or even a few months, to an inhospitable and frightening jungle. A piece of property is abandoned, weeks grow up, a window is smashed. Adults stop scolding rowdy children; the children, emboldened, become more rowdy. Families move out, unattached adults move in. Teenagers gather in front of the corner store. The merchant asks them to move; they refuse. Fights occur. Litter accumulates. People start drinking in front of the grocery; in time, an inebriate slumps to the sidewalk and is allowed to sleep it off. Pedestrians are approached by panhandlers.

At this point it is not inevitable that serious crime will flourish or violent attacks on strangers will occur. But many residents will think that crime, especially violent crime, is on the rise, and they will modify their behavior accordingly. They will use the streets less often, and when on the streets will stay apart from their fellows, moving with averted eyes, silent lips, and hurried steps. 'Don't get involved.' For some residents, this growing atomization will matter little, because the neighborhood is not their 'home' but 'the place where they live.' Their interests are elsewhere; they are cosmopolitans. but it will matter greatly to other people, whose lives derive meaning and satisfaction from local attachments rather than worldly involvement; for them, the neighborhood will cease to exist except for a few reliable friends whom they arrange to meet.

Such an area is vulnerable to criminal invasion. Though it is not inevitable, it is more likely that here, rather than in places where people are confident they can regulate public behavior by informal controls, drugs will change hands, prostitutes will solicit, and cars will be stripped. That the drunks will be robbed by boys who do it as a lark, and the prostitutes' customers will be robbed by men who do it purposefully and perhaps violently. That muggings will occur.

Among those who often find it difficult to move away from this are the elderly. Surveys of citizens suggest that the elderly are much less likely to be the victims of crime than younger persons, and some have inferred from this that the well-known fear of crime voiced by the elderly is an exaggeration: perhaps we ought not to design special programs to protect older persons; perhaps we should even try to talk them out of their mistaken fears. This argument misses the point. The prospect of a confrontation with an obstreperous teenager or a drunken panhandler can be as fear-inducing for defenseless persons as the prospect of meeting an actual robber; indeed, to a defenseless person, the two kinds of confrontation are often indistinguishable. Moreover, the lower rate at which the elderly are victimized is a measure of the steps they have already taken—chiefly, staying behind locked doors— to minimize the risks they face. Young men are more frequently attacked than older women, not because they are easier or more lucrative targets but because they are on the streets more.

Nor is the connection between disorderliness and fear made only by the elderly. Susan Estrich, of the Harvard Law School, has recently gathered together a number of surveys on the sources of public fear. One, done in Portland, Oregon, indicated that three fourths of the adults interviewed cross to the other side of a street when they see a gang of teenagers; another survey in Baltimore, discovered that nearly half would cross the street to avoid even a single strange youth. When an interviewer asked people in a housing project where the most dangerous spot was, they mentioned a place where young persons gathered to drink and play music, despite the fact that not a single crime had occurred there. In Boston public housing projects, the greatest fear was expressed by persons living in he buildings where disorderliness and incivility, not crime, were the greatest. Knowing this helps one understand the significance of such otherwise harmless displays as subway graffiti. As Nathan Glazer has written, the proliferation of graffiti, even when not obscene, confronts the subway rider with the 'inescapable knowledge that the environment he must endure for an hour or more a day is uncontrolled and uncontrollable, and that anyone can invade it to do whatever damage and mischief the mind suggests.'

In response to fear, people avoid one another, weakening controls. Sometimes they call the police. Patrol cars arrive, an occasional arrest occurs, but crime continues and disorder is not abated. Citizens complain to the police chief, but he explains that his department is low on personnel and that the courts do not punish petty or first-time offenders. To the residents, the police who arrive in squad cars are either ineffective or uncaring; to the police, the residents are animals who deserve each other. The citizens may soon stop calling the police, because 'they can't do anything.'

The process we call urban decay has occurred for centuries in every city. But what is happening today is different in at least two important respects. First, in the period before, say, World War II, city dwellers—because of money costs, transportation difficulties, familial and church connections—could rarely move away from neighborhood problems. When movement did occur, it tended to be along public-transit routes. Now mobility has become exceptionally easy for all but the poorest or those who are blocked by racial prejudice. Earlier crime waves had a kind of built-in self-correcting mechanism: the determination of a neighborhood or community to reassert control over its turf. Areas in Chicago, New York, and Boston would experience crime and gang wars, and then normalcy would return, as the families for whom no alternative residences were possible reclaimed their authority over the streets.

Second, the police in this earlier period assisted in that reassertion of authority by acting, sometimes violently, on behalf of the community. Young toughs were roughed up, people were arrested 'on suspicion' or for vagrancy, and prostitutes and petty thieves were routed. 'Rights' were something enjoyed by decent folk, and perhaps also by the serious professional criminal, who avoided violence and could afford a lawyer.

This pattern of policing was not an aberration or the result of occasional excess. From the earliest days of the nation, the police function was seen primarily as that of a night watchman: to maintain order against the chief threats to order—fire, wild animals, and disreputable behavior. Solving crimes was viewed not as a police responsibility but as a private one. In the March, 1969, *Atlantic* one of us (Wilson) wrote a brief account of how the police role had slowly changed from maintaining order to fighting crimes. The change began with the creation of private detectives (often ex-criminals), who worked on a contingency-fee basis for individuals who had suffered losses. In time, the detectives were absorbed into municipal police agencies and paid a regular salary; simultaneously, the responsibility for prosecuting thieves was shifted from the aggrieved private citizen to the professional prosecutor. This process was not complete in most places until the twentieth century.

In the 1960s, when urban riots were a major problem, social scientists began to explore carefully the order-maintenance function of the police, and to suggest ways of improving it—not to make streets safer (its original function) but to reduce the incidence of mass violence. Order-maintenance became, to a degree, coterminous with 'community relations.' But, as the crime wave that began in the early 1960s continued without abatement throughout the decade and into the 1970s, attention shifted to the role of the police as crime-fighters. Studies of police behavior ceased, by and large, to be accounts of the order-maintenance function and became, instead, efforts to propose and test ways whereby the police could solve more crimes, make more arrests, and gather better evidence. If these things could be done, social scientists assumed, citizens would be less fearful.

A great deal was accomplished during this transition, as both police chiefs and outside experts emphasized the crime-fighting function in their plans, in the allocation of resources, and in deployment of personnel. The police may well have become better crime-fighters as a result. And doubtless they remained aware of their responsibility for order. But the link between order-maintenance and crime-prevention, so obvious to earlier generations, was forgotten.

That link is similar to the process whereby one broken window becomes many. The citizen who fears the ill-smelling drunk, the rowdy teenager, or the importuning beggar is not merely expressing his distaste for unseemly behaviour; he is also giving voice to a bit of folk wisdom that happens to be a correct generalization—namely, that serious street crime flourishes in areas in which disorderly behavior goes unchecked. The unchecked panhandler is, in effect, the first broken window. Muggers and robbers, whether opportunistic or professional, believe they reduce their chances of being caught or even identified if they operate on streets where potential victims are already intimidated by prevailing conditions. If the neighborhood cannot keep a bothersome panhandler from annoying passersby, the thief may reason, it is even less likely to call the police to identify a potential mugger or to interfere if the mugging actually takes place.

Some police administrators concede that this process occurs, but argue that motorized-patrol officers can deal with it as effectively as foot-patrol officers. We are not so sure. In theory, an officer in a squad car can observe as much as an officer on foot; in theory, the former can talk to as many people as the latter. But the reality of police–citizen encounters is powerfully altered by the automobile. An officer on foot cannot separate himself from the street people; if he is approached, only his uniform and his personality can help him manage whatever is about to happen. And he can never be certain what that will be—a request for directions, a plea for help, an angry denunciation, a teasing remark, a confused babble, a threatening gesture.

In a car, an officer is more likely to deal with street people by rolling down the window and looking at them. The door and the window exclude the approaching citizen; they are a barrier. Some officers take advantage of this barrier, perhaps unconsciously, by acting differently if in the car than they would on foot. We have seen this countless times. The police car pulls up to a corner where teenagers are gathered. The window is rolled down. The officer stares at the youths. They stare back. The officer says to one, 'C'mere.' He saunters over, conveying to his friends by his elaborately casual style the idea that he is not intimidated by authority. 'What's you name?' 'Chuck.' 'Chuck who?' 'Chuck Jones.' 'What'ya doing, Chuck?' 'Nothin'.' 'Got a P.O. [parole officer]?' 'Nah.' 'Sure?' 'Yeah.' 'Stay out of trouble, Chuckie.' Meanwhile, the other boys laugh and exchange comments among themselves, probably at the officer's expense. The officer stares harder. He cannot be certain what is being said, nor can he join in and, by displaying his own skill at street banter, prove that he cannot be 'put down.' In the process, the officer has learned almost nothing, and the boys have decided the officer is an alien force who can safely be disregarded, even mocked.

Our experience is that most citizens like to talk to a police officer. Such exchanges give them a sense of importance, provide them with the basis for gossip, and allow them to explain to the authorities what is worrying them (whereby they gain a modest but significant sense of having 'done something' about the problem). You approach a person on foot more easily, and talk to him more readily, than you do a person in a car. Moreover, you can more easily retain some anonymity if you draw an officer aside for a private chat. Suppose you want to pass on a tip about who is stealing handbags, or who offered to sell you a stolen TV. In the inner city, the culprit, in all likelihood, lives nearby. To walk up to a marked patrol car and lean in the window is to convey a visible signal that you are a 'fink.'

The essence of the police role in maintaining order is to reinforce the informal control mechanisms of the community itself. The police cannot, without committing extraordinary resources, provide a substitute for that informal control. On the other hand, to reinforce those natural forces the police must accommodate them. And therein lies the problem.

Should police activity on the street be shaped, in important ways, by the standards of the neighborhood rather than by the rules of state? Over the past two decades, the shirt of police from order-maintenance to law-enforcement has brought them increasingly under the influence of legal restrictions, provoked by media complaints and enforced by court decisions and departmental orders. As a consequence, the order-maintenance functions of the police are now governed by rules developed to control police relations with suspected criminals. This is, we think, an entirely new development. For centuries, the role of the police as watchmen was judged primarily not in terms of its compliance with appropriate procedures but rather in terms of its attaining a desired objective. The objective was order, an inherently ambiguous term but a condition that people in a given community recognized when they saw it. The means were the same as those the community itself would employ, if its members were sufficiently determined, courageous, and authoritative. Detecting and apprehending criminals, by contrast, was a means to an end, not an end in itself; a judicial determination of guilt or innocence was the hoped-for result of the law-enforcement mode. From the first, the police were expected to follow rules defining that process, though states differed in how stringent the rules should be. The criminal-apprehension process was always understood to involve individual rights, the violation of which was unacceptable because it meant that the violating officer would be acting as a judge and jury—and that was not his job. Guilt or innocence was to be determined by universal standards under special procedures.

Ordinarily, no judge or jury ever sees the persons caught up in a dispute over the appropriate level of neighborhood order. That is true not only because most cases are handled informally on the street but also because no universal standards are available to settle arguments over disorder, and thus a judge may not be any wiser or more effective than a police officer. Until quite recently in many states, and even today in some places, the police make arrests on such charges as 'suspicious person' or 'vagrancy' or 'public drunkenness'—charges with scarcely any legal meaning. These charges exist not because society wants judges to punish vagrants or drunks but because it wants an officer to have the legal tools to remove undesirable persons from a neighborhood when informal efforts to preserve order in the streets have failed.

Once we begin to think of all aspects of police work as involving the application of universal rules under special procedures, we inevitably ask what constituties an 'undesirable person' and why we should 'criminalize' vagrancy or drunkenness. A strong and commendable desire to see that people are treated fairly makes us worry about allowing the police to rout persons who are undesirable by some vague or parochial standard. A growing and not-so-commendable utilitarianism leads us to doubt that any behavior that does not 'hurt' another person should be made illegal. And thus many of us who watch over the police are reluctant to allow them to perform, in the only way they can, a function that every neighborhood desperately wants them to perform.

This wish to 'decriminalize' disreputable behavior that 'harms no one'—and thus remove the ultimate sanction the police can employ to maintain neighborhood order—is, we think, a mistake. Arresting a single drunk or a single vagrant who has harmed no identifiable person seems unjust, and in a sense it is. But failing to do anything about a score of drunks or a hundred vagrants may destroy an entire community. A particular rule that seems to make sense in the individual case makes no sense when it is made a universal rule and applied to all cases. It makes no sense because it fails to take into account the connection between one broken window left untended and a thousand broken windows. Of course, agencies other than the police could attend to the problems posed by drunks or the mentally ill, but in most communities—especially where the 'deinstitutionalization' movement has been strong—they do not.

The concern about equity is more serious. We might agree that certain behavior makes one person more undesirable than another, but how do we ensure that age or skin color or national origin or harmless mannerisms will not also become the basis for distinguishing the undesirable from the desirable? How do we ensure, in short, that the police do not become the agents of neighborhood bigotry?

We can offer no wholly satisfactory answer to this important question. We are not confident that there *is* a satisfactory answer, except to hope that by their selection, training, and supervision, the police will be inculcated with a clear sense of the outer limit of their discretionary authority. That limit, roughly, is this—the police exist to help regulate behavior, not to maintain the racial or ethnic purity of a neighborhood.

Consider the case of the Robert Taylor Homes in Chicago, one of the largest public-housing projects in the country. It is home for nearly 20,000 people, all black, and extends over ninety-two acres along South State Street. It was named after a distinguished black who had been, during the 1940s, chairman of the Chicago Housing Authority. Not long after it opened, in 1962, relations between project residents and the police deteriorated badly. The citizens felt that the police were insensitive or brutal; the police, in turn, complained of unprovoked attacks on them. Some Chicago officers tell of times when they were afraid to enter the Homes. Crime rates soared.

Today, the atmosphere has changed. Police–citizen relations have improved—apparently, both sides learned something from the earlier experience. Recently, a boy stole a purse and ran off. Several young persons who saw the theft voluntarily passed along to the police information on the identity and residence of the thief, and they did this publicly, with friends and neighbors looking on. But problems persist, chief among them the presence of youth gangs that terrorize residents and recruit members in the project. The people expect the police to 'do something' about this, and the police are determined to do just that.

But do what? Though the police can obviously make arrests whenever a gang member breaks the law, a gang can form, recruit, and congregate without breaking the law. And only a tiny fraction of gang-related crimes can be solved by an arrest; thus, if an arrest is the only recourse for the police, the residents' fears will go unassuaged. The police will soon feel helpless, and the residents will again believe that the police 'do nothing.' What the police in fact do is to chase known gang members out of the project. In the words of one officer, 'We kick ass.' Project residents both know and approve of this. The tacit police–citizen alliance in the project is reinforced by the police view that the cops and the gangs are the two rival sources of power in the area, and that the gangs are not going to win.

None of this is easily reconciled with any conception of due process or fair treatment. Since both residents and gang members are black, race is not a factor. But it could be. Suppose a white project confronted a black gang, or vice versa. We would be apprehensive about the police taking sides. But the substantive problem remains the same: how can the police strengthen the informal social-control mechanisms of natural communities in order to minimize fear in public places? Law enforcement, per se, is no answer. A gang can weaken or destroy a community by standing about in a menacing fashion and speaking rudely to passersby without breaking the law.

We have difficulty thinking about such matters, not simply because the ethical and legal issues are so complex but because we have become accustomed to thinking of the law in essentially individualistic terms. The law defines *my* rights, punishes *his* behavior, and is applied by *that* officer because of *this* harm. We assume, in thinking this way, that what is good for the individual will be good for the community, and what doesn't matter when it happens to one person won't matter if it happens to many. Ordinarily, those are plausible assumptions. But in cases where behavior that is tolerable to one person is intolerable to many others, the reactions of the others— fear, withdrawal, flight—may ultimately make matters worse for everyone, including the individual who first professed his indifference.

It may be their greater sensitivity to communal as opposed to individual needs that helps explain why the residents of small communities are more satisfied with their police than are the residents of similar neighborhoods in big cities. Elinor Ostrom and her co-workers at Indiana University compared the perception of police services in two poor, all-black Illinois towns—Phoenix and East Chicago Heights— with those of three comparable all-black neighborhoods in Chicago. The level of criminal victimization and the quality of police–community relations appeared to be about the same in the towns and the Chicago neighborhoods. But the citizens living in their own villages were much more likely than those living in the Chicago neighborhoods to say that they do not stay at home for fear of crime, to agree that the local police have 'the right to take any action necessary' to deal with problems, and to agree that the police 'look out for the needs of the average citizen.' It is possible that the residents and the police of the small towns saw themselves as engaged in a collaborative effort to maintain a certain standard of communal life, whereas those of the big city felt themselves to be simply requesting and supplying particular services on an individual basis.

If this is true, how should a wise police chief deploy his meager forces? The first answer is that nobody knows for certain, and the most prudent course of action would be to try further variations on the Newark experiment, to see more precisely what works in what kinds of neighborhoods. The second answer is also a hedge—many aspects of order-maintenance in neighborhoods can probably best be handled in ways that involve the police minimally, if at all. A busy, bustling shopping center and a quiet, well-tended suburb may need almost no visible police presence. In both cases, the ratio of respectable to disreputable people is ordinarily so high as to make informal social control effective.

Even in areas that are in jeopardy from disorderly elements, citizen action without substantial police involvement may be sufficient. Meetings between teenagers who like to hand out on a particular corner and adults who want to use that corner might well lead to an amicable agreement on a set of rules about how many people can be allowed to congregate, where, and when.

Where no understanding is possible—or if possible, not observed—citizen patrols may be a sufficient response. There are two traditions of communal involvement in maintaining order. One, that of the 'community watchmen,' is as old as the first settlement of the New World. Until well into the nineteenth century, volunteer watchmen, not policemen, patrolled their communities to keep order. They did so, by and large, without taking the law into their own hands—without, that is, punishing persons or using force. Their presence deterred disorder or alerted the community to disorder that could not be deterred. There are hundreds of such efforts today in communities all across the nation. Perhaps the best known is that of the Guardian Angels, a group of unarmed young persons in distinctive berets and T-shirts, who first came to public attention when they began patrolling the New York City subways but who claim now to have chapters in more than thirty American cities. Unfortunately, we have little information about the effect of these groups on crime. It is possible, however, that whatever their effect on crime, citizens find their presence reassuring, and that they thus contribute to maintaining a sense of order and civility.

The second tradition is that of the 'vigilante.' Rarely a feature of the settled communities of the East, it was primarily to be found in those frontier towns that grew up in advance of the reach of government. More than 350 vigilante groups are known to have existed; their distinctive feature was that their members did take the law into their own hands, by acting as judge, jury, and often executioner as well as policeman. Today, the vigilante movement is conspicuous by its rarity, despite the great fear expressed by citizens that the older cities are becoming 'urban frontiers.' But some community-watchmen groups have skirted the line, and others may cross it in the future. An ambiguous case, reported in *The Wall Street Journal*, involved a citizens' patrol in the Silver Lake area of Belleville, New Jersey. A leader told the reporter, 'We look for outsiders.' If a few teenagers from outside the neighborhood enter it, 'we ask them their business,' he said. 'If they say they're going down the street to see Mrs. Jones, fine, we let them pass. but then we follow them down the block to make sure they're really going to see Mrs. Jones.'

Though citizens can do a great deal, the police are plainly the key to order-maintenance. For one thing, many communities, such as the Robert Taylor Homes, cannot do the job by themselves. For another, no citizen in a neighborhood, even an organized one, is likely to feel the sense of responsibility that wearing a badge confers. Psychologists have done many studies on why people fail to go to the aid of persons being attacked or seeking help, and they have learned that the cause is not 'apathy' or 'selfishness' but the absence of some plausible grounds for feeling that one must personally accept responsibility. Ironically, avoiding responsibility is easier when a lot of people are standing about. On streets and in public places, where order is so important, many people are likely to be 'around,' a fact that reduces the chance of any one person acting as the agent of the community. The police officer's uniform singles him out as a person who must accept responsibility if asked. In addition, officers, more easily than their fellow citizens, can be expected to distinguish between what is necessary to protect the safety of the street and what merely protects its ethnic purity.

But the police forces of America are losing, not gaining, members. Some cities have suffered substantial cuts in the number of officers available for duty. These cuts are not likely to be reversed in the near future. Therefore, each department must assign its existing officers with great care. Some neighborhoods are so demoralized and crime-ridden as to make foot patrol useless; the best the police can do with limited resources is respond to the enormous number of calls for service. Other neighborhoods are so stable and serene as to make foot patrol unnecessary. The key is to identify neighborhoods at the tipping point—where the public order is deteriorating but not unreclaimable, where the streets are used frequently but by apprehensive people, where a window is likely to be broken at any time, and must quickly be fixed if all are not to be shattered.

Most police departments do not have ways of systematically identifying such areas and assigning officers to them. Officers are assigned on the basis of crime rates (meaning that marginally threatened areas are often stripped so that police can investigate crimes in areas where the situation is hopeless) or on the basis of calls for service (despite the fact that most citizens do not call the police when they are merely frightened or annoyed). To allocate patrol wisely, the department must look at the neighborhoods and decide, from first-hand evidence, where an additional officer will make the greatest difference in promoting a sense of safety.

One way to stretch limited police resources is being tried in some public-housing projects. Tenant organizations hire off-duty police officers for patrol work in their buildings. The costs are not high (at least not per resident), the officer likes the additional income, and the residents feel safer. Such arrangements are probably more successful than hiring private watchmen, and the Newark experiment helps us understand why. A private security guard may deter crime or misconduct by his presence, and he may go to the aid of persons needing help, but he may well not intervene—that is, control or drive away—someone challenging community standards. Being a sworn officer—a 'real cop'—seems to give one the confidence, the sense of duty, and the aura of authority necessary to perform this difficult task.

Patrol officers might be encouraged to go to and from duty stations on public transportation and, while on the bus or subway car, enforce rules about smoking, drinking, disorderly conduct, and the like. The enforcement need involve nothing more than ejecting the offender (the offense, after all, is not one with which a booking officer or a judge wishes to be bothered). Perhaps the random but relentless maintenance of standards on buses would lead to conditions on buses that approximate the level of civility we now take for granted on airplanes.

But the most important requirement is to think that to maintain order in precarious situations is a vital job. The police know this is one of their functions, and they also believe, correctly, that it cannot be done to the exclusion of criminal investigation and responding to calls. We may have encouraged them to suppose, however, on the basis of our oft-repeated concerns about serious, violent crime, that they will be judged exclusively on their capacity as crime-fighters. To the extent that this is the case, police administrators will continue to concentrate police personnel in the highest-crime areas (though not necessarily in the areas most vulnerable to criminal invasion), emphasize their training in the law and criminal apprehension (and not their training in managing street life), and join too quickly in campaigns to decriminalize 'harmless' behavior (though public drunkenness, street prostitution, and pornographic displays can destroy a community more quickly than any team of professional burglars).

Above all, we must return to out long-abandoned view that the police ought to protect communities as well as individuals. Our crime statistics and victimization surveys measure individual losses, but they do not measure communal losses. Just as physicians now recognize the importance of fostering health rather than simply treating illness, so the police—and the rest of us—ought to recognize the importance of maintaining, intact, communities without broken windows.

Part V

Crime control II: Discipline and governmentality

INTRODUCTION

In 'black letter' discourse, crime is a self-evident fact, its meaning inherent in the actions of a particular individual, from which the consequences flow according to the due process of law. In fact, as will have emerged from the readings to date, things are rather more complicated. Far from having an absolute character, crime is a socially constructed and historically contingent phenomenon. Definitions of acts as 'criminal' or 'legal' must be viewed as tentative and capable of redefinition.

Furthermore, the institutions, authorities and procedures which provide any society with its mechanism for controlling and preventing crime cannot merely be taken at face value as methods of dealing with the particular behaviours of specific individuals. Such measures reflect wider concerns about the existing social order and, as the readings in this section indicate, they are a crucial part of the processes for exerting control, regulation and *discipline* over 'society' and for the *governance* of the soul of individuals and whole populations.

It is widely acknowledged that Michel Foucault's book *Discipline and Punish* (1977) provided criminology with a new theoretical language with which to analyse the practices of punishment in modernity as well as providing the discipline with a greater awareness of its own status as a power/knowledge apparatus related to these very practices. According to Foucault, the 'disciplinary society' emerged in Western Europe in the early nineteenth century. He emphasized that the methods of dealing with criminals in the modern penitentiaries were part of a wider process of disciplining and regimentation in society. The criminal was no longer regarded merely as somebody who had broken the law and had to be punished. Now the criminal/prisoner required close supervision and expert intervention with the view to returning 'him' to normality. Not surprisingly, Foucault was fascinated with Jeremy Bentham's plan for the 'Panopticon'. This confirmed his belief that prison was intended to be an instrument acting with precision upon its individual subjects.

According to Foucault, the prison was just one island in a 'carceral archipelago' of disciplinary institutions which included schools, hospitals and asylums, and barracks, and extending through a 'carceral continuum' to the home and the workplace. In this process the traditional disciplinary mechanisms of the law and custom were powerfully supplemented by new fields of knowledge (including medicine, psychiatry, pedagogy, criminology) and new bodies of experts. As Foucault argues in the first reading included here, the crucial role of the modern prison was to pioneer and legitimize a method of dealing with 'deviants' from prescribed norms which could then be generalized to 'the entire social body'. This theme is taken up in the next three readings which are explicitly influenced by Foucault's work.

Shearing and Stenning are interested in the mechanisms through which the disciplinary society achieves social control. They contrast the essentially *moral* basis of the traditional criminal justice state (including the prison system) with the more *instrumental* and *amoral* character of control methods which operate in the ever growing private sector. Here the aim is not to reform individuals but to restrict the opportunities for crime. Using Disney World as a case-study, they show how such 'non-carceral' but unmistakably 'disciplinary' control measures are embedded in the structures of modern social practice.

The reading by Malcolm Feeley and Jonathan Simon argues that the last decades of the twentieth century have witnessed the emergence of a new penological discourse. This discourse in essence is a managerialist and *actuarialist* approach to the problem of crime and its control. It is not interested in philosophising about or assessing the respective merits of deterrence, just deserts, and individual rehabilitation. Rather it is committed to the effective management of the criminal justice system and its component parts. Cost-effectiveness, efficient forms of custody and control, competition and organizational targets and outputs are the concerns of the new managerial regime. However, Feeley and Simon do recognize that this new systems approach overlaps with more general populist authoritarian discourses on how to manage (and punish) problem populations.

In the second of our readings from Michel Foucault, this French philosopher's second major contribution to the rethinking of criminology is presented in brief. From 1978 until 1984 when he died, Foucault's work explored a new theme, that of governance and governmentality. This tentative work was concerned with the relations between two axes of governance, namely both the forms of rule by which various authorities govern populations and the technologies of the governance of the self through which individuals work on themselves to shape their own subjectivity. The concept of governance thus concerns not simply the actions of the state but relates more generally to all the efforts to guide and direct the conduct of others.

The governmentality literature which has emerged in the wake of Foucault's initial thoughts provides a challenging framework for analysing how crime is problematized and controlled. This body of work focuses on 'the present' and avoids both reductionist and totalising analyses. Instead their anatomy of contemporary practices focuses on how particular modes of exercising power depend on specific ways of thinking ('rationalities') and of acting ('technologies') as well as ways of subjectifying individuals and governing populations. The readings by O'Malley, Garland and Merry represent some of the most interesting engagements with the reconfigured criminological field which Foucault's writing on governmentality opens up.

Pat O'Malley begins by plotting the rise in recent decades of post-disciplinary risk-based technologies of power and control. However, he also counters overly deterministic readings of the growth of actuarial risk management technologies of governance and in turn highlights the 'survival' of older punitive and correctional technologies. O'Malley argues against explanations which focus on increased efficiency as an evolutionary criterion for emerging technologies of power. Instead he suggests that the forms taken by such technologies are primarily determined by the character and success of the political programmes with which they are aligned. Situational crime prevention is explored as a prime example of a neo-liberal, *prudentialist* risk management discourse. Throughout O'Malley's analysis emphasis is placed on the primacy of politics: indeed the 'success' of situational crime prevention compared with other criminological technologies is explained in terms of its broader political and ideological effects (and particularly its attraction to rationalist, neo-conservative and New Right programmes).

David Garland's work represents the most influential critical engagement with the ideas of Foucault in contemporary criminology. Garland provides a sociological overview of the major trends in crime control (and more broadly the culture of control) in late modern societies. His starting point is that crime is now a routine part of modern consciousness and rather than being viewed as something to be eradicated, it is now increasingly viewed as something to be managed. Garland also suggests that the myth of the power of the sovereign state has been severely damaged. This combined normality of high crime rates and the recognition of the reality of the limitations of the state's criminal justice agencies have created a major new predicament for contemporary govern-ments. Garland focuses particularly on the state's ambivalent and volatile response to this predicament in crime control. Two major strategies of crime control are identified. First we witness the emergence of the 'rational choice' adaptive strategies associated with multi-agency crime prevention partner-ships and those technologies associated with 'the new criminologies of everyday life' in which the normality of the criminal and the crime event are accepted and the limitations of state solutions to the problem are taken for granted. These pragmatic adaptive preventive strategies are also predicated on what has been termed a strategy of responsibilization whereby the state seeks to act upon crime not in a direct fashion through state agencies but by acting indirectly and activating action by non-state agencies and groups. Second, in sharp contrast to these adaptive strategies, we find a recurring recourse to punitive display which Garland characterizes as strategies of denial drawing on a punitive, sovereign response. In this second set of control strategies the criminal is viewed as the pathological other to be ostentatiously punished and expelled from society, chiefly via mass incarceration. Both strategies, preventive and punitive, are viewed as symptoms of the eclipse of the social democratically inspired 'solidarity project and its penal-welfare strategy.

In the next reading, Sally Engle Merry draws on the governmentality literature to analyse the different techniques for governing gender violence in contemporary society. She argues that the new urban social order depends on a complex and intersecting mix of systems of punishment, discipline and security. In particular, Merry argues that contemporary urban orders are increasingly based on the governance of space (rather than the punishment of offences or the discipline of offenders). Alongside the well-documented rise of privatized security systems and consumer-policed spaces such as shopping malls, Merry analyses the growing deployment of spatial forms of govern-mentality in gender violence situations. She suggests that security through the use of protection orders represents the most innovative features of con-temporary efforts to diminish wife battering and may open up the possibility of more democratic forms of spatial governance for the protection of vulnerable populations. However the selective deployment of this governmental technique also reflects the structural inequalities linked to class and ethnicity as well as gender.

36

The carceral

Michel Foucault

[. . .] [I]n penal justice, the prison transformed the punitive procedure into a penitentiary technique; the carceral archipelago transported this technique from the penal
institution to the entire social body. With several important results.

1   This vast mechanism established a slow, continuous, imperceptible gradation
that made it possible to pass naturally from disorder to offence and back from a
transgression of the law to a slight departure from a rule, an average, a demand, a
norm. In the classical period, despite a certain common reference to offence in
general, the order of the crime, the order of sin and the order of bad conduct
remained separate in so far as they related to separate criteria and authorities (court,
penitence, confinement). Incarceration with its mechanisms of surveillance and
punishment functioned, on the contrary, according to a principle of relative continuity. The continuity of the institutions themselves, which were linked to one
another (public assistance with the orphanage, the reformatory, the penitentiary, the
disciplinary battalion, the prison; the school with the charitable society, the workshop, the almshouse, the penitentiary convent; the workers' estate with the hospital
and the prison). A continuity of the punitive criteria and mechanisms, which on the
basis of a mere deviation gradually strengthened the rules and increased the punishment. A continuous gradation of the established, specialized and competent
authorities (in the order of knowledge and in the order of power) which, without
resort to arbitrariness, but strictly according to the regulations, by means of observation and assessment hierarchized, differentiated, judged, punished and moved
gradually from the correction of irregularities to the punishment of crime. The
'carceral' with its many diffuse or compact forms, its institutions of supervision or
constraint, of discreet surveillance and insistent coercion, assured the communication
of punishments according to quality and quantity; it connected in series or disposed
according to subtle divisions the minor and the serious penalties, the mild and the
strict forms of treatment, bad marks and light sentences. You will end up in the
convict-ship, the slightest indiscipline seems to say; and the harshest of prisons says
to the prisoners condemned to life: I shall note the slightest irregularity in your

From *Discipline and Punish* (trans. Alan Sheridan), pp. 298–308. (London: Allen
Lane, 1977.)

conduct. The generality of the punitive function that the eighteenth century sought in the 'ideological' technique of representations and signs now had as its support the extension, the material framework, complex, dispersed, but coherent, of the various carceral mechanisms. As a result, a certain significant generality moved between the least irregularity and the greatest crime; it was no longer the offence, the attack on the common interest, it was the departure from the norm, the anomaly; it was this that haunted the school, the court, the asylum or the prison. It generalized in the sphere of meaning the function that the carceral generalized in the sphere of tactics. Replacing the adversary of the sovereign, the social enemy was transformed into a deviant, who brought with him the multiple danger of disorder, crime and madness. The carceral network linked, through innumerable relations, the two long, multiple series of the punitive and the abnormal.

2   The carceral, with its far-reaching networks, allows the recruitment of major 'delinquents'. It organizes what might be called 'disciplinary careers' in which, through various exclusions and rejections, a whole process is set in motion. In the classical period, there opened up in the confines or interstices of society the confused, tolerant and dangerous domain of the 'outlaw' or at least of that which eluded the direct hold of power: an uncertain space that was for criminality a training ground and a region of refuge; there poverty, unemployment, pursued innocence, cunning, the struggle against the powerful, the refusal of obligations and laws, and organized crime all came together as chance and fortune would dictate; it was the domain of adventure that Gil Blas, Sheppard or Mandrin, each in his own way, inhabited. Through the play of disciplinary differentiations and divisions, the nineteenth century constructed rigorous channels which, within the system, inculcated docility and produced delinquency by the same mechanisms. There was a sort of disciplinary 'training', continuous and compelling, that had something of the pedagogical curriculum and something of the professional network. Careers emerged from it, as secure, as predictable, as those of public life: assistance associations, residential apprenticeships, penal colonies, disciplinary battalions, prisons, hospitals, almshouses. These networks were already well mapped out at the beginning of the nineteenth century:

> Our benevolent establishments present an admirably coordinated whole by means of which the indigent does not remain a moment without help from the cradle to the grave. Follow the course of the unfortunate man: you will see him born among foundlings; from there he passes to the nursery, then to an orphanage; at the age of six he goes off to primary school and later to adult schools. If he cannot work, he is placed on the list of the charity offices of his district, and if he falls ill he may choose between twelve hospitals . . . Lastly, when the poor Parisian reaches the end of his career, seven almshouses await his age and often their salubrious régime has prolonged his useless days well beyond those of the rich man. (Moreau de Jonnès, quoted in Touquet)

The carceral network does not cast the unassimilable into a confused hell; there is no outside. It takes back with one hand what it seems to exclude with the other. It saves everything, including what it punishes. It is unwilling to waste even what it has decided to disqualify. In this panoptic society of which incarceration is the omnipresent armature, the delinquent is not outside the law; he is, from the very outset, in the law, at the very heart of the law, or at least in the midst of those mechanisms that transfer the individual imperceptibly from discipline to the law, from deviation to offence. Although it is true that prison punishes delinquency, delinquency is for the most part produced in and by an incarceration which, ultimately, prison perpetuates in its turn. The prison is merely the natural consequence, no more than a higher degree, of that hierarchy laid down step by step. The delinquent is an institutional product. It is no use being surprised, therefore, that in a considerable proportion of cases the biography of convicts passes through all these mechanisms and establishments, whose purpose, it is widely believed, is to lead away from prison. That one should find in them what one might call the index of an irrepressibly delinquent 'character': the prisoner condemned to hard labour was meticulously produced by a childhood spent in a reformatory, according to the lines of force of the generalized carceral system. Conversely, the lyricism of marginality may find inspiration in the image of the 'outlaw', the great social nomad, who prowls on the confines of a docile, frightened order. But it is not on the fringes of society and through successive exiles that criminality is born, but by means of ever more closely placed insertions, under ever more insistent surveillance, by an accumulation of disciplinary coercion. In short, the carceral archipelago assures, in the depths of the social body, the formation of delinquency on the basis of subtle illegalities, the overlapping of the latter by the former and the establishment of a specified criminality.

3 But perhaps the most important effect of the carceral system and of its extension well beyond legal imprisonment is that it succeeds in making the power to punish natural and legitimate, in lowering at least the threshold of tolerance to penality. It tends to efface what may be exorbitant in the exercise of punishment. It does this by playing the two registers in which it is deployed – the legal register of justice and the extra-legal register of discipline – against one another. In effect, the great continuity of the carceral system throughout the law and its sentences gives a sort of legal sanction to the disciplinary mechanisms, to the decisions and judgements that they enforce. Throughout this network, which comprises so many 'regional' institutions, relatively autonomous and independent, is transmitted, with the 'prison-form', the model of justice itself. The regulations of the disciplinary establishments may reproduce the law, the punishments imitate the verdicts and penalties, the surveillance repeat the police model; and, above all these multiple establishments, the prison, which in relation to them is a pure form, unadulterated and unmitigated, gives them a sort of official sanction. The carceral, with its long gradation stretching from the convictship or imprisonment with hard labour to diffuse, slight limitations, communicates a type of power that the law validates and that justice uses as its favourite weapon. How could the disciplines and the power that functions in them appear arbitrary, when they merely operate the mechanisms of justice itself, even with a view to mitigating their intensity? When, by generalizing its effects and transmitting it to every level, it makes it possible to avoid its full rigour? Carceral continuity and the fusion of the prison-form make it possible to legalize, or in any case to legitimate disciplinary power, which thus avoids any element of excess or abuse it may entail.

But, conversely, the carceral pyramid gives to the power to inflict legal punishment a context in which it appears to be free of all excess and all violence. In the subtle gradation of the apparatuses of discipline and of the successive 'embeddings' that they involve, the prison does not at all represent the unleashing of a different kind of power, but simply an additional degree in the intensity of a mechanism that has continued to operate since the earliest forms of legal punishment. Between the latest institution of 'rehabilitation', where one is taken in order to avoid prison, and the prison where one is sent after a definable offence, the difference is (and must be) scarcely perceptible. There is a strict economy that has the effect of rendering as discreet as possible the singular power to punish. There is nothing in it now that recalls the former excess of sovereign power when it revenged its authority on the tortured body of those about to be executed. Prison continues, on those who are entrusted to it, a work begun elsewhere, which the whole of society pursues on each individual through innumerable mechanisms of discipline. By means of a carceral continuum, the authority that sentences infiltrates all those other authorities that supervise, transform, correct, improve. It might even be said that nothing really distinguishes them any more except the singularly 'dangerous' character of the delinquents, the gravity of their departures from normal behaviour and the necessary solemnity of the ritual. But, in its function, the power to punish is not essentially different from that of curing or educating. It receives from them, and from their lesser, smaller task, a sanction from below; but one that is no less important for that, since it is the sanction of technique and rationality. The carceral 'naturalizes' the legal power to punish, as it 'legalizes' the technical power to discipline. In thus homogenizing them, effacing what may be violent in one and arbitrary in the other, attenuating the effects of revolt that they may both arouse, thus depriving excess in either of any purpose, circulating the same calculated, mechanical and discreet methods from one to the other, the carceral makes it possible to carry out that great 'economy' of power whose formula the eighteenth century had sought, when the problem of the accumulation and useful administration of men first emerged.

By operating at every level of the social body and by mingling ceaselessly the art of rectifying and the right to punish, the universality of the carceral lowers the level from which it becomes natural and acceptable to be punished. The question is often posed as to how, before and after the Revolution, a new foundation was given to the right to punish. And no doubt the answer is to be found in the theory of the contract. But it is perhaps more important to ask the reverse question: how were people made to accept the power to punish, or quite simply, when punished, tolerate being so. The theory of the contract can only answer this question by the fiction of a juridical subject giving to others the power to exercise over him the right that he himself possesses over them. It is highly probable that the great carceral continuum, which provides a communication between the power of discipline and the power of the law, and extends without interruption from the smallest coercions to the longest penal detention, constituted the technical and real, immediately material counterpart of that chimerical granting of the right to punish.

4 With this new economy of power, the carceral system, which is its basic instrument, permitted the emergence of a new form of 'law': a mixture of legality and nature, prescription and constitution, the norm. This had a whole series of effects: the internal dislocation of the judicial power or at least of its functioning; an increasing difficulty in judging, as if one were ashamed to pass sentence; a furious desire on the part of the judges to judge, assess, diagnose, recognize the normal and abnormal and claim the honour of curing or rehabilitating. In view of this, it is useless to believe in the good or bad consciences of judges, or even of their unconscious. Their immense 'appetite for medicine' which is constantly manifested – from their appeal to psychiatric experts, to their attention to the chatter of criminology –

expresses the major fact that the power they exercise has been 'denatured'; that it is at a certain level governed by laws; that at another, more fundamental level it functions as a normative power; it is the economy of power that they exercise, and not that of their scruples or their humanism, that makes them pass 'therapeutic' sentences and recommend 'rehabilitating' periods of imprisonment. But, conversely, if the judges accept ever more reluctantly to condemn for the sake of condemning, the activity of judging has increased precisely to the extent that the normalizing power has spread. Borne along by the omnipresence of the mechanisms of discipline, basing itself on all the carceral apparatuses, it has become one of the major functions of our society. The judges of normality are present everywhere. We are in the society of the teacher–judge, the doctor–judge, the educator–judge, the 'social worker'– judge; it is on them that the universal reign of the normative is based; and each individual, wherever he may find himself, subjects to it his body, his gestures, his behaviour, his aptitudes, his achievements. The carceral network, in its compact or disseminated forms, with its systems of insertion, distribution, surveillance, observation, has been the greatest support, in modern society, of the normalizing power.

5   The carceral texture of society assures both the real capture of the body and its perpetual observation; it is, by its very nature, the apparatus of punishment that conforms most completely to the new economy of power and the instrument for the formation of knowledge that this very economy needs. Its panoptic functioning enables it to play this double role. By virtue of its methods of fixing, dividing, recording, it has been one of the simplest, crudest, also most concrete, but perhaps most indispensable conditions for the development of this immense activity of examination that has objectified human behaviour. If, after the age of 'inquisitorial' justice, we have entered the age of 'examinatory' justice, if, in an even more general way, the method of examination has been able to spread so widely throughout society, and to give rise in part to the sciences of man, one of the great instruments for this has been the multiplicity and close overlapping of the various mechanisms of incarceration. I am not saying that the human sciences emerged from the prison. But, if they have been able to be formed and to produce so many profound changes in the episteme, it is because they have been conveyed by a specific and new modality of power: a certain policy of the body, a certain way of rendering the group of men docile and useful. This policy required the involvement of definite relations of knowledge in relations of power; it called for a technique of overlapping subjection and objectification; it brought with it new procedures of individualization. The carceral network constituted one of the armatures of this power–knowledge that has made the human sciences historically possible. Knowable man (soul, individuality, consciousness, conduct, whatever it is called) is the object–effect of this analytical investment, of this domination–observation.

6   This no doubt explains the extreme solidity of the prison, that slight invention that was nevertheless decried from the outset. If it had been no more than an instrument of rejection or repression in the service of a state apparatus, it would have been easier to alter its more overt forms or to find a more acceptable substitute for it. But, rooted as it was in mechanisms and strategies of power, it could meet any attempt to transform it with a great force of inertia. One fact is characteristic: when it is a question of altering the system of imprisonment, opposition does not come from the judicial institutions alone; resistance is to be found not in the prison as

penal sanction, but in the prison with all its determinations, links and extra-judicial results; in the prison as the relay in a general network of disciplines and surveillances; in the prison as it functions in a panoptic regime. This does not mean that it cannot be altered, nor that it is once and for all indispensable to our kind of society. One may, on the contrary, cite the two processes which, in the very continuity of the processes that make the prison function, are capable of exercising considerable restraint on its use and of transforming its internal functioning. And no doubt these processes have already begun to a large degree. The first is that which reduces the utility (or increases its inconveniences) of a delinquency accommodated as a specific illegality, locked up and supervised; thus the growth of great national or international illegalities directly linked to the political and economic apparatuses (financial illegalities, information services, arms and drugs trafficking, property speculation) makes it clear that the somewhat rustic and conspicuous work force of delinquency is proving ineffective; or again, on a smaller scale, as soon as the economic levy on sexual pleasure is carried out more efficiently by the sale of contraceptives, or obliquely through publications, films or shows, the archaic hierarchy of prostitution loses much of its former usefulness. The second process is the growth of the disciplinary networks, the multiplication of their exchanges with the penal apparatus, the ever more important powers that are given them, the ever more massive transference to them of judicial functions; now, as medicine, psychology, education, public assistance, 'social work' assume an ever greater share of the powers of supervision and assessment, the penal apparatus will be able, in turn, to become medicalized, psychologized, educationalized; and by the same token that turning-point represented by the prison becomes less useful when, through the gap between its penitentiary discourse and its effect of consolidating delinquency, it articulates the penal power and the disciplinary power. In the midst of all these mechanisms of normalization, which are becoming ever more rigorous in their application, the specificity of the prison and its role as link are losing something of their purpose.

If there is an overall political issue around the prison, it is not therefore whether it is to be corrective or not; whether the judges, the psychiatrists or the sociologists are to exercise more power in it than the administrators or supervisors; it is not even whether we should have prison or something other than prison. At present, the problem lies rather in the steep rise in the use of these mechanisms of normalization and the wide-ranging powers which, through the proliferation of new disciplines, they bring with them. In 1836, a correspondent wrote to *La Phalange*:

> Moralists, philosophers, legislators, flatterers of civilization, this is the plan of your Paris, neatly ordered and arranged, here is the improved plan in which all like things are gathered together. At the centre, and within a first enclosure: hospitals for all diseases, almshouses for all types of poverty, madhouses, prisons, convict-prisons for men, women and children. Around the first enclosure, barracks, court-rooms, police stations, houses for prison warders, scaffolds, houses for the executioner and his assistants. At the four corners, the Chamber of Deputies, the Chamber of Peers, the Institute and the Royal Palace. Outside, there are the various services that supply the central enclosure, commerce, with its swindlers and its bankruptcies; industry and its furious struggles; the press, with its sophisms; the gambling dens; prostitution, the people dying of hunger or wallowing in debauchery, always ready to lend an ear to the voice of the Genius of Revolutions; the heartless rich . . . Lastly the ruthless war of all against all. (*La Phalange*, 10 August 1836)

I shall stop with this anonymous text. We are now far away from the country of tortures, dotted with wheels, gibbets, gallows, pillories; we are far, too, from that dream of the reformers, less than fifty years before: the city of punishments in which a thousand small theatres would have provided an endless multicoloured representation of justice in which the punishments, meticulously produced on decorative scaffolds, would have constituted the permanent festival of the penal code. The carceral city, with its imaginary 'geo-politics', is governed by quite different principles. The extract from *La Phalange* reminds us of some of the more important ones: that at the centre of this city, and as if to hold it in place, there is, not the 'centre of power', not a network of forces, but a multiple network of diverse elements – walls, space, institution, rules, discourse; that the model of the carceral city is not, therefore, the body of the king, with the powers that emanate from it, nor the contractual meeting of wills from which a body that was both individual and collective was born, but a strategic distribution of elements of different natures and levels. That the prison is not the daughter of laws, codes or the judicial apparatus; that it is not subordinated to the court and the docile or clumsy instrument of the sentences that it hands out and of the results that it would like to achieve; that it is the court that is external and subordinate to the prison. That in the central position that it occupies, it is not alone, but linked to a whole series of 'carceral' mechanisms which seem distinct enough – since they are intended to alleviate pain, to cure, to comfort – but which all tend, like the prison, to exercise a power of normalization. That these mechanisms are applied not to transgressions against a 'central' law, but to the apparatus of production – 'commerce' and 'industry' – to a whole multiplicity of illegalities, in all their diversity of nature and origin, their specific role in profit and the different ways in which they are dealt with by the punitive mechanisms. And that ultimately what presides over all these mechanisms is not the unitary functioning of an apparatus or an institution, but the necessity of combat and the rules of strategy. That, consequently, the notions of institutions of repression, rejection, exclusion, marginalization, are not adequate to describe, at the very centre of the carceral city, the formation of the insidious leniencies, unavowable petty cruelties, small acts of cunning, calculated methods, techniques, 'sciences' that permit the fabrication of the disciplinary individual. In this central and centralized humanity, the effect and instrument of complex power relations, bodies and forces subjected by multiple mechanisms of 'incarceration', objects for discourses that are in themselves elements for this strategy, we must hear the distant roar of battle.

[. . .]

37

From the Panopticon to Disney World: The development of discipline

Clifford D. Shearing and Philip C. Stenning

In the literature on punishment an interesting and important debate has recently surfaced on the question of whether modern penal developments in the criminal justice system represent an extension of discipline (in the sense in which Foucault used the term) or a move away from it. In an influential article published in 1979, Cohen argued that modern penal practices provide evidence of a significant 'dispersal of social control', in which the community is increasingly being involved in its administration. He also claimed, however, that this dispersal of social control is 'merely a continuation of the overall pattern established in the nineteenth century' (p. 359), and described by Foucault, in which corporal punishment (based on the administration of pain and torture to the body) was replaced by carceral punishment (based on the exercise of sustained discipline over the soul).

In an incisive critique of Cohen's thesis, Bottoms has recently sought to show – successfully in our view – that while Cohen's conclusion that modern penal developments represent a significant dispersal of social control is correct, his conclusion that these developments are an extension of disciplinary punishment is not. Specifically, Bottoms argued that the most significant recent developments in penal practice – the greatly increased use of the fine, the growth of community service orders and the modern resort to compensation and related matters – are not essentially disciplinary in character. In making this argument, Bottoms makes the point that these new modes of punishment lack the element of 'soul-training' which is the essential hallmark of disciplinary carceral punishment. He went on to speculate that this move away from disciplinary punishment within the criminal justice system may have been made possible, and encouraged, because more effective preventative social control measures are being implemented within the general society outside the criminal justice system. This latter system, the argument goes, is increasingly being regarded only as a 'last resort' in social control, and as a result 'juridical' rather than disciplinary carceral punishments are being resorted to within it (Bottoms, 1983: 187–8, 191, 195).

From *Perspectives in Criminal Law* (eds A. Doob and E. Greenspan), pp. 335-49. (Ontario: Canada Law Book Inc., 1985.)

Thus far, Bottoms's argument is entirely consistent with similar arguments we have made in our explanations of the implications for social control of the modern growth of private security and private control systems (Shearing and Stenning, 1983). These, we have contended, are preventative rather than punitive in character, rely heavily on strategies of disciplinary control, and make resort to the more punitively orientated public criminal justice system only as a last resort when their own strategies have failed to achieve their instrumentally conceived objectives.

Bottoms, however, went on to argue that we, too, are wrong to characterize such private control systems as disciplinary in the Foucauldian sense. This, he wrote, was because the systems we described lack the essential ingredient of discipline, which he characterized as '"the mechanics of training" upon the bodies and souls of individuals' (Bottoms, 1983: 182). Work by Mathiesen (1980, 1983), in which he characterized modern trends away from individualism as the organizing focus of social control, and towards 'surveillance of whole categories of people' as 'a change from open to hidden discipline', was criticized by Bottoms for the same reasons (Bottoms, 1983: 181–2). In both cases, he argued that the mere extension of *surveillance*, without the accompanying individualized soul-training, does not constitute 'discipline' as Foucault intended the term.

The explicit assumption which Bottoms makes in thus characterizing modern non-penal systems of social control as not 'disciplinary', is that 'discipline' necessarily involves individualized soul-training. In this essay, we shall seek to argue that the concept of 'discipline', as used by Foucault, is much broader than this, and is appropriate to describe many modern forms of social control which do not apparently have individualized soul-training as their primary organizing focus. More particularly, we shall argue that the identification of discipline with individualized soul-training reflects a failure adequately to distinguish between Foucault's generic concept of discipline and his more historically specific examination of it in the context of carceral punishment. Having made this argument, the essay will conclude with an examination of a popular modern exemplar of non-carceral disciplinary social control which, we believe, represents an important indication of what the 'social control apparatus of society is actually getting up to' (Cohen, 1979: 339).

DISCIPLINE AND CARCERAL PUNISHMENT

Central to Foucault's argument in *Discipline and Punish* is his contention that discipline as a generic form of power should be distinguished from the particular strategies through which it is expressed at any particular time.

> 'Discipline' may be identified neither with an institution nor with an apparatus; it is a type of power, a modality for its exercise, comprising a whole set of instruments, techniques, procedures, levels of application, targets; it is a 'physics' or anatomy of power, technology. (1977: 215)

This distinction between discipline, as a type of power, and its particular expression, is important for it allows for the possibility of the evolution of discipline through a series of different concrete expressions. Given this distinction it becomes apparent that carceral punishment, as exemplified in Bentham's Panopticon, should be seen as an instance of discipline that seeks compliance through individual soul-training. It is, however, only one possible expression, albeit the one that occupied Foucault's attention.

What, then, are the essential characteristics of 'discipline' as a generic concept? There can be no doubt that training of one sort or another is an objective if not an explicit element of 'discipline'. Indeed, the very derivation of the word (from the Latin *disciplina* = instruction, tuition) confirms this. The nature of such training, however, and the manner in which it is accomplished, will vary accordingly to the context in which discipline is applied. Of this we shall say more in a moment. For Foucault, there was another essential characteristic of discipline – namely, that it is a type of power that is embedded in, and dispersed through, the micro relations that constitute society. Unlike monarchical power (which is expressed through terror and torture) it is not located outside and above the social relations to be controlled but is integrated into them. As it is part of the social fabric it is everywhere, and yet it is nowhere, because it does not have an identifiable locus.

> disciplines have to bring into play the power relations, not above but inside the very texture of the multiplicity, as discretely as possible. . . . (1977: 220)

It is this embedded character that defines the Panopticon as an exemplar for discipline.

> [The Panopticon] is an important mechanism, for it automizes and disindividualizes power. Power has its principle not so much in a person as in a certain concerted distribution of bodies, surfaces, lights, gazes; in an arrangement whose internal mechanisms produce the relation in which individuals are caught up. The ceremonies, the rituals, the marks by which the sovereign's surplus power was manifested are useless. There is a machinery that assures dissymmetry, disequilibrium, difference. Consequently, it does not matter who exercises power. Any individual taken almost at random, can operate the machine. . . . (1977: 202)

The embedded nature of discipline makes it especially suitable as a preventative mode of control, as the surveillance (that is its basis) becomes part of the very relations to be controlled. Foucault illustrates this in discussing discipline in the context of the workshop:

> The discipline of the workshop, while remaining a way of enforcing respect for the regulations and authorities, of preventing thefts and losses, tends to increase aptitudes, speeds, output and therefore profits; it still exerts a moral influence over behavior, but more and more it treats actions in terms of their results, introduces bodies into a machinery, forces into an economy. (1977: 210)

It is precisely because of this embedded character of discipline that its nature varies according to the context in which it is applied, and it is for this reason that, when applied in the context of carceral punishment, one of its distinctive elements is that of individualized soul-training. This is because the context of carceral punishment (unlike that, for instance, of the factory, the hospital or the workshop) is essentially a moral one rather than a primarily instrumental one. It is perhaps because Foucault was primarily concerned to explain 'the birth of the prison' in *Discipline and Punish*, that the elements of carceral discipline have so easily come to be thought to be the fundamental elements of *all* discipline. As we shall try to illustrate, however, when applied in a context which is primarily instrumental rather than moral, the elements of discipline are significantly different.

INSTRUMENTAL AND MORAL DISCIPLINE

The three models of control that Foucault identifies (monarchical, juridical and carceral), while fundamentally different in disciplinary terms, all share a moral foundation that defines them as 'justice' systems. Foucault, in his analysis of these types of control, tended to take this feature for granted as it was common to all three models. As a result, if one works from within Foucault's framework in studying contemporary control, although one's attention will be directed towards discipline, the issue of whether the moral foundation of social control is changing will tend not to be considered. This is evident in the work of all the participants in the debate we have reviewed. Yet if contemporary control, especially as it appears in the private sector, is to be understood, it is precisely this issue (as the quotation above about disciplinary control in the work place suggests) that needs to be addressed. What makes private control different from traditional criminal justice is not its disciplinary character, which it shares with carceral control, but the challenge it offers to the moral foundation of the order-maintenance process (Shearing and Stenning, 1983).

Within criminal justice 'order' is fundamentally a moral phenomenon and its maintenance a moral process. Accordingly, social order (and its enforcement) tends to be defined in absolute terms: one proper order expressing 'natural justice'. Within criminal justice the premise that shapes order maintenance is that order is the expression of a community of morally righteous people. Thus, the criminal process is concerned with the rightness and wrongness of acts and the goodness and badness of people. It defines the boundaries of moral order by stigmatizing certain acts and persons as morally tainted (Durkheim). Its methods are indignation, retribution and redemption. Each of the models of punishment Foucault identified represents a different set of strategies for doing this.

Every aspect of the criminal process is structured and shaped by its moral, absolutist foundation. Within it, discipline is a technology of power used to achieve this moral purpose. There is no better illustration of this than the carceral regime which targets the soul, the moral centre of the human being, so as to provide for its moral reformation. Not surprisingly, therefore, individualized soul-training is the essential hallmark of carceral discipline.

Private control, in sharp contrast, rejects a moral conception of order and the control process. Private security executives, for example, not only reject, as Wilson does, the present possibility of moral reform but reject the very idea of moral reform as a basis for control. Within private control, order is conceived primarily in instrumental rather than moral terms. Order is simply the set of conditions most conducive to achieving fundamental community objectives. Thus in a business corporation, for instance, order is usually whatever maximizes profit.

In contrasting their definition of order with that of criminal justice, private control systems stress that for them 'theft' is not a moral category and consequently does not deserve, or require, a moral response. Within private control the instrumental language of profit and loss replaces the moral language of criminal justice. This is not merely terminological (different terms for the same objects) but a reconstitution of the social world. 'Loss' refers not simply to theft but includes, among other things, the cost of attempting to control theft. This redefinition has important implications for the way in which control is exercised and thus for order. For example, theft will not be subject to control if the cost of doing so is likely to be greater than the initial loss.

Where moral rhetoric appears in private control it does so not as principles that guide the order-maintenance process (as it does in judicial decision-making) but simply as a control strategy. For example, employees may be given a lecture on morality not because control is conceived of in moral terms but because it creates attitudes that are good for profit. In such a context, training, as an element of discipline, need be neither individualized nor particularly directed at the soul. Indeed, from the point of view of the evolution of discipline, perhaps the most important consequence of the shift to an instrumental focus has been the move away from a concern with individual reformation to the control of the opportunities that permit breaches of order to occur. Accordingly, within private control it is prevention through the reduction of opportunities for disorder that is the primary focus of attention (Shearing and Stenning, 1982). This directs attention away from traditional offenders to a new class of delinquents: those who create opportunities for disorder. It is thus, to use banking as an illustration, not the employee who steals who is the primary focus of the control system's attention but the teller who creates the opportunity for the theft by neglecting to secure his/her cash drawer.

This transformation of the preventative thrust within discipline has important implications for other aspects of disciplinary control. The most visible is the change in the nature of surveillance as attention shifts from the morally culpable individual to the *categories* of people who create opportunities for disorder (Mathiesen, 1983; Rule et al., 1983).

Although this focus on opportunities creates a need for mass surveillance it does not eliminate carefully pinpointed surveillance. Its purpose, however, changes; it is no longer soul-training, as such, but rather 'tuning up the machine' (of which the human operator merely constitutes one part). While such scrutiny may, for this reason, focus on individuals, it is just as likely to target system deficiencies, for instance, in the paper systems that provide for ongoing surveillance, as well as retrospective surveillance, through the paper trails that they create.

In summary, the emergence of an explicitly instrumental focus in control has changed the nature of disciplinary power while reinforcing its embedded features. Thus surveillance, while changing both its focus and its purpose, has become increasingly embedded in other structures and functions. For example, the surveillance which Oscar Newman sought to achieve through 'defensible space' is embedded both in the structure of the physical environment, as well as in the social relations it facilitates.

Finally, we may note that an instrumental focus implies a variety of orders, each reflecting the fact that different communities have different objectives. Thus, within private control systems, we find not one conception of order but many; not one societal order but many community-based orders.

PRIVATE NON-CARCERAL DISCIPLINE

In seeking to identify the carceral model, and in explicating its relationship to disciplinary control, Foucault realized that, at any point in time, the actual control mechanisms in force would reflect the influences of both established and developing forms (1977: 130). Thus in order to identify the nature and direction of these forms he turned to the ideas and projects of influential reformers. Hence his use of the Panopticon as an exemplar of the disciplinary form as expressed through carceral strategies.

This approach suggests that in seeking to understand contemporary control we should direct our attention to strategies in arenas relatively immune from the influence of the carceral model. As public sector control has been dominated over the past century by the soul-training of the carceral model we are likely to find that the control strategies within this arena will reflect a mix of both established and newer forms, so that although it will be possible to identify disciplinary initiatives, we are not likely to find exemplary instances of contemporary embedded control here. The reverse, however, is likely to be true with respect to private control systems which, because they were in decline for most of the nineteenth and the first half of the twentieth centuries, are remarkably free of carceral overtones (Spitzer and Scull, 1977; Shearing and Stenning, 1981, 1983). Their contemporary manifestations, however, display precisely the embedded features that characterize disciplinary control (Shearing and Stenning, 1982: 101). Thus, in seeking an exemplar of contemporary discipline, we turn to the private arena.
[. . .]

DISNEY WORLD: AN EXEMPLAR OF INSTRUMENTAL DISCIPLINE

As the discussion to this point has indicated, research on private security has already confirmed the development of a contemporary form of discipline outside of the moral restraints of criminal justice and begun to identify some of its distinguishing features. To elucidate the notion of instrumental discipline we contrast it with moral discipline by identifying the analytic equivalents of the carceral project and the Panopticon so as to highlight the nature of the changes that have been occurring in the development of discipline. As the identification of order with profit provides the most explicit example of an instrumental order, corporate control is an appropriate equivalent to the carceral model. As the features of corporate control are highly developed in the recreational facilities operated by Disney Productions and as these facilities are so widely known (directly through visits or indirectly through media coverage and Disney advertising), Disney World, in Orlando, Florida, provides a suitable exemplar to set against the Panopticon. In order to avoid lengthy descriptions of security strategies we will draw our illustrations from consumer controls which every visitor to Disney World encounters.

The essential features of Disney's control system become apparent the moment the visitor enters Disney World. As one arrives by car one is greeted by a series of smiling young people who, with the aid of clearly visible road markings, direct one to one's parking spot, remind one to lock one's car and to remember its location and then direct one to await the rubber wheeled train that will convey visitors away from the parking lot. At the boarding location one is directed to stand safely behind guard rails and to board the train in an orderly fashion. While climbing on board one is reminded to remember the name of the parking area and the row number in which one is parked (for instance, 'Donald Duck, 1'). Once on the train one is encouraged to protect oneself from injury by keeping one's body within the bounds of the carriage and to do the same for children in one's care. Before disembarking one is told how to get from the train back to the monorail platform and where to wait for the train to the parking lot on one's return. At each transition from one stage of one's journey to the next one is wished a happy day and a 'good time' at Disney World (this begins as one drives in and is directed by road signs to tune one's car radio to the Disney radio network).

[. . .]

It will be apparent from the above that Disney Productions is able to handle large crowds of visitors in a most orderly fashion. Potential trouble is anticipated and prevented. Opportunities for disorder are minimized by constant instruction, by physical barriers which severely limit the choice of action available and by the surveillance of omnipresent employees who detect and rectify the slightest deviation.

The vehicles that carry people between locations are an important component of the system of physical barriers. Throughout Disney World vehicles are used as barriers. This is particularly apparent in the Epcot Center, the newest Disney facility, where many exhibits are accessible only via special vehicles which automatically secure one once they begin moving.

Control strategies are embedded in both environmental features and structural relations. In both cases control structures and activities have other functions which are highlighted so that the control function is overshadowed. None the less, control is pervasive. For example, virtually every pool, fountain and flower garden serves both as an aesthetic object and to direct visitors away from, or towards, particular locations. Similarly, every Disney Productions employee, while visibly and primarily engaged in other functions, is also engaged in the maintenance of order. This integration of functions is real and not simply an appearance: beauty *is* created, safety *is* protected, employees *are* helpful. The effect is, however, to embed the control function into the 'woodwork' where its presence is unnoticed but its effects are ever present.

A critical consequence of this process of embedding control in other structures is that control becomes consensual. It is effected with the willing cooperation of those being controlled so that the controlled become, as Foucault (1977: 170) has observed, the source of their own control. Thus, for example, the batching that keeps families together provides for family unity while at the same time ensuring that parents will be available to control their children. By seeking a definition of order within Disney World that can convincingly be presented as being in the interest of visitors, order maintenance is established as a voluntary activity which allows coercion to be reduced to a minimum. Thus, adult visitors willingly submit to a variety of devices that increase the flow of consumers through Disney World, such as being corralled on the monorail platform, so as to ensure the safety of their children. Furthermore, while doing so they gratefully acknowledge the concern Disney Productions has for their family, thereby legitimating its authority, not only in the particular situation in question, but in others as well. Thus, while profit ultimately underlies the order Disney Productions seeks to maintain, it is pursued in conjunction with other objectives that will encourage the willing compliance of visitors in maintaining Disney profits. This approach to profit-making, which seeks a coincidence of corporate and individual interests (employee and consumer alike), extends beyond the control function and reflects a business philosophy to be applied to all corporate operations (Peters and Waterman).

The coercive edge of Disney's control system is seldom far from the surface, however, and becomes visible the moment the Disney-visitor consensus breaks down, that is, when a visitor attempts to exercise a choice that is incompatible with the Disney order. It is apparent in the physical barriers that forcefully prevent certain activities as well as in the action of employees who detect breaches of order. This can be illustrated by an incident that occurred during a visit to Disney World by Shearing and his daughter, during the course of which she developed a blister on her heel. To avoid further irritation she removed her shoes and proceeded to walk barefooted. They had not progressed ten yards before they were approached by a very personable security guard dressed as a Bahamian police officer, with white pith helmet and white gloves that perfectly suited the theme of the area they were moving through (so that he, at first, appeared more like a scenic prop than a security person), who informed them that walking barefoot was, 'for the safety of visitors', not permitted. [After explaining] that, given the blister, the safety of this visitor was likely to be better secured by remaining barefooted, at least on the walkways, they were informed that their safety and how best to protect it was a matter for Disney Productions to determine while they were on Disney property and that unless they complied he would be compelled to escort them out of Disney World. Shearing's daughter, on learning that failure to comply with the security guard's instruction would deprive her of the pleasures of Disney World, quickly decided that she would prefer to further injure her heel and remain on Disney property. As this example illustrates, the source of Disney Productions' power rests both in the physical coercion it can bring to bear and in its capacity to induce cooperation by depriving visitors of a resource that they value.

[. . .]

As we have hinted throughout this discussion, training is a pervasive feature of the control system of Disney Productions. It is not, however, the redemptive soul-training of the carceral project but an ever-present flow of directions for, and definitions of, order directed at every visitor. Unlike carceral training, these messages do not require detailed knowledge of the individual. They are, on the contrary, for anyone and everyone. Messages are, none the less, often conveyed to single individuals or small groups of friends and relatives. For example, in some of the newer exhibits, the vehicles that take one through swivel and turn so that one's gaze can be precisely directed. Similarly, each seat is fitted with individual sets of speakers that talk directly to one, thus permitting a seductive sense of intimacy while simultaneously imparting a uniform message.

In summary, within Disney World control is embedded, preventative, subtle, cooperative and apparently non-coercive and consensual. It focuses on categories, requires no knowledge of the individual and employs pervasive surveillance. Thus, although disciplinary, it is distinctively non-carceral. Its order is instrumental and determined by the interests of Disney Productions rather than moral and absolute. As anyone who has visited Disney World knows, it is extraordinarily effective.

CONCLUSIONS

While this new instrumental discipline is rapidly becoming a dominant force in social control in this year, 1984, it is as different from the Orwellian totalitarian nightmare as it is from the carceral regime. Surveillance is pervasive but it is the antithesis of the blatant control of the Orwellian state: its source is not government and its vehicle is not Big Brother. The order of instrumental discipline is not the unitary order of a central state but diffuse and separate orders defined by private authorities responsible for the feudal-like domains of Disney World, condominium estates, commercial complexes and the like. Within contemporary discipline, control is as fine-grained as Orwell imagined but its features are very different.

In this auspicious year it is thus, paradoxically, not to Orwell's socialist-inspired Utopia that we must look for a picture of contemporary control but to the capitalist-inspired disciplinary model conceived of by Huxley who, in his *Brave New World*, painted a picture of consensually based control that bears a striking resemblance to the disciplinary control of Disney World and other corporate control systems. Within Huxley's imaginary world people are seduced into conformity by the pleasures offered by the drug 'soma' rather than coerced into compliance by threat of Big Brother, just as people are today seduced to conform by the pleasures of consuming the goods that corporate power has to offer.

The contrasts between morally based justice and instrumental control, carceral punishment and corporate control, the Panopticon and Disney World and Orwell's and Huxley's visions [are] succinctly captured by the novelist Beryl Bainbridge's observations about a recent journey she made retracing J.B. Priestley's celebrated trip around Britain. She notes how during his travels in 1933 the centre of the cities and towns he visited were defined by either a church or a centre of government (depicting the coalition between Church and state in the production of order that characterizes morally based regimes).

During her more recent trip one of the changes that struck her most forcibly was the transformation that had taken place in the centre of cities and towns. These were now identified not by churches or town halls, but by shopping centres; often vaulted glass-roofed structures that she found reminiscent of the cathedrals they had replaced both in their awe-inspiring architecture and in the hush that she found they sometimes created. What was worshipped in these contemporary cathedrals, she noted, was not an absolute moral order but something much more mundane: people were 'worshipping shopping' and through it, we would add, the private authorities, the order and the corporate power their worship makes possible.

REFERENCES

Bottoms, A.E. (1983) 'Neglected features of contemporary penal systems', in D. Garland and P. Young (eds), *The Power to Punish: Contemporary Penality and Social Analysis*. Atlantic Highlands, NJ: Humanities. p. 166.

Cohen, S. (1979) 'The punitive city: notes on the dispersal of social control', *Contemporary Crises*, 3(4): 339.

Foucault, M. (1977) *Discipline and Punish: the Birth of the Prison*. New York: Vintage Books.

Mathiesen, T. (1980) 'The future of social control systems – the case of Norway', *International Journal of the Sociology of Law*, 8: 149.

Mathiesen, T. (1983) 'The future of social control systems – the case of Norway', in D. Garland and P. Young (eds), *The Power to Punish: Contemporary Penality and Social Analysis*. Atlantic Highlands, NJ: Humanities. p. 130.

Newman, O. (1972) *Defensible Space: Crime Prevention through Urban Design*. New York: Macmillan.

Peters, T. and Waterman, R.H., Jr. (1982) *In Search of Excellence: Lessons from America's Best-run Companies*. New York: Warner Books.

Priestley, J.B. (1934) *English Journey: Being a Rambling but Truthful Account of What One Man Saw and Heard and Felt During a Journey Through England the Autumn of the Year 1933*. London: Heinemann & Gollancz.

Rule, J.B., McAdam, D., Stearns, L. and Uglow, D. (1983) 'Documentary identification and mass surveillance in the United States', *Social Problems*, 31(2): 222.

Shearing, C.D. and Stenning P.C. (1981) 'Private security: its growth and implications', in M. Tonry and N. Morris (eds), *Crime and Justice – an Annual Review of Research*, vol. 3. Chicago: University of Chicago Press. p. 193.

Shearing, C.D. and Stenning, P.C. (1982) 'Snowflakes or good pinches? Private security's contribution to modern policing', in R. Donelan (ed.), *The Maintenance of Order in Society*. Ottawa: Canadian Police College.

Shearing, C.D. and Stenning, P.C. (1983) 'Private security: implications for social control', *Social Problems* 30(5): 493.

Spitzer, S. and Scull, A. (1977) 'Privatization and capitalist development: the case of the private police', *Social Problems*, 25(1): 18.

38

The new penology

Malcolm M. Feeley and Jonathan Simon

DISTINGUISHING FEATURES OF THE NEW PENOLOGY

What we call the new penology is not a theory of crime or criminology. Its uniqueness lies less in conceptual integration than in a common focus on certain problems and a shared way of framing issues. This strategic formation of knowledge and power offers managers of the system a more or less coherent picture of the challenges they face and the kinds of solutions that are most likely to work. While we cannot reduce it to a set of principles, we can point to some of its most salient features.

The new discourse

A central feature of the new discourse is the replacement of a moral or clinical description of the individual with an actuarial language of probabilistic calculations and statistical distributions applied to populations. Although social utility analysis or actuarial thinking is commonplace enough in modern life – it frames policy considerations of all sorts – in recent years this mode of thinking has gained ascendancy in legal discourse, a system of reasoning that traditionally has employed the language of morality and been focused on individuals (Simon, 1988). For instance, this new mode of reasoning is found increasingly in tort law, where traditional fault and negligence standards – which require a focus on the individual and are based upon notions of individual responsibility – have given way to strict liability and no-fault. These new doctrines rest upon actuarial ways of thinking about how to 'manage' accidents and public safety. They employ the language of social utility and management, not individual responsibility (Simon, 1987; Steiner, 1987). [. . .]

Although crime policy, criminal procedure and criminal sanctioning have been influenced by such social utility analysis, there is no body of commentary on the criminal law that is equivalent to the body of social utility analysis for tort law

From *Criminology*, 1992, 30(4): 452–74.

doctrine. Nor has strict liability in the criminal law achieved anything like the acceptance of related no-fault principles in tort law. Perhaps because the criminal law is so firmly rooted in a focus on the individual, these developments have come late to criminal law and penology.

Scholars of both European and North American penal strategies have noted the recent and rising trend of the penal system to target categories and subpopulations rather than individuals (Bottoms, 1983; Cohen, 1985; Mathiesen, 1983; Reichman, 1986). This reflects, at least in part, the fact that actuarial forms of representation promote quantification as a way of visualizing populations.

Crime statistics have been a part of the discourse of the state for over 200 years, but the advance of statistical methods permits the formation of concepts and strategies that allow direct relations between penal strategy and the population. Earlier generations used statistics to map the responses of normatively defined groups to punishment; today one talks of 'high-rate offenders', 'career criminals', and other categories defined by the distribution itself. Rather than simply extending the capacity of the system to rehabilitate or control crime, actuarial classification has come increasingly to define the correctional enterprise itself.

The importance of actuarial language in the system will come as no surprise to anyone who has spent time observing it. Its significance, however, is often lost in the more spectacular shift in emphasis from rehabilitation to crime control. No doubt, a new and more punitive attitude toward the proper role of punishment has emerged in recent years, and it is manifest in a shift in the language of statutes, internal procedures and academic scholarship. Yet looking across the past several decades, it appears that the pendulum-like swings of penal attitude moved independently of the actuarial language that has steadily crept into the discourse.

The discourse of the new penology is not simply one of greater quantification; it is also characterized by an emphasis on the systemic and on formal rationality. While the history of systems theory and operations research has yet to be written, their progression from business administration to the military and, in the 1960s, to domestic public policy must be counted as among the most significant of current intellectual trends. [. . .]

Some of the most astute observers identified this change near the outset and understood that it was distinct from the concurrent rightward shift in penal thinking. Jacobs (1977) noted the rise at Stateville Penitentiary of what he called a 'managerial' perspective during the mid-1970s. The regime of Warden Brierton was characterized, according to Jacobs, by a focus on tighter administrative control through the gathering and distribution of statistical information about the functioning of the prison. Throughout the 1980s this perspective grew considerably within the correctional system. Jacobs presciently noted that the managerial perspective might succeed where traditional and reform administrations had failed because it was capable of handling the greatly increased demands for rationality and accountability coming from the courts and the political system.

The new objectives

The new penology is neither about punishing nor about rehabilitating individuals. It is about identifying and managing unruly groups. It is concerned with the rationality not of individual behavior or even community organization, but of managerial processes. Its goal is not to eliminate crime but to make it tolerable through systemic coordination.

One measure of the shift away from trying to normalize offenders and toward trying to manage them is seen in the declining significance of recidivism. Under the old penology, recidivism was a nearly universal criterion for assessing success or failure of penal programs. Under the new penology, recidivism rates continue to be important, but their significance has changed. The word itself seems to be used less often precisely because it carries a normative connotation that reintegrating offenders into the community is the major objective. High rates of parolees being returned to prison once indicated program failure; now they are offered as evidence of efficiency and effectiveness of parole as a control apparatus.

It is possible that recidivism is dropping out of the vocabulary as an adjustment to harsh realities and is a way of avoiding charges of institutional failure. [. . .] However, in shifting to emphasize the virtues of return as an indication of *effective* control, the new penology reshapes one's understanding of the functions of the penal sanction. By emphasizing correctional programs in terms of aggregate control and system management rather than individual success and failure, the new penology lowers one's expectations about the criminal sanction. These redefined objectives are reinforced by the new discourses discussed above which take deviance as a given, mute aspirations for individual reformation, and seek to classify, sort and manage dangerous groups efficiently.

The waning of concern over recidivism reveals fundamental changes in the very penal processes that recidivism once was used to evaluate. For example, although parole and probation have long been justified as means of reintegrating offenders into the community [. . .] increasingly they are being perceived as cost-effective ways of imposing long-term management on the dangerous. Instead of treating revocation of parole and probation as a mechanism to short-circuit the supervision process when the risks to public safety become unacceptable, the system now treats revocation as a cost-effective way to police and sanction a chronically troublesome population. In such an operation, recidivism is either irrelevant or, as suggested above, is stood on its head and transformed into an indicator of success in a new form of law enforcement.

The importance that recidivism once had in evaluating the performance of corrections is now being taken up by measures of system functioning. Heydebrand and Seron (1990) have noted a tendency in courts and other social agencies toward decoupling performance evaluation from external social objectives. Instead of social norms like the elimination of crime, reintegration into the community, or public safety, institutions begin to measure their own outputs as indicators of performance. Thus, courts may look at docket flow. Similarly, parole agencies may shift evaluations of performance to, say the time elapsed between arrests and due process hearings. In much the same way, many schools have come to focus on standardized test performance rather than on reading or mathematics, and some have begun to see teaching itself as the process of teaching students how to take such tests (Heydebrand and Seron, 1990: 190–4; Lipsky, 1980: 4–53).

Such technocratic rationalization tends to insulate institutions from the messy, hard-to-control demands of the social world. By limiting their exposure to indicators that they can control, managers ensure that their problems will have solutions. No doubt this tendency in the new penology is, in part, a response to the acceleration of demands for rationality and accountability in punishment coming from the courts and legislatures during the 1970s (Jacobs, 1977). It also reflects the lowered expectations for the penal system that result from failures to accomplish more ambitious promises of the past. Yet in the end, the inclination of the system to measure its success against its own production processes helps lock the system into a mode of operation that has only an attenuated connection with the *social* purposes of punishment. In the long term it becomes more difficult to evaluate an institution critically if there are no references to substantive social ends.

The new objectives also inevitably permeate through the courts into thinking about rights. The new penology replaces consideration of fault with predictions of dangerousness and safety management and, in so doing, modifies traditional individual-oriented doctrines of criminal procedure. [. . .]

New techniques

These altered, lowered expectations manifest themselves in the development of more cost-effective forms of custody and control and in new technologies to identify and classify risk. Among them are low frills, no-service custodial centers; various forms of electronic monitoring systems that impose a form of custody without walls; and new statistical techniques for assessing risk and predicting dangerousness. These new forms of control are not anchored in aspirations to rehabilitate, reintegrate, retrain, provide employment, or the like. They are justified in more blunt terms: variable detention depending upon risk assessment.

Perhaps the clearest example of the new penology's method is the theory of incapacitation, which has become the predominant utilitarian model of punishment (Greenwood, 1982; Moore et al., 1984). Incapacitation promises to reduce the effects of crime in society not by altering either offender or social context, but by rearranging the distribution of offenders in society. If the prison can do nothing else, incapacitation theory holds, it can detain offenders for a time and thus delay their resumption of criminal activity. According to the theory, if such delays are sustained for enough time and for enough offenders, significant aggregate effects in crime can take place although individual destinies are only marginally altered.

These aggregate effects can be further intensified, in some accounts, by a strategy of selective incapacitation. This approach proposes a sentencing scheme in which lengths of sentence depend not upon the nature of the criminal offense or upon an assessment of the character of the offender, but upon risk profiles. Its objectives are to identify high-risk offenders and to maintain long-term control over them while investing in shorter terms and less intrusive control over lower risk offenders. [. . .]

The new penology in perspective

The correctional practices emerging from the shifts we identified above present a kind of 'custodial continuum'. But unlike the 'correctional continuum' discussed in the 1960s, this new custodial continuum does not design penal measures for the particular needs of the individual or the community. Rather, it sorts individuals into groups according to the degree of control warranted by their risk profiles.

At one extreme the prison provides maximum security at a high cost for those who pose the greatest risks, and at the other probation provides low-cost surveillance for low-risk offenders. In between stretches a growing range of intermediate supervisory and surveillance techniques. The management concerns of the new penology – in contrast to the transformative concerns of the old – are displayed especially clearly in justifications for various new intermediate sanctions.

What we call the new penology is only beginning to take coherent shape. Although most of what we have stressed as its central elements – statistical prediction, concern with groups, strategies of management – have a long history in penology, in recent years they have come to the fore, and their functions have coalesced and expanded to form a new strategic approach. Discussing the new penology in terms of discourse, objective and technique risks a certain repetitiveness. Indeed, all three are closely linked, and while none can be assigned priority as the cause of the others, each entails and facilitates the others.

Thus, one can speak of normalizing individuals, but when the emphasis is on separating people into distinct and independent categories the idea of the 'normal' itself becomes obscured if not irrelevant. If the 'norm' can no longer function as a relevant criterion of success for the organizations of criminal justice, it is not surprising that evaluation turns to indicators of internal system performance. The focus of the system on the efficiency of its own outputs, in turn, places a premium on those methods (e.g., risk screening, sorting and monitoring) that fit wholly within the bureaucratic capacities of the apparatus.

But the same story can be told in a different order. The steady bureaucratization of the correctional apparatus during the 1950s and 1960s shifted the target from individuals, who did not fit easily into centralized administration, to categories or classes, which do. But once the focus is on categories of offenders rather than individuals, methods naturally shift toward mechanisms of appraising and arranging groups rather than intervening in the lives of individuals. In the end the search for causal order is at least premature.

In the section below we explore the contours of some of the new patterns represented by these developments, and in so doing suggest that the enterprise is by now relatively well established.

NEW FUNCTIONS AND TRADITIONAL FORMS

Someday, perhaps, the new penology will have its own Jeremy Bentham or Zebulon Brockway [. . .], some gigantic figure who can stamp his or her own sense of order on the messy results of incremental change. For now it is better not to think of it so much as a theory or program conceived in full by any particular actors in the system, but as an interpretative net that can help reveal in the present some of the directions the future may take. The test of such a net, to which we now turn, is not its elegance as a model but whether it enables one to grasp a wide set of developments in an enlightening way (in short, does it catch fish?). Below we re-examine three of the major features of the contemporary penal landscape in light of our argument –

the expansion of the penal sanction, the rise of drug testing and innovation within the criminal process – and relate them to our thesis.

The expansion of penal sanctions

During the past decade the number of people covered by penal sanctions has expanded significantly. Because of its high costs, the growth of prison populations has drawn the greatest attention, but probation and parole have increased at a proportionate or faster rate. The importance of these other sanctions goes beyond their ability to stretch penal resources; they expand and redistribute the use of imprisonment. Probation and parole violations now constitute a major source of prison inmates, and negotiations over probation revocation are replacing plea bargaining as modes of disposition (Greenspan, 1988; Messinger and Berecochea, 1990).

Many probation and parole revocations are triggered by events, like failing a drug test, that are driven by parole procedures themselves (Simon, 1990; Zimring and Hawkins, 1991). The increased flow of probationers and parolees into prisons is expanding the prison population and changing the nature of the prison. Increasingly, prisons are short-term holding pens for violators deemed too dangerous to remain on the streets. To the extent the prison is organized to receive such people, its correctional mission is replaced by a management function, a warehouse for the highest risk classes of offenders.

From the perspective of the new penology, the growth of community corrections in the shadow of imprisonment is not surprising. The new penology does not regard prison as a special institution capable of making a difference in the individuals who pass through it. Rather, it functions as but one of several custodial options. The actuarial logic of the new penology dictates an expansion of the continuum of control for more efficient risk management. [. . .]

Thus, community-based sanctions can be understood in terms of risk management rather than rehabilitative or correctional aspirations. Rather than instruments of reintegrating offenders into the community, they function as mechanisms to maintain control, often through frequent drug testing, over low-risk offenders for whom the more secure forms of custody are judged too expensive or unnecessary. [. . .]

Drugs and punishment

Drug use and its detection and control have become central concerns of the penal system. No one observing the system today can fail to be struck by the increasingly tough laws directed against users and traffickers, well-publicized data that suggest that a majority of arrestees are drug users, and the increasing proportion of drug offenders sent to prison.

In one sense, of course, the emphasis on drugs marks a continuity with the past thirty years of correctional history. Drug treatment and drug testing were hallmarks of the rehabilitative model in the 1950s and 1960s. The recent upsurge of concern with drugs may be attributed to the hardening of social attitudes toward drug use (especially in marked contrast to the tolerant 1970s), the introduction of virulent new drug products, like crack cocaine, and the disintegrating social conditions of the urban poor.

Without dismissing the relevance of these continuities and explanations for change, it is important to note that there are distinctive changes in the role of drugs in the current system that reflect the logic of the new penology. In place of the traditional emphasis on treatment and eradication, today's practices track drug use as a kind of risk indicator. The widespread evidence of drug use in the offending population leads not to new theories of crime causation but to more efficient ways of identifying those at highest risk of offending. With drug use so prevalent that it is found in a majority of arrestees in some large cities [. . .], it can hardly mark a special type of individual deviance. From the perspective of the new penology, drug use is not so much a measure of individual acts of deviance as it is a mechanism for classifying the offender within a risk group.

Thus, one finds in the correctional system today a much greater emphasis on drug testing than on drug treatment. This may reflect the normal kinds of gaps in policy as well as difficulty in treating relatively new forms of drug abuse. Yet, testing serves functions in the new penology even in the absence of a treatment option. By marking the distribution of risk within the offender population under surveillance, testing makes possible greater coordination of scarce penal resources.

Testing also fills the gap left by the decline of traditional intervention strategies. [. . .] If nothing else, testing provide[s] parole (and probably probation) agents [with] a means to document compliance with their own internal performance requirements. [. . .] Testing provides both an occasion for requiring the parolee to show up in the parole office and a purpose for meeting. The results of tests have become a network of fact and explanation for use in a decision-making process that requires accountability but provides little substantive basis for distinguishing among offenders.

Innovation

Our description may seem to imply the onset of a reactive age in which penal managers strive to manage populations of marginal citizens with no concomitant effort toward integration into mainstream society. This may seem hard to square with the myriad new and innovative technologies introduced over the past decade. Indeed the media, which for years have portrayed the correctional system as a failure, have recently enthusiastically reported on these innovations: boot camps, electronic surveillance, high security 'campuses' for drug users, house arrest, intensive parole and probation, and drug treatment programs.

Although some of the new proposals are presented in terms of the 'old penology' and emphasize individuals, normalization and rehabilitation, it is risky to come to any firm conviction about how these innovations will turn out. If historians of punishment have provided any clear lessons, it is that reforms evolve in ways quite different from the aims of their proponents (Foucault, 1977; Rothman, 1971). Thus, we wonder if these most recent innovations won't be recast in the terms outlined in this paper. Many of these innovations are compatible with the imperatives of the new penology, that is, managing a permanently dangerous population while maintaining the system at a minimum cost.

One of the current innovations most in vogue with the press and politicians is correctional 'boot camps'. These are minimum security custodial facilities, usually for youthful first offenders, designed on the model of a training center for military personnel, complete with barracks, physical exercise and tough drill sergeants. Boot camps are portrayed as providing discipline and pride to young offenders brought up in the unrestrained culture of poverty (as though physical fitness could fill the gap left by the weakening of families, schools, neighborhoods, and other social organizations in the inner city).

The camps borrow explicitly from a military model of discipline, which has influenced penality from at least the eighteenth century. No doubt the image of inmates smartly dressed in uniforms performing drills and calisthenics appeals to long-standing ideals of order in post-Enlightenment culture. But in its proposed application to correction, the military model is even less appropriate now than when it was rejected in the nineteenth century; indeed, today's boot camps are more a simulation of discipline than the real thing.

In the nineteenth century the military model was superseded by another model of discipline, the factory. Inmates were controlled by making them work at hard industrial labor (Ignatieff, 1978; Rothman, 1971). It was assumed that forced labor would inculcate in offenders the discipline required of factory laborers, so that they might earn their keep while in custody and join the ranks of the usefully employed when released. One can argue that this model did not work very well, but at least it was coherent. The model of discipline through labor suited our capitalist democracy in a way the model of a militarized citizenry did not.

The recent decline of employment opportunities among the populations of urban poor most at risk for conventional crime involvement has left the applicability of industrial discipline in doubt. But the substitution of the boot camp for vocational training is even less plausible. Even if the typical 90-day regime of training envisioned by proponents of boot camps is effective in reorienting its subjects, at best it can only produce soldiers without a company to join. Indeed, the grim vision of the effect of boot camp is that it will be effective for those who will subsequently put their lessons of discipline and organization to use in the street gangs and drug distribution networks. However, despite the earnestness with which the boot camp metaphor is touted, we suspect that the camps will be little more than holding pens for managing a short-term, mid-range risk population.

Drug testing and electronic monitors being tried in experimental 'intensive supervision' and 'house arrest' programs are justified in rehabilitative terms, but both sorts of programs lack a foundation in today's social and economic realities. The drug treatment programs in the 1960s encompassed a regime of coercive treatment: 'inpatient' custody in secured settings followed by community supervision and reintegration [. . .]. The record suggests that these programs had enduring effects for at least some of those who participated in them (Anglin et al., 1990). Today's proposals are similar, but it remains to be seen whether they can be effective in the absence of long-term treatment facilities, community-based follow-up, and prospects for viable conventional lifestyles and employment opportunities. In the meantime it is obvious that they can also serve the imperative of reducing the costs of correctional jurisdiction while maintaining some check on the offender population.

Our point is not to belittle the stated aspirations of current proposals or to argue that drug treatment programs cannot work. Indeed, we anticipate that drug treatment and rehabilitation will become increasingly attractive as the cost of long-term custody increases. However, given the emergence of the management concerns of the new penology, we question whether these innovations will embrace the long-term perspective of earlier successful treatment programs, and we suspect that they will emerge as control processes for managing and recycling selected risk populations. If so, these new programs will extend still further the capacity of the new penology. The undeniable attractiveness of boot camps, house arrest, secure drug 'centers', and the like, is that they promise to provide secure custody in a more flexible format and at less cost than traditional correctional facilities. Indeed, some of them are envisioned as private contract facilities that can be expanded or reduced with relative ease. Further, they hold out the promise of expanding the range of low- and mid-level custodial alternatives, thereby facilitating the transfer of offenders now held in more expensive, higher security facilities that have been so favored in recent years. Tougher eligibility requirements, including job offers, stable residency and promises of sponsorship in the community, can be used to screen out 'higher risk' categories for non-custodial release programs (Petersilia, 1987). Thus, despite the lingering language of rehabilitation and reintegration, the programs generated under the new penology can best be understood in terms of managing costs and controlling dangerous populations rather than social or personal transformation.

SOCIAL BASES OF THE NEW PENOLOGY

The point of these reinterpretations is not to show that shifts in the way the penal enterprise is understood and discussed inexorably determine how the system will take shape. What actually emerges in corrections over the near and distant future will depend on how this understanding itself is shaped by the pressures of demographic, economic and political factors. Still, such factors rarely operate as pure forces. They are filtered through and expressed in terms in which the problems are understood. Thus, the strategic field we call the new penology itself will help shape the future.

The new discourse of crime

Like the old penology, traditional 'sociological' criminology has focused on the relationship between individuals and communities. Its central concerns have been the causes and correlates of delinquent and criminal behavior, and it has sought to develop intervention strategies designed to correct delinquents and decrease the likelihood of deviant behavior. Thus, it has focused on the family and the workplace as important influences of socialization and control.

The new penology has an affinity with a new 'actuarial' criminology, which eschews these traditional concerns of criminology. Instead of training in sociology or social work, increasingly the new criminologists are trained in operations research and systems analysis. This new approach is not a criminology at all, but an applied branch of systems theory. This shift in training and orientation has been accompanied by a shift in interest. A concern with successful intervention strategies, the province of the former, is replaced by models designed to optimize public safety through the management of aggregates, which is the province of the latter.

In one important sense this new criminology is simply a consequence of steady improvements in the quantitative rigor with which crime is studied. No doubt the amassing of a statistical picture of crime and the criminal justice system has improved researchers' ability to speak realistically about the distribution of crimes and the fairness of procedures. But, we submit, it has also contributed to a shift, a reconceptualization, in the way crime is understood as a social problem. The new techniques and the new language have facilitated reconceptualization of the way issues are framed and policies pursued. Sociological criminology tended to emphasize crime as a relationship between the individual and the normative expectations of his or her community (Bennett, 1981). Policies premised on this perspective addressed problems of reintegration, including the mismatch among individual motivation, normative orientation and social opportunity structures. In contrast, actuarial criminology highlights the interaction of criminal justice institutions and specific segments of the population. Policy discussions framed in its terms emphasize the management of high-risk groups and make less salient the qualities of individual delinquents and their communities.

Indeed, even the use of predictive statistics by pioneers like Ernest Burgess (1936) reflected sociological criminology's emphasis on normalization. Burgess's statistics (and those of most other quantitative criminologists before the 1960s) measured the activity of subjects defined by a specifiable set of individual or social factors (e.g., alcoholism, unemployment etc.). In the actuarial criminology of today, by contrast, the numbers generate the subject itself (e.g., the high-rate offender of incapacitation research). In short, criminals are no longer the organizing referent (or logos) of criminology. Instead, criminology has become a subfield of a generalized public policy analysis discourse. This new criminal knowledge aims at rationalizing the operation of the systems that manage criminals, not dealing with criminality. The same techniques that can be used to improve the circulation of baggage in airports or delivery of food to troops can be used to improve the penal system's efficiency.

The discourse of poverty and the underclass

The new penology may also be seen as responsive to the emergence of a new understanding of poverty in America. The term *underclass* is used [. . .] to characterize a segment of society that is viewed as permanently excluded from social mobility and economic integration. The term is used to refer to a largely black and Hispanic population living in concentrated zones of poverty in central cities, separated physically and institutionally from the suburban locus of mainstream social and economic life in America.

In contrast to groups whose members are deemed employable, even if they may be temporarily out of work, the underclass is understood as a permanently marginal population, without literacy, without skills and without hope; a self-perpetuating and pathological segment of society that is not integratable into the larger whole, even as a reserve labor pool (Wilson, 1987). Conceived of this way, the underclass is also a dangerous class, not only for what any particular member may or may not do, but more generally for collective potential misbehavior. It is treated as a high-risk group that must be managed for the protection of the rest of society. Indeed, it is this managerial task that provides one of the most powerful sources for the imperative of preventative management in the new penology. The concept of 'underclass' makes clear why correctional officials increasingly regard as a bad joke the claim that their goal is to reintegrate offenders back into their communities.

Reintegration and rehabilitation inevitably imply a norm against which deviant subjects are evaluated. As Allen (1981) perceived [. . .], rehabilitation as a project can only survive if public confidence in the viability and appropriateness of such norms endures. Allen viewed the decline of the rehabilitative ideal as a result of the cultural revolts of the 1960s, which undermined the capacity of the American middle classes to justify their norms and the imposition of those norms on others. It is this decline in social will, rather than empirical evidence of the failure of penal programs to rehabilitate, that, in Allen's analysis, doomed the rehabilitative ideal.

Whatever significance cultural radicalism may have had in initiating the break-up of the old penology in the mid-1970s, the emergence of the new penology in the 1980s reflects the influence of a more despairing view of poverty and the prospects for achieving equality (views that can hardly be blamed on the Left). Rehabilitating offenders, or any kind of reintegration strategy, can only make sense if the larger community from which offenders come is viewed as sharing a common normative universe with the communities of the middle classes – especially those values and expectations derived from the labor market. The concept of an underclass, with its connotation of a permanent marginality for whole portions of the population, has rendered the old penology incoherent and laid the groundwork for a strategic field that emphasizes low-cost management of a permanent offender population.

The connection between the new penality and the (re)emergent term *underclass* also is illustrated by studies of American jails. For instance, [. . .] Irwin's 1985 book *The Jail*, is subtitled *Managing the Underclass in American Society*. His thesis is that 'prisoners in jails share two essential characteristics: detachment and disrepute' (p. 2). For Irwin, the function of jail is to manage the underclass, which he reports is also referred to as 'rabble', 'disorganized', 'disorderly', and the 'lowest class of people'.

In one rough version of Irwin's analysis, the jail can be viewed as a means of controlling the most disruptive and unsightly members of the underclass. But in another version, it can be conceived of as an emergency service net for those who are in the most desperate straits. As other social services have shrunk, increasingly this task falls on the jail.

Whichever version one selects, few of those familiar with the jails in America's urban centers find it meaningful to characterize them only as facilities for 'pre-trial detention' or for serving 'short-term sentences'. Although not literally false, this characterization misses the broader function of the jail. The high rates of those released without charges filed, the turnstile-like frequency with which some people reappear, and the pathological characteristics of a high proportion of the inmates lead many to agree with Irwin that the jail is best understood as a social management instrument rather than an institution for effecting the purported aims of the criminal process.

Social management, not individualized justice, is also emphasized in other discussions of the criminal process. Long-time public defender James M. Doyle (1992) offers the metaphors 'colonial', 'White Man's burden', and 'Third World', in an essay drawing parallels between the careers of criminal justice officials and colonial administrators. Both, he argues, are convinced that they are menaced by both inscrutable, malign natives and ignorant, distant, policy-makers. They believe they are hamstrung by crazy legalities. Young Assistant District Attorneys, like young Assistant District Commissioners, hurriedly seize, then vehemently defend, a conventional wisdom as a protection against these threats. They pledge themselves to a professional code that sees the world in which people are divided into various collectives. Where they might have seen individuals, they see races, types and colors instead. Like the colonialists before them, they embrace a 'rigidly binomial opposition of "ours" and "theirs"'. In the criminal justice system as on the frontiers of empire 'the impersonal communal idea of being a White Man' rules; it becomes 'a very concrete way of being-in-the-world, a way of taking hold of reality, language and thought'. (1992: 74)

Sustaining his metaphor, Doyle parallels the corrupting influence of the White Man's effort to 'manage' Third World natives with those of the criminal justice professionals' effort to handle cases. He concludes, 'we have paid too much attention to the superficial exotic charms by which the reports of the colonial and criminal justice White Man entertain us, too little to the darker strains they also share' (1992: 126).

Whether one prefers Irwin's notion of underclass or Doyle's 'colonial' and 'Third World' metaphors, both resonate with our notion of the new penology. They vividly explain who is being managed and why. But in providing an explanation of these relationships, there is a danger that the terms will reify the problem, that they will suggest the problem is inevitable and permanent. Indeed, it is this belief, we maintain, that has contributed to the lowered expectations of the new penology – away from an aspiration to affect individual lives through rehabilitative and transformative efforts and toward the more 'realistic' task of monitoring and managing intractable groups.

The hardening of poverty in contemporary America reinforces this view. When combined with a pessimistic analysis implied by the term *underclass*, the structural barriers that maintain the large islands of Third World misery in America's major cities can lead to the conclusion that such conditions are inevitable and impervious to social policy intervention. This, in turn, can push corrections ever further toward a self-understanding based on the imperative of herding a specific population that cannot be disaggregated and transformed but only maintained – a kind of waste management function.

[. . .]

REFERENCES

Allen, F. (1981) *The Decline of the Rehabilitative Idea*. New Haven, CT: Yale University Press.

Anglin, D., Speckhart, G. and Piper Deschenes, E. (1990) *Examining the Effects of Narcotics Addiction*. Los Angeles: UCLA Neuropsychiatric Institute, Drug Abuse Research Group.

Bennett, J. (1981) *Oral History and Delinquency: the Rhetoric of Criminology*. Chicago: University of Chicago Press.

Bottoms, A. (1983) 'Neglected features of contemporary penal systems', in D. Garland and P. Young (eds), *The Power to Punish*. London: Heinemann.

Burgess, E.W. (1936) 'Protecting the public by parole and parole prediction', *Journal of Criminal Law and Criminology*, 27: 491–502.

Cohen, S. (1985) *Visions of Social Control: Crime, Punishment and Classification*. Cambridge: Polity.

Doyle, J.M. (1992) '"It's the Third World down there": The colonialist vocation and American criminal justice', *Harvard Civil Rights – Civil Liberties Law Review*, 27: 71–126.

Foucault, M. (1977) *Discipline and Punish*. New York: Pantheon.

Greenspan, R. (1988) 'The transformation of criminal due process in the administrative state', Paper prepared for delivery at the annual meeting of the Law and Society Association, Vail, Colorado, June 1988.

Greenwood, P. (1982) *Selective Incapacitation*. Santa Monica, CA: Rand.

Heydebrand, W. and Seron, C. (1990) *Rationalizing Justice: the Political Economy and Federal District Courts*. New York: State University of New York Press.

Ignatieff, M. (1978) *A Just Measure of Pain: the Penitentiary in the Industrial Revolution, 1750–1850*. London: Macmillan.

Irwin, J. (1985) *The Jail: Managing the Underclass in American Society*. Berkeley, CA: University of California Press.

Jacobs, J.B. (1977) *Stateville: the Penitentiary in Mass Society*. Chicago: University of Chicago Press.

Lipsky, M. (1980) *Street Level Bureaucrats*. New York: Russell Sage Foundation.

Mathiesen, T. (1983) 'The future of control systems – the case of Norway', in D. Garland and P. Young (eds), *The Power to Punish*. London: Heinemann.

Messinger, S. and Berecochea, J. (1990) 'Don't stay too long but do come back soon'. Proceedings, Conference on Growth and Its Influence on Correctional Policy, Center for the Study of Law and Society, University of California at Berkeley.

Moore, M.H., Estrich, S.R., McGillis, D. and Spelman, W. (1984) *Dangerous Offenders: the Elusive Target of Justice*. Cambridge, MA: Harvard University Press.

Petersilia, J. (1987) *Expanding Options for Criminal Sentencing*. Santa Monica, CA: Rand.

Reichman, N. (1986) 'Managing crime risks: toward an insurance-based model of social control', *Research in Law, Deviance and Social Control*, 8: 151–72.

Rothman, D. (1971) *The Discovery of the Asylum: Social Order and Disorder in the New Republic*. Boston, MA: Little, Brown.

Simon, J. (1987) 'The emergence of a risk society: insurance law and the state', *Socialist Review*, 95: 61–89.

Simon, J. (1988) 'The ideological effect of actuarial practices', *Law and Society Review*, 22: 771–800.

Simon, J. (1990) 'From discipline to management: strategies of control in parole supervision, 1890–1900'. PhD dissertation, Jurisprudence and Social Policy Program, University of California at Berkeley.

Steiner, H.J. (1987) *Moral Vision and Social Vision in the Court: a Study of Tort Accident Law*. Madison, WI: University of Wisconsin Press.

Wilson, W.J. (1987) *The Truly Disadvantaged: the Inner City, the Underclass, and Public Policy*. Chicago: University of Chicago Press.

Zimring, F. and Hawkins, G. (1991) *The Scale of Imprisonment*. Chicago: University of Chicago Press.

39

Governmentality

Michel Foucault

[. . .] What I would like to undertake is something I would term a history of 'governmentality.' By this word I mean three things:

1. The ensemble formed by the institutions, procedures, analyses, and reflections, the calculations and tactics that allow the exercise of this very specific albeit complex form of power, which has as its target population, as its principal form of knowledge political economy, and as its essential technical means apparatuses of security.
2. The tendency that, over a long period and throughout the West, has steadily led toward the preeminence over all other forms (sovereignty, discipline, and so on) of this type of power—which may be termed 'government'—resulting, on the one hand, in the formation of a whole series of specific governmental apparatuses, and, on the other, in the development of a whole complex of knowledges [*savoirs*].
3. The process or, rather, the result of the process through which the state of justice of the Middle Ages transformed into the administrative state during the fifteenth and sixteenth centuries and gradually becomes 'governmentalized.'

We all know the fascination that the love, or horror, of the state exercises today; we know how much attention is paid to the genesis of the state, its history, its advance, its power, abuses, and soon. The excessive value attributed to the problem of the state is expressed, basically, in two ways: the one form, immediate, affective, and tragic, is the lyricism of the cold monster we see confronting us. But there is a second way of overvaluing the problem of the state, one that is paradoxical because it is apparently reductionist: it is the form of analysis that consists in reducing the state to a certain number of functions, such as the development of productive forces and the reproduction of relations of production, and yet this reductionist vision of the relative importance of the state's role nevertheless invariably renders it absolutely essential as a target needing to be attacked and a privileged position needing to be occupied. But the state, no more probably today than at any other time in its history,

From *Power* Vol. 3. (ed. J.D. Faubion), pp. 219–222. (New York: New Press.)

does not have this unity, this individuality, this rigorous functionality, nor, to speak frankly, this importance. Maybe, after all, the state is no more than a composite reality and a mythicized abstraction, whose importance is a lot more limited than many of us think. Maybe what is really important for our modernity—that is, for our present—is not so much the statization [*étatisation*] of society, as the 'governmentalization' of the state.

We live in the era of a 'governmentality' first discovered in the eighteenth century. This governmentalization of the state is a singularly paradoxical phenomenon: if in fact the problems of governmentality and the techniques of government have become the only political issue, the only real space for political struggle and contestation, this is because the governmentalization of the state is, at the same time, what has permitted the state to survive. It is possible to suppose that if the state is what it is today, this is so precisely thanks to this governmentality, which is at once internal and external to the state—since it is the tactics of government that make possible the continual definition and redefinition of what is within the competence of the state and what is not, the public versus the private, and so on. Thus, the state can only be understood in its survival and its limits on the basis of the general tactics of governmentality.

And maybe we could even, albeit in a very global, rough, and inexact fashion, reconstitute the great forms, the great economies of power in the West in the following way. First came the state of justice, born in a territoriality of feudal type and corresponding in large part to a society of the law—customary laws and written laws—with a whole game of engagements and litigations. Second, the administrative state, born in the fifteenth and sixteenth centuries in a frontier and no longer feudal territoriality, an administrative state than corresponds to a society of regulations and disciplines. Finally, the state of government, which is no longer essentially defined by its territoriality, by the surface it occupies, but by a mass: the mass of the population, with its volume, its density, with the territory that it covers, to be sure, but only in a sense as one of its components. And this state of government, which is grounded in its population and which refers and has resort to the instrumentality of economic knowledge, would correspond to a society controlled by apparatuses of security.

There, if you like, are certain pointers [*propos*] for positioning this phenomenon—which I believe to be important—of governmentality. I will try further to show how such governmentality is born, in one part, out of an archaic model, that of the Christian pastoral, and secondly, while drawing support from a diplomatico-military model, or better, technics, and finally, thirdly, how governmentality could not have assumed the dimensions it has except thanks to a series of quite particular instruments, whose formation is precisely contemporary with the art of government, and which one could call, in the old sense of the term, that of the twelfth and thirteenth centuries, the police. The pastoral, the new diplomatico-military technics, and finally the police, I believe, were the three elements from which the phenomenon of the governmentalization of the state, so fundamental in the history of the West, could be produced.

40

Risk, power and crime prevention

Pat O'Malley

[. . .]

RISK-BASED SOCIETY

Almost the defining property of Foucault's conception of disciplinary power is that it works through and upon the individual, and constitutes the individual as an object of knowledge. In the disciplines, the central technique is that of normalization in the specific sense of creating or specifying a general rule (norm) in terms of which individual uniqueness can be recognized, characterized and then standardized. Normalization in the disciplinary sense thus implies 'correction' of the individual, and the development of a causal knowledge of deviance and normalization. Thus, in the prison, Foucault (1977) saw discipline as acting directly and coercively upon the individual, producing thereby 'a biographical knowledge and a technique for correcting individual lives' which should follow the delinquent's life course 'back not only to the circumstances but also to the causes of his crime' (Foucault 1977:251–2).

Rejection of the focus upon individuals and on causation therefore would reflect not merely a redirection of particular policies but rather a shift away from the disciplinary technology of power itself. In the field of crime and crime management, a number of commentators have noted the development of programs and policies based on the regulation of behaviours and their consequences – in which 'actuarial' (Cohen 1985) or 'insurance' based (Reichman 1986; Hogg 1989) assumptions and techniques are brought into play. Perhaps the most striking statement of the changes implied has been provided by Cohen (1985) who observes that the conception of a mind-control society envisaged in Orwell's *1984* is mistaken, for although such key Foucauldian elements as surveillance continue to develop, there is little or no concern with individuals as such. Thus in situational crime prevention, one of the fastest growing techniques of crime control, concern is with the spatial and temporal aspects

From *Economy and Society*, 1992, 21:3. pp. 361–374.

of crime, though out in terms of the opportunities for crime rather than its causal or biographical origins:

> What is being monitored is behaviour (or the physiological correlates of emotion and behaviour). No one is interested in inner thoughts . . . 'the game is up' for all policies directed to the criminal as an individual, either in terms of detection (blaming and punishing) or causation (finding motivational or causal chains). . . . The talk now is about 'spatial' and 'temporal' aspects of crime, about systems, behaviour sequences, ecology, defensible space . . . target hardening . . .
>
> (Cohen 1985:146–8)

[. . .]

SITUATIONAL CRIME PREVENTION AS RISK MANAGEMENT

[. . .] Situational crime prevention may be understood as quintessentially 'actuarial'. It deals hardly at all with individual offenders, is uninterested in the causes of crime, and generally is hostile or at best agnostic toward correctionalism. Its concern is with crime control as risk management (Reichman 1986). [. . .] Situational crime prevention is enjoying a period of extraordinary success in Britain, the United States, Australia and elsewhere – at least in the political sense of its influence as a program of crime control. Certainly it is tempting to follow earlier arguments and regard this as due to the increased efficiency of actuarial techniques. But the rapidity of its rise to prominence can scarcely be attributed to evidence of its superiority over correctionalism and causal/social criminologies. Rather what emerges, as might be expected from Cohen's (1985) original account of the 'politics of failure', is a political struggle over the definition and the criteria of failure and success. [. . .]

Such debates are endless. The reveal only that the politics of success and failure normally are struggles over the status of criteria, and can rarely be reduced to any universally accepted scale of efficiency. If this is the case, then the question of why situational crime prevention has proven so influential a technique will need to be answered in terms of its relationship to political programs and strategies, and especially to those currently in ascendance. I believe that the broader political and ideological effects of situational crime prevention reveal that its attractions to economic rationalist, neo-conservative and New Right programs provide such an answer (although not unrelated attractions to police forces are also significant). The primary attractions, I will argue, link directly with core ideological assumptions of the New Right, and through these with the two directions of population management – increasing punitiveness with respect to offenders, and with respect to victims, the displacement of socialized risk management with privatized prudentialism. While it is by no means the case that this is the only possible construction of situational crime prevention (others will be discussed briefly toward the end of this paper), for a variety of reasons it is a particularly durable and readily mobilized version under current conditions.

NEO-CONSERVATIVE READING OF CRIME PREVENTION

Situational crime prevention and the offender

Situational crime prevention destroys the disciplines' biographical individual as a category of criminological knowledge, but the criminal does not disappear. Opportunities only exist in relation to potential criminals who convert open windows into windows of opportunity for crime. To install such an agent, situational crime prevention replaces the biographical criminal with a polar opposition – the abstract and universal 'abiographical' individual – the 'rational choice' actor [. . .].

However, while abstract and abiographic, this rational choice individual nevertheless is clearly structured. It thinks in cost-benefit terms – weighing up the risks, potential gains and potential costs, and then committing an offence only when the benefits are perceived to outweigh the losses. This construction may be thought of as having a source very close to the foundations of actuarialism. It is of course the amoral rational choice individual beloved of classical economics, the *homo economicus* which inhabits the world of insurance – the home base of risk management discourses, and an industry closely connected with the promotion of situational crime prevention (O'Malley 1991).

This same being, but invested with additional moral and political characteristics is the denizen of neo-conservative and New Right discourses. It single-mindedly pursues the entrepreneurial ideal, as an atomistic being it is 'naturally free', self-reliant, and responsible (Gamble 1988). It is the underlying form of the human being that the Right would liberate from the debilitating 'public benefit' shackles of the welfare state which have progressively been imposed upon it especially since the end of the Second World War (Levitas 1986). Indeed, the demolition of socialized risk management and the restoration of social conditions approximating 'freedom' of the responsible individual is central to neo-conservative thinking about crime.

> When the traditional family is undermined, as it has been, self reliance tends to be lost and responsibility tends to disappear, both to be replaced by a dependence often long term, on the government and manipulation by social engineers. It also provides the setting which leads young people to the treadmill of drug abuse and crime.
>
> (Liberal Party of Australia 1988:15)

Already it is possible to see how it might be that the neo-conservatives who are concerned to dismantle so much that Simon understands as actuarialism, might nevertheless embrace and foster the actuarialism of situational crime prevention. But there are other reasons as well.

Situational crime prevention's rejection of concern with biographical-causal approaches to understanding crime, and the focus on the targets of crime rather than on offenders, combine to deflect attention from the social foundations of offending. This effect is achieved in the case of the rational choice model by its rejection of or agnosticism toward conditions which may have given rise to the offenders' action, but also and especially by constructing the offender as abstract, universal and rational. [. . .] Such abstract and universal, equal and voluntary individuals are free to act in a perfectly 'rational' self-interested fashion, maximizing gains and minimizing costs. They are free to commit crime or not to commit crime.

This latter point suggests that not only is the knowledge of the criminal disarticulated from a critique of society, but in turn, both of these may be disarticulated from the reaction to the offender. As Foucault made clear, what he saw as the 'criminological labyrinth' was constructed around the assumption that crime is caused, and that cause reduces responsibility (1977:252). Elimination of cause from the discourse of crime obviously restores responsibility and this has its effects on punishment. Thus the logical corollary of situational crime prevention from the point of view of a New Right discourse, is a policy of punitive or just desserts sentencing, rather than a program of sentencing for reform. Compatibility of crime prevention thinking with these models is furthered by the argument that salutary punishment in the form of imprisonment incapacitates offenders and thus acts directly as a means of behavioural crime prevention.

Thus the criminal becomes individually responsible for our concern with offenders as such ceases with that knowledge. In consequence, any class, race, gender or similar foundations of crime, especially as identified by causal criminology, are automatically excluded from consideration except in their role as risk-enhancing factors. If bothered with at all they are taken to be predictive of behaviours, not explanatory of meaningful actions.

This shift in understanding eschews also the moral dimensions of the sociological criminologies, condemned to the status of 'failures' by situational crime prevention theorists [. . .]. Out with them go their respective agendas linking crime and social justice – for example that of strain theory and its concerns with relative deprivation and inequality of opportunity, and the appreciative recognition of cultural variability and of the impact of material degradation of the inner city poor that was the hallmark of ecological analysis. Academically as well as politically and administratively, it now becomes respectable to regard criminals as unconstrained agents, and to regard a crime control policy as divorced from questions of social justice.

Finally, the 'politics of failure' provide a technical glass to justify punitiveness. If correction and deterrence do not work, then sanctions based on these ideas must be swept away. What is left for the offender but punishment, retribution and incapacitation?

Situational crime prevention and the victim

If situational crime prevention short-circuits the link between criminality and social justice, then it might be expected that the victim of crime moves more into the centre of concern. In some sense this is undoubtedly the case, as the rhetoric of 'protecting the public' rings loud throughout this program (e.g. Home Office 1990). However, just as the offenders are disconnected from the political dimensions of their existence, so too are the victims, for victims like offenders are to be understood as rational choice actors, responsible and free individuals.

Prevention now becomes the responsibility of the victim. This view is by no means the construct of academic reflection but permeates crime prevention thinking at all levels. At one level, this position emerges no doubt because it reduces pressure on police forces, which have not noticeably reduced crime victimization and which are therefore vulnerable to political pressure for this reason. Thus a senior official of the Australian insurance Council has noted: 'Severely restricted police resources and the sheer frequency of crime, means that any improvement in the situation will rely heavily on property owners accepting responsibility for their own property and valuables' (Hall 1986:243).

At broader political levels similar arguments are being presented for much the same reasons. Responding to news that crime rates in Britain have reached record levels, 'the Prime Minister, Mrs Thatcher, blamed a large portion of the crimes on the victims' carelessness. "We have to be careful that we ourselves don't make it easy for the criminal" she said' (*Age* 28 September 1990).

Not only does responsibility and thus critique shift, but so too do costs. Privatization of security practice and costs – to be seen in the trend toward private security agencies, security devices, domestic security practices, neighbourhood watch schemes (with attendant insurance underwriting) – generate the rudiments of a user pays system of policing security. Closer to the heart of neo-conservatism, the rational choice public will come to see the justice in this:

> The general public's apathy about self-protection arises mainly from ignorance of the means of protection, and a perception that somebody else – 'the Government' or insurance companies – bears most of the cost of theft and vandalism. The community is beginning to realise however that crime rates are rising despite increased penalties, that the judicial system cannot cope, and that it is the individual who eventually foots the bill for crime through increased taxes for expanded police forces and more jails, and through higher insurance premiums.
>
> (Geason and Wilson 1989: 9)

In this process, security becomes the responsibility of the private individuals who through the pursuit of self-interest, and liberated from enervating reliance on 'the state' to provide for them will participate in the creation of the new order.

Putting these points together, it can be seen that in this construction of situational crime prevention there is no conflict between risk management *per se* and punitiveness. Quite to the contrary, in the privatization of the actuarial techniques are the same notions of individual responsibility and rational choice that are present in the justification for expanding punitiveness. Reliance on the state, even for protection against crime, is not to be encouraged. Quite literally therefore it represents the expression in one field of the New Right ideal of the Strong State and the Free Market, combining to provide crime control in a period when the threat of crime generated by the Right's own market oriented practices can be expected to increase.

CRIME PREVENTION AND SOCIAL JUSTICE

The discussion of situational crime prevention thus far has been one-sided, for it has deliberately focused on developments illustrative of the ways in which risk-based and punitive techniques may be rendered compatible and mutually reinforcing under neo-conservatism. It will not have escaped recognition that situational crime prevention is by no means *necessarily* associated with neo-conservatism. The French Bonnemaison program for example incorporates much that is focused on social justice (King 1988). Likewise, in the Australian state of Victoria situational crime prevention is integrated quite explicitly with a government focus on social justice and is shaped accordingly (Sandon 1991a, 1991b; Victoria Police 1991). Thus with respect to the status of women, an issue on which situational crime prevention has been soundly criticized, such policies have extended well beyond narrowly defensive and privatized risk bearing, and have embedded preventative techniques in socializing reforms, being 'concentrated on reducing violence against women by targeting the involvement of the community to change male behaviour and attitudes, empower women in unsafe situations and change community perceptions and understandings about violence toward women' (Thurgood 1991).

Clearly this social justice contextualization of situational crime prevention conflicts considerably with the behavioural regulation model reviewed above and criticized by Cohen. Not only is this because of the focus on changing people's attitudes and 'inner states', but also because it reflects a series of value assertions and policy directions which are remote from rational choice individualism. Such articulation between situational crime prevention and collective responses to crime as an issue of *social justice* of course reflects precisely that social risk-based model actively discarded by conservatives, and which was highlighted by the analyses of Simon *et al.* Articulation of situational crime prevention with social justice is intelligible in terms of the construction of risk as shared among large sectors of the populace – a precondition of socialized actuarialism. Thus with the welfare model, 'The concept of social risk makes it possible for insurance technologies to be applied to social problems in a way which can be presented as creative simultaneously of social justice and social solidarity' (Gordon 1991:40).

It is therefore intelligible that risk-based techniques may be allied to socializing political programs through their discursive construction in terms of shared risk. Conversely it is equally clear that it may be articulated with a conservative political program through discursive construction in terms of rational choice individuals. As witnessed, this construction fosters the combination of a variety of disciplinary, punitive, and risk-based techniques in order to achieve effects consistent with neo-conservative programs.

[. . .]

REFERENCES

Cohen, Stanley (1985) *Visions of Social Control: Crime, Punishment and Classification*, London: Polity Press.
Foucault, Michel (1977) *Discipline and Punish*, London: Peregrine Books.
Gamble, Andrew (1988) *The Free Economy and the Strong State*, London: Macmillan.
Geason, Susan and Wilson, Paul (1989) *Crime Prevention: Theory and Practice*, Canberra: Australian Institute of Criminology.
Gordon, Colin (1991) 'Governmental rationality: An introduction', in G. Burchell, C. Gordon and P. Miller (eds), *The Foucault Effect. Studies in Governmentality*, London: Harvester/Wheatsheaf.
Hall, John (1986) 'Burglary: The insurance industry viewpoint', in S. Mukherjee (ed.), *Burglary. A Social Reality*, Canberra: AIC.
Hogg, Russell (1989) 'Criminal justice and social control: Contemporary development in Australia', *Journal of Studies in Justice* 2:89–122.

Home Office (1990) *Crime, Justice and Protecting The Public*, London: HMSO.

King, Michael (1988) *How to Make Social Crime Prevention Work: The French Experience*, London: NACRO Occasional Paper.

Levitas, Ruth (1986) 'Introduction. Ideology and the New Right', in Ruth Levitas (ed.), *The Ideology of the New Right*, Oxford: Basil Blackwell.

O'Malley, Pat (1991) 'Legal networks and domestic security', *Studies in Law, Politics and Society* 11:181–91.

Reichman, Nancy (1986) 'Managing crime risks: Toward an insurance based model of social control', *Research in Law and Social Control* 8:151–72.

Sandon, Mal (1991a) *Safety and Security*, Melbourne: Ministry of Policy and Emergency Services (Victoria).

Sandon, Mal (1991b) *Ministerial Statement: Safety, Security and Women*, Melbourne: Parliament of Victoria.

Thurgood, Pat (1991) 'Safety, security and women', Paper Presented at the Crime Prevention seminar, Ministry of Police and Emergency Services, Melbourne, 30 August.

41

'Governmentality' and the problem of crime: Foucault, criminology, sociology

David Garland

[. . .]

INTRODUCTION

[. . .]

   At a time when criminologists are trying to come to terms with a reconfigured criminological field (see Feeley and Simon, 1992; Garland, 1996), the governmentality literature offers a powerful framework for analysing how crime is problematized and controlled. It is focused upon the present, and particularly upon the shift from 'welfarist' to 'neo-liberal' politics. It avoids reductionist or totalizing analyses, encouraging instead an open-ended, positive account of practices of governance in specific fields. It aims to anatomize contemporary practices, revealing the ways in which their modes of exercising power depend upon specific ways of thinking (rationalities) and specific ways of acting (technologies) as well as upon specific ways of 'subjectifying' individuals and governing populations. It also problematizes these practices by subjecting them to a 'genealogical' analysis—a tracing of their historical lineages that aims to undermine their 'naturalness' and open up a space for alternative possibilities.

   [. . .]

The governmentality literature does not offer a general thesis that can be 'applied' to the field of crime control. Nor does it provide a unified account of the present—such as 'postmodernity' or 'risk society'—under which can be subsumed the facts of criminal policy or the developmental tendencies of the criminal justice system. It does, however, isolate a series of objects of analysis, and suggest certain lines of enquiry that strike me as having great potential for researching and interpreting current developments in this field.

From *Theoretical Criminology*, 1997, 1:2. pp. 173–214.

Pat O'Malley (1996) and Kevin Stenson (1993) have already suggested ways in which crime prevention and community policing can be illuminated by reference to this framework, and O'Malley's claim that neo-liberal social policy is increasingly promoting 'prudentialism' and 'the responsible individual' helps make sense of the expansion of the demand for private security, and the declining influence of 'social criminologies'. Similarly, Feeley and Simon's account of 'the new penology' points to the increasing influence of 'managerialism', 'risk-management' and 'actuarial justice' in US criminal justice (see Feeley and Simon, 1992, 1994; Simon and Feeley, 1995). In the following pages, I sketch some further ways in which an analytic of 'governmentality' might deepen our understanding of contemporary crime control and criminal justice.

Rationalities of crime control

The idea of a 'governmental rationality' is of crucial importance in pointing us towards a quite specific dimension of crime control that otherwise goes unnoticed. The dimension it identifies is not quite that of policy statements, nor the legitimatory rhetorics that are used by officials to gloss the practice of institutions. Nor is it precisely the same thing as the criminological theories or the reform programmes that influence these practices. The idea of 'governmental rationalities' refers instead to the ways of thinking and styles of reasoning that are embodied in a particular set of practices. It points to the forms of rationality that organize these practices, and supply them with their objectives and knowledge and forms of reflexivity.

Rationalities are thus *practical* rather than theoretical or discursive entities. They are forged in the business of problem solving and attempting to make things work. Consequently they manifest a logic of practice, rather than of analysis, and tend to bear the hallmarks of the institutional settings out of which they emerged.[1]

If we use this idea of 'rationalities' to think about crime control, it prompts questions such as the following: How have authorities understood their role in relation to the problem of crime? How has the problem of governing crime been problematized and rationalized? Through what technologies and assemblages, and using what forms of knowledge, have authorities exercised governance in this area?

It seems plausible to suggest that in recent decades the governance of crime has come to be problematized in new ways, partly in reaction to chronically high crime rates and the failure of criminal justice controls (Garland, 1996), and partly under the influence of broader shifts away from welfarist styles of government towards neo-liberal ones.

It also seems plausible to argue that, in response to this emergent field of problems and political forces, a new rationality for the governance of crime is coming into existence, together with a new rationality for the governance of criminal justice. Described in very broad terms, this is a governmental style that is organized around *economic* forms of reasoning, in contrast to the social and legal forms that have predominated for most of the 20th century.

By an 'economic' rationality, I don't mean simply that value-for-money considerations and fiscal restraint have nowadays become prominent and explicit aspects of crime control discourse and practice—though this is certainly a feature of the contemporary scene. I mean to point to (i) the increasing reliance upon an *analytical language* of risks and rewards, rationality, choice, probability, targeting and the demand and supply of opportunities—a language that translates 'economic' forms of reasoning and calculation into the criminological field; (ii) the increasing importance of *objectives* such as compensation, cost-control, harm-reduction, economy, efficiency and effectiveness; and (iii) the increasing resort to *technologies* such as audit, fiscal control, market competition and devolved management to control penal decision-making.

For example, the now recurring image of the 'rational criminal' and the concern to govern this figure by manipulating incentives and risks, replicates the standard thought-patterns of economic analysis. So, too, does the image of the victim as a supplier of criminal opportunities, and the idealized figure of *homo prudents* (Adams, 1995; O'Malley, 1996) projected by crime prevention literature and insurance contracts. These new ways of thinking strip away the sociological and psychological layers in which 20th-century criminology had clothed its conception of the criminal offender, and try to rethink the dynamics of crime and punishment in pseudo-economic terms.[2]

This kind of thinking developed first in the private sector—in the practices of insurance companies, private security firms and commercial enterprises, concerned to reduce those costs of crime that fall on them. Commercial and insurance-based thinking about crime control focuses upon reducing or displacing the costs of crime, upon prevention rather than punishment and upon minimizing risk rather than ensuring justice. Commercially situated attempts to control 'reactive risk', 'morale hazard' and 'risk compensation' (see Adams, 1995; Heimer, 1985; Litton, 1990) or to weigh the costs of crime against the cost—to the enterprise—of its prevention or prosecution, led to the elaboration of this style of reasoning about crime and its control. Only later, in the 1980s, did it begin to influence state agencies and practices, most of which are in the control of professional groups allied to social and legal ways of conceiving the problem of crime.

This way of thinking also draws upon other sources. One such source is the work of Gary Becker (1968) and other economic analysts of crime, whose ideas have recently been imported into the language of criminal policy (Cook, 1986; van Dijk, 1994). Another is the cluster of criminological theories—rational choice theory, routine activity theory, and the various approaches that view crime as a matter of opportunity—which I have described elsewhere as 'the new criminologies of everyday life' (Garland, 1996). In contrast to older criminologies, which assumed that the individual offender could be differentiated and corrected, these theoretical frameworks view crime as a normal, mundane event, requiring no special disposition or abnormality on the part of the offender. Crime is viewed as a routine phenomenon, as something that happens in the course of events, rather than a disruption of normality that has to be specially explained. The everyday conduct of economic and social life supplies countless opportunities for illegitimate transactions. Viewed en masse, criminal events are regular, predictable, systematic, in the way that road traffic accidents are. It follows that action upon crime should cease to be primarily action upon deviant individuals and become instead action designed to govern social and economic routines.[3]

Since this emergence, these theories have received considerable critical scrutiny, usually from the point of view of rival criminological traditions whose proponents complain that the new theories fail to get to the root causes of crime, or else that they take too superficial a view of human nature and of criminal conduct. In contrast to that kind of critique, the aim of the Foucauldian approach is to address the substance of these discourses and the practical programmes that they support. It aims to pay careful attention to what they say, how they say it, and to the complex of pre-conditions that make these statements sayable, and which govern their emergence, functioning and transformation. It aims to describe how agents, knowledges, powers and techniques are assembled into specific apparatuses for the exercise of these new ways of governing crime, thus making these ways of thinking into practical ways of acting. And though this approach will tend to imply a critical stance—insofar as it is describing modes of exercising power and of projecting forms of subjectivity that are otherwise hidden—it seeks to maintain the neutral gaze of an analyst rather than the hostile glare of a rival with competing claims to truth. This strikes me as a valuable way of coming to terms with the new configuration of crime control that is currently emerging, the very newness of which tends to undercut our conventional stock of 'critical' and 'progressive' positions, most of which derive from an earlier period of the history of the field.

The criminogenic situation

One of the effects of the new criminologies discussed above has been to bring into view—and therefore into existence for the purposes of knowledge and of govern-ment—an entity that one might call *the criminogenic situation*. This constitutes a new site of intervention for governmental practices, a new practicable object, quite distinct from the individual delinquents and legal subjects that previously formed the targets for crime control. Moreover, the criminogenic situation is like 'the economy' or 'the population' in being a domain with its own internal dynamics and processes. It is populated by active human subjects whose interests and actions shape these processes, and it has functional ends of its own that are easily disturbed by heavy-handed regulation.

Criminogenic situations are commonplace in modern society. They take a variety of forms and come in all shapes and sizes: unsupervised car-parks, town squares late at night, deserted neighbourhoods, poorly-lit streets, shopping malls, football games, but stops, subway stations, etc. Their status as more or less 'criminogenic'—as hot spots of crime or low-rate, secure areas—are established by reference to local police statistics, victim surveys and crime pattern analysis. Their fundamental dynamics can be represented by a few simple parameters—the presence of valuable targets and criminally-inclined individuals, and the absence of effective guardians or situational controls—that emulate the commodity/buyer/price formulae of neo-classical economics. A new body of research on 'situational crime prevention'—offering phenomenological descriptions of situations that 'invite' crime, 'natural histories' of criminal events and 'environmental risk indexes' that calculate vulnerability—has begun to develop a working knowledge of this variable entity.

'The criminogenic situation' poses difficulties for government because it gener-ally has a commercial or social value of its own which sets limits upon crime control. Precisely because crime occurs in the course of routine social and economic trans-actions, and crime-reducing intervention must seek to preserve 'normal life' and 'business as usual'. The characteristic modes of intervening involve the implantation of non-intrusive controls in the situation itself, or else attempts to modify the interests and the incentives of the actors involved (see Shearing and Stenning, 1985). The situation can be 'governed', but it cannot be completely or coercively controlled. Practices of situational governance must operate lightly and unobtrusively, working with and through the actors involved. The aim is to align the actors' objectives with those of the authorities; to make them active partners in the business of security and crime control. In this way the situation is allowed to retain its 'natural' character, but is made more secure against the occurrence of criminal events. The parallels with the problems of 'securing' economic processes through 'liberal' government suggest themselves forcefully.

This analysis also calls to mind Foucault's suggestion that the forms of modern power might be viewed as a 'triangle of sovereignty-discipline-government'. Thus we find, coexisting on the terrain of crime control, three practicable objects and three forms of exercising power in respect of them: (i) the *legal subject*, governed by sovereign command and obliged to obey or be punished; (ii) the *criminal delinquent*, governed by discipline and required to conform or be corrected; and now (iii) the *criminogenic situation*, governed by the manipulation of interests and the promotion of mechanisms of self-regulation. Each of these stands for a particular way of acting upon the problem of crime, supported by a complex of laws, institutional practices and forms of expertise, and each way of acting commands the support of particular groups (the judiciary, the social work establishment, the new crime prevention agencies, etc.). The interweaving of these different modes of 'governing crime' produces an intricate web of policies and practices that cannot be reduced to a single formula. There is no phased historical progression from 'sovereign punishment' to 'discipline' to 'government at a distance', nor is there an easy or coherent relationship between these different conceptions and practices of crime control. In any concrete conjuncture the field of crime control will manifest an uneven (and often incoherent) combination of these modes of action, the specific 'mix' depending upon the balance of power between the different groups involved, as well as the residues of past practices and institutional arrangements. The value of Foucault's analysis (which is both genealogical and typological) is that it allows us to analyse the crime control field as *a field of power relations and subjectifications* and draws attention to the impact of new knowledges and technologies upon the power relations between governmental actors as well as between the rulers and the ruled.

The attempt to govern criminogenic situations has led to a set of new objectives—the reduction of crime and the fear of crime, the promotion of a culture of security consciousness, the enhancement of public safety, etc.—which are seen to be best achieved by acting through (rather than acting upon) the actors involved. This gives rise to a 'responsibilization strategy' whereby state authorities (typically the police or the Home Office) seek to enlist other agencies and individuals to form a chain of coordinated action that reaches into criminogenic situations, prompting crime-control conduct on the part of 'responsibilized' actors (see Garland, 1996). Central to this strategy is the attempt to ensure that all the agencies and individuals who are in a position to contribute to these crime-reducing ends come to see it as being in their interests to do so. 'Government' is thus extended and enhanced by the creation of 'governors' and 'guardians' in the space between the state and the offender.

Whereas older strategies sought to govern crime directly, through the specialist apparatus of criminal justice, this new approach entails a more indirect form of government-at-a-distance, involving 'inter-agency' cooperation and the responsibilization of private individuals and organizations. This practice of enlisting and enrolment, of seeking to build chains of action and to instil crime-conscious attitudes, gives rise, in turn, to the development of new forms of knowledge and expertise—about the problems of coordinated action, about the costs of crime and ways to reduce them, about technologies of situational prevention. Complex assemblages (composed of specific combinations of agents, knowledges, techniques and practices) are thus pieced together in an attempt to translate the new rationalities and programmes into practical effects. There has been a real spurt of inventiveness at the level of security technologies [. . .] partly due to government interest in the project, and partly because of the formation of a market in security which speeds up the development and the (very unequal) distribution of such devices.

The criminal justice system as an entity to be governed

A striking feature of the present period is the degree to which official attention has become focused not just upon the government of crime, but also upon the problem of governing criminal justice. Rises in the flow of cases through the criminal justice system, resulting in crowded court calendars and overcrowded prisons, prompted government concern about new problems such as costs, efficiency and coordination in criminal justice. This, in turn, led to the development of techniques for representing and controlling these problems. Over time, there was a transformation in the way that 'criminal justice' was understood. What was previously viewed as a loosely coupled series of independent agencies—police, prosecution, courts, prison, probation, each with its own objectives and working ideologies, each with its own sphere of autonomous action—came to be seen instead as a 'system'. This 'system' is an entity which can be known and governed. It has become a practicable object of government, with the Home Office increasingly constituting itself as a centre of calculation and management, oriented to that governmental task.

The system's processes and internal dynamics have been theorized, using concepts and tools borrowed from 'systems management'. Models have been constructed to simulate the workings of the system. Monitoring devices, auditing requirements and decision-making guidelines have been implanted at key points so that the flow of cases can be predicted and controlled from a central point in a way that was quite impossible before. Similarly, the day-to-day practice of practitioners working in the various agencies has been standardized and subjected to greater managerial control by the use of 'government-at-a-distance' techniques (budgetary limits, national standards, 'gatekeeping' guidelines) by which the central authorities exert broad control over decision-making while still leaving a space for the exercise of localized judgement on the part of individual professionals.

As many commentators have pointed out—see Peters (1986), Heydebrand and Seron (1990), Tuck (1991), Feeley and Simon (1992), Walker (1993)—the rendering of criminal justice into a 'system' that can be known and centrally governed presupposes a new way of thinking about the processes involved. The focus of attention is shifted from individuals to aggregates, from specific cases to population flows, and from individualized justice to the management of resources. The discretionary powers of professionals are curtailed, and their jurisdictions are narrowed. The system is rendered more homogeneous, more knowable and more governable. There is a centralization of powers and a shift from a patchwork of particular expertise to a more homogenized field of risk- and resource-management. Precisely because of these curtailments and centralized controls, this development has provoked resistance from some of the professional groups involved. The judiciary is especially forceful in its opposition to this attempt to 'systematize' and govern its conduct, and the need 'to treat the merits of the individual case' is used as a counter-claim by judges and social workers alike.

Active subjects

Crime control practices embody a conception of the subjects they seek to govern. For most of the 20th century, the subjects of crime control have been the 'individual delinquent' and the 'legal subject'. The new economic rationality attempts to make up new kinds of individuals, or rather, to create and impart new forms of subjectivity, which individuals and organizations will adopt for themselves.

One new form of 'subjectification' is the responsibilized, security-conscious crime preventing subject—*homo prudens*—analysed by O'Malley (1992) and Adams (1995). A related, though opposed, figure is what has been called 'situational man' (see Clarke and Cornish, 1986). Situational man is criminology's version of the economic subject of interest. He (or less often, she) is a moderately rational, self-interested individual, unfettered by any moral compass or super-ego controls; a consumer who is alert to criminal opportunities and responsive to situational inducements.

The questions to be asked of subjects of this kind are not 'how did their attitudes and personalities come to be abnormal?' or 'how can they be corrected?' but rather 'how do such persons reason and act in criminogenic situations?', 'how do they choose?' and 'how can their actions be channelled away from crime by modifying situational controls?'

Unlike the 'crime-preventing subject', situational man is not a preferred form of subjectivity that is promoted and projected by the authorities. It is an assumption about the real subjectivity of already-formed individuals. But in assuming the reality of situational man, the authorities begin to give substance to it, projecting it on to live men and women, and 'making people up' in this form. Thus research is conducted into the reasoning processes of burglars or robbers, offenders are officially identified as career criminals, sentencers shape their sentences on the basis of these perceptions, and convicted offenders are treated as entrepreneurial actors rather than as subjects of need or candidates for rehabilitative treatment.

Penal technologies of the self

In contemporary prison and probation regimes one sees a similar characterization of the criminal subject, and a determined effort to assimilate individual offenders to its terms by means of new 'technologies of the self'. Techniques of correction stress the offender's responsibility for his or her criminal actions and insist that he or she must 'address' and 'take responsibility' for them. This is not merely a reversion to an older punitive mode which assumes that the offender has the attributes of a free-willed legal subject. On the contrary. Instead of assuming that all adult individuals are 'naturally' capable of responsible, self-directed action and moral agency, contemporary penal regimes treat this as a problem to be remedied by procedures that actively seek to 'subjectify' and to 'responsibilize' individuals.[4]

[. . .]

The new stress upon the offender's 'autonomy' and 'responsibility' can also be seen in recent policy on community penalties and the idea of 'punishment in the community'. Part of the appeal of probation and community service and monetary penalties is that they avoid the 'objectifying' tendencies of imprisonment and organize a form of penal control in which the offender is enlisted in the process of his or her own control. Instead of removing the individual into the near-total control of a custodial enclosure, these community measures seek to insert regulatory devices into the offender's natural habitat and daily routines, producing a light framework of supervision but leaving plenty of opportunity for the offender to practice self-control. Techniques such as intermittent supervision and reporting, electronic monitoring, tracking, drug-testing and attendance for work, are used, as are alliances with other sources of social control (such as the family, landladies, employers, bail hostel workers, etc.), to try to build an environment conductive to self-control and the practice of a responsibilized freedom.[5]

No doubt there are other lines of research which a governmentality analytic would help to open up for criminologists. The 'neo-liberal' strategies involved in the 'privatization' or 'contracting out' of crime-control functions; the new linkages being formed between 'public' and 'private' forms of crime control; the impact of insurance upon criminal behaviour and the conduct of victims; and the shift in police policy towards a more generic concern with the promotion of security and good order, reminiscent of the older programme of 'police', are some that come to mind. And of course historical work on the development of crime control, criminal justice and a professionalized police has much to learn from the genealogical writings of Foucault and Foucauldian scholars such as Dean (1991), Burchell (1991) and Pasquino (1991). But I hope I have said enough to suggest that the field of crime control is certainly one in which 'governmental' analyses can be effectively and productively employed.

The present article is written in the hope of encouraging such work, and suggesting lines of enquiry. However, and in anticipation of such work being done, it might be useful to point to some of the limitations of this analytical scheme, and some of the problems that inhere in the governmentality literature. Analytical frameworks are most effectively deployed with a degree of self-consciousness about their boundaries and blind-spots. The governmentality approach has been developed to address particular kinds of questions in a particular kind of way. Some of its objects of analysis—such as the rationalities of rule, and the self-problematizing activities of rulers—were simply not visible prior to the development of Foucault's approach. Other theoretical objects, as I will argue, are rather less distinctive, and may be compatible with other, more developed, traditions of research. Some of its methodological protocols—such as the requirement to study programmes in their own terms—strike me as well founded. Others—such as its apparent hostility to causal analysis and explanation—seem to me much less convincing. Some of its key concepts—such as the idea of 'governing through freedom'—are illuminating when properly deployed, but are easily misused and misunderstood. Finally, the idea of a 'history of the present' is attractive but also ambiguous. My own preferred usage would be to think of this as an approach concerned to produce a critical, historical and sociological account of contemporary practices but it can also be regarded as a rather more philosophical (or 'archaeological') enterprise concerned less with contemporary practices than with the 'absent conditions' or 'historical a prioris' that make these practices possible. This suggests something of a tension between the reconstruction of governmental rationalities and the construction of a history of the present. Writers in the governmentality literature usually claim to be doing both, but the latter task requires a broader, more sociological agenda than the former. To understand the present, one must establish not just the rationalities that structure practices of government, but also the ways in which these practices sometimes diverge from the pattern implicit in these rationalities.

[. . .]

NOTES

1 To talk of a style of practical reasoning as a 'rationality' is perhaps to imply more analytical coherence than it actually possesses. Specific rationalities tend to emerge following the success of particular modes of problem solving. They become exemplars, and are the subject of imitation and analogous application. The actors who develop these ways of thinking and acting rarely articulate them in a coherent form. Instead, they become habits of mind and of action which only later are articulated as an explicit framework. Inevitably then, there is much room for argument about the veracity of such post hoc reconstructions.

2 One effect of this, of course, is to facilitate recourse to a simplified moral discourse about crime and punishment. If crime is a matter of simple rational choice, then we can 'understand less and condemn more' as Prime Minister John Major put it in 1993.

3 [. . .] This 'economic' reasoning about crime—nicely typified by the various Audit Commission Reports on policing, prosecution and the processing of young offenders [. . .]—is by no means uncontested. One sees it most fully realized in practices that deal with 'shallow end' offences and offenders. In respect of violent, sexual or serious crime, economic and risk-based reasoning tends to give way to a more absolutist discourse of public protection and punishment in which cost considerations are deemed irrelevant (see Garland, 1996).

4 This points up an important contradiction in contemporary criminal justice. The legal framework, which dominates current sentencing practice, assumes the truth of the fiction that individuals who are not mentally ill are therefore 'responsible' and proceeds to deal with them on this basis. The prison authorities, on the other hand, recognize that many offenders lack the learned capacity for responsible action and put into place a machinery for creating and reinforcing this absent capacity—a machinery which no doubt fails much of the time. The responsible offender is thus conjured in and out of existence by the different working ideologies of criminal justice agencies.

[. . .]

5 Simon (1993) provides an excellent analysis of how US parole officers try to introduce a measure of structure and routine into the 'disorganized' lives of their (workless) clients.

REFERENCES

Adams, J. (1995) *Risk*. London: UCL Press.

Barry, A., T. Osborne and N. Rose (1993) *Economy and society Special Issue on Liberalism and Governmentality*. London: Routledge.

Barry, A., T. Osborne and N. Rose (eds) (1996) *Foucault and Political Reason. Liberalism, Neo-liberalism and Rationalities of Government*. Chicago: Chicago University Press.

Becker, G. (1968) 'Crime and Punishment: An Economic Approach', *Journal of Political Economy* 76:128–47.

Burchell, G. (1991) 'Peculiar Interests: Civil Society and Governing the System of Natural Liberty', in G. Burchell, C. Gordon and P. Miller (eds) *The Foucault Effect. Studies in Governmentality*, pp. 119–50. Hemel Hempstead: Harvester Wheatsheaf.

Clarke, R. and D. Cornish (1986) 'Introduction', in R. Clarke and D. Cornish (eds) *The Reasoning Criminal: Rational Choice Perspectives on Offending*, New York: Springer-Verlag.

Cook, P.J. (1986) 'The Demand and Supply of Criminal Opportunities', *Crime and Justice* 9:1–27.

Dean, M. (1991) *The Constitution of Poverty: Towards a Genealogy of Liberal Governance*. London: Routledge.

Dean, M. (1994) *Critical and Effective Histories: Foucault's Methods and Historical Sociology*. London: Routledge.

Durkheim, E. (1973) *Moral Education*. New York: Free Press.

Feeley, M. and J. Simon (1992) 'The New Penology: Notes on the Emerging Strategy of Corrections and its Implication', *Criminology* 30:449–74.

Feeley, M. and J. Simon (1994) 'Actuarial Justice: The Emerging New Criminal Law', in D. Nelkin (ed.) *The Futures of Criminology*. London: Sage.

Foucault, M. (1977) *Discipline and Punish*. London: Allen Lane.

Garland, D. (1996) 'The Limits of the Sovereign State: Strategies of Crime Control in Contemporary Society', *British Journal of Criminology* 36(4):445–71.

Heimer, C. (1985) *Reactive Risk and Rational Action: Managing Moral Hazard in Insurance Contracts*. Berkeley: University of California Press.

Heydebrand, W. and Seron, C. (1990) *Rationalizing Justice*. Albany: SUNY Press.

Hunt, A. and G. Wickham (1994) *Foucault and Law*. London: Pluto Press.

Litton, R.A. (1990) *Crime and Crime Prevention for Insurance Practice*. Aldershot: Avebury.

O'Malley, P. (1992) 'Risk, Power and Crime Prevention', *Economy and Society* 21(3):252–75.

O'Malley, P. (1996) 'Risk and Responsibility', in A. Barry, T. Osborne and N. Rose (eds) *Foucault and Political Reason*. Chicago: Chicago University Press.

Pasquino, P. (1991) 'Theatrum Politicum: The Genealogy of Capital – Police and the State of Prosperity', in G. Burchell, C. Gordon and P. Miller (eds) *The Foucault Effect*. Hemel Hempstead: Harvester Wheatsheaf.

Peters, A.A.G. (1986) 'Main Currents in Criminal Law Theory', in J.J. van Dijk et al. (eds) *Criminal Law in Action*. Arnhem: Gouda Quint.

Shearing, C. and P. Stenning (1985) 'From the Panopticon to Disneyworld: The Development of Discipline', in A. Doob and E. Greenspan (eds) *Perspectives in Criminal Law*. Aurora: Canada Law Book Co.

Simon, J. (1988) 'The Ideological Effects of Actuarial Practices', *Law and Society Review* 22:772–800.

Simon, J. (1993) *Poor Discipline: Parole and the Social Control of the Underclass, 1890–1990*. Chicago: University of Chicago Press.

Simon, J. and M. Feeley (1995) 'True Crime: The New Penology and Public Discourse on Crime', in T. Blomberg and S. Cohen (eds) *Punishment and Social Control*. New York: Walter de Gruyter.

Stenson, K. (1993) 'Community Policing as a Governmental Technology', in A. Barry, T. Osborne and N. Rose (eds) *Economy and Society Special Issue on Liberalism and Governmentality*. London: Routledge.

Tuck, M. (1991) 'Community and the Criminal Justice System', *Policy Studies* 12(3):22–37.

van Dijk, J.J.M. (1994) 'Understanding Crime Rates: On the Interactions between the Rational Choices of Victims and Offenders', *British Journal of Criminology* 34(2):105–21.

Walker, S. (1993) *Taming the System: The Control of Discretion in Criminal Justice, 1950–1990*. New York: Oxford University Press.

42

Spatial governmentality and the new urban social order: Controlling gender violence through law

Sally Engle Merry

[. . .]

Although modern penality is largely structured around the process of retraining the soul rather than corporal punishment, as Foucault argued in his study of the emergence of the prison (1979), recent scholarship has highlighted another regime of governance: control through the management of space. New forms of spatially organized crime control characterize contemporary cities, from the explosion of gated communities (Caldeira 1999) to 'prostitution free zones' as a regulatory strategy for the sex trade (Perry and Sanchez 1998; Sanchez 1997a, 1997b) to 'violence free zones' as a way of diminishing communal conflict in India. Spatialized strategies have been applied to the control of alcohol consumption (Valverde 1998) and the regulation of smoking. In the 1970s, concerns about fear of crime in the United States expanded from a focus on catching offenders to removing 'incivilities' in public spaces (Merry 1981; Wilson and Kelling 1982). This meant creating spaces that appeared safe to urbanites by removing people who looked dangerous or activities that seemed to reveal social disorder such as homeless people or abandoned trash. New community-policing strategies toward youths emphasize moving potentially criminal youths to other areas rather than prosecuting them (Ericson and Haggerty 1999:168).

These are all examples of new regulatory mechanisms that target spaces rather than persons. They exclude offensive behavior from specified places rather than attempting to correct or reform offenders. The regulation of space through architectural design and security devices is generally understood as a complement to disciplinary penality but fundamentally different in its logic and technologies (Ewick 1997; Shearing and Stenning 1985; Shields 1989; Simon 1988; Valverde et al. 1999). While disciplinary mechanisms endeavor to normalize the deviant behavior of individuals, these new mechanisms focus on governing populations as a whole (O'Malley 1993; Simon 1988). [. . .]

From *American Anthropologist*, 2001, 103:1. pp. 16–29.

A focus on managing risk rather than enforcing moral norms has transformed police practices in recent years (Ericson and Haggerty 1997, 1999; O'Malley 1999a:138–139). This approach seeks to produce security rather than to prevent crime—to reduce the risk of crime rather than to eliminate it. Order is defined by actuarial calculations of tolerable risk rather than by consensus and conformity to norms (Simon 1988). New policing strategies seek to diminish risks through the production of knowledge about potential offenders (Ericson and Haggerty 1997). In general, modern democratic countries have experienced a pluralizing of policing, which joins private and community-based strategies that focus on protection of space with public strategies that detect and punish offenders (Bayley and Shearing 1996).

New mechanisms of social ordering based on spatial regulation have been labeled spatial governmentality (Perry 2000; Perry and Sanchez 1998). They differ substantially from disciplinary forms of regulation in logic and techniques of punishment. Disciplinary regulation focuses on the regulation of persons through incarceration or treatment, while spatial mechanisms concentrate on the regulation of space through excluding offensive behavior. Spatial forms of regulation focus on concealing or displacing offensive activities rather than eliminating them. Their target is a population rather than individuals. [. . .]

Spatialized regulation is always also temporal as well. Regulations excluding offensive behavior usually specify time as well as place. Systems such as curfews designate both where and when persons can appear. Spatial regulations may interdict particular kinds of persons from an area only during certain times, such as business hours, or prohibit behavior, such as drinking, only after a certain time at night (see Valverde 1998). [. . .]

Although spatial forms of governmentality are not exclusively urban, they have taken on particular importance in modern cities. In addition to features of size, scale, heterogeneity, and anonymity, many contemporary cities are characterized by sharp economic inequalities, major differences in levels of development, global labor and capital flows, and a shift to neoliberal forms of governance (see Low 1999). As states endeavor to govern more while spending less, they have adopted mechanisms that build on individual self-governance and guarded spaces. They establish areas to which only people seen as capable of self-governance have access and incarcerate those who cannot be reformed. People are encouraged to participate in their own self-governance, whether by voluntarily passing through metal-detector machines in airports or organizing into community watch brigades (Bayley and Shearing 1996).

In the United States, this has meant an increasing focus on self-management along with the rapid expansion of prison populations. There has been an enormous increase in the number of prisoners over the last decade as well as a turn to more severe punishments, including the revival of the death penalty. Within the neoliberal regime of individual responsibility and accountability, populations are divided between those understood as capable of self-management and those not. Managing spaces and incarcerating offenders are therefore complementary rather than opposing strategies. These complementary strategies are the product of the vast economic inequalities dividing urban populations in the United States. In American cities, spatial strategies are typically used by the wealthy to exclude the poor, while those who fail to respect these islands of safety are incarcerated. Private organizations pursue similar strategies, developing systems of private policing and governance that parallel those of the state (Valverde et al. 1999). This transformation seems to be characteristic of cities outside the United States as well (see Low 1999; Caldeira 1999). Indeed, contemporary urbanism is shaped not only be features of size, scale, and anonymity but also by globally produced inequalities and transnationally circulating notions of governance.

[. . .] The turn to more spatialized systems reflects despair about the possibilities of reform and the difficulties of reincorporating offenders into the contemporary order of labor (see Simon 1993a). The new systems promote safety for the privileged few by excluding those who are dangerous rather than promoting safety for the collectivity by seeking to reform those who offend. Constructing safe, policed spaces requires resources that are not available to everyone. These strategies are limited to those who can mobilize them—typically people located in more privileged positions in class, racial, and gender hierarchies. New walled towns within cities allow wealthier individuals to retreat into privately secured spaces and abandon the public arena (see Perry 2000). With the shift to community policing and private police, the affluent acquire greater safety than the poor (Bayley and Shearing 1996).

The expansion of spatial governmentality diminishes the scope of collective responsibility for producing social order characteristic of governance in the modern state. Some persons are defined as hopeless, deserving exclusion rather than correction and reintegration. The collectivity takes less responsibility for the excluded. Prisons are increasingly seen as holding pens rather than places of education, training, and reform.

Although spatial governmentality is generally described as a system that provides safety for those who can afford it while abandoning the poor to unregulated public spaces, in this article I describe a different use of spatial governance: the spatial exclusion of batterers from the life space of their victims. This is not an instance of creating a collective safe space but, instead, of protecting a person by prohibiting access to her home or workplace. This approach emphasizes the safety of the victim rather than the punishment or reform of the offender. Unlike the more recognized uses of spatial governance, this initiative endeavors to protect poor women as well as rich women. It represents the use of spatial systems of governance that benefit more than the wealthy and privileged. Like other forms of spatial governmentality, however, this regime typically controls the disadvantaged rather than the privileged. People subject to restraining orders for gender violence are typically poor men very similar to, and often identical with, those generally controlled by the forms of spatial governmentality developed by the wealthy. It is not that these are the only men who batter, but these are usually the only ones who end up in the restraining order process.

The use of spatial control in gender violence situations is relatively new. It took a powerful social movement many years to develop this legal protection for battered women. Punishing batterers for the crime of assault is an old practice; providing legal restrictions on their movements to create a safe space for victims is much newer (Pleck 1987). A concerted social movement of feminist activists beginning in the late 1960s argued for the applicability of protective orders for such situations. Commonly referred to as temporary restraining orders (TROs), these orders supplement more conventional strategies for punishing batterers. TROs are court orders that require the person who batters (usually but not always male) to stay away from his victim (usually but not always female) under penalty of criminal prosecution. In the United States, protective orders were used for domestic abuse situations beginning in the 1970s, about the same time as refuges and shelters were being promoted by the battered-women's movement (Schechter 1982). Both provide a safe space for the victim rather than seeking to reform or punish the offender. It was not until the late 1980s that activists succeeded in persuading courts and police to use these protective orders widely. Requests for civil protective orders for battering grew dramatically in the 1990s. My research documents the explosion of these cases in a small town in Hawai'i in the late 1980s and 1990s, a pattern replicated in other parts of the country during the same time period. Although I am describing spatial governmentality in a small town rather than a major city, restraining orders were developed in large urban areas and spread to smaller cities and towns.

Although spatial mechanisms may reduce women's risk of attack from their batterers, they only protect a victim from a specified offender for a limited period of time. They do not establish public safety zones that exclude people with histories of battering. Nor is there intensive surveillance of people with hazardous risk profiles for battering. Such proactive risk-minimization strategies are increasingly common in modern policing strategies that target high-risk populations for special surveillance (Ericson and Haggerty 1999), but the protection of poor women from their batterers has not evoked a similar investment of state resources. Indeed, it is only the consistent political pressure of battered-women's advocates that has succeeded in developing and extending this mechanism for governing batterers.

The article is based on a decade of ethnographic research in a town in Hawai'i, [. . .] The town, Hilo, has 45,000 inhabitants and serves as the hub of a large agricultural region dotted with vast sugar cane plantations, the recent collapse of which has exacerbated problems of unemployment and poverty. [. . .]

THEORIZING SPATIAL GOVERNMENTALITY

The concept of spatial governmentality derives from Foucault's elaboration of the notion of governmentality, a neologism that incorporates both government and rationality (1991). Governmentality refers to the rationalities and mentalities of governance and the range of tactics and strategies that produce social order. It focuses on the 'how' of governance (its arts and techniques) rather than the 'why' (its goals and values). Techniques of governmentality are applied to the art of governing the self as well as that of governing society. Nikolas Rose defines governmentality as 'the deliberations, strategies, tactics and devices employed by authorities for making up and acting upon a population and its constituents to ensure good and avert ill . . .' (Rose 1996:328; see also Miller and Rose 1990; Rose and Miller 1992; Rose and Valverde 1998).

Considerable research on governmentality has delineated a rough historical sequence from eighteenth-century mechanisms that act primarily on the body, such as exile or dramatic physical punishment, to a modern, nineteenth-century system of social control that relies on reforming the soul of the individual and normalizing rule breakers, to a late-twentieth-century postmodern form of social control that targets categories of people using actuarial techniques to assess the characteristics of populations and develops specific locales designed for prevention rather than the normalization of offenders (Simon 1993b). The modern system relies on disciplinary technologies to forge the modern subject at work as well as in the family. The postmodern system is premised on a postindustrial subjectivity of consumption, choice, introspection about feelings, and flexibility. It draws on the therapeutic mechanisms widespread by the close of the twentieth century. The contemporary use of therapy to acquire self-governance, to learn to manage feelings, to rethink the costs and benefits of violence against intimates, and to focus on choice represents a new technology of governance characteristic of postindustrial society (Rose 1990, 1996; Simon 1993a). Therapies of various kinds seek to gain the subject's compliance in a regime of change. Instead of inducing change through discipline and habit, these approaches focus on insight and choice. The subject is encouraged to understand why she feels and acts as she does and brought to see that she could make different choices that would be better for her. An important facet of therapeutic interventions is, therefore, an emphasis on self-governance, on establishing control over feelings, and on making choices about actions. These systems focus not on regimes of punishment and correction but on inducing consent through coercion—on forcing people to participate in remaking themselves, taking responsibility for themselves, and developing their capacity to control their emotional lives and actions. Foucault refers to this form of power as 'a biopolitics of the population' in contrast to disciplinary power that works on deviant individuals (O'Malley 1993:160). These transformations are part of a transnational movement toward self-management and neoliberal governance rather than the particular features of urban environments.

At the same time, there has been an elaboration of mechanisms that promote security by diminishing risks. Risk-based techniques such as social insurance, workers' compensation, and income tax are examples of security-focused technologies of governance. They offer more efficient ways of exercising power since they tolerate individual deviance but produce order by dividing the population into categories organized around differential degrees of risk (O'Malley 1992; Simon 1988). Risk-based approaches fall within the sphere of neoliberal techniques of governance, which Valverde et al. describe as the downloading of risk management to individuals and families, 'responsibilization,' empowerment, and consumer choice (1999:19). Responsibilization involves the inculcation and shaping of responsibility for good health and good order within the home, the family, and the individual by means of expert knowledges (Rose 1999:74).

Foucault was unclear about whether these three forms of governance, organized by a logic of punishment, discipline, and security, represented a sequence or a coexisting triangle (Foucault 1991:102). He suggests that there has been a rough historical development from feudal forms of the state based on sovereignty and law to an administrative state characterized by regulation and discipline to a governmental state defined not simply by its territory but by its population and economic administration and controlled by the apparatuses of security (1991:104). Then he argues that sovereignty, discipline, and government do not replace each other but constitute a triangle with its primary target the population and its essential mechanism the apparatus of security (1991:102). The triangle suggests mutual interdependence and connection rather than displacement, but Foucault never developed this concept nor its implications for the interpenetration of law, normalization, and discipline (see Hunt and Wickham 1994:67). Empirical research suggests a relationship of growth and layering among these forms of governance rather than a process of displacement. For example, the study of alcohol regulation suggests the historical accretion of governance practices and their mutual redefinition of one another rather than a series of stages (Valverde 1998:177).

Patrick O'Malley questions the evolutionary assumptions behind the thesis of a sequence of forms of governance from punishment to discipline to security. New strategies are developed not just because they are more efficient, but also because they belong to political programs developed in moral and political struggles oriented either toward neoconservative or social justice agendas (O'Malley 1992, 1996; O'Malley and Palmer 1996). For example, Alan Hunt demonstrates how new forms of governance of others and of the self arise out of social movements for moral reform (1999). These movements for moral regulation, often focusing on demands for new patterns of drug consumption or sexual behavior, are spearheaded by particular actors located in the state, in organizations, or in communities who articulate a crisis and a solution in a way that resonates with broader social trends and discourses (Hunt 1999:10). Changes in forms of governance are agentic and contested parts of the political and social process. Indeed, in the case of gender violence, it is clear that the new deployment of spatial governmentality—the use of restraining orders—was the result of sustained political activism.

Many forms of governmentality have a spatial component. Foucault recognized a critical role for spatial ordering in his analysis of systems of discipline in the nineteenth century, but he saw its role largely as a frame for ordering and confining bodies and as a structure of surveillance (1979). In contemporary society, spatialized forms of ordering are connected to the recent intensification of consumption as a mode of identity formation along with neo-liberal approaches to government. In contemporary cities, there is increasing focus on managing the spaces people occupy rather than managing the people themselves. Systems of providing security through the private regulation of spaces reveal the emergence of postcarceral forms of discipline that do not focus on individualized soul training (Shearing and Stenning 1985:336). Instead, these new forms of regulation depend on creating spaces characterized by the consensual, participatory governance of selves (Ewick 1997; O'Malley and Palmer 1996; Rose 1996; Shearing and Stenning 1985; Shields 1989; Simon 1993a). These systems rely on selves who see themselves as choice-making consumers, defining themselves through the way they acquire commodities and choose spouses, children, and work (Miller and Rose 1990). As Rose argues, in liberal democracies of the postwar period, citizens are to regulate themselves, to become active participants in the process rather than objects of domination (1990:10). Citizen subjects are educated and solicited into an alliance between personal objectives and institutional goals, creating the phenomenon Rose calls 'government at a distance' (Rose 1999).

Disney World and the shopping mall represent locales for such participatory regulation in which the self is made and makes itself in ways structured by the private regulation of the space. These forms of regulation rely on the state only minimally and are largely maintained through private security forces. The space itself creates expectations of behavior and consumption. These systems are not targeted at reforming the individual or transforming his or her soul; instead they operate on populations, inducing cooperation without individualizing the object of regulation. Private control lacks a moral conception of order and is concerned only with what works; it is preventative rather than punishing (Shearing and Stenning 1985:339). This shift to an instrumental focus means a move away from concern with individual reform to control over opportunities for breaches of order. Spatial governmentality works not by containing disruptive populations but by excluding them from particular places. The shopping mall, the prototype of spatial governmentality, is also the product of market-based technologies for shaping and controlling identity and behavior. As subjects become consumers, 'the autonomous citizens regulate themselves through organizing their lives around the market' (O'Malley 1993:172– 173). The individual invested with rights is replaced by the individual who defines himself or herself by consumption. This control is promotive rather than reactive, voluntary rather than coercive, based more on choice than constraint. Power appears to disappear behind individual choice (Ewick 1997:81). Systems of private regulation are backed by formal legal processes, which will remove those who cannot govern themselves.

Thus, the newer systems coexist with morally reformist carceral systems, each defined by whom and what it excludes (Ewick 1997; see also O'Malley 1992). The prison system survives and expands along with nonpunitive systems, which manage the opportunities for behaviors rather than the behaviors themselves. Outside the space marked by the absence of penal power, there is a world of unemployed, insane, socially marginal people subjected to the penal power of police and prisons (Ewick 1997:83). Although there is a tendency to understand these changes as sequential rather than co-present, Ewick notes that the spatial system of ordering founded in consumption depends on an expanding carceral system for those excluded from participation in the shopping mall order of individual choice (1997). As in the control of gender-based violence, spatial forms of ordering operate against a backdrop of punishment.

PUNISHMENT/THERAPY/SAFETY: APPROACHES TO GENDER VIOLENCE.

From a governmentality perspective, there are three distinct forms of governance: punishment, discipline, and security. One is based on punishing offenders, one on reforming offenders through therapy and training, and one on keeping offenders away from victims through spatial separation. All three are used in dealing with gender-based violence in cities in North America. [. . .]

PUNISHMENT/PRISON

[. . .]
Beginning in the 1970s, feminist activists pressed for a greater use of punishment in gender violence cases, advocating mandatory police arrests, no-drop prosecution, and mandatory incarceration. Historically, under the legal doctrine of coverture, the family had been defined as a private sphere under the authority of the husband rather than the state (see Fineman and Mykitiuk 1994). Although coverture was generally eliminated by the late nineteenth century in the United States, its legacy is a reluctance to intervene legally in the family in ways that challenge male authority. The law intervenes in gender violence incidents less readily than in other cases of assault. Until recently, violence within families was treated as a social problem reflective of poverty rather than as a criminal offense. [. . .]

Gender violence cases did appear in court in the past in Hilo, and offenders were generally found guilty and fined, but the numbers were small. [. . .] Between 1971 and 1976, there were between one and nine cases of gender violence in Hilo courts every year and between 1980 and 1986, fewer than twenty a year. By 1998 the number had increased 25 times to 538 cases a year and the caseload in 2000 is likely to be even higher. [. . .] Fragmentary data from other parts of the United States reveal a similar staggering growth in the number of criminal cases of domestic violence in the courts since the mid-1980s. These changes are a result of demands for a more activist police force and mandatory arrest policies along with no-drop prosecution.

This increase in cases has not translated into a significant increase in punishment. Instead, it has served to funnel offenders into an array of services and subject them to ongoing supervision by the courts. [. . .]

DISCIPLINE/REFORM

Disciplinary techniques work on persons rather than actions, seeking to reform them through rehabilitation and repentance. Disciplinary systems incorporate a broad range of therapeutic and group discussion techniques ranging from batterer's intervention programs to alcoholics-anonymous-style self-help meetings (see Rose 1990; Valverde 1998). Some are designed to reform by forcing the body to follow an orderly sequence of activities in work and everyday life, while others reform through introspection and insight, requiring consent from the subject of transformation. [. . .] In the late twentieth century, the criminal justice system in the United States has increasingly turned to introspective forms of discipline and self-management (Simon 1993a).

In the 1990s, this model dominated batterer reform efforts in Hilo as well as in the rest of the United States. Feminist-inspired batterer intervention programs grew out of discussions by battered women in Duluth, Minnesota, in the 1980s, which emphasized that battering needs to be understood in terms of power and control (Pence and Paymar 1993). This model focused on undermining the cultural support for male privilege and violence against women by exploring men's feelings and beliefs and encouraging men to analyze their own behavior during battering events. Violence against women was understood as an aspect of patriarchy. A dominant feature of group discussions was changing beliefs about men's entitlement to make authoritative decisions and back them up with violence.

The Duluth model came to Hawai'i in the 1980s. Men convicted of spouse abuse or under a TRO were required to attend the Alternatives to Violence (ATV) program started in Hilo in 1986. ATV offers violence control training for men and a support group for women. Men are required to attend weekly two-hour group discussions for six months. In groups of 10 to 15 men and 2 facilitators, participants talk about their use of violence to control their partners. Discussions stress the importance of egalitarian relations between men and women and the value of settling differences by negotiation rather than by force. The men are taught that treating their partners with respect rather than violence will win them a more loving, trusting, and sexually fulfilling relationship and forge warmer relations with their children. [. . .]

If men fail to attend the program, the staff informs their probation officers. Those whose attendance is a stipulation of a criminal spouse abuse conviction face revocation of their probation. Those required to attend as a condition of a TRO are guilty of contempt of court—a criminal offense—and their case is sent to the prosecutor. In practice, these men are typically sent back to ATV rather than receiving a jail sentence or other criminal penalty, but the threat of jail time is frequently articulated by judges during court hearings. Thus, attendance at this psychoeducational program is enforced by the threat of prison. The program emphasizes training in self-management of violence, but failure to accomplish this task results in the return to a regime of punishment, at least in theory. In practice, nonparticipants are typically sent back to the program. Only after new violations are they sent to jail.

The men attending this program are largely poor, unemployed, and relatively uneducated. [. . .] Men and women in the violence control program and women's support groups frequently talked about poverty, welfare, and survival by fishing, hunting, and odd construction jobs. ATV clients are also substantially less educated than town residents, with the men even less educated than the women. [. . .] Thus, the men sent to the violence control program, as well as the women they batter, are significantly poorer and less educated that the town overall.
[. . .]

SECURITY/SPATIAL MECHANISMS

Security techniques are those that seek to minimize the harm wreaked by offenders by containing or diminishing the risks they post to others. They focus on protecting victims or potential victims and spreading the cost of harms to a larger group through insurance systems. Security technologies assess risks, anticipate and prevent risks, and analyze factors that produce risk. Their target is an entire population rather than particular individuals, and the goal is not reform but security for the population as a whole. Foucault sees security as a specific principle of political method and practice capable of being combined with sovereignty and discipline (Gordon 1991:20). The method of security deals in a series of possible and probable events, calculates comparative costs, and, instead of demarcating the permissible and forbidden, specifies a mean and possible range of variation. Sovereignty works on a territory, discipline focuses on the individual, and security addresses itself to a population. From the eighteenth century on, security is increasingly the dominant component of modern governmental rationality. Hunt and Wickham suggest that Foucault's term *security* can be better translated as "welfare," emphasizing the focus on individuals as subjects of the state (1994:54). The emphasis on security technologies represents, Gordon argues, Foucault's most important extension of the analysis of discipline beyond the framework of *Discipline and Punish* (1991:20).
[. . .]

In the domain of gender violence, security techniques are designed to protect victims instead of seeking to reform offenders. They did not emerge in the field of gender violence until the battered-women's movement of the 1970s (Schechter 1982). Although there was some use of 'peace bonds' in earlier years, leaders of the battered-women's movement began to press for a system of restraining orders rooted in the civil law system in the early 1970s. A 1973 article describes a New York statute for a family court proceeding that allowed a victim to receive a protective order without having to bring criminal charges. This order was backed by a penalty of prison for its violation (Field and Field 1973:238). During this period of initial experimentation, there was worry about the lack of a right to counsel and protection against self-incrimination for the defendant in this civil proceeding. On the other hand, some applauded the way this legal mechanism could invoke the authority of the law in a noncriminal context. In 1976, Pennsylvania became the first state to pass legislation authorizing judges to issue domestic violence restraining orders; in 1978, Massachusetts followed suit (Ptacek 1999:48). In Hawai'i, a law providing for Ex-Parte Temporary Restraining Orders for victims of domestic violence was passed in 1979. Thus, the use of protective orders for domestic violence represented a new legal mechanism developed in the 1970s, which disseminated rapidly across the U.S.

This is the most innovative feature of contemporary American efforts to diminish wife battering. It is fundamentally a spatial mechanism since it simply separates the man and the woman. Shelters, which provide places of refuge for battered women, are similarly novel inventions of the battered-women's movement of the 1970s, although they build on older patterns of safe houses and helpful neighbors and relatives. Neither of these interventions makes an effort to reform the batterer, but seek only to keep him away from the victim.

THE TRO PROCESS IN HILO

The development of this legal mechanism means that gender violence incidents arrive in the legal system through two quite different processes: a criminal process of arrest and conviction or a civil process of issuing a temporary restraining order. The first leads to a trial and potential criminal conviction, the second to a family court hearing that could result in the issuance of a TRO. Both are activated largely by the complaint of an injured party, although a police officer may be summoned by a neighbor, relative, or friend. TROs are almost always issued at the request of an individual petitioner. Although the first process is a criminal one and the second a civil one, in practice there are many connections between the two. Criminal cases are often handled through plea bargaining between the prosecutor and defense attorney rather than trial. Defendants typically receive the same sentences as TRO respondents. Moreover, a civil case can be converted into a criminal case if there is a violation of the conditions of the order. [. . .]

The number of requests for TROs has increased dramatically since the early 1970s. Between 1971 and 1978, there were 7 protective orders or 'peace bonds' issued in Hilo for domestic violence situations. By 1985, however, the year a new, more stringent spouse abuse law went into effect, there were 250 in one year. In 1990 there were 338 and by 1999, 471 from an area of perhaps 70,000 residents. Although there has been a doubling of population in the last twenty years, TRO petitions have increased far more rapidly [. . .].

Observations of the domestic violence calendar during the 1990s indicate that most defendants are men and most victims are women. The women who bring these cases to the court are primarily young, in their 20s and 30s, and nonprofessional workers or nonworkers. Their ethnic identities reflect the local population, including white, Portuguese, Filipino, Japanese, Hawaiian, Hawaiian/Chinese, and Puerto Rican individuals. Because of the high rate of intermarriage among these groups, the majority have multiple ethnicities. Most are "local," although a significant minority are people from the mainland, many of whom follow alternative lifestyles such as that of the pioneer/survivalist aspiring to live off the land. A few support themselves by cultivating marijuana. Most of the people have low incomes and often are not working.

At the hearing, victims are almost always accompanied by a woman advocate from ATV. The man appears alone, although there is always a male advocate from the ATV program present in the waiting area of the court and willing to talk to the men. The Family Court judge reads the written account provided by the victim, asks the accused if he or she acknowledges the charge, and takes testimony if the accused denies all violence. If the accused accepts the charge or the evidence is persuasive, the judge issues a TRO for a period of months with a series of conditions. If there are no children and a desire by both to separate, the respondent is told to stay away from the petitioner and both are told to have no further contact. This is called a no-contact TRO. If they have children but the victim wishes no contact, the judge will arrange visitation or custody for the children and specify no contact between the adults. If they wish to continue the relationship and/or to live together, the judge usually issues a contact TRO but also sends them to ATV, requiring either the accused or both parties to participate in the program. The contact order allows the respondent to be with the petitioner but prohibits him from using violence against her. Observations of 130 cases in the early 1990s indicated that slightly under half (42%) of petitioners requested and received contact TROs.

At the hearing, the judge points out that any violation of the conditions of the protective order is a misdemeanor, punishable by a jail sentence of up to one year and/or a fine of $2,000. He frequently schedules a review hearing in a month or two to monitor the situation, particularly for the contact restraining orders, and to make sure that the conditions of the TRO are being fulfilled. He also requires the respondent to surrender any guns in his possession to the local police officer for the duration of the TRO.

The Family Court judge's concerns are twofold: first, to stop the violence and second, to protect the children involved. The judge endeavors to convey a clear message that violence is against the law and that it is bad for children. Any indication of violence or abuse against children elicits an immediate referral to Children's Protective Services. Protective orders commonly include the requirement to seek treatment as well as the obligation to refrain from violence and, in no-contact orders, to stay away. The judge is much more likely to refer a couple to the batterer intervention program when the woman requests a contact TRO than when she wishes no contact. When a woman requesting a TRO says she wishes to stay with her partner and they have children, the judge usually makes a referral to ATV.

These legal orders are sometimes viewed uneasily by judges. Since they begin as an emergency intervention, they impose restrictions on individuals who are initially absent from the hearing. Because they are civil proceedings rather than criminal, defendants do not have the right to an attorney if they cannot afford one. Yet, if a person violates the terms of a TRO, he is guilty of contempt of court and can be prosecuted for a criminal violation and theoretically face a prison sentence. Although in practice this is rare, in theory it remains a possibility. In Hilo, a violation based on a violent incident typically led to a new arrest, while a violation based on the failure to attend ATV typically led to being resentenced back to the program.

A second difficulty with the TRO in gender violence cases is its limited enforceability. It relies on the respondent's acquiescence or an effective police response. In the hands of a skeptical batterer, it is no more powerful than the policing behind it.

With a no-contact TRO, a respondent is in violation if he simply appears at the plaintiff's house or workplace. The police should remove him and charge him with a violation of order. Thus, the efficacy of the order depends on the willingness of the police to appear and take the violator away.

But a no-contact order does not fit well with the exigencies of everyday life. A woman may wish to see her partner to exchange children, to ask for financial help, or simply because she is lonely and wishes to consider restarting the relationship. If she allows him into her house, she is violating the TRO and he is risking criminal penalties. In order to avoid these difficulties, many women request a contact TRO initially or ask to change the no-contact order to a contact one a few months after the incident. Under a contact order, the petitioner and respondent can be together, but he is prohibited from using violence against her. There is no spatial segregation. In many cases, women want the continuation of the relationship without the violence.

A third difficulty is that a woman with a contact restraining order is little better off than a woman without one. A new act of violence simply places the batterer at risk of being arrested for that violence, as he would be in any case. Some judges have expressed discomfort with the contact TRO, arguing that it is too hard to enforce and should be eliminated. Without spatial and temporal separation, the TRO is a fragile form of governance. The Family Court judge in Hilo tried to persuade petitioners to ask for no-contact TROs. Nevertheless, almost half the TROs issued in Hilo were contact orders.

A final difficulty with the TRO system occurs when the parties succeed in persuading a judge to issue mutual restraining orders. If both parties file for restraining orders against each other and if a judge issues both, then any time they are together both are guilty of a legal infraction. Since it is common for an incident of wife battering to include mutual blows, such an outcome can appear logical to a judge. Yet, the result is an enforcement quagmire, since both are equally, and indistinguishably, guilty at the moment of contact. A related problem is the use of TROs to deal with custody disputes. The party who retains custody of the children with a TRO has an advantage in keeping the children during subsequent divorce proceedings. Consequently, a person contemplating divorce may take out a restraining order on his or her partner in order to be in possession of the children at the time of the divorce decree.

On the other hand, this is a mechanism that focuses on the safety of the woman without waiting until the man has been reformed. Because murdered wives are often found with restraining orders, such orders are often considered of little value. Yet, many of the men I talked to took the order seriously and, although they were angry at being kicked out of their houses, did stay away. Women felt comforted by the presence of this legal document, even though many were still harassed by their batterers at home and at work. Furthermore, the no-contact TRO shifts the evidentiary burden away from the woman, releasing her from the necessity of testifying against her batterer in his presence. His presence alone is a proscribed location constitutes adequate evidence of a criminal offense. The skyrocketing use of this mechanism in the 1980s and 1990s indicates its popularity with battered women. It offers what many victims want: separation from their batterer, or even prohibition of violence while they remain together, along with a program of reform. Whether or not this mechanism is always effective, it encapsulates the desires of many battered women who do not want their abusers punished, but reformed or gone. Its novelty is that it foregrounds the security of the victim rather than the reform or punishment of the offender. This spatialized form of governance represents a popular new addition to legal relief for battered women.

It is possible to imagine other expansions of this logic of security for the problem of wife battering. Women could subscribe to battering insurance programs, which would provide funds for emergency housing and moving costs to relocate to a different area. Violence free zones could be established where a person with a history of battering would be excluded. Batterers could be required to wear monitors that would emit a sound when they enter a prohibited zone. Obviously there are difficulties with aspects of these ideas, but they suggest the possibilities of governance based on security and the regulation of space rather than the regulation of persons.

CONCLUSIONS

Although Hilo is a small town, its changing practices of managing wife battering parallel those of big cities and exemplify shifting forms of governance in contemporary industrialized cities. In Hilo, as in many larger cities, responsibility for control of violence against women has shifted from kin and neighbors to the state. It is the law, rather than the family, to which these battered women turn. Such a decision is not easy and is often discouraged by kin and friends. Yet, the skyrocketing number of complaints shows that the turn to the law is happening in Hilo as well as elsewhere in the United States.

In Hilo as well as in large industrial cities, processes of spatial governmentality are shaped by inequalities linked to class and ethnicity. Yet, spatial governmentality does not simply increase the control over the poor, but also can increase the safety of all women. Many who write about risk society fear that it is a slide into a big brother state, but there may be possibilities for these new mechanisms when they are democratically distributed. It took a protracted struggle led by a powerful social movement to develop and implement a legal innovation that benefits poor women. Many judges still question its validity as a legal procedure, and police are often lax in enforcing it. Overworked prosecutors ignore TRO violations. Yet, the creation and implementation of this spatial mechanism of governmentality at least reveals the possibility of more democratic forms of spatial governance for the protection of vulnerable populations.

On the other hand, those who end up with TROs or in batterer treatment programs are typically the poorest and least educated segments of the male population, disproportionately members of colonized and disadvantaged communities. Protecting women from battering provides ways to enhance discipline over men who are already the target of state systems of control. Almost one half (46%) of the men in the batterer intervention program said they had been arrested for an offense other than abuse. Wealthier men in Hilo also beat their wives (although this is hard to find out in any systematic way), but they very rarely appear in criminal court or batterer intervention programs and only slightly more often in Family Court. It is largely poor men who are controlled. This example shows that spatial forms of governance do not simply protect the rich and abandon the poor, but that the target of control remains the poor. Wealthy batterers often escape.

The example also reveals the interlocking and layered nature of the mechanisms of punishment, discipline, and security. Each operates only in conjunction with the others and can only be understood within the matrix created by the whole system. None would function the same alone. Men would not attend ATV unless required to; two days in jail would have little impact on helping men to rethink masculinity; simply staying away from one victim still leaves a batterer free to hit the next one. Spatial separation without criminal penalties for violating it has little effect. Governmentality does not shift from one system to the next—from punishment to reform to risk management. Instead, there is a pattern of growth and layering in which the new is added to the old, which then redefines the meanings and operation of the new. There are clearly new dimensions of social ordering in contemporary cities, which are spatial; yet even Disney World does not control behavior without the threat of arrest and punishment. Punishment forms the bedrock for the newer technologies of reform and security. This is not an evolutionary relationship, but an intersecting one. Spatialized control technologies focused on security and risk management are intimately linked to forms of punishment and discipline.

The adoption of new forms of spatial governmentality is part of a complex reconfiguration of governance in the postmodern world. These changes are fostered by globalization. Globalization distributes not only commodities and images, but also modes of governance. The invention of the TRO for gender violence was quickly followed by its rapid spread through the United States. There is now a global diffusion of batterer intervention programs, no-drop policies, and restraining orders. Practices in Hilo are brought by activists from other parts of the country, while judges and officials concerned about controlling gender violence face budget pressures found elsewhere in North America to do less and accomplish more. The Hilo judiciary has, like many other U.S. jurisdictions, focused on developing self-management training for offenders in conjunction with spatially based systems of deterrence in place of more costly systems of punishment. Along with neoliberal approaches to governance, these new technologies of spatial governmentality now circulate globally within cities large and small.

[. . .]

REFERENCES

Bayley, David H., and Clifford D. Shearing 1996 The Future of Policing. Law and Society Review 30:585–606.
Blomley, Nick, and Jeff Sommers 1999 Mapping Urban Space: Governmentality and Cartographic Struggles in Inner City Vancouver. *In* Governable Places: Readings on Governmentality and Crime Control. Russell Smandych, ed. pp. 261–287. Aldershot, UK: Ashgate/Dartmouth.
Burchell, Graham, Colin Gordon, and Peter Miller, eds. 1991 The Foucault Effect: Studies in Governmentality. Chicago: University of Chicago Press.
Caldeira, Teresa P.R. 1999 Fortified Enclaves: The New Urban Segregation. *In* Theorizing the City: The New Urban Anthropology Reader. Setha M. Low, ed. pp. 83–110. New Brunswick, NJ: Rutgers University Press.
Ericson, Richard V., and Kevin D. Haggerty 1997 Policing the Risk Society. Toronto: University of Toronto Press.

Ericson, Richard V., and Kevin D. Haggerty 1999 Governing the Young. *In* Governable Places: Readings on governmentality and Crime Control. Russell Smandych, ed. Pp. 163–191. Aldershot, UK: Ashgate/Dartmouth.

Ewick, Patricia 1997 Punishment, Power, and Justice. *In* Justice and Power in Socio-Legal Studies. Bryant G. Garth and Austin Sarat, eds. Pp. 36–54. Chicago: Northwestern University Press.

Field, Martha H., and Henry F. Field 1973 Marital Violence and the Criminal Process: Neither Justice Nor Peace. Social Science Review 47: 221–240.

Fineman, Martha, and Rotanne Mykitiuk, eds. 1994 Feminist Perspectives on Gender Violence. New York: Routledge.

Foucault Michel 1979 Discipline and Punish: The Birth of the Prison. New York: Vintage.

Foucault Michel 1991 Governmentality. *In* The Foucault Effect: Studies in Governmentality. Graham Burchell, Colin Gordon, and Peter Miller, eds. Pp. 87–105. Chicago: University of Chicago Press.

Garland, David 1999 Crime Control, Governmentality and Sovereignty. *In* Governable Places: Readings on Governmentality and Crime Control. Russell Smandych, ed. pp. 15–45. Aldershot, UK: Ashgate/Dartmouth.

Gordon, Colin 1991 Governmental Rationality: An Introduction. *In* The Foucault Effect: Studies in Governmentality. Graham Burchell, Colin Gordon, and Peter Miller, eds. Pp. 1–53. Chicago: University of Chicago Press.

Healy, Kerry and Christine Smith, with Chris O'Sullivan 1998 Batterer Intervention: Program Approaches and Criminal Justice Strategies. Issues and Practices. U.S. Department of Justice, Office of Justice Programs, National Institute of Justice. Electronic document. http://www.ncjrs.org/textfiles/168638.txt.

Hunt, Alan 1999 Governing Morals: A Social History of Moral Regulation. Cambridge: Cambridge University Press.

Hunt, Alan, and Gary Wickham 1994 Foucault and Law: Towards a Sociology of Law as Governance. London: Pluto Press.

Low, Setha M., ed. 1999 Theorizing the City: The New Urban Anthropology Reader. New Brunswick, NJ: Rutgers University Press.

Merry, Sally Engle 1981 Urban Danger: Life in a Neighborhood of Strangers. Philadelphia, PA: Temple University Press.

Merry, Sally Engle 1995 Gender Violence and Legally Engendered Selves. Identities: Global Studies in Culture and Power 2:49–73.

Merry, Sally Engle 2000 Colonizing Hawai'i: The Cultural Power of Law. Princeton, NJ: Princeton University Press.

Miller, Peter, and Nikolas Rose 1990 Governing Economic Life. Economy and Society 19:1–27.

O'Malley, Pat 1992 Risk, Power and Crime Prevention. Economy and Society 21:252–275.

O'Malley Pat 1993 Containing Our Excitement: Commodity Culture and the Crisis of Discipline. Research in Law, Politics, and Society 13:151–172.

O'Malley Pat 1996 Indigenous Governance. Economy and Society 25:310–326.

O'Malley Pat 1999a Governmentality and the Risk Society. Economy and Society 28:138–148.

O'Malley, Pat, and Darren Palmer 1996 Post Keynsian Policing. Economy and Society 25:137–155.

Pence, Ellen, and Michael Paymar 1993 Education Groups for Men Who Batter: The Duluth Model. New York: Springer.

Perry, Richard 2000 Governmentalities in City-Scapes: Introduction to the Symposium. Symposium on City-Spaces and Arts of Government. Polar: Political and Legal Anthropology Review 23(1):65–73.

Perry, Richard Warren, and Lisa Erin Sanchez 1998 Transactions in the Flesh: Toward an Embodied Sexual Reason. *In* Studies in Law, Politics, and Society, vol. 18. Austin Sarat and Patricia Ewick, eds. Pp. 29–76. Stamford, CT: JAI Press.

Pleck, Elizabeth Hafkin 1987 Domestic Tyranny: The Making of Social Policy against Family Violence from Colonial Times to the Present. New York: Oxford University Press.

Ptacek, James 1999 Battered Women in the Courtroom: The Power of Judicial Responses. Boston: Northeastern University Press.

Rose, Nikolas 1990 Governing the Soul: The Shaping of the Private Self. London: Routledge.

Rose, Nikolas 1996 The Death of the Social? Re-Figuring the Territory of Government. Economy and Society 25:327–356.

Rose, Nikolas 1999 Predicaments of Freedom. Cambridge: Cambridge University Press.

Rose, Nikolas, and Peter Miller 1992 Political Power beyond the State: Problematics of Government. British Journal of Sociology 43:173–205.

Rose, Nikolas, and Mariana Valverde 1998 Governed by Law? Social and Legal Studies 7:541–551.

Rosenbaum, Michael D. 1998 To Break the Shell without Scrambling the Egg) An Empirical Analysis of the Impact of Intervention into Violent Families. Stanford Law and Policy Review 9:409–427.

Sanchez, Lisa 1997a Boundaries of Legitimacy: Sex, Violence, Citizenship, and Community in a Local Sexual Economy. Law and Social Inquiry 22:543–581.

Sanchez, Lisa 1997b Spatial Practices and Bodily Maneuvers: Negotiating at the Margins of a Local Sexual Economy. Polar: Political and Legal Anthropology Review 20(2):47–62.

Schechter, Susan 1982 Women and male Violence: The Visions and Struggles of the Battered Women's Movement. Boston: South End Press.

Shearing, Clifford D., and Philip C. Stenning 1985 From the Panopticon to Disney World: The Development of Discipline. *In* Perspectives in Criminal Law. Anthony N. Doob and Edward L. Greenspan, Q.C., eds. Pp. 335–349. Aurora, ON: Canada Law Book, Inc.

Shields, Rob 1989 Social Spatialization and the Built Environment: The West Edmonton Mall. Society and Space 7:147–164.

Shumway, David R. 1989 Michel Foucault. Boston: Twayne Publishers.

Simon, Jonathan 1988 The Ideological Effects of Actuarial Practices. Law and Society Review 22:771–800.

Simon, Jonathan 1993a Poor discipline: Parole and the Social Control of the Underclass, 1890–1990. Chicago: University of Chicago Press.

Simon, Jonathan 1993b From Confinement to Waste Management: The Postmoderniza-tion of Social Control. Focus on Law Studies 8:4–7.

St. Joan, Jacqueline 1997 Sex, Sense, and Sensibility: Trespassing into the Culture of Domestic Abuse. Harvard Women's Law Journal 20:263–308.

Valverde, Mariana 1998 Diseases of the Will: Alcohol and the Dilemmas of Freedom. Cambridge: Cambridge University Press.

Valverde, Mariana, Ron Levi, Clifford Shearing, Mary Condon, and Pat O'Malley 1999 Democracy in Governance: A Socio-Legal Framework. A Report for the Law Commission of Canada on Law and Governance Relationships. Toronto.

Wilson, James Q., and George L. Kelling 1982 Broken Windows: The Police and Neighborhood Safety. Atlantic Monthly, March: 29–38.

Part VI

Future tense: Criminological transformations

The readings in this section map the shifts in criminology at the beginning of a new millennium. As many of the readings in part five of this reader indicate, the sheer scale of the transformation of 'the social' currently underway calls into question criminology's traditional assumptions, rationales, ways of thinking and purpose.

Carol Smart's contribution poses a stark question: what has criminology, of any kind, got to offer feminist analysis? She takes those who adhere to realist thinking to task because it anchors its proponents to a flawed and discredited positivist paradigm. Criminologists still believe that they can 'discover' both the causes of and solutions to 'crime'. Conventional criminology's obsession with 'the real' leads Smart to argue that feminist scholars should relocate themselves wholeheartedly within wider, more ambitious theoretical debates, particularly those emanating from postmodernism. Criminology responded to Smarts' intervention with considerable hostility. Indeed it seemed that for criminologists of a variety of persuasions one of the key tasks was to protect criminology from the postmodern. Much more valued was exploring Gidden's conceptualisation of late modernity and/or Beck's 'risk society'.

Kathleen Daly's sweeping overview seeks to extend the debate triggered by Smart by attempting to demonstrate the far-reaching effects posed to feminist criminology by developments such as critical race theory and postmodern/poststructuralist theorizing. She assesses the contributions and limitations of three modes of analysis – 'class-race-gender', 'doing gender' and 'sexed bodies' – for feminist criminology.

The next cluster of readings concentrate on the criminological consequences of the extensive globalization of economic, political and cultural activities that is producing new harms across the world. The rapid change accompanying certain globalizations are bringing serious risks of global economic instability as a result of unregulated neo-liberal markets and the equally serious risk of political and social disorder and mounting violence resultant from the decline of traditional forms of governance and the fragmentation of social relations. Manuel Castells' contribution represents one of the first attempts to detail the new criminal threats that are being unleashed by wider socio-economic, political and cultural transformations. He notes that geo-political change and economic shifts have facilitated the emergence of 'joined up' globalized criminal networks and new forms of highly profitable crime. Many of the developments he points to can be confirmed if one reads recent reports released by transnational law enforcement bodies. There is increasing acceptance by governments, particularly after the 11 September 2001 attacks on New York, that organised global criminal activity has the potential to corrupt democratic institutions, undermine the rule of law and human rights and embed itself within conventional modes of economic exchange. Interestingly, Castells also recognizes the relationship between the rise of 'Crime PLC' and the cultural realm noting how particular cultural identities nurture and protect the new criminal networks and the impact of the media's glamourization of 'live fast, die young' criminals and the life choices and life chances of disaffected youth in many societies.

Stan Cohen pushes our discussion towards human rights and the new global (dis)order. In the course of his discussion of human rights abuses and crimes of the state, he questions the core concerns of traditional criminology. He notes how for example criminologists have devoted time and effort to analysing the state of crime and virtually ignored the criminological significance of the crimes of the state. With one or two notable exceptions criminologists have been remarkably silent on the genocide, ethnic cleansing, extra-judicial killings and violations of human rights that are occurring in many parts of the world. Cohen provides us with an important case study of how key criminological concepts can be deployed to analyse and explain the state inspired criminal events and actions that will define the twenty-first century.

Mike Davis offers us a chilling vision of the possible dystopian future for cities in the twenty-first century, drawing especially on developments in regulation, surveillance and repression in Los Angeles immediately after the urban disorders of 1992. This reading is a brutal reminder of the persistence of modes of brutal, coercive control which exist alongside the new, more subtle modes of governance and ordering in contemporary 'cityscapes'. Davis highlights how technologies of regulation, surveillance and repression in 'post'-Blade Runner LA are designed to stabilize class, racial and generational relations across the chasm of the new inequalities and in the context of accelerating social polarization and spatial apartheid. In line with most of the readings in this section, Davis highlights the new culture of fear and the obsession with (privatized) safety and security which lies at the heart of the city and of the new modes of governance in contemporary neo-liberal societies. Davis' work represents a productive dialogue between social theory and science fiction, and in the course of this dialogue, his analysis opens up a new criminological imaginary, albeit predicated upon a vision of a profoundly dystopian/pessimistic urban future for us all.

The next two readings explore the notion of 'risk society' that is claimed to be one of the hallmark of late/post modernity. Jock Young's critically acclaimed thesis on crime and late modernity documents the shift from an inclusive, stable, homogenous society to an exclusive society of constant change, multiple social divisions and authoritarian forms of social control. Young is fascinated by how citizens have no choice but to attempt to manage and negotiate a multitude of risks unleashed by late/post modernity. Like Giddens and Beck he argues for a balanced reading of risk society, one which also acknowledges the appearance of more risks associated with a quantum leap in levels of crime and disorder but also recognizes that there is greater public awareness of and sensitivity about risks. A progressive politics of crime can be built around the fact that the public in late modern societies have higher expectations than previously and lower toleration of unacceptable anti-social behaviour and attitudes.

Hollway and Jefferson deepen our discussion of the nature and meaning of 'risk society' by exploring how 'fear of crime' is handled and explained. They argue that to date core concepts such as 'fear', 'crime', 'risk' and 'anxiety' remain under-theorised in the available literature. In addition, they identify serious limitations with the identification of the rationally calculating 'subject' who apprehends and makes sense of the many risks characteristic of late modern societies. Hollway and Jefferson wish to compose a more psycho-social understanding and utilize the psychoanalytic concept of 'anxiety' to introduce a 'subject' whose principal source of meaning and action is the dynamic unconscious rather than cognitive reason. This psychosocial criminology demands a critical rethinking of questions of 'fear' and 'risk'.

The final reading by Ferrell points towards the possibilities of a fully fledged cultural criminology, something which is hinted at in previous readings. Drawing on cultural studies, postmodernism, interactionist sociology and the ethno-graphic tradition, cultural criminology spotlights issues of image, meaning and the representation in the interchange between crime and crime control. In its interdisciplinary scope, its conscious attempt to connect with cutting edge developments in other parts of the academy, the focus on the hyper-mediated construction of crime and control issues and the centring of the impact of culture shocks on crime, cultural criminology holds out intriguing research and theoretical possibilities for students of crime.

43

Feminist approaches to criminology or postmodern woman meets atavistic man

Carol Smart

[. . .]

It is a story that has been told many times, although most effectively in *The New Criminology* (Taylor et al., 1973) that criminology is an applied discipline which searches for the causes of crime in order to eradicate the problem. Admittedly, criminology as a subject embraces much more than this. For example, it tends to focus also on the operations of the criminal justice system, the relationship between the police and communities or systems of punishment. However, such topics fit just as easily under the rubric of the sociology of law or even philosophy. What is unique about criminology, indeed its defining characteristic, is the central question of the *causes* of crime and the ultimate focus of the 'offender' rather than on mechanisms of discipline and regulation which go beyond the limits of the field of crime. It is this defining characteristic with which I wish to take issue here. Arguably, it is this which creates a kind of vortex in this area of intellectual endeavour. It is the ultimate question against which criminology is judged. Can the causes of crime be identified and explained? Moreover, once identified, can they be modified?

Criminologies of the traditional schools have been unashamedly interventionist in aim if not always in practice. This goal was criticized by the radical criminologists of the 1970s for being oppressive, conservative and narrowly partisan (that is, on the side of the state and/or powerful). Moreover, the radicals argued that the traditional criminologists had, in any case, got their theories wrong. Crime, it was argued, could not be explained by chromosomal imbalance, hereditary factors, working-class membership, racial difference, intelligence and so on. So, among the many errors of traditional criminology, the two main ones to be identified were an inherent conservatism and inadequate theorization. The repudiation of these errors was condensed into the most critically damning term of abuse – positivist. To be positivist embodied everything that was bad. Positivism, like functionalism, had to be sought out, exposed and eliminated. Now, in some respects I would agree with this; but the

From *Feminist Perspectives in Criminology* (eds A. Morris and L. Gelsthorpe), pp. 71–84. (Milton Keynes: Open University Press, 1990.)

problem we face is whether critical criminologies or the more recent left realist criminologies have transcended the problem of positivism or whether they have merely projected it on to their political opponents while assuming that they themselves are untainted.

I would argue that positivism is misconstrued if its main problem is seen as its connection to a conservative politics or a biological determinism. The problem of positivism is arguably less transparent than this and lies in the basic presumption that we can establish a verifiable knowledge or truth about events: in particular, that we can establish a causal explanation which will in turn provide us with objective methods for intervening in the events defined as problematic. Given this formulation, positivism may be, at the level of political orientation, either socialist or reactionary. The problem of positivism is, therefore, not redeemed by the espousal of left politics. Positivism poses an epistemological problem; it is not a simple problem of party membership.

It is this problem of epistemology which has begun to attract the attention of feminist scholarship (the postmodern woman of my title). Feminism is now raising significant questions about the status and power of knowledge (Harding, 1986; Weedon, 1987) and formulating challenges to modes of totalizing or grand theorizing which impose a uniformity of perspective and ignore the immense diversity of subjectivities of women and men. This has in turn led to a questioning of whether 'scientific' work can ever provide a basis for intervention as positivism would presuppose. This is not to argue that intervention is inevitably undesirable or impossible, but rather to challenge the modernist assumption that, once we have the theory ('master' narrative, (Kellner, 1988)) which will explain all forms of social behaviour, we will also know what to do and that the rightness of this 'doing' will be verifiable and transparent.

THE CONTINUING SEARCH FOR THE THEORY, THE CAUSE AND THE SOLUTION

It is useful to concentrate on the work of Jock Young as a main exponent of left realism in criminology. His work is particularly significant because, unlike many other left thinkers, he has remained inside criminology and, while acknowledging many of the problems of his earlier stance in critical criminology, has sustained a commitment to the core element of the subject. That is to say he addresses the question of the causes of crime and the associated problems of attempting to devise policies to reduce crime. For example, he states:

> It is time for us to *compete* in policy terms . . . the major task of radical criminology is to seek a solution to the problem of crime and that of a socialist policy is to substantially reduce the crime rate. (1986: 28, emphasis in the original)

This is compelling stuff but it is precisely what I want to argue is problematic about the new forms of radical criminology for feminism. It might be useful initially to outline Young's position before highlighting some of the problems it poses.

As part of his call for a left realist criminology, Young (1986) constructs a version of the recent history of post-war criminology. He sees it as a series of crises and failures (and in this respect we are at one). He points to the positivist heritage of post-war criminology in Britain which, in his account, amounts to a faith in medicine and cure and/or a reliance on biologically determinist explanations of crime. He sees the influence of North American criminology in a positive light, [. . .] and then turns to the work of the 'new criminologists' in Britain who constructed a political paradigm in which to reappraise criminal behaviour. He is, however, critical of the idealism of this work and interprets it as the 'seedbed' of more radical work to come rather than a real challenge to mainstream orthodoxy or an adequate account in and of itself.

The failures of the criminological enterprise overall which Young identifies are twofold. The first is the failure 'really' to explain criminal behaviour. The theories are always flawed either ontologically or politically. The second is the failure to solve the problem of crime or even to stem its rise. These are not two separate failures, however, as the failure to stop crime is 'proof' of the failure of the theories to explain the causes of crime. [. . .] It is through this linkage between theory and policy that the positivism of the left realists comes to light. The problem is not that there is a commitment to reducing the misery to which crime is often wedded, nor is the problem that socialists (and feminists) want policies which are less punitive and oppressive. The problem is that science is held to have the answer if only it is scientific enough. Here is revealed the faith in the totalizing theory, the 'master' narrative which will eventually – when sufficient scales have fallen from our eyes or sufficient connections have been made – allow us to see things for what they really are.

To return to Young's story, we pick up the unfolding of criminology at the point of intervention by the new criminologists. Young points out that while this intervention may have excited the academic criminologists there was simultaneously another revolution in mainstream criminology. This revolution was the transformation of traditional criminology from a discipline concerned with causes and cures to one concerned with administrative efficiency and methods of containment. Young argues that mainstream criminology has given up the search for causes, the goal of the meta-narrative of criminal causation. It has gone wholeheartedly over to the state and merely provides techniques of control and manipulation. Again it is important to highlight the linkages in Young's argument. On the one hand, he is critical of what he calls administrative criminology because it has become (even more transparently?) an extension of the state (or a disciplinary mechanism). But the reason for this is identified as the abandonment of the search for the causes (a search which was, according to Young, in any case misdirected). The thesis, therefore, is that to abandon the search for the causes is to become prey to reactionary forces. This, it seems to me, is to ignore completely the debates which have been going on within sociology and cultural theory about the problems of grand and totalizing theories. And such ideas are coming not from the right but precisely from the subjects which such theoretical enterprises have subjugated, that is, lesbians and gays, black women and men, Asian women and men, feminists and so on. I shall briefly consider aspects of this debate before returning to the specific problem of feminism in criminology.

THE DEBATE OVER POSTMODERNISM

There is now a considerable literature on postmodernism and a number of scholars are particularly concerned to explore the consequences of this development for sociology (Bauman, 1988; Kellner, 1988; Smart, 1989) and for feminism (Fraser and Nicholson, 1988; Harding, 1986; Weedon, 1987). The concept of postmodernism derives from outside the social sciences, from the fields of architecture and art (Rose, 1988). Bauman (1988) argues that we should not assume that postmodernism is simply another word for post-industrialism or post-capitalism. It has a specific meaning and a specific significance, especially for a discipline like sociology (and by extension criminology), one which challenges the very existence of such an enterprise. Postmodernism refers to a mode of thinking which threatens to overturn the basic premises of modernism within which sociology has been nurtured.

Briefly, the modern age has been identified by Foucault (1973) as beginning at the start of the nineteenth century. The rise of modernity marks the eclipsing of Classical thought and, most importantly, heralds the centring of the conception of 'man' as the knowing actor who is author of his own actions and knowledge (that is, the liberal subject) and who simultaneously becomes the object of (human) scientific enquiry. Modernism is, however, more than the moment in which the human subject is constituted and transformed. It is a world view, a way of seeing and interpreting, a science which holds the promise that it can reveal the truth about human behaviour. The human sciences, at the moment of constituting the human subject, make her knowable – a site of investigation. What secrets there are will succumb to better knowledge, more rigorous methodologies, or more accurate typologizing. Implicit in the modernist paradigm is the idea that there is progress. What we do not know now, we will know tomorrow. It presumes that it is only a matter of time before science can explain all from the broad sweep of societal change to the motivations of the child molester. And because progress is presumed to be good and inevitable, science inevitably serves progress. Knowledge becomes nothing if it is not knowledge for something. Knowledge must be applied or applicable – even if we do not know how to apply it now, there is the hope that one day we will find a use for it (space travel did after all justify itself for we do now have non-stick frying pans).

Modernity has now become associated with some of the most deep-seated intellectual problems of the end of the twentieth century. It is seen as synonymous with racism, sexism, Euro-centredness and the attempt to reduce cultural and sexual differences to one dominant set of values and knowledge. Modernism is the intellectual mode of Western thought which has been identified as male or phallogocentric (for example, by Duchen, 1986 and Gilligan, 1982) and as white or Eurocentric (for example, by Dixon, 1976 and Harding, 1987). It is also seen as an exhausted mode, one which has failed to live up to its promise and which is losing credibility. As Bauman argues:

> Nobody but the most rabid of the diehards believes today that the western mode of life, either the actual one or one idealized ('utopianized') in the intellectual mode has more than a sporting chance of ever becoming universal . . . The search for the universal standards has suddenly become gratuitous . . . Impracticality erodes interest. The task of establishing universal standards of truth, morality, taste does not seem that much important. (1988: 220–1)

Clinging to modernist thought, in this account, is not only antediluvian; it is also politically suspect. It presumes that sociology (which for brevity's sake I shall take to include criminology in this section) as a way of knowing the world is superior, more objective, more truthful than other knowledges. However, it is easier said than done to shake off the grip of a way of knowing which is almost all one knows. In turn, this reflects a dilemma which has always plagued sociology. If we say we do not know (in the modernist sense) then we seem to be succumbing to the forces of the right who have always said we knew nothing – or, at least, that we were good for nothing.

The irony is, as Bauman (1988) points out, that we are damned if we do and also if we do not. He points to the way in which sociology has little choice but to recognize the failure of its originating paradigm. On the one hand, doubts cannot be wished away and we cannot pretend that sociology produces the goods that the post-war welfare state required of it. On the other hand, governments already know this. We cannot keep it a secret. State funding of sociological research is already much reduced and what will be funded is narrowly restricted to meet governmental aims. It may have been possible in the past to claim that more money was necessary or that a larger study was imperative before conclusions could be drawn but now we know (and they know) that conclusions, in the sense of final definitive statements, cannot be drawn. The point is whether we argue that all the studies that have been carried out to date have been inadequate or whether we reappraise the very idea that we will find solutions. Young, for example, is scathing about a major study carried out on 400 schoolboys by West (1969). He points out that this was one of the largest and most expensive pieces of criminological work to be carried out in Britain. Yet, he argues disparagingly, it could only come up with a link between delinquency and poverty and no real causes. For Young the problem is the intellectual bankruptcy of the positivist paradigm. From where I stand he is right, but, as I shall argue below, the problem is that he locates himself inside exactly the same paradigm.

THE VORTEX THAT IS CRIMINOLOGY

It is, then, interesting that Young acknowledges many of the problems outlined above, although he does not do so from a postmodern stance. Rather he is situated inside the modernist problematic itself. He acknowledges that mainstream criminology has given up the search for causes and the 'master' narrative. He also recognizes the power of governments to diminish an academic enterprise which they no longer have use for. Hence, to keep their jobs, criminologists have had to give up promising the solutions and knuckle down to oiling the wheels. He is rightly critical of this, but, rather than seeing the broad implications of this development, these criminolog*ists* are depicted as capitalist lackeys while criminolog*y* as an enterprise can be saved from such political impurity by a reassertion of a modernist faith. While applauding Young's resistance to the logic of the market which has infected much of criminology (and sociology), I am doubtful that a backward looking, almost nostalgic, *cri de coeur* for the theory that will answer everything is very convincing. Yet Young can see nothing positive in challenging the modernist mode of thought; he only sees capitulation. The way to resist is apparently to proclaim that suffering is real and that we still need a 'scientific' solution for it.

In so doing Young claims the moral high ground for the realists, since to contradict the intellectual content of the argument appears to be a denial of misery and a negation of the very constituencies for whom he now speaks. So, let me make it plain that the challenge to modernist thought, with its positivist overtones which are apparent in criminology, does not entail a denial of poverty, inequality, repression, racism, sexual violence and so on. Rather it denies that the intellectual can divine the answer to these through the demand for more scientific activity and bigger and better theories.

The problem which faces criminology is not insignificant, however, and, arguably, its dilemma is even more fundamental than that facing sociology. The whole *raison d'être* of criminology is that it addresses crime. It categorizes a vast range of activities and treats them as if they were all subject to the same laws – whether laws of human behaviour, genetic inheritance, economic rationality, development or the like. The argument within criminology has always been between those who give primacy to one form of explanation rather than another. The thing that criminology cannot do is deconstruct crime. It cannot locate rape or child sexual abuse in the domain of sexuality or theft in the domain of economic activity or drug use in the domain of health. To do so would be to abandon criminology to sociology; but more importantly it would involve abandoning the idea of a unified problem which requires a unified response – at least, at the theoretical level. However, left realist criminology does not seem prepared for this: see, for example, Young, 1986: 27–8.

FEMINIST INTERVENTION INTO CRIMINOLOGY

[. . .] the core enterprise of criminology is profoundly problematic. However, it is important to acknowledge that it is not just criminology which is inevitably challenged by the more general reappraisal of modernist thinking. My argument is not that criminology alone is vulnerable to the question of whether or not such a knowledge project is tenable. But criminology does occupy a particularly significant position in this debate because both traditional and realist criminological thinking are especially wedded to the positivist paradigm of modernism. This makes it particularly important for feminist work to challenge the core of criminology and to avoid isolation from some of the major theoretical and political questions which are engaging feminist scholarship elsewhere. It might, therefore, be useful to consider schematically a range of feminist contributions to criminology to see the extent to which feminism has resisted or succumbed to the vortex.

Feminist empiricism

Sandra Harding (1986, 1987) has provided a useful conceptual framework for mapping the development of feminist thought in the social sciences. She refers to feminist empiricism, standpoint feminism and postmodern feminism. By feminist empiricism she means that work which has criticized the claims to objectivity made by mainstream social science. Feminist empiricism points out that what has passed for science is in fact the world perceived from the perspective of men, what looks like objectivity is really sexism and that the kinds of questions social science has traditionally asked have systematically excluded women and the interests of women. Feminist empiricism, therefore, claims that a truly objective science would not be androcentric but would take account of both genders. What is required under this model is that social scientists live up to their proclaimed codes of objectivity. Under this schema, empirical practice is critiqued but empiricism remains intact. Such a perspective is not particularly threatening to the established order. It facilitates the study of female offenders to fill the gaps in existing knowledge; men can go on studying men and the relevances of men as long as they acknowledge that it is men and not humanity they are addressing.

In criminology there has been a growth in the study of female offenders (for example, Carlen, 1988; Eaton, 1986; Heidensohn, 1985). It would be unjust to suggest that these have merely followed the basic tenets of mainstream empirical work, but a motivating element in all of these has been to do studies on women. But, as Dorothy Smith pointed out in 1973, to direct research at women without revising traditional assumptions about methodology and epistemology can result in making women a mere addendum to the main project of studying men. It also leaves unchallenged the way men are studied.

Harding sees a radical potential in feminist empiricism, however. She argues that the fact that feminists identify different areas for study (for example, wife abuse rather than delinquency) has brought a whole range of new issues on to the agenda. It is also the case that feminists who subscribe to empiricism have challenged the way we arrive at the goal of objective knowledge. Hence different kinds of methods are espoused, note is taken of the power relationship between researcher and researched and so on (Stanley and Wise, 1983). The move towards ethnographic research is an example of this (although this is not, of course, peculiar to feminist work).

It is perhaps important at this stage to differentiate between empiricism and empirical work. Harding's categories refer to epistemological stances rather than practices (although the two are not unrelated). Empiricism is a stance which proclaims the possibility of objective and true knowledge which can be arrived at and tested against clearly identified procedures. Mainstream criminology, having followed these tenets, claimed to have discovered valid truths about women's criminal behaviour (and, of course, men's). The initial reaction of feminism to this claim was to reinterpret this truth as a patriarchal lie. It was argued that the methods used had been tainted with bias and so the outcome was inevitably faulty (Smart, 1986). This left open the presumption that the methods could be retained if the biases were removed because the ideal of a true or real science was posited as the alternative to the biased one.

Empirical research does not have to be attached to empiricism, however. To engage with women, to interview them, to document their oral histories, to participate with them, does not automatically mean that one upholds the ideal of empiricism. To be critical of empiricism is not to reject empirical work *per se*. However, some of the empirical studies, generated under the goal of collecting more knowledge about women, which feminist empiricism engendered presented a different sort of problem for the project of a feminist criminology.

This problem was the thorny question of discrimination. The early feminist contributions did not only challenge the objectivity of criminological thought; they challenged the idea of an objective judiciary and criminal justice system. Hence there grew up a major preoccupation with revealing the truth or otherwise of equality before the law in a range of empirical studies. Some studies seemed to find that the police or courts treated women and girls more leniently than men and boys. Others found the opposite. Then there were discoveries that much depended on the nature of the offence or the length of previous record or whether the offender was married or not (see, for example, Farrington and Morris, 1983). As Gelsthorpe (1986) has pointed out, the search for straightforward sexism was more difficult than anyone imagined at first. It was, of course, a false trail in as much as it was anticipated that forms of oppression (whether sexual or racial or other) could be identified in a few simple criteria which could then be established (or not) in following a ritual procedure. So in this respect the (with the benefit of hindsight) overly simplistic approach of early feminist work in this field has created an obstacle to further developments.

The other drawback to this type of research is the one which has been highlighted by MacKinnon (1987). She argues that any approach which focuses on equality and inequality always presumes that the norm is men. Hence studies of the criminal justice system always compare the treatment of women with men and men remain the standard against which all are judged. This has led to two problems. The first arouses a facile, yet widespread, reaction that if one has the audacity to compare women to men in circumstances where men are more favourably treated, then in those instances where they are treated less favourably one must, *ipso facto*, also be requiring the standard of treatment for women to be reduced. Hence, in comparing how the courts treat men and women, the response is inevitably the threat that if women want equality they must have it in full and so some feminists want women to be sent in their droves to dirty, violent and overcrowded prisons for long periods of time. This is what Lahey (1985) has called 'equality with a vengeance'.

The second problem goes beyond the transparent difficulties of treating women as if they were men to the level of the symbolic. Basically the equality paradigm always reaffirms the centrality of men. Men continue to constitute the norm, the unproblematic, the natural social actor. Women are thus always seen as interlopers into a world already organized by others. This has been well established in areas like employment law where the equality argument has been seen unintentionally to reproduce men as the ideal employees, with women struggling to make the grade (Kenney, 1986). Underlying such an approach in any case is the presumption that law is fundamentally a neutral object inside a liberal regime, thus wholly misconstruing the nature of power and the power of law (Smart, 1989). Law does not stand outside gender relations and adjudicate upon them. Law is part of these relations and is always already gendered in its principles and practices. We cannot separate out one practice – called discrimination – and ask for it to cease to be gendered as it would be a meaningless request. This is not to say we cannot object to certain principles and practices but we need to think carefully before we continue to sustain a conceptual framework which either prioritizes men as the norm, or assumes that genderlessness (or gender-blindness) is either possible or desirable.

Standpoint feminism

The second category identified by Harding is standpoint feminism. The epistemological basis of this form of feminist knowledge is experience. However, not just any experience is deemed to be equally valuable or valid. *Feminist* experience is achieved through a struggle against oppression; it is, therefore, argued to be more complete and less distorted than the perspective of the ruling group of men. A feminist standpoint then is not just the experience of women, but of women *reflexively* engaged in struggle (intellectual and political). In this process it is argued that a more accurate or fuller version of reality is achieved. This stance does not divide knowledge from values and politics but sees knowledge arising from engagement.

Arguably, standpoint feminism does not feature strongly in feminist criminology except in quite specific areas of concern like rape, sexual assault and wife abuse. It is undoubtedly the influence of feminists engaged at a political level with these forms of oppression that has begun to transform some areas of criminological thinking. Hence the work of Rape Crisis Centres [. . .] has been vital in proffering an alternative 'truth' about rape and women's experience of the criminal justice system. However, as far as mainstream criminology is concerned we should perhaps not be too optimistic about this since the accounts provided by such organizations have only been partially accepted and, even then, as a consequence of substantiation by more orthodox accounts (Blair, 1985; Chambers and Millar, 1983).

Taking experience as a starting-point and testing ground has only made a partial entry into criminology and, interestingly, where it has entered has been in the domain of left realism. It is here we find the resort to experience (that is, women's experience of crime) a constant referent and justification. Women's fear of rape and violence is used in this context to argue that rape and violence must be treated as serious problems. The question that this poses is whether we now have a feminist realist criminology or whether left realism (and consequently criminology as a whole) has been revitalized by the energies and concerns of a politically active women's movement. If we consider texts like *Well-Founded Fear* (Hanmer and Saunders, 1984) or *Leaving Violent Men* (Binney et al., 1981), we find that the motivating drive is the desire to let women's experiences be told. These experiences are not meant to stand alongside the experiences of the police or violent men; they represent the expression of subjugation which will replace the dominant account. Hanmer and Saunders outline methodological procedures for tapping into this experience and produce what Harding has referred to as a 'successor science'. As she argues, 'the adoption of this standpoint is fundamentally a moral and political act of commitment to understanding the world from the perspective of the socially subjugated' (1986: 149). In fact, it goes beyond this as the researchers, as feminists, also inhabit the world of the socially subjugated. It is not an act of empathy as such but a shared knowledge.

The real issue remains unresolved, however. For while feminist work is generating another sort of knowledge (for example, other ways of accounting for violence), feminist work which fits under the umbrella of left realist criminology does not embrace the full scope of what Young has called for. [. . .] This is because standpoint feminism has not taken masculinity as a focus of investigation. Precisely because standpoint feminism in this area has arisen from a grassroots concern to protect women and to reveal the victimization of women, it has not been sympathetic to the study of masculinity(ies). Indeed, it would argue that we have heard enough from that quarter and that any attempt by feminists to turn their attention away from women is to neglect the very real problems that women still face. So the feminist realists (if we can use this term for the sake of argument) are on quite a different trajectory from the left realists. It may be convenient to the Left to support the work of feminists in this area but it is unclear to me where this unholy 'alliance' is going analytically. Like the protracted debate about the marriage of Marxism and feminism, we may find that this alliance ends in annulment.

Feminist postmodernism

It would be a mistake to depict feminist postmodernism as the third stage or synthesis of feminist empiricism and standpoint feminism. Feminist postmodernism does not try to resolve the problems of other positions; rather it starts from a different place and proceeds in other directions. Much postmodern analysis is rooted in philosophy and aesthetics (Fekete, 1988; Lyotard, 1986; Rorty, 1985) but in the case of feminism it started in political practice. It began with the separate demises of sisterhood and of Marxism.

By the demise of sisterhood, I mean the realization that women were not all white, middle-class and of Anglo-Saxon, Protestant extract. Feminism resisted this realization by invoking notions of womanhood as a core essence to unite women (under the leadership of the said white, middle-class and Protestant women). However, black feminists, lesbian feminists, Third World feminists, aboriginal feminists and many others simply refused to swallow the story. To put it simply, they knew power when they saw it exercised. Feminism had to abandon its early framework and to start to look for other ways of thinking which did not subjugate other subjectivities. But at the same time, feminism came to recognize that individual women did not have unitary selves. Debates over sexuality, pornography and desire began to undo the idea of the true self and gave way to notions of fractured subjectivities. These developments were much influenced by the work of Foucault and psychoanalytic theory but they cannot be dismissed simply as a 'fad' because the recognition of the inadequacy of the feminist paradigm was not imposed by the intellectuals but arose out of a series of painful struggles for understanding combined with a progressive political stance.

The other key element in this development was the demise of Marxism as a rigorously policed grid of analysis, adherence to which had meant the promise of the total explanation or master narrative. Again, feminist practice revealed the inadequacy of the grand theoretical project of Marxism quite early in the second wave. But the struggle to retain the paradigm lasted much longer. None the less it is now realized that we cannot keep adding bits of Marxist orthodoxy to try to explain all the awkward silences. While many Marxian values may be retained, the idea and the promise of the totalizing theory have gradually loosened their grip.

The core element of feminist postmodernism is the rejection of the one reality which arises from 'the falsely universalizing perspective of the master' (Harding, 1987: 188). But unlike standpoint feminism it does not seek to impose a different unitary reality. Rather it refers to subjugated knowledges, which tell different stories and have different specificities. Thus the aim of feminism ceases to be the establishment of the feminist truth and becomes the deconstruction of truth and analysis of the power effects which claims to truth entail. So there is a shift away from treating knowledge as ultimately objective or, at least, the final standard and hence able to reveal the concealed truth, towards recognizing that knowledge is part of power and that power is ubiquitous. Feminist knowledge, therefore, becomes part of a multiplicity of resistances. Take, for example, feminist interventions in the area of rape. This is an area which I have explored in detail elsewhere (Smart, 1989) but for the sake of this discussion I wish to rely on the work of Woodhull (1988). Woodhull, in an article on sexuality and Foucault, argues against a traditional feminist mode of explanation for rape. She concentrates on Brownmiller's (1975) approach which seeks to explain rape in terms of the physiological differences between men and women. Woodhull's argument is that in explaining rape in this way, Brownmiller puts sex and biology outside the social, as preceding all power relations. What is missing is an understanding of how sexual difference and the meanings of different bits of bodies are constructed. Woodhull argues:

> If we are seriously to come to terms with rape, we must explain how the vagina comes to be coded – and experienced – as a place of emptiness and vulnerability, the penis as a weapon, and intercourse as violation, rather than naturalize these processes through references to 'basic' physiology. (1988: 171)

So it becomes a concern of feminism to explore how women's bodies have become saturated with (hetero)sex, how codes of sexualized meaning are reproduced and sustained and to begin (or continue) the deconstruction of these meanings.

This is just one example of how postmodernism is influencing feminist practice (for others, see Diamond and Quinby, 1988; Fraser and Nicholson, 1988; Jardine, 1985; Weedon, 1987) and it is clear that the ramifications of the epistemological crisis of modernism are far from being fully mapped or exhaustively considered as yet. We are in no position to judge what shapes feminism will take in the next decade or so. However, it might be interesting to consider, albeit prematurely, what all this means for criminology.

CONCLUDING REMARKS

It is a feature of postmodernism that questions posed within a modernist frame are turned about. So, for a long time, we have been asking 'what does feminism have to contribute to criminology (or sociology)?'. Feminism has been knocking at the door of established disciplines hoping to be let in on equal terms. These established disciplines have largely looked down their noses (metaphorically speaking) and found feminism wanting. Feminism has been required to become more objective, more substantive, more scientific, more anything before a grudging entry could be granted. But now the established disciplines are themselves looking rather insecure (Bauman, 1988) and, as the door is opening, we must ask whether feminism really does want to enter.

Perhaps it is now apt to rephrase the traditional question to read 'what has criminology got to offer feminism?' Feminism is now a broadly based scholarship and political practice. Its concerns range from questions of philosophy to representations to engagement; it is, therefore, no longer in the supplicant position of an Olivia Twist. On the contrary, we have already seen that a lot of feminist work has revitalized radical criminology. It might be that criminology needs feminism more than the converse. Of course, many criminologists, especially the traditional variety, will find this preposterous; but perhaps they had better look to who their students are and who their students are reading.

It is clear that if mainstream criminology remains unchanged it will follow the path that Young has outlined into greater and greater complicity with mechanisms of discipline. However, the path of radical criminology seems wedded to the modernist enterprise and is, as yet, unaffected by the epistemological sea-changes which have touched feminism and other discourses. Under such circumstances, it is very hard to see what criminology has to offer to feminism.

REFERENCES

Bauman, Z. (1988) 'Is there a postmodern sociology?', *Theory, Culture and Society*, 5(2/3): 217–38.

Binney, V., Harknell, G. and Nixon, J. (1981) *Leaving Violent Men: a Study of Refuges and Housing for Battered Women*. Leeds: Women's Aid Federation.

Blair, I. (1985) *Investigating Rape: a New Approach for the Police*. London: Croom Helm.

Brownmiller, S. (1975) *Against Our Will: Men, Women and Rape*. London: Secker and Warburg.

Carlen, P. (1988) *Women, Crime and Poverty*. Milton Keynes: Open University Press.

Chambers, G. and Millar, A. (1983) *Investigating Sexual Assault*. Scottish Office Social Research Study. Edinburgh: HMSO.

Diamond, I. and Quinby, L. (eds) (1988) *Feminism and Foucault*: Boston, MA: Northeastern University Press.

Dixon, V. (1976) 'World views and research methodology', in L. King, V. Dixon and W. Nobles (eds), *African Philosophy: Assumptions and Paradigms for Research on Black Persons*. Los Angeles: Fanon Centre.

Duchen, C. (1986) *Feminism in France*. London: Routledge.

Eaton, M. (1986) *Justice for Women? Family, Court and Social Control*. Milton Keynes: Open University Press.

Farrington, D. and Morris, A. (1983) 'Sex, sentencing and reconviction', *British Journal of Criminology*, 23(3): 229–48.

Fekete, J. (1988) *Life After Postmodernism*. London: Macmillan.

Foucault, M. (1973) *The Order of Things*. New York: Vintage Books.

Fraser, N. and Nicholson, L. (1988) 'Social criticism without philosophy: an encounter between feminism and postmodernism', *Theory, Culture and Society*, 5(2/3): 373–94.

Gelsthorpe, L. (1986) 'Towards a sceptical look at sexism', *International Journal of the Sociology of Law*. 14(2): 125–52.

Gilligan, C. (1982) *In a Different Voice*. London: Harvard University Press.

Hanmer, J. and Saunders, S. (1984) *Well-Founded Fear: a Community Study of Violence to Women*. London: Hutchinson.

Harding, S. (ed.) (1986) *The Science Question in Feminism*. Milton Keynes: Open University Press.

Harding, S. (ed.) (1987) *Feminism and Methodology*. Milton Keynes: Open University Press.

Heidensohn, F. (1985) *Women and Crime*. Basingstoke: Macmillan.

Jardine, A. (1985) *Gynsis*: London: Cornell University Press.

Kellner, D. (1988) 'Postmodernism as social theory: some challenges and problems', *Theory, Culture and Society*, 5(2/3): 239–70.

Kenney, S.J. (1986) 'Reproductive hazards in the workplace: the law and sexual difference', *International Journal of the Sociology of Law*, 14(3/4): 393–444.

Lahey, K. (1985) '. . . until women themselves have told all that they have to tell . . .' *Osgood Hall Law Journal*, 23(3): 519–41.

Lyotard, J. (1986) *The Postmodern Condition*. Manchester: Manchester University Press.

MacKinnon, C. (1987) *Feminism Unmodified: Discourses on Life and Law*. Cambridge, MA: Harvard University Press.

Rorty, R. (1985) 'Habermas and Lyotard on postmodernity', in R. Bernstein (ed.), *Habermas and Modernity*. Cambridge: Polity.

Rose, G. (1988) 'Architecture to philosophy – the postmodern complicity', *Theory, Culture and Society*, 5(2/3): 357–72.

Smart, C. (1986) 'Feminism and law: some problems of analysis and strategy', *International Journal of the Sociology of Law*, 14(1): 109–23.

Smart, C. (1989) *Feminism and the Power of Law*. London: Routledge.

Smith, D. (1973) 'Women's perspective as a radical critique of sociology', *Sociological Inquiry*, 14(1): 7–13.

Stanley, L. and Wise, S. (1983) *Breaking Out: Feminist Consciousness and Feminist Research*. London: Routledge.

Taylor, I., Walton, P. and Young, J. (1973) *The New Criminology*. London: Routledge.

Weedon, C. (1987) *Feminist Practice and Poststructuralist Theory*. Oxford: Basil Blackwell.

West, D. (1969) *Present Conduct and Future Delinquency*. London: Heinemann.

Woodhull, W. (1988) 'Sexuality, power and the question of rape', in I. Diamond and L. Quinby (eds), *Feminism and Foucault*. Boston: Northeastern University Press.

Young, J. (1986) 'The failure of criminology: the need for a radical realism', in R. Matthews and J. Young (eds) *Confronting Crime*. London: Sage.

44

Different ways of conceptualizing sex/gender in feminist theory and their implications for criminology

Kathleen Daly

[. . .]

In the 1970s and 1980s feminist research on Real Women challenged the andro-centrism of the field, as scholars filled knowledge gaps about women law-breakers, victims and criminal justice workers. By the 1990s, several scholars signalled a shift in interest from Real Women to The Woman of criminological or legal discourse (see Smart, 1990a, 1992). This reflected a move toward postmodern thinking on crime, courts and prisons, which is evident in the works of Bertrand (1994), Howe (1990, 1994), Smart (1995), Worrall (1990), and A. Young (1990, 1996). While sympathetic to postmodern texts, others have not wanted to abandon Real Women; they include Cain (1989), Carlen (1985, 1988), Carrington (1990), Daly (1992), Joe and Chesney-Lind (1995), and Maher and Daly (1996). Those studying violence against women may be especially resistant to letting go of Real Women because their voices and experiences have only recently been 'named' (compare Marcus, 1992 and Hawkesworth, 1989; see Radford et al., 1996). I am, of course, simplifying here, but I do so to highlight where feminist debate remains keen, both within and outside criminology, on the politics of knowledge. By retaining Real Women, feminists may take 'the ground of specifically *moral* claims against domination—the avenging of strength through moral critique' (Brown, 1991:75). Real Women can be mobilized as 'our subject that harbors truth, and our truth that opposes power' (p. 77). But for others, Real Women, their moral grounds and 'truths', must be set aside (Smart, 1990b, as discussed below). Concurring with Smart, Brown asks

> What is it about feminism that fears the replacement of truth with politics . . . privileged knowledge with a cacophony of unequal voices clamoring for position?
>
> (Brown, 1991:73)

From *Theoretical Criminology*, 1997, 1:1. pp. 25–53.

A good deal, many reply (e.g. di Leonardo, 1991; di Stefano, 1990; Harding, 1987). And that is why the knowledge problem continues to be contentious for feminist theory and politics. One response has been sketched by Smart (1995:230–2), who now admits that while we 'need to address this Woman of legal [or criminological] discourse, . . . this kind of analysis alone gives me cause for concern'. She suggests that discourse analysis of, for example, 'the raped woman is of little value unless we are also talking to women who have been raped' (p. 231). To Smart, this is not the same as asserting some truth about Real Women, but rather to be cognizant that 'women discursively construct themselves' (p. 231).

Let me summarize and reflect on my argument in this first section. I identified problems resulting from a dominance of the humanities in feminist work: theoretical imperialism, insufficient attention to and a misreading of social science enquiry, and analyzing women's 'differences' solely in linguistic or discursive terms. I would not wish to claim superiority of 'the empirical' or of social science enquiry. Such a position does not reflect what I have learned from feminist work in philosophy, literature and media studies. Nor does it reflect my interests to develop inter-disciplinary 'hybrid knowledges' that break down disciplinary boundaries (Seidman, 1994:2). It is to say that social science research has a key role to play in feminist knowledge and that empirical enquiry can be as radical and subversive as deconstruction.

THREE MODES OF FEMINIST ENQUIRY

The challenges to feminist theory in the 1980s, both by women marginalized by its terms and by postmodern texts, were not isolated. They were part of a general mood to unsettle social theory and to re-engage a critique of positivist social science (Seidman, 1994). Thus, we would expect to see reworkings of old concepts and the emergence of new ones. Two ways of reconceptualizing sex/gender in feminist enquiry—'class-race-gender' and 'doing gender'—have been developed by feminists in the social sciences, especially those in sociology. 'Sexed bodies' has been developed by feminists in philosophy, and more generally, by re-reading of Foucault.

Class-race-gender

My work has been most influenced by class-race-gender or what I have come to term *multiple inequalities* (Daly, 1993; 1995a). In the 1980s, it was not French men but black women whose critique of feminist thought had the greater influence on my thinking. Class-race-gender need not be interpreted literally to mean a sole focus on these three relations; its meaning can be stretched to include others, e.g. age, sexuality and physical ability. For many scholars, the term retains an allegiance, though not complete fealty, to notions of determining structures of inequality. For example, Pat Carlen (1994:139–40) suggests the need to theorize inequalities that 'both recognizes and denies structuralism'. The term varies in application across and within the disciplines: from statistical analyses of wages and law-breaking for particular sub-groups (e.g. King, 1988; Simpson, 1991) to biographical and auto-biographical storytelling forms (e.g. Abrams, 1991; Lorde, 1984; Pratt, 1984;

Williams, 1991). In the US, class-race-gender is used to denote a more inclusive college-level curricula (see, for example, Belkhir et al., 1994 and the new journal, *Race, Sex & Class*), and it has become a popular title in marketing readers in women's studies (e.g. Andersen and Collins, 1992; Jagger and Rothenberg, 1993; Ruiz and DuBois, 1994). While, on balance, curricular change and new readers are a good thing, they are but a small slice of a wider class-race-gender project.

Class-race-gender conceptualizes inequalities, not as additive and discrete, but as intersecting, interlocking and contingent. In the US, class-race-gender emerged from the struggles of black women in the Civil Rights Movement; it came into academic institutions (and especially sociology) in the late 1970s through articles and books by women of color. This early body of work not only critiqued ethnocentrism in feminist theory, but also established a rhetorical ground for women of color (see, e.g. Baca Zinn et al., 1986; Combahee River Collective, 1979; Dill, 1983).

Conceptualizing multiple relations of inequality has only just begun (for a recent effort in criminology, see Schwartz and Milovanovic, 1995). It will not take the same form as previous efforts to theorize 'systems of inequality' (as in relationships of capitalism and patriarchy). And while its proponents often claim its 'greater inclusiveness', we should expect that like other ideas, it is 'condemned to be haunted by a voice from the margins . . . awakening us to what has been excluded, effaced, damaged' (Bordo, 1990:138). Like others (e.g. Anthias and Yuval-Davis, 1992; Collins, 1993) I see the project as mapping the salience and contingency of gender, class, race-ethnicity, and the like, both separately and together, For Floya Anthias and Niro Yuval-Davis (1992:99), this means 'specify[ing] the mechanisms by which different forms of exclusion and subordination operate'. For Patricia Hill Collins (1990:226–7), it means showing how social relations operate in a matrix of domination at three levels: personal, group and systemic. Authors' uses of terms such as *power* and *social structure* may vary: they range from earlier, more deterministic understandings of power as something individuals 'possess' in varying degrees, depending on their location in social structures external to them (e.g. Davis, 1981) to recent understandings, which are more context-dependent. These recent ways of conceptualizing social structure as fluid pose major challenges to previous understandings of power, subordination and human emancipation (see Collins, 1990; Henry and Milovanovic, 1996: Chs. 2–3; Yeatman, 1995).

Bordo (1990:145) observes that the 'analytics of class and race . . . do not seem to be undergoing the same deconstruction' as gender and women. I would agree: relatively less intellectual discussion has been devoted to showing the lack of a unified referent for racial and class categories compared to those for gender. One reason is an under-theorization of race-ethnicity and its links to other social relations, e.g. the 'gendering' of race or the 'racializing' of gender. This is one of several building blocks in developing a class-race-gender analysis in criminology, but as yet, movement has been slow. Discomfort levels are high, not coincidentally because criminologists are so 'white' and advantaged, while the subjects of their crime theories more often are not (despite some attention to organizational crime). Moreover, scholars of color in criminology have only recently been in a position to challenge the white-centred assumptions of the field and to develop anti-racist theoretical and research agendas (see Russell, 1992; Walker and Brown, 1995; Young and Greene, 1995).

There are many ways to work with the idea of multiple inequalities. One is to use it to transform research and writing practices in the social sciences (see Daly,

1993, 1994). For example, to show how racial discrimination 'works', one could use Richard Delgado's (1989) method of presenting multiple accounts of the 'same event'. In this case, Delgado describes what happened when a black man was interviewed for a job at a law school. The multiple perspectives of the participants, as orchestrated by Delgado, bring the white reader into the story in such a way that racial discrimination toward the black man becomes visible to the white reader as part of his/her routine interpretations and practices. Delgado offers a nuanced picture of how race relations routinely work to disadvantage black job applicants through the organizational frame of 'neutral' job criteria. This kind of multi-perspectival approach could also be used by authors in communicating research findings and, as such, class-race-gender can be a vehicle by which to develop collaborations across academic-community locations and identities (see Austin, 1992; Daly and Stephens, 1995).

To date, class-race-gender has been most vividly revealed through literary and storytelling forms (see, for example, Bell, 1987; Delgado, 1989; Jordan, 1985; Lubiano, 1992; Pratt, 1984; Williams, 1991). Unlike a good deal of traditional social science, these works reveal (1) the shifting salience of race, class, gender, nation and sexuality, and the like as one moves through space and time, and (2) the different world-views or lenses that participants bring to social encounters. A major question is whether one can bring these literary or storytelling forms into research practices in sociology and criminology. It may be possible, if researchers use narrative modes of reasoning (see Richardson, 1990; Stivers, 1993; Ewick and Silbey, 1995).

The contribution of class-race-gender to criminology is an insistence that everyone is located in a matrix of multiple social relations, i.e. that race and gender are just as relevant to an analysis of white men as they are to black women. With an emphasis on contingency, one can explore the varied positions of 'black women'—as offenders, victims, and mothers and wives of offenders and victims—to 'white justice' (Daly 1995b). And as Lisa Maher (1995: Ch. 9) demonstrates in her ethnographic research on women drug-users in New York City, one can reveal varied angles of vision for African- and European-American women and Latinas in neighborhood drug markets. Class-race-gender can also be used to politicize and problematize knowledge in collaboration with others. In this regard, Collins (1993) is right to emphasize the piecing together of work by different scholars as bits in a wider mosaic; the quest to theorize the 'totality' of multiple inequalities is ill-founded. One set of theoretical problems, discussed by Anthias and Yuval-Davis (1992:17), is how to relate the 'different ontological spheres' of class, race and gender divisions, while simultaneously showing the ways they intermesh in concrete situations. Another challenge is to identify new vocabularies to discuss multiple, intersecting or interlocking inequalities. Otherwise, we may easily slip into additive, mechanical analyses of power, oppression and the heaping of disadvantage and advantage.

DOING GENDER

Candace West and Donald Zimmerman (1987) coined the construct 'doing gender' to describe gender as a 'situated accomplishment':

> [Gender is not the] property of individuals . . . [but rather] an emergent feature of social
> situations: . . . an outcome of and a rationale for . . . social arrangements . . . a means of
> legitimating [a] fundamental division . . . of society. [Gender is] a routine, methodical,
> and recurring accomplishment (p. 126) . . . not a set of traits, nor a variable, nor a role
> [but] itself constituted through interaction. (p. 129)

R.W. Connell (1987, 1995) and James Messerschmidt (1993) have developed linkages between 'doing gender' (more precisely, 'doing masculinity') and gender relations of power. Susan Martin and Nancy Jurik (1996) have also utilized 'doing gender' in their analysis of women and gender in justice system occupations. All four authors have elements of 'class-race-gender' in their work. They view structure as ordering interaction, and interaction as producing structure, drawing on Anthony Giddens' (1984) efforts to transcend the sociological dualism of interaction and social structure.

In 1995, West and Fenstermaker published 'Doing Difference', in which they attempt to incorporate 'doing gender' with 'class-race-gender'. Rather than viewing each relation of class or race or gender as a 'structure of oppression', they propose that the whole be viewed as 'experience'. Thus, every social encounter, no matter who the participants are, can be conceptualized as being classed, raced and gendered. The terms used in 'doing gender' are extended without modification to 'doing race' or class. For example, the authors say that

> the accomplishment of race (like gender) does not necessarily mean 'living up' to
> normative conceptions of attitudes and activities appropriate to a particular race
> category; rather, it means engaging in action at the risk of race assessment.
> (West and Fenstermaker, 1995:23–4)

Later that year, several scholars replied to West and Fenstermaker's article (Collins et al., 1995). Critics objected that it ignored power and oppression, as it did resistance and conflict (Collins et al., 1995:491–4, 497–502).

What vexed the critics, in part, was that the 'isms' of inequality—racism, classism, etc.—were not sufficiently addressed with West and Fenstermaker's version of social constructionism. Also vexing was that gender or race, etc. could be viewed merely as an accomplishment or performance. In this regard, Barrie Thorne (1995:498–9) noted similarities between 'doing gender' and Judith Butler's (1990) discussion of gender as the performance of sex; both, in her view, neglected the importance of seeing gender (and other social relations) as extending 'deep into the unconscious . . . and outward into social structure and material interests'.

Some feminist skepticism toward 'doing gender' lies in a desire to retain 'structures of power' that both precede and are produced by gender or race, etc. as 'accomplishments'. Whether sex and gender are understood to be produced in interaction or in discourse, feminist critiques (specifically, by sociologists) are based on retaining some semblance of social structure or materialism. As we shall see, some feminists using 'sexed bodies' also wish to include a form of materialism ('materiality'), but its constituents are the body and sexual difference.

Messerschmidt (1993:85) applied 'doing gender' in his analysis of crime as 'a resource for doing masculinity in specific social settings . . .';

Crime . . . may be invoked as a practice through which masculinities (and men and women) are differentiated from one another. . . . [It] is a resource that may be summoned when men lack other resources to accomplish gender.

(p. 85)

Whereas West and Zimmerman (1987:137) had focused on how the doing of gender 'creat[es] differences between . . . women and men' that materialize as 'essential sexual natures' (p. 138), Messerschmidt suggested that the doing of gender also produces multiple forms of masculinity and crime.

One problem Messerschmidt encounters is how to conceptualize crime as a gendered line of social action without once again establishing boys and men as the norm, differentiating themselves from all that is 'feminine'. Although masculine subjectivity and lines of action may be described with these terms (see Jefferson, 1994), it is disputable that feminine subjectivity and lines of action could be. Specifically, would the claim that crime is a 'resource for doing femininity'—for women and girls 'to create differences from men and boys or to separate from all that is masculine'—have any cultural resonance? Probably not. But nor should theories necessarily have to employ symmetrical sex/gender terms. That is to say, arguments that crime is a resource or situation where masculinities are produced may be useful: they normalize crime but problematize men and masculinity.

In applying 'doing gender' to criminological research, scholars will have to let go of thinking about gender or race etc. as attributes of persons and examine how situations and social practices produce qualities and identities associated with membership in particular social categories. Despite the creative efforts of some to employ doing gender in quantitative analyses of self-reported delinquency (e.g. Simpson and Elis, 1995), it is better suited to analyses of social interaction. Researchers will need to be mindful that categories taken from theorizing masculinity may be inappropriately applied to femininity. Gender categories are not neutral, and the terms used to describe men and women 'doing gender' are not likely to be interchangeable. These are major points for those using the 'sexed bodies' construct.

Sexed Bodies

Gatens (1996:67) observes that 'there is probably no simple explanation for the recent proliferation of writings concerning the body'. She credits Foucault's work on the (male) body as a site of disciplinary practices, coupled with that of feminist social scientists, who showed that even the most privileged women have not attained equality with men in the 'public sphere'. Perhaps feminists would need to face, yet again but in different ways, 'questions of corporeal specificity' (p. 68). The trick, Gatens suggests, is to acknowledge 'historical realities . . . without resorting to biological essentialism' (p. 69):

The present capacities of female bodies are, by and large, very different from the present capacities of male bodies. It is important to create the means of articulating the historical realities of sexual difference without thereby reifying these differences.

(p. 69)

Feminists have been analyzing a large philosophical literature on 'the body' and its connection with 'the mind' (see, for example, Butler, 1993; Gatens, 1996; Grosz, 1994, 1995). Sexed bodies is theorized in several ways: some emphasize the discursive construction of 'sex', including cultural inscription on bodies, whereas others work at the edges of the 'materiality of sex' and 'culture'. For the moment, I will focus on the latter in reviewing three interrelated themes: the sex/gender distinction, power as productive of gender and sexual difference, and dualisms in western philosophy.

Sex/gender. In 1983 Gatens challenged the familiar distinction between sex (the biological categories of 'male' and 'female') and gender (the social categories of 'masculinity' and 'femininity' that are linked to sex) (reprinted in Gatens, 1996: Ch. 1). She was critical of the assumption that 'the mind of either sex is initially a neutral, passive entity, a blank slate on which are inscribed various social "lessons"'. The 'alleged *neutrality* of the body, the postulated *arbitrary* connection between femininity and the female body, masculinity and the male body' troubled Gatens because it 'encourage[s] . . . a neutralization of sexual difference and sexual politics . . . and the naive solution of resocialization' (p. 4, Gaten's emphasis). Moreover, by denying sex-specific corporeality, key differences are overlooked 'between feminine behavior or experience that is lived out by a female subject and feminine behavior or experience that is lived out by a male subject (and vice versa with masculine behavior)' (p. 9).

Power. Drawing on but moving beyond Foucault's account of 'the manner in which the micropolitical operations of power produce socially appropriate bodies', Gatens (1996:70) proposes that we view gender as

> not the effect of ideology or cultural values but as the way in which power takes hold of and constructs bodies in particular ways. . . . The sexed body can no longer be conceived as the unproblematic biological and factual base upon which gender is inscribed, but must itself be recognized as constructed by discourses and practices that take the body both as their target and as their vehicle of expression.

Gaten's conceptualization of gender as 'the way in which power takes hold of bodies and constructs them in particular ways' raises questions for the relationship between social construction and materiality, which Butler (1993) takes up:

> To claim that sex is already gendered, already constructed, is not yet to explain in which way the 'materiality' of sex is forcibly produced. What are the constraints by which bodies are materialized as 'sexed', and how are we to understand the 'matter' of sex? . . .
>
> (p. xi)

Butler proposes a 'return to the notion of matter, not as site or surface, but as a process of materialization' (p. 9) and suggests we should ask, 'Through what regulatory norms is sex itself materialized?' (p. 10).

Dualisms. Elizabeth Grosz (1994) argues that current understandings of 'the body' reflect dualisms in western thinking, and by rethinking 'the body', subjectivity can be reconceptualized. She rejects the view of the body as 'natural' or having a 'presocial' existence and, simultaneously, she rejects the view of the body as '*purely* a social, cultural, and signifying effect lacking its own weighty materiality' (p. 21,

Grosz's emphasis). (As such, she takes issue with feminist approaches she terms egalitarian and social constructionist.) She wants to

> ... deny that there is the 'real' material body on the one hand and its various cultural and historical representations on the other. .... These representations and cultural inscriptions quite literally constitute bodies and help to produce them as such.
>
> (p. x)

Grosz uses the metaphor of a moibus strip to suggest the 'inflection of mind into body and body into mind . . . the torsion of the one into the other . . . [the] uncontrollable drift of the inside into the outside and outside into the inside' (p. xii). Terms such as 'embodied subjectivity' and 'physical corporeality' (p. 22) might be used to characterize this inflection.

Why are sexed bodies and corporeality important? When viewing the mind as 'linked to, perhaps even part of, the body' and 'bodies themselves as always sexually (and racially) distinct, . . . then [we can see that] the very forms that subjectivity takes are not generalizable'. We therefore cannot assume 'universalist ideals of humanism' nor can we produce and evaluate knowledges that are not 'sexually determinate, limited, finite' (Grosz, 1994:20).

'Sexed bodies' is excellent for revealing the 'neutralization and neutering of . . . [sex] specificity' and with it the 'cultural and intellectual effacement of women' (Grosz, 1994:ix). Its practitioners are on weaker ground, however, when they attempt to connect, in a theoretical sense, sexual difference and racial, cultural and class divisions. Grosz suggests that interconnections be viewed as 'interlocking'— using similar terms as Collins (1990) and West and Fenstermaker (1995)—and like these theorists, she is concerned that class, race, etc. should not be conceived as 'autonomous structures which then require external connections' (p. 20). A major difference is what is being explained. For Collins, it is inequality and oppression; for Grosz, it is sexual difference and multiple subjectivities.

Grosz argues (1994:18) that scholars working with a sexed bodies construct share 'a commitment to a notion of the fundamental, irreducible differences between the sexes' and while they acknowledge that 'class and race differences may divide women, sexual differences demand social recognition and representation'. Arguing against those who say that theirs is an essentialist analysis, Grosz suggests that the task is to undermine the dichotomy between 'sex as an essentialist and gender as a constructionist category' (p. 18).

Grosz and colleagues' work on sexed bodies is one way the construct can be used. Another emphasizes cultural inscription *on* the body (see review in Howe, 1994:194–205). The work I shall consider is Carol Smart's (1990b) on the production of sexed bodies in legal discourse.

Smart is interested in how 'law constructs and reconstructs masculinity and femininity, and maleness and femaleness' that produce a 'commonsense perception of difference' (p. 201). One sees affinity between Smart's claim that legal discourse produces gender and that of West and Zimmerman for whom situations produce gender; but there are key differences. Smart wants to consider how 'law constructs sexed (and not simply gendered) subjectivities' (p. 202), that is, 'the sexed body' (p. 203). She does so by examining rape and rape trials. Smart's (1990b) article was published at around the same time that analyses of the 'matter' or 'materiality of sex' were emerging; this may explain why she does not engage with authors like Grosz who viewed 'sexed bodies' neither as natural nor as signifying effects of culture. Instead, Smart analyzes the sexed body as produced both by legal and feminist discourse: the 'natural' sexed woman, who during a rape trial becomes a victimized sexed body. In feminist discourse this is the body of the eternal victim, whereas in legal discourse, it is the deserving victim (pp. 207–8). Smart cautions that it will be difficult for feminists to 'construct rape differently' because the effort to 'deconstruct the biological/sexed woman is silenced by the apparition of law's sexed woman to whose survival it is unwillingly tied' (p. 208). In other words, feminist efforts to challenge rape law will be thwarted by law's discursive power.

'Sexed bodies' can contribute to criminology in several ways. We can see that gender categories 'neuter' sexual difference, both in research and in policy. For research, we might explore how the 'sensual attractions' of crime (Katz, 1988) are differently available to and 'experienced' by male/female bodies and masculine/feminine subjectivities. We could analyze the variable production of sexed (and racialized, etc.) bodies across many types of harms (not just rape) or for other sites of legal regulation such as family law. We could take Howe's (1994) theoretical lead by investigating women's bodies as the object of penality. For policy, 'sexed bodies' is useful for showing that reputedly gender-neutral policies are tied to specific male bodies. Sexed bodies may worry some feminists because the construct seems to revisit the spectre of biologism and body types that has long haunted criminology. This need not be the case. Sexed bodies calls attention to how we 'experience' sexual difference and its relationship to gender. It also calls attention to dualisms in western philosophy and how dualisms such as reason/emotion, mind/body and male/female are constituted in and through law, science and criminology.

A problem with sexed bodies is the strong temptation to see social life primarily through a lens of sexual difference. It is not just that feminist analyses may unwittingly collude with say, legal discourse in 'reifying these differences' (Gatens, 1996:69), as Smart's (1990b) analysis reveals so well. Not that for those who take 'phallocentric culture' as the start point, the recommended strategy of 'thinking outside the confining concept of the natural/sexed woman' (Smart, 1990b:208) may be foreclosed by its own terms. From an empirical point of view, the problem is that claims such as 'the utterances of judges constantly reaffirm [the natural/sexed woman]' and 'almost every rape trial tells the same story' (Smart, 1990b:205–6) are theoretical claims. While they may help us see a pattern of discursive power, they should be seen as open to empirical enquiry not asserted as ahistorical discursive 'fact' (see Carrington, 1994 on this point). A second problem is that variation and particularlity in sexed bodies (e.g. by race or age, etc.) is posited by theorists but not explored with care. As a consequence, sex and gender are foregrounded whereas other socially relevant divisions are accorded secondary status.

CONCLUSION

I have highlighted the different contributions and trajectories that class-race-gender, doing gender and sexed bodies take, but I have also endeavored to identify points of convergence. 'Class-race-gender' and 'doing gender' share a common sociological heritage, the former emphasizing social relations of inequality and the latter, the production of social categories in interaction. Thus, scholars have drawn from each to get around the sociological 'macro-micro level' problem and the structure–agency dualism. Most feminist scholars today are concerned with linking sex/gender to other social relations and with making particular (not generic) claims about women or men. Those working with 'class-race-gender' have begun to articulate what the linkages might look like and to conduct empirical research along these lines. Those working with 'sexed bodies' continue to challenge the thinking of 'class-race-gender' and 'doing gender' analysts by emphasizing that sexual difference is qualitatively different from other social categories and divisions. The 'sexed bodies' construct takes several forms: one relies on discursive power inscribing 'sex' on bodies (e.g. Butler, 1990), and another aims to bring a 'materiality' to the cultural construction of 'the body' (e.g. Bordo, 1993; Butler, 1993; Grosz, 1994).

REFERENCES

Abrams, Kathryn (1991) 'Hearing the Call of Stories', *California Law Review* 79(4):971–1052.

Anthias, Floya and Nira Yuval-Davis (1992) *Racialized Boundaries: Race, Nation, Gender, Colour and Class and the Anti-Racist Struggle.* New York: Routledge.

Austin, Regina (1992) '"The Black Community," Its Lawbreakers, and a Politics of Identification', *Southern California Law Review* 65:1769–1817.

Baca Zinn, Maxine, Lynn Weber Cannon, Elizabeth Higginbotham, and Bonnie Thornton Dill (1986) 'The Costs of Exclusionary Practices in Women's Studies', *Signs: Journal of Women in Culture and Society* 11(2):290–303.

Beirne, Piers and James W. Messerschmidt (1995, 2nd edn) *Criminology.* San Diego: Harcourt Brace Jovanovich.

Belkhir, Jean, Suzanne Griffith, Christine Sleeter and Carl Allsup (1994) 'Race, Sex, Class & Multicultural Education: Women's Angle of Vision', *Race, Sex & Class* 1(2):7–22.

Bell, Derrick (1987) *And We Are Not Saved.* New York: Basic Books.

Bertrand, Marie-Andree (1994) '1893–1993: From La Donna Delinquente to a Postmodern Deconstruction of the "Woman Question" in Social Control Theory', *The Journal of Human Justice* 5(2):43–57.

Bordo, Susan (1990) 'Feminism, Postmodernism, and Gender-Scepticism', in Linda J. Nicholson (ed.) *Feminism/Postmodernism*, pp. 133–56. New York: Routledge.

Bordo, Susan (1993) *Unbearable Weight: Feminism, Western Culture, and the Body.* Berkeley: University of California Press.

Brown, Wendy (1991) 'Feminist Hesitations, Postmodern Exposures', *differences: A Journal of Feminist Cultural Studies* 3(1):63–84.

Butler, Judith (1990) *Gender Trouble: Feminism and the Subversion of Identity.* New York: Routledge.

Butler, Judith (1993) *Bodies That Matter: On the Discursive Limits of "Sex".* New York: Routledge.

Butler, Judith and Joan W. Scott (eds) (1992) *Feminists Theorize the Political.* New York: Routledge.

Cain, Maureen (ed.) (1989) *Growing Up Good.* Newbury Park: Sage.

Carlen, Pat (ed.) (1985) *Criminal Women: Autobiographical Accounts.* Cambridge: Polity Press.

Carlen, Pat (1988) *Women, Crime and Poverty*. Philadelphia: Open University Press.

Carlen, Pat (1994) 'Gender, Class, Racism, and Criminal Justice: Against Global and Gender-Centric Theories, For Poststructuralist Perspectives', in George S. Bridges and Martha A. Myers (eds) *Inequality and Social Control*, pp. 134–44. Boulder: Westview Press.

Carrington, Kerry (1990) 'Aboriginal Girls and Juvenile Justice: What Justice? What Justice', *Journal for Social Justice Studies* 3:1–18.

Carrington, Kerry (1994) 'Postmodern and Feminist Criminologies: Disconnecting Discourses?', *International Journal of the Sociology of Law* 22:261–77.

Collins, Patricia Hill (1990) *Black Feminist Thought: Knowledge, Consciousness, and the Politics of Empowerment*. London: Unwin Hyman.

Collins, Patricia Hill (1993) 'Toward a New Vision: Race, Class, and Gender as Categories of Analysis and Connection', *Race, Sex, and Class* 1(1):25–45.

Collins, Patricia Hill, Lionel A. Maldonado, Dana Y. Takagi, Barrie Thorne, Lynn Weber and Howard Winant (1995) 'Symposium: On West and Fenstermaker's "Doing Difference"', *Gender & Society* 9(4):491–506.

Combahee River Collective (1979) 'The Combahee River Collective Statement', in Zillah Eisenstein (ed.) *Capitalist Patriarchy and the Case for Socialist Feminism*, pp. 362–72. New York: Monthly Review Press.

Connell, R.W. (1987) *Gender and Power*. Stanford: Stanford University Press.

Connell, R.W. (1995) *Masculinities*. St Leonards, NSW: Allen & Unwin.

Daly, Kathleen (1992) 'Women's Pathways to Felony Court: Feminist Theories of Lawbreaking and Problems of Representation', *Southern California Review of Law and Women's Studies* 2(1):11–52.

Daly, Kathleen (1993) 'Class-Race-Gender: Sloganeering in Search of Meaning', *Social Justice* 20(1–2):56–71.

Daly, Kathleen (1994) 'Criminal Law and Justice System Practices as Racist, White, and Racialized', *Washington & Lee Law Review* 51(2):431–64.

Daly, Kathleen (1995a) 'Where Feminists Fear to Tread? Working in the Research Trenches of Class-Race-Gender', paper presented at the annual meeting of the British Criminology Conference, Loughborough, July.

Daly, Kathleen (1995b) 'Black Women, White Justice', paper presented to the Law and Society Summer Institute, Niagara-on-the-Lake, Ontario, June.

Daly, Kathleen and Deborah Stephens (1995) 'The "Dark Figure" of Criminology: Toward a Black and Multi-Ethnic Feminist Agenda for Theory and Research', in Nicole Hahn Rafter and Frances Heidensohn (eds) *International Feminist Perspectives in Criminology*, pp. 189–215. Philadelphia: Open University Press.

Davis, Angela (1981) *Women, Race, and Class*, New York: Vintage.

Delgado, Richard (1989) 'Storytelling for Oppositionists and Others: A Plea for Narrative', *Michigan Law Review* 87:2411–41.

di Leonardo, Micaela (1991) 'Introduction', in Micaela di Leonardo (ed.) *Gender at the Crossroads of Knowledge: Feminist Anthropology in the Postmodern Era*, pp. 1–48. Berkeley: University of California Press.

Dill, Bonnie Thornton (1983) 'Race, Class, and Gender: Prospects for an All-Inclusive Sisterhood', *Feminist Studies* 9:131–50.

di Stefano, Christine (1990) 'Dilemmas of Difference: Feminism, Modernity, and Postmodernism', in Linda J. Nicholson (ed.) *Feminism/Postmodernism*, pp. 63–82. New York: Routledge.

Epstein, Steven (1994) 'A Queer Encounter: Sociology and the Study of Sexuality', *Sociological Theory* 12:188–202.

Ewick, Patricia and Susan S. Silbey (1995) 'Subversive Stones and Hegemonic Tales: Toward a Sociology of Narrative', *Law & Society Review* 29(2):197–226.

Gatens, Moira (1996) *Imaginary Bodies: Ethics, Power, and Corporeality*. New York: Routledge.

Giddens, Anthony (1984) *The Constitution of Society: Outline of the Theory of Structuration*. Oxford: Polity Press.

Grosz, Elizabeth (1990) 'A Note on Essentialism and Difference', in Sneja Gunew (ed.) *Feminist Knowledge: Critique and Construct*, pp. 332–44. London: Routledge.

Grosz, Elizabeth (1994) *Volatile Bodies: Toward a Corporeal Feminism*. St Leonards, NSW: Allen & Unwin.

Harding, Sandra (1987) 'The Instability of the Analytical Categories of Feminist Theory', in Sandra Harding and Jean F. O'Barr (eds) *Sex and Scientific Inquiry*, pp. 283–302. Chicago: University of Chicago Press.

Hawkesworth, Mary E. (1989) 'Knowers, Knowing, Known: Feminist Theory and Claims of Truth', *Signs: Journal of Women in Culture and Society* 14(3):533–57.

Henry, Stuart and Dragan Milovanovic (1996) *Constitutive Criminology: Beyond Postmodernism*. London: Sage.

hooks, bell (1981) *Ain't I a Woman? Black Women and Feminism*. Boston: South End Press.

Howe, Adrian (1990) 'Prologue to a History of Women's Imprisonment: In Search of a Feminist Perspective', *Social Justice* 17(2):5–22.

Howe, Adrian (1994) *Discipline and Critique: Towards a Feminist Analysis of Penality*. New York: Routledge.

Jaggar, Alison and Paula Rothenberg (eds) (1993, 3rd edn) *Feminist Frameworks*. New York: McGraw-Hill.

Jefferson, Tony (1994) 'Theorizing Masculine Subjectivity', in Tim Newburn and Elizabeth A. Stanko (eds) *Just Boys Doing Business? Men, Masculinities and Crime*, pp. 10–31. New York: Routledge.

Joe, Karen A. and Meda Chesney-Lind (1995) '"Just Every Mother's Angel": An Analysis of Gender and Ethnic Variations in Youth Gang Membership', *Gender & Society* 9(4):408–30.

Jordan, June (1985) 'Report from the Bahamas', in June Jordan (ed.) *On Call: Political Essays*, pp. 39–49. Boston: South End Press.

Katz, Jonathan (1988) *Seductions of Crime: Moral and Sensual Attractions of Doing Evil*. New York: Basic Books.

King, Deborah K. (1988) 'Multiple Jeopardy, Multiple Consciousness: The Context of a Black Feminist Ideology', *Signs: Journal of Women in Culture and Society* 14(1):42–72.

Lemert, Charles C. (1994) 'Post-Structuralism and Sociology', in Steven Seidman (ed.) *The Postmodern Turn: New Perspectives on Social Theory*, pp. 265–81. New York: Cambridge University Press.

Lorde, Audre (1984) *Sister Outsider*. Trumansburg, NY: The Crossing Press.

Lubiano, Wahneema (1992) 'Black Ladies, Welfare Queens, and State Minstrels: Ideological War by Narrative Means', in Toni Morrison (ed.) *Race-ing Justice, Engendering Power*, pp. 323–63. New York: Pantheon.

Maher, Lisa (1995) 'Dope Girls: Gender, Race and Class in the Drug Economy', PhD Thesis, Rutgers University, New Jersey.

Maher, Lisa and Kathleen Daly (1996) 'Women in the Street-Level Drug Economy: Continuity or Change?', *Criminology* 34(4): in press.

Marcus, Sharon (1992) 'Fighting Bodies, Fighting Words: A Theory and Politics of Rape Prevention', in Judith Butler and Joan W. Scott (eds) *Feminists Theorize the Political*, pp. 385–403. New York: Routledge.

Martin, Jane Roland (1994) 'Methodological Essentialism, False Difference, and other Dangerous Traps', *Signs: Journal of women in Culture and Society* 19(3):630–57.

Martin, Susan E. and Nancy C. Jurik (1996) *Doing Justice, Doing Gender*. Newbury Park: Sage.

Messerschmidt, James W. (1993) *Masculinities and Crime: Critique and Reconceptualization of Theory*. Lanham, MD: Rowman & Littlefield Publishers.

Naffine, Ngaire (1994) 'Introduction', in Ngaire Naffine (ed.) *Gender, Crime and Feminism*, pp. xi–xxx. Brookfield, VT: Dartmouth Publishing Company.

Nicholson, Linda (ed.) (1990) *Feminism/Postmodernism*. New York: Routledge.

Norris, Christopher (1992) *Uncritical Theory: Postmodernism, Intellectuals and the Gulf War*. London: Lawrence & Wishart.

Pratt, Minnie Bruce (1984) 'Identity: Skin Blood Heart', in Elly Bulkin, Minnie Bruce Pratt and Barbara Smith (eds) *Yours in Struggle*, pp. 11–63. Ithaca, NY: Firebrand Books.

Price, Barbara Raffel and Natalie J. Sokoloff (eds) (1995, 2nd edn) *The Criminal Justice System and Women*. New York: McGraw-Hill.

Radford, Jill, Liz Kelly and Marianne Hester (1996) 'Introduction', in Marianne Hester, Liz Kelly and Jill Radford (eds) *Women, Violence and Male Power*, pp. 1–16. Philadelphia: Open University Press.

Rich, Adrienne (1979) 'Disloyal to Civilization: Feminism, Racism, Gynophobia', in Adrienne Rich (ed.) *On Lies, Secrets, and Silence*, pp. 275–310. New York: Norton.

Richardson, Laurel (1990) 'Narrative and Sociology', *Journal of Contemporary Ethnography* 19(1):116–35.

Roseneil, Sasha (1995) 'The Coming of Age of Feminist Sociology: Some Issues of Practice and Theory for the Next Twenty Years', *British Journal of Sociology* 46(2):191–205.

Ruiz, Vicki L. and Ellen Carol DuBois (eds) (1994, 2nd edn) *Unequal Sisters*. New York: Routledge.

Russell, Katheryn K. (1992) 'Development of a Black Criminology and Role of the Black Criminologist', *Justice Quarterly* 9:667–83.

Schwartz, Martin D. and David O. Friedrichs (1994) 'Postmodern Thought and Criminological Discontent: New Metaphors for Understanding Violence', *Criminology* 32(2):221–46.

Schwartz, Martin D. and Dragan Milovanovic (eds) (1995) *Race, Gender, and Class in Criminology: The Intersections*. New York: Garland.

Scott, Joan W. (1992) '"Experience"', in Judith Butler and Joan W. Scott (eds) *Feminists Theorize the Political*, pp. 22–40. New York: Routledge.

Seidman, Steven (1994) 'Introduction', in Steven Seidman (ed.) *The Postmodern Turn: New Perspectives on Social Theory*, pp. 1–23. New York: Cambridge University Press.

Simpson, Sally S. (1991) 'Caste, Class, and Violent Crime: Explaining Differences in Female Offending', *Criminology* 29(1):115–35.

Simpson, Sally S. and Lori Elis (1995) 'Doing Gender: Sorting Out the Caste and Crime Conundrum', *Criminology* 33(1): 47–81.

Smart, Carol (1989) *Feminism and the Power of Law*. New York: Routledge.

Smart, Carol (1990a) 'Feminist Approaches to Criminology, or Postmodern Woman Meets Atavistic Man', in Loraine Gelsthorpe and Allison Morris (eds) *Feminist Perspectives in Criminology*, pp. 70–84. Philadelphia: Open University Press.

Smart, Carol (1990b) 'Law's Power, the Sexed Body, and Feminist Discourse', *Journal of Law and Society* 17:194–210.

Smart, Carol (1992) 'The Woman of Legal Discourse', *Social and Legal Studies* 1(1):29–44.

Smart, Carol (1995) *Law, Crime and Sexuality: Essays in Feminism*. London: Sage.

Spivak, Gayatri Chakravorty (1992) 'French Feminism Revisited: Ethics and Politics', in Judith Butler and Joan W. Scott (eds) *Feminists Theorize the Political*, pp. 54–85. New York: Routledge.

Stivers, Camilla (1993) 'Reflections on the Role of Personal Narrative in Social Science', *Signs: Journal of Women in Culture and Society* 18(2):408–25.

Thorne, Barrie (1995) Symposium participant, *Gender & Society* 9(4):497–9.

Vogel, Lise (1991) 'Telling Tales: Historians of Our Own Lives', *Journal of Women's History* 2(winter):89–101.

Walker, Samuel and Molly Brown (1995) 'A Pale Reflection of Reality: The Neglect of Racial and Ethnic Minorities in Introductory Criminal Justice Textbooks', *Journal of Criminal Justice Education* 6(1):61–83.

West, Candace and Sarah Fenstermaker (1995) 'Doing Difference', *Gender & Society* 9(1):8–37.

West, Candace and Don H. Zimmerman (1987) 'Doing Gender', *Gender & Society* 1(2):125–51.

Williams, Patricia J. (1991) *The Alchemy of Race and Rights: Diary of a Law Professor*. Cambridge: Harvard University Press.

Worrall, Anne (1990) *Offending Women*. New York: Routledge.

Yeatman, Anna (1995) 'Interlocking Oppressions', in Barbara Caine and Rosemary Pringle (eds) *Transitions: New Australian Feminisms*, pp. 42–56. Sydney: Allen & Unwin.

Young, Alison (1990) *Femininity in Dissent*. London: Routledge.

Young, Alison (1996) *Imagining Crime*. London: Sage.

Young, Iris Marion (1994) 'Gender as Seriality: Thinking About Women as a Social Collective', *Signs: Journal of Women In Culture and Society* 19(3):713–38.

Young, Vernetta D. and Helen Taylor Greene (1995) 'Pedagogical Reconstruction: Incorporating African-American Perspectives into the Curriculum', *Journal of Criminal Justice Education* 6(1):85–104.

45

The global criminal economy

Manuel Castells

[. . .]

Crime is as old as humankind. But the global crime, the networking of powerful criminal organizations, and their associates, in shared activities throughout the planet, is a new phenomenon that profoundly affects international and national economies, politics, security, and, ultimately, societies at large. The Sicilian *Cosa Nostra* (and its associates, *La Camorra*, *Ndrangheta*, and *Sacra Corona Unita*), the American Mafia, the Colombian cartels, the Mexican cartels, the Nigerian criminal networks, the Japanese *Yakuza*, the Chinese Triads, the constellation of Russian *Mafiyas*, the Turkish heroin traffickers, the Jamaican Posses, and a myriad of regional and local criminal groupings in all countries, have come together in a global, diversified network, that permeates boundaries and links up ventures of all sorts. While drugs traffic is the most important segment of this worldwide industry, arms deals also represent a high-value market. In addition, is everything that receives added value precisely from its prohibition in a given institutional environment: smuggling of everything from everywhere to everywhere, including radioactive material, human organs, and illegal immigrants; prostitution; gambling; loan-sharking; kidnapping; racketeering and extortion; counterfeiting of goods, bank notes, financial documents, credit cards, and identity cards; killers for hire; traffic of sensitive information, technology, or art objects; international sales of stolen goods; or even dumping garbage illegally from one country into another [. . .]. Extortion is also practiced on an international scale; for instance, by the *Yakuza* on Japanese corporations abroad. At the heart of the system, there is money laundering by the hundreds of billions (maybe trillions) of dollars. Complex financial schemes and international trade networks link up the criminal economy to the formal economy, thus deeply penetrating financial markets, and constituting a critical, volatile element in a fragile global economy. The economies *and politics* of many countries (such as Italy, Russia, the former Soviet Union republics, Colombia, Mexico, Bolivia, Peru, Venezuela, Turkey, Afghanistan, Burma, Thailand, but also Japan [. . .], Taiwan, Hong Kong, and a multiplicity of small countries which include Luxembourg and Austria) cannot be understood without considering the dynamics of criminal

From *End of Millennium*, 1998. (Blackwell: Oxford.)

networks present in their daily workings. The flexible connection of these criminal activities in international networks constitutes an essential feature of the new global economy, and of the social/political dynamics of the Information Age. There is general acknowledgment of the importance and reality of this phenomenon, and a wealth of evidence, mainly from well-documented journalists' reports, and the conferences of international organizations. Yet, the phenomenon is largely ignored by social scientists, when it comes to understanding economies and societies, with the arguments that data are not truly reliable, and that sensationalism taints interpretation. I take exception to these views. If a phenomenon is acknowledged as a fundamental dimension of our societies, indeed of the new, globalized system, we must use whatever evidence is available to explore the connection between these criminal activities and societies and economies at large.

ORGANIZATIONAL GLOBALIZATION OF CRIME, CULTURAL IDENTIFICATION OF CRIMINALS

In the past two decades, criminal organizations have increasingly set up their operations transnationally, taking advantage of economic globalization and new communication and transportation technologies. Their strategy is to base their management and production functions in low-risk areas, where they have relative control of the institutional environment, while targeting as preferential markets those areas with the most affluent demand, so that higher prices can be charged. This is clearly the case for the drug cartels, whether it is cocaine in Colombia and the Andean region, or opium/heroin from the South-East Asian Golden Triangle, or from Afghanistan and Central Asia. But it is also the essential mechanism in weapons trade or traffic in radioactive material. Using their relative impunity in Russia and the former Soviet Union republics during the transition period, criminal networks, both Russian/ex-Soviet and from all around the world, took control of a significant amount of military and nuclear supplies to be offered to the highest bidder in the chaotic post-Cold War international scene. This internationalization of criminal activities induces organized crime from different countries to establish strategic alliances to cooperate, rather than fight, on each other's turf, through subcontracting arrangements, and joint ventures, whose business practice closely follows the organizational logic of what I identified as 'the network enterprise,' characteristic of the Information Age [. . .]. Furthermore, the bulk of the proceedings of these activities are by definition globalized, through their laundering via global financial markets.

Estimates of profits and financial flows originating in the criminal economy vary wildly and are not fully reliable. Yet they are indicative of the staggering size of the phenomenon we are describing. The 1994 United Nations Conference on Global Organized Crime estimated that global trade in drugs amounted to about US$ 500 billion a year; that is, it was larger than the global trade in oil. Overall profits from all kinds of activities were put as high as US$ 750 billion a year. Other estimates mention the figure of US$ 1 trillion a year in 1993, which was about the same size as the US federal budget at that time. In a very conservative estimate, the G-7 Financial Task Force declared in April 1990 that at least US$ 120 billion a year in drug money were laundered in the world's financial system. The OECD reported in 1993 the laundering of at least US$ 85 billion a year from drug traffic profits. Sterling considers plausible the figure of US$ 500 billion as the likely global turnover of 'narcodollars.' A substantial proportion of profits is laundered (with a commission for the launderers of between 15 and 25 percent of nominal dollars price), and about half of the laundered money, at least in the case of the Sicilian Mafia, is reinvested in legitimate activities. This continuity between profits from criminal activities and their investment in legitimate activities makes it impossible to limit the economic impact of global crime to the former, since the latter play a major role in ensuring, and covering up, the overall dynamics of the system. Furthermore, enforcement of deals also combines the skillful manipulation of legal procedures and financial systems in each country and internationally, with the selective use of violence, and widespread corruption of government officials, bankers, bureaucrats, and law-enforcement personnel.

At the sources of global crime, there are nationally, regionally, and ethnically rooted organizations, most of them with a long history, linked to the culture of specific countries and regions, with their ideology, their codes of honor, and their bonding mechanisms. These culturally based criminal organizations do not disappear in the new, global networks. On the contrary, their global networking allows traditional criminal organizations to survive, and prosper, by escaping the controls of a given state at a difficult time. Thus, the American Mafia, after considerably suffering from devastating strikes from the FBI in the 1980s, is being revived in the 1990s by an influx of Sicilian Mafia, and by alliances with the Chinese Triads, the Russian *Mafiyas*, and a variety of ethnic mobs.

The Sicilian Mafia is still one of the most powerful criminal organizations in the world, using its historical control over the South of Italy, and its deep penetration of the Italian state. Its links with the Italian Christian Democratic Party (including, allegedly, to Andreotti, the towering figure of the party for almost half a century) allowed the Mafia to extend its presence to the entire country, to link up with the banking system, and, through it, with the entire political and business elite of the country, even coming very close to the Vatican through the Banco Ambrosiano which appears to have been under Mafia influence. In 1987, an agreement between the Sicilian Mafia and the Medellin cartel opened the way to swap heroin from Asia/Europe for cocaine from Colombia. Thus, the Colombians could enter the heroin market in the United States, shared until then between the Sicilian and American Mafias and the Chinese Triads. While using the Sicilian infrastructure, Colombian cartels could distribute their cocaine in Europe, paying a share to the Sicilians. This was only the best documented of a series of international moves by the Sicilian Mafia, which included a deep penetration of Germany's criminal markets, and major speculative takeovers of Soviet property and currency during the transition period [. . .].

When the Italian state tried to regain its autonomy by confronting the Mafia, once the grip of the Christian Democrats and other traditional parties over the country was shaken in the early 1990s, the Mafia's reaction reached unprecedented brutality, including the killing of some leading figures in the anti-crime operations in Italy, most notably Judges Falcone and Borsalino. Popular reaction, exposure in the media, and the partial crumbling of corrupt Italian politics, weakened considerably the power of the Mafia in Italy itself, with the capture and imprisonment of its bloody *capo di tutti capi* Toto Riina. Yet the increased internationalization of Mafia activities in the 1990s allowed a new round of prosperity for its members, even if they had to relinquish some (but not most) of their control over local societies and government institutions in Italy.

In this internationalization process, the Italian Mafia coincides with the Chinese Triads, currently one of the largest and best articulated networks of criminal organizations in the world, [. . .].

The Japanese *Yakuza* (the *Boryokudan*, that is 'the violent ones') has a quasi-legal existence in Japan, and is openly present in a wide array of businesses and political activities (usually ultra-nationalistic political associations). The most important gangs are *Yamagachi-gumi*, with 26,000 members in 944 networked gangs; *Inagawa-kai*, with 8,600 members; and *Sumiyoshi-kai*, with over 7,000 members. They also originated in the protection networks created by disaffected *samurai* among the poor population of cities in the early stages of Japanese urbanization in the nineteenth century. As with the other organizations, protection turned into preying on their own members. For a long time, the Japanese *Yakuza* felt so secure at home that its international activities were limited to smuggling weapons from the US into Japan, and to providing women sex slaves from other Asian countries to Japanese brothels and night clubs. Yet, they followed the globalization of Japanese corporations, and went into exporting to the United States their customary practice of blackmail and extortion of corporations, intimidating Japanese executives abroad by sending in their *Sokaiya* (violent *provocateurs*). They also imitated Japanese firms by investing heavily in real estate, particularly in America, and by manipulating stocks in financial markets. To operate in the United States and Europe, they made a number of deals with the Sicilian and American Mafias, as well as with various Russian criminal groups.

The dramatic expansion of several Russian criminal networks has made headline news in the whole world in the 1990s. Although some leaders of this underworld relate to the old Russian tradition of *vorovskoi mir* ("thieves' community' or "thieves' world'), organized crime in contemporary Russia and the ex-Soviet republics is the result of the chaotic, uncontrolled transition from statism to wild capitalism. Members of the Soviet *nomenklatura*, exceedingly entrepreneurial 'capitalists' aspiring to become 'end of millennium robber barons,' and a myriad of ethnic mobs (with the Chechens as the most brutal and villified), constituted criminal networks in the wasteland created by the collapse of the Soviet Union. From there, they expanded throughout the world, linking up with organized crime everywhere, converging or competing, sharing profits with or killing each other, depending upon circumstances.

Emerging from drug traffic in Latin America, the Medellin and Cali cartels in Colombia, the Tamaulipas and Tijuana cartels in Mexico, and similar groups almost in every Latin American country, organized a network of production, management, and distribution activities that linked up agricultural production areas, chemical laboratories, storage facilities, and transportation systems for export to affluent markets. These cartels focused almost exclusively on drug traffic, originally cocaine, but later they added marijuana, heroin, and chemical drugs. They set up their enforcement units, and their autonomous money-laundering schemes. They also favored penetration of police, judicial systems, and politicians, in a vast network of influence and corruption that changed Latin American politics, and will exercise its lasting influence for years to come. By their very essence, these cartels (actually made up of a coordinated network of smaller producers, under the control of cartel leaders through violence, finance, and distribution capability) were internationalized from the outset. They aimed essentially at exports to the United States, later to Europe, then to the whole world. Their strategies were, in fact, a peculiar adaptation of IMF-inspired export-oriented, growth policies toward the actual ability of some Latin American regions to complete in the high-technology environment of the new global economy. They linked up with national/local crime organizations in America and Europe to distribute their merchandise. And they set up a vast financial and commercial empire of money-laundering operations that, more than any other criminal organization, deeply penetrated the global financial system. Colombian and Latin American drug traffickers, as their Sicilian, Chinese, Japanese, or Russian counterparts, are also deeply rooted in their national, cultural identity. Pablo Escobar, the leader of the Medellin cartel made famous his slogan: 'I prefer a tomb in Colombia than a prison in the United States.' He succeeded in fulfilling his wish. His attitude, and similar attitudes among Latin America's drug kingpins reflect an obvious opportunism, since they are confident of their relative control over judges, police, and the penal system in their own countries. But there is undoubtedly something else, a more specific cultural component in their stand against the United States, and in their attachment to their regions and nations, a theme on which I will elaborate below.

The nationally and ethnically based criminal organizations that I have cited are the most notorious, but they are not, by any means, the only ones in the global scene. Turkish organized crime (enjoying significant influence in Turkey's politics and law-enforcement agencies) is a major player in the traditional Balkan route that brings heroin into Europe, a route now used for all kinds of additional traffic. Diversified Nigerian criminal networks have become a force to reckon with, not only in Nigeria and in Africa (where they subcontract their knowledge of the field to international cartels), but in the world arena, where they excel, for instance, in credit-card fraud. In every country, and in every region, gangs, and networks of gangs, are now aware of their chances of linking up with broader chains of activities in this underworld that has a dominant presence in many neighborhoods, cities, and regions, and that has even been able to buy most of the assets of some small countries, such as the island nation of Aruba, off the Venezuelan coast.

From these local, national, and ethnic bases, rooted in identity, and relying on interpersonal relationships of trust/distrust (naturally enforced with machine guns), criminal organizations engage in a wide range of activities. Drug traffic is the paramount business, to the point that the legalization of drugs is probably the greatest threat that organized crime would have to confront. But they can rely on the political blindness, and misplaced morality, of societies that do not come to terms with the bottom line of the problem: demand drives supply. The source of drug addiction, and therefore of most crimes in the world, lies in the psychological injuries inflicted on people by everyday life in our societies. Therefore, there will be mass consumption of drugs, for the foreseeable future, regardless of repression. And global organized crime will find ways to supply this demand, making it a most profitable business, and the mother of most other crimes.

Yet, besides drug trafficking, the criminal economy has expanded its realm to an extraordinary diversity of operations, making it an increasingly diversified, and interconnected, global industry. The 1994 United Nations Conference on Transnational Crime listed the main activities in which this kind of organized crime is engaged, *in addition to drug traffic.*

1. *Weapons trafficking* This is, of course, a multi-billion dollar business whose boundaries with the legal export of arms are not easy to determine. The critical matter in the business is the identity of the end-user, barred by international agreements or geopolitical considerations from receiving certain types of weapons. In some cases, these are states under an international embargo (such as Iran, Iraq, Libya, Bosnia, or Serbia). In other instances, they are guerrilla groups, or parties involved in a civil war. Still others are terrorist groups, and criminal organizations. The United States and the Soviet Union created the main supply of war weaponry in the world by providing it generously to various warring parties to influence them in their geopolitical games. After the end of the Cold War, weapons were left in often unreliable hands, which used their stocks to feed the market. Other deals originate in semi-legal exports from arms-producing countries, such as France, the UK, China, the Czech Republic, Spain, or Israel. [. . .]

2. *Trafficking of nuclear material* This involves the smuggling of nuclear weapons grade material, for eventual use in building these weapons and/or blackmailing by threatening their use. The disintegration of the Soviet Union provided a major opportunity for supplying this kind of material. Germany has been, in the 1990s, at the forefront of this kind of traffic, as criminal networks from the former Warsaw Pact countries have been smuggling nuclear material on behalf of international agents, sometimes in reckless ways, including carrying extremely radioactive items in the pockets of the smuggler. [. . .]

3. *Smuggling of illegal immigrants.* The combination of misery around the world, displacement of populations, and dynamism in the core economies pushes millions of people to emigrate. On the other hand, increased border controls, particularly in the affluent societies, try to stem the immigration flow. These contradictory trends provide an exceptional opportunity to criminal organizations to tap into an immense market: 'coyote' traffic on a global scale. [. . .] It also keeps many of them in bondage for a long time to repay their debt with a high interest. It exposes them, as well, to fraud, abuse, violence, and death. Furthermore, by threatening to overwhelm channels of lawful immigration, it triggers a xenophobic backlash which, manipulated by demagogic politicians, is destroying cultural tolerance and feelings of solidarity in most countries.

4. *Trafficking in women and children* Global tourism has become closely linked with a global prostitution industry, particularly active in Asia, where it is often under the control of the Triads and the *Yakuza*. It increasingly affects children as well [. . .]. In addition to child abuse and exploitation, there is also a growing industry in child adoption, particularly in Latin America, with destination to the United States. [. . .]

5. *Trafficking in body parts* According to the United Nations 1994 report, there have been confirmed reports of such trafficking in Argentina, Brazil, Honduras, Mexico, and Peru, largely with destination to German, Swiss, and Italian buyers. In Argentina, there have been examples of the removal of corneas of patients who were declared brain dead after fabricated brain scans. The problem seems to be serious in Russia, mainly because of thousands of unclaimed bodies in the morgues: [. . .] Traffic seems to be particularly important in India and in Egypt, with destination to wealthy Middle Eastern patients. Most of these organs are voluntarily sold by people, either alive (one kidney, one eye), or by their families once they are dead. Yet, because of national and international legislation, the

traffic is indeed illegal, and handled by smuggling networks, whose ultimate clients are, naturally, leading hospitals around the world. This is one of the links between global poverty and high technology.

6. *Money laundering* The whole criminal system only makes business sense if the profits generated can be used and reinvested in the legal economy. This has become increasingly complicated given the staggering volume of these profits. This is why money laundering is the matrix of global crime, and its most direct connecting point to global capitalism. Money laundering involves three stages. The first, and most delicate, requires the placement of cash into the financial system through banks or other financial institutions. In some instances, banks are located in countries with little control. Panama, Aruba, the Cayman Islands, the Bahamas, St Maertens, Vanuatu, but also Luxembourg and Austria (although in these two countries things are changing lately) are often cited in police reports as key entry points for dirty money into the financial system. In the leading economies, however, cash transactions over a certain sum (10,000 dollars in the US) must be reported. Thus, deposits operate through a large number of $9,999 (or less) transactions, a process called 'smurfing.' The second stage is 'layering'; that is, separating funds from their source to avoid detection by future audits. What is critical here is the globalization of financial markets, and the availability of electronic transfer funds in seconds. Together with currency swaps, investments in different stocks, and use of some of this 'dirty money' as collateral for loans from legitimate funds, the speed and diversity of transactions makes it extremely difficult to detect the origin of these funds. Evidence of this difficulty is the very small amount of funds seized in the main capitalist countries. The third stage is 'integration'; that is, the introduction of laundered capital into the legal economy, usually in real estate or stocks, and generally using the weakest entry points of the legal economy, in countries with no or little anti-money-laundering legislation. After this integration, criminally-generated profits join the whirlwind of global financial flows.

The key to the success and expansion of global crime in the 1990s is the flexibility and versatility of their organization. *Networking is their form of operation*, both internally, in each criminal organization (for example, the Sicilian Mafia, the Cali cartel), and in relation to other criminal organizations. Distribution networks operate on the basis of autonomous local gangs, to which they supply goods and services, and from which they receive cash. Each major criminal organization has its own means of enforcing deals. Ruthless violence (including intimidation, torture, kidnapping of family members, killings) are, of course, part of the routine, often subcontracted to contract killers. But more important is the 'security apparatus' of organized crime, the network of law-enforcement agents, judges, and politicians, who are on the payroll. Once they enter this system, they are captive for life. While judicial tactics of plea bargains and crime witness-protection schemes have helped the repression of organized crime, particularly in America and Italy, the increasing ability of criminal leaders to find safe havens, and the global reach of killers-for-hire, are considerably limiting the effectiveness of classic repression methods of 1950s America and 1980s Italy.

This need to escape police repression based on nation-states makes *strategic alliances between criminal networks* essential in their new mode of operation. No one organization can by itself link up throughout the globe. Moreover, it cannot extend its international reach without entering the traditional territory of another criminal power. This is why, in strictly business logic, criminal organizations respect each other, and find points of convergence across national boundaries and turfs. Most of the killings are intranational: Russians killing Russians, Sicilians killing Sicilians, the Medellin cartel and the Cali cartel members killing each other, precisely to control their local/national base from which they can operate comfortably. It is this combination of flexible networking between local turfs, rooted in tradition and identity, in a favourable institutional environment, and the global reach provided by strategic alliances, that explains the organizational strength of global crime. It makes it a fundamental actor in the economy and society of the Information Age. [. . .]

[. . .]

THE IMPACT OF GLOBAL CRIME ON ECONOMY, POLITICS, AND CULTURE

Money laundering, and its derivatives, have become a significant and troubling component of global financial flows and stock markets. The size of these capitals, while unknown, is likely to be considerable. But more important is their mobility. To avoid tracking, capital originating in the criminal economy shifts constantly from financial institution to financial institution, from currency to currency, from stock to stock, from investment in real estate to investment in entertainment. Because of its volatility, and its willingness to take high risks, criminal capital follows, and amplifies, speculative turbulences in financial markets. Thus, it has become an important source of destabilization of international finance and capital markets.

Criminal activity has also a powerful direct effect on a number of national economies. In some cases, the size of its capital overwhelms the economy of small countries. In other cases, such as Colombia, Peru, Bolivia, or Nigeria, it represents an amount sizeable enough to condition macroeconomic processes, becoming decisive in specific regions or sectors. Still in other countries, such as Russia or Italy, its penetration of business and institutions transforms the economic environment, making it unpredictable, and favouring investment strategies focused on short-term returns. Even in economies as large and solid as Japan, financial crises can be triggered by criminal maneuvers, as was the case in 1995 of the savings and loans defaults, for hundreds of billions of dollars, as a result of bad loans forced on some bankers by the *Yakuza*. The distorting effects of the unseen criminal economy on monetary policies, and on economic policies at large, make it even more difficult to control nationally based economic processes in a globalized economy, one component of which has no official existence.

The impact of crime on state institutions and politics is even greater. State sovereignty, already battered by the processes of globalization and identification, is directly threatened by flexible networks of crime that bypass controls and assume a level of risk that no other organizations are capable of absorbing [. . .]. The technological and organizational opportunity to set up global networks has transformed, and empowered, organized crime. For a long time, its fundamental strategy was to penetrate national and local state institutions in its home country, in order to protect its activities. The Sicilian Mafia, the Japanese *Yakuza*, the Hong Kong-based, or Taiwan-based, or Bangkok-based Triads, the Colombian cartels relied on their capacity to build over time a deep connection with segments of national and regional states, both with bureaucrats and with politicians. This is still an important element in the operational procedures of organized crime: it can only survive on the basis of corruption and intimidation of state personnel and, sometimes, of state institutions. However, in recent times, globalization has added a decisive twist to the institutional strategy of organized crime. Safe, or relatively safe, houses have been found around the planet: small (Aruba), medium (Colombia), large (Mexico) or extra-large (Russia), among many others. Besides, the high mobility and extreme flexibility of the networks makes it possible to evade national regulations and the rigid procedures of international police cooperation. Thus, the consolidation of the European Union has handed organized crime a wonderful opportunity to take advantage of contradictions between national legislations and of the reluctance of most police forces to relinquish their independence. Thus, Germany has become a major operational center for the Sicilian Mafia, Galicia is a major staging point for the Colombian cartels, and The Netherlands harbors important nodes of heroin traffic of the Chinese Triads. When pressure from the state, and from international forces (usually US intelligence agencies), becomes excessive in a given country, even in a region that was 'safe' for organized crime (for example, the significant repression of crime in Sicily in 1995–6, or in Medellin and Cali in 1994–6), the flexibility of the network allows it to shift its organizational geometry, moving supply bases, altering transportation routes, and finding new places of residence for their bosses, increasingly in respectable countries, such as Switzerland, Spain, and Austria. As for the real thing, that is the money, it circulates safely in the flows of computerized financial transactions, managed from offshore banking bases that direct its swirling in time and space.

Furthermore, escaping police control through networking and globalization allows organized crime to keep its grip on its national bases. For instance, in the mid-1990s, while the Colombian cartels (particularly Medellin) suffered serious blows, Colombian drug traffickers survived by modifying their organization and decentralizing their structure. In fact, they were never a hierarchical, consolidated cartel, but a loose association of exporters, including, in Cali, for instance, over 200 independent organizations. Thus, when some leaders become too inconvenient (as, for example, Rodriguez Gacha, or Escobar), or are eliminated, these networks find new arrangements, new power relationships, and new, albeit unstable, forms of cooperation. By emphasizing local flexibility and international complexity, the criminal economy adapts itself to the desperate control attempts by rigid, nationally bound state institutions, that, for the time being, know they are losing the battle. With it, they are also losing an essential component of state sovereignty *and legitimacy*: its ability to impose law and order.

In a desperate reaction to the growing power of organized crime, democratic states, in self-defense, resort to measures that curtail, and will curtail, democratic liberties. Furthermore, since immigrant networks are often used by organized crime to penetrate societies, the excessive, and unjust, association between immigration and crime triggers xenophobic feelings in public opinion, undermining the tolerance and capacity of coexistence that our increasingly multi-ethnic societies desperately need. With the nation-state under siege, and with national societies and economies already insecure from their intertwining with transnational networks of capital and people, the growing influence of global crime may induce a substantial retrenchment of democratic rights, values, and institutions.

The state is not only being bypassed from outside by organized crime. It is disintegrating from within. Besides the ability of criminals to bribe and/or intimidate police, judges, and government officials, there is a more insidious and devastating penetration: *the corruption of democratic politics*. The increasingly important financial needs of political candidates and parties create a golden opportunity for organized crime to offer support in critical moments of political campaigns. Any movement in this direction will haunt the politician for ever. Furthermore, the domination of the democratic process by scandal politics, character assassination, and image-making also offers organized crime a privileged terrain of political influence [. . .]. By luring politicians into sex, drugs, and money, or fabricating allegations as necessary, organized crime has created a wide network of intelligence and extortion, which traffics influence against silence. In the 1990s, the politics of many countries, not only in Latin America, have been dominated by scandals and crises induced by the direct or indirect connection between organized crime and politics. But in addition to these known, or suspected, cases of political corruption, the pervasiveness of scandal politics suggests the possibility that organized crime has discretely positioned itself in the world of politics and media in a number of countries, for instance in Japan (*Yakuza*), or Italy (Sicilian Mafia).

The influence of global crime also reaches the *cultural realm* in more subtle ways. On the one hand, cultural identity nurtures most of these criminal networks, and provides the codes and bonding that build trust and communication within each network. This complicity does not preclude violence against their own kind. On the contrary, most violence is within the network. Yet there is a broader level of sharing and understanding in the criminal organization, that builds on history, culture, and tradition, and generates its own legitimizing ideology. This has been documented in numerous studies of the Sicilian and American Mafias, since their resistance to French occupation in the eighteenth century, or among the Chinese Triads, which originated in southern resistance to northern invaders, and then developed as a brotherhood in foreign lands. In my brief description of the Colombian cartels I have given a glimpse of their deep rooting in regional culture, and in their rural past, which they tried to revive. As for Russian crime, which is probably the most cosmopolitan in its projection, it is also embedded in Russian culture and institutions. In fact, the more organized crime becomes global, the more its most important components emphasize their cultural identity, so as not to disappear in the whirlwind of the space of flows. In so doing, they preserve their ethnic, cultural, and, where possible, territorial bases. This is their strength. Criminal networks are probably in advance of multinational corporations in their decisive ability to combine cultural identity and global business.

However, the main cultural impact of global crime networks on societies at large, beyond the expression of their own cultural identity, is in *the new culture they induce*. In many contexts, daring, successful criminals have become role models for a young generation that does not see an easy way out of poverty, and certainly no chance of enjoying consumption and live adventure. From Russia to Colombia, observers emphasize the fascination of local youth for the mafiosi. In a world of exclusion, and in the midst of a crisis of political legitimacy, the boundary between protest, patterns of immediate gratification, adventure, and crime becomes increasingly blurred. Perhaps Garcia Marquez, better than anyone else, has captured the 'culture of urgency' of young killers in the world of organized crime. In his non-fiction book *Noticia de un secuestro* (1996), he describes the fatalism and negativism of young killers. For them, there is no hope in society, and everything, particularly politics and politicians, is rotten. Life itself has no meaning, and their life has no future. They know they will die soon. So, only the moment counts, the immediate consumption, good clothing, good life, on the run, together with the satisfaction of inducing fear, of feeling powerful with their guns. Just one supreme value: their families, and in particular their mother, for whom they would do anything. And their religious beliefs, particularly for specific saints that would help in bad moments. In striking literary terms, Garcia Marquez recounts the phenomenon that many social scientists around the world have observed: young criminals are caught between their enthusiasm for life and the realization of their limits. Thus, they compress life into a few instants, to live it fully, and then disappear. For those brief moments of existence, the breaking of the rules, and the feeling of empowerment, compensates for the monotone display of a longer, but miserable life. Their values are, to a large extent, shared by many other youngsters, albeit in less extreme forms.

The diffusion of the culture of organized crime is reinforced by the pervasiveness of the everyday life of the criminal world in the media. People around the world are probably more acquainted with the media version of the working conditions and psyche of 'hit men' and drug traffickers than with the dynamics of financial markets where people invest their money. The collective fascination of the entire planet with action movies where the protagonists are the players in organized crime cannot be explained just by the repressed urge for violence in our psychological make up. It may well indicate the cultural breakdown of traditional moral order, and the implicit recognition of a new society, made up of communal identity and unruly competition, of which global crime is a condensed expression.

46

Beyond Blade Runner: Urban control. The ecology of fear

Mike Davis

1. BEYOND BLADE RUNNER

Every American city has its official insignia and slogan, some have municipal mascots, colors, songs, birds, trees, even rocks. But Los Angeles alone has adopted an official Nightmare.

In 1988, after three years of debate, a galaxy of corporate and civic leaders submitted to Mayor Bradley a detailed strategic plan for Southern California's future. Although most of *L.A. 2000: A City for the Future* is devoted to hyperbolic rhetoric about Los Angeles' irresistible rise as a 'world crossroads,' a section in the epilogue (written by historian Kevin Starr) considers what might happen if the city fails to create a new 'dominant establishment' to manage its extraordinary ethnic diversity. 'There is, of course, the *Blade Runner* scenario: the fusion of individual cultures into a demotic poly-glotism ominous with unresolved hostilities.' [. . .]

With Warner Bros.' release of the original (more hard-boiled) director's cut a few months after the 1992 Los Angeles uprising, Ridley Scott's 1982 film version of the Philip K. Dick story ('Do Androids Dream of Electric Sheep?') reasserts its sovereignty over our increasingly troubled sleep. Virtually all ruminations about the future of Los Angeles now take for granted the dark imagery of *Blade Runner* as a possible, if not inevitable, terminal point of the land of sunshine.

Yet for all of *Blade Runner's* glamor as the star of sci-fi dystopias, I find it strangely anachronistic and surprisingly unprescient. [. . .] What remains is recognizably the same vista or urban gigantism that Fritz Lang celebrated in *Metropolis* (1931).

The sinister, man-made Everest of the Tyrell Corporation, as well as all the souped-up rocket-squad-cars darting around the air space, are obvious progenies—albeit now swaddled in darkness—of the famous skyscraper city of the bourgeoisie in *Metropolis*. [. . .]

From Open Magazine Pamphlet Series, Pamphlet 23 (second printing 1994).

Blade Runner, in other words, remains yet another edition of this core modernist vision—alternately utopia or dystopia, *ville radieuse* or Gotham City—of the future metropolis as Monster Manhattan. [. . .]

Ridley Scott's particular 'gigantesque caricature' may capture ethno-centric anxieties about poly-glottism run amock but it fails to imaginatively engage the real Los Angeles landscape—especially the great unbroken plains of aging bungalows, dingbats and ranch-style homes—as it socially and physically erodes into the 21st century.

In my recent book on Los Angeles (*City of Quartz*, 1990) I enumerate various tendencies toward the militarization of this landscape. Events since the uprising of Spring 1992—including a deepening recession, corporate flight, savage budget cuts, a soaring homicide rate (despite the black gang truce), and a huge spree of gun-buying in the suburbs—only confirm that social polarization and spatial apartheid are accelerating. As the Endless Summer comes to an end, it seems quite possible that Los Angeles 2019 could well stand in a dystopian relationship to any ideal of the democratic city.

But what kind of cityscape, if not *Blade Runner*, would this malign evolution of inequality produce? Instead of seeing the future merely as a grotesque, Wellsian magnification of technology and architecture, I have tried to carefully extrapolate existing spatial tendencies in order to glimpse their emergent pattern. William Gibson, in *Neuromancer* and other novels, has provided stunning examples of how realist, 'extrapolative' science fiction can operate as prefigurative social theory, as well as an anticipatory opposition politics to the cyber-fascism lurking over the next horizon.

In what follows, I offer a 'Gibsonian' map to a future Los Angeles that is already half-born. Paradoxically, the literal map itself [. . .], although inspired by a vision of Marxism-for-cyberpunks, looks like nothing so much as that venerable 'combination of half-moon and dart board' that Ernest W. Burgess of the University of Chicago long ago made 'the most famous diagram in social science.'

For those unfamiliar with the legacy of the Chicago School of Sociology and their canonical study of the 'North American city,' let me just say that Burgess' dart board represents the five concentric zones into which the struggle for the survival of the fittest (as imagined by Social Darwinists) supposedly sorts urban social classes and housing types. It portrays a 'human ecology' organized by biological forces of invasion, competition, succession and symbiosis. My remapping of the urban structure takes Burgess back to the future. It preserves such 'ecological' determinants as income, land value, class and race, but adds a decisive new factor: fear.

2. SCANSCAPE

Is there any need to explain *why* fear eats the soul of Los Angeles?

The current obsession with personal safety and social insulation is only exceeded by the middle-class dread of progressive taxation. In the face of unemployment and homelessness on scales not seen since 1938, a bipartisan consensus insists that the budget must be balanced and entitlements reduced. Refusing to make any further public investment in the remediation of underlying social conditions, we are forced

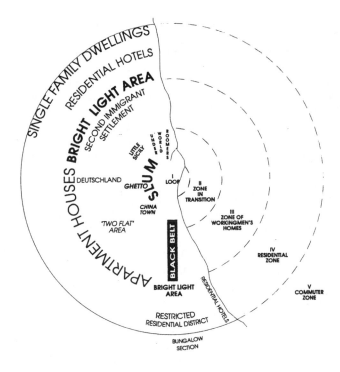

instead to make increasing private investments in physical security. The rhetoric of urban reform persists, but the substance is extinct. 'Rebuilding L.A.' simply means padding the bunker.

As city life, in consequence, grows more feral, the different social milieux adopt security strategies and technologies according to their means. Like Burgess' original dart board, the resulting pattern condenses into concentric zones. The bull's eye is Downtown.

In another essay I have recounted in detail how a secretive, emergency committee of Downtown's leading corporate landowners (the so-called Committee of 25) responded to the perceived threat of the 1965 Watts Rebellion. Warned by law-enforcement authorities that a black 'inundation' of the central city was imminent, the Committee of 25 abandoned redevelopment efforts in the old office and retail core. They then used the city's power of eminent domain to raze neighborhoods and create a new financial core a few blocks further west. The city's redevelopment agency, acting virtually as their private planner, bailed out the Committee of 25's sunk investments in the old business district by offering huge discounts, far below market value, on parcels in the new core.

Key to the success of the entire strategy (celebrated as Downtown L.A.'s 'renaissance') was the physical segregation of the new core and its land values behind a rampart of regarded palisades, concrete pillars and freeway walls. Traditional pedestrian connections between Bunker Hill and the old core were removed, and foot traffic in the new financial district was elevated above the street on pedways whose access was controlled by the security systems of individual skyscrapers. This radical privatization of Downtown public space—with its ominous racial undertones—occurred without significant public debate or protest.

Last year's riots, moreover, have only seemed to vindicate the foresight of Fortress Downtown's designers. While windows were being smashed throughout the old business district along Broadway and Spring streets, Bunker Hill lived up to its name. By flicking a few switches on their command consoles, the security staffs of the great bank towers were able to cut off all access to their expensive real estate. Bullet-proof steel doors rolled down over street-level entrances, escalators instantly stopped and electronic locks sealed off pedestrian passageways. As the *Los Angeles Business Journal* recently pointed out in a special report, the riot-tested success of corporate Downtown's defenses has only stimulated demand for new and higher levels of physical security.

In the first place, the boundary between architecture and law enforcement is further eroded. The LAPD have become central players in the Downtown design process. No major project now breaks ground without their participation, and in some cases, like the recent debate over the provision of public toilets in parks and subway stations (which they opposed), they openly exercise veto power.

Secondly, video monitoring of Downtown's redeveloped zones has been extended to parking structures, private sidewalks, plazas, and so on. This comprehensive surveillance constitutes a virtual *scanscape*—a space of protective visibility that increasingly defines where white-collar office workers and middle-class tourists feel safe Downtown. Inevitably the workplace or shopping mall video camera will become linked with home security systems, personal 'panic buttons,' car alarms, cellular phones, and the like, in a seamless continuity of surveillance over daily routine. Indeed, yuppies' lifestyles soon may be defined by the ability to afford *electronic guardian angels* to watch over them. [. . .]

Thirdly, tall buildings are becoming increasingly sentient and packed with deadly firepower. The skyscraper with a computer brain in *Die Hard I* (actually F. Scott Johnson's Fox-Pereira Tower) anticipates a possible genre of architectural anti-heroes as *intelligent buildings* alternately battle evil or become its pawns. The sensory system of the average office tower already includes panoptic vision, smell, sensitivity to temperature and humidity, motion detection, and, in some cases, hearing. Some architects now predict the day when the building's own AI security computer will be able to automatically screen and identify its human population, and, even perhaps, respond to their emotional states (fear, panic, etc.). Without dispatching security personnel, the building itself will manage crises both minor (like ordering street people out of the building or preventing them from using toilets) and major (like trapping burglars in an elevator).

When all else fails, the smart building will become a combination of bunker and fire-base. [. . .]

3. FREE FIRE ZONE

Beyond the scanscape of the fortified core is the halo of barrios and ghettos that surround Downtown Los Angeles. In Burgess' original Chicago-inspired schema this was the 'zone in transition:' the boarding house and tenement streets, intermixed with old industry and transportation infrastructure, that sheltered new immigrant families and single male laborers. Los Angeles' inner ring of freeway-sliced Latino neighborhoods still recapitulate these classical functions. Here in Boyle and Lincoln Heights, Central-Vernon and MacArthur Park are the ports of entry for the region's poorest immigrants, as well as the low-wage labor reservoir for Downtown's hotels and garment sweatshops. Residential densities, just as in the Burgess diagram, are the highest in the city. [. . .]

Finally, just as in Chicago in 1927, this tenement zone ('where an inordinately large number of children are crowded into a small area') remains the classic breeding ground of teenage street gangs (over one-hundred according to L.A. school district intelligence). But while 'Gangland' in 1920s Chicago was theorized as essentially *interstitial* to the social organization of the city—'as better residential districts recede before the encroachments of business and industry, the gang develops as one manifestation of the economic, moral, and cultural frontier which marks the interstice'—a gang map of Los Angeles today is coextensive with the geography of social class. Tribalized teenage violence now spills out of the inner ring into the older suburban zones; the Boyz are now in the 'Hood where Ozzie and Harriet used to live.

For all that, however, the inner ring remains the most dangerous sector of the city. Ramparts Division of the LAPD, which patrols the salient just west of Downtown, regularly investigates more homicides than any other neighborhood police jurisdiction in the nation. Nearby MacArthur Park, once the jewel in the crown of L.A.'s park system, is now a free-fire zone where crack dealers and street gangs settle their scores with shotguns and Uzis. Thirty people were murdered there in 1990.

By their own admission the overwhelmed inner-city detachments of the LAPD are unable to keep track of all the bodies on the street, much less deal with common burglaries, car thefts or gang-organized protection rackets. Lacking the resources or political clout of more affluent neighborhoods, the desperate population of the inner ring is left to its own devices. As a last resort they have turned to Messieurs Smith and Wesson, whose name follows 'protected by . . .' on many a porch.

Slumlords, meanwhile, are mounting their own private reign of terror against drug-dealers and petty criminals. Faced with new laws authorizing the seizure of drug-infested properties, they are hiring goon squads and armed mercenaries to 'exterminate' crime in their tenements. [. . .]

Apart from these rent-a-thugs, the Inner City also spawns a vast cottage industry that manufacturers bars and grates for home protection. Indeed most of the bungalows in the inner ring now tend to resemble cages in a zoo. As in a George Romero movie, working-class families must now lock themselves in every night from the zombified city outside. One inadvertent consequence has been the terrifying frequency with which fires immolate entire families trapped helpless in their barred homes.

The *prison cell house* has many resonances in the landscape of the inner city. Before the Spring uprising most liquor stores, borrowing from the precedent of pawn-shops, had completely caged in the area behind the counter, with firearms discretely hidden at strategic locations. Even local greasy spoons were beginning to exchange hamburgers for money through bullet-proof acrylic turnstiles. Windowless concrete-block buildings, with rough surfaces exposed to deter graffiti, have spread across the streetscape like acne during the last decade. Now insurance companies may make such *riot-proof bunkers* virtually obligatory in the rebuilding of many districts.

Local intermediate and secondary schools, meanwhile, have become even more indistinguishable from jails. As per capita education spending has plummeted in Los Angeles, scarce resources have been absorbed in fortifying school grounds and hiring armed security police. Teenagers complain bitterly about overcrowded classrooms and demoralized teachers on decaying campuses that have become little more than daytime detention centers for an abandoned generation. The schoolyard, meanwhile, has become a killing field. [. . .]

Federally subsidized and public housing projects, for their part, are coming to resemble the infamous 'strategic hamlets' that were used to incarcerate the rural population of Vietnam. Although no L.A. housing project is yet as technologically sophisticated as Chicago's Cabrini-Green, where retinal scans (c.f., the opening sequence of *Blade Runner*) are used to check i.d.s, police exercise increasing control over freedom of movement. Like peasants in a rebel countryside, public housing residents of every age are stopped and searched at will, and their homes broken into without court warrants. [. . .]

In a city with the nation's worst housing shortage, project residents, fearful of eviction, are increasingly reluctant to claim any of their constitutional protections against unlawful search or seizure. Meanwhile national guidelines approved by Housing Secretary Jack Kemp (and almost certain to be continued in the Clinton administration) allow housing authorities to evict *families* of alleged drug-dealers or felons. This opens the door to a policy of *collective punishment* as practiced, for example, by the Israelis against Palestinian communities on the West Bank.

4. THE HALF-MOONS OF REPRESSION

In the original Burgess diagram, the 'half-moons' of ethnic enclaves ('Deutschland,' 'Little Sicily,' 'the Black Belt,' etc.) and specialized architectural ecologies ('residential hotels,' 'the two flat area,' etc.) cut across the 'dart board' of the city's fundamental socio-economic patterning. In contemporary metropolitan Los Angeles, a new species of special enclave is emerging in sympathetic synchronization to the militarization of the landscape. For want of a better generic appellation, we might call them 'social control districts' (SCDs). They merge the sanctions of the criminal or civil code with land-use planning to create what Michel Foucault would undoubtedly have recognized as further instances of the evolution of the 'disciplinary order' of the twentieth-century city.
[. . .]

Currently existing SCDs (simultaneously 'real and ideal') can be distinguished according to their juridical mode of spatial 'discipline.' *Abatement* districts, currently enforced against graffiti and prostitution in sign-posted areas of Los Angeles and West Hollywood, extend the traditional police power over nuisance (the legal fount of all zoning) from noxious industry to noxious behavior. Because they are self-financed by the fines collected or special sales taxes levied (on spray paints, for example), abatement districts allow homeowner or merchant groups to target intensified law enforcement against specific local social problems.

Enhancement districts, represented all over Southern California by the 'drug-free zones' surrounding public schools, add extra federal/state penalties or 'enhancements' to crimes committed within a specified radius of public institutions. *Containment* districts are designed to quarantine potentially epidemic social problems, ranging from the insect illegal immigrant, the Mediterranean fruit fly, to the ever increasing masses of homeless Angelenos. Although Downtown L.A.'s 'homeless containment zone' lacks the precise, if surreal, sign-posting of the state Department of Agriculture's 'Medfly Quarantine Zone,' it is nonetheless one of the most dramatic examples of a SCD. By city policy, the spillover of homeless encampments into surrounding council districts, or into the tonier precincts of the Downtown scanscape, is prevented by their 'containment' (official term) within the over-crowded Skid row area known as Central City East (or the 'Nickle' to its inhabitants). Although the recession-driven explosion in the homeless population has inexorably leaked street people into the alleys and vacant lots of nearby inner-ring neighborhoods, the LAPD maintains its pitiless policy of driving them back into the squalor of the Nickle.

The obverse strategy, of course, is the formal *exclusion* of the homeless and other pariah groups from public spaces. A spate of Southland cities, from Orange County to Santa Barbara, and even including the 'Peoples' Republic of Santa Monica,' recently have passed 'anti-camping' ordinances to banish the homeless from their sight. Meanwhile Los Angeles and Pomona are emulating the small city of San Fernando (Richie Valens' hometown) in banning gang members from parks. These 'Gang Free Parks' reinforce non-spatialized sanctions against gang membership (especially the recent Street Terrorism Enforcement and Prevention Act or STEP) as examples of 'status criminalization' where group membership, even in the absence of a specific criminal act, has been outlawed.

Status crime, by its very nature, involves projections of middle-class or conservative fantasies about the nature of the 'dangerous classes.' Thus in the 19th century the bourgeoisie crusaded against a largely phantasmagorical 'tramp menace,' and, in the 20th century, against a hallucinatory domestic 'red menace.' In the middle 1980s, however, the ghost of Cotton Mather suddenly reappeared in suburban Southern California. Allegations that local daycare centers were actually covens of satanic perversion wrenched us back to the seventeenth century and the Salem witch trials. In the course of the McMartin Preschool molestation case— ultimately the longest and most expensive such ordeal in American history—children testified about molester-teachers who flew around on broomsticks and other manifestations of the Evil One.

One legacy of the accompanying collective hysteria, which undoubtedly mined huge veins of displaced parental guilt, was the little city of San Dimas' creation of the nation's first 'child molestation exclusion zone.' This Twin-Peaks-like suburb in the eastern San Gabriel Valley was sign-posted from stem to stern with the warning: 'Hands Off! Our children are photographed and fingerprinted for their own protection.' I don't know if the armies of lurking pedophiles in the mountains above San Dimas were actually deterred by these warnings, but any mapping of contemporary urban space must acknowledge the existence of such dark, Lynchian zones where the *social imaginary* discharges its fantasies.

Meanwhile, post-riot Southern California seems on the verge of creating yet more SCDs. On the one hand, the arrival of the federal 'Weed and Seed' program,

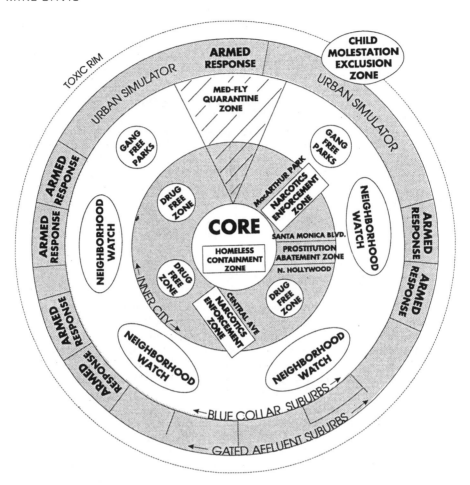

The ecology of fear

linking community development funds to anti-gang repression, provides a new set of incentives for neighborhoods to adopt exclusion and/or enhancement strategies. As many activists have warned, 'Weed and Seed' is like a police-state caricature of the 1960s War on Poverty, with the Justice Dept. transformed into the manager of urban redevelopment. The poor will be forced to cooperate with their own criminalization as a precondition for urban aid. On the other hand, emerging technologies may give conservatives, and probably neo-liberals as well, a real opportunity to test cost-saving proposals for *community imprisonment* as an alternative to expensive pro-grams of prison construction. Led by Heritage Institute ideologue Charles Murray—whose polemic against social spending for the poor, *Losing Ground* (1984), was the most potent manifesto of the Reagan era—conservative theorists are exploring the practicalities of the *carceral city* depicted in sci-fi fantasies like *Escape from New York* [. . .].

Murray's concept, [. . .] is that 'drug free zones for the majority' may require social-refuse heaps for the criminalized minority. 'If the result of implementing these policies [landlords' and employers' unrestricted right to discriminate in the selection of tenants and workers] is to concentrate the bad apples into a few hyper-violent, antisocial neighborhoods, so be it.' But how will the underclass be effectively confined to its own 'hyper-violent' super-SCDs and kept out of the drug-free shangri-las of the overclass?

One possibility is the systematic establishment of discrete *security gateways* that will use some bio-metric criterion, universally registered, to screen crowds and bypassers. [. . .]

Another emerging technology is the police utilization of LANDSAT satellites linked to Geographical Information Systems (GIS). Almost certainly by the end of the decade the largest U.S. metropolitan areas, including Los Angeles, will be using geosynchronous LANDSAT systems to manage traffic congestion and oversee physical planning. The same LANDSAT-GIS capability can be cost-shared and time-shared with police departments to surveil the movements of tens of thousands of electronically tagged individuals and their automobiles.

Although such monitoring is immediately intended to safeguard expensive sports cars and other toys of the rich, it will be entirely possible to use the same technology to pull the equivalent of an electronic handcuff on the activities of entire urban social strata. Drug offenders and gang members can be 'bar-coded' and paroled to the omniscient scrutiny of a satellite that will track their 24-hour itineraries and automatically sound an alarm if they stray outside the borders of their *surveillance district*. With such powerful Orwellian technologies for social control, community confinement and the confinement of communities may ultimately mean the same thing.

5. THE NEIGHBORS ARE WATCHING

[. . .]

The Neighborhood Watch program, comprising more than 5,500 crime-surveillance block clubs from San Pedro to Sylmar, is the LAPD's most important innovation in urban policing. Throughout what Burgess called the 'Zone of Workingmen's Homes,' which in Los Angeles comprises the owner-occupied neighborhoods of the central city as well as older blue-collar suburbs in the San Fernando and San Gabriel valleys, a huge network of watchful neighbors provides a security system that is midway between the besieged, gun-toting anomie of the inner ring and the private police forces of more affluent, gated suburbs.

Neighborhood Watch, now emulated by hundreds of North American and even European cities, from Rosemead to London, was the brainchild of former police chief Ed Davis. In the aftermath of the 1965–71 cycle of unrest in Southcentral and East L.A., Davis envisioned the program as the anchor of a larger 'Basic Car' strategy designed to rebuild community support for the LAPD by establishing a territorial identity between patrol units and neighborhoods. [. . .]

According to LAPD spokesperson Sgt. Christopher West,

Neighborhood Watch block clubs are intended to increase local solidarity and self-confidence in the face of crime. Spurred by their block captains, neighbors become more vigilant in the protection of each other's property and well-being. Suspicious behavior is immediately reported and home-owners meet regularly with patrol officers to plan crime prevention tactics.

An off-duty officer in a Winchell's Donut Shop was more picturesque. 'Neighbour-hood Watch is supposed to work like a wagon train in an old-fashioned cowboy movie. The neighbors are the settlers, and the goal is to get them to circle their wagons and fight off the Indians until the cavalry—that is to say, the LAPD—can ride to their rescue.'

Needless to say, this Wild West analogy has its dark sides. Who, for example, gets to decide what behavior is 'suspicious' or who looks like an 'Indian'? The obvious danger in any program that conscripts thousands of citizens to become police informers under the official slogan 'Be on the Look Out for Strangers' is that it inevitably stigmatizes innocent groups. Inner-city teenagers are especially vulnerable to this flagrant stereotyping and harassment.

[. . .]

Critics also worry that Neighborhood Watch does double-duty as a captive constituency for partisan politics. As Sergeant West acknowledged, 'block captains are appointed by patrol officers and the program does obviously tend to attract the most pro-police elements of the population.' These pro-police activists, moreover, tend to be demographically or culturally unrepresentative of their neighborhoods. In poor, young Latino areas, Watch captains are frequently elderly, residual Anglos. In areas where renters are a majority, the pro-police activists are typically homeowners or landlords. [. . .]

6. MINI-CITADELS AND GERONCRATS

When I first began to study gated communities in Southern California in the mid-1980s, it was a trend largely confined to very wealthy neighborhoods or new developments on the distant metropolitan frontier (e.g., the areas Burgess described as the 'restricted residential district' or the 'commuter zone'). Since the Spring 1992 rebellion, however, dozens of ordinary residential neighborhoods in Los Angeles have demanded the right to gate themselves off from the rest of the city. As one newspaper put it, 'The 1980s had their boom in mini-malls; the 1990s may bring a bull market in mini-citadels.'

Although crime and safety are the ostensible issues, increased equity may be the deeper motive. Some realtors have estimated that 'gatedness' can raise home values by as much as 40 percent over ten years. As communities—including black middle-class areas like Windsor Village and Baldwin Hills Estates—race to reap this windfall, Burgess' 'Residential Zone IV' begins to look like a fortified honeycomb, with each residential neighborhood now encased in its own walled cell. In most cases, the local homeowners' associations also contract 'armed response' private policing from one of the several multi-national security firms that specialize in residential security. Obviously this only further widens the 'security differential' between the inner city and the suburbs.

'Empty-nest' households are especially passionate advocates of restricted-access neighborhoods, and there is an important sense in which Los Angeles is not merely being polarized between rich and poor, but more specifically between the young poor and the old rich. Furthermore, the 1990 Census showed that metropolitan Los Angeles has the greatest discrepancy in the nation between household size and home size. On the Westside and Hollywood Hills, where 'mansionization' has been in vogue, older, smaller Anglo households occupy ever bigger homes, while in the rest of the city large Latino families are being crammed into diminishing floor-space.

California as a whole is an incipient gerontocracy, and any post-*Blade-Runner* dystopia must take account of the explosive fusion of class, ethnic and generational contradictions. [. . .]

7. PARALLEL UNIVERSES

Burgess and his students, who took 1920s Chicago as a vast research laboratory, never had any doubts about the 'raw reality' of the phenomena that they were systematically studying. Empirical method was matched to empirical reality. The image or mythography of the city did not intervene as a significant stratum in its own right. Nor did the Chicago School pay any attention to the critical role of the Columbian Exposition as an ideal-type for the city's planned development. Although the 1892 and 1933 Chicago World's Fairs were theme parks *avant l'lettre*, urban sociology could not yet make conceptual space for the city as *simulation*.

Today there is no way around the problem. The contemporary city simulates or hallucinates itself in at least two decisive senses. First, in the age of electronic culture and economy, the city redoubles itself through the complex architecture of its information and media networks. [. . .]

If so, *urban cyberspace*—as the simulation of the city's information order—will be experienced as even more segregated, and devoid of true public space, than the traditional built city. Southcentral L.A., for instance, is a data and media black hole, without local cable programming or links to major data systems. Just as it became a housing/jobs ghetto in the early twentieth century industrial city, it is now evolving into an *electronic ghetto* within the emerging *information city*.

Secondly, social fantasy is increasingly embodied in simulacral landscapes—theme parks, 'historic' districts and malls—that are partitioned off from the rest of the metropolis. All the post-modern philosopher kings (Baudrillard, Eco, etc), of course, agree that Los Angeles is the world capital of 'hyper-reality.' Traditionally its major theme parks have been primarily architectural simulations of the movies or television. [. . .]

Today, however, the city itself—or rather its idealization—has become the subject of simulation. With the recent decline of the military aerospace industry in Southern California, the tourism/hotel/entertainment sector has become the single largest regional employer. But tourists are increasingly reluctant to venture into the perceived dangers of Los Angeles' 'urban jungle.' [. . .]

MCA and Disney believe the solution is to recreate vital bits of the city within the secure confines of fortress hotels and walled theme parks. As a result, *artificial Los Angeles* is gradually coming into being. In essence, it is an archipelago of well-guarded corporate cashpoints where affluent tourists can relax, spend lots of money, and have 'fun' again. A largely invisible army of low-wage service workers, who themselves live in virtual bantustans like the Santa Ana barrio (Disneyland) or Lennox (LAX) *barrios*, keep the machinery of simulation running smoothly. [. . .]

8. HOLLYWOOD(S): POWERS OF SIMULATION

[. . .]

The HOLLYWOOD in the imagination of the world's movie public, therefore, was kept tenuously anchored to its namesake location by regular rituals (premieres, the Academy Awards, etc.) and the magical investment of a dozen or so places (the Bowl, Graumann's, etc.) as tourist shrines. But over the last generation, as the real Hollywood has become a hyper-violent slum, the rituals have ceased and the magic has waned. As the linkages between historic signifier and its signified decayed, the opportunity arose to resurrect HOLLYWOOD in a safer neighborhood. Thus in Orlando, Disney created a stunning Art Deco mirage of MGM's golden age, while arch-competitor MCA countered with its own idealized versions of Hollywood Boulevard and Rodeo Drive at Universal Studios Florida.

Meanwhile, the elopement of Disney and HOLLYWOOD to Florida further depressed real-estate back in real-time Hollywood. After bitter battles with local home-owners, the major landowners were able to win city authorization for a $1 billion facelift of Hollywood Boulevard. In their scheme, the Boulevard would be transformed into a gated, linear theme park, anchored by mega-entertainment complexes at each end. But while the redevelopers were still negotiating with potential investors, MCA pulled the rug out from under Hollywood Redux with the announcement that its nearby tax-dodge enclave, Universal City, would construct a parallel urban reality called 'CityWalk.'

Designed by master illusionist Jon Jerde, CityWalk is an 'idealized reality,' the best features of Olvera Street, Hollywood and the West side synthesized in 'easy, bite-sized pieces' for consumption by tourists and residents who 'don't need the excitement of dodging bullets . . . in the Third World country' that Los Angeles has become. [. . .]

Hollywood redevelopers immediately responded to construction of CityWalk with a $4.3 million beautification plan that includes paving Hollywood Blvd. with 'glitz' made from recycled glass. But even spruced up and glitzified there is almost no way that the old Boulevard can compete with the hyper-real perfection on Universal's hill. As its MCA proprietors have taken pains to emphasize, CityWalk is 'not a mall' but a 'revolution in urban design . . . a new kind of neighborhood'—an urban simulator. Indeed, some critics wonder if it isn't the moral equivalent of the neutron bomb: the city emptied of all lived human experience. With its fake fossil candy wrappers and other deceits, CityWalk sneeringly mocks us as it erases any trace of our real joy, pain or labor.

9. THE TOXIC RIM

Where does the nightmare end? Burgess was not greatly interested in urban boundaries. His Chicago dart board simply fades into the 'commuter zone' and, beyond, into the Corn Belt. The city limits of Dystopia, however, are an intrinsically fascinating problem. In *Blade Runner*, it will be recalled, the dark megalopolis improbably yielded, at its outer edge, to Ecotopia—evergreen forests and boundless wilderness.

No such happy ending will be possible in the coming Los Angeles of 2019. Post-modern geographer Edward Soja has observed that Southern California is already bounded, along an almost unbroken desert perimeter, by huge military air bases, bombing ranges and desert warfare reservations. Now a second, equally ominous circumference clearly is being drawn around this pentagon desert. Choking on its own wastes, with its landfills overflowing and its coastal waters polluted, Los Angeles is preparing to export its garbage and hazardous land-uses to the Eastern Mojave and Baja California. Instead of reducing its production of dangerous waste, the city is simply planning to 'regionalize' their disposal.

This emergent *Toxic Rim* includes giant landfills at Eagle Mountain (the former Kaiser open-pit iron mine) and possibly near Adelanto (defunct Air Force base), the controversial radioactive waste dump in Ward Valley near Needles, and the relo-cation of such polluting industries as furniture manufacture and metal-plating to Tijuana's *maquiladora* belt. The environmental consequences may be almost catastrophic.

The proposed 300,000 barrels of nuclear waste, for example, in the unlined trenches of the Ward Valley nuclear dump will remain lethal for 10,000 years. They will pose the perennial risk of leaking radioactive tritium into the nearby Colorado River, thereby poisoning the irreplaceable water source for much of southern California. For its part, the immense landfill at Eagle Mountain—2.5 miles long, 1 mile wide, and 2,000 feet deep—will not only contaminate the water table but also create a toxic shroud of air pollution over much of eastern Riverside County. Meanwhile, the flight of hazardous industries across the Border, eventually including a large segment of Los Angeles' petrochemical production, will increase the possibility of Bhopal-like catastrophes.

In sum, the formation of this waste-belt will accelerate the environmental degradation of the entire American West (and part of Mexico). Today a third of the trees in Southern California's mountains already have been suffocated by smog, and animal species are rapidly dying off throughout the polluted Mojave Desert. Tomorrow, Los Angeles' radioactive and carcinogenic wastes may be killing life as far away as Utah or Sonora. The Toxic Rim will be a zone of extinction.

10. BEFORE WE WAKE . . .

Finally, leaving behind all the Burgessian diagrams and analogies, what will be the real fate of Los Angeles? Can emergent technologies of surveillance and repression stabilize class and racial relations across the chasm of the new inequality? Will the ecology of fear become the natural order of the 21st-century American city? Will razor-wire and security cameras someday be as sentimentally redolent of suburban life as white-picket fences and dogs named Spot?

A global perspective may be useful. Los Angeles in 2019 will be the core of a metro-galaxy of 22–24 million people in Southern and Baja Californias. Together with Tokyo, Sao Paulo, Mexico City, and Shanghai, it will comprise a new evolutionary form: mega-cities of 20–30 million inhabitants. It is important to emphasize that we are not merely talking about larger specimens of an old, familiar type, but an absolutely original, and unexpected, phyla of social life.

No one knows, in fact, whether physical and biological systems of this magnitude and complexity are actually sustainable. Many experts believe that the Third World mega-cities, at least, will eventually precipitate environmental holocausts and/or implode in urban .civil wars. Indeed, the contemporary 'New World Order' certainly offers enough grim examples of total societal disintegration—from Bosnia to Somalia—to underscore realistic fears of a mega-city apocalypse.

If Tokyo proves an exception, despite inevitable natural disasters, it will only be by dint of extraordinary levels of public investment, private affluence and social discipline (and because Japan is culturally a highly urban rather than suburban society). In the recent past, however, Los Angeles has begun to resemble Sao Paulo and Mexico City more than post-modern Tokyo-Yokohama.

It may be theoretically possible, of course, for a Democratic administration in Washington over the next decade to being to reverse American urban decay with massive new public works. But it will remain extraordinarily difficult to secure Congressional support for reinvestment to the Bos-Wash and Southern California urban cores as long as the Reagan-era deficit remains the dominant issue in domestic politics. Indeed the principal legacy of the Perot movement—the most successful electoral insurgency in 75 years—may be precisely the fiscal Gordian knot it has managed to tie around any resolution of the urban crisis.

If hopes of urban reform, now guardedly raised by the Clinton landslide, are once again dashed, it will only accelerate the dystopic tendencies described in this pamphlet. For in the specific case of Los Angeles, where recession has already wiped out a fifth of the region's manufacturing jobs, there is little private-sector help in sight. Even the most traditionally optimistic business-school econometric models now predict a 'Texas-style' regional slump lasting until 1997, while forecasters at the Southern California Association of Governments talk about steady-state unemployment rates of 10–12 percent for the next *twenty years*.

As the golden dream withers, so also may faith in non-violent social reform. If last year's riots set a precedent, anomic neighborhood violence may begin to be transmuted into more organized political violence. Both cops and gangmembers already talk with chilling matter-of-factness about the inevitability of some manner of urban guerrilla warfare. And in spite of all the new residential walls and scanscapes—even the future police eye in the sky—sprawling Los Angeles is a metropolis uniquely vulnerable to strategic sabotage.

As the examples of Belfast, Beirut and, more recently, Palermo and Lima have demonstrated, the car bomb is the weapon of anonymous urban terror *par excellence* (or, as one counter-insurgency expert once put it, 'the poor man's substitute for an airforce'). Car bombs have reduced half of Beirut to debris, wiped out a neighborhood known as 'Lima's Beverly Hills,' and massacred Italy's most heavily guarded public officials.

If the British Army, uniquely, was finally able to prevent car bombers from entering Belfast, it was only after years of effort and the construction of an immense security cage around the entire city center. A comparable preventative effort in Los Angeles—e.g. closing the freeways and heavily fortifying all the public utilities, oil refineries and pipelines, and commercial centers—would not only cost tens of billions but also dissolve the city as a functioning entity.

The Los Angeles freeway system, in effect, guarantees to the future urban terrorist what the tropical rainforest or Andean Peak offers to the rural *guerrillero*: ideal terrain.

If we continue to allow our central cities to degenerate into criminalized Third Worlds, all the ingenious security technology, present and future, will not safeguard the anxious middle class. The sound of that first car bomb on Rodeo Drive or in front of City Hall will wake us from our mere bad dream and confront us with our real nightmare.

47

Human rights and crimes of the state: The culture of denial

Stanley Cohen

[. . .]
It would be ludicrous to claim that Western criminology over the past decades has completely ignored the subject of state crime or the broader discourse of human rights. [. . .] [T]he subject has often been raised and then its implications conveniently repressed. This is a process strangely reminiscent of my substantive interest in the sociology of denial: how information is known but its implications are not acknowledged.

The first significant confrontation with the subject came in the early phase of radical criminology in the late 1960s. That favourite debate of the times – 'who are the *real* criminals?' – naturally turned attention from street crime to white-collar/ corporate crime and then to the wider notion of 'crimes of the powerful'. The particular context of the Vietnam War, pushed our slogans ('Hey, hey LBJ! How many kids have you killed today?') explicitly in the direction of 'crimes of the state'.

In criminology, this sentiment was expressed in the much cited paper by the Schwendingers (1970) entitled 'Defenders of order or guardians of human rights?'. Looking back at this text, it appears a missed opportunity to deal with the core issues of state crime.

Quite rightly, the Schwendingers saw themselves going in the same direction, but a step further than Sutherland by invoking the criterion of *social injury* to define crime. In the case of white-collar crime, this mandated us to go beyond criminal law into the areas of civil and administrative law. The Schwendingers then noted that if Sutherland had consistently followed what they rightly call his 'ethical' rather than legal categorization, he should also have arrived at those other socially injurious actions which are not defined as either criminal or civil law violations. So far, so good. But their argument then goes awry.

First, they cite as examples of other socially injurious action (their only examples) 'genocide and economic exploitation'. Now, besides the fact that these are

From *Australian and New Zealand Journal of Criminology*, 1993, 26(2): 97–115.

hardly morally equivalent categories, genocide is crucially different from economic exploitation. It is recognized in current political discourse as crime by the state; it is clearly illegal by internal state laws; and since the Nuremberg Judgements and the 1948 UN Convention Against Genocide, it is a 'crime' according to international law. Genocide belongs to the same conceptual universe as 'war crimes' and 'crimes against humanity'. By any known criteria, genocide is more self-evidently criminal than economic exploitation.

The Schwendingers make no such distinctions nor try to establish the criminality of human rights violations. Instead they launch into a moral crusade against imperialistic war, racism, sexism and economic exploitation. We might agree with their ideology and we might even use the term 'crime' rhetorically to describe racism, sexism and economic exploitation. This type of 1960s rhetoric indeed anticipates the current third and fourth generation 'social rights'. A more restricted and literal use of the concept 'state crime', however, is both more defensible and useful. If we come from the discourse of human rights, this covers what is known in the jargon (for once, not euphemistic) as 'gross' violations of human rights – genocide, mass political killings, state terrorism, torture, disappearances. If we come from the discourse of criminology, we are talking about clear criminal offences – murder, rape, espionage, kidnapping, assault.

I don't want to get into definitional quibbles. Enough to say that the extension of criminology into the terrain of state crimes can be justified without our object of study becoming simply everything we might not like at the time. Let us see what happened after that mid-1960s to mid-1970s phase when questions about state crimes and human rights were placed on the criminological agenda by the radicals.

What mostly happened was that the human rights connection became lost. In the discourse of critical criminology, the putative connection between crime and politics took two different directions, both quite removed from the idea of state crime.

The first was the short-lived notion of the criminal as proto-revolutionary actor and the extension of this to all forms of deviance. This whole enterprise – referred to as the 'politicization of deviance' – was soon abandoned and eventually denounced as naive, romantic and sentimental. The second connection – which turned out the more productive – was the focus on the criminalizing power of the state. This led to the whole revisionist discourse on the sociology of law, social control and punishment that has remained so salient and powerful.

But neither direction leads anywhere near towards talking about state crimes. The subject simply faded away from criminological view in the mid-1970s to mid-1980s. By the time left realist criminology appeared, we [had moved] entirely from 'crimes of the state' back to the 'state of crime'. Today, the subject has re-appeared from two contexts, one *external* to the discipline, the other *internal*.

The *external* context is the incremental growth of the international human rights movement itself. Emerging from the United Nations Charter and the great declarations and conventions of the next decade, from international governmental organizations such as UNESCO and the Council of Europe, from fledgling pressure groups such as Amnesty International to the vast current list of national and international non-governmental organizations, the human rights movement has become a major institutional force. Pushed by the rhetorical use of 'human rights' by the Carter Administration about Latin America and its critique of the Soviet Union, the ideal of human rights took on a powerful life of its own. It has become a secular religion.

This discourse, of course, is very dense, complex and contradictory [. . .] 'Human Rights' has become a slogan raised from most extraordinary different directions. Progressive forces and organizations like Amnesty can enlist famous rock stars to perform in defence of international human rights. Right wing pressure groups in the USA can unseat politicians and defeat Supreme Court nominations by invoking the human rights of the unborn foetus. Civil liberties groups defend pornography on the grounds of freedom of speech and the women's movement attacks this freedom as an assault on the human rights of women. Nations with the most appalling record of state violence and terror can self-righteously join together in the UN to condemn other nations for their human rights violations. Some human rights activists are awarded the Nobel Peace Prize, others are jailed, tortured, have disappeared or been assassinated. The human rights of one group are held sacred, the rights of another totally ignored . . . and so on.

But whatever the concept of human rights means, it has become a dominant narrative. Arguably, with the so-called death of the old meta-narratives of Marxism, liberalism and the Cold War, human rights will become *the* normative political language of the future. I have no time to go into its conceptual ambiguities – the difference between civil and human rights, the relationship between political and human rights work, the tension between universalism and cultural relativism. Nor can I raise the numerous policy issues of policing, enforcement and international law. One of the most salient issues for criminologists, raised dramatically by the current horrors in the former Yugoslavia, is the long-proposed establishment of an international criminal tribunal.

So this is one way – from the outside – that criminologists as citizens who read the news, must have become aware of the subject of human rights violations and crimes of the state. Not that you know about this awareness if you just read criminological texts. There is, however, one *internal* way in which the subject has been registered in criminology. This is through the growth of victimology.

There are many obvious echoes of human rights issues in victimological literature – whether in the feminist debate about female victims of male sexualized violence; in talking about children and children's rights; in the concern about victims of corporate crime, ecological abuse, etc. Some students (Karmen, 1990) find these echoes only in 'radical' rather than 'conservative' or 'liberal' victimology. The conservative tendency is concerned with victims of street crime, making offenders accountable, encouraging self reliance and advocating retributive justice. The liberal tendency includes white-collar crime, is concerned with making the victim 'whole' and advocates restitution and reconciliation. Only the radical tendency extends to all forms of human suffering and sees law and the criminal justice system as implicated in this suffering.

This distinction, though, between conservative, liberal and radical tendencies, is not always clear. And in the context of one crucial subject – what happens to state criminals such as torturers after democratization or a change in regime – the distinction breaks down altogether. Here, it is the 'radicals' who call for punishment and retributive justice, while it is the 'conservatives' who invoke ideals such as reconciliation to call for impunity.

In any event, these external and internal inputs are slowly making their way into criminology. In the mainstream, this can be seen in recent standard textbooks which explicitly deal with the subject of state crime, and others which consider the human rights definition of crime.

In the radical stream, there is Barak's recent (1991) volume *Crimes By the Capitalist State*. The editor makes a strong case for including state criminality in the field of criminology – both on the grounds that the consequences of state crimes are more widespread and destructive than traditional crime and because this would be a logical extension of the already accepted move into the field of white-collar crime. The overall tone of the volume, though, is too redolent of the 1960s debates: general ideas about discrimination and abuse of political and economic power, the focus only on capitalism and the disproportionate attention on worldwide low intensity warfare by the USA (CIA, counter-insurgency etc.).

Despite this recent interest, major gaps in the criminological discourse remain.

(a) First, there is little understanding that a major source of criminalization at national and international levels draws on the rhetoric of human rights. Significant waves of moral enterprise and criminalization over the last decade are derived not from the old middle-class morality, the Protestant ethic nor the interests of corporate capitalism, but from the feminist, ecological and human rights movements. A major part of criminology is supposed to be the study of law making – criminalization – but we pay little attention to the driving force behind so many new laws: the demand for protection from 'abuses of power'. The radical slogans of the 1960s have become the commonplace of any government and inter-government forum. Alongside our standard research on domestic legislatures and ministries of justice, we should see what our foreign ministries are doing – at the Council of Europe, the United Nations, etc.

(b) Another important defect in recent literature is its American focus. It is pre-occupied with 'exposures' – of the CIA (e.g. drug running in Vietnam), FBI surveillance methods, the global drug wars, international arms dealing, etc. This results in a certain ethnocentrism, but also allows the derivative subjects (political economy, globalization, state propaganda, illegal clandestine operations, counter-intelligence) to be denied as being 'normal politics' (like the white-collar crime issue allowed the denial of 'normal business'). For my purposes here, I want to stress not the politicality of the subject but its criminality. For this, we don't need theories of the state, we need merely to pick up the latest Amnesty Annual Report.

(c) If we have missed something about law making, we have ignored even more the facts of victimization. Again, there is a ritualistic acknowledgement of the damage, harm and violence that are the obvious consequences of state crime – and then we return to easier topics. It is as if we don't want to face these facts; as if – to anticipate the substance of the second part of [this chapter] – we have denied their implications. I am aware that phrases such as 'crimes of the twentieth century' sound bombastic – but for vast populations of the world, this is a fair characterization of those 'gross violations of human rights': genocide, mass political killings, disappearances, torture, rape by agents of state.

This terrible record is known but (as I will show) simultaneously not known. Take genocides and mass political killings only: the Turkish genocide of at least a million Armenians; the Holocaust against six million Jews and the hundreds of thousands of political opponents, gypsies and others; the millions killed under

Stalin's regime; the tribal and religious massacres in Burundi, Bengal and Paraguay; the mass political killings in East Timor and Uganda; the 'autogenocide' in Cambodia; the 'ethnic cleansing' in Bosnia; the death squads and disappearances in Argentina, Guatemala, El Salvador. Or take torture – a practice supposedly eradicated from Europe by the beginning of the nineteenth century and now routinely used in two-thirds of the world.

To add up the deaths, injuries and destruction from all these sources and then compare this to the cumulative results of homicide, assault, property crime and sexual crime in even the highest crime countries of the world, is too tendentious an exercise, too insulting to the intelligence. One cannot calibrate human suffering in this way.

But criminologists do, after all, talk about offence 'seriousness'. The standard literature in this area – and allied debates on culpability, harm, responsibility and the 'just deserts' model – already compares street crime with white-collar crime. A current important contribution (von Hirsch and Jareborg, 1991) tries to gauge criminal harm by using a 'living-standard analysis'. Von Hirsch and his colleague have argued ingeniously that criminal acts can be ranked by a complicated scale of 'degrees of intrusion' on different kinds of legally protected interests: physical integrity; material support and amenity; freedom from humiliation; privacy and autonomy.

What von Hirsch calls 'interests' are strikingly close to what are also called 'human rights'. His examples, however, come only from the standard criminological terrain of citizen against citizen. Including corporate crime would extend the list to (business) organizations against citizen. This is certainly an interesting and worthwhile exercise. It allows, for example, the ranking of forcible rape by a stranger as very grave because this is so demeaning and gross an attack against the 'freedom from humiliation' interest; therefore rape at gun point becomes more serious than armed robbery; date rape comes lower on the cumulative scale on grounds that threat to bodily safety is eliminated, and so on.

But neither crimes of state nor the wider category of 'political crime' are mentioned. There is no logical reason why the identity of the offender should be assumed to be fixed as citizen against citizen, rather than state agent against citizen when talking about, say, murder, assault or rape. In fact, there are good *moral* reasons why any grading of seriousness should take this into account – in particular, the fact that the very agent responsible for upholding law, is actually responsible for the crime. And there is a good *empirical* reason: that for large parts of the world's population, state agents (or paramilitary groups, vigilantes or terrorists) are the normal violators of your 'legally protected interests'.

I don't want to oversimplify the many conceptual objections and obstacles that criminologists will legitimately raise to my glib appeal to include state crime in our frame of reference. Most such objections fall under two categories.

First, there are the equivalent arguments to those used in the field of corporate crime – that the state is not an actor and that individual criminal responsibility cannot be identified. For corporate crime, this objection has been disposed of often enough, most recently (and to my mind convincingly) by Braithwaite and Fisse (1990). The corporation engages in rational goal-seeking behaviour; it can act; it can have intentions; it can commit crimes. This is just as (though more complicatedly) true for the state.

The second objection (again paralleled from Sutherland onwards in the case of corporate crime) is that the resultant action is not 'really' crime. Here, the counter-arguments are complicated and come from a number of different directions: (i) an appeal to international law and conventions on such concepts as 'war crimes' or 'crimes against humanity'; (ii) a demonstration that these acts are illegal by domestic criminal law and fit all criteria of 'crime'; (iii) and even if the acts in question are legal by internal state jurisdiction, then the question arises of how this legal legitimation occurs. We have to remember (perhaps by inscribing this on our consciousness each morning) that state crimes are not just the unlicensed terror of totalitarian or fascist regimes, police states, dictatorships or military juntas. And in even the most extreme of these regimes, such as Nazi Germany, the discourse of legality is used (Muller, 1991).

One of the clearest and most eloquent texts for understanding these symbiotic issues of responsibility and criminality, is the 1985 trial in Argentina of the former military junta members responsible for the mass killings, atrocities, disappearances of the 'dirty war'. Reports of this trial (e.g. by Amnesty International) should be on all criminology reading lists.

The reasons why we don't make these connections are less logical than epistemological. The political discourse of the atrocity is, as I will soon show, designed to hide its presence from awareness. This is not a matter of secrecy, in the sense of lack of access to information, but an unwillingness to confront anomalous or disturbing information. Take the example of torture. Democratic-type societies – the French in Algeria (Maran, 1989); the British in Northern Ireland; the Israelis in the Occupied Territories (Cohen, 1991) – could all proclaim their adherence to international conventions and domestic laws against torture. This called for a complex discourse of denial that what they were doing constituted torture. No, it was something else, 'special procedures' or 'moderate physical pressure'. So something happened – but it was not illegal. In more totalitarian societies (with no accountability, no free press, no independent judiciary) denial is simpler – you do it, but say you do not. Nothing happened.

The standard vocabulary of official (government) denial weaves its way – at times simultaneously, at times sequentially – through a complete spiral of denial. First you try 'it didn't happen'. There was no massacre, no one was tortured. But then the media, human rights organizations and victims show that it does happen: here are the graves; we have the photos; look at the autopsy reports. So you have to say that what happened was not what it looks to be but really something else: a 'transfer of population', 'collateral damage', 'self-defence'. And then – the crucial subtext – what happened anyway was completely justified – protecting national security, part of the war against terrorism. So:

- It doesn't happen here.
- If it does, 'it' is something else.
- Even if it is what you say it is, it is justified.

Faced with this spiral of denial, criminologists may not be expected to respond very differently from ordinary citizens. But the debate is only a little more complex and dramatic than debates about whether white-collar crime is really crime. I say more 'dramatic' because we are forced back not just to questions about what is normal business, but what is the normal state. Take, for example, the question of jurisdiction and punishment. Precisely because we expect so little from domestic and international law as sanctions against gross state crimes (against our own or other citizens), we seldom frame human rights violations in criminal terms. Talking about the limitations in the 1948 UN Convention Against Genocide and in the UN Charter itself, the anthropologist Leo Kuper remarks with characteristic irony that an unstated assumption of the international discourse is that:

> the sovereign territorial state claims, as an integral part of its sovereignty, the right to commit genocide or engage in genocidal massacres against people under its rule, and that the United Nations for all practical purposes, defends this right. (Kuper, 1981: 161)

Obviously, this is very complex territory – more complex that I can even hint at here – and it is understandable why mainstream criminology is reluctant to become too immersed in these debates. Their absence in 'left realist' criminology is stranger to explain. After all, the ontological base here is a realist philosophy which starts with harm, victimization, seriousness, suffering and supposed indifference to all this by the adolescent left idealism of the 1960s.

I will return to some possible explanations for this blindsight. On one level, this is nothing more sinister than a Western ethnocentrism preoccupied with its own national concerns and secure in the great achievement of liberal capitalism; the separation of crime from the state. On another more interesting level, this stems from the universal tendency to see only what is convenient to see.

THE CULTURE OF DENIAL

Let me now turn to my substantive topic – denial. How did I get to this subject?

During the decade in which I have lived in Israel, but especially the past five years of the *intifada* (the uprising of Palestinians in the Occupied Territories), I have been puzzled by the apparent lack of overt reaction (dissent, criticism, protest) in just those sectors of Israeli society [which] one would expect to be reacting more. In the face of clear information about what's going on – escalating levels of violence and repression, beatings, torture, daily humiliations, collective punishment (curfews, house demolition, deportations), death-squad-type killings by army undercover units – the level of shame, outrage and protest is not psychologically or morally appropriate.

Of course there are no objective scales of psychological or moral 'appropriateness'. But many observers, inside and outside the country, have sensed that this part of the public should find [things] more disturbing and be prepared to act accordingly.

Remember that I am talking not about that clear majority of the population who support these measures and would not object to even more severe repression. My object of study is the minority: the enlightened, educated middle class, responsive to messages of peace and co-existence, first to condemn human rights violations everywhere else in the world.

Note that unlike most societies where gross human rights violations occur, the facts are both private and public knowledge. Nearly everyone has direct personal knowledge, especially from army service. These are not conscripts or mercenary soldiers drawn from the underclass; everybody serves (including the middle class liberals) or has a husband, son, cousin or neighbour in reserve duty. There is a relatively open press, liberal in tone, which regularly and clearly exposes what is happening in the Occupied Territories. No one – least of all the group which interests me – can say those terrible (though, as I will show, complicated) words 'I didn't know'.

It is way beyond my scope to discuss the special reasons in Israel for denial, passivity or indifference. These are part of a complex political history – of being Jewish, of Zionism, of fear and insecurity. I mention this case only because it led me to comparisons, to looking for similarities and differences in other societies. I went back to my experience of growing up in apartheid South Africa. More fatefully, I turned to the emblematic events of this century: the Holocaust 'texts' about the good Germans who knew what was happening; the lawyers and doctors who colluded; the ordinary people who passed by the concentration camps every day and claimed not to know what was happening; the politicians in Europe and America who did not believe what they were told. Then from this one historical event, I went to the contemporary horrors reported every day in the mass media and documented by human rights reports – about Bosnia, Peru, Guatemala, Burma, Uganda . . .

All this – and the relevant social scientific literature – led me back to versions of the same universal question. This is not Milgram's famous question of how ordinary people will behave in terrible ways, but rather how ordinary, even good people, will not react appropriately to knowledge of the terrible. Why, when faced by knowledge of others' suffering and pain – particularly the suffering and pain resulting from what are called 'human rights violations' – does 'reaction' so often take the form of denial, avoidance, passivity, indifference, rationalization or collusion?

I have mentioned the official state discourse: the pure denials (it didn't happen, they are lying, the media are biased, the world community is just picking on us) and the pure justifications (deterrence, self-defence, national security, ideology, information gathering). But my concern is not the actor but rather (back, in a curious way, to labelling theory!) the audience. In the triangle of human suffering so familiar to criminologists – the victim, to whom things are done; the perpetrator, who is actively causing the suffering; the observer who sees and knows – my interest lies in this third corner: the audience, the observers, the bystanders.

For my purposes here, I want to consider a specific group of observers – not those whose avoidance derives from (crudely speaking) their *support* for the action. If they see nothing morally wrong or emotionally disturbing in what is happening, why should they do anything? In this sense, their denial or passivity is 'easy' to explain. My interest is more in the subgroup who are ideologically predisposed to be against what is happening, to be disturbed by what they know. How do they react to their knowledge of the terrible?

Before presenting some lines of enquiry into this subject, let me note an important distinction which I won't have time to follow through. In talking about the denial of atrocities or human rights violations, there is a world of difference between reacting to your own government's actions as distinct from what might be happening in a distant country. My response, say, as an Australian, to newspaper revelations about the treatment of Aborigines in custody, follows different lines from my response to sitting in Melbourne and reading a human rights report about death squads in El Salvador.

[. . .] First, I will list some of the more useful bodies of literature which deal – directly, but more often obliquely – with the general phenomenon of denial. Then I will give a preliminary classification of the major forms of denial. Finally, I will note a few questions from my fieldwork on human rights organizations. Through interviews, analysis of publications, educational material advertisements and campaign evaluations, I am trying to understand how human rights messages are disseminated and received.

This last part of the work is a study in communication. The *sender* is the international human rights community (directly or through the mass media). The *audience* is our real and metaphorical bystanders. The *message* is something like this (to quote from an actual Amnesty International advert in Britain in 1991):

> *Brazil has solved the Problem of how to keep kids off the street. Kill Them.*

What bodies of literature might be of relevance?

1   The psychology of denial

Orthodox psychoanalysis sees denial as an unconscious defence mechanism for coping with guilt and other disturbing psychic realities. Freud originally distinguished between 'repression' which applies to defences against internal instinctual demands and 'denial' (or what he called 'disavowal') which applies to defences against the claims of external reality.

With a few exceptions, pure psychoanalytic theory has paid much less attention to denial in this sense than repression (but see Edelstein, 1989). We have to look in the more applied fields of psychoanalysis (or its derivatives) for studies about the denial of external information. This yields a mass of useful material. There is the rich literature on the denial of knowledge about fatal disease (especially cancer and more recently, AIDS) affecting self or loved ones. More familiar to criminologists, there is the literature on family violence and pathology: spouse abuse, child abuse, incest etc. The concept of denial is standard to describe a mother's reaction on 'discovering' that her husband had been sexually abusing their daughter for many years: 'I didn't notice anything'. In this case, the concept implies that in fact the mother did 'know' – how could she not have? – but that this knowledge was too unbearable to confront.

The subject of denial has also been dealt with by cognitive psychology and information theory. Of particular interest is the 'denial paradox': in order to use the term 'denial' to describe a person's statement 'I didn't know', you have to assume that he or she knew or knows about what it is he or she claims not to know (otherwise the term 'denial' is inappropriate).

Cognitive psychologists have used the language of information processing, selective perception, filtering, attention span etc., to understand the phenomenon of how we notice and simultaneously do not notice (Goleman, 1985). Some have even argued that the neurological phenomenon of 'blindsight' suggests a startling possibility: that one part of the mind may know just what it is doing, while the part that supposedly knows, remains oblivious of this.

We are all familiar, from basic social psychology, with the notion of cognitive bias: the selection of information to fit existing perceptual frames. At the extreme, information which is too threatening to absorb is shut out altogether. The mind somehow grasps what is going on, but rushes a protective filter into place, steering information away from what threatens. Information slips into a kind of 'black hole of the mind' – a blind zone of blocked attention and self-deception. Attention is thus diverted from facts or their meaning. Thus, the 'vital lies' sustained by family members about violence, incest, sexual abuse, infidelity, unhappiness. Lies continue unrevealed, covered up by the family's silence, collusion, alibis and conspiracies (Goleman, 1985).

Similar processes have been well documented outside both the social psychology laboratory and intimate settings like the family. The litany by observers of atrocities is all too familiar: 'we didn't see anything', 'no one told us', 'it looked different at the time'.

In addition to psychoanalytical and cognitive theory, there is also the tradition in philosophical psychology concerned with questions of self-knowledge and self-deception. The Sartrean notion of 'bad faith' is of particular interest in implying – contrary to psychoanalytical theory – that the denial is indeed conscious.

2 Bystanders and rescuers

Another body of literature more obviously relevant (and more familiar to criminologists) derives from the victimological focus on the bystander. The classic 'bystander effect' has become a cliché: how witnesses to a crime will somehow disassociate themselves from what is happening and not help the victim. The prototype is the famous Kitty Genovese case. (One night in New York in 1964, a young woman, Kitty Genovese, was savagely assaulted in the street just before reaching her apartment. Her assailant attacked her over a period of forty minutes while she struggled, battered and screaming, to reach her apartment. Her screams and calls for help were heard by at least 38 neighbours who, from their own windows saw or heard her struggle. No one intervened directly or by calling the police. Eventually a patrol car arrived – too late to save her life.)

Studies of the bystander effect (Sheleff, 1978) suggest that intervention is less likely to occur under three conditions:

1 *Diffusion of responsibility* – so many others are watching, why should I be the one to intervene? Besides, it's none of my business.
2 *Inability to identify with the victim* – even if I see someone as a victim, I won't act if I cannot sympathize or emphathize with their suffering. We help our family, friends, nation, in-group – not those excluded from our moral universe (*Journal of Social Issues*, 1990). In fact, those who are outside out moral universe may be blamed for their predicament (the common experience of women victims of sexual violence). If full responsibility is laid on the political out-group (they provoked us, they had it coming), this releases you from your obligation to respond.

3   *Inability to conceive of effective intervention* – even if you do not erect barriers of denial, even if you feel genuine moral or psychological unease ('I feel so awful about what's going on in Bosnia', 'I just can't get those pictures from Somalia out of my mind'), this will not necessarily result in intervention. Observers will not act if they do not know what to do, if they feel powerless and helpless themselves, if they don't see any reward in helping, or if they fear punishment if they help.

These processes are of obvious relevance to my work on human rights violations. There are immediate and literal 'bystanders': all massacres, disappearances and atrocities have their witnesses. And there are also metaphorical bystanders; remember the reader looking at the Amnesty adverts about street kids being killed in Brazil or dissidents being tortured in Turkey: Is this really my problem? Can I identify with these victims? What can I do about it anyway?

The obverse of the bystander effect has generated its own special discourse. Just as interesting as the social bases of indifference, are the conditions under which people are aroused to intervene – often at great personal cost and risk. There is a vast ranging literature here: experimental studies on the social psychology of altruism and pro-social behaviour; the sociology of charity and philanthropy; philosophical and economic discussions of altruism (notably attempts to reconcile the phenomenon to rational choice theory); historical studies of helping, rescuing, altruism, the Good Samaritan. The best known of this work deals with rescuers of Jews in Nazi Europe (Oliner and Oliner, 1988).

3   Neutralization theory

More familiar ground to criminologists is the body of literature known as 'motivational accounts' or 'vocabulary of motives' theory. The application of this theory in Sykes and Matza's (1957) 'techniques of neutralization' paper is a criminological classic. [. . .]

The theory assumes that motivational accounts which actors (offenders) give of their (deviant) behaviour must be acceptable to their audience (or audiences). Moreover, accounts are not just *post facto* improvisations, but are drawn upon in advance from the cultural pool of motivational vocabularies available to actors and observers (and honoured by systems of legality and morality). Remember Sykes and Matza's original list; each technique of neutralization is a way of denying the moral bind of the law and the blame attached to the offence: denial of injury ('no one got hurt'); denial of victim ('they started it'; 'it's all their fault'); denial of responsibility ('I didn't mean to do it', 'they made me do it'); condemnation of the condemners ('they are just as bad') and appeal to higher loyalties (friends, gang, family, neighbourhood).

Something very strange happens if we apply this list not to the techniques for denying or neutralizing conventional delinquency but to human rights violations and state crimes. For Sykes and Matza's point was precisely that delinquents are *not* 'political' in the sense implied by subcultural theory; that is, they are not committed to an alternative value system nor do they withdraw legitimacy from conventional values. The necessity for verbal neutralization shows precisely the continuing bind of conventional values.

But exactly the same techniques appear in the manifestly political discourse of human rights violations – whether in collective political trials (note, for example, the Nuremberg trials or the Argentinian junta trial) or official government responses to human rights reports (a genre which I am studying) or media debates about war crimes and human rights abuses. I will return soon to 'literal denial', that first twist of the denial spiral which I identified earlier (it didn't happen, it can't happen here, they are all liars). Neutralization comes into play when you acknowledge (admit) that something happened – but either refuse to accept the category of acts to which it is assigned ('crime' or 'massacre') or present it as morally justified. Here are the original neutralization techniques, with corresponding examples from the realm of human rights violations.

- *Denial of injury* – they exaggerate, they don't feel it, they are used to violence, see what they do to each other.
- *Denial of victim* – they started it, look what they've done to us; they are the terrorists, we are just defending ourselves, we are the real victims.
- *Denial of responsibility* – here, instead of the criminal versions of psychological incapacity or diminished responsibility (I didn't know what I was doing. I blacked out, etc.) we find a denial of individual moral responsibility on the grounds of obedience: I was following orders, only doing my duty, just a cog in the machine. (For individual offenders like the ordinary soldier, this is the most pervasive and powerful of all denial systems).
- *Condemnation of the condemners* – here, the politics are obviously more explicit than in the original delinquency context. Instead of condemning the police for being corrupt and biased or teachers for being hypocrites, we have the vast discourse of official denial used by the modern state to protect its public image: the whole world is picking on us; they are using double standards to judge us; it's worse elsewhere (Syria, Iraq, Guatemala or wherever is convenient to name); they are condemning us only because of their anti-semitism (the Israeli version), their hostility to Islam (the Arab version), their racism and cultural imperialism in imposing Western values (all Third World tyrannies).
- *Appeal to higher loyalty* – the original subdued 'ideology' is now total and self-righteous justification. The appeal to the army, the nation, the *volk*, the sacred mission, the higher cause – whether the revolution, 'history', the purity of Islam, Zionism, the defence of the free world or state security. As the tragic events of the last few years show, despite the end of the cold war, the end of history and the decline of meta narratives, there is no shortage of 'higher loyalties', old and new.

Let us remember the implications of accounts theory for our subject. Built into the offender's action, is the knowledge that certain accounts will be accepted. Soldiers on trial for, say, killing a peaceful demonstrator, can offer the account of 'obeying orders' because this will be honoured by the legal system and the wider public. This honouring is, of course, not a simple matter: Were the orders clear? Did the soldier suspect that the order was illegal? Where in the chain of command did the order originate from? These, and other ambiguities, make up the stuff of legal, moral and political discourses of denial.

I have no time here to apply each of these theoretical frameworks – psycho-analysis, cognitive psychology, bystander theory, motivational accounts etc. – to my case study of reactions to knowledge of human rights violations and state crimes. (There are obviously also many other relevant fields: political socialization and mobilization, mass media analysis, collective memory). For illustration only, let me list some elementary forms of denial which these theories might illuminate.

I will distinguish three forms of denial, each of which operates at (i) the indi-vidual or psychic level and (ii) at the organized, political, collective or official level.

1   Denial of the past

At the individual level, there are the complex psychic mechanisms which allow us to 'forget' unpleasant, threatening or terrible information. Memories of what we have done or seen or known are selected out and filtered.

At the collective level, there are the organized attempts to cover up the record of past atrocities. The most dramatic and successful example in the modern era is the eighty years of organized denial by successive Turkish governments of the 1915–17 genocide against the Armenians – in which some one and half million people lost their lives (Hovanissian, 1986). This denial has been sustained by deliberate propa-ganda, lying and cover-ups, forging of documents, suppression of archives and bribing of scholars. The West, especially the USA, has colluded by not referring to the massacres in the UN, ignoring memorial ceremonies and by surrendering to Turkish pressure in NATO and other arenas of strategic cooperation.

The less successful example, of course, is the so-called 'revisionist' history of holocaust of European Jews, dismissed as a 'hoax' or a 'myth'.

At both levels, we can approach the process of denial through its opposite: the attempt to recover or uncover the past. At the individual level, the entire psycho-analytic procedure itself is a massive onslaught on individual denial and self-deception. At the political level, there is the opening of collective memory, the painful coming to terms with the past, the literal and metaphorical digging up of graves when regimes change and try to exorcise their history.

2   Literal denial

Here we enter the grey area sketched out by psychoanalysis and cognitive theory. In what senses can we be said to 'know' about something we profess not to know about? If we do shut something out of knowledge, is this unconscious or conscious? Under what conditions (for example, information overload or desensitization) is such denial likely to take place?

There are many different versions of literal denial, some of which appear to be wholly individual, others which are clearly structured by the massive resources of the state. We didn't know, we didn't see anything, it couldn't have happened without us knowing (or it could have happened without us knowing). Or: things like this can't happen here, people like us don't do things like this. Or: you can't believe the source of your knowledge: – victims, sympathizers, human rights monitors, journalists are biased, partial or ignorant.

The psychological ambiguities of 'literal denial' and their political implications are nicely illustrated by the psychoanalyst John Steiner's re-interpretation of the Oedipus drama (Steiner, 1985, 1990).

The standard version of the legend is a tragedy in which Oedipus is a victim of fate who bravely pursues the truth. At the beginning he does not know the truth (that he has killed his father, that he had sexual relations with his mother); at the end he does. This is taken as a paradigm for the therapeutic process itself: the patient in analysis to whom, gradually and painfully, the secrets of the unconscious are revealed. But alongside this version, Steiner shows, Sophocles also conveys a quite different message in the original drama: the message is that the main characters in the play must have been aware of the identity of Oedipus and realized that he had committed patricide and incest. There is a deliberate ambiguity throughout the text about the nature of this awareness – just how much did each character know? Each of the participants (including Oedipus himself) and especially the various court officials, had (good) different reasons for denying their knowledge, for staging a cover-up. The Oedipus story is not at all about the discovery of truth, but the denial of truth – a cover-up like Watergate, Iran Contra. Thus the question: how much did Nixon or Bush 'know'?

The ambiguity about how conscious or unconscious our knowledge is, how much we are aware of what we say we are unaware, is nicely captured in Steiner's title 'Turning a Blind Eye'. This suggests the possibility of *simultaneously* knowing and not knowing. We are not talking about the simple lie or fraud where facts are accessible but lead to a conclusion which is knowingly evaded. This, of course, is standard in the organized government cover-up: bodies are burnt, evidence is concealed, officials are given detailed instructions on how to lie. Rather, we are talking about the more common situation where 'we are vaguely aware that we choose not to look at the facts without being conscious of what it is we are evading' (Steiner, 1985: 61).

3 Implicatory denial

The forms of denial that we conceptualize as excuses, justifications, rationalizations or neutralizations, do not assert that the event did not happen. They seek to negotiate or impose a different construction of the event from what might appear the case. At the individual level, you know and admit to what you have done, seen or heard about. At the organized level, the event is also registered but is subjected to cultural reconstruction (for example, through euphemistic, technical or legalistic terminology). The point is to deny the implications – psychological and moral – of what is known. The common linguistic structure is 'yes, but'. Yes, detainees are being tortured but there is no other way to obtain information. Yes, Bosnian women are being raped, but what can a mere individual thousands of miles away do about it?

'Denial of Responsibility', as I noted earlier, is one of the most common forms of implicatory denial. The sociology of 'crimes of obedience' has received sustained attention, notably by Kelman and Hamilton (1989). The anatomy of obedience and conformity – the frightening degree to which ordinary people are willing to inflict great psychological and physical harm to others – was originally revealed by Milgram's famous experiment. Kelman and Hamilton begin from history rather than a university laboratory: the famous case of Lieutenant Calley and the My Lai massacre during the Vietnam War in May 1968 when a platoon of American soldiers massacred some 400 civilians. From this case and other 'guilt free' or 'sanctioned' massacres, they extract a rather stable set of conditions under which crimes of obedience will occur.

1   *Authorization*: when acts are ordered, encouraged, or tacitly approved by those in authority, then normal moral principles are replaced by the duty to obey.
2   *Routinization*: the first step is often difficult, but when you pass the initial moral and psychological barrier, then the pressure to continue is powerful. You become involved without considering the implications; it's all in a day's work. This tendency is re-inforced by special vocabularies and euphemisms ('surgical strike') or a simple sense of routine. (Asked about what he thought he was doing, Calley replied in one of the most chilling sentences of all times: 'It was no big deal').
3   *Dehumanization*: when the qualities of being human are deprived from the other, then the usual principles of morality do not apply. The enemy is described as animals, monsters, gooks, sub-humans. A whole language excludes them from your shared moral universe.

The conditions under which perpetrators behave can be translated into the very bystander rationalizations which allow the action in the first place and then deny its implications afterwards. As Kelman and Hamilton show in their analysis of successive public opinion surveys (in which people were asked both to imagine how they would react to a My Lai situation themselves and to judge the actual perpetrators), obedience and authorization are powerful justifications. And observers as well as offenders are subject to desensitization (the bombardment by horror stories from the media to a point that you cannot absorb them any more and they are no longer 'news') and dehumanization.

My research on human rights organizations (national and international) deals with their attempts to overcome these barriers of denial. What is the difference between working in your own country and trying to arouse an international audience in distant and different places? What messages work best in mobilizing public action (whether going to a demonstration, donating money or joining an organization like Amnesty International)? Does focusing on a country work better than raising an issue (such as torture or the death penalty)? And which countries or which issues? Are some techniques of confronting denial – for example, inducing guilt or representing the horrors more vividly – counter-productive? Is there competition for the human rights message within the same audiences (for example, from the environmental movement)? . . .

CONCLUSION

[. . .]

Instead of a conclusion, let me instead end with two footnotes. One raises – dare I say – some meta-theoretical issues; the other introduces a little optimism into an otherwise bleak story.

Meta theory

I mentioned the strange neglect of these issues by new realist criminologists and suggested that what is at stake is their sense of reality. But 'reality' is not a word used too easily these days – or if used, only politically correct in inverted commas. This is the legacy of post-structuralism, deconstructionism and postmodernism. There are a number of trends in postmodernist theory which – usually unwittingly – impinge on the human rights discourse. Let me mention a few such meta issues:

First, there is the question of moral relativism. This is the familiar claim – now supposedly finally vindicated – that if there is no universal, foundational base for morality (the death of meta-narratives), then it is impossible to stake out universal values (such as those enshrined in human rights standards). Then comes the derivative claim that such values and standards are Western, ethnocentric, individualistic, alien and imposed.

Now, whatever the historical record, this claim has some strange political implications. The standard and age-old government denials of the applicability of international human rights norms – we are different, we face special problems, the world doesn't understand us – now acquire a new philosophical dignity. And further, the condemners are condemned for being ethnocentric and imperialist.

A similar problem comes from the assertion that local struggles for human rights lose their meaning because they are informed by the very universal foundations and master narratives now so thoroughly discredited or tarnished. This is again a complex debate; I side with those who argue that no amount of deconstructive scepticism should deny the force with which we defend these values. It is surely a bizarre sight for Western progressives to be telling human rights activists from the Third World or Eastern Europe that their struggle is, after all, not worth the candle.

A second problem is posed by the proclaimed end of history. This is the current round of the old 'end of ideology' game: the collapse of international socialism finally proving the triumph of Western democratic capitalism. Besides the poverty of the case itself, it can make little sense for those still living between death squads, famine, disease and violence. For them, history is not over. But even if one meta narrative has won and there is nothing left for 'history' in the industrialized world, then how does this world react to what is happening elsewhere? Why – if not because of racism, selfishness, greed, and the type of denial I've talked about – do the victors not devote more resources to achieve these values elsewhere?

A third postmodernist theme is even more directly relevant to my subject here – and potentially even more destructive. This is the attack on all modes of rational enquiry which work with positivist categories of reality. The human rights movement can live without absolute, foundational values. But it cannot live with a theory which denies any way of knowing what has really happened. All of us who carried the anti-positivist banners of the 1960s are responsible for the emergent epistemological circus.

[. . .] On 29 March 1991, shortly after the cessation of hostilities in the Gulf War – just as thousands were lying dead and maimed in Iraq, the country's infra-structure deliberately destroyed by savage bombing, the Kurds abandoned to their fate – the high priest of postmodernism, Jean Baudrillard, published an article entitled 'The Gulf War Has Not Taken Place' (Baudrillard, 1991b). The 'true belligerents' he argued, are those who thrive on the ideology of the truth of this war.

He was only being consistent with an article he wrote a few days before the war (Baudrillard, 1991a) in which he predicted that it would never happen. The war existed only as a figment of media simulation, of imaginary scenarios that exceeded all limits of real world facticity. The war, Baudrillard had solemnly declared, was strictly unthinkable except as an exchange of threats so exorbitant that it would guarantee that the event would not take place. The 'thing' would happen only in the minds of its audience, as an extension of the video games imagery which had filled our screens during the long build up. Dependent as we all were – prime time viewers as well as generals – on these computer generated images, we might as well drop all self-deluding distinctions between screen events and 'reality'.

Given this 'prediction', it was unlikely that Baudrillard would be proved wrong if the war really did break out. So indeed the 'war' – a free floating signifier, devoid of referential bearing – did not happen. To complain that he was caught out by events only shows our theoretical naïveté, our nostalgia for the old truth-telling discourses.

What does one make of all this? I take my cue from Christopher Norris (1992), who has devoted a splendid polemical book to attacking Baudrillard's theses on the Gulf War. Norris is by no means a philistine critic or an unregenerated 'positivist'. He is the author of altogether sympathetic studies of Derrida and deconstructionism. And he concedes that Baudrillard makes some shrewd observations about how the war was presented by its managers and the media: the meaningless statistical data to create a illusory sense of factual reporting, the absurd claims about 'precision targeting', and 'clever bombs' to convince us that the mass destruction of civilian lives were either not happening (literal denial) or were accidental (denial of responsibility).

But Norris is now appalled by the precious nonsense to which the fashionable tracks of postmodernism have led. What disturbs him is how seriously these ideas were taken, 'to the point where Baudrillard can deliver his ludicrous theses on the Gulf War without fear of subsequent exposure as a charlatan or of finding these theses resoundingly disconfirmed by the course of real-world events' (Norris, 1992: 17).

It is beyond my scope and competence to consider Norris's explanation for how these ideas emerged and just where they lost their plausibility. He places particular importance on the curious ascendancy of literary theory as a paradigm for other areas of study. There is the bland assumption that because every text involves some kind of narrative interest, therefore there is no way to distinguish factual, historical or documentary material on the one hand from fictive, imaginary or simulated material on the other. With no possible access to truth or historical record, we are asked, Norris shows, to inhabit a realm of unanchored persuasive utterances where rhetoric goes all the way down and where nothing could count as an argument against what the media or governments would have us currently believe.

This re-definition of history finds strange echoes, as Norris notes, among the right wing revisionist historians of the holocaust, 'those for whom it clearly comes as good news that past events can only be interpreted according to present consensus values, or ideas of what currently and contingently counts as "good in the way of belief"' (Norris, 1992: 21). In the case of current events, like the Gulf War, we are left with no resources to deal with the obvious contradictions between official propaganda and personal witness (for example, about the bombing of the Amiriyah civilian air raid shelter). The cult following of these ideas by some intellectuals reflects, as Norris suggests, their lack of desire to make any political judgement, their cynical acquiescence in the war. If the war was so unreal, so completely beyond our competence to judge as informed observers, then we can say nothing to challenge the official (media sponsored) version of events.

My point in raising this example is simple. If the Turkish government can deny that the Armenian genocide happened; if revisionist historians and neo-Nazis deny that the Holocaust took place; if powerful states all around the world today can systematically deny the systematic violations of human rights they are carrying out – then we know that we're in bad shape. But we're in even worse shape when the intellectual *avant garde* invent a form of denial so profound, that serious people – including progressives – will have to debate whether the Gulf War actually took place or not.

Acknowledgement

I promised a more optimistic second footnote. This is not to cheer you up, but just to be honest. Denial has it opposites. What has to be understood are the conditions under which denial does not occur, in which the truth (even if this concept is disappearing down the postmodern black hole) is acknowledged, not just its existence but its moral implications.

After all, in the Milgram experiment, somewhere around 30 per cent of the subjects (depending on the conditions) did not push the button. In Kelman and Hamilton's public opinion surveys, again another 30 per cent would not obey orders to shoot innocent women and children. In the middle of even the most grotesque of state crimes, such as genocide, there are extraordinary tales of courage, rescuing and resistance. Acts of altruism, compassion and pro-social behaviour are woven into the social fabric. Above all, there is the whole human rights movement itself, which over the last three decades has mobilized an extraordinary number of people into wholly selfless behaviour to alleviate the suffering of others – whether by giving money, writing to a prisoner of conscience or joining a campaign.

In my initial interviews with human rights organizations, I was surprised to hear a sense of optimism. Yes, there are some people (referred to in the trade as the 'ostriches') who do not want to know. But most organizations were certain that their potential pool has not been reached. I mentioned to one of my interviewees the cynical notion of 'compassion fatigue' – that people are just too tired to respond, they can't bear seeing any more pictures of the homeless in the streets, victims of AIDS, children starving in Somalia, refugees in Bosnia. Her response was that the concept was a journalistic invention; what there is, is media fatigue.

This is where we return to the state of hyper-reality which postmodernist theories have so well exposed. The question is right open: Will the type of manipulation and simulation seen in the Gulf War dominate, creating indeed a culture of denial? Or can we conceive of a flow of information which will allow people to acknowledge reality and act accordingly?

This might seem a pretentious question for us humble criminologists to consider, but I hope that you will allow me to get away with it.

REFERENCES

Barak, G. (ed.) (1991) *Crimes by the Capitalist State: an Introduction to State Criminality*. Albany: State University of New York Press.

Baudrillard, J. (1991a) 'The Reality Gulf', *Guardian*, 11 January.

Baudrillard, J. (1991b) 'La guerre du Golfe n'a pas eu lieu', *Libération*, 29 March.

Braithwaite, J. and Fisse, B. (1990) 'On the plausibility of corporate crime theory', in W. Laufer and F. Adler (eds), *Advances in Criminological Theory*, vol. II. New Brunswick, NJ: Transaction Books.

Cohen, S. (1991) 'Talking about torture in Israel', *Tikkun*, 6(6): 22–30, 89–90.

Edelstein, E.L. et al. (eds) (1989) *Denial: a Clarification of Concepts and Research*. New York: Plenum Press.

Goleman, D. (1985) *Vital Lies, Simple Truths: On the Psychology of Self Deception*. New York: Simon and Schuster.

Hovanissian, R.G. (ed.) (1986) *The Armenian Genocide in Perspective*. New Brunswick, NJ: Transaction Books.

Karmen, A. (1990) *Crime Victims: an Introduction to Victimology*. California: Brooks Cole.

Kelman, H.C. and Hamilton, V.L. (1989) *Crimes of Obedience*. New Haven, CT: Yale University Press.

Kuper, L. (1981) *Genocide*. Harmondsworth: Penguin Books.

Maran, R. (1989) *Torture: the Role of Ideology in the French-Algerian War*. New York: Praeger.

Muller, I. (1991) *Hitler's Justice: the Courts of the Third Reich*. Cambridge, MA: Harvard University Press.

Norris, C. (1992) *Uncritical Theory: Postmodernism, Intellectuals and the Gulf War*. London: Lawrence and Wishart.

Oliner, S. and Oliner, P. (1988) *The Altruistic Personality: Rescuers of Jews in Nazi Europe*. New York: Free Press.

Schwendinger, H. and Schwendinger, J. (1970) 'Defenders of order or guardians of human rights', *Issues in Criminology*, 7: 72–81.

Sheleff, L. (1978) *The Bystander*, Lexington, MA.

Steiner, J. (1985) 'Turning a blind eye: the cover up for Oedipus', *International Review of Psycho-Analysis*, 12: 161–72.

Steiner, J. (1990) 'The retreat from truth to omnipotence in Sophocles' *Oedipus at Colonus*', *International Review of Psycho-Analysis*, 17: 227–37.

Sykes, G. and Matza, D. (1957) 'Techniques of neutralization: a theory of delinquency', *American Sociology Review*, 22: 664–70.

Von Hirsch, A. and Jareborg, N. (1991) 'Gauging criminal harm: a living-standard analysis', *Oxford Journal of Legal Studies*, II(1): 1–38.

48

The exclusive society: Social exclusion, crime and difference in late modernity

Jock Young

[. . .]
A major motif of social control in late modern society is actuarialism. This involves, [. . .] a transition where there is a concern less with justice than with harm minimization and where causes of crime and deviance are not seen as the vital clue to the solution to the problem of crime. The actuarial stance is calculative of risk. It is wary and probabilistic, it is not concerned with causes but with probabilities, not with justice but with harm minimization, it does not seek a world free of crime but one where the best practices of damage limitation have been put in place; not a utopia but a series of gated havens in a hostile world. The actuarial stance reflects the fact that risk both to individuals and collectivities has increased, crime has become a normalized part of everyday life, the offender is seemingly everywhere in the street and in high office, within the poor parts of town but also in those institutions which were set up to rehabilitate and protect, within the public world of encounters with strangers but within the family itself in relationships between husband and wife and parent and child. We are wary of scoutmasters, policemen, hitchhikers, babysitters, husbands, dates, stepfathers and stepmothers, people who care for the elderly – the 'other' is everywhere and not restricted to criminals and outsiders. Its causes are increasingly unsure and this uncertainty is compounded by its seeming ubiquitousness. Both individuals *and* institutions face the problems of sorting out the safe from the risky and doing so in ways which are no longer cast iron and certain but merely probabilistic.

Rules themselves have become problematic in a pluralistic society where rules overlap to be sure but are never identical between one group and the other; they change over time and have changed, *without doubt*, within the lifetime of everyone. So it is no longer a question of right and wrong, more what is the likelihood of your rules being broken, and when the unit of risk becomes your chance of victimage, assessment of individual responsibility becomes less and less relevant. If you are the manager of a shopping mall or a mother seeking to protect her family, whether the

From *The Exclusive Society*, 1999. (Sage: London.)

likely transgressor is mad or bad, following rules or being unable to engage in rule-following behaviour, is of little consequence. Thus the line between free will and determinism becomes not only blurred but in a sense irrelevant. *You want above all to avoid trouble rather than to understand it.* You want to minimize risk rather than morally condemn behaviour.

[. . .]

For Anthony Giddens the concept of a risk society is concerned with the nature of risks in late modern society and with what he calls 'the calculative attitude' which individuals and collectivities develop in *response* to such risk:

> To live in the 'world' produced by high modernity has the feeling of riding a juggernaut. It is not just that more or less continuous and profound processes of change occur; rather, change does not consistently conform either to human expectation or to human control. The anticipation that the social and natural environments would increasingly be subject to rational ordering has not proved to be valid. . . .
>
> Providential reason – the idea that increased secular understanding of the nature of things intrinsically leads to a safer and more rewarding existence for human beings – carries residues of conceptions of fate deriving from pre-modern eras. Notions of fate may of course have a sombre cast, but they always imply that a course of events is in some way preordained. In circumstances of modernity, traditional notions of fate may still exist, but for the most part these are inconsistent with an outlook in which risk becomes a fundamental element. To accept risk as risk . . . is to acknowledge that no aspects of our activities follow a predestined course, and all are open to contingent happenings. In this sense it is quite accurate to characterise modernity, as Ulrich Beck does, as a 'risk society', a phrase which refers to more than just the fact that modern social life introduces new forms of danger which humanity has to face. Living in the 'risk society' means living with a calculative attitude to the open possibilities of action, positive and negative, with which, as individuals and globally, we are confronted in a continuous way in our contemporary social existence. (1991, p. 28)

What I want to do is discuss the basis of such a notion of risk in the area of crime and deviance and how this results in a 'calculative' or 'actuarial' attitude in individuals, in institutions and in the criminal justice system itself.

LIVING WITH STRANGERS: THE SIX COMPONENTS OF RISK

A 'real' rise in risk

[. . .] the vast majority of countries in the developed world have experienced a rise in crime in the last 30 years. Such a crime rate has been accompanied by a penumbra of incivilities and crime had become increasingly internecine in its nature so that predatory behaviour and disorder is more and more implosive within each neighbourhood and social group.

Revelation

The mass media, the pressure group activities – and even the criminological researcher – have presented to the public a wider range of crime and on a greater scale than ever before. National crime surveys inform us that we can at least double (if not quadruple) the official crime rate, pressure groups indicate abuse occurring within the family often as much (if not more) than in the world outside, institutions which serve to protect and safeguard the vulnerable are seen to be sites of crime (from homes for the elderly to the orphanages of the Christian Brothers or the Sisters of Mercy), police and prisons are exposed as prime sites of corruption, violence and drug dealing. And on top of this, the illicit activities of white collar and corporate criminals are every day presented on our televisions and in our newspapers. No doubt some of this is inaccurate and a proportion misleading and mischievous, but the world which we *experience* as risky is *revealed* as risky on a wider and wider scale in all areas and parts of the social fabric.

Rising expectations

Risk is not a fixed objective thing: it rises or falls as our tolerance of a particular behaviour or practice changes. The change in public attitudes over the last 30 years has shown every indication of the 'civilizing influence' of a greater demand for a refinement in our behaviour towards each other and for an enhanced quality of life. Indeed the rising demand for law and order, which is often seen negatively as a sign of growing public authoritarianism may, more positively, be viewed as increasing demands for security, safety and civility in everyday life. One look at the area of violence confirms this, where a whole array of crimes have become a major focus of public concern: for example domestic violence, rape, child abuse and violence against animals. The entry of women into public life, consequent on their incorporation into the labour force, is no doubt a major influence on this, with rising demands being made on the level of civility both in public spaces and within the home. The area of public space is of interest in this respect in that it represents an area where women, because of increased economic and social equality, place themselves more at risk from male abuse but also demand more propriety. The greater use of pubs by women is a humdrum example of this two-way process, and is encouraged by the brewers for precisely these reasons.

Reserve

The greater mobility of people in modern society results in a decline of communities where people live most of their life and which centre around their workplace. This results in a significant drop in information, about neighbours, acquaintances, or chance encounters in the street. One has less direct knowledge of fellow citizens and this, together with living in a much more heterogeneous society, leads to much less *predictability* of behaviour. Unpredictability combined with risk generates a greater wariness in an actuarial stance towards others.

Reflexivity: the uncertainty of uncertainty

A key aspect of the late modern world, over and above the sensitization to risk, is the problematization of risk itself. Not only is the metropolis an uncertain world of dangers, but the level of risk itself is uncertain. In contrast to the modern world of predictable anxieties and dangers it is a world of uncertainty in that each level of risk will be questioned by experts and public alike. The fears come and go: carjacking, BSE, AIDS, road rage. They flicker on the screen of consciousness, something is going on but we are not sure who or what to believe. Whereas experts once concurred, they now seem to make a point of disagreement. From global warming to the ozone layer, from BSE to satanic child abuse, disagreement is the norm to an extent that the experts themselves begin to look shaky and to purvey just another opinion. But this is not a phantasmagoria, as some writers would have it (e.g. Furedi, 1997); city life is scarcely an Arcadian dream: if there was not a rational core of unease the images would not be able to find any purchase in the public consciousness.

Refraction

The mass media carry a plethora of images of crime and deviance gleaned from across the world. These media commodities are characterized like all news by their atypical nature – they are 'news' because they surprise and shock. Without doubt such imagery in its sheer quantity and in its garishness must cause 'fear' of crime disproportional to actual risk. Yet it is only one factor out of six, but it is often presented as *the* factor which determines public assessment of risk – as if fear were merely a metaphenomenon of television viewing.

UMWELT AND THE MANAGEMENT OF RISK

The awareness of risk generates an actuarial attitude in the citizen of late modernity. This is an attitude of wariness, of calculation and of reflectiveness. Some of these calculations will involve seeking for opportunities: urban life is full of excitement and pleasure as well as risk. The citizens of all the great First World megalopolises – London, New York, Paris, for example – share the same habits of reserve, of abrasiveness with strangers, of 'ducking and diving': of avoiding trouble and seeking gain.

Anthony Giddens discusses the way in which human beings generate around themselves a feeling of bodily and psychic ease. 'If we mostly seem less fragile,' he notes, 'than we really are . . . it is because of long-term learning processes whereby potential threats are avoided or immobilized' (1991, p. 127). He builds on Goffman's notion of an *Umwelt*: a core of accomplished normality with which individuals and groups surround themselves. Taking inspiration from studies of animal behaviour, Goffman begins the section of *Relations in Public* designated 'normal appearances' with this remarkable imagery of the *Umwelt*:

> Individuals, whether in human or animal form, exhibit two basic modes of activity. They go about their business grazing, gazing, mothering, digesting, building, resting, playing, placidly attending to easily managed matters at hand. Or, fully mobilized, a fury of intent, alarmed, they get ready to attack or to stalk or to flee. Physiology itself is patterned to coincide with this duality.

> The individual mediates between these two tendencies with a very pretty capacity for dissociated vigilance. Smells, sounds, sights, touches, pressures – in various combinations, depending on the species – provide a running reading of the situation, a constant monitoring of what surrounds. But by a wonder of adaptation these readings can be done out of the furthest corner of whatever is serving for an eye, leaving the individual himself free to focus his main attention on the non-emergencies around him. Matters that the actor has become accustomed to will receive a flick or a shadow of concern, one that decays as soon as he obtains a microsecond of confirmation that everything is in order; should something really prove to be 'up', prior activity can be dropped and full orientation mobilized, followed by coping behaviour. . . . (1971, p. 238)

The *Umwelt* has two dimensions: the area which one feels secure in and the area in which one is aware; the area of apprehension. The lioness sleeps tranquilly on the veldt, her eye every now and then taking in the activities in the distance. In human society it is a moving bubble which shrinks and expands wherever one is: whether, for example, one is at home or in the urban street. The nature of the *Umwelt* varies by social category. It is strongly gendered: Goffman noted that the *Umwelt* of women differed from men. Clearly, recognizing predatory sexual signs as well as signals of possible violence from men both in public and in the home is an important part of the social repertoire of women. Anyone who has conducted a criminal victimization survey knows that it is possible to identify and differentiate, 'blind', between women and men merely by looking at their avoidance behaviour patterns. Researchers talk of the 'curfew' at night of urban women (see Painter et al., 1989). The *Umwelt* is strongly racialized: ethnic groups are aware of areas of safety and danger and in racist discourse, minorities are represented as signals of fear and danger to the majority population. It has strong dimensions of age: schoolchildren have a vivid sense of space and safety (see Anderson et al., 1994); whilst street gangs and home boys actively police their turf, providing both security for themselves and alarm for others. Lastly, *Umwelt* is, of course, crucially constituted by class: the middle class by virtue of the cost of area, by the use of motor car, by private club and fancy restaurant seek to separate themselves from the undesirables, the 'dangerous classes', even when in transit through the busy city centres of Manhattan and London.

The signs of danger need not be crime itself or the threat of it, but more subtle perceptions of possible risk and the escalation of danger. Goffman was perhaps the first academic to note the problem of incivilities, way ahead of Wilson and Kelling's famous 'Broken Windows' [. . .] Thus:

> When an individual finds persons in his presence acting improperly or appearing out of place, he can read this as evidence that although the peculiarity itself may not be a threat to him, still, those who are peculiar in one regard may well be peculiar in other ways, too, some of which may be threatening. For the individual, then, impropriety on the part of others may function as an alarming sign. Thus, the minor civilities of everyday life can function as an early warning system; conventional courtesies are seen as mere convention, but non-performance can cause alarm. (1971, p. 241)

He cites an example of sexual harassment which graphically indicates the continuum nature of crime. This is from Meredith Tax's article in *Women's Liberation: Notes from the Second Year*:

> A young woman is walking down a city street. She is excruciatingly aware of her
> appearance and of the reaction to it (imagined or real) of every person she meets. She
> walks through a group of construction workers who are eating lunch in a line along the
> pavement. Her stomach tightens with terror and revulsion; her face becomes contorted
> into a grimace of self-control and fake unawareness; her walk and carriage become stiff
> and dehumanized. No matter what they say to her, it will be unbearable. She knows that
> they will not physically assault her or hurt her. They will only do so metaphorically.
> What they will do is impinge on her. They will use her body with their eyes. They will
> evaluate her market price. They will comment on her defects or compare them to those of
> other passers-by. They will make her a participant in their fantasies without asking if she
> is willing. They will make her feel ridiculous, or grotesquely sexual, or hideously ugly.
> Above all, they will make her feel like a thing. (Tax, 1970, p. 12)

Goffman is convinced that the condition of 'uneventfulness' is a moral right of a
citizen (see 1971, p. 240); such a level of trust is part of the nature of civilized life.
And he detects an overall deterioration in this quality of life:

> The vulnerability of public life is what we are coming more and more to see, if only
> because we are becoming more aware of the areas of intricacies of mutual trust
> presupposed in public order. Certainly circumstances can arise which undermine the case
> that individuals have within their *Umwelt*. Some of these circumstances are currently
> found in the semi-public places within slum housing developments. . . . Certainly the
> great public forums of our society, the downtown areas of our cities, can come to be
> uneasy places. Militantly sustained antagonisms between diffusely intermingled major
> population segments – young and old, male and female, white and black, impoverished
> and well-off – can cause those in public gatherings to distrust (and to fear they are
> distrusted by) the persons standing next to them. The forms of civil inattention, of
> persons circumspectly treating one another with polite and glancing concern while each
> goes about his own separate business, may be maintained, but behind these normal
> appearances individuals can come to be at the ready, poised to flee or to fight back if
> necessary. And in place of unconcern there can be alarm – until, that is, the streets are
> redefined as naturally precarious places, and a high level of risk becomes routine. (1971,
> pp. 331–2)

The area of security, of the *Umwelt*, shrinks apace . . . : it shrinks because of actual
risk but also, as we saw in the last section, because sensitivity to risk rises whilst
knowledge of others diminishes. But what can one say of the area of apprehension?
Here the paradox of a drop in knowledge of immediates is associated with a
globalization of knowledge of the wider outside world. *The area of security, of the*
Umwelt, *thus decreases whilst at the same time the area of apprehension vastly
increases.*

Lastly, there is another side of *Umwelt*, not touched upon by Goffman, but with
obvious relevance and with parallels in animal behaviour. The lioness gazing
fleetingly across the veldt is mapping out not only an area of security and one of
apprehension but also looking for indications of prey and the possibilities of
predation. In human terms the city is not only an area of security and insecurity but
of opportunities for excitement, interest, gain and action. The *Soft City* of Jonathan
Raban is an emporium of possibility as well as a labyrinth of danger.

RECALCITRANT MODERNITY AND THE CRITICS OF RISK

There is a body of thought which sees fear of crime and perceptions of likely risk as a phenomenon quite separate from the actual risk of crime itself. Indeed 'fear' of crime is regarded sometimes as a problem autonomous from crime. Fear and concern about crime then become metaphors for other types of urban unease (e.g. urban development), or a displacement of other fears (e.g. racism, psychological difficulties). The 'real' or 'true' fears are separated from crime itself and this exercise is achieved by contrasting the 'gap' between the 'real' risk of crime and the evidence of 'disproportionate' fears. Women and old people are the most frequently cited examples of evidence that such a disproportionality exists. This is not the place to enter into a discussion of the concealment of risks of crime against these groups either by underreporting or by avoidance behaviour which, so to speak, 'artificially' lowers the rates. I have analysed this extensively elsewhere (see Young, 1988, 1992). What is vital to reiterate, however, is that groups vary in their evaluation of the grossness of crime and that each item or risk is weighted differently by them. Women tend to view violence with greater abhorrence than men, but it is grotesque masculinism to suggest that because they worry more about violence, they are suffering from a form of irrationality which necessitates an expert unravelling their 'real' causes of discontent.

Crime, then, is refracted through the subculture of a group; it can never be perceived 'objectively' as naive 'realists' and their critics seem to believe. But there is more to it than this: within the notion of crime as a metaphor for other forms of urban unease is implicit the belief that crime is somehow *separate* from the other problems of society. Yet in fact, as numerous theorists have pointed out, crime is part of a continuum with other forms of antisocial behaviour and, indeed, as radical criminologists have never ceased to argue, the values which underlie much criminal behaviour are not distinct from conventional values but are closely related to them (see, e.g. Currie, 1997). To talk, then, of crime as a metaphor for urban unease is a bit like saying that fires is a metaphor for heat; that it is somehow unrelated, but excessive heat is the real problem and that the fascination with these flames that flicker around us is merely a distraction brought upon us, no doubt, by the mass media and the crime control industry (e.g. Baer and Chambliss, 1997).

My argument is that because human behaviour is always a subject of evaluation and assessment there can be no one-to-one relationship between 'risk' and 'fear': arguments which are based simply on the level of correlation, for or against, are positivist blind alleys which lead nowhere. What is necessary is to enter into the subculture in order to discover the significance of crime within it. To conduct qualitative research on the group is the only way to work out lines of causality (Sayer, 1984). In some cases almost metaphorical relationships will be found (but even here they are metaphors grounded in reality), in others the relationship will be stark and close (see Young, 1992).

Human evaluation takes time, it does not happen in an instant, as if we were talking of particles colliding with each other in the physical sciences. This mistake befuddles the debate about public attitudes to crime in the present period, particularly in the United States. Even such sophisticated commentators as Simon and Feeley can construct a false puzzle about public attitudes to crime:

What accounts for such intense fear? And what accounts for the dramatic increase in fear in recent years? Shifts in levels of fear of crime are not well-understood, and the answers to such questions are both complex and incomplete. But one important piece of the puzzle is well-charted if not well-understood: the intensity of public concern with crime is not directly or strongly related to the magnitude of crime. Indeed in recent years, concern about crime has increased despite a decline in overall rates of victimization. To be sure, some groups have experiences significant increases; young people from twelve to fifteen years of age, for example, experienced a 34 percent increase in violent crime victimizations during the 1980s. And citizens of our poorest inner-city neighborhoods, in particular young African-American males, have experienced significant increases in violence over the past decade. Still, the groundswell of support for more and more punitive crime measures in recent years has come after a decade of steady or declining crime rates for suburban middle-class whites, that segment of the population from which the strongest support for new get-tough measures comes. Why is this group which in other respects seems relatively insensitive to the well-being of people in communities distanced from themselves by poverty and race, and which is otherwise so sceptical of increases in government expenditures, so responsive to threats that in an objective sense affect them less now than at any time in recent memory? And why, when they generally resist increased government spending, are they willing to support vast new expenditures for crime control measures of dubious efficacy?

Fear by itself is an inherently unsatisfying explanation for the formation of recent crime policy. Indeed, it is difficult to explain the fear itself, in its own right. And the very lack of any clear correspondence between objective risk and fear suggests that discourse, including the discourse of crime and penality, must be fundamental input to fear itself, along with factors such as neighborhood disorder, economic anxiety, and changes in racial demographics. (1995, p. 154)

I have quoted this at length, although such views are echoed regularly elsewhere (e.g. Chambliss, 1994a, 1994b; Platt, 1996) because it most thoroughly describes this perplexity. Briefly in response to this it should be noted that a central plank of the conundrum is that in the recent years the crime rate for the United States has levelled: for example the homicide rate (one of the more reliable statistics) was 10.2 per 100,000 in 1974 and 9.5 in 1993. In between this it has fluctuated, sometimes being as low as 8.0 (1985). William Chambliss quite correctly posited that the FBI has often capitalized on these fluctuations by claiming increases in violence when over the longer period there was, if anything, a slight decline (see Chambliss, 1994b). This rosy positivistic vision is dependent on public memory being extremely short, yet it is undoubtedly longer than these authors allow for. Any middle-aged person in the United States will be only too aware that over the last third of the century (the period that concerns us here) there has been a dramatic increase in violence. [. . .] Could it not be that the American public is sick to its back teeth with this inordinate slaughter of its young people? Could it not be that they are willing to back intemperate policy and imprisonment in order, they hope, to achieve some abatement of the problem?

THE PROGRESSIVE MOMENT OF LATE MODERNITY

The critics of risk portray the risk of crime as greatly exaggerated, and the public as cultural dupes manipulated by the mass media and the risk control industries. They have a rather irritating habit of talking learnedly of the transition to late modernity whilst still feeling it necessary, in a good old-fashioned modernist tone, to inform their readers what are the 'real' risk rates and the 'real' causes of public fears. They fail to take on board two of the key elements of late modernity: public reflexivity about risk and a deep-rooted scepticism about experts.

The critics of risk take their arguments too far. The emergence of a risk society, as the development of late modernity itself, is a contradictory phenomenon. For the greater public awareness of risk is part and parcel of what are essentially progressive and democratic processes occurring throughout the world in the late twentieth century. The first is that of environmentalism, the Green movement. The awareness of the dangers of pollution in the atmosphere, in food, in our drinking water, in the city and on the beach, is undoubtedly a great step forward. Secondly, there is a greater repugnance of violence, an awareness of the hidden violence against children and women, in particular, and of violence against the other species that inhabit our planet, both domesticated animals and wildlife. Here both feminism and Green politics have made their mark. The above two demands are subsumed by a more general desire that citizenship should encompass a degree of control of the world that surrounds us, from the quality of life in the streets of our cities to the accountability of public bodies. Lastly, we have become increasingly sceptical of experts both in their right to define *our* problems and their ability to provide solutions. Three major political strands lie behind this greater awareness of risk: the Green movement, feminism and libertarianism. Thus, talk of 'risk' rates, debate about safety and security, scepticism about figures and political turmoil about solutions can scarcely be regarded as an abnegation of politics, as authors such as Frank Furedi would have it. 'Risk rates' have become a democratic currency, part of a reflexive audit of our affairs. To hinge the question on whether they have actually risen and whether they are phrased in an alarmist fashion fundamentally misses the point. In some instances they have risen, in many cases they are exaggerated, but what is important is that the base line of evaluation has increased as has the demand for a higher quality of life. The point is that we are increasing our level of social scrutiny and demand. Furthermore, the very existence of a debate about the levels of risk, of which the writers on risk are part, is *in itself* one of the great gains of late modernity. It is not so much that modernity has failed to keep its promise to provide a risk-free society as that late modernity has *taken seriously* this promise, has demanded more and realized the greater difficulty of its accomplishment.

[. . .]

REFERENCES

Anderson, S., Kinsey, R., Loader, I and smith, C. (1994) *Cautionary Tales*, Aldershot: Gower.

Baer, J. and Chambliss, W. (1997) 'Generating fear: the politics of crime reporting', *Crime Law and Social Change* 27, pp. 87–107.

Chambliss, W. (1994a) 'Profiling the ghetto underclass: the politics of law and order enforcement', *Social Problems* 41(2), pp. 177–194.

Chambliss, W. (1994b) 'Don't confuse me with facts – 'Clinton just say no'', *New Left Review* 204, pp. 113–128.

Currie, E. (1997) 'Market, crime and community', *Theoretical Criminology* 1(2), pp. 147–172.

Furedi, F. (1997) *The Culture of Fear*, London: Cassell.

Giddens, A. (1991) *Modernity and Self-Identity*, Cambridge: Polity.

Goffman, E. (1971) *Relations in Public*, London: Allen Lane.

Painter, K., Lea, J., Woodhouse, T. and Young, J. (1989) *The Hammersmith and Fulham Crime Survey*, Middlesex University: Centre for Criminology.

Platt, A. (1976) 'The Politics of Law and Order', *Social Justice*, 21(3), pp. 3–13.

Sayer, A. (1984) *Method in Social Science: A Realist Approach*, London: Hutchinson.

Simon, J. and Feeley, M. (1995) 'True crime: the new penology and public discourse on crime' in T. Blomberg and S. Cohen (eds) *Punishment and Social Control*, New York: Aldine de Gruyter.

Tax, M. (1970) 'The woman and her mind: the story of everyday life' in A. Koedt and S. Firestone (eds) *Women's Liberation: Notes from the Second Year*, New York: Justice Books.

Young, J. (1992) 'Ten points of realism' in J. Young and R. Matthews (eds) *Rethinking Criminology*, London: Sage.

49

The risk society in an age of anxiety: Situating fear of crime

Wendy Hollway and Tony Jefferson

[. . .]

FEAR OF CRIME, MODERNITY AND RISK

In *The Risk Society* Beck uses risk as the central analytical tool for understanding the social forms characteristic of modernization and late modernity (which he calls reflexive modernity). The influence of 'the culture of scientism' (Beck 1992:3) is central to the risk society because

> the consequences of scientific and industrial development [are] a set of risks and hazards which are no longer limited in time and space and for which no-one can be held accountable. (Beck 1992:2)

This unknowability has profound effects on the social world in its entirety, including on relevant forms of control and resistance.

For Beck, the new moral questions are about the allocation of risks, rather than the allocation of wealth (Douglas 1994:45). The importance of Beck's arguments, for us, is that risk is understood as pervasive in late modernity. When fear of crime and risk of victimization are considered in this light, they can no longer be looked at in isolation, but must be addressed in the political context of how multifarious risks are known and regulated.

Beck draws a distinction between, for example, the risk of job loss, which is clear through 'independent knowledge', and the risk of DDT in the tea people drink, where 'their victimization is not determinable by their own cognitive means', but depends on external [expert scientific] knowledge (Beck 1992:53). This issue is not primarily one of individual risk perception (though risk analysis has construed it as such, Douglas 1986), but a political question: in whose hands lies the representation

From *British Journal of Sociology*, 1997. 48:2. pp. 252–266.

of different categories of risk such as environmental hazards or, what interests us, risk of criminal victimization, and with what political effects?

For Douglas, situating it comparatively, risk is always a political and moral issue

> The theme, well known to anthropologists, is that at all places at all times the universe is moralized and politicized. Disasters that befoul the air and soil and poison the water are generally turned to political account: someone already unpopular is going to be blamed for it. (Douglas 1994:5)

Misfortunes have always been significant through social regulative systems of blame. However, the notion of risk is a modern production 'that admirably serves the forensic needs of the new global culture' (Douglas 1994:22). The sub-discipline of risk perception, she points out, arose in the 1960s as a result of the risk from new technologies, and was concerned with the issue of public tolerance for risks (Douglas 1986:19). Risk is about 'trying to turn uncertainties into probabilities' (Douglas 1986:42), thus making them accessible to impersonal administrative regulation, based on scientific principles, which evacuate the moral and political realm.

By creating a language of risk through using the concept of probability, science has accomplished a transformation of the language of misfortune and danger, with the implication that calculating individuals then modify their behaviour according to rational decisions. Risks then become ascertainable and thus, in principle, individuals are able to banish uncertainty

> How much risk is a matter for experts, but it is taken for granted that the matter is ascertainable. Anyone who insists that there is a high degree of uncertainty is taken to be opting out of accountability. (Douglas 1994:30)

However, the moral and political dimension of blaming is not banished by the modern risk discourse, rather it is expressed in the modern claim that 'real blaming' is possible, a claim that Douglas regards as a fantasy (1994:7). Douglas contests the claim of scientific rationality and certainty. In comparing 'primitive' and 'modern' reasoning about blame, she argues that the modern belief in probabilistic risk analysis functions rather like the primitive denial of natural death; that is as a defence against uncertainty (Douglas 1994:3). In practice, cultures of blame, whether 'primitive' or 'modern', fulfil social regulation functions. Douglas identifies two primary ones: victim blaming which facilitates internal social control and outsider blaming which enhances loyalty (Douglas 1986:59). Fear of crime, which is essentially fear of crime by outsiders, fits neatly into the latter category. In this way, Douglas locates the modern belief in real blaming and the wider dominance of a probabilistic risk discourse firmly in the political and moral realm of modernity's search for order and certainty.

The desire to eliminate uncertainty, evident in the modern quest for mathematically calculated risks with 'blame' scientifically assigned, is also at the heart of Bauman's conceptualization of modernity. For him, modernity's task of tasks is the production of order

> Among the multitude of impossible tasks that modernity set itself and that made modernity into what it is, the task of order (more precisely and most importantly, of order as a task) stands out – as the least possible among the impossible and the least disposable among the indispensable; indeed, as the archetype for all other tasks, one that renders all other tasks mere metaphors of itself. (Bauman 1991:4)

According to Bauman, this struggle for order, always doomed to be lost, is essentially a flight from the ambivalence at the heart of order's opposite, namely, chaos. Thus the central elements of the modernist project – the 'legislative ambitions of philosophical reason', the 'gardening ambitions of the state' and the 'ordering ambitions of applied sciences' were all pitted against the threat of 'underdetermination/ ambivalence/contingency' and 'made its elimination one of the main *foci imaginarii* of social order' (Bauman 1991:15–16).

Thus whether the present is best conceptualized as late or postmodernity, it presents threats to beliefs in certainty and order which are central in the 'great modern campaign against ambivalence', which Bauman regards as the most important feature of the human condition (1991:16). While Bauman believes that we have to get used to the idea of 'living without foundations' under conditions of *'admitted contingency'* (ibid.), we would stress the psychological difficulty of such an achievement. While conditions characteristic of the risk society coexist with the defences against anxiety precipitated by uncertainty, people will be drawn to discourses and practices which appear to offer the hope of order or control.

Within this conceptualization of modernity, the war against crime is but one of the 'multitude of local battles for order' within the ceaseless (and unwinnable) 'war against chaos' (Bauman 1991:11). Arguably, criminology's contribution to the modernist project has been to produce a never-ending supply of blameable scapegoats; the dishonest, inhumane, disorderly criminal 'Other' to society's truthful, humane, orderly 'self'. As Bauman argues, the practices of classification/segregation; for example the production of the *stranger*, were central to the project of order-building. Probably the two most significant 'strangers' in modern societies are the 'criminal' and the 'racial' (leaving aside the question of women as 'other'). Certainly fear of the alarming increase in juvenile crime in early nineteenth-century London, as well as the fear of 'King Mob', produced the most significant modern agency of social control, the new police. Thereafter, nearly two centuries of police 'ordering' practices have produced a galaxy of 'folk devils'.[1] Though different at different times, these folk devils tend to share certain features which make the fear of crime discourse such a powerful modernist tool in the quest for order, in contrast to Beck's unknowable risks of late modernity.

First, the risks focused on in fear of crime discourse tend to have individual identifiable victims and individual identifiable offenders. This makes them *knowable*. Indeed, where crimes do not have a knowable victim (for example, tax evasion) or an easily identifiable offender (for example dumping toxic waste) they tend not to become part of 'fear of crime' [. . .]. Second, offenders tend to be relatively powerless (given the power of the powerful to resist the criminal label). This makes them *decisionable (actionable)*. Third, offenders tend to be 'strangers', rather than known others, which helps explain why the key measure of fear of crime is premised so unselfconsciously on 'stranger danger'. Crimes between familiars therefore tend not to get treated as crimes. This blaming of the outsider builds loyalty and this assists social cohesion, as Douglas reminds us. It also renders the problem potentially *controllable* (even though the supply of 'criminals' is apparently endless).

FEAR OF CRIME, ANXIETY AND THE MISSING SUBJECT

Despite the highly sociological nature of his analysis of late modernity, Giddens depends centrally on the concept of anxiety, which for him is an inevitable part of the human condition. Giddens does not assume a simple link between anxiety and actual risk or between anxiety and the risk culture. Neither does he assume that high anxiety is a product of modernity: 'the modern age is not specifically one of high anxiety . . . but the content and form of prevalent anxiety certainly have become altered' (Giddens 1991:32). The later modern settings which provide this content and form are to do with disembedding, reflexivity and 'circumstances of uncertainty and multiple choice' (Giddens, 1991:3). These distinguish them both from a traditional order characterized by 'the sureties of tradition and habit' and from the ideal of modernity, 'the certitude of rational knowledge' (1991:2). In such circumstances 'trust and risk have particular application' (1991:3).

Following Winnicott, Giddens sees trust as normally vested in caretakers in early life and as providing 'a sort of emotional inoculation against existential anxieties' (1991:39). If it weren't for this trust, which is variably achieved over the course of a child's development, 'every human individual could . . . be overwhelmed by anxieties about risks which are implied by the very business of living' (ibid.).

Basically Giddens is arguing that 'anxiety has to be understood in relation to the overall security system the individual develops, rather than only as a situationally specific phenomenon connected to particular risks or dangers' (1991:41). The value of this argument for us is twofold. First, anxiety is not a produce of the social but a psychic phenomenon which will affect the way that actual risk is experienced, and thus the way that positions within fear/risk discourses, such as fear of crime, get reproduced. Second, circumstances of individual history as well as contemporary social position in relation to risk and crime will variably affect people's fear of crime.

In all four of the above accounts – Beck, Douglas, Bauman and Giddens – a subject is inferred who apprehends and makes sense of the risks characterizing late modern society, but this subject is not developed (except partially in Giddens). In each case, the desire for certainty, or the wish to avoid uncertainty, is a central feature of this late-modern subject, stemming from late modernity's 'globalization of doubt' (Beck 1992:21). In Beck, consequences for the subject stem primarily from the unknowability of the hazard, which makes control impossible and means that 'hazards can be projected onto all other objects of daily life' (op. cit.:54). In other words, because we have no means of being sure where risk and safety lie, nothing can be trusted and anxiety, therefore, potentially finds a location in any area of daily life. In Douglas' account, the desire for certainty translates into the 'moral concern' of 'real blaming'; 'the belief that any misfortune must have a cause; a perpetrator to blame, from whom to extract compensation' (1994:16). Thus 'real blaming' can be seen as a defence against uncertainty, produced and reproduced at the cultural level. Likewise in Bauman, the denial of ambivalence functions as a defence against uncertainty. In Giddens, trust and anxiety are central explanatory concepts. In each case, concepts are brought into play which require a psychodynamic theory for their elaboration: projection (of fear), defence against uncertainty, denial of ambivalence, trust and anxiety. All of these concepts, which cohere around anxiety and defences against anxiety, have been elaborated within psychoanalytic theory.

THE ANXIOUS SUBJECT IN FEAR OF CRIME

The introduction of psychological-level concepts which contradict the assumption of a rational calculating subject is evident in each of the major social theories of risk which we have introduced, but they are only developed in Giddens' work. The need for such a conceptualization is also apparent from empirical and feminist work. An example of the former is Nicholson's interview study of burglary victims (1994), whose theme was the seriousness of the trauma suffered as a result of house break-ins which, although they resulted in stolen property, had not involved any physical threats. In the case of feminist work on violence against women, including rape, there is an insistence on traumatic effects which operate at a deep level and persist over time (Roberts 1989). Again, these subjects, traumatized victims of crime, are rarely theorized, and then inadequately.

The psychoanalytic concept of anxiety has the virtue of being part of a sophisticated and coherent body of theory which is based on a subject whose primary source of meaning and action is the dynamic unconscious, rather than cognitive reason. The desire for certainty and the related fantasy of controlling external forces are derived from psychic sources to do with the universal condition of anxiety, which none the less manifests differently in particular historical periods and places (Brennan 1993). The creative and imaginative forms which defences against anxiety take can explain the fact that the subject is not simply a product of the social environment. Whatever is repressed because it is threatening to the integrity of the self (thereby provoking anxiety) does not disappear but manifests in indirect ways; for example through displacement onto another arena in a person's life or indeed onto another person or idea or group. We are arguing that to understand the growth and impact of a fear of crime discourse, given the many other competing fear/risk discourses currently available, we must theorize the passage of this discourse through individual psyches – the reasons for its take-up by at least many individuals – which has enabled it to be reproduced in the way we have seen in the cultural, political and organizational spheres.

The following case examples are based on data drawn from an early stage of our fieldwork interviewing. We use material from two contrasting interviewees to provide an illustration of how subjects are variably invested in a fear of crime discourse.

Bob is a middle-aged man who lost his job, partly as a result of an industrial accident which has left him in pain and contributed to his general ill-health. His wife is also unemployed and they have lived for six years in a council house, with their nine-year-old son, on a high-crime estate on the outskirts of North city. Within the last year they have had their one and only burglary, occurring when they had gone out shopping, in which a TV, video and three tapes were stolen. Their neighbour saw local boys running away from the house. They are still preoccupied with this break-in, to the extent that they mostly arrange their daily life so that one of them is always at home. They don't go away and rarely go out together because the worry spoils their excursion (they can't afford it either). They have intentionally replaced their TV and video with such old and cheap models that they would not be worth stealing. Bob sleeps poorly and at the slightest sound is up to make a tour of the windows to check for intruders. He lies awake thinking about which tactics he would use to overpower intruders (he is army trained and claims to have no fear for his own physical safety).

Most external commentators, slipping into the language of risk analysis, would conclude that the fear of crime which appears to be governing the life of this family is out of proportion to the risk. If risk is made up of 'not only the probability of an event but the magnitude of its outcome' (Douglas 1994:31), there would seem to be little at stake: nothing valuable in the house, no history of violent burglary on the estate. Why then are Bob and his wife preoccupied with another burglary? The social constructionist, or discourse determinist, answer would be drawn to the fact that Bob can recite a catalogue of burglaries on households in the nearby streets, which feed into the reproduction of the fear of crime discourse on this estate. We wish rather to ask: 'why is fear of crime so dominant as a discourse and how does this get reproduced through the meanings that Bob (and many but not all others) make of their lives?

Fear of crime (in this case fear of burglary) is an unconscious displacement of other fears which are far more intractable and do not display the modern characteristics of knowability and decisionability (or actionability) which add up to the belief in ones capacity to control the external world. These other fears, in Bob's case, might be fear of physical incapacity and ageing; fear of the meaninglessness of his current existence; fear of an unfamiliar and potentially hostile world outside the home. The fear of crime discourse has certain effects which promote control, in contrast to uncertainty, thereby paradoxically functioning as a defence against more threatening anxieties. First, his take up of a position as potential victim in the fear of crime discourse keeps him at home, which is the place he feels most safe. Second, it provides a knowable location for his fears: nothing worse than local kids whom he believes, as in his night-time fantasies, he can deal with if they do intrude. This provides him with an imaginary sense of mastery which must be in short supply for an unemployed and ailing man whose wife has to continuously sit with him in case he has a fit, who has constant headaches, who no longer feels able to do any practical jobs in the house or garden. Third, it provides an external rationale for behaviour (like never going away and rarely going out) which, if it were seen in purely economic terms might well reflect on him personally as failed breadwinner.

Paradoxically then, a rampant 'fear of crime' discourse which might on the face of it be thought to exacerbate fears, could actually serve unconsciously as a relatively reassuring site for displaced anxieties which otherwise would be too threatening to cope with. In a late-modern world of uncertainty, ambivalence, chaos even; of risks that are omnipresent but invisible, fear of crime might provide some rather modern reassurances: the knowability of the criminal (local kids); the decisionability of response (don't leave the house empty); the mastery or control of anxiety (I can physically overpower the intruder); the externality of the source of misfortune and the consequent opportunity for 'real blaming' (the 'other', not myself, is responsible for my predicament).

A second respondent, Joe, demonstrates a different positioning within the fear of crime discourse. Also middle-aged and unemployed, he has worked only briefly after his seven-year apprenticeship ended in the mid 1970s. Like Bob he has a fund of stories of crime on the estate, much of it directly witnessed: kids breaking into empty houses; youngsters knocking up dealers for their 'draw'; stolen cars and motorbikes being raced dangerously around the narrow roads. However, the worst that has happened to him is a stolen puppy. Despite the omnipresent criminal activity, he doesn't expect personally to become a victim, nor is he afraid to walk the estate at any time of the day or night – beliefs that do not prevent him taking a range of precautions like garaging his car off the estate and installing security lights.[2]

Like Bob he thinks the estate is 'terrible' and getting worse, but, unlike Bob, he would never move. Coming from a large family, having lived there from early childhood, knowing and being known by almost 'everybody', being active in the community as boys' soccer coach and Working Men's Club secretary, this estate is where he belongs, and where he has 'respect', a word he uses fondly to remember his dead father's reputation. He loves the fact that 'all' the local youngsters know him by name – even if he has to shout them down from the roofs of local empty houses. In so far as he is concerned about crime, he worries for his children: that the youngest might get knocked down by a stolen car; that the older teenage stepson might be the driver.

Joe's is then a history of feeling connected; to a large family, many of whom still live locally; and to a community which has provided the parameters of his whole life. He has known little else, neither in the worlds of work, family not leisure, and appears to want for little else. One of his deepest regrets is that his large family does not all get together on ritual occasions; one of his greatest satisfactions was becoming an 'adoptive' grandfather for his eldest stepson's first child. This world, in which family and community play a central role, is essentially a local world, a known world, and in principle, therefore, a controllable world. His stepson might be teetering on the brink of crime, the local youngsters might do far worse things than youngsters dared to do 'in his day', but, according to Joe, measures such as an evening youth club could potentially make the difference.

Joe's individual biography and his consequent 'emotional inoculation against existential anxieties' does not render him immune to the take-up and reproduction of a fear of crime discourse (hence his security measures), but it does mean that fear of crime does not act as a magnet for other anxieties. Thus Joe has no need of the unconscious displacement apparent in Bob's story. Being fit and healthy, being active in the community, being known and respected: these give Joe a feeling of being in control, of having some influence. The fear of crime discourse has little purchase on his local, estate-based life because it achieves no additional meaning as a defence against other unnameable fears and anxieties.

CONCLUSION

In this paper we have developed a double critique of existing approaches to fear of crime. First we argued the need to render the debate more social by resituating it within larger debates about the nature of late-modern societies. Second we stressed the importance of a more complex psychic dimension to 'fearful' subjects than has been provided so far. In rethinking questions of 'fear' and 'risk' against the broader canvas of modernity, we concluded that fear of crime is a peculiarly apt discourse within the modernist quest for order since the risks it signifies, unlike other late modern risks, are *knowable, decisionable (actionable)*, and potentially *controllable*. In an age of uncertainty, discourses that appear to promise a resolution to ambivalence by producing identifiable victims and blameable villains are likely to figure prominently in the State's ceaseless attempts to impost social order. Thus the figure of the 'criminal' becomes a convenient folk devil and the fear of crime discourse a satisfying location for anxieties generated more widely. However, how particular individuals identify with fear of crime discourses depends on their unique biographies, especially their histories of anxiety and how they have come to handle the circumstances of their lives in the light of these. Thus the impact of fear of crime discourses, even on high-crime estates where criminal victimization is commonplace, is a variable affair that does not reduce to social group membership, incivilities and official risk rates.

NOTES

1 If the criminal is a salient 'folk devil', the late-modern context of uncertainty and a multitude of unaccountable, uncontrollable risks perhaps begin to explain the contemporary prevalence of moral panics and the ever-growing litany of society's folk devils. Crises have become endemic, uncontrollable. The inability of modern governments to contain and control the manifold crises that beset them makes 'crisis management' arguably the key art of government and moral panics a key discursive strategy in their management. In this connection, the crises that the contemporary manifestation of fear of crime is supposed to manage stem from soaring crime rates and concerns about violence against women. Feminist concerns with violence against women, from the 1970s on, led to more political pressure about women's safety and fears, thus indirectly contributing to fear of crime discourses.

2 Joe has recently started to keep a baseball bat under his bed, deciding it was a good idea after discovering that his stepson did so. These precautionary measures taken together suggest that Joe is a cautious man, but his life is not changed in significant ways by his fear of crime.

REFERENCES

Bauman, Z. 1991 *Modernity and Ambivalence*, Cambridge: Polity Press.
Beck, U. 1992 *The Risk Society*. London: Sage.
Brennan, T. 1993 *History After Lacan*, London: Routledge.
Douglas, M. 1986 *Risk Acceptability According to the Social Sciences*, London: Routledge and Kegan Paul.
Douglas, M. 1994 *Risk and Blame: Essays in Cultural Theory*, London: Routledge.
Giddens, A. 1991 *Modernity and Self Identity*, Cambridge: Polity Press.
Nicholson, P. 1994 *The Experience of Being Burgled: A Psychological Study of the Impact of Domestic Burglary on Victims*, Sheffield: University of Sheffield.
Roberts, C. 1989 *Women and Rape*, Brighton: Harvester Wheatsheaf.

50

Cultural criminology

Jeff Ferrell

[. . .]

INTRODUCTION

The concept of 'cultural criminology' denotes both specific perspectives and broader orientations that have emerged in criminology, sociology, and criminal justice over the past few years. Most specifically, 'cultural criminology' represents a perspective developed by Ferrell & Sanders (1995), and likewise employed by Redhead (1995) and others (Kane 1998a), that interweaves particular intellectual threads to explore the convergence of cultural and criminal processes in contemporary social life. More broadly, the notion of cultural criminology references the increasing analytic attention that many criminologists now give to popular culture constructions, and especially mass media constructions, of crime and crime control. It in turn highlights the emergence of this general area of media and cultural inquiry as a relatively distinct domain within criminology, as evidenced, for example, by the number of recently published collections undertaking explorations of media, culture and crime (Anderson & Howard 1998, Bailey & Hale 1998, Barak 1994a, Ferrell & Sanders 1995, Ferrell & Websdale 1999, Kidd-Hewitt & Osborne 1995, Potter & Kappeler 1998). Most broadly, the existence of a concept such as cultural criminology underscores the steady seepage in recent years of cultural and media analysis into the traditional domains of criminological inquiry, such that criminological conferences and journals increasingly provide room and legitimacy for such analysis under any number of conventional headings, from juvenile delinquency and corporate crime to policing and domestic violence.
   [. . .]

CONTEMPORARY AREAS OF INQUIRY

[. . .] Cultural criminological research and analysis have emerged in the past few years within a number of overlapping substantive areas. The first two of these can be

From *Annual Review of Sociology*, 1999. 25. pp. 395–418.

characterized by an overly simple but perhaps informative dichotomy between 'crime as culture' and 'culture as crime.' The third broad area incorporates the variety of ways in which media dynamics construct the reality of crime and crime control; the fourth explores the social politics of crime and culture and the intellectual politics of cultural criminology.

Crime as Culture

To speak of crime as culture is to acknowledge at a minimum that much of what we label criminal behavior is at the same time subcultural behavior, collectively organized around networks of symbol, ritual, and shared meaning. Put simply, it is to adopt the subculture as a basic unit of criminological analysis. While this general insight is hardly a new one, cultural criminology develops it in a number of directions. Bringing a postmodern sensibility to their understanding of deviant and criminal subcultures, cultural criminologists argue that such subcultures incorporate—indeed, are defined by—elaborate conventions of argot, appearance, aesthetics, and stylized presentation of self and thus operate as repositories of collective meaning and representation for their members. Within these subcultures as in other arenas of crime, form shapes content, image frames identity. Taken into a mediated world of increasingly dislocated communication and dispersed meaning, this insight further implies that deviant and criminal subcultures may now be exploding into universes of symbolic communication that in many ways transcend time and space. For computer hackers, graffiti writers, drug runners, and others, a mix of widespread spatial dislocation and precise normative organization implies subcultures defined less by face-to-face interaction than by shared, if second-hand, symbolic codes (Gelder & Thornton 1997:473–550).

Understandably, then, much research in this area of cultural criminology has focused on the dispersed dynamics of subcultural style. Following from Hebdige's (1979) classic exploration of 'subculture: the meaning of style,' cultural criminologists have investigated style as defining both the internal characteristics of deviant and criminal subcultures and external constructions of them. Miller (1995), for example, has documented the many ways in which gang symbolism and style exist as the medium of meaning for both street gang members and the probation officers who attempt to control them. Reading gang styles as emblematic of gang immersion and gang defiance, enforcing court orders prohibiting gang clothing, confiscating gang paraphernalia, and displaying their confiscated collections on their own office walls, the probation officers in Miller's study construct the meanings of gang style as surely as do the gang members themselves. Likewise, Ferrell (1996) has shown how contemporary hip hop graffiti exists essentially as a 'crime of style' for graffiti writers, who operate and evaluate one another within complex stylistic and symbolic conventions, but also for media institutions and legal and political authorities who perceive graffiti as violating the 'aesthetics of authority' essential to their ongoing control of urban environments. More broadly, Ferrell (in Ferrell & Sanders 1995:169–89) has explored style as the tissue connecting cultural and criminal practices and has examined the ways in which subcultural style shapes not only aesthetic communities, but official and unofficial reactions to subcultural identity. Finally, Lyng & Bracey (1995) have documented the multiply ironic process by which the style of the outlaw biker sub-culture came first to signify class-based cultural resistance, next to elicit the sorts of media reactions and legal controls that in fact amplified and confirmed its meaning, and finally to be appropriated and commodified in such a way as to void its political potential. Significantly, these and other studies (Cosgrove 1984) echo and confirm the integrative methodological framework outlined above by demonstrating that the importance of style resides not within the dynamics of criminal subcultures, nor in media and political constructions of its meaning, but in the contested interplay of the two.

If subcultures of crime and deviance are defined by their aesthetic and symbolic organization, cultural criminology has also begun to show that they are defined by intensities of collective experience and emotion as well. Building on Katz's (1988) wide-ranging exploration of the sensually seductive 'foreground' of criminality, cultural criminologists like Lyng (1990, 1998) and Ferrell (1996) have utilized *verstehen*-oriented methodologies to document the experiences of 'edgework' and 'the adrenalin rush'—immediate, incandescent integrations of risk, danger, and skill—that shape participation and membership in deviant and criminal subcultures. Discovered across a range of illicit subcultures (Presdee 1994, O'Malley & Mugford 1994, Tunnell 1992:45, Wright & Decker 1994:117), these intense and often ritualized moments of pleasure and excitement define the experience of subcultural membership and, by members' own accounts, seduce them into continued sub-cultural participation. Significantly for a sociology of these subcultural practices, research (Lyng & Snow 1986) shows that experiences of edgework and adrenalin exist as collectively constructed endeavors, encased in shared vocabularies of motive and meaning (Mills 1940, Cressey 1954). Thus, while these experiences certainly suggest a sociology of the body and the emotions, and further *verstehen*-oriented explorations of deviant and criminal subcultures as 'affectually determined' (Weber 1978:9) domains, they also reveal the ways in which collective intensities of experience, like collective conventions of style, construct shared subcultural meaning.

Culture as Crime

The notion of 'culture as crime' denotes the reconstruction of cultural enterprise as criminal endeavor—through, for example, the public labeling of popular culture products as criminogenic, or the criminalization of cultural producers through media or legal channels. In contemporary society, such reconstructions pervade popular culture and transcend traditional 'high' and 'low' cultural boundaries. Art photographers Robert Mapplethorpe and Jock Sturges, for example, have faced highly orchestrated campaigns accusing them of producing obscene or pornographic images; in addition, an art center exhibiting Mapplethorpe's photographs was indicted on charges of 'pandering obscenity,' and Sturges's studio was raided by local police and the FBI (Dubin 1992). Punk and heavy metal bands, and associated record companies, distributors, and retail outlets, have encountered obscenity rulings, civil and criminal suits, high-profile police raids, and police interference with concerts. Performers, producers, distributors, and retailers of rap and 'gangsta rap' music have likewise faced arrest and conviction on obscenity charges, legal confiscation of albums, highly publicized protests, boycotts, hearings organized by political figures and police officials, and ongoing media campaigns and legal proceedings accusing them of promoting—indeed, directly causing—crime and delinquency (Hamm & Ferrell 1994). More broadly, a variety of television programs, films, and cartoons have been targeted by public campaigns alleging that they incite delinquency, spin off 'copy-cat' crimes, and otherwise serve as criminogenic social forces (Ferrell 1998, Nyberg 1998).

These many cases certainly fall within the purview of cultural criminology because the targets of criminalization—photographers, musicians, television writers, and their products—are 'cultural' in nature, but equally so because their criminalization itself unfolds as a cultural process. When contemporary culture personas and performances are criminalized, they are primarily criminalized through the mass media, through their presentation and re-presentation as criminal in the realm of sound bites, shock images, news conferences, and newspaper headlines. This mediated spiral, in which media-produced popular culture forms and figures are in turn criminalized by means of the media, leads once again into a complex hall of mirrors. It generates not only images, but images of images—that is, attempts by lawyers, police officials, religious leaders, media workers, and others to craft criminalized images of those images previously crafted by artists, musicians, and film makers. Thus, the criminalization of popular culture is itself a popular, and cultural, enterprise, standing in opposition to popular culture less than participating in it, and helping to construct the very meanings and effects to which it allegedly responds. Given this, cultural criminologists have begun to widen the notion of 'criminalization' to include more than the simple creation and application of criminal law. Increasingly, they investigate the larger process of 'cultural criminalization' (Ferrell 1998:80–82), the mediated reconstruction of meaning and perception around issues of culture and crime. In some cases, this cultural criminalization stands as an end in itself, successfully dehumanizing or delegitimating those targeted, though no formal legal charges are brought against them. In other cases, cultural criminalization helps construct a perceptual context in which direct criminal charges can more easily follow. In either scenario, though, media dynamics drive and define the criminalization of popular culture.

The mediated context of criminalization is a political one as well. The contemporary criminalization of popular culture has emerged as part of larger 'culture wars' (Bolton 1992) waged by political conservatives and cultural reactionaries. Controversies over the criminal or criminogenic characteristics of art photographers and rap musicians have resulted less from spontaneous public concern than from the sorts of well-funded and politically sophisticated campaigns that have similarly targeted the National Endowment for the Arts and its support of feminist/gay/lesbian performance artists and film festivals. In this light it is less than surprising that contemporary cultural criminalization is aimed time and again at marginal(ized) subcultures—radical punk musicians, politically militant black rap groups, lesbian and gay visual and performance artists—whose stylized celebration of and confrontation with their marginality threaten particular patterns of moral and legal control. Cultural criminalization in this sense exposes yet another set of linkages between subcultural styles and symbols and mediated constructions and reconstructions of these as criminal or criminogenic. In addition, as a process conducted largely in the public realm, cultural criminalization contributes to popular perceptions and panics, and thus to the further marginalization of those who are its focus. If successful, it constructs a degree of social discomfort that reflects off the face of popular culture and into the practice of everyday life.

Media Constructions of Crime and Crime Control

The mediated criminalization of popular culture exists, of course, as but one of many media processes that construct the meanings of crime and crime control. As noted in earlier discussions of textual methodologies, cultural criminology incorporates a wealth of research on mediated characterizations of crime and crime control, ranging across historical and contemporary texts and investigating images generated in newspaper reporting, popular film, television news and entertainment programming, popular music, comic books, and the cyber-spaces of the Internet. Further, cultural criminologists have begun to explore the complex institutional interconnections between the criminal justice system and the mass media. Researchers like Chermak (1995, 1997, 1998) and Sanders & Lyon (1995) have documented not only the mass media's heavy reliance on criminal justice sources for imagery and information on crime, but more importantly, the reciprocal relationship that undergirds this reliance. Working within organizational imperatives of efficiency and routinization, media institutions regularly rely on data selectively provided by policing and court agencies. In so doing, they highlight for the public issues chosen by criminal justice institutions and framed by criminal justice imperatives, and they in turn contribute to the political agendas of the criminal justice system and to the generation of public support for these agendas. In a relatively nonconspiratorial but nonetheless powerful fashion, media and criminal justice organizations thus coordinate their day-to-day operations and cooperate in constructing circumscribed understandings of crime and crime control.

A large body of research in cultural criminology examines the nature of these understandings and the public dynamics of their production. Like cultural criminology generally, much of the research here (Adler & Adler 1994, Goode & Ben-Yehuda 1994, Hollywood 1997, Jenkins 1992, Sparks 1995, Thornton 1994) builds on the classic analytic models of cultural studies and interactionist sociology, as embodied in concepts such as moral entrepreneurship and moral enterprise in the creation of crime and deviance (Becker 1963), and the invention of folk devils as a means of generating moral panic (Cohen 1972/1980) around issues of crime and deviance. Exploring the epistemic frameworks surrounding everyday understandings of crime controversies, this research (Fishman 1978, Best 1995, Acland 1995, Reinarman 1994, Reinarman & Duskin 1992, Websdale 1996) problematizes and unpacks taken-for-granted assumptions regarding the prevalence of criminality and the particular characteristics of criminals, and the research traces these assumptions to the interrelated workings of interest groups, media institutions, and criminal justice organizations.

Emerging scholarship in cultural criminology also offers useful reconceptualizations and refinements of these analytic models. McRobbie & Thornton (1995), for example, argue that the essential concepts of 'moral panic' and 'folk devils' must be reconsidered in multi-mediated societies; with the proliferation of media channels and the saturation of media markets, moral panics have become both dangerous endeavors and marketable commodities, and folk devils now find themselves both stigmatized and lionized in mainstream media and alternative media alike. Similarly, Jenkins's (1999) recent work has begun to refine understandings of crime and justice issues as social and cultural constructions. Building on his earlier, meticulous deconstructions of drug panics, serial homicide scares, and other constructed crime controversies, Jenkins (1994a,b) argues that attention must be paid to the media and political dynamics underlying 'unconstructed' crime as well. Jenkins explores the failure to frame activities such as anti-abortion violence as criminal terrorism, situates this failure within active media and political processes, and thus questions the meaning of that for which no criminal meaning is provided.

Through all of this, cultural criminologists further emphasize that in the process of constructing crime and crime control as social concerns and political controversies, the media also construct them as entertainment. Revisiting the classic cultural studies/new criminology notion of 'policing the crisis' (Hall et al 1978), Sparks (1995; see 1992), for example, characterizes the production and perception of crime and policing imagery in television crime dramas as a process of 'entertaining the crisis.' Intertwined with mediated moral panic over crime and crime waves, amplified fear of street crime and stranger violence, and politically popular concern for the harm done to crime victims, then, is the pleasure found in consuming mediated crime imagery and crime drama. To the extent that the mass media constructs crime as entertainment, we are thus offered not only selective images and agendas, but the ironic mechanism for amusing ourselves to death (Postman 1986) by way of our own collective pain, misery, and fear. Given this, contemporary media scholarship in cultural criminology focuses as much on popular film, popular music, and television entertainment programming as on the mediated manufacture of news and information, and it investigates the collapsing boundaries between such categories. Recent work in this area targets especially the popularity of 'reality' crime programs (Fishman & Cavender 1998). With their mix of street footage, theatrical staging, and patrol-car sermonizing, reality crime programs such as 'C.O.P.S.,' 'L.A.P.D,' and 'True Stories of the Highway Patrol' generate conventional, though at times contradictory, images of crime and policing. Along with talk shows devoted largely to crime and deviance topics, they in turn spin off secondary merchandising schemes, legal suits over videotaped police chases and televised invasions of privacy, and criminal activities allegedly induced by the programs themselves. Such dynamics demonstrate the entangled reality of crime, crime news, and crime entertainment, and suggest that as mediated crime constructions come to be defined as real, 'they are real in their consequences' (Thomas 1966:301).

The Politics of Culture, Crime, and Cultural Criminology

Clearly, a common thread connects the many domains into which cultural criminology inquires: the presence of power relations, and the emergence of social control, at the intersections of culture and crime. The stylistic practices and symbolic codes of illicit subcultures are made the object of legal surveillance and control or, alternatively, are appropriated, commodified, and sanitized within a vast machinery of consumption. Sophisticated media and criminal justice 'culture wars' are launched against alternative forms of art, music, and entertainment, thereby criminalizing the personalities and performances involve, marginalizing them from idealized notions of decency and community and, at the extreme, silencing the political critiques they present. Ongoing media constructions of crime and crime control emerge out of an alliance of convenience between media institutions and criminal justice agencies, serve to promote and legitimate broader political agendas regarding crime control, and in turn function to both trivialize and dramatize the meaning of crime.

Increasingly, then, it is television crime shows and big budget detective movies, nightly newscasts and morning newspaper headlines, recurrent campaigns against the real and imagined crimes of the disenfranchised that constitute Foucault's (in Cohen 1979:339) 'Hundreds of tiny theatres of punishment'—theatres in which young people, ethnic minorities, lesbians and gays, and other play villains deserving of penalty and public outrage.

At the same time, cultural criminologists emphasize and explore the various forms that resistance to this complex web of social control may take. As Sparks (1992, 1995) and others argue, the audiences for media constructions of crime are diverse in both their composition and their readings of these constructions; they recontextualize, remake, and even reverse mass media meanings as they incorporate them into their daily lives and interactions. Varieties of resistance also emerge among those groups more specifically targeted within the practice of mediated control. Artists and musicians caught up in contemporary 'culture wars' have refused governmental awards, resigned high-profile positions, won legal judgements, organized alternative media outlets and performances, and otherwise produced public counter-attacks (Ferrell 1998). Within other marginalized subcultures, personal and group style certainly exists as stigmata, inviting outside surveillance and control, but at the same time is valued as a badge of honor and resistance made all the more meaningful by its enduring defiance of outside authority (Hebdige 1988). Likewise, as Lyng (1990, 1998) and Ferrell (1996) emphasize, those immersed in moments of illicit edgework and adrenalin construct resistance doubly. First, by combining in such moments high levels of risk with precise skills and practiced artistry, those involved invent an identity, a sense of crafted self, that resists the usual degradations of subordinate status and deskilled, alienated labor. Second, as these moments become more dangerous because targeted by campaigns of criminalization and enforcement, participants in them find an enhancement and amplification of the edgy excitement they provide, and in so doing transform political pressure into personal and collective pleasure. In investigating the intersections of culture and crime for power relations and emerging forms of social control, then, cultural criminologists carry on the tradition of cultural studies (Hall & Jefferson 1976) by examining the many forms of resistance that emerge there as well.

Moreover, cultural criminology itself operates as a sort of intellectual resistance, as a diverse counter-reading and counter-discourse on, and critical 'intervention' (Pfohl & Gordon 1986:94) into, conventional constructions of crime. In deconstructing moments of mediated panic over crime, cultural criminologists work to expose the political processes behind seemingly spontaneous social concerns and to dismantle the recurring and often essentialist metaphors of disease, invasion, and decay on which crime panics are built (Brownstein 1995, 1996, Reinarman 1994, Reinarman & Duskin 1992, Murji 1999). Beyond this, Barak (1988, 1994a) argues for an activist 'newsmaking criminology' in which criminologists integrate themselves into the ongoing mediated construction of crime, develop as part of their role in this process alternative images and understandings of crime issues, and in so doing produce what constitutive criminologists (Henry & Milovanovic 1991, Barak 1995) call a 'replacement discourse' regarding crime and crime control. Much of cultural criminology's ethnographic work in subcultural domains functions similarly, as a critical move away from the 'official definitions of reality' (Hagedorn 1990:244) produced by the media and the criminal justice system and reproduced by a 'courthouse criminology' (see Polsky 1969) that relies on these sources. By attentively documenting the lived realities of groups whom conventional crime constructions have marginalized, and in turn documenting the situated politics of this marginalization process, cultural criminologists attempt to deconstruct the official demonization of various 'outsiders' (Becker 1963)—from rural domestic violence victims (Websdale 1998) to urban graffiti writers (Ferrell 1996, Sanchez-Tranquilino 1995), gay hustlers (Pettiway 1996), and homeless heroin addicts (Bourgois et al 1997)— and to produce alternative understandings of them. Approaching this task from the other direction, Hamm (1993) and others likewise venture inside the worlds of particularly violent criminals to document dangerous nuances of meaning and style often invisible in official reporting on such groups. In its politics as in its theory and method, then, cultural criminology integrates subcultural ethnography with media and institutional analysis to produce an alternative image of crime.

TRAJECTORIES OF CULTURAL CRIMINOLOGY

In describing an emergent orientation like cultural criminology, it is perhaps appropriate to close with a brief consideration of its unfinished edges. The following short discussions are therefore meant to be neither systematic nor exhaustive; they simply suggest some of what is emerging, and what might productively emerge, as cultural criminology continues to develop.

Situated Media, Situated Audiences

The dynamic integration of subcultural crime constructions and media crime constructions has surfaced time and again in this essay as one of cultural criminology's essential insights. This insight further implies that the everyday notion of 'media' must be expanded to include those media that take shape within and among the various subcultures of crime, deviance, and crime control. As noted in the above methodological discussions, various illicit subcultures certainly come into regular contact with the mass media, but in so doing appropriate and reinvent mass media channels, products, and meanings. Further, illicit subcultures regularly invent their own media of communication; as McRobbie & Thornton (1995:559) point out, even the interests of 'folk devils' are increasingly 'defended by their own niche and micromedia.' Thus, alternative and marginalized youth subcultures self-produce a wealth of zines (alternative magazines) and websites; street gang members construct elaborate edifices of communication out of particular clothing styles, colors, and hand signs; and graffiti writers develop a continent-wide network of freight train graffiti that mirrors existing hobo train graffiti in its ability to link distant subcultural members within a shared symbolic community. As also suggested in above discussions, multiple, fluid audiences likewise witness efflorescences of crime and crime control in their everyday existence, consume a multitude of crime images packaged as news and entertainment, and in turn remake the meaning of these encounters within the symbolic interaction of their own lives. Investigating the linkages between 'media' and crime, then, means investigating the many situations in which these linkages emerge, and moreover the situated place of media, audience, and meaning within criminal worlds (see Vaughan 1998). Ultimately, perhaps, this investigation suggests blurring the analytic boundary between producer and audience—recognizing, in other words, that a variety of groups both produce and consume contested images of crime—and moving ahead to explore the many microcircuits of meaning that collectively construct the reality of crime.

The Media and Culture of Policing

Increasingly, the production and consumption of mediated meaning frames not only the reality of crime, but of crime control as well. Contemporary policing can in fact hardly be understood apart from its interpenetration with media at all levels. As 'reality' crime and policing television programs shape public perceptions of policing, serve as controversial tools of officer recruitment and suspect apprehension, and engender legal suits over their effects on street-level policing, citizens shoot video footage of police conduct and misconduct—some of which finds its way, full-circle, onto news and 'reality' programs. Meanwhile, within the police subculture itself, surveillance cameras and on-board patrol car cameras capture the practices of police officers and citizens alike and, as Websdale (1999) documents, police crime files themselves take shape as 'situated media substrates' which, like surveillance and patrol car footage, regularly become building blocks for subsequent mass media images of policing. The policing of a postmodern world emerges as a complex set of visual and semiotic practices, an expanding spiral of mediated social control (Manning 1998, 1999a,b).

From the view of cultural criminology, policing must in turn be understood as a set of practices situated, like criminal practices, within subcultural conventions of meaning, symbolism, and style. In this regard, Kraska & Kappeler (1995:85) integrate perspectives from police studies, feminist literature, and critical theory to explore the subcultural ideologies, situated dynamics, and broader 'cultural and structural context' within which police deviance and police sexual violence against women develop. Perhaps most interesting here, in light of the reflexive methodologies discussed above, is Kraska's (1998) grounded investigation of police paramilitary units. Immersing himself and his emotions in a situation of police paramilitary violence, Kraska details the stylized subcultural status afforded by particular forms of weaponry and clothing, and he documents the deep-seated ideological and affective states that define the collective meaning of such situations. With crime control as with crime, subcultural and media dynamics construct experience and perception.

Crime and Cultural Space

Many of the everyday situations in which crime and policing are played out, and in fact many of the most visible contemporary controversies surrounding crime and policing issues, involve the contestation of cultural space. Incorporating perspectives from cultural studies, cultural geography, and postmodern geography (Merrifield & Swyngedouw 1997, Scott & Soja 1996, Davis 1992), the notion of cultural space references the process by which meaning is constructed and contested in public domains (Ferrell 1997). This process intertwines with a variety of crime and crime control situations. Homeless populations declare by their public presence the scandal of inequality, and they are in turn hounded and herded by a host of loitering, vagrancy, trespass, public lodging, and public nuisance statutes. 'Gutter punks' invest downtown street corners with disheveled style, 'skate punks' and skateboarders convert walkways and parking garages into playgrounds, Latino/a street 'cruisers' create mobile subcultures out of dropped frames and polished chrome—and face in response aggressive enforcement of laws regarding trespass, curfew, public sleeping, and even car stereo volume. Street gangs carve out collective cultural space from shared styles and public rituals; criminal justice officials prohibit and confiscate stylized clothing, enforce prohibitions against public gatherings by 'known' gang members, and orchestrate public gang 'round-ups.' Graffiti writers remake the visual landscapes and symbolic codes of public life, but they do so in the face of increasing criminal sanctions, high-tech surveillance systems, and nationally coordinated legal campaigns designed to remove them and their markings from public life.

As with the mediated campaigns of cultural criminalization discussed above, these conflicts over crime and cultural space regularly emerge around the marginalized subcultures of young people, ethnic minorities, and other groups, and thus they raise essential issues of identity and authenticity (Sanchez-Tranquilino 1995). Such conflicts in turn incorporate a complex criminalization of these subcultures as part of a systematic effort to erase their self-constructed public images, to substitute in their place symbols of homogeneity and consensus, and thereby to restore and expand the 'aesthetics of authority' noted in above discussions. Ultimately, these disparate conflicts over crime and cultural space reveal the common thread of contested public meaning, and something of the work of control in the age of cultural reproduction.

Bodies, Emotions, and Cultural Criminology

Perhaps the most critical of situations, the most intimate of cultural spaces in which crime and crime control intersect are those in and around the physical and emotional self (Pfohl 1990). Throughout this essay such situations have been seen: the development of subcultural style as marker of identity and locus of criminalization; the fleeting experience of edgework and adrenalin rushes, heightened by risk of legal apprehension; the utilization of researchers' own experiences and emotions in the study of crime and policing. These situations suggest that other moments merit the attention of cultural criminology as well, from gang girls' construction of identity through hair, makeup, and discourse (Mendoza-Denton 1996) and phone fantasy workers' invocation of sexuality and emotion (Mattley 1998), to the contested media and body politics of AIDS (Kane 1998b, Watney 1987, Young 1996:175–206). Together, these and other situations in turn suggest a criminology of the skin (see Kushner 1994)—a criminology that can account for crime and crime control in terms of pleasure, fear, and excitement and that can confront the deformities of sexuality and power, control and resistance that emerge in these inside spaces. They also demand the ongoing refinement of the reflexive, *verstehen*-oriented methodologies and epistemologies described above—of ways of investigating and knowing that are at the same time embodied and affective (Scheper-Hughes 1994), closer to the intimate meaning of crime and yet never close enough.

CONCLUSIONS

As an emerging perspective within criminology, sociology, and criminal justice, cultural criminology draws from a wide range of intellectual orientations. Revisiting and perhaps reinventing existing paradigms in cultural studies, the 'new' criminology, interactionist sociology, and critical theory; integrating insights from postmodern, feminist, and constructionist thought; and incorporating aspects of newsmaking, constitutive, and other evolving criminologies, cultural criminology seek less to synthesize or subsume these various perspectives than to engage them in a critical, multifaceted exploration of culture and crime. Linking these diverse intellectual dimensions, and their attendant methodologies of ethnography and media/ textual analysis, is cultural criminology's overarching concern with the meaning of crime and crime control. Some three decades ago, Cohen (1988:68, 1971:19) wrote of 'placing on the agenda' of a culturally informed criminology issues of 'subjective meaning,' and of deviance and crime as 'meaningful action.' Cultural criminology embraces and expands this agenda by exploring the complex construction, attribution, and appropriation of meaning that occurs within and between media and political formations, illicit subcultures, and audiences around matters of crime and crime control. In so doing, cultural criminology likewise highlights the inevitability of the image. Inside the stylized rhythms of a criminal subculture, reading a newspaper crime report or persuing a police file, caught between the panic and pleasure of crime, 'there is no escape from the politics of representation' (Hall 1993:111).

[. . .]

REFERENCES

Acland C.R. 1995. *Youth, Murder, Spectacle: The Cultural Politics of 'Youth in Crisis'*. Boulder, CO: Westview.

Adler P.A., Adler P. eds. 1994. *Constructions of Deviance: Social Power, Context, and Interaction*. Belmont, CA: Wadsworth.

Anderson S.E., Howard, G.J. eds. 1998. *Interrogating Popular Culture: Deviance, Justice, and social Order*. Guilderland, NY: Harrow & Heston.

Bailey F.Y., Hale D.C. eds. 1998. *Popular Culture, Crime, and Justice*. Belmont, CA: West/Wadsworth.

Barak G. 1988. Newsmaking criminology: reflections on the media, intellectuals, and crime. *Justice Q.* 5:565–87.

Barak G. ed. 1994a. *Media, Process, and the Social Construction of Crime: Studies in Newsmaking Criminology*. New York: Garland.

Barak G. 1995, Media, crime, and justice: a case for constitutive criminology. See Ferrell & Sanders 1995, pp. 142–66.

Becker H.S. 1963. *Outsiders: Studies in the Sociology of Deviance*. New York: Free Press.

Best J. ed. 1995. *Images of Issues: Typifying Contemporary Social Problems*. New York: Aldine de Gruyter. 2nd ed.

Bolton R, ed. 1992. *Culture Wars: Documents from the Recent Controversies in the Arts*. New York: New Press.

Bourgois P., Lettiere M., Quesada J. 1997. Social misery and the sanctions of substance abuse: confronting HIV risk among homeless heroin addicts in San Francisco. *Soc. Probl.* 44:155–73.

Brownstein H.H. 1995. The media and the construction of random drug violence. See Ferrell & Sanders 1995, pp. 45–65.

Brownstein H.H. 1996. *The Rise and Fall of a Violent Crime Wave: Crack Cocaine and the Social Construction of a Crime Problem*. Guilderland, NY: Harrow & Heston.

Chermak S. 1995. *Victims in the News: Crime and the American News Media*. Boulder, CO: Westview.

Chermak S. 1997. The presentation of drugs in the news media: the news sources involved in the construction of social problems. *Justice Q.* 14:687–718.

Chermak S.M. 1998. Police, courts, and corrections in the media. See Bailey & Hale 1998, pp. 87–99.

Cohen S. ed. 1971. *Images of Deviance*. Harmondsworth, UK: Penguin.

Cohen S. 1972/1980. *Folk Devils and Moral Panics*. London: Macgibbon & Kee.

Cohen S. 1979. The punitive city: notes on the dispersal of social control. *Contemp. Crises*. 3:339–63.

Cohen S. 1988. *Against Criminology*. New Brunswick, NJ: Transaction.

Cosgrove S. 1984. The zoot-suit and style warfare. *Radical Am.* 18:38–51.

Cressey D. 1954. The differential association theory and compulsive crime. *J. Crim. Law Criminol.* 45:49–64.

Davis M. 1992. *City of Quartz*. New York: Vintage.

Dubin S. 1992. *Arresting Images: Impolitic Art and Uncivil Actions*. London: Routledge.

Ferrell J. 1996. *Crimes of Style: Urban Graffiti and the Politics of Criminality*. Boston: Northeastern Univ. Press.

Ferrell J. 1997. Youth, crime, and cultural space. *Soc. Justice* 24:21–38.

Ferrell J. 1998. Criminalizing popular culture. See Bailey & Hale 1998, pp. 71–83.

Ferrell J., Sanders C.R., eds. 1995. *Cultural Criminology*. Boston: Northeastern Univ. Press.

Ferrell J., Websdale N. eds. 1999. *Making Trouble: Cultural Constructions of Crime, Deviance, and Control*. Hawthorne, NY: Aldine de Gruyter.

Fishman M. 1978. Crime waves as ideology. *Soc. Probl.* 25:531–43.

Fishman M., Cavender G. eds. 1998. *Entertaining Crime: Television Reality Programs*. Hawthorne, NY: Aldine de Gruyter.

Gelder K., Thornton S. eds. 1997. *The Subcultures Reader*. London: Routledge.

Goode E., Ben-Yehuda N. 1994. *Moral Panics*. Cambridge, MA: Blackwell.

Hagedorn J.M. 1990. Black in the field again: gang research in the nineties. In *Gangs in America*, ed. C.R. Huff, pp. 240–59. Newbury Park, CA: Sage.

Hall S. 1993. What is this 'black' in black popular culture? *Soc. Justice* 20:104–14.

Hall S., Critcher C., Jefferson T., Clarke J., Roberts B. 1978. *Policing the Crisis: Mugging, the State, and Law and Order*. Houndmills, UK: MacMillan.

Hall S., Jefferson T. eds. 1976. *Resistance Through Rituals: Youth Subcultures in Post-War Britain*. London: Hutchinson.

Hamm M.S. 1993. *American Skinheads: The Criminology and Control of Hate Crime.* Westport, CT: Praeger.

Hamm M.S., Ferrell J. 1994. Rap, cops, and crime: clarifying the 'cop killer' controversy. *ACJS Today* 13:1, 3, 29.

Hebdige D. 1979. *Subculture: The Meaning of Style.* London: Methuen.

Hebdige D. 1988. *Hiding in the Light.* London: Routledge.

Henry S., Milovanovic D. 1991. Constitutive criminology: the maturation of critical theory. *Criminology* 29:293–315.

Hollywood B. 1997. Dancing in the dark: ecstasy, the dance culture, and moral panic in post ceasefire Northern Ireland. *Crit. Criminol.* 8:62–77.

Jenkins P. 1992. *Intimate Enemies: Moral Panics in Contemporary Great Britain.* Hawthorne, NY: Aldine de Gruyter.

Jenkins P. 1994a. *Using Murder: The social Construction of Serial Homicide.* Hawthorne, NY: Aldine de Gruyter.

Jenkins P. 1994b. 'The Ice Age': the social construction of a drug panic. *Justice Q.* 11:7–31.

Jenkins P. 1999. Fighting terrorism as if women mattered: anti-abortion violence as unconstructed terrorism. See Ferrell & Websdale 1999, pp. 319–46.

Kane S. 1998a. Reversing the ethnographic gaze: experiments in cultural criminology. See Ferrell & Hamm 1998, pp. 132–45.

Kane S. 1998b. *AIDS Alibis: Sex, Drugs and Crime in the Americas.* Philadelphia: Temple Univ. Press.

Katz J. 1988. *Seductions of Crime: Moral and Sensual Attractions in Doing Evil,* NY: Basic Books.

Kidd-Hewitt D., Osborne R. eds. 1995. *Crime and the Media: The Post-Modern Spectacle.* London: Pluto.

Kraska P.B. 1998. Enjoying militarism: political/personal dilemmas in studying U.S. police paramilitary units. See Ferrell & Hamm 1998, pp. 88–110.

Kraska P.B., Kappeler V.E. 1995. To serve and pursue: exploring police sexual violence against women. *Justice Q.* 12:85–111.

Kushner T. 1994. A socialism of the skin. *Nation* 259:9–14.

Lyng S. 1990. Edgework: a social psychological analysis of voluntary risk taking. *Am. J. Social.* 95:851–86.

Lyng S. 1998. Dangerous methods: risk taking and the research process. See Ferrell & Hamm 1998, pp. 221–51.

Lyng S., Bracey M.L. 1995. Squaring the one percent: biker style and the selling of cultural resistance. See Ferrell & Sanders 1995. pp. 235–76.

Lyng S., Snow D. 1986. Vocabularies of motive and high-risk behavior: the case of skydiving. In *Advances in Group Processes,* ed. E. Lawler, pp. 157–79. Greenwich, CT: JAI.

Manning P.K. 1998. Media loops. See Bailey & Hale 1998, pp. 25–39.

Manning P.K. 1999a. Semiotics and social justice. In *Social Justice/Criminal Justice,* ed. B.A. Arrigo, pp. 131–49. Belmont, CA: West/Wadsworth.

Manning P.K. 1999b. Reflections: the visual as a mode of social control. See Ferrell & Websdale 1999, pp. 255–75.

Mattley C. 1998. (Dis)courtesy stigma: fieldwork among phone fantasy workers. See Ferrell & Hamm 1998, pp. 146–58.

McRobbie A., Thornton S.L. 1995. Rethinking 'moral panic' for multi-mediated social worlds. *Br. J. Sociol.* 46:559–574.

Mendoza-Denton N. 1996. 'Muy macha': gender and ideology in gang-girls' discourse about makeup. *Ethnos* 61:47–63.

Merrifield A., Swyngedouw E. eds. 1997. *The Urbanization of Injustice*. Washington Square. NY: New York Univ. Press.

Miller J.A. 1995. Struggles over the symbolic: gang style and the meanings of social control. See Ferrell & Sanders 1995, pp. 213–34.

Mills C.W. 1940. Situated actions and vocabularies of motive. *Am. Sociol. Rev.* 5:904–13.

Murji K. 1999. Wild life: constructions and representations of yardies. See Ferrell & Websdale 1999, pp. 179–201

Nyberg A.K. 1998. Comic books and juvenile delinquency: a historical perspective. See Bailey & Hale 1998, pp. 61–70.

O'Malley P., Mugford S. 1994. Crime, excitement, and modernity. See Barak 1994b, pp. 189–211.

Pettiway L.E. 1996. *Honey. Honey, Miss Thang: Being Black, Gay, and on the Streets.* Philadelphia: Temple Univ. Press.

Pfohl S. 1990. Welcome to the Parasite Cafe: postmodernity as a social problem. *Soc. Probl.* 37:421–42.

Pfohl S., Gordon A. 1986. Criminological displacements: a sociological deconstruction. *Soc. Probl.* 33:94–113.

Polsky N. 1969. *Hustlers, Beats, and Others*. Garden City, NY: Anchor.

Postman N. 1986. *Amusing Ourselves to Death*. London: Heinemann.

Potter G.W., Kappeler, V.E. eds. 1998. *Constructing Crime: Perspectives on Making News and Social Problems*. Prospect Heights. IL: Waveland.

Presdee M. 1994. Young people, culture, and the construction of crime: doing wrong versus doing crime. See Barak 1994b, pp. 179–87.

Redhead S. 1995. *Unpopular Cultures: The Birth of Law and Popular Culture.* Manchester, UK: Manchester Univ. Press.

Reinarman C. 1994. The social construction of drug scares. See Adler & Adler 1994, pp. 92–104.

Reinarman C., Duskin C. 1992. Dominant ideology and drugs in the media. *Intern. J. Drug Pol.* 3:6–15.

Sanchez-Tranquilino M. 1995. Space, power, and youth culture: Mexican American graffiti and Chicano murals in East Los Angeles, 1972–1978. In *Looking High and Low: Art and Cultural Identity*, ed. B.J. Bright, L. Bakewell, pp. 55–88. Tucson, AZ: Univ. Ariz. Press.

Sanders C.R., Lyon E. 1995. Repetitive retribution: media images and the cultural construction of criminal justice. See Ferrell & Sanders 1995, pp. 25–44.

Scheper-Hughes N. 1994. Embodied knowledge: thinking with the body in critical medical anthropology. In *Assessing Cultural Anthropology*, ed. R. Borofsky, pp. 229–42. New York: McGraw-Hill.

Scott A., Soja E. eds. 1996. *The City: Los Angeles and Urban Theory at the End of the Twentieth Century*. Berkeley: Univ. Calif. Press.

Sparks R. 1992. *Television and the Drama of Crime: Moral Tales and the Place of Crime in Public Life*. Buckingham, UK: Open Univ. Press.

Sparks R. 1995. Entertaining the crisis: television and moral enterprise. See Kidd-Hewitt & Osborne 1995, pp. 49–66.

Thomas W.I. 1966. The relation of research to the social process. In *W.I. Thomas on Social Organization and Social Personality*, ed. M. Janowitz, pp. 289–305. Chicago: Univ. Chicago Press.

Thornton S. 1994. Moral panic, the media, and British rave culture. In *Microphone Fiends: Youth Music and Youth Culture*, eds. A. Ross, T. Rose, pp. 176–92. New York: Routledge.

Tunnell K.D. 1992. *Choosing Crime: The Criminal Calculus of Property Offenders*. Chicago: Nelson-Hall.

Vaughn D. 1998. Rational choice, situated action, and the social control of organizations. *Law Soc. Rev.* 32:501–39.

Watney S. 1987. *Policing Desire: Pornography, AIDS and the Media*. Minneapolis: Univ. Minn. Press.

Weber M. 1978. *Economy and Society*. Berkeley: Univ. Calif. Press.

Websdale N. 1996. Predators: the social construction of 'stranger-danger' in Washington State as a form of patriarchal ideology. *Women Crim. Justice* 7:43–68.

Websdale N. 1998. *Rural Women Battering and the Justice System: An Ethnography*. Thousand Oaks, CA: Sage.

Websdale N. 1999. Police homicide files as situated media substrates. See Ferrell & Websdale 1999, pp. 277–300.

Wright R., Decker S. 1994. *Burglars on the Job*. Boston: Northeastern Univ. Press.

Young A. 1996. *Imagining Crime: Textual Outlaws and Criminal Conversations*. London: Sage.

Young J. 1971. The role of the police as amplifiers of deviancy, negotiators of reality and translators of fantasy. In *Images of Deviance*, ed. S. Cohen, pp. 27–61. Harmondsworth, UK: Penguin.

Name index

Subject index